GARDEN OF ZOLA

GRAHAM KING

GARDEN OF ZOLA

Emile Zola and his Novels for English Readers

COMMUNICA-EUROPA

© Graham King   1978

First published in 1978
by Barrie and Jenkins Ltd,
24 Highbury Crescent, London N5 1RX

ISBN   0 214 20403 0

Printed in Great Britain by
UNWIN BROTHERS LIMITED,
The Gresham Press,
Old Woking, Surrey

To Lyn Curry

Contents

List of illustrations

In the list above, item 31 should be deleted and the subsequent numbers altered accordingly.

Acknowledgements

I must acknowledge my indebtedness to the many authors, translators and publishers in respect of quotations and extracts in this book; in particular Airmont Publishing Co., Avon Publications, Bantam Books, Chatto & Windus, Citadel Press, Elek Books Ltd, Granada Publishing Co., Grove Press, Hamish Hamilton Ltd, Harper & Row, Howell, Soskin, Hutchinson & Co., John Calder, Julien Press, New American Library, New English Library, Oxford University Press, Penguin Books Ltd, Prentice-Hall Inc., Princeton University Press and William Heinemann Ltd. It has been found impossible to trace all copyright holders, and I apologise for credits thus omitted; if informed of the fact such omissions will be gladly rectified in future editions.

I also wish to record my gratitude to many patient friends for their encouragement; to Michael Thomas for his reassurance; to James Moore for his enthusiasm; and finally to Rupert Murdoch for his generous help, without which I doubt this book would exist.

G. P. K.

Introduction

A great deal has already been written about the man who wrote so much, sometimes reverent, sometimes hostile, occasionally detached, frequently repetitious, at times illuminating — but rarely, to my knowledge, with the general reader in mind.

And now, another book about Emile Zola.

I doubt whether this book will add much to what is already known about Zola and his work except my own opinions, and perhaps some fresh evaluations from the viewpoint of an English reader. But what seems to me to be missing from the long shelves of Zola studies is a complete, accurate and readable book for the *general* reader — one that might be picked up and read with pleasure, interest and enlightenment by someone with an enquiring mind wanting nothing more than to make the acquaintance of one of the most remarkable writers of modern times. Whether the present book will fill such a gap will depend on the reactions of individual readers, but that is my hope.

Many writers of greater sensibility and judgement, and far abler than myself, have shone a lamp into the dark corner where, for half a century longer than he could possibly deserve, Zola has been confined, and their efforts have encouraged the rediscovery of a whole pleasure-ground of reading enjoyment.

Since picking up a battered copy of *Germinal* many years ago, I have come to regard Zola's writings with a comforting familiarity. For a reason I have never been able properly to determine, not only *Germinal* but a great many of Zola's other novels have struck in me some sympathetic chord, a curiously presistent harmony. Indeed, the memory of my original reading of *Germinal* evokes emotions quite beyond even those stirred from between the covers of a particularly inspiriting book; an experience, incidentally, shared by Henry James when he re-read *The Debacle*:

I have been rereading it, I confess, with a certain timidity, the dread of perhaps impairing the deep impression received at the time of its appearance. I recall the effect it then produced on me as a really luxurious act of submission. It was early in the summer; the heat was oppressive, and one could but recline, in the lightest of garments, in a great dim room and give one's self up. I like to think of the conditions and the emotion, which melt for me together into the memory I fear to imperil.

(*Atlantic Monthly*, August 1903)

Emile Zola has given me enormous enjoyment through his novels. I feel I owe him something for this, although the way I've chosen to pay the debt may seem misguided to many. But it is rather more involved than that, for I have debit and credit accounts with a hundred-odd translators, too. For the reader who has no French, and must read Zola in whatever English-language versions which come his way, what ought to be a delightful ramble through his novels becomes an obstacle course over treacherous, although occasionally rewarding, terrain. In the past couple of decades the situation for Zola's English readers has vastly improved, but in the matter of translations one is just as likely to pick up glass as diamond, regardless of the excellence of the original. Obviously, some guidance here can only be helpful.

Just as one may walk unconducted through a strange city or a museum yet still enjoy the experience immensely, so one may read a novel unguided, and with no apparent lack of pleasure. Few readers, however, would dispute the benefit of a friendly pilot if the aim of both is to enlarge and enrich the reading experience, and this is where a critical commentary succeeds or fails. But does it help the reader of *Nana* to know how Zola went about collecting information on prostitution in Paris? Does the fact that Zola was emerging from the throes of a deep depression when he wrote *Joy of Life* add anything to the reader's understanding and enjoyment of the novel? If the reader is made aware of the structural composition of *L'Assommoir* does he read it with greater perception than if he is not? Considered separately these questions are open to debate. But in the broadest sense my experience is that a knowledge of the circumstances surrounding the writing of a novel, of its author and his intentions, of its critical and public acceptance, can satisfy, either in advance or in retrospect, questions a curious reader might want to ask. In the event, I have in this book attempted to contribute a commentary on each of the novels with the hope that I can assist with their comprehension and perhaps even extend the area of enjoyment for the reader. But even if I do little or no more than encourage the reading of a single novel of Zola's, I shall be happy.

The composition of this book is somewhat of a gamble: part biography, part criticism, part commentary, and with a number of side journeys into areas I considered to be of special interest. Despite the volume of documentation there still remain gaps in what is known about the novelist's life, and if at times I yield to conjecture I hope the departure is made clear. Zola's literary life was marked by a phenomenal output, and I find that none of it can be easily discounted or readily ignored. Being an admirer of Zola doesn't oblige me to admire everything he wrote, only to understand why some of his novels are better than others and why — in the case of the half-dozen the world might not have missed — they were written at all.

I have been a regular literary companion of Zola's for many years, and for the past year I feel I have lived with him. The experience, as fascinating as it was exhausting, has left me in no doubt of Zola's greatness.

Emile Zola never knew anything but the sequestered life of a dedicated

...nce.

...la, above all, was confused about what he was attempting. His theories and philosophies were self-created to fill a void left by his rejection of Christian dogma and other accepted philosophies. We have travelled some way since Zola formulated them, and today they are about as quaint as bustles and bone corsets, and just as constricting to free expression. Zola's genius, fortunately, triumphed. As he wrote his novels from the careful plans he always prepared, they persisted in assuming a life of their own; characters would develop and influence each other, an event would precipitate consequences unforeseen by the novelist, and so forth; his fantasy world would begin to take control.

...ritical opprobrium as the result of confusing Zola's theories with his fiction, ...unjustified, is easy to understand. What is more difficult to comprehend ...ast outpouring of literary bias and bigotry that has, at times, taken on the ...ions of an industry. Academics have competed with one another in ... to expose alleged weaknesses in Zola's style. Remarks by the ... less than perceptive Henry James who, while declaring Zola a ... said that the *Rougon-Macquart* novels were 'perhaps the most ...y imitation of observation that we possess', tended to become ...ble doctrine, to be passed from one generation of scholars on to

...mon and persisting criticism is that Zola lacked insight. ...his monumental and profoundly perceptive study of a

writer. Although his early years of poverty served as a valuable apprenticeship in that he stored up observations on the lives of the poor and a compassion for the dispossessed that were to assist him later on, he was never a soldier, never a womaniser; he never knew the trials of selling one's muscle and sweat, the itch to travel, the desire to live life to the full. Havelock Ellis wrote that 'life only came to him as the sights, sounds and smells that reached his garret window. His soul seems to have been starved at the centre, and to have encamped at the sensory periphery.' Yet for all that, on the evidence of the books he left behind, his incredible broadness of vision and understanding is all the more remarkable. It was his powerful artist's vision which transformed his largely second-hand experiences into vivid, intensely personal fictions. From hazy boyhood memories of Aix-en-Provence and tourist brochures — because at the time he couldn't afford the railway fare for on-the-spot observations — he created Plassans, a town which hummed with life and intrigue in *The Conquest of Plassans*. From a garden catalogue and a visit to a horticultural show he dreamed up the abandoned, intoxicating jungle of *Le Paradou* for *The Abbé Mouret's Sin*. He never slept with a prostitute yet he breathed life into the most famous fictional courtesan of them all, *Nana*. A single descent down a coal mine was sufficient to stimulate the creation of the haunting, man-eating Voreaux in *Germinal*.

Emile Zola was also one of the great literary pioneers of the last two centuries. Because of his audacity and honesty, no subject matter was thereafter taboo to the novelist. He wrote the first major novel about the lives and plight of ordinary working people. As a social reformer he courageously kicked every sacred cow in French life: church, army, financiers, politicians, middle-class pretensions. He dramatically broke time-honoured linguistic bonds by demonstrating that a novel — *L'Assommoir* — could be written in the everyday language of the people, and be poetry at the same time. He added a new dimension to descriptive prose by integrating the environment with his characters and narrative. Any one of these innovations is an achievement that would fulfil any artist.

Only a few determined readers have ever read the twenty volumes of Zola's *Rougon-Macquart* chronicle from the first word to the last. The chronicle is not a family saga in the style of Galsworthy, nor a single narrative in twelve volumes like Anthony Powell's *The Music of Time*, nor is it a collection of loosely related tales like Balzac's *Comédie humaine*. It is, as Zola himself once put it, a vast symphony, in which individual novels are musical phrases, a superbly planned literary symphony with varying tempos and shadings and recurring themes all building up to a tremendous climax. The *Rougon-Macquart* chronicle, whatever its faults and despite its detractors, stands as one of the greatest living monuments in modern literature. Even if it did not include three undisputed masterpieces and a dozen other novels of awesome accomplishment, the *Rougon-Macquart* would still remain as an epic of creative effort that has no parallel in contemporary fiction. Much fun has been made at Zola's expense over the unarguably earnest, naïve and even stodgy methods by which he produced his books. He found writing a grim and often despairing task. The verbal fancies that flew effortlessly from the pens of lesser writers he had to grub from a quarry, and, true, sometimes it shows. But only a writer whose typewriter is often clogged with clay can fully appreciate the hellish frustration of knowing that a passage that took him a four-hour slog could have been dashed off by others with so little effort the comparison is derisory. I know how it.feels, and this may explain in part the affinity I feel with Zola.

If Zola *made* history at the close of the century by his intervention in the Dreyfus case, he was also one of its most colourful recorders. What emerges during the reading of his *Rougon-Macquart* novels is one of the most intimate and vivid pictures of Louis-Napoleon's Second Empire between 1851 and 1870 available to us today. He recorded not only the bustling, gaudy and extravagant face of this 'upstart empire' but, almost alone among writers and historians, poked about in its dungpiles and into hidden corners where the seeds of socialism and reform were germinating. Behind the creamy façades of Haussmann's rebuilt Paris flourished sordid flesh-pots and infernos of poverty so unspeakable as to make Doré's London a paradise by comparison.

The essence of an age is not necessarily best conveyed by the works of historians, who frequently fail to bridge the gap between knowledge and understanding. Zola's documentary-based fictional picture of the Second Empire, however, enables the reader not only to know but to comprehend and *feel* what life was like during that repressive regime. Only the possession of a profoundly compassionate nature could have enabled him to convey this with such force. But the novelist was also gifted with remarkable intuition. In *The Ladies' Paradise* you have the blueprint for the retail monolith, the twentieth-century department store, years before its time. In the realm of the class struggle and in the conflict between the socialist and capitalist systems, one marvels again and again at Zola's astonishing insight. He was the first Western novelist to use fiction to draw attention to the excesses of capitalism and to foresee — in *Germinal,* written in 1885 — the inevitable rise of socialism in capitalist societies and problems that have become today's political hot potatoes: the increasing deployment of terrorism for political ends, and the inherent threat to private enterprise by corporate organisations.

If Zola was called the 'poet of the cesspit' he was also the 'poet of Paris', his lyricism drawing inspiration from its marble façades to the most miserable slum streets, from its elegant department stores to its teeming markets, from the prostitutes on the boulevards to the hot-house apartments of the upper middle classes. Yes, he was a poet, often dark, violent and bitter, but just as often with a lyricism that soared beyond the real to the surreal. A poet, a supreme artist, a brilliant technician, painstaking craftsman, futurologist, reformer — Zola was all of these.

Zola was fortunate in that he found himself ideally placed to ride the crest of a literary wave of tidal proportions. When his first novel was published in 1866

se of idealism and religion
this new line of least resistance. Flaubert had demonstrated the
potential of realism, but the discoveries of Darwin and the mat
philosophy of scientific determinism added fresh justification to th
explain human behaviour in physiological rather than superr
The scientific method appealed to artists and writers, lost in th
romanticism and unreality. The painters Courbert and M
way out by following a path of scientific realism, to be fol
the prose writers, Zola among them.

But what was missing from realist fiction was th
and the imagination of earlier writers unham
and despite his original intentions this is just
Zola was a novelist of the masses and for
this new audience for fiction without

English readers were not introdu
with the publication of *L'Assomm*
The Drunkard. To readers ac
Eliot, the brutal frankness
shock to the sensibilitie
pornographer had p
not shun even ordu.
mushrooming popular.
result of a prosecution in
Thereafter, even the expu

writer. Although his early years of poverty served as a valuable apprenticeship *his sentiment* in that he stored up observations on the lives of the poor and a compassion for *is in the* the dispossessed that were to assist him later on, he was never a soldier, never a *novels* womaniser; he never knew the trials of selling one's muscle and sweat, the itch to travel, the desire to live life to the full. Havelock Ellis wrote that 'life only came to him as the sights, sounds and smells that reached his garret window. His soul seems to have been starved at the centre, and to have encamped at the sensory periphery.' Yet for all that, on the evidence of the books he left behind, his incredible broadness of vision and understanding is all the more remarkable. It was his powerful artist's vision which transformed his largely second-hand experiences into vivid, intensely personal fictions. From hazy boyhood memories of Aix-en-Provence and tourist brochures — because at the time he couldn't afford the railway fare for on-the-spot observations — he created Plassans, a town which hummed with life and intrigue in *The Conquest of Plassans*. From a garden catalogue and a visit to a horticultural show he dreamed up the abandoned, intoxicating jungle of *Le Paradou* for *The Abbé Mouret's Sin*. He never slept with a prostitute yet he breathed life into the most famous fictional courtesan of them all, *Nana*. A single descent down a coal mine was sufficient to stimulate the creation of the haunting, man-eating Voreaux in *Germinal*.

Emile Zola was also one of the great literary pioneers of the last two centuries. Because of his audacity and honesty, no subject matter was thereafter taboo to the novelist. He wrote the first major novel about the lives and plight of ordinary working people. As a social reformer he courageously kicked every sacred cow in French life: church, army, financiers, politicians, middle-class pretensions. He dramatically broke time-honoured linguistic bonds by demonstrating that a novel — *L'Assommoir* — could be written in the everyday language of the people, and be poetry at the same time. He added a new dimension to descriptive prose by integrating the environment with his characters and narrative. Any one of these innovations is an achievement that would fulfil any artist.

Only a few determined readers have ever read the twenty volumes of Zola's *Rougon-Macquart* chronicle from the first word to the last. The chronicle is not a family saga in the style of Galsworthy, nor a single narrative in twelve volumes like Anthony Powell's *The Music of Time*, nor is it a collection of loosely related tales like Balzac's *Comédie humaine*. It is, as Zola himself once put it, a vast symphony, in which individual novels are musical phrases, a superbly planned literary symphony with varying tempos and shadings and recurring themes all building up to a tremendous climax. The *Rougon-Macquart* chronicle, whatever its faults and despite its detractors, stands as one of the greatest living monuments in modern literature. Even if it did not include three undisputed masterpieces and a dozen other novels of awesome accomplishment, the *Rougon-Macquart* would still remain as an epic of creative effort that has no parallel in contemporary fiction. Much fun has been made at Zola's expense over the unarguably earnest, naïve and even stodgy methods by which he produced his books. He found writing a grim and often despairing task. The verbal fancies that flew effortlessly from the pens of lesser writers he had to grub from a quarry, and, true, sometimes it shows. But only a writer whose typewriter is often clogged with clay can fully appreciate the hellish frustration of knowing that a passage that took him a four-hour slog could have been dashed off by others with so little effort the comparison is derisory. I know how it feels, and this may explain in part the affinity I feel with Zola.

If Zola *made* history at the close of the century by his intervention in the Dreyfus case, he was also one of its most colourful recorders. What emerges during the reading of his *Rougon-Macquart* novels is one of the most intimate and vivid pictures of Louis-Napoleon's Second Empire between 1851 and 1870 available to us today. He recorded not only the bustling, gaudy and extravagant face of this 'upstart empire' but, almost alone among writers and historians, poked about in its dungpiles and into hidden corners where the seeds of socialism and reform were germinating. Behind the creamy façades of Haussmann's rebuilt Paris flourished sordid flesh-pots and infernos of poverty so unspeakable as to make Doré's London a paradise by comparison.

The essence of an age is not necessarily best conveyed by the works of historians, who frequently fail to bridge the gap between knowledge and understanding. Zola's documentary-based fictional picture of the Second Empire, however, enables the reader not only to know but to comprehend and *feel* what life was like during that repressive regime. Only the possession of a profoundly compassionate nature could have enabled him to convey this with such force. But the novelist was also gifted with remarkable intuition. In *The Ladies' Paradise* you have the blueprint for the retail monolith, the twentieth-century department store, years before its time. In the realm of the class struggle and in the conflict between the socialist and capitalist systems, one marvels again and again at Zola's astonishing insight. He was the first Western novelist to use fiction to draw attention to the excesses of capitalism and to foresee — in *Germinal*, written in 1885 — the inevitable rise of socialism in capitalist societies and problems that have become today's political hot potatoes: the increasing deployment of terrorism for political ends, and the inherent threat to private enterprise by corporate organisations.

If Zola was called the 'poet of the cesspit' he was also the 'poet of Paris', his lyricism drawing inspiration from its marble façades to the most miserable slum streets, from its elegant department stores to its teeming markets, from the prostitutes on the boulevards to the hot-house apartments of the upper middle classes. Yes, he was a poet, often dark, violent and bitter, but just as often with a lyricism that soared beyond the real to the surreal. A poet, a supreme artist, a brilliant technician, painstaking craftsman, futurologist, reformer — Zola was all of these.

Zola was fortunate in that he found himself ideally placed to ride the crest of a literary wave of tidal proportions. When his first novel was published in 1866 complex family and a crumbling empire, he is accused of not adding to our understanding of the human condition, of failing to enlarge our experience and enrich out lives. The trouble with Zola, wrote one distinguished critic, was that he was a man 'of defective sensibility, of defective intelligence...who, for all his glibness, his air of knowing all the answers...had a standard of intelligence in many respects no higher than that of a Hyde Park orator'.

In France Zola, until recently, was regarded with the deference accorded an unfashionable antique, while his position in Britain is a curious void. Although for a quarter of a century during his life he was one of the most influential, most creative writers in France, and although his continuing influence on twentieth-century fiction is undeniable, he had never cut much ice among critics and academics in this country. In textbooks and studies of French literature, when he is not ignored, he is placed in third rank, while writers of infinitely lesser talent continue to be rehabilitated. Looking for the enigmatical the literary intelligensia miss his genius for simplicity. Because his novels were bestsellers they are assumed to be shallow. Even the Marxists perversely disown him, for he tended to show man as an impossibly tiny figure, eternally helpless on the vast canvas of life. Nor was Zola ever a darling of the trendies, or of the *Zeitgeist*, an essential factor, it seems, in the apparatus of modern book publishing which increasingly ransacks the literary archives for mediocrity and allows, in the case of contemporary fiction, formidable reputations to be built on two or three overpraised novels.

The question, however, cannot be avoided; it won't go away: How many novelists in the last half-century can claim to have rivalled Zola's achievement in fiction?

Fortunately, good fiction seems to have the property of attracting readers, and it is to the public, the ordinary reader, that we owe a debt for Zola's English-language revival in the 1950s. Now, twenty years later, most of the novelist's finest work is freely available in excellent translations. In that time, many millions of readers have made the acquaintance of this outstanding literary personality. The publishers involved in the enterprise have been surprised, stunned even, by the public's appetite for Zola's fiction. *Germinal,* for example, still sells 10,000 copies a year in England alone, and has done so since 1954 — a performance few contemporary novels can match.

Why this should be so undoubtedly reflects on the novel's greatness, but as many of his lesser novels have racked up similar sales figures it is not entirely the answer. Nor is it literary fashion, for other revivals have been short-lived. Trollope, for instance, had a brief revival in the 1940s, a relapse, then a further revival in the 1970s, stimulated by a television series. Wells, Bennett and Kipling are more recently arrived ghosts, but their visitations, I suspect, will be ephemeral.

Part of the reason for Zola's enduring popularity among readers — and, interestingly, *young* readers — is that his life, and life's work, is of special relevance today. Consider, for a moment, mankind's current conditions: doubts and fears about the future; the exploitation of whole sections of society; the cruelly persistent gap between the haves and the have-nots, with wanton waste flaunted only a few jet hours away from wide-scale grinding poverty; graft and corruption in the highest places — these global symptoms may be pessimistic but they're broadly accurate.

But they are not unique to the 1970s. They are, in fact, strikingly similar to the problems that confronted thinking people in France a century ago. The search for alternative systems of government and the threat of violent overthrow have, even in solidly based societies, never been more real. This gives fresh relevance to situations Zola recounts in many of his novels and we can read of the frustrations and aspirations of his revolutionaries with more understanding than could his readers during the first half of the twentieth-century. To the average European taking a Zola novel from the lending library in the past, conspiring revolutionaries were too distant to have any impact; not any more. Other parallels abound: national financial scandals, political instability, the churches abandoned by the masses, scientists and the professionals in contradiction and confusion. The Watergate affair in the U.S. was no less a squalid national conspiracy than was the Dreyfus conspiracy of the 1890s.

Zola's answer — in the absence of a vigilant and investigative press — was to search for a literary method to help solve the problems of mankind: a daunting and possibly misguided task. His blind attachment to naturalism and utopianism has a long history of ridicule, but his intentions were humanistic. Did he discredit any trend towards a reformist fiction to the extent that it is now totally beyond recall? It would of course be wrong, in a world where reality can no longer be taken for granted, to return to an antique form like naturalism when we should be searching for a new mode of creative expression more relevant to today's needs, but I find it ironic that, where Zola used the techniques of journalism to give fiction strong links with reality, today's journalists have harnessed the techniques of fiction to widen the appeal of factual reporting.

But there is another aspect of Zola that commends itself to our age — he came giant-size in sheer effort and in the scope of his vision.

Who can fail to be thrilled by his brave and lonely undertaking? A self-imposed task spanning over twenty years of mind-numbing application? Isn't that what we want today — the literary hero? But where is the grandness? Where are today's marvellous literary memorials to a lifetime's generosity of time and talent?

And then, perhaps Zola's naturalist and determinist philosophies aren't so *passé* after all. Since his death literature has, like the other arts, undergone an intensive period of experimentation, of reaching towards some ultimate. This will, of course, never cease. But from any contemporary viewpoint, fiction has reached a baffling, if temporary, dead-end.

The modern novel is light-years apart from realism, as much the product of the university-trained mind as was the pre-realist fiction of the eighteenth-century. The novels that win most critical praise today are not the relevant, well-researched and competently crafted books that occasionally crack through the academic apparatus to become bestsellers, but trivial, bewildering soliloquies in which the characters perform in a hazy limbo; the settings are indeterminate, the thoughts are commonplace and the speech has little touch with reality. One has only to read reviews of novels for a few months to arrive at the conclusion that a competently written novel which spun an interesting narrative around some current social problem or other would be very speedily dispatched with the critical bullet. The critically praised novels, and those that win the prizes, are invariably those that baffle and frustrate the reader, thus further endangering the species. The number of novels in the past decade which have won some prize or award, achieved a sale of less than 10,000, and have then been forgotten, is surely high enough to demand a reappraisal of the fiction critic's place in today's society. If they claim to influence literary standards then they must accept responsibility.

But not all. Writers of original fiction are themselves probably less in command of their craft and traditions than at any time during the past couple of hundred years, preferring retirement in which to contemplate the dangling carrot of a hoped-for bestseller which will send them off on a flight from the taxman. From the moment they finish a manuscript their affairs are in the hands of agents, publishers, editors, accountants, critics and publicists. Their withdrawal from the hurly-burly of publishing is almost complete; their feeble voices impotent against the wall of economic and academic judgement.

With a large proportion of contemporary novelists alienated from their potential audience by their preoccupation with technique and style, and the polarization of critical and public taste, it is illuminating to review the work of a writer who was, for many years, the world's best-selling novelist. Emile Zola's achievement is many-faceted. His books were so closely linked to the people and the social movements of his time that his work is a living mirror, surpassing in interest and objectivity most accounts of the second half of the nineteenth-century produced by historians. The majority of his novels are characterised by fascinating, gripping narratives which, whether in the original, translated, hacked about or bowdlerised, held the interest of millions of people of all classes, and still do. Yet there was no lack of craft, style or invention in his work; he explored new literary frontiers and at least three of his bestsellers are timeless masterpieces of fiction.

Has the shock value of Zola's frank language been completely dissipated by the effects of contemporary liberation, when in what many might call an excess of frankness readers can view, in their living-room, a human being killed, a woman giving birth, simulated fornication – in addition to any amount of good, wholesome smut? Certainly it must be difficult for today's reader to appreciate the explosive impact his ruthless exposés made on a society conditioned to live in ignorance of injustice, vice and all kinds of inhumanity. Zola diagnosed the

easier than to appreciate the demographics of this injustice, complaints of his society and slashed great holes in the illusory curtains hung up by the middle classes, using anything but genteel language. Then it was easy to ignore a poor, crushed and inarticulate laundress on the streets, but almost impossible to ignore Zola's story about her. But it is to his eternal credit, and a measure of the power of his artistic insight, that his account of Gervaise in *L'Assommoir* is no less harrowing, his chronicle of the miners in *Germinal* no less chilling, his story of Serge and Albine in *The Abbe Mouret's Sin* no less thought-provoking today than they were a century ago. And for the linguistic liberation we enjoy today not a little of the credit is owed to Emile Zola.

This study is mainly based on the English translations of Zola's works. It is primarily written for those readers who do not know French or who, knowing some French, prefer, as I do, to read a good translation rather than to read the original, more slowly and somewhat laboriously. Relying largely on translations has sharpened my awareness of their variable quality, and this book features, for the first time I believe, a comprehensive listing of all the principal English-language translations of the novels published in Britain and America from 1878 to the present day, together with comparative comments on their readability and faithfulness to the original.

Generally, I have avoided the use of French wherever possible, and the titles of all the novels have been rendered into English throughout the book. A standardised list of these titles will be found at the end of this Introduction, while alternative published titles may be found in Chapter 22.

I have used a great many excerpts and passages from the novels to illustrate various points, but hope their inclusion will be additionally justified by the pleasure I'm sure they will give the reader. Each excerpt is followed by a number in parenthesis; by referring to this number in the listing of translations in Chapter 22 the translation may be identified. For example (40) appearing below an excerpt indicates that it is the translation of *L'Assommoir* by L.W. Tancock, done in 1970, and published by Penguin Books Ltd in London and New York.

To have footnoted the hundreds of references involved in the writing of this work would have, to my mind, imposed an unnecessary burden on the general reader for whom this book is intended. I trust to be allowed the favour of acknowledging my considerable debt to previous Zola biographers, critics and researchers collectively in the bibliographical notes at the end of this volume.

Graham King
September, 1977
London

The Novels of Emile Zola

The purpose of this list of Zola's novels is to establish *standardised* English-language titles for each of them, by which they will be referred throughout this book. Many of the novels have alternative titles which are given in the comprehensive list in Chapter 22. This list gives the date of original publication in France, the original French title, and the standard English title.

Early Novels

1865	*La Confession de Claude*	*Claude's Confessions*
1866	*Le Voeu d'une morte*	*A Dead Woman's Wish*
1867	*Les Mystères de Marseille*	*Mysteries of Marseilles*
1867	*Thérèse Raquin*	*Thérèse Raquin*
1868	*Madeleine Férat*	*Madeleine Férat*

The Rougon-Macquart Chronicle

1871	*La Fortune des Rougon*	*The Fortune of the Rougons*
1872	*La Curée*	*The Kill*
1873	*Le Ventre de Paris*	*The Belly of Paris*
1874	*La Conquête de Plassans*	*The Conquest of Plassans*
1875	*La Faute de l'abbé Mouret*	*The Abbé Mouret's Sin*
1876	*Son Excellence Eugène Rougon*	*His Excellency*
1877	*L'Assommoir*	*L'Assommoir*
1878	*Une Page d'amour*	*A Love Episode*
1880	*Nana*	*Nana*
1882	*Pot-Bouille*	*Piping Hot!*
1883	*Au Bonheur des dames*	*The Ladies' Paradise*
1884	*La Joie de vivre*	*Joy of Life*
1885	*Germinal*	*Germinal*
1886	*L'Oeuvre*	*The Masterpiece*
1887	*La Terre*	*Earth*
1888	*Le Rêve*	*The Dream*
1890	*La Bête humaine*	*The Beast in Man*

1891	*L'Argent*	*Money*
1892	*La Débâcle*	*The Debacle*
1893	*Le Docteur Pascal*	*Doctor Pascal*

The Three Cities Trilogy

1894	*Lourdes*	*Lourdes*
1896	*Rome*	*Rome*
1898	*Paris*	*Paris*

The Four Gospels Tetralogy

1899	*Fécondité*	*Fruitfulness*
1901	*Travail*	*Labour*
1903	*Vérité*	*Truth*
—	*Justice (unwritten)*	*Justice*

Other Works

1864	*Contes à Ninon*	*Stories for Ninon*
1874	*Nouveaux Contes à Ninon*	*New Stories for Ninon*
1866	*Mes haines*	*My Hates*
1880	*Le Roman expérimental*	*The Experimental Novel*

1

Casting the Mould

A biographer searching for some portentous trivia associated with the birth of his subject is saved, in the case of Emile Edouard Charles Antoine Zola, a good deal of trouble. The future novelist was born in Paris on 2 April 1840, in a fourth-floor apartment at 10 Rue Saint-Joseph, a narrow street of bookshops, publishers and newspaper offices, and on the site of an old cemetery reputed to contain the remains of Molière and La Fontaine. The little furnished flat was dark and noisy and the emergence of the infant, pale and underweight, was accompanied by the yells of the newsvendors below as the papers ran their afternoon editions. It was an appropriate backdrop for the first appearance of the boy who, fifty years later, would be described as a 'river of ink'. Within six weeks the baby had been baptised and vaccinated, parental tributes to religion and science; in due course their son was to attack one and embrace the other.

For several months it was touch and go, and in an effort to improve the baby's sickly condition he was wet-nursed by a woman at Dourdan, his mother's birthplace. At two he contracted meningitis and at three he was still so frail his parents were unable to take him with them when they moved to the Provençal town of Aix, where François Zola, his father, had plans to build a canal.

François – formerly Francesco – Zola was a man of many talents, an unpredictable romantic, impetuous and energetic, and a footloose adventurer. His family origins were Venetian and Dalmatian, and his ancestors had followed either soldiering or religion; one distant forbear, Giovanni Battista Zolla of Brescia, was a saint and martyr. None of the Zolla or Zola family appear to have been sons of the soil, which is curious, for the surname literally means 'clod of earth'. François's mother was an intruder from Corfu, an island of sailors, which may have accounted for his wanderlust.

As a young subaltern in the Venetian army, François's early travels were hardly by choice, and when Venetia was annexed by Austria in 1815 he abandoned the army for engineering. At about this time, too, he discovered another talent: writing. Although this flair was confined to technical works, one engineering treatise did win him a nomination for the Royal Academy of Padua.

But the military blood in François's veins still ran strong and he found

1

himself, in his late thirties, a lieutenant in the newly created Foreign Legion in Algeria. Although he served satisfactorily, he resigned under a cloud. Now an acting quartermaster, he had fallen heavily for the wife of a German legionnaire and, at her suggestion, had 'borrowed' 1,500 francs from the till of the company store. He'd intended to replace the money but his mistress had other plans, and embarked with it on a repatriation ship to Germany. To make matters worse the distracted François attempted suicide by drowning, but whether the impulse was from his lost love or the missing money his superiors could never establish. In the event he was exonerated, but the incident marked the end of his military career.

In 1833 the ex-soldier arrived in Marseilles, and returned to his professional calling of civil engineer. There he conceived the idea of constructing a new harbour, and laboured for three years on the plans only to be turned down by the authorities after months of fruitless lobbying. François's visionary imagination soon overcame the effects of this disappointment, however, and he turned his attentions to the water supply problems of Aix, the ancient capital of Provence, eighteen miles north of Marseilles. Once the headquarters of the Romans in Gaul, Aix was a somnolent oasis in the centre of a hot plain, a mile or so from the River Arc. For 800 years the town had been the scene of endless battles between Romans, Teutons, Visigoths, Franks, Lombards and Saracens, all fighting at various times for control of the only water supply in the region.

By the early nineteenth century Aix was a very parched town during summer. It had now grown to be an important centre of trade and industry of about 25,000 people, yet still relied on three ancient fountains, two of which dried to a trickle during the frequent droughts. François soon saw that by building a series of dams in the nearby hills and linking them to the town by a system of canals, Aix could have as much water as it wanted, right through the driest summers. It was an ingenious scheme and therefore strange that, when the engineer announced his plans to supply Aix with permanent water, he met with unexpected opposition. If the provincial Frenchman of his day was conservative, the Provençal Frenchman was totally inert. It took a man of François's tireless energy to overcome the municipal stonewalling to form the company that would build the dams and canal, the *Société du Canal Zola*. But before work could begin, planning permission had to be obtained from a dozen different authorities – a nightmare jungle of patronage, favours, graft and greed. Prime Minister Thiers was a great help – Aix was his home town – but his influence waxed and waned according to whether his government was in or out of office. Then there were the landowners, suspicious and grasping; each had to be approached for permission to allow the canal through their property; and, finally, money had to be raised.

All this inevitably took François to Paris where, while waiting for the complicated negotiations to be completed, he designed an earth-moving machine to help build the new fortifications around the city. Its success won him some helpful patronage among government ministers, but a hundred details were still bogged down in Provence. During his five-year stay in Paris about the only piece of luck to come his way was nineteen-year-old Emilie-Aurélie Aubert, whom he met and married in 1838. Emile was born two years later and the family finally settled down in Aix in 1843.

After eight years of negotiation, plans for the Zola Canal were finally accepted, and blasting actually commenced late in 1846. Six months later its creator was dead with pleurisy. 'The treacherous mistral', one contemporary writer put it, 'smote him with her icy hands.' It was a bitterly cold March day and on a rush coach trip to Marseilles François had begun to cough. On reaching the Hôtel de la Méditerranée he collapsed, weakened no doubt by previous bouts of recurring malaria. Emilie was sent for and arrived the next day with Emile. In a few days it was all over, but the waiting, in that strange room, with the tumultuous life of the bustling port going on outside as though nothing was happening, made such a lasting impression on the child that the memory of it was evoked, many years later, in *A Love Episode*:

> Her husband's illness, which was to prove fatal, had developed quite suddenly, the day after their arrival, just as they were about to go out together. She knew not a single street, she could not even have said in what district she was living; and for a whole week she had stayed shut up with the dying man, listening to the roar of the Paris traffic under her windows, feeling as lonely, as forsaken, as utterly lost as if she were in the depths of a wilderness. When she had set foot outside again for the first time, she was a widow. The thought of that great bare room, full of medicine bottles and unpacked trunks, still sent a shudder running through her. (45)

Back in Aix several days later, six-year-old Emile was the chief mourner at the elaborate funeral. He had little idea of where the strange procession was going, and certainly no idea of the misfortunes ahead of him. A daguerreotype taken of him at this time captures a solemn, plump-faced little boy in a velvet suit, full-lipped and with one eye raised slightly above the other, a legacy of the attack of meningitis which almost killed him three years before. The face in the photograph reflects none of the confusion of influences and incidents that had intruded into his six years. He was obsessively shy, and lisped, an impediment François had tried to correct with long coaching lessons on his knee; otherwise Emile hardly knew his father, who was absent from their big house in the Impasse Sylvacanne more often than not. It was in this house, just before his father's death, that Emile was the victim of homosexual molestation by a young servant. The facts of this incident, which was the subject of a Marseilles police report made out in 1845, were completely unknown until 1929 when the report was accidentally discovered in the police archives and then deliberately and sensationally disclosed. The servant, a twelve-year-old Algerian youth named Mustapha, was committed for indecent conduct with Emile. The experience can only have added to the child's insecurity and feelings of confusion after his father's death. Later in his life Zola was to allude to experiences of homosexuality at his school in Aix – probably some form of schoolboy initiation – but the sum of these experiences scarred him with a violent loathing for any activity of a homosexual nature, a scar still evident in the very last novel he wrote.

After the death of François the *Société du Canal Zola* was manipulated into liquidation, its assets acquired cheaply by one of the original financiers, and refloated as a new company. The construction of the scheme went ahead, as the Canal d'Aix, based on François's plans, but Madame Zola, along with all the other shareholders, received nothing. Although quite blameless in the affair she had to cope not only with penury but with abuse from the shareholders and creditors as well. The swindle was to affect Emile for most of his life and two of his Rougon-Macquart novels deal exclusively and bitterly with property speculators and financial sharks.

The Zolas were forced to move to the poorer part of Aix, where the bewildered boy became an innocent pawn in his mother's grim refusal to come to terms with their new poverty. Humiliated, Madame Zola resolved not to be degraded to the level of her destitute neighbours, mostly labourers, gypsies and assorted foreigners. The humble house was kept secure against dirt, dust, gossip and other children. The family had few friends and vistors were rare. The household now included Madame Zola's father and mother, the latter from hard-as-nails peasant stock and by many accounts a daunting character; even at seventy she had not a single grey hair on her head. It was a gloomy Borstal-like place for Emile, but to his mother the home was an island of manners and culture in a threatening sea infested with ignorance and strong drink. The effect of all this on the lonely boy cannot be underestimated. The son of a foreigner, he was discouraged from playing with the local children, and constantly admonished to study his schoolbooks. He lived in an atmosphere of rancour and hate and, not surprisingly, eventually came to despise the neighbours himself. Doubtless he began to think of himself as somebody special, for he was constantly lectured on his responsibilities in preparation for his future role of family breadwinner. All the while the circumstances of their downfall ate into his mother's pride like a canker. She grew bitter at any thought or mention of their former bourgeois neighbours, who still enjoyed their confortable, respectable lives. And the Zolas' new neighbours, outraged by the family's lofty condescensions, effectively completed their isolation.

With our knowledge of Zola's childhood years, it is tempting to see his great achievement in maturity not as the result of random accidents of fate, but as a logical progression of circumstances of the kind he could quite easily have fictionalised in one of his novels. Zola's father, despite his enormous energy and great talents, was a failure – although it would be more accurate to describe him as downright unlucky. He was largely ignored throughout his life, and his sudden death plunged his widow and young son into a poverty they were ill-equipped to cope with. At six, Emile's dreams and hopes were abruptly transformed into realities and disillusionment. Through his father he became sharply aware of what it was like to be denied due recognition and success. The forced move from the comfortable, rambling, rose-covered house in the Impasse Sylvacanne, with its great garden and pleasant, mellow streets, to the wrong side of the tracks in Aix, must have demonstrated to the boy the material consequences of failure in the eyes of society. It is interesting that an analysis of

Zola's fictional fathers, who appear as characters in his novels, reveals few if any who are 'ideal' in the sense of fulfilling their parental obligations. When they are not improvident and irresponsible they either leave home, become ill, go mad, commit suicide or die. Nor do any of Zola's fictional fathers resemble his own in any way, with the exception of those who die early, leaving orphans. Pauline is such an orphan in *Joy of Life*; Angélique, in *The Dream*; Sandoz's wife, in *The Masterpiece*; and the heroines of two early novels, *Therese Raquin* and *Madeleine Ferat*, are both orphans. The pattern is so consistent that it must be ascribed to the author's refusal – for the greater part of his life – to come to terms with the facts about his father's bad luck, which Zola equated with failure. In this, of course, he is being less than fair to his father's unusual potential, for only his untimely death robbed him of certain success, considerable wealth and widespread recognition. Early in his career Zola campaigned for and won a belated and grudging recognition, but from his correspondence the motive was not so much to honour his father's memory as to extract revenge from the ungrateful and unjust authorities of his own suffering as a child. The episode left an indelible mark on Emile; what he feared most of all throughout his life was failure. However irrational his reasoning, he knew all about its dire consequences.

It was no consolation to young Emile that he was spoiled; in fact he was almost deified by his mother as the future saviour who would restore the family fortunes. He was kept indoors like a valuable pet and only with reluctance was he finally dispatched to school at the age of seven, when he still didn't know the alphabet. At the Pension Notre-Dame, a small preparatory school, he was placed in the care of a Monsieur Isoard, who imparted kindliness to the boy but very little else. But Emile soon proved to be an inquisitive child, and while lagging in his lessons was active and full of initiative; what he really excelled at was playing hookey and wandering in the fields on the outskirts of the town. In contrast to the exciting days when his father was alive, his days now were dull and disciplined. When he wrote, in *Claude's Confessions*, 'My years at school were years of tears' he was probably referring to this period.

As Emile entered his teens his education became Madame Zola's major preoccupation. Her long-standing claims for compensation for her husband's canal scheme were eventually settled in part, and with this money and a bursary, and by moving to an even smaller house in the centre of the town, she was just able to send the boy to the Collège Bourbon, a local high school. Although Emile's scholastic record was studded with numerous prizes and distinctions, the standards of the school were, by some accounts, rather indifferent, and the lack of a really sound education was to plague Zola in various ways for the rest of his life. The school, with perhaps a few changes, is described in a passage from *The Masterpiece*.

> First it was the school itself they talked about; the mouldering ex-convent stretching away up to the town ramparts; its two playgrounds with their huge plane trees; the muddy pond covered with green slime in which they had learned to swim; the downstairs classrooms where the damp ran down the walls; the refectory that

always reeked of cooking and washing-up water; the juniors' dormitory, known as 'the chamber of horrors', and the sick-bay with its gentle, soothing nuns in their black habits and white coifs! What a to-do there'd been when Sister Angèle, the one who played such havoc with the hearts of the seniors, ran away with Hermeline, the fat boy in the top form who was so much in love that he used deliberately to cut his fingers so as to be able to go up and have her dress them for him! (70)

At first Emile's performance was spectacular, and his mother must have glowed with pride when he carried off five prizes at the end of his first year. This was of no particular importance to the boy, however. Having established the fact that he was capable of brilliance he promptly resumed the daydreaming which had characterised his years at the junior school. He began to write, preferring creation to memorising lessons. Many successful authors have remembered their first schoolboy attempts at writing: usually short stories, tentative essays in the expression of their personal feelings, eight-line poems and so on. Not so with Zola, who, typically as it later turned out, began with a full-scale romantic novel set in the Middle Ages. The manuscript, like almost everything he wrote in his lifetime, still exists, but it is impossible to evaluate its worth because it is completely illegible. But it wasn't the unexpected academic success nor the emerging urge to write that made his years at the Bourbon so enjoyable; for the first time in his life, Emile had *friends*!

During the early months of his first year at the college he had suffered the cruel mocking of the other students, who made fun of his foreign-sounding accent, shortsightedness and puny size. Pale, meek and subservient, Emile badly needed a protector, and his life changed dramatically when one finally turned up at his side: Paul Cézanne. Paul, older, bigger and stronger than most of the other boys, was the answer to Emile's wistful prayers. He possessed a range of invective and used it with peasant bluntness. He was moody and occasionally violent, and more than a match for any school bully. The two were soon inseparable, and when they were joined by another friend, Baptistin Baille, the trio became known as the 'Three Inseparables'. For each of them this friendship was to have lasting value and significance. Some indication of the happy new dimension it added to the boy's life is reflected in a passage from *The Masterpiece* in which Sandoz (Zola) and Claude (Cézanne) are recounting some of the practical jokes they played during their schooldays.

Next they talked about the 'rags' and those ridiculous practical jokes the memory of which could still reduce them to helpless mirth. Oh, the morning when they lit the stove with the boots of the boy who used to supply the whole class with snuff, 'Bones-the-Day-Boy', otherwise known as 'Death-warmed-Up', he was so thin! And that winter evening when they stole the matches from the chapel to smoke dried chestnut leaves in their home-made pipes. It was Sandoz who did it, and he now admitted how scared he had been as he scrambled down from the choir in the dark. Then there was the day Claude tried roasting hornets in the bottom of his desk, because he had heard they were good to eat that way, and filled the place with such dense, acrid smoke that the usher had dashed in with a water-jug, thinking the desk was on fire. The onion fields they had robbed when out on school walks, and the windows they had broken and thought themselves very smart if the damaged pane looked anything like a map in the atlas; Greek lessons printed in large letters on the blackboard and rattled off by all the dunces without the master discovering how they did it; the playground benches sawn off and carried like corpses round the pond, in a

6

long procession, complete with dirges. This last affair had been a great joke. Dubuche, as the priest, had slipped into the pond when he tried to fill his cap with 'holy' water. But the best joke of all, and the funniest, was the time when Pouillaud tied all the dormitory chamber-pots to one long string and then in the morning – it was the last day of term – raced along the corridor and down three flights of stairs dragging this long trail of domestic china clanking and smashing itself to atoms in his wake!   (70)

The trio also found common ground in the countryside, and tramped for miles, observing, declaiming poetry, reading, planning and even composing plays, poems and short stories of their own. One – by the sixteen-year-old Emile – survives: *La Fée amoureuse*, a sentimental love story which was later published in the collection, *Stories for Ninon*. On these weekend jaunts into the Provençal countryside, wandering across fields of baked, red earth, up the slopes of stony hills and through forests of thorny scrub, the trio would sometimes swim in one of the mountain streams, afterwards lying naked on the sandy banks under the hot sun. Cézanne would often take a sketchbook with him, filling it with impressions of the varied landscape, while Emile's pocket would frequently bulge with a volume of romantic verse. Again, from *The Masterpiece*, Zola fondly recalls these carefree days:

> In summer especially their dream was the Viorne, the mountain torrent that waters the low-lying meadows of Plassans. When they were about twelve they had a passion for playing about in the deeper portions of the stream; they swam like fish and would spend whole days, stark naked, lying on the burning sand, then diving back into the water, spending hours grubbing for water-plants or watching for eels. They practically lived in the river, and the combination of pure water and sunshine seemed to prolong their childhood, so that even when they were already young men they still sounded like a trio of laughing urchins as they ambled back into Plassans on a sultry July evening after a day on the river.... The memory of those country walks always brought tears to their eyes. They went along the long white roads once more, roads covered with dust like a thick fall of snow and ringing with the tramp of their heavy boots; they cut across the fields again and roamed for miles where the soil was rusty-red with iron deposits, and there was not a cloud in the sky, not a shadow, apart from stunted olive trees and the sparse foliage of almonds. They recalled their homecomings, the delicious sense of weariness, their boasting about having walked even farther than last time, the thrill it gave them to feel they were carried over the ground by sheer momentum, their bodies spurred into action and their minds lulled into numbness by some outrageous army ditty.   (70)

So cramped by his mother, so repressed by her disciplinary regime, Emile must have experienced a sense of soaring relief during his hikes in the fields and hills around Aix. His dormant senses reeled at the delights that surrounded him – the sights and the smells, the rich sensual feel of dank grass, the hot excitement of a sun-parched rock, or the dazzle of scorched fields shimmering into the distance... the acrid odour of a disturbed bog, the fugitive smell of advancing rain on the wind... the menacing rumble of distant thunder. One spot, the narrow Infernet Gorge near his father's canal, had a particular fascination for him, with its rugged, sun-hardened cliffs and deep clefts like cutlass scars, remote and silent and disturbed only by the calls of hovering eagles. From here he could observe the effects of light on the patterned plain around Aix, and his emerging visual awareness delighted in the ever-changing atmospheric effects. The cloud shapes and their shadows on the rolling landscape, the morning mists and distant dust-drifts which hazily formed and reformed during hot afternoons, all this, with his discovery of Hugo, Musset and Lamartine, gave wings to his romantic imagination. It was like a school for the senses, and it is thus no accident that Zola's mature writing is imbued with an unusually vivid feeling for atmosphere.

Away from his home, in the down-at-heel streets of the poor district through which he hurried, in the hot fields of the countryside, Emile must have been shocked at the explicit goings-on of the Provençal peasantry. His mother's constant moralising and her gentle, sexless affection were no preparation for a chance encounter with a couple copulating in the hay, or, for that matter, a planned encounter between bull and cow. With a maternally induced innocence, youthful romantic ideals and his own retarded though dawning sexuality, Emile's mind must have at times been in considerable conflict when grappling with the realities of procreation and promiscuity. In letters written several years later to Cézanne and Baille, it is clear that he idealised love in the form of a girl he'd admired distantly in Aix; in his cold room in the Latin Quarter of Paris he warmed himself with memories of her, and dreamed... although not, apparently, of physical contact. 'I turn my eyes from the dungheap', he wrote, 'to rest them on the roses. I prefer roses, useless though they are.' An illustration of a young girl accompanying a *La Revue Illustrée* article published in 1887 entitled, 'Emile Zola's First Love', appears to identify the object of Zola's youthful affections as Louise Solari, the sister of sculptor Philippe Solari, one of the future novelist's companions. As an extremely shy young man, with his foreign-sounding speech, it is probable that Emile was something of a joke among the girls of Aix, rather than an object of their desire. Provençal courtship began, by tradition, as a dusk affair; the lovestruck couple were nevertheless expected to keep walking. Merely sitting down on a park bench could be construed as seduction. Unfortunately Emile's yearning for even this upright form of love's endeavour was more cerebral than real, although the frequent sight of the heavily cloaked couples no doubt sent him into endless fits of romantic dreaming. These ambiguous frustrations, these confused, ignored cries from the well-springs of his sexuality, were the source of much of the sexual imagery, erotic and overwrought, that was to be a compelling and sometimes disturbing feature of his mature writing.

At seventeen a great turning point came in Emile's life. The small settlement from the Canal Company had been spent on his schooling and the family resources were now exhausted, forcing yet another move, this time to a dingy, two-roomed cottage in the Rue Mazarine. Then Madame Aubert, his grandmother, suddenly died. Misery and distress now stared the small family in the face. To Madame Zola it was unthinkable that they should sink any lower on the social scale of Aix and, stifling her pride, she went to Paris in a desperate attempt to seek help from any of her husband's former patrons she could find. It wasn't easy, but at last, in February 1858, she wrote to Emile instructing him to sell the furniture for whatever it would fetch and come at once to Paris, with her aged father.

The money from the sale of the family's remaining chattels barely covered two third-class coach tickets to Paris for Emile and his grandfather. It was a depressing time for the boy, his life brutally disrupted for the second time. He'd been to Paris only once before, to stay with his Uncle Adolphe in one of the poor parts of the city. It had been frightening and exciting, but after the drabness of the narrow, crowded streets, and the noise, the stink and the poverty, he had been glad to return to the hot, open fields around Aix. Now, glimpsed through the grimy windows of the coach, it was all slipping away, this beautiful countryside he'd grown to love and understand, his childhood and boyhood, his friends and the deep security of the only real friendship he'd ever known – all to be exchanged for the unknown terrors of the great northern city.

After a long and uncomfortable journey, Emile arrived in Paris on a bleak February day in 1858 to rejoin his mother. Immediately, they moved into a shabby hotel at 63 Rue Monsieur-le-Prince, a few doors away, strangely enough, from the house in which Oliver Wendell Holmes had studied medicine thirty years before. From the scruffy Latin Quarter neighbourhood Zola wandered wide-eyed across the Seine to the north, where spectacular wonders were taking shape. Paris of the late 1850s was an old body on an operating table, convulsing in shock from the savagery of the surgery being undertaken upon it. The ruthless repression of Louis-Napoleon's Second Empire, founded seven years before, was partly disguised by great Exhibitions and magnificent ceremonies and especially by the rebuilding and transformation of Paris into a modern metropolis, with new avenues wide enough to take a marching army; parks, squares and bridges; and row upon row of splendid houses and public buildings. The activity was feverish and its excitement infectious. Vast areas of old Paris were being destroyed to conform to the ideas of Barón Haussmann, the master planner. Thousands of families in the poorer districts lost their homes and shops; a hundred thousand labourers toiled among the rubble; thousands of speculators, attracted by the billions of francs involved, made fortunes overnight. The capital seethed with action, graft and corruption. And Emile was stunned by it all.

Through his father's friends Madame Zola managed to secure a place for her son at the Lycée St Louis on the Boulevard St Michel, a two-minute walk from their new apartment. There, Emile was to study for the *baccalaureat*, or Bachelor of Arts diploma, which was the passport to a university and the professions. But he couldn't cog into the academic machinery, preferring to read George Sand, Rabelais and Montaigne than listen to the lectures. With the exception of French composition he found the course impossibly difficult; the prize-winner from Aix was now a dunce.

Emile's only respite from his slum surroundings and the drudgery of school was his correspondence with Cézanne and Baille in Aix. He exchanged poems with them. Cézanne's lines were robust and lusty, while Emile's were fragile and pretentious, as in a poem, *To My Friend Paul*, proclaiming that his friendship with Cézanne – who at the time was discovering the charms of young women – was superior to any love he might have for the opposite sex. Part of it reads:

> But though my worthless hands, sweet-scented crown,
> Did not for a loved one weave your flowers,
> If I've not intertwined capricious verses
> To draw a passing smile from two bright eyes,
> My humble garland, it's that I elect
> One heart before the heart of a lady fair,
> A noble and kind heart, on which this day
> I set you, a brief comfort in his trials.
> Go forth and find my friend. His manly chest
> I place above a frivolous bosom.
> You will gleam brighter on his coat of black
> Than among the jewels of an enchanting corsage.

The young poet expressed his feelings rather more satisfactorily by actually journeying to Aix to see his friends during the summer holidays. For two months the trio wandered over the hills and among the groves of olives and almonds, swimming whenever possible in the River Arc, drinking vermouth and talking interminably of their literary and artistic ambitions. For Emile, the holiday provided one of the most delightful memories of his life.

Soon after his return to Paris he fell dangerously ill with encephalitis. For several days he was delirious, followed by weeks of painful recovery during which his mouth was so ulcerated he couldn't speak. His convalescence took two months, but in a well-tended sickbed, in a world of caressing daydreams, it also afforded an escape from the pressing problems which at times threatened to overcome him. Unfortunately his long absence from school and general disinterest in his studies culminated in his failing the *baccalauréat* examination. Concerned at his personal contribution to his mother's money worries, he decided to skip a year's classes and try for the diploma anyway. On the first day of the Sorbonne examination he began well, effortlessly flying through the physics, chemistry and mathematics papers. But calamity awaited him the next day, which was devoted to oral tests in languages and literature. Emile not only failed, he failed miserably. So, apparently, did his memory and his nerves. The date of the death of Charlemagne, a date which every French schoolboy must know, eluded him. He stumbled, numb-lipped, through the German reading test. And a confused misinterpretation of a simple La Fontaine fable eventually ended the painful interview with the examining professor. Emile Zola received an *O* for literature.

Two months later, in November, he tried again, this time at the University of Marseilles. His performance was even more lamentable, failing so badly in the written tests that he abandoned the oral. He must have returned to Paris with a heavy heart. In a letter to Paul Cézanne he mourns: 'I failed to complete my studies; I can't even speak good French; I'm a total ignoramus!' His mother had been forced to move to an even more squalid apartment, a tiny attic in the Rue Saint-Jacques, where the water in the bedroom jug froze on winter nights. He was nineteen, penniless, in a city he neither knew nor liked, without friends, without qualifications, connections or prospects. And knowing that all his mother's sacrifices had been in vain was a weight he could hardly bear. He was even more depressed about the position which was eventually found for him by an old friend of his father's. Desperate for some link with literature he had tried to apprentice himself to a printer, but without success. Now, he trudged daily to the customs offices by the docks to a clerical job at sixty francs a month, which barely paid for his boot leather.

It was either the end, or the most humiliating of beginnings, he couldn't tell which. He could only see blackness. 'I am destined to rot on the straw of an office chair,' he wrote to Cézanne...

2

Dream World

On 16 April 1860, Zola wrote again to Cézanne, in an even more despairing tone.

> My new life is monotony itself. I go to the office at 9 a.m. and until 4 make records of customs declarations, copy correspondence, etc. – or rather I read the newspaper, yawn, pace up and down, etc., etc. All very sad. But the moment I leave, I shake myself like a wet bird, light my pipe, breathe, live. I turn over in my mind long poems, long dramas, long novels. I wait for summer that I might find an outlet for my creative spirit. Good God! I want to publish a volume of poetry and dedicate it to you.

But it wasn't only the boredom that was getting Zola down. Despite his job he was still dependent on his mother. Of his sixty francs a month, his small hotel room took a third, meals were a franc apiece, and his personal needs and clothing took forty francs. Only her meagre weekly hand-outs enabled him to survive, and he was both deeply troubled and humiliated. At one stage he even considered joining the army for the 1,500 francs bounty so that he might repay her.

He was equally dependent on his friends in Aix for the survival of his spirit. 'Since my arrival in Paris I haven't had a moment's happiness,' he told Cézanne. 'I see nobody and sit by my fireplace with my sad thoughts, sometimes with my fine dreams. But now and again I'm cheerful; that's when I think of you and Baille. I know that whatever our situation, we'll treasure the same sentiments, and that consoles me.'

For two months he endured the mental paralysis brought on by the long hours at a desk calculating dues on bills of lading and adding up figures, then left. The job at the customs office by the Canal St Martin had been a disaster, and also a warning; at times he'd felt like a drowning man and fought as though his very life was at stake. He became intensely annoyed with Baille, who had accused him of failing to come to grips with reality and to aim at some kind of career. Baille had also made some disparaging remarks about Emile's poetic aspirations. 'You call them crazy,' Zola replied, 'and claim that you won't be so foolish as to expire in some attic merely for applause, as poets do.' Later, he took the conservative Baille to task again. 'The word *position* occurs several times in your letters, and it makes me angry... Those eight letters have the touch of the prosperous grocer about them... Are you really sincere? Do you no longer dream of liberty?... Are all your aspirations limited by material success?' In Paris, Emile was surrounded by the results of the rat race, 'insignificant, dull people', and with a perception astonishing for his age realised that to capitulate to society's pressures at this stage would spell the end of his dreams and ambitions. As it was, he could hardly escape the feeling that life was passing him by as though he didn't matter. Paris was in the grip of rebuilding fever, railway madness and speculating mania, and throbbed like a giant engine. The European power game was in full swing: in a series of lightning moves Austria attacked Sardinia, France attacked Austria, Prussia mobilised against France, which won Nice and Savoy; France and England declared war on China, Spain went to war against Morocco; Garibaldi marched into Naples, Victor Emmanuel invaded the Papal States and Christians were massacred in Syria; in the New World, Abraham Lincoln was elected President of the United States. It is doubtful whether this martial mayhem made any impression on the young man, immersed in his own troubles, but he could not but have been affected by the burgeoning mood of advance and discovery: Darwin's *Origin of Species*, Mill's *On Liberty* and Marx's *Criticism of the Political Economy* were all published in 1859, as were Dickens's *Tale of Two Cities* and George Eliot's *Adam Bede*. Until now he had suffered a life of rigorously enforced respectability in a household dominated by two women where sex and drink were taboo; his domestic imprisonment and his own shyness had severely limited social contact. But within him was stirring a greedy, unsatisfied appetite for life, and his energies and ambitions sought some outlet. To Cézanne he confided, 'I dreamed the other day that I had written a beautiful book, a magnificent book, which you had illustrated with your beautiful, magnificent drawings. Our names gleamed in golden letters, united on the title page, a brotherhood of genius inseparable in posterity. Sadly, it is still only a dream.'

Soon, Zola was quite alone; his mother was forced to move to a boarding-house and he was left to fend off imminent starvation by himself. His lodgings became poorer and his possessions, as he pawned them, fewer. He began to be a regular visitor to the local *mont-de-piété*, exchanging anything he could spare for cash. Now a victim of the most extreme poverty, living only to exist through the day and another night, he sank into a stupor of the kind George Orwell described so vividly in his *Down and Out in Paris and London*. Living on bread and watery soup, occasionally a penny piece of pork, Zola drifted through the seasons, the hunger-induced inertia confining him for long periods in his room, in bed for warmth, with a day now and then wandering listlessly among the bookstalls along the Seine. As he sank down through the strata of Parisian destitution his lodgings rose, but in elevation only, for the cheapest rooms were always attics, stifling in summer, freezing in winter.

There were days, of course, when he was compelled to look inside himself, and he was discouraged at the prospect: 'I believe in nothing, least of all myself.

On some days I think I have no mind at all, when I wonder how I ever allowed myself to have ambitions.' His failure at school still haunted him and there was hardly a day that he wasn't made aware of his ignorance. Whenever he passed the Lycée he turned his head and hurried on, ashamed and afraid he'd be recognised. Relations with his mother grew strained, too. The occasions when they shared a frugal meal together became rare; the silences, during which Madame Zola would stare at her son in reproach, became longer. And, watching his mother bent over her atrociously paid needlework, Emile constantly reproached himself.

With what little energy and spirit he could summon up he continued to write verse, though his efforts were tangled in a web of confusion. Two short poems had already been published the year before, in 1859: *La Fée amoureuse*, a fairy story in a medieval setting, and 'Le Canal Zola'; neither had provoked the slightest comment from the public or given satisfaction to the writer, in whom was dawning a recognition that there could be little future in a form which commanded no audience. But he persisted, spasmodically, and began to write longer poems in keeping with his vague and fading ambition to become the poet of his age. He had finished one, *Rodolpho*, during his stay in Aix, just before his second attempt at the *baccalauréat*; another, *Le Carnet de Danse*, a vaporous love story, survives only because it was later included in his first book, *Stories for Ninon*. His new project was an epic poem in three parts to be called *La Chaîne des êtres*, which would describe human life from its evolution through to its demise and replacement by a superior race of beings. That it was never finished reflects the extent of his confusion and disillusionment, which would have been complete had his verse been subjected to critical evaluation; for there is no avoiding the fact that it was uniformly hackneyed and banal. The young poet was blind to this, however, and hopeful, if not exactly buoyant: 'I have few illusions, Paul,' he wrote to Cézanne. 'I know I can only stammer. But I'll find a way.'

Emile's dependence upon Cézanne at this time has something of the quality of his own mother's smothering concern for him after she was widowed. He spent hours over his correspondence with the emerging artist, chiding, cheering, encouraging, counselling and clucking over him like a broody hen. The value of this reassuring stimulation to Cézanne was inestimable, but the link of friendship was also a lifeline for Emile. 'Like a shipwrecked man clinging to a floating plank I've been clinging to you, dear old Paul. You have understood me, your nature has been sympathetic to mine. In you I have found a friend, and give thanks to heaven.'

Pining for Cézanne, dreaming of the day when they might take up their friendship where they had left off at Aix, Emile increasingly put pressure on the young artist to come to Paris. In a letter written on 24 October he attempts to lure him to the capital with enticing descriptions of artist's models:

Chaillan [an art student] says that the models are approachable, though not of the freshest quality. One draws them by day and cuddles them by night – though the term cuddle is perhaps too mild. You pay them so much to pose by day, and so much for the pose by night. The figleaf is unknown in the studios. The models undress as they do at home, and the love of art checks what other emotions might be excited by their nakedness. Come and see.

Finally, in the spring of 1861, Emile's strategy was successful, and Cézanne arrived unexpectedly in Paris with his father. Zola's ecstasy bubbles over in a letter to Baille, written on the day of his arrival. '*I've seen Paul!!!* I've seen Paul. Do you understand? Do you understand the music in these three words? He came this morning, Sunday, and shouted several times to me from the stairs. I was half asleep. I opened my door shaking with delight, and we embraced furiously.'

The well-to-do Cézanne, with his annuity of 125 francs a month, must have been shocked on joining Zola. His leaving home had been the subject of a long-standing family row into which even Zola had been drawn; Cézanne's family saw him as the greatest threat to what they hoped would be their son's great career in banking. Now, after gagging at the revolting eating places which his friend frequented, buffeted by the crowds in the narrow streets and appalled by Emile's sloppy habits, even he must have wondered whether the domestic acrimony and the journey had been worthwhile. But after visits to the Louvre and the Luxembourg, where he gazed in silent awe at the huge academic paintings, his resolve and enthusiasm partially returned. He began attending a life class, started several paintings and met Monet and Pissarro, witnessing, incidentally, the first gropings towards the new Impressionism which were dramatically to change the course of Western art.

It was not long, however, before Cézanne's lack of confidence threw him into periods of black disillusionment. He grew depressed and frustrated by what he saw as the unattainable: the immense paintings, the Old Masters, the painstaking techniques, the detail and the craft of academic art. Even Zola's gentle encouragement failed to break through his surliness, and relations between them became strained. Zola unburdened himself one evening. 'I hardly ever see you,' he complained. 'In the mornings you go to the life class, and I remain in my room to write. We lunch separately. We see one another for an hour or two on those days when you work here, otherwise you're away painting. You have supper by yourself and go to bed early. It's not like it was at Aix, is it?'

Cézanne, distracted only momentarily, merely grunted.

Some of the ill feeling that abraded their close friendship doubtless arose from Zola's envy of Cézanne's middle-class security when he was one remove from starvation and had no resources other than an occasional guilt-laden hand-out from his mother – a fact to which the single-minded artist appeared sublimely indifferent. Nor had Cézanne suffered the deprivations that he had: a lost father, a lost fortune, disrupted schooling, not to mention the loss of his beloved Aix countryside. But despite this Zola never stopped begging Cézanne to stay in Paris. Time and time again he argued with him when he wanted to give up and return to his home in Aix. On one occasion Zola asked him to paint his portrait, desperate for some pretext to ensure that Cézanne would stay a

15

little longer; in the end, however, it had almost the reverse effect. One day Zola went to his room to find a grim-faced Cézanne packing his trunk.

'I'm leaving tomorrow,' Cézanne said, matter-of-factly.

'But what about my portrait?' Zola asked.

Cézanne pointed to a ripped-up canvas in the corner of the room. 'There it is. I was working on it and it got worse and worse. So now it's finished. And I'm off.'

Zola stayed with him through the day and well into the night, until Cézanne relented and agreed to stay on. But it was only a patch on the cracks that were opening up in the artist's confidence. The incident also shook Zola's faith in his friend's ability to realise his genius as a painter. 'Paul may have the genius of a great painter,' he wrote to Baille, 'but he will never have the genius to become one.'

Cézanne departed a few months later, in September, convinced that his stay in Paris had been a total failure.

Alone again, Zola's breadline diet generated little energy, but sometimes he simply had to escape from the crowded, dingy streets. He was fascinated by Les Halles, the vast market area, and would spend entire days wandering among the stalls, taking in the sounds and smells of the place. He would also catch an occasional whiff of the countryside by tramping beyond Montmartre, where mills still turned in the wind and where there was hay and clover to lie in, and sometimes sunshine to bask in, to read Montaigne and Shakespeare. He was particularly fond of the country around Vitry-sur-Seine, where the river and trees reminded him of Aix, and during the autumn of 1861 frequently spent a day there.

It was also autumn for his romantic notions which, only a few months before, had enabled him to turn a tiny, mean seventh-floor attic room on the Rue Saint-Victor into a penthouse of his dreams. 'I'm going to furnish it in the modern style,' he wrote, 'with a divan, piano, an ornamental iron stove... and on the balcony I shall have flowers and a birdcage and a fountain.' The only part of the dream that came true was that he could view half of Paris from his window; by winter he was reduced to trapping sparrows to cook and eat.

For all his penurious misery, however, he was free, his only responsibility being to continue to exist. Every minute of every day was his; he could spend whole days in contemplation; hours at a time observing details of Parisian life: the absinthe dens, the *camaraderie* of the students, the painted faces of the promenading prostitutes, the shocking squalor and poverty around him. It was all etched deeply in his memory. He was seeing the results of corruption and indifference at first hand. That he should have conceived, at this lowest point in his life, a compassion for the poor and oppressed and a hatred for the society that condoned the dreadful conditions is hardly surprising; in a similar way Charles Dickens's childhood job labelling pots in a blacking warehouse provided the source of the bitterness which, when later fused with sympathy and his genius for writing, made him into one of England's most potent reformers.

This wretched period also served to allow Zola's pent-up creative urge, now face to face with the cruel realities of life, to orientate itself. Like his romanticism, his belief in verse as his chosen form of expression was receiving a series of painful shocks. It became obvious to him that in the previous decade there had been a dramatic decline in published verse, and publishers and public alike were much more interested in topical writing and popular fiction. Poetry, Zola concluded sadly, had little future, and he could see no way to forge it into a more effective form of expression.

As he began to be aware of contemporary writing, painting, architecture and drama, he was greeted by a scene of vapid mediocrity. In the years of his schooldays, in the repressive early years of the Second Empire, life was being made increasingly difficult for artists and writers of any stature. There was stage censorship, the forced closing down of dozens of newspapers, police vetting of cartoons (which is why Daumier's vast output of caricatures and cartoons of the period deal with the frailties of mankind rather than with the insanities of politics) and, perhaps worst of all, every copy of every book sold had to bear the stamped approval of the local police office. Writers were frequently prosecuted, recalcitrant academics dismissed, and many were imprisoned or driven into exile. Flaubert was prosecuted and fined for writing *Madame Bovary*, Baudelaire for *Les Fleurs du mal* and the Goncourts for quoting, in an article published in *Le Paris*, two innocent lines about Venus from a sixteenth-century poem. What remained in the country was an emasculated, trivial, muck-raking press; 'approved' artists such as Meissonier and Vernet, music by Offenbach, and dreary fiction by writers such as Feuillet and Paul de Kock. The young Zola, who should have awakened to a creative sunrise, was opening his new eyes to a grey fog.

At the close of 1861 he at last became agonisingly aware of the dark pit into which he had descended. Having sampled some of the city's scurviest attics he finally reached the last stopping place before the street and the banks of the Seine, the terminal refuge of the destitute. It was the filthiest kind of hotel in the Rue Soufflot, a louse-infested lodging-house packed with thieves and prostitutes and where drunken parties, fights and police raids were nightly occurrences. He was now constantly ill, cold and hungry. 'I feel a heaviness in my belly and in my bowels,' he noted. 'My insides worry me, and so does the future.' After Cézanne's departure he grew morose, and was reduced to delivering visiting cards to earn a franc for his daily meal. But for all his discomforts and disappointments, the hole into which he had fallen was a little like Pandora's box: it still contained hope. Working at night when he could afford a candle, he was becoming surer in his writing; it was the one belief that kept him going – that soon he would find some direction for his creative impulse. With renewed determination he set about writing a long essay on the relationship of science and civilisation with poetry.

It is difficult to imagine that a youth, living alone among the flesh-pots of the Latin Quarter of Paris for two years, could have avoided sexual experience of some kind. In this area Zola was, with his upbringing and his mantle of romantic ideals, understandably reticent, and there are few clues to work on. In an early letter to Cézanne, written in February 1858, he infers that he has passed through a hard school 'of real love-making', details of which could not be imparted through the mails but would have to wait until they met again – but this was probably just youthful braggadocio. Zola seems to have tangled with the idea, certainly, but preferred to veil his need in protective conceit. Among all the lost girls of the gutter he would choose one, he confided once, 'to bathe all that is soiled in her with love'. But unless we read more into his subsequent fictional autobiography than we ought, there is little evidence to suggest he did other than wait for his tarnished angel in vain. In *Claude's Confessions*, published in 1865, he describes Claude's (his?) efforts to rehabilitate a fallen woman, Laurence, attempting to implant in her his own idealism. He fails, but with his ideals in a state of disarray he unexpectedly triumphs over the mistress of a student who lives in an adjoining room. The fifteen-year-old Marie shows Claude (or Zola) that love does exist; then dies. Friends of the novelist later attested that Marie was a fictional counterpart of Berthe, Zola's first mistress, but the truth remains obscured. Whatever the truth – whether Marie was a conquest or merely the creation of his observation and imagination – some sexual experience, possibly a squalid encounter of some kind, would help to explain Zola's subsequent discomfiture when dealing with aspects of physical love in his fiction, which is invariably brutalised, humiliating and overstated.

As 1862 dawned, it seemed at last that the tide of personal misfortune was turning. Some poems were accepted for publication in *Le Travail*, an obscure provincial satirical journal, the editor of which was twenty-year-old Georges Clemenceau. And then, through an old doctor friend of his father's, he was promised a job with a big publishing firm. Zola grabbed at the opportunity with gratitude, although not without deep misgivings. His youth had gone, lost forever, it seemed, with his ideals, dreams and hopes. In their place was a deep-felt hostility to society, its crudities and hypocrisies, injustices and evils – and so rotten that it affronted him to know that it had won the two-year battle to force him to compete and live the bourgeois life.

Zola's dream world ended for reasons as enigmatical and complex as those which induced him into this suspended state in the first place. Discomfort and starvation, certainly. He had at last learned to live with the world's grim realities without turning away in fear and confusion. There were also intimations of a new direction his creative spirit might follow, of an outlet for his dammed-up energies. And a new determination revitalised him: he resolved to pull himself up by his own bootlaces. But first, of course, he needed that job to buy the bootlaces.

The romantic poet's time had come; the time for his metamorphosis. It was to be a remarkable metamorphosis, and in defiance of nature in that the idealistic butterfly, after gently flitting through a flowery world of romanticism, was to emerge through a chrysalis transition as an indefatigable worm, to gnaw its way through the rotten refuse of French society and expose the skeleton of corruption, vice and injustice.

3

The Confused Rebel

'*Four hostile newspapers are more to be feared than a thousand bayonets*' – Napoleon Bonaparte (Napoleon III's uncle)

Despite the difficulties of book publishing in the repressive climate of the Second Empire, the black clouds occasionally disgorged a shower of golden rain. In the four years from its tumultuous reception on the bookstalls in 1862, Hugo's *Les Misérables* earned for its author an advance of 300,000 francs, and half a million francs profit for Lacroix, his publisher; for such rewards hundreds of publishers were prepared to overcome the most incredible obstacles Napoleon III's regime seemed to want to put in their way. Printer's devils were constantly on the streets, delivering proofs of newspapers, journals and books to the police censors and collecting them after they'd been blue-pencilled, running from office to office, from type-foundry to the printers, from the printers to the binders, from the binders to the warehouses, from the publishers to the booksellers; it was a scene of intense industry that belied the vapidity of the product upon which most of them were engaged.

In the hurly-burly of all this activity was Louis Hachette, a former student teacher who had steered his missionary zeal for education into publishing to found the now world-famous firm of Hachette's. Beginning with school textbooks, he branched out into dictionaries, Latin and Greek classics, and various cultured journals. By 1850 he was publishing cheap modern novels, romances and guide-books. In 1862 Hachette's was one of the biggest publishers in Paris and it was in February of that year that Zola, now twenty-two, found himself in the firm's packing department at a salary of 100 francs a month. This wage, on which he barely managed to live, nevertheless enabled him to buy a new black frock-coat and move from the pestiferous Rue Soufflot to better quarters, in what is now the Impasse Royer-Collard.

In the packing room at Hachette's, illuminated only by the gloomy light filtering through grime-encrusted window-panes, the young writer was at last making contact with commercial literature. Observing the books flow across the packing table provided him with a first-hand lesson in practical publishing, on how literature was expertly tailored to the market; and the fact that volumes of poetry were vastly outnumbered by works of popular fiction didn't go unnoticed. Although the work was menial, Zola found the bookish atmosphere stimulating, and occasionally, in the building, he would recognise some of

France's most celebrated men of letters: Taine, Lamartine and Sainte-Beuve among them. He wasn't, however, overwhelmed by this; what surprised him was the servility of many of Hachette's authors, and the continual complaining and pettiness of others.

Physically, Zola was maturing at last. The few extra francs in his pocket went directly to his stomach and as his health returned the boyish frame soon gave way to a broad-shouldered stockiness. A little of the weight went to his face, too; a studio photograph at the time shows him with a square forehead above a round face, tapering slightly to a small chin, deeply cleft under the lower lip. The upper lip, downturned enough to give him an air of melancholy, is full and sensual. A luxuriant head of dark hair falls about his ears and a beard covers his chin and neck, though shaved off the face; his moustache, a shade lopsided, looks as though it has been stuck on in a hurry. But of all the features, the dark eyes command most attention, with an intensity that not even his short-sightedness can diffuse. He is now, by the way, a French citizen; his application for naturalisation was granted in October 1862, and he received his military call-up number six months later: 495. This numbered marble weighed like a cannonball in the lives of most young Frenchmen but fortunately – unlike Baille's – Zola's was never called.

On most evenings, after his meal, he would sit down in his room to work away at his writing. He was not a facile writer; putting his thoughts on paper was always a slow and painful struggle. His mind was like a battlefield, a mass of ideas in conflict; they would charge across his consciousness in a chaotic rush, evading all attempts to discipline them into some sort of order, leaving him stunned and inarticulate, without a single word written on the page. Agonisingly aware of his clumsiness, it is not surprising that he found it difficult to show his work to others. One Saturday evening, however, his stirring ambitions overcame his reticence and he left a carefully written copy of his poetic trilogy, *The Comedy of Love*, on Louis Hachette's desk. The old publisher read it the following Monday morning and sent for its author, to whom he explained in a kindly manner that it was not quite the thing the firm was looking for. 'Stick to prose, my boy,' was his advice. But Hachette was sufficiently impressed, not only by his employee's talent, but also by his ideas for a new magazine, to double Zola's salary to 200 francs a month.

More to the point as far as his career was concerned was the old man's invitation, some months later, to write a short story for one of the firm's juvenile magazines. The result was *Sister of the Poor*, a children's fable about a poor girl whose kindness was rewarded with a magic coin which had the power to reproduce itself. Unfortunately, in those sensitive times, Zola's pointedly accurate descriptions of poverty in Paris were thought to be too revolutionary, and the story was refused. Zola was not too disappointed, however; the commission indicated that the discerning Hachette thought him good enough to write publishable prose, and added fresh impetus to his efforts.

Late in 1862, Zola was overjoyed to have his two close friends join him in Paris. It had taken a year for Cézanne's father to realise that his son was totally unsuited for a career in the family banking business at Aix, so now he returned to study at the École des Beaux-Arts and the Académie Suisse, and with a fresh determination to become a successful artist. Baille arrived too, at about the same time, to take a course at the École Polytechnique, to be followed later in the year by yet another schoolfriend from Aix, Marius Roux. Having his friends close by did more than anything else to help mend Zola's shattered life and to restore his confidence. He had moved to a rooming house in what is now the Rue Daguerre, and soon moved again to a larger apartment in the Rue des Feuillantines with his mother, where every Thursday evening the four young men met for tea and earnest discussion. Most of the talk revolved around art and literature, but especially painting. On some evenings Zola would accompany Cézanne to the studios of several of the painters: Degas, Monet, Pissarro, Fantin-Latour and Manet; and at weekends the pair would hike to Aulnay and the Vallée-aux-Loups to sit by Chalot Pond which Cézanne liked to sketch, talking excitedly about plans to challenge the supremacy of the academic artists.

By 1863 art had been painted into a dark and lifeless corner. The fashionable paintings of the period, the prize-winning canvases, were vast, funereal panoramas, composed and sketched out by the master, worked on for a year or two by up to a dozen assistants, varnished with umber to produce an Old Master effect and finally showcased in a gilded, highly ornamented frame weighing up to half a ton. This was the official art of the Second Empire and over the years it had become so entrenched, and its supporters so powerful, that a painting exhibiting any departure from the approved style, or showing any originality at all, was derided and suppressed. So closed were the ranks of the Academicians that few artists cared to challenge them; those who did so earned nothing but ridicule and risked permanent banishment from the salons and galleries of Paris. But on his rounds of the studios of the rebels, Zola sensed that their canvases, unorthodox, thrilling and vibrating with light and colour, represented much more than a glove thrown at the Academicians; what he was witnessing was a momentous and profound departure from the artistic tradition. And here he was, right in the front line, waiting for the battle to begin! He wasn't an artist, but that hardly mattered; their cause was his.

The young writer was now constantly with Paul Cézanne, who had decided to take a crack at the Salon in April. The annual Salon exhibition was the biggest art event in France, and his chances of having a painting hung were laughable. But this wasn't the point; as he confided to Zola during one of their Sunday hikes, 'My friend, revolution is in the air!' At the mention of the word the writer's nostrils quivered at the imagined smell of gunsmoke. His critical position on the new art was still somewhat equivocal; no matter – he would look and learn as much as possible, and become its defender.

The selection jury of the Salon had in the past thrown out works by Corot, Courbet, Millet and Daumier, so few could plead surprise when every one of the canvases by the revolutionary painters was summarily rejected by the 1863 jury. Paintings by Manet, Fantin-Latour, Jongkind, Whistler, Legros,

21

Bracquemond, Harpignies – and, of course, Cézanne – were all returned with the customary *R* chalked on the backs. By now, however, the numbers of the rejected artists had swollen to a large and influential group – of the 5,000 works submitted in 1863, 2,800 were rejected – and they were not without their enthusiastic supporters. Their outcry this year was so vociferous it reached the Palace, and Napoleon III, prodded by the Empress, visited the Salon, thought the rejected paintings worthy of exhibition, and by imperial decree established the *Salon des Refusés* – the 'Salon of the Rejected'. The result was that 600 canvases, sculptures, drawings and prints were displayed in a separate exhibition in the Palais de l'Industrie. The public, led by the critics, came by the thousand to laugh at and mock these strange paintings which to their eyes were like the work of children: rough, naïve and unfinished. The loudest criticism was reserved for Manet's *Déjeuner sur l'herbe*, an unorthodox composition painted in bright outdoor colours which dramatically broke with convention by showing clothed men and a naked woman together. Far from being an innovation, the blending of clothed and unclothed figures was a common practice among the Old Masters, including Titian and Raphael, but middle-class Paris, encouraged by the critics, preferred or pretended to be outraged.

Zola never forgot the scene at the *Salon des Refusés* and, twelve years later, set it down in his novel, *The Masterpiece*. He describes how he and Cézanne follow the amused crowd into the exhibition.

> The Exhibition of the Rejected was well arranged. The officially accepted pictures were no better displayed. The doorways were hung with antique tapestries, there were red velvet cushions on the benches and the skylights were shaded with canvas blinds. At first glance down the long series of rooms it looked the same as the official Salon, with the same gold frames, the same splashes of colour. But what was not immediately apparent was the atmosphere of life and gaiety, the presence of brightness and youth. The crowd, already dense, was growing by the minute, for visitors were deserting the official Salon for this one, encouraged by curiosity and eager to pass judgement on the judges, convinced they were going to be vastly entertained. The rooms were already hot; a fine dust rose from the floor, and by four the place would be stifling.

Then they reach the painting the crowd has come to mock, the *Lunch on the Grass*:

> ...As the visitors entered the door he could see their jaws gape, their eyes contract, their faces expand. Opposite, several young men collapsed into contortions, as though someone was tickling them. One woman fell on to a bench, her knees clamped together, choking and trying to get her breath back. Rumours of this excruciatingly comic picture had been spreading everywhere, and new visitors kept jostling into the room with shouts of 'Where is it?' 'Over there!' 'Good Lord, what a joke!' Witty remarks flew about at the expense of the painting; for it was the subject that amused and baffled them – it was so insane, so ludicrous, it made them sick with laughing. 'Look, the lady is too hot, and the gentleman too cold, because he's put on his coat.' 'No – she's blue, so he must have just pulled her out of the pond!'

The exciting weeks of the *Salon des Refusés* stimulated Zola's rebellious spirit and influences of all kinds began to crowd into his fertile and receptive mind. Gustave Flaubert's *Salammbo* had appeared on the bookstalls in 1862 and was greeted with critical contempt. Flaubert had survived a rough time from both the critics and the public five years before with *Madame Bovary*, destined to revolutionise the art of the novel it had scandalised the country with its depressingly true picture of middle-class society, and even attracted a prosecution for obscenity. But it was greedily read by the young generation, and to writers like Zola, the reviled, misunderstood, persecuted Flaubert became a hero and an inspiration.

The Goncourts, too, the collaborating brothers Edmond and Jules, were experimenting with a new style of novel in which observation and experience were dissected, as light was dissected by the Impressionist painters. The result was a pattern of details, a gallery of word-pictures, momentary impressions of connecting and conflicting incidents. They abandoned the ideal of creating a unified composition; theirs was the novel of sensations, colour, movement and personal experience.

Zola was now reading voluminously and developing his own literary theories. Realism, to him, was nothing more than an accurate representation of real life, possessing none of the distortions of classic or romantic literature. Art, he concluded in 1864, was 'a corner of nature seen through a temperament'. Then, in January the following year, his literary progress took a further step. In the preface to their new novel, *Germinie Lacerteux*, the Goncourts laid down the first principles of what was to emerge as naturalism: the contemporary novel, they said, must be true to life and have its basis in science rather than in abstract philosophies; it must reflect a detached observation of society, recognise the working class, and convey a compassion for humanity.

Another powerful influence on the young writer was the philosopher and literary historian Hippolyte Taine (1828-93) who in the early 1860s reached the peak of a controversial career by leading a movement to sever French literature from its romantic past and to thrust it into the new scientific age. Taine was also the leading exponent of the determinist philosophy – expounded in his *History of English Literature*, published at the end of 1863 – a philosophy towards which Zola had been groping and which was suddenly delivered into his open arms. At twenty, Zola had believed in a God Almighty who created him, guided him, and who endowed him with a free will; and that his soul was immortal. 'But if', he explained, 'I am asked whether I believe in the divinity of Jesus Christ, I confess I hesitate to reply...' Taine's scientific determinism was an attractive alternative to his doubts about dogma and supernatural powers, for it embodied the theory that all actions, including moral choices, are *entirely* determined by influences and causes which already exist. Most people adopt a half-way stance by accepting that some actions are beyond free will, that heredity can influence an individual character, and that outside causes can precipitate inexplicable actions. But these people also believe that man ultimately has a free will and is therefore responsible, whatever the mitigating factors, for all his actions. In the law of most societies insanity is the sole mitigating factor which can exonerate man from his behaviour. Scientific determinism, however, rejects all this and sees God or some supreme being as a kind of computer in which every action of every human being at all times is programmed, predictable and thus causally explicable. The doctrine is not without its primal logic, but as with Taine, and later with Zola, it tends to seduce its followers into the creation of secondary theories which are patently absurd.

For the moment, though, these liberating ideas were confined to Zola's thinking. As for his writing, the transition from romantic to realist was far from complete and he was still picking over the tail-ends of the fantasies he'd been weaving over the past few years, some of which he'd managed to get published in obscure journals. He approached several publishers with a collection of these stories, including Hetzel and Lacroix, a small firm on the Boulevard Montmartre which specialised in foreign translations, French classics and leftist writers, and whose authors included Jules Verne. Leaving the manuscript with the monocled Lacroix, who promised to read it although without any intention of doing so, Zola waited impatiently for several weeks for an enthusiastic note from the publisher. When nothing arrived, far from being intimidated by the silence, he badgered Lacroix until his persistence was rewarded, and the collection, under the title *Stories for Ninon*, appeared late in 1864.

For the aspiring author the act of publication was the vindication of years of agonising labour for which no amount of money could compensate. It was just as well, for contracts with maiden authors at that time were designed neither to enrich nor encourage. It certainly didn't matter to Zola, who was overjoyed; his voice at last was a public voice. It didn't matter, either, that *Stories for Ninon* wasn't a sensation; as a published author he now had a new key to try in the doors that had previously been locked to him, and in the months that followed he found his writing increasingly accepted by newspapers and journals where it had been refused before. 'The struggle was brief,' he wrote to the young poet Valabregue in Aix, in a letter which reflects his excitement, 'and I'm amazed I wasn't more bruised. I am on the threshold, the battlefield is wide open, yet I may still very well break my neck!' He concluded the letter with the exhortation, 'Get ready to write an article about me.'

Zola was now the publicity chief at Hachette's, growing familiar with the world of journalism, and writing until late every night. His pen flew over sheets of paper at a scorching pace. Each week he wrote up to 150 lines for the *Petit Journal* for twenty francs an article, and there were much longer pieces to write for the *Salut public* of Lyons for which he was paid between fifty and sixty francs – thus equalling his salary at Hachette's. But while the money was welcome it was a public he wanted most, and it was well known that in the *Petit Journal*, which was a penny newspaper with a circulation of 200,000, contributors climbed to popularity very quickly.

The pieces he wrote were lively and bristling with opinion; readers often disagreed with him but he *was* being noticed, and this was vital to his professional ego. In 1865 he found himself caught up in the controversy over the Goncourts' novel, *Germinie Lacerteux*. To Parisian readers it was

24

unexpectedly realistic, perhaps too true a reflection of their own lives, protected as they had been by mirrors covered almost entirely by ornament. The theme was age-old: a poor, pretty servant girl is exploited and humiliated to finish up as a degraded piece of human flotsam. What was new was the way in which the story was told, with accurate and often cruel observations. Zola saw the novel as a masterpiece and immediately leapt into print to defend it, no doubt enviously, as it was the kind of book he wished he had written himself. Controversy seemed to be his natural element, for his article attracted nearly as much attention as the book. The priority of his intentions at the time were as clear-cut as his opinions: 'One is to make myself well-known; the second is to increase my revenue. May Heaven help me!' This latter was rather an empty appeal, for the young writer was developing an extraordinary facility to help himself; in fact the book-keeping side of Zola is already evident even at this early stage of his career. While it was never to be an obsession – understandable in people who have known real poverty – it was unquestionably a major preoccupation. It has been said of his fictional characters that an accurate accounting can be made of every sou that passes through their pockets.

In the spring of 1865 Zola fell in love with a *grisette*, a seamstress. One account has it that the girl was deserted by her student lover and collapsed in a fit of hysterical weeping, which attracted the sympathetic attentions of the young writer. Profusely grateful for his comfort the young lady returned the inexperienced Zola's kindness in a manner so passionate and intimate as to completely knock him off his feet. What seems more likely is that no woman of his own age had ever loved Zola until now, so it was not surprising that the spark of his compassion soon roared into a forest fire of desire. Everything, even his writing, was abandoned for this woman; he wrapped her in a smothering blanket of gratitude and concern; and for weeks he was distracted, demented, and thought of nothing, nobody else, but Alexandrine-Gabrielle Meley.

Alexandrine was a year older than Emile; tall, dark-haired and pallid, with intense, black eyes set beneath sensuous, heavy lids and fine, expressive eyebrows. Her birth certificate testifies that she was born out of wedlock to teenage parents but otherwise her background is obscure. She apparently lived with her mother, who worked as a florist until her death in 1850, and then with a guardian, and that is about all that is known about her. A story persists that for many weeks Zola was tormented by the thought that Alexandrine's former lover might return to rob him of his mistress and his new-found happiness. Despite her protestations of faithfulness, this unreasonable fear nagged in his brain and brought on fevers of doubt and worry and a prolonged bout of insomnia. It is suggested that this resulted in a neurosis which remained with him for many years, for the idea of the former lover returning to claim his woman provides the foundation for many of the plots in his novels. It is a central theme in *L'Assommoir,* and a vital ingredient in the plots of *Earth* and *The Beast on Man,* but nowhere is it more allegedly autobiographical than in one of his early novels, *Madeleine Ferat.* If we are to believe the plot of this novel has its foundations in real life, Alexandrine's former lover returned but confounded Zola's neurotic anxiety by not being in the least put out by the transfer of her affections to the young writer.

About a year after their first meeting the couple moved to the Rue de Vaugirard, where Alexandrine lived, to be joined by Zola's mother. At first distant, Madame Zola soon saw in Alexandrine a careful and competent housewife who was invariably cheerful and completely devoted to her son, and the two women quickly became friends. If there was any conflict at all it was in Emile's own mind; however gracious his mother's acceptance of Alexandrine he doubtless experienced pangs of guilt, knowing her standards of morality, for having introduced a mistress into the family household. He may also have had second thoughts about the relationship, but although it was not planned as a selfish move he clearly came out on the winning side domestically, for now he had two women to care for him. In some ways this was just as well, for the work-load he now took upon himself was nothing short of crushing.

Zola's relationship with Alexandrine might well have been consummated on Christmas Eve 1865, for that is the date inscribed in the copy he gave her of his second book, *Claude's Confessions*. Published by Lacroix, the novel appeared in October 1865. I've already mentioned its autobiographical aspect in the previous chapter: Claude, a young poet in Paris, meets a drab prostitute, worn out before her time. Out of compassion he spends a night with her and, as she has no home, decides to let her share his room and to help her regain her self-respect. Unfortunately the woman is past all hope, and instead of being rescued drags her young benefactor down with her to the gutter. Despite this, Claude falls in love with her, and it isn't until she prostitutes herself to one of his friends in his presence that he awakes to his love-blinded life of squalor. Horrified, he flees from Paris to his family home in the country in an attempt to recapture his lost innocence. The author drifts into the skin of Claude from time to time, but more often into the character's mind, for the novel may be read as a chronicle of Zola's four-year struggle to reconcile his dreams and ideals with reality; as with Claude's unsuccessful efforts to redeem the prostitute, Zola fails also. By the end of the book we are left in little doubt that the rose-tinted spectacles have been abandoned, and that forever after Zola will see the world as it really is.

Claude's Confessions wasn't really the novel Zola wanted to write at all. As he was grinding out the closing chapters, the Goncourts' *Germinie Lacerteux* had appeared, written with the uncompromising realism he might have wished for his own book, the concept of which now seemed to him decadently romantic. The gap between what he was doing and what he wanted to do exasperated the young author intensely, and the extent of his frustration is revealed in the blatant opportunism he resorted to in promoting his novel. At first it looked as though *Claude's Confessions* might provoke the kind of public scandal that had greeted *Madam Bovary* and *Germinie Lacerteux*. One or two critics expressed their dislike of the novel's 'hideous realism' but more promising was the reaction of the police censor, who debated whether or not to prosecute the young writer. In the Censor's Report of 2 December 1865, the following opinion is recorded:

> The author has exaggerated certain passages describing lustful passions. . . He forgets that the youthful mind is not likely to be improved by smearing its imagination, and that a book which sets out to convey a moral should avoid anything suggesting pornography.

To Zola's delight, although not unmixed with some fear, the police opened a file on him, searched his lodgings and made enquiries about him at Hachette's. But then, to his great disappointment, the authorities decided not to take any action; notwithstanding its racy boudoir scenes it was not, in the final opinion of the censor, a novel which threatened the morality of the public, and its author's ambitions seemed to be literary rather than political. The book was cleared for general distribution, and the crestfallen writer remained as uncontroversial as ever.

The chances that *Claude's Confessions*, with its modest edition of 1,500 copies, might still be the subject of a scandal were remote, but Zola persisted, using every trick he'd learned in the publicity department at Hachette's. With a mounting flair for self-advertisement he wrote dozens of imploring letters to critics and literary acquaintances, sometimes even including directions as to how he'd like the review written. He sent a review copy to *Le Figaro* accompanied by a spuriously self-effacing note: 'Sir, I hope you will find the space to mention this small volume in your pages,' he wrote, adding, 'I would even prefer to see it abused than merely have pleasantries written about it.' A number of reviewers did pan the book, although not quite in the manner Zola had in mind. Whatever the shortcomings of the novel – and privately its author admitted there were many – he nonetheless defended it at every opportunity. His over-reaction to the least criticism reflected his deep need for some concrete form of opposition, some tangible display of anger or fear by the literary establishment, scared out of its wits by this rebel invader. Much of this probably sprang from his own disillusionment over the novel, and he needed the attacks to buoy up his ego. When they failed to eventuate, he imagined them. 'I am feared and abused,' he wrote shortly after the book's publication. 'Today I have been classed among those writers who are dangerous to read.'

Perhaps owing something to its author's strenuous efforts to drum up attention, *Claude's Confessions* sold out, earning Zola 450 francs, the equivalent of a month's income from all his sources. But with his self-absorption in promoting his own book and because of the unwelcome attentions of the police, relations at Hachette's had become strained. Louis Hachette had died the previous year, and Zola had lost a protector, for the old man had continued to encourage him up until his death. The young employee's literary efforts were not greeted with anything like the same enthusiasm by the executives who took over, however; indeed, they were even discouraged. One particular incident finally led to a breaking point. When sending out a new Hachette book for review, Zola was not above enclosing a copy of his own. This led one reviewer to accredit the firm with *Confessions*, which he went on to dismiss in a most condescending manner. It was an attribution the directors of Hachette's didn't care for at all, and the young author was asked to write a letter of retraction to the newspaper concerned. Shortly after this incident it was politely put to Zola that his talents were being wasted. 'You know,' one of the directors told him, 'Your salary here is 200 francs a month. For someone of your talent it's ridiculous! You would do much better to take up literature full-time, not only for profit, but think of the glory!' The prompting couldn't have come at a more opportune time; with two published books behind him Zola was ready, in spirit at least, to make writing his career, but in those uncertain times it must have taken considerable courage to make the decision to abandon a regular salary. At any rate, at the end of 1865, he sent in a letter of resignation, the practical nature of which was a little uncharacteristic of the rebel its writer professed to be. The terms were that Hachette's would allow him six weeks' grace to the termination of his employment and that, for a fee of course, he could continue to push the firm's books through his newspaper reviews.

The Paris into which Zola now launched himself as a full-time writer was, despite its hectic atmosphere, a lot less forbidding and threatening than when he'd arrived there. Once stifled and overwhelmed in its feverish coils, he now felt himself a giant. He could see the city now for what it was: a vast compost heap, fermenting with ideas and activity, glittering with jewels for the taking The rebuilding, the speculation, the graft and corruption that had characterised the early years of the Second Empire, continued unabated, and the schemers, carpetbaggers and adventurers still flowed into Paris in an unceasing flood. Almost hourly, the thunder of a new demolition racked the city; each week whole blocks of shoulder-to-shoulder slum tenements, rat-holes of disease, vice, ignorance and poverty, were reduced to rubble. New boulevards continued to slice through the patchwork of the old quarters. Like the spokes of a gigantic wheel, twelve wide avenues radiated from the Opera House, already rising grandly from its imperial foundations. And beneath this steaming compost heap, snaking sinuously under the railway networks, canals the ninety miles of new roadworks already chaotic with cabs, hansoms, ornate victorias and lumbering delivery vans, ran a vast complex of sewers: great tunnels, arches and dripping caverns that would become one of the unseen marvels of European civilisation. Paris was bursting. Yet stonemasons, bricklayers, roofers, labourers and tradesmen of all kinds still poured in from the provinces by the thousand to spend their pay-packets in the noisy, gas-lit cafés and on whatever entertainment they could find. For almost every kind of human activity it was an era of fantastic opportunity. Newspapers, in particular, were quick to seize their share of all this wealth. Advanced machinery and big steam presses had speeded up output, and it was obvious that fortunes could be made by newspapers achieving big circulations. The race was on for readers; not only by the proprietors and publishers, but by writers, too, eager for a public and publicity. Zola was one of them, driven paradoxically by his own lack of confidence, for only by hearing the tumult, by sniffing the smoke of controversy, by basking in the admiration of millions, could he ever acknowledge success.

At a far deeper level there could have been another source for the young writer's craving for public approval: his father's failure. Acclaim and fame might help expunge the guilt Zola had carried on behalf of his father since childhood. Even now the bureaucrats in Aix were gnawing at the family pride; the authorities there planned to remove the name *Zola* from his father's canal. That a bronze tablet was to be removed from the wall of one of the canal dams was of small concern; but what Emile interpreted as an act that publicly recognised his father's failure disturbed and infuriated him. To the son the slur was the spur to over-achievement; whatever happened, however he did it, somehow he would be successful, celebrated and famous. One day, he thought, letters would arrive at his door addressed to *Emile Zola, France.*

4

First Steps
on a Long Journey

From the moment he handed in his notice at Hachette's, Zola wasted no time in setting himself up as a journalist. He had had his eyes on *L'Evenement*, a new cheap daily paper put out by the publisher of *Le Figaro*, Henri de Villemessant, and now he wrote to him with an idea. One of the popular features of the paper was a chat column about the theatrical world; Zola suggested that he should write a similar column but about books and authors. It would include advance notices of new books, brief reviews, pre-publication extracts and gossip. The idea appealed to Villemessant and, two days after leaving Hachette's, at the end of January 1866, Zola began work on *L'Événement* for 500 francs a month, more than twice his previous salary. The generous pay undoubtedly pleased the young writer, who could now justly regard himself as an up-and-coming – even influential – journalist. And an affluent one, too; the apartment in the Rue de Vaugirard boasted five rooms and a balcony that overlooked the Luxembourg Gardens.

By working for *L'Événement*, Zola had chosen one of the most 'commercial' newspapers in Paris, for its resourceful publisher could have easily held his own on Fleet Street today. Paunchy, double-chinned, florid, an ex-actor and ex-singer, Villemessant had founded *Le Figaro* in 1854. But in the ensuing decade he'd watched a new public emerge from the pretensions and opulence of the Second Empire, a new race of society loungers with nothing to do but recycle mischievous gossip and idle their days away in the fashionable parts of the city. All this artificiality was pandered to by the energetic Villemessant who was constantly searching for novelties with which to appeal to the *salon* crowd. One of his journals had literally been on the nose; it was sprayed with perfume as it issued from the presses. Another of his innovations was the miscellany, or gossip column; and he also invented the 'star reporter', which was doubtless behind the success of *Le Figaro* and later his new paper, *L'Événement*. Villemessant was also prone to run his newspapers like a circus; his announcements to readers were certainly those of a sideshow barker. His introduction of Zola had something of a theatrical ordeal by fire touch about it:

To spy on a new book, even before it is published if possible; to give a brief and impartial judgement; to know everything about the world of books. . . this is the role of M. Émile Zola. If my performer succeeds, well and good. If he fails, nothing is simpler – I drop his act from my vaudeville.

Sacked journalists were never called into the editor's office to be dismissed; Villemessant merely made them a present of a walking-stick.

Zola's act, however, was a good one. He was quite philosophical about writing in order to eat. 'I don't write all this stuff simply for the love of the public, he commented shortly after joining the paper. 'The question of money has a good deal to do with it.' But he knew also there were valuable long-term benefits. His literary connections were increasing all the time and at *L'Événement* the young recruit was thrown in among the best.

Within a month Zola was also the art critic at *L'Événement*. Although in this role he has been criticised as a purveyor of other men's opinions and as the fortunate opportunist who happened to be in the right place at the right time, few can question his courageous forthrightness when it was most needed. Without a Zola the entrenched Academicians would have made life much more difficult, perhaps impossible, for the emerging school of revolutionary artists. And though his appreciation for the new art was perhaps stimulated more by the rebel painters themselves than by contemplative appraisal of their work and intentions, his intuition was rarely at fault; with the exception of Cézanne and to some extent Degas, he recognised the potential of every great artist of his time well before their general acceptance, and often alone.

Remembering the controversy that had surrounded the *Salon des Refusés* of 1863, the young journalist suggested to Villesmessant a series of sixteen articles on the 1866 Salon. He had a shrewd idea there would be fireworks, and indeed he had already attempted to light some by helping Cézanne write a letter to the Director of the Beaux-Arts insisting that the *Salon des Refusés* be reopened, only to be turned down. The publisher immediately saw the circulation potential in the mild scandal the articles were certain to provoke, and eagerly commissioned his fledgling critic. He soon realised, however, that in Zola he had grabbed a tiger by the tail, for in the first two articles, published at the end of April just before the opening of the Salon exhibition to the public, the official jury was mercilessly flayed and denounced as a bunch of pompous nobodies, petty intriguers and partially blind octogenarians.

The articles were aimed at, in Zola's words, 'those who amputate art and present to the crowd only a mutilated corpse'. The Salon, he complained, 'is not the work of artists, but that of a jury, who reject and accept with indifference. . . artists of a past age who deny new ideas, and artists of the present who grip their modest success between their teeth and growl like dogs, threatening anyone who comes near'. He concluded derisively: 'Art has had its face washed, its hair carefully combed. The fashionable ladies who visit the Salon will find everything as neat and as clear as a mirror. They could do their hair in the canvases. . .'

However naïve and insensitive his artistic eye, Zola's colourful and audacious condemnation of the academic, and his championing of the new, was a blast of cold, fresh air in the stuffy closeness of the Salon, an impudent wedge driven into the enemy camp. Villemessant certainly had his scandal; members of the jury howled with rage and some wanted to fight a duel with his critic. But Zola had only just got into his stride, and devoted the next article to defending and praising Manet, the most ridiculed artist of them all. Readers of *L'Événement* were baffled and indignant, and letters of protest landed on the publisher's desk by the dozen. Thousands cancelled their subscriptions. Undismayed, Zola followed with an article acclaiming Monet, and another which made no bones about the favouritism shown by the Salon jury. At this point, painfully aware that the carefully planned scandal had got out of hand, Villemessant politely requested his critic to wrap up the series with a final article. In this piece the impudent reviewer defended his praise for Manet as an artist of power and originality, poured scorn on those who preferred fashion and convention to truth, and prophesied oblivion for the popular academic artists of the day.

There is little question that the impulse behind this remarkable and historic series of articles was Zola's own heightened instinct for controversy and drama, but the extraordinary perception displayed in his opinions is quite astonishing for one so young. What impressed Zola about the art he promoted was its vigour and originality; he did not have an eye for subtleties, nor did elegance of expression excite him. Interesting, too, is that in these articles we can see the foundation of all Zola's subsequent literary and art criticism: and almost unerring eye for true originality, a deep belief in the correctness of his opinions, and the honest, even courageous, expression of them. Rarely does his criticism vacillate with reservations; on the contrary, it is often extravagantly outspoken and occasionally even abusive. Another feature revealed in the articles is his ability to capture the colourful and memorable phrase. His role as an art critic, he said, was to 'search for men in the company of eunuchs'.

The seven articles were a personal triumph for him, and when he wrote in the preface to the collected articles published later in book form (*My Hates*, 1866): 'I felt so misunderstood, so much hate about me, there were times when my pen would fall from my hand in pure despair,' he was being less than honest. Zola probably loved every second of the controversy he'd sparked off. His pen was that of a controversialist, his opinions those of the *provocateur*.

Less satisfactory, though, was the effect of the articles on his career at *L'Événement*, which began to go downhill. Another of his ideas, that of writing a serial story for the paper, was a dismal failure. The story, *A Dead Woman's Wish*, never reached its final chapter. Finally, because his name was associated with the Salon scandal and his views so detested by the readers, Zola was asked to sign future articles with a pseudonym. After just a year with *L'Événement*, as it was about to merge with *Le Figaro*, Zola fell out with the publisher, and left.

The loss of his regular 500 francs a month was a disaster. He had lived up to every sou of his salary only too well; he'd moved again to the high-rent Right Bank, to Batignolles, leasing a fine house near the Avenue Clichy with the silhouetted windmills of Montmartre on the right and with an almost rural panorama of vineyards, gardens and smallholdings stretching away to the north-west. Finding another job wasn't easy. Word had got around that the highly opinionated writer attracted more trouble than he was worth and he was forced, during 1867, to accept any kind of literary hackwork for whatever payment he could squeeze from unenthusiastic publishers. It was a trial for Alexandrine, not knowing from one week to the next where the money to exist might come from, but she coped with considerable courage. On one occasion even their furniture was seized by impatient creditors.

Once again Zola tasted the corrosive sourness of poverty, while all around Paris seemed at times to burst with wealth. The mounting deficiencies of the Empire regime were hidden behind bigger and bigger displays of almost ferocious grandeur. At one imperial ball, when a labourer was lucky to earn eighty francs a month, 25,000 francs was spent on the floral decorations alone. Preparations for the forthcoming Exposition Universelle, to which would come all the crowned heads of Europe, were being made on an undreamed-of scale while half the population struggled to earn enough to eat. The polarisation of France had probably never been more complete.

One day a form of salvation walked in the door in the person of the proprietor of a small Marseilles newspaper, *Le Messager de Provence*, carrying a huge bundle of legal documents from the files of the Aix and Marseilles law courts, and representing some of the more sensational cases that had been tried there. Using this material, Zola was to breathe life into the criminal *causes célèbres* by rewriting them in a racy, lurid style, a practice still favoured by newspapers today. It was hackwork, but Zola had little alternative but to accept the commission for he desperately needed the 200 francs a month it offered. The series of stories ran under the title of *Mysteries of Marseilles*, and serialisation began in March 1867, to run for nine months; later the same year it was published as a novel, a rather dreary catalogue of man's follies, and one which the author, in later life, was happy to forget. Nor was his first attempt at theatrical drama one of his happiest memories. Lured into squeezing the juiceless pulp of the *Mysteries* to provide the story for a stage play, Zola collaborated with his old school friend Marius Roux in a production that opened in the provincial capital with disastrous results; he travelled down to Marseilles for the opening night and returned the next day, deeply disappointed at its dismal reception.

But three significant benefits did emerge from *Mysteries of Marseilles*. The first was that Zola was made aware of the advantages of newspaper serialisation to introduce novels to the public; henceforth every word of fiction he ever wrote in his life appeared first as a serial. Another, and perhaps the most important benefit, was the evolution of the novelist's work method. Faced with the huge pile of documents that at times threatened to engulf him, Zola learned how to accumulate and assemble a vast collection of facts; to filter them for the details he needed; and to organise them around his chosen theme. The discipline, as he was to discover, was a vital prerequisite to a monumental literary enterprise he would undertake in two years time. And, finally, working on the profitable but dreary crime stories during the mornings allowed him to begin another novel, *Thérèse Raquin*, in the afternoons.

'Putrid literature...a mass of blood and mud!' wrote Louis Ulbach in *Le Figaro* of *Thérèse Raquin* in January 1868, when it appeared in book form. As often happens the outraged reaction served as good publicity and sales were so promising that Zola seized the opportunity to extend the controversy. He answered his critics – although in fact they were very few – in a somewhat conceited preface to the second edition of the novel, heavy with the hallmarks of Zola's polemical style: naïve astonishment and blatant sarcasm. 'The critics greeted this novel with cries of indignation,' he wrote:

> Some virtuous people in equally virtuous newspapers professed disgust, picking up the book with tongs to throw it on the fire. Even the tatty little news-sheets, specialising in below-stairs scandal, held their noses, complaining of smuttiness. I do not complain, however, at this reception – on the contrary I am amused to find that my colleagues have the sensitivity of young girls – but what I do object to is that not one of these prudish critics who blushed when reading *Thérèse Raquin* appears to have understood the novel at all. If they had, then no doubt they would have blushed much more, but at least I would have had the satisfaction of knowing they were upset for the right reason.

The young novelist then went on to explain his intentions, and the essay is interesting for in it Zola summarises his 'scientific' method. It is also notable that he uses the term *naturalism* for the first time.

> In *Thérèse Raquin* my intention was to study temperament, not character. That is the essence of the novel. I selected characters dominated by nerves and blood, without free will, drawn to each act of their lives by the immutable laws of their flesh. Thérèse and Laurent are human animals, nothing more. I have tried to follow, step by step, the urges of passion and instinct and the mental disturbance resulting from emotional crisis. My two characters love only from a physical need; the murder they commit is a result of their adultery...and what I have had to call their remorse is really only an organic disorder, a rebellion of the nervous system driven to breaking point. The soul is totally absent, I freely admit, since that is how I intended it to be.

Thérèse and Laurent, then, are Zola's laboratory specimens – 'a highly sexed man and an unsatisfied woman, dissected to reveal their animal natures' – and thrown into the crucible of a violent drama to be observed with scrupulous detachment. 'I have performed', Zola concluded, 'on these two living bodies, the analytical work that surgeons perform on corpses.

Here, in the form of a synopsis of the story of *Thérèse Raquin*, is a brief report on Zola's so-called scientific observations.

Thérèse is an orphan, about twenty, who has for many years lived with her aunt, Madame Raquin, and her spoiled, sickly son, Camille. They live above a haberdashery shop run by the old lady in a dark, damp, squalid alley, the Pont-Neuf Passage. Although Thérèse has inherited hot blood from her Algerian mother, the cloistered, gloomy ordinariness of the household numbs her passions, which even the inevitable arranged, loveless marriage with her cousin Camille fails to bring to life.

That evening, Thérèse, instead of going into her room, which was on the left of the staircase, went into her cousin's, which was on the right. That was all the change that took place in her life that day. And the next day when the married couple came down, Camille still had his languid tiredness, his saintly, egoistical self-possession. Thérèse still had a look of quiet indifference and terrifying calm. (7)

Three uneventful years pass until, one evening, Camille brings home a former schoolfriend, Laurent. The visitor's presence troubles Thérèse, for he is of red-blooded peasant stock, handsome and sensual. Although she feels a presentiment of some disaster they become firm friends and Laurent resolves to make her his mistress. A brutal seduction is all that is needed to release the love-starved girl's latent desire and she succumbs to a love affair with a reckless abandon that completely hooks Laurent.

For nearly a year the lovers meet often in a delirium of happiness. Thérèse comes alive, and her beauty blooms. As for Laurent, his mistress has 'insulated herself into every fibre of his body.' Thérèse begins the process of hating her impotent husband:

When she got into her bed, she found the sheets cold and damp. Shivers of repugnance passed through her still burning limbs. Camille was not long in going to sleep, and Thérèse for a long time looked at the pale face stupidly sleeping on the pillow with its wide-open mouth. She moved away from him, stifling a desire to stuff her closed fist in that mouth. (7)

It isn't long, of course, before Camille is found to be in the way of the lovers' blissful future, and Laurent decides to kill the unfortunate husband. A plan is conceived to remove him during one of their Sunday outings to Saint-Ouen, a river resort. While they are out in a dinghy, on a deserted stretch of the river, Laurent throws Camille overboard and when he is drowned, he and Thérèse throw themselves in the water too, pretending it to be a tragic mishap. The scheme is successful and they escape detection, but that night their hand-clasp becomes the guilty bond of two murderers.

He felt the hand tremble, but it did not move back, on the contrary, it caressed his hand roughly. Their hands were burning hot, one in the other; the moist palms stuck together and their fingers, tightly clasped, were bruised at each lurch of the cab. It seemed to Laurent and Thérèse that the blood of each was going to the heart of the other, passing through their joined hands; these hands became a blazing fire on which their life was boiling. Their fierce hand-clasp, in the silence of the night, was like a crushing weight thrown on to Camille's head to keep him under water. (7)

For the satisfaction of knowing that Camille really is dead, Laurent forces himself to visit the morgue each day, in the hope of identifying the victim's drowned corpse. When he does, however, the satisfaction curdles to terror, and he leaves the morgue followed by the persistent smell of death.

Far from uniting the lovers, the event kills all desire between them. Two years pass, during which both of them suffer increasingly from dreadful hallucinations and horrible visions of the dead man. Believing that together they will defeat these guilty apparitions, they propose to marry – even if only for a good night's sleep. But the nuptials are a disaster; on their wedding night Camille's ghost comes between them, and they find they cannot bear to sleep

35

together nor to touch each other. When, many nights later, they finally do throw themselves on the bed in utter exhaustion, they are fully clothed.

Suddenly, Madame Raquin, whose grief at the death of her son has been almost unendurable, is paralysed by a stroke. She cannot move a muscle, and is mute. Both Thérèse and Laurent want to escape from each other and from the invalid, but they have no money. Only the value of the shop, which will be theirs on the old lady's death, nails them to the unhappy household. Their frustration breeds desperation and anger; ugly quarrels erupt, and finally physical violence; Thérèse is beaten almost every night. During one of these quarrels, in which the former lovers blame one another for their misery, Madame Raquin learns the terrible truth about her son's death. Unable to escape, unable to tell anyone, her despair is absolute. All she can do is watch with vengeful eyes the gradual disintegration of Camille's killers, which proceeds with mounting horror until, during the calm which descends before the final, desperate act, the exhausted pair make plans to kill each other. The outcome is pure Greek tragedy.

Thérèse Raquin duly appeared as a serial in *L'Artiste*, a periodical claiming a blue-blood readership which included even Empress Eugénie. Unfortunately the imperial patronage required the excision of certain passages. These were, however, reinstated in the subsequent book version published by Lacroix in October 1867, which was so successful that the book went into a second edition at the beginning of 1868. It has been, over the years, and possibly still is, one of Zola's most popular stories, and several different adaptations for the stage have been made from it.

All the elements which distinguish Zola's later work are present in *Thérèse Raquin*: the remorseless build-up of intensity; the extravagantly coloured extra-dimensional impressionism; the dark symbolism and that razor-narrow path along the precipice of over-statement, on which the novelist took a great deal of exercise. The book introduced a new facet into the nature of fictional violence, but its overall effect was to advance beyond previously reached limits. Progressing from the realism of the Goncourts' *Germinie Lacerteux*, Zola's approach is wholly materialistic; his two main characters have no 'souls'. They live by their animal instincts alone and, like animals, have no moral consciences. Interestingly, even the author could not completely hide his repugnance for the characters he created, which may have something to do with the fact that the plot of the novel has its origins in a real-life crime. This began with the adulterous affair between a farmer's wife and a horse dealer and the attempted poisoning of their respective partners, and concluded on Christmas Day 1861 with the shooting of the woman's husband. The horse trader was arrested, and confessed; the farmer's wife, after letters implicating her were found, was also charged and convicted. Zola used the crime as the basis for a short story, 'Un Mariage d'Amour', which was accepted by *Le Figaro* towards the end of 1866. He was so attracted by the theme that passion can drive people to any lengths – even murder – that he expanded the same material for *Thérèse Raquin*, though making one important change. In his novel the murderers are not caught by

36

instead punished by a life of nightmares and eventual homicidal madness. His belief that the passions of one human being for another can generate every animal instinct is explored more searchingly, and with masterly handling, in two later novels, *Earth* and *The Beast in Man*. There are many original aspects of *Thérèse Raquin* which place it considerably above most melodramas of this kind. In essence it is a thriller and a precursor of dozens of novels and films using the same theme of lust, murder and the destructive potential of joint guilt; *The Postman Always Rings Twice* and *Double Indemnity* are two close parallels that come instantly to mind. Its simplicity is deceiving. There are only four major characters and four minor characters. Long descriptive passages are entirely absent but the descriptive prose which is rationed out is hauntingly effective. The construction is as tight as a drum, proceeding from one logical step to the next, threading its way through the ironies Zola distributes through the narrative to leaven the grim, often nightmarish drama. The constant irony is the presence in the household, every Thursday evening, of a group of very dull and boring friends. Over the years the tragic events and deceptions take place right under their unsuspecting noses, yet one of them is moved to say, just before the dénouement, 'It's so comfortable, this house, that one never thinks of going.' To which another guest adds, 'That's right. This room smells of honest people; that's why we all feel so much at home.'

If it lacks an epic quality and finer shadings, *Thérèse Raquin* is nevertheless a little masterpiece of the storyteller's art.

In *Madeleine Férat*, Zola's next novel, two lovers are similarly destroyed by a ghost which comes between them, although this time the intruder who completes the triangular time-bomb is real flesh and blood. The 'ghost' is actually a weird idea – the author's belief that a woman's first love affair can leave an ineffaceable imprint upon her sufficient to blight all her subsequent relationships with men. The blurb on a paperback version of the novel sums it up in twenty-two words: *He married his mistress. Could her past be wiped out? Can a woman escape the stigma of nights spent with another man?*

It is one of the flaws in Zola's working methods that, on rather too many occasions, he seems to borrow the ideas of others with uncritical enthusiasm. As a result he was rarely stuck for an idea, but the practice led him often on to the thin ice of credulity. In *Madeleine Férat*, for example, he transplants an intriguing theory gleaned initially from Jules Michelet's *L'Amour* and followed up in a treatise on heredity by a Dr Prosper Lucas. Although neither Michelet nor Lucas were oracles on the subject of love, Zola accepted their theory as scientific truth, and proceeded to treat it as a natural law governing the actions of his heroine, Madeleine. Briefly – Zola expounds it over several pages – the notion is that a woman remains inescapably tied to her first lover not merely by bonds of affection, remorse or memory, but *organically* and regardless of her new ties, however powerful. If a woman should meet her first lover again she would be unable to resist returning to him if that should be his desire.

Moreover, the theory went on, a woman, once impregnated, carries the seeds of that first impregnation for any length of time, and even should she have a child by a subsequent partner, the child would inherit the characteristics of the first lover. It's all preposterously difficult to swallow, but Zola did.

There could be, of course, a personal reason for Zola's credulity: the obsession which supposedly erupted at the start of his love affair with Alexandrine, the unreasonable fear that he would lose her to her former lover, a medical student, should he return. The experience made him quite ill, we are told, and imprinted the wild theory more deeply in his mind, despite the fact that no such catastrophe happened, nor was even threatened. Jacques, in the novel, is also a medical student, but the autobiographical echoes don't end there. Both the author and his hero, Guillaume, were teased and bullied at school; both fled into a dream world in their youth to escape the vicissitudes of reality. In the character of Monsier de Viargue we find Mosieur Zola, the author's father; both were aliens and visionaries; both had only sons who suffered from their fathers' untimely deaths. Madeleine, of course, is an idealised Alexandrine; the verisimilitude was so striking at the time that many of the novelist's friends and colleagues were convinced that the fictional trio consisted of Zola and Alexandrine with Cézanne as Alexandrine's first lover.

This obsession about the strange power of the first lover formed the theme of a three-act stage play Zola had written in 1865. He had hawked it around the theatres without success. But he had constantly pondered its theme and, after completing *Thérèse Raquin*, set about translating the drama into prose. The result was a story published as a serial under the title *Shame*, only to be discontinued following a fuss by the paper's subscribers. Zola then passed the manuscript to Lacroix for publication as a novel, for which there was absolutely no demand from either the booksellers or the public. Zola fumed at this massive indifference until, hearing the merest whisper of a rumour that the imperial censor disapproved of *Madeleine Férat*, he set about to try and make capital out of it. With his publisher as anxious as he was for publicity, the ambitious author wrote a press release setting himself up as a martyr to bureaucracy. Lacroix, for his part, was to be ready to flood the bookstalls with the new novel the moment the fuse was lit. It was a damp squib. Nothing happened: the censor wasn't really interested and neither were the newspapers, although this didn't prevent Zola from writing to Marius Roux, 'All the newspapers are talking about it!'

In the novel nobody talked about, Guillaume, the young hero, is a fugitive from life; a shy, introspective dreamer. In a scruffy Paris hotel he meets Madeleine who has just been deserted by her lover, who has left for overseas to take up a commission as an army doctor. The two lonely people find a bond in their disappointments and in time become lovers. Guillaume idolises Madeleine and she returns his love and affection; and several months pass in this state of happy bliss.

But then a cloud appears on Madeleine's horizon. Staying one night at a country hotel during a violent storm she is disturbed that circumstances have orced them to occupy the very room in which she had made love to the other man, many months before. The coincidence chills her with foreboding. Then, oon after, back in Paris, Guillaume comes home one day distraught with the ews that his closest friend has been reported drowned. It transpires that this ld school friend, who was like a brother to him, is Jacques, who – can you guess? – was also Madeleine's former lover. Guillaume doesn't know this, owever, and apart from Madeleine's disquiet no harm has been done, for she eeps the secret to herself. They marry and live peacefully in the country, and a hild is born to complete their happiness.

Three years later, amazingly, Jacques turns up. He hadn't drowned at all. He eets Guillaume by accident, and is invited home. Madeleine shuts herself way in a room during his visit but when he leaves, after being questioned by er husband about her unsocial behaviour, breaks down and admits the ormer liaison. Both are terribly upset by the dark coincidence but common ense prevails and, realising they love each other, attempt to shake off the ursuing ghost by fleeing to Paris. They leave late at night and, half-way on heir journey, decide to put up at an inn. It is only when Madeleine looks round the room while Guillaume is stabling the horses that she discovers that his room, too, was a former love-nest of hers. In mounting consternation she ecognises objects in the room – and even finds the message '*J'aime Jacques*' crawled on a piece of furniture by her finger dipped in ink.

But hang on! Jacques's return journey has been interrupted, too, and he is lso staying at the inn. He sees Madeleine, though not Guillaume, because the anic-stricken woman drives him away. When her husband returns, she tells im everything, and again they flee. But their devotion crumbles in the ghostly resence of Jacques.

> If her heart no longer loved Jacques, the fatal memory of her flesh was unchanged. She was his for ever. In vain had the love emotion faded out, the bodily effect of that possession had thereby lost none of its potency. The marks of the liaison which had made a woman of a girl had survived her love. Even though all she now felt for him was a dull hatred, she was still Jacques' wife. Guillaume's caresses, five years of other embraces, had never sufficed to purge her limbs of the man who had first entered there, to take her puberty. She was shaped, fashioned by the male, for all time, and a crowd might have tried in vain with their kisses to fade out those first kisses she had known. Her husband possessed merely her heart. Her body was no longer to be given, she could only lend it. (13)

Even their little daughter Lucy seems to have some of Jacques's facial haracteristics, and Guillaume also begins to notice certain of his friend's nannerisms in his wife. The situation finally gets beyond them when juillaume wakes up one night to Madeleine's moans, only to find that she is usting after her former lover in her sleep:

> One night, hearing her moaning, Guillaume thought she must be ill. Sitting up in bed, he drew back a little, the better to see her features in the night-light's glimmer. They were alone in their bedroom, this night, Lucy's cot having already been put back in the room next to theirs. Madeleine was now no longer groaning. Leaning over her,

Guillaume anxiously peered at her features. By sitting up, he had drawn th
bedclothes away and partially uncovered her bare shoulders. He then suddenly sa
that mother-of-pearl skin ripple with an under-current of spasm, and the scarlet lip
of the young woman who lay beside him were parted in a smile of great tendernes
Yet Madeleine was sound asleep. Suddenly, a nervous shock seemed to convulse he
She moaned again, but the moan was soft and poignant. The skin of her bosom wa
faintly suffused with blood. Choking, she began to mutter. 'Jacques, Jacques!' h
heard in a low voice. She sighed faintly.
    Pale, frozen at heart, Guillaume slipped from the bed. His bare feet sank into th
thick pile of the rug. Stooping down, in the shelter of the bed-curtains, he sa
Madeleine jerking. It gripped him with horror as if he had witnessed some monstrou
perversity. For nearly two minutes, he gaped at her, unable to look away, listenin
despite himself to the young woman's mutterings. She had now thrown back th
bedclothes and held her arms wide, continuously repeating that name, ever fainte
yet ever caressing.
    It was too much; Guillaume was outraged. For a moment he felt he must strangl
this wretched woman, so replete she was with the other man, so turgid with bodi
lust.   (13

Something has to be done, obviously, so Madeleine decides to seek ou
Jacques in Paris, explain things, and ask him to go away out of their lives
Jacques, you see, knows his friend Guillaume is married, though not t
Madeleine, and he knows Madeleine is married, though not to Guillaume! Bu
the moment his ex-mistress steps into his room her former feelings flood bac
and within minutes she is the victim of her fatal flesh and captive in Jacques'
bed. As she swoons in illicit ecstasy the clock strikes twelve.

    Humiliated and overwhelmed by her traitorous body, Madeleine flees bac
to her family, resolved to kill herself in some way. But at their country home
fresh tragedy awaits her. Lucy, who had been ill from smallpox, died while sh
was away in Paris. At exactly twelve o'clock. As in *Thérèse Raquin*, the finale is i
the finest tradition of Greek tragedy.

    One feature crops up rather too frequently in this synopsis of the story, an
that is 'coincidence'. The succession of coincidences is the chief critica
objection to this novel as a realist work. As with so much of Zola's fiction
romance and fantasy triumph over the naturalist trappings. If we can forge
Zola's pseudo-scientific intentions, *Madeleine Férat* is an exciting, engrossin
drama of tormented passions, enlivened with perceptive observations. It is
measure of the novelist's emerging powers that he almost tricks us int
accepting his absurd theory of the indissoluble tie, although all conviction flie
out of the window when Lucy expires at the very moment her mothe
experiences her adulterous orgasm.

    Although in many ways it is a less satisfactory novel than *Thérèse Raqui*
Madeleine Férat is a far more complete and rounded work. As character
Thérèse, Camille and Laurent in the former novel are quite simplistic, an
carry conviction only because they are supported by a narrative which rarel
flags. They are like objects passing by in a swift-flowing stream; we are nev
able to examine them closely. Madeleine and Guillaume, on the other hand, ar
each exposed in some depth; for the first time Zola had created two characte
who are individually believable in a far from convincing setting. Without the

40

Madeleine Férat would be in danger of sinking out of sight in the slush of its improbable melodrama.

The writing of both these novels provided valuable experience to Zola in deploying realism as a fictional device by giving him the chance to observe how his imagined characters performed in real settings. There was also another benefit, a fortuitous guiding light in the confused greyness of his literary intentions. He had sent copies of *Thérèse Raquin* and *Madeleine Férat* to the critic Hippolyte Taine, for review. But instead of reviewing them, Taine – whom Zola revered – wrote him two long and thoughtful letters advising the young author to discard the intensely dramatised miniatures of domestic life and apply himself instead to the larger canvas and wider horizons of contemporary life and social movements; to have as his models Balzac and Shakespeare; to see mankind rather than a man, singular. The advice could not have come at a more opportune moment; it was the crystal implanted in Zola's mind, super-saturated with drifting, swirling ideas, which was to seed the crystallisation of the *Rougon-Macquart* chronicle.

At the close of 1868 the novelist was wretchedly hard-pressed for money, but having crossed the Seine he had no intention of returning to the Left Bank with its painful memories of poverty of a more hopeless kind. If he was poor in pocket, his life was enriched by an ever-widening circle of friends, which now included Pissarro and Degas among the painters; Duranty, a young writer; and the Goncourt brothers, whom he visited regularly at their home in Auteuil. The gulf between him and the two brothers, Edmond, sombre and gentle, and the elegant Jules, was vast. He had debts up to his ears; they had money to squander. Although he admired them greatly he could not suppress the opinion that they were snobs and spoiled dilettantes to whom writing was almost a hobby. To Zola the brothers were always polite and attentive but as aloof as priests with private incomes.

The writers among Zola's friends were now beginning to outnumber the painters, although he still frequented the artists' unofficial 'club', the Café Guerbois on the Avenue de Clichy. The old regulars – Monet, Degas, Fantin-Latour, Pissarro and Cézanne – had been joined by Frédéric Bazille, who shared a studio with Monet, the landscapist Guillemet, and the sole female artist of the group, Berthe Morisot. Zola had become very close to Manet, who had painted his portrait; in return he dedicated *Madeleine Férat* to the artist. The dedication contains the merest note of wistfulness, as though Zola wished to reaffirm a friendship to which he would, as the world of fiction overtook him, contribute less and less:

TO EDOUARD MANET

The day when, with an indignant voice, I undertook the defence of your talent, I did not know you. There were fools who then dared to say we were two friends in search of notoriety. Since these fools placed our hands one in the other, may our hands remain for ever united. The crowd willed that you should have my friendship; this friendship is now complete and durable, and as a public proof of it, I dedicate to you this book.

Émile Zola

41

With Cézanne, however, relations were becoming decidedly strained. In the summer of 1866 they had spent a long holiday together at Bennecourt, a nearby country village on the Seine, perhaps hoping to recapture flashes of their youthful idealism. But it had passed forever; they had been blooded, in those few years, into a world harsher by light-years from their idyllic life at Aix. Subsequently the novelist found himself more and more irritated by Cézanne, who seemed to be progressively retreating into himself. Zola had already tasted success of a kind; he was moving ahead fast and it would be only a matter of time before he 'arrived'. The artist, on the other hand, was bogged down with problems and seemed to be making no headway at all. Zola, with his pathological dislike of failure, jumped too soon to the conclusion that his distressed friend was doomed to be defeated. Cézanne, certainly, didn't make things easier with his surly outspokenness and untidy appearance, and no doubt the novelist found him an embarrassment as he began to move among more sophisticated people, many of whom made no secret of their dislike for the rough, crude bohemian.

Of all the rebel artists, only Cézanne was rejected by the 1868 Salon. A tolerant jury hung works by Manet (even his portrait of the Salon's arch-enemy, Zola), Pissarro, Renoir, Monet, Sisley and Solari, and the event was proclaimed a breakthrough by the dissidents, so long held at bay. Zola covered the Salon for *L'Événement Illustré*, now published by a new proprietor. He wrote that Manet's victory was now complete, and that

> the classical landscape is dead, killed by life and truth... Our (new) landscapists set out at dawn, painting boxes on their backs, happily like hunters who love the open air... they are personal interpreters, translating truths in original languages; they remain true while preserving their individuality. They are above all human, and mix their humanity in the smallest tuft of painted foliage. That is why their works will live.

Zola was now twenty-eight, a walking storm of conflict, tense and serious, racked by money worries and consumed by bouts of ferocious energy. His new philosophy of hopeful materialism gave him a feeling of confidence and security, and he began to see salvation as the coming to terms with the real, tangible things of the world, the exploitation of all the new scientific discoveries. 'Humanity will glide exultantly over the sheer slopes of science,' he wrote.

Of more immediate significance, however, is a sentence he added to the preface of the second edition of *Thérèse Raquin* in April 1868: 'What is required now of the writer of a new novel is that he should view society with a wider vision, paint all its many and varied aspects, and in particular write clearly and naturally.'

These are the words of a writer preparing himself for a task attempted, but never before achieved, in the history of literature.

5

An End
and a Beginning

By the close of 1868, The Goncourt brothers had revised their first impression of Zola as a stiffish and superficial young man. In December that year they recorded in their famous diary that he was, on the contrary, a person with a most complex personality... 'a rebellious victim of some malady of the heart... a disturbed, profound, reserved and complicated man...'

They were even more impressed when, one afternoon, in a burst of unaccustomed loquacity, the young writer poured out some incredibly ambitious plans for a master work he intended to write: a long series of novels, perhaps as many as ten, peopled by multitudes of characters and holding a mirror to all the machinery that was changing society – capitalism, government, religion, industry and warfare. It would take him, he told them, five years to write.

'If only', the novelist complained, 'some publisher would back my talent with a five-year, 30,000 franc contract!'

Unfortunately, as Zola worked away on his great scheme during the winter and spring of 1869, the only news from publishers was bad. Neither *Thérèse Raquin* nor *Madeleine Férat* were likely to justify third editions, and Lacroix, so he heard, was on the brink of bankruptcy. There was no other way to keep the wolf from the door than accept any kind of ill-paid journalistic hackwork. He fretted at dissipating so much creative energy on ephemeral dross, for the more he developed his cycle of novels the more exciting the project became. It is fascinating to glimpse the novelist's first thoughts on an enterprise which – although he did not know it at the time – was to take up all but ten years of his long professional life. Here they are, the first hardly visible strands of what was to become an enormous web of facts, incidents, characters, ideas and words – nearly five million of them:

I wish to paint, at the opening of a century of truth and liberty, a family which throws itself toward the immediate good, and which is defeated by its own impulsiveness and by the fatal convulsions of a world in torment.
The study will simply analyse the world as it is. I will only state facts. It will be a study of man placed in an environment, with no sermonising. If my work must have a purpose, it shall be to tell the human truth, to display the human machinery, revealing the concealed springs of heredity and the influences of the environment.

43

I must have passion, keeping a single and sustained breath in my work which, rising from the first page, will carry the reader to the last.

The novels should be massed into chapters, logically constructed... instead of multiplying scenes too much I will choose a limited number and study them thoroughly and deeply... I must animate everything with the breath of passion.

I must adopt, above all, a philosophical discipline, not for show but to provide direction for my work. Materialism will be ideal.

A drama must grab the public by the throat. They may get angry, but they don't forget. If not nightmares, I must give them something they'll remember...

Zola was now forging the literary philosophy for his life's work. Already, in a very short time, he had thrust himself to the forefront of a new school of fiction.

The French classic novelists had written through an almost environmentless character, man in limbo. As the world he lived in had always been there, would always be there and would always remain the same, there was no point in describing it. The character in these novels was *Life*, with an unchangeable identity.

Then came the 'slice of life' realists, Flaubert and Goncourt, whose novels dealt with particular cases, individual case histories, accepting and reporting reality as it was. But while he enthusiastically endorsed the Goncourts' theories of realism, Zola felt the need to develop them, objecting especially to the lack of poetry and passion in the realist outlook. He wanted to generalise first and then get down to particular cases selected to fit into his generalisation.

Naturalism to Zola was, like realism, the re-creation of reality. But this was achieved not by merely reflecting what was seen and heard, but by translating reactions, feelings and experiences with any appropriate technique: symbolism, lyrical expression or personalised reporting. Naturalism was also a method for the times. The new social movements, economic pressures, the emerging power of labour and of the state – none of these could be adequately dealt with by the existing schools of fiction. A new world was demanding a new approach, and a writer ignoring these demands was clearly writing of and in the past. Zola wanted above all to bridge the gap between the old and the new and yet still be read and understood by the public. To write an unread book was, to Zola, to achieve nothing.

The setting for his chronicle of a family would be one he knew intimately: the Second Empire, which began with a *coup d'etat* in 1851, a national takeover masterminded by a group of clever opportunists with Napoleon III at their head. It ushered in a strange, schizoid society. The Imperial Court lived aloof in its own world, a non-stop pageant of extravagant splendour which was rebuilding Paris into a glittering showpiece but doing nothing to alleviate the misery and poverty of its citizens; while the rest of the population lived in another world, one enduring the shockwaves of momentous social upheavals and from the collision of scientific advances, new technologies and emerging industries with the old order. The great gap in between was the rich hunting-ground for packs of rapacious adventurers, a breeding ground for incompetence and corruption. The Empire, Zola saw, was a structure that was all façade, one with such rotten foundations and design that it was doomed to crack apart and crash to ruins through the depredations of the busy worms and termites within its fabric. Nothing could suit his purpose better.

Zola's own construction, by contrast, was going to last. Its foundations, as 1869 progressed, were beginning to look as though intended for a really colossal edifice. As he had shown in the epic poems of his youth – one ran into thousands of couplets; another had a theme embracing all creation – he was not intimidated by the size of a project. Most writers display considerable courage when they sit down to spend a year or so writing a single book. Unless they are fortunate, they have no guarantee the book will be published; or, if it is, whether it will meet with public approval, scorn, or, worse, indifference. That the book might provide bread for its author is a hope only nurtured during hysterically optimistic moments. Yet Zola was planning a cycle of ten novels, each linked but self-contained, which would grow to twenty novels, a complex saga involving over a thousand characters and hundreds of plots and sub-plots, all meticulously planned and researched, a literary continuum that would span more years of its author's life than of the Empire he was writing about.

Much of the inspiration for the gargantuan scale of his design lay in Zola's often acknowledged admiration of Balzac. The wild, erratic romantic, the passionate lover and wry chronicler of life, was Zola's literary hero, and although they shared few things in common, one was a prodigious energy and the other was a fascination for power and size. Towards the end of 1866 Zola had been invited to contribute a lecture to a national scientific congress at Aix. His subject was a survey of the novel, beginning with the Greek romances and ending with a round of unrestrained applause for Balzac. From that date one might say the germ of his Second Empire epic was placed in his mind, and he went on to make a close study of the master's works.

Zola's borrowing from Balzac was, however, far from uncritical. In his methodical way he carefully summarised the differences in their outlook. The basis of Balzac's *Comédie humaine*, he wrote, was, with its all-embracing, frameless theme and two thousand characters, a history of morals. Zola, though, saw his frame of reference more restrained; his portrait was to be of a family, not all contemporary society, and the reactions of its members to their environment. He would have laws, not principles: laws of heredity and atavism. He would not, like Balzac, put forward decisions on the affairs of mankind, nor would he be political, philosophical or moral. He would observe, and seek reasons, but not conclusions. He would reveal the truth about his fictional family by exposing the interior mechanisms which directed them. Balzac was a romantic, drawing the substance of his novels almost exclusively from his experience and intuition. Far from being a precise planner he was often grossly disorganised; even the idea of *La Comédie humaine* came to him in a flash of inspiration rather than as the result of prolonged thought. Balzac's undisciplined collection of stories was, despite its unifying title, never finished: it may have been complete in his head, but among his notes titles exist for which there are no stories; sketches and drafts exist for which there are no completed manuscripts. He was notorious for massive alterations and additions to printers' proofs, and endlessly rejigged chapters and passages from one end of a book to the other. Balzac's contribution to Zola's project, and to literature, was predominantly *scale*, for no writer has surpassed the sheer size and range of his highly original creation: a world, if you like, of his own. Yet no individual novel of his can be called a masterpiece, and very few books from his tremendous output are commonly read today. Balzac's reputation rests on his total achievement, on the richness and vitality of all his writing, and upon the legend of his own colourful life.

While Zola shared his hero's capacity for big thinking, he was, unlike Balzac, a meticulous planner. He would tackle the challenge of his epic cycle with the thoroughness of a military campaign, with detailed observations and field work, disciplining and drilling his facts and characters, plots and ideas, to fit neatly into his preconceived plan. The secret of success, he felt, was all in the plan. From his hazy conception it grew, step by step, like an architect's structural design, into the plan of a formal framework in which the novelist's imagination could freely wander as he built upwards, changing, adding and modifying as he wished.

Zola now put his mind to the fabrication of the great structure. His inner soliloquies are set down in the preliminary notes for the first of the novels and now, over a century later, we can listen as he methodically argues with himself:

> As a writer I must dominate. To dominate, I must present a certainty, a truth. Taine says all great writing must be founded on a philosophy. Therefore I must search for a philosophy, a law which embraces all things. It will be new, which means it must draw on contemporary thinking. The most forward thinking today is in the realm of science. Thus my philosophy will be based on science.

Like many of his contemporaries, the novelist was caught up in predicament and doubt. His experiences during the previous five years had amply demonstrated to him that the world was real flesh and blood and not an illusion created by religion. Moreover he believed the Catholic Church was an essential cog in the exploitative and unjust society he saw around him; it sat on the rights of the ruling classes, fat and complacent, an enemy of free thinking and liberty. Science, though, was making breathtaking strides; every day there was some new discovery. In this decade alone, Zola could point out Pasteur's germ theory, Lister's antiseptic surgery, the Transatlantic cable, the cell theory, dynamite and bicycles. In the past few months margarine, celluloid and washing machines had been invented, and as he pondered on these scientific marvels, preparations were at that moment being made for the opening of the greatest engineering triumph of the century, the Suez Canal. What next! Science had made more impact on civilisation in half a century than religion had in a millennium. All society had to do to secure its future was to exploit science for the common good.

For to Zola, the novel was not just the greatest art form, but an instrument with the power to bring about social reforms and even to inspire the dawn of the age of scientific enlightenment he dreamed about. On his battlefield, science would be pitted against religion, labour against capital, education against oppression. Although some of Zola's characters were to be among the most famous in literature, he was rarely to be as concerned with their minds as with external influences on his creations. His characters are placed in an environment and totally at the mercy of it. Earlier in the century and before, the classic novelists displayed brilliant insight into the workings of their characters' minds, with which they were almost completely preoccupied. But the harsh realities of the nineteenth century could not be ignored; it was an age of change, of new and pressing dilemmas, of stunning discoveries. The conscientious novelist could not ignore the impact these changes and problems had made on every man, woman and child, increasingly trapped in a world not of their own making. Zola's involvement with the material aspects of life reflects this, and also reveals his need, in common with the people he wrote about, for something enduring, something solid, in a world of changing values.

One area of discovery which especially intrigued the novelist was the emerging science of genetics. That heredity might furnish a suitable stock upon which he could graft fictional themes had been in his mind for some time; it was, he shrewdly noted, more scientifically based than those other poor, overworked literary devices, Fate and Coincidence. Increasingly, he found himself in the medical, physiology and neurology departments of the Bibliothèque Impèriale in Paris, though not so much in search of a philosophy as a formula, a catalyst, to unite all the elements of the grand scheme that was so vividly in his mind.

Although Gregor Mendel's famous laws of heredity were published in 1866 and 1869 they were not recognised even by biologists until the turn of the century, so it is fairly certain Zola was unaware of them. But the possibility that human behaviour might be controlled by hereditary influences was confirmed for Zola when he read Dr Prosper Lucas's *Traité de l'hérédité naturelle*, which had appeared in 1850. At that time, ideas on heredity were so speculative that it suited Zola perfectly to use them as the muscles on the skeleton of his project; he could add his own imaginative extensions to the theories of the scientists without too much fear of ridicule or contradiction (which turned out to be good strategy; many of the wild theories were not refuted until after Zola's death!). The various heredity theories were also simpler and more believable than the complex laws of temperament he'd used in *Thérèse Raquin* and *Madeleine Férat*. And their scope seemed unlimited; in genetics, permutations are immeasurably complex; in the span of three generations alone there can be over a thousand factors influencing a single result.

It is true that Zola had previously grasped and utilised pseudo-scientific theories without proper comprehension, but the evidence suggests that he entertained no great faith in the then fashionable notions on heredity. His background reading was comprehensive and he merely accepted the ideas for what they were: speculations, spoons with which to stir his own inventiveness. In any case, they obviously helped him get his teeth into his project, and the use

47

of genetic theories was to prove a valuable device for disciplining and identifying his vast cast of characters.

Running through Zola's work, though, is one theory to which particular exception is taken, and the reason will quickly become clear. This is the theory of 'organic lesions' which suggests that a wider range of attributes and defects than we accept today could be transmitted from parent to child and to future generations. A child conceived in drunkenness, for instance, is very likely to become an alcoholic, or at least be prone to alcoholism. Physiological damage to the brain and nervous system could not only be transmitted, but even be predicted by studying the medical history of an individual's antecedents. As Zola accepted that human behaviour was the exact sum of heredity and environmental influences, one might therefore predict, given the necessary facts, the likely future behaviour of any individual. The theory is intriguing, if spurious, and one can see why it appealed to the novelist as a vehicle in which to contain and blend the motives for the behaviour of his multitudinous, related characters. That, in the event, this wild notion had so little effect on the quality of the concept and characterisation of his novels is attributable to many factors which will become obvious as we go along. One of the most important of them, however, is that while Zola's characters may be subordinated to his genetic theories, they are rarely absolutely so (in only one novel, *The Beast in Man*, is a character completely the victim of his genes) and, far from being puppets activated by hereditary strings, they are subjected to varied environmental influences. Squalid living conditions, poverty, official corruption, injustice, neighbourhood and family relationships – all these play a part in determining the behaviour of the characters in Zola's fiction.

Zola's choice of the Second Empire as the setting for his proposed cycle of novels was profound, and also personal. He had grown up in its materialistic hustling; he had witnessed its contempt for human rights and its arrogant rape of Paris; he had sensed the brittle unease of its rulers and had heard the snarling of its pack of predators; and all this had left deep scars on his impressionable mind. Now he had to create a fictional family through whom all his feelings and observations could be projected. He had in mind a family which combined two distinct branches, one of which would be legitimate, the other illegitimate. The members of the first branch would be clever, and assert their superiority by exploiting the members of the second branch, who would represent the dispossessed working class, fighting for survival and doomed by blood and circumstance to be defeated.

The title of his chronicle was chosen with great care, to reflect the legitimate and illegitimate branches of the family tree. The novelist placed a curious importance on the names of his characters: to him there was a complementary bond between a man and his name. Illogical as the notion is we commonly prejudge someone by their name. For some reason, possibly emanating from childhood, I have an aversion for people named Raymond or Ronald; a blockage that is often instantly overcome and replaced by pleasure as soon as I neet them. Zola would pore for hours over directories and lexicons until his intuition rewarded him with a name that fitted the character he had in mind.

The names Zola finally chose were *Rougon* and *Macquart*. The Rougons were to be the legitimate, privileged branch of the family. It was the surname of one of the novelist's fellow students of the Aix Lycée, the grandson of a former mayor, which had stuck in Zola's mind. It was not an uncommon name in southern France and has a pleasant sonority, almost the ring of a cash register about it. Just as fitting was the name he chose for his illegitimate characters: Macquart, which is undeniably squat and ugly, whether read or said, with an implication of vulgarity and low breeding. The complete title of his work was *The Rougon-Macquart: the Natural and Social History of a Family under the Second Empire*.

Zola summarised his plans for the family in a statement included as a preface to the first novel of the cycle, part of which reads:

> *I wish to show how a family, a small group of human beings, conducts itself in the society in which it is placed, flowering and giving birth to ten, twenty individuals who appear at first glance to be very dissimilar but who, upon examination, are seen to be intimately bound one to the other. Heredity has its laws, like gravity.*
>
> *By taking into account the twin question of temperaments and environments, I shall attempt to find and trace the thread which leads mathematically from one individual to the other. And when I have all the threads, when I hold the whole social group in my hands, I shall show this group in action in a single period of history. At the same time I shall analyse the total will of its individual members and the overall driving force of the whole body.*
>
> *The prime characteristic of the Rougon-Macquart family, the group I propose to study, is its overflow of appetites, the revolutionising feature of our age, which encourages excessive self-indulgence. Physiologically, these appetites are the gradual results of accidents to the nervous system and blood which occur in humans as a consequence to some previous organic lesion, and which determine the sentiments, desires and passions of each according to environmental influences; in other words, all those instinctive human manifestations we refer to as virtues and vices. Historically, these appetites originate with the people, spread through contemporary society and climb to every level from the impulse generated in the lower classes as they progress in their social development; and thus, through their individual dramas, they document the history of the Second Empire.*

The *Rougon-Macquart* springs, like a cluster of plants, from the soil. To grow, the plants need death and decay to feed upon. Some plants have an advantage and outgrow the others, stunting and eventually choking them so that they die, to create more nourishment. Then they, too, die or are cut down, replenishing the soil for yet another regenerative cycle of germination, growth, death, decay and rebirth. This primal cycle, which is as much human as vegetable, provides the basic theme for the *Rougon-Macquart*. Fittingly, it is introduced in the first pages of the first book in the novel-cycle:

The earth, which had been glutted with corpses for more than a century, literally perspired with death; and it had been necessary to open a new burial-ground at the other end of the town. The old cemetery, long abandoned, had been gradually purified by the dark, thick-set vegetation which used to sprout over it every spring. This rich soil, in which the gravediggers could no longer delve without turning up some human remains, possessed a most formidable fertility. The tall weeds, which overtopped the walls after the May rains and the June sunshine, were plainly visible from the high road; while inside, the place presented the appearance of a deep

49

DIAGRAM OF THE ROUGON-MACQUART GENEALOGICAL-TREE.

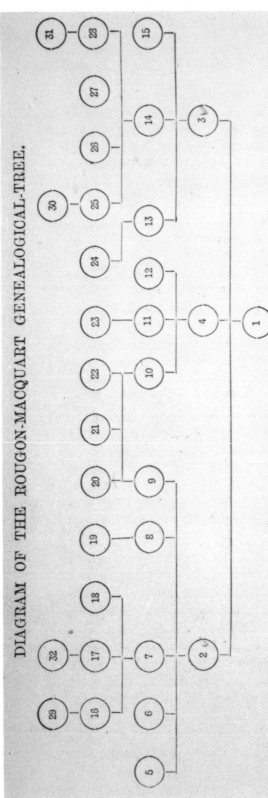

First Generation.

1. ADÉLAÏDE FOUQUE, called AUNT DIDE, born in 1768, married in 1786 to Rougon, a placid, lubberly gardener; bears him a son in 1787; loses her husband in 1788; takes in 1789 a lover, Macquart, a smuggler, addicted to drink and half crazed; bears him a son in 1789, and a daughter in 1791; goes mad, and is sent to the Asylum of Les Tulettes in 1851; dies there of cerebral congestion in 1873 at 105 years of age. Supplies the original neurosis.

Second Generation.

by her a son in 1840, a daughter in 1847; loses his wife in 1854; has a natural son in 1853 by a work-girl, Rosalie Chavaille, counting consumptives and epileptics among her forerunners; remarried in 1865 to Renée Beraud Du Chatel, who dies childless in 1864. An adjunction of characteristics, moral prepotency of his father, physical likeness to his mother. Her ambition, modified by his father's appetites. A clerk, then a speculator. Still alive in Paris, directing a newspaper.

8. SIDONIE ROUGON, born in 1818,

there deserted by him; is married in 1852 to a workman, Coupeau, who comes of an alcoholic stock; has a daughter by him; dies of misery and drink in 1869. Prepotency of her father. Conceived in drunkenness. Is lame. A washerwoman.

15. JEAN MACQUART, born in 1831, married in 1867 to Françoise Mouche, who dies childless in 1870; remarried in 1871 to Mélanie Vial, a sturdy, healthy peasant-girl, by whom he has a son, and who is again *enceinte*. Innateness, as with Pascal and Hélène. First a peasant, then a soldier, then peasant again,

ness to her mother. Heredity of a form of neurosis developing into idiocy. Still alive at St. Eutrope with her brother Serge.

23. JEANNE GRANDJEAN, born in 1842, dies of a nervous complaint in 1855. Reverting heredity, skipping two generations. Physical and moral resemblance to Adélaïde Fouque.

24. PAULINE QUÉNU, born in 1852, never marries. An equilibrious blending of characteristics. Moral and physical resemblance to her father and mother. An example of honesty. Still alive at Bonneville.

ceiver of taxes.

3. ANTOINE MACQUART, born in 1789; a soldier in 1809; married in 1829 to a market dealer, Josephine Gavaudan, a vigorous, industrious, but intemperate woman; has three children by her; loses her in 1851; dies himself in 1873 from spontaneous combustion, brought about by alcoholism. A fusion of characteristics. Moral prepotency of and physical likeness to his father. A soldier, then a basket-maker, afterwards lives idle on his income.

4. URSULE MACQUART, born in 1791, married in 1810 to a journeyman-hatter, Mouret, a healthy man with a well-balanced mind. Bears him 3 children, dies of consumption in 1840. An adjunction of character-istics, her mother predominating morally and physically.

Third Generation.

5. EUGÈNE ROUGON, born in 1811, married in 1857 to Véronique Beulin d'Orchères, by whom he has no children. A fusion of characteris-tics. Prepotency and ambition of his father. Physical likeness to his mother. A politician. At one time Cabinet Minister. Still alive in Paris, a deputy.

6. PASCAL ROUGON, born in 1813, never marries, has a posthumous child by Clotilde Rougon in 1874; dies of heart disease on November 7, 1873. Innateness, a combination in which the physical and moral characteris-tics of the parents are so blended that nothing of them appears manifest in the offspring. A doctor.

7. ARISTIDE ROUGON, *alias* SACCARD, born in 1815, married in 1836 to Angèle Sicardot, the calm, dreamy-minded daughter of an officer; has

Œuvre du Sacrement.

9. MARTHE ROUGON, born in 1820, married in 1840 to her cousin François Mouret, bears him three children, dies in 1864 from a ner-vous disease. Reverting heredity, skipping one generation. Hysteria. Moral and physical likeness to Adélaïde Fouque. Resembles her husband.

10. FRANÇOIS MOURET, born in 1817, married in 1840 to Marthe Rougon, who bears him 3 children; dies mad in 1864 in a conflagration kindled by himself. Prepotency of his father. Physical likeness to his mother. Resembles his wife. At first a wine-merchant, then lives on his income.

11. HÉLÈNE MOURET, born in 1824, married in 1841 to Grandjean, a puny man, inclined to phthisis, who dies in 1853; has a daughter by him in 1842; remarried in 1857 to M. Rambaud, by whom she has no children. Innateness as in Pascal Roujon's case. Still living, at Marseilles, in retirement with her second husband.

12. SILVÈRE MOURET, born in 1834; shot dead by a gendarme in 1851. Prepotency of his mother. Innate-ness with regard to physical re-semblance.

13. LISA MACQUART, born in 1827, married in 1852 to Quénu, a healthy man with a well-balanced mind. Bears him a daughter, dies in 1863 from decomposition of the blood. Prepotency of and physical likeness to her mother. Keeps a large pork-butcher's shop at the Paris markets.

14. GERVAISE MACQUART, born in 1828, has three sons by her lover Lantier, who counts paralytics among his ancestors; is taken to Paris, and

teristics. Moral prepotency of his father, physical likeness to his mother. Idle, inclined to spending unearned money.

17. CLOTILDE ROUGON, *alias* SACCARD, born in 1847, has a son by Pascal Rougon in 1874. Prepotency of her mother. Reverting heredity, the moral and physical character-istics of her maternal grandfather preponderant. Still alive at Plassans.

18. VICTOR ROUGON, *alias* SACCARD, born in 1853. Adjunction of character istics. Physical resemblance to his father. Has disappeared.

19. ANGÉLIQUE ROUGON, born in 1851, married in 1869 to Félicien de Hautecœur, and dies the same day of a complaint never determined. Innateness: no resemblance to the ma-ternal side. No information as to her father.

20. OCTAVE MOURET, born in 1840, mar-ried in 1865 to Madame Hédouin, who dies the same year; remarried in 1869 to Denise Baudu, a healthy girl with a well-balanced mind, by whom he has a boy and a girl, still too young to be classified. Prepo-tency of his father. Physical re-semblance to his uncle, Eugène Rougon. Indirect heredity. Es-tablishes and directs 'The Ladies' Paradise.' Still alive in Paris.

21. SERGE MOURET, born in 1841. A dissemination of characteristics; moral and physical resemblance to his mother. Has his father's brain, influenced by the diseased condition of his mother. Heredity of a form of neurosis developing into mysti-cism. A priest, still alive at St. Eutrope.

22. DÉSIRÉE MOURET, born in 1844. Prepotency of and physical like-

25. JACQUES LANTIER, born in 1844, killed in an accident in 1870. Pre-potency of his mother. Physical likeness to his father. Heredity of alcoholism, developing into homi-cidal mania. An example of crime. An engine-driver.

27. ÉTIENNE LANTIER, born in 1846. A dissemination of characteristics. Physical resemblance, first to his mother, afterwards to his father. A miner. Still alive, transported to Noumea, there married, with children, it is said, who cannot, however, be classified.

23. ANNA COUPEAU, *alias* NANA, born in 1852, gives birth to a child, Louis, in 1867, loses him in 1870, dies herself of small-pox a few days later. A blending of characteris-tics. Moral prepotency of her father. Physical resemblance to her mother's first lover, Lantier. Heredity of alcoholism developing into mental and physical perver-sion. An example of vice.

Fifth Generation.

29. CHARLES ROUGON, *alias* SACCARD, born in 1857, dies of haemorrhage in 1873. Reverting heredity skipping three generations. Physical and moral resemblance to Adélaïde Fouque. The last outcome of an exhausted stock.

30. JACQUES LOUIS LANTIER, born in 1860, a case of hydrocephalus, dies in 1869. Prepotency of his father, whom he physically resembles.

31. LOUIS COUPEAU, *called* LOUISET, born in 1867, dies of small-pox in 1870. Prepotency of his mother, whom he physically resembles.

32. THE UNKNOWN CHILD will be born in 1874. What will it be?

sombre green sea studded with large blossoms of singular brilliancy. Under the shade of the close-set stalks the very sap seemed, as it were, to boil and ooze out from the damp soil. . .
The trees and vegetation, in their vigorous growth, had rapidly assimilated the decomposing matter in the old cemetery of Saint-Mittre; while the malaria rising from the human remains had been greedily absorbed by the flowers and fruits; so that eventually the only odour one could detect, in passing by this accumulation of putrefaction, was that arising from the strong smell of the wild gillyflowers. It was merely a question of a few summers.   (14)

One can't help noting, in this description of exotic profusion, that there are some disturbing undercurrents in the symbolism. And there is another premonitory clue: 'It was merely a question of a few summers', pointing to the ephemerality of the family and its members, its rapid rise and sure fall, its total dependence on the fertility, the sustaining power of the Second Empire. When the Empire falls and becomes barren, so will the individuals who suck its juices.

The family, then, all the progeny of a common ancestor, falls into clear divisions. The Rougons, the legitimate branch, are driving, ambitious, sometimes brilliant, instinctively motivated by greed. They will provide the spoilers, the exploiters and opportunists and will spawn politicians, bankers and speculators.

The Macquarts, the illegitimate branch, are the exploited workers, always saddled with the burden of their low origins, invariably preoccupied in a fight against the predatory forces which threaten to obliterate them. Nevertheless they contribute some outstanding individuals – an artist, for instance, a revolutionary, a soldier and even a courtesan – but they are all doomed to degradation.

The two sides of the Rougon-Macquart family will, by intermarriage, establish a third line – the Mouret branch – which will occupy the centre of the tree. Its members will constitute a bourgeois group who will prosper for a time but never escape the consequences of their bond of blood with the others.

These divisions, Zola considered, would be logically achieved by choosing a suitable progenitor whose children would issue from two separate unions. Adélaide Föuqué, born in 1768, is the common ancestress of all the Rougons and Macquarts in the chronicle. She is an impetuous and intense woman with an unstable, hysterical temperament. At eighteen she marries a farmer named Rougon, a poor but very ambitious man by whom she has a son before he dies two years later. The son is Pierre Rougon who eventually marries to establish the Rougon branch of the family. Adélaide, who is often referred to in the novels as Tante or Aunt Dide, then takes up with a delinquent, half-crazy alcoholic smuggler named Macquart, by whom she has a son, Antoine, and a daughter, Ursule. Antoine, who develops into a cunning idler like his father, founds the Macquart side of the family; while Ursule marries a hatter, Mouret, who, although infusing some sanity into the line, cannot obliterate the strain of madness contributed by his wife, with the result that their children are either middle-class nobodies or sad neurotics. All the children, then, inherit the highly emotional and avaricious characteristics of their ancestress, although

52

this manifests itself in different ways; on the legitimate Rougon side the descendants are ambitious and astute, whereas the illegitimate Macquart progeny, their mental instability compounded by the father's violent and felonious nature, tend to be extreme neurotic types ranging from genius to homicidal maniac.

The family, as such, is never a community. Throughout the novels they rarely meet. No family photograph could ever have been taken. Indeed, one half of the family seems completely unaware of the other. It is perhaps the most estranged family in the history of fiction and, in a way, provides the antithesis of the classic family saga. The individual members repel, rather than attract one another. This was, of course, Zola's clear intention, to create and study a family of *individuals*, linked by inherited characteristics and only occasionally by involvement with each other. As a general rule, each novel is monopolised by a different single descendant and, interestingly, only five of the eventual twenty novels are concerned exclusively with the Rougon side of the family.

Zola was a man who, if he went on a journey, wanted to know every inch of the route. Timetables and maps would be consulted, officials would be badgered for information, reassurance coaxed from friends. Similarly, in his writing, the novelist would not set his pen on the first page of a book until it had been planned almost to the last detail. It was, I suppose, an indication of his insecurity, and deep doubts about his abilities; the humility, perhaps, of genius. When the critic Sainte-Beuve chided him for using a particular Paris street in *Thérèse Raquin* which was inaccurately described, Zola had been really stung. But there would be no slip-up, if he could help it, in the *Rougon-Macquart*. Every member of the family was named at the outset (with the exception of five, Victor Saccard, Angélique Rougon, Jacques Lantier and the fifth generation children Louis Coupeau and Jacques-Louis Lantier, who were all created later as the project was enlarged) and placed on a genealogical tree, each accompanied by a biography and detailed notes on temperament and medical history.

The fine spring days were melting into the hot Parisian summer of 1869 when Zola took his still unfinished plan for the cycle of ten novels to his publisher. He told Lacroix he would write them at the rate of two a year and that they were his to publish in return for a guaranteed 500 francs a month and a contract for five years. Lacroix hadn't done too badly out of his ambitious author and had great faith in him. The idea appealed and he readily agreed, but the eventual contract reflected more on the publisher's financial troubles than his enthusiasm. Although the agreement allowed Zola to draw his 500 francs a month in advance of delivering the manuscript of his first novel, the author in return had to sign a promissory note for 500 francs each time he collected. This procedure was to continue until the total amount was covered by royalties on sales and income from serial rights. Zola was soon to regret that he ever signed it.

The following months, though, were months of contentment. The novelist, his mistress and his mother moved once more, this time to a three-up, three-down house on the Rue Condamine in upper Montmartre, with its own entrance and tiny garden. It wasn't as grand as it sounds, for the rooms were so cramped that when Zola proudly bought a piano, part of the wall of one of the rooms had to be demolished to fit it in. But the house was quiet, and perfect for the isolation the novelist needed to concentrate on the immense undertaking before him. The 500 francs he drew from Lacroix each month added to the feeling of contentment and, even before he had finished the first novel, the newspaper *Le Siècle* had indicated an interest in the serialisation rights.

In September, Zola was paid a visit by a young writer and poet who was to become the first of his disciples, Paul Alexis. They sat for a while in the tiny, narrow dining-room and drank tea before adjourning to a little pavilion in the garden to talk. The heart and mind of the impressionable Alexis was completely captured at the fateful meeting, during which, under the stars, he felt the great *Rougon-Macquart* work germinating from the very ground beneath him. 'The moment we shook hands', he wrote later, 'I knew the die was cast, that I had just given him my whole heart, and that I could expect in return the solid affection of an elder brother.' Alexis also came from Aix, from Zola's old school in fact, and had followed the older man's career with the enthusiasm of a sports fan. He had ambitions to be a published writer and soon became a regular visitor to the Zola house when he would join the other guests on the lawn – Duranty, Roux, occasionally Cézanne – to hear their host read selections from his latest chapter. Alexis was transfixed by the masterly control displayed in the writing, the organisation of events, the startling realism of the characters. It is not surprising that Alexis became for Zola during the following years what Boswell was to Dr Johnson.

As the summer of 1870 approached, Zola and Alexandrine decided to get married. Their friends were hardly surprised. Zola, they joked, had finally become what he secretly wanted to be: a little bourgeoisie. The relationship had developed into a fulfilling union and neither saw any reason why their attachment shouldn't be permanent. Accordingly, on 31 May, they became man and wife before a small circle of friends, Cézanne, Baille, Solari and Valabrègue, the party celebrating afterwards at a Montmartre restaurant. With her poor, working-class background and lack of education, it was obviously an event of the greatest importance to Alexandrine, and she must have derived great satisfaction from her marriage to a man whose work she may have little understood but which she loyally believed would someday confer greatness upon them both. But Zola drew benefits from the union, too. In a later novel he refers to his belief that a creative artist needs affection to safeguard his peace of mind, and marriage to provide him with a refuge. The times were becoming increasingly uncertain; the sabre-rattling between France and Prussia grew louder each day, and both countries were going through all the motions preparatory to a war. But this was not the only source of Zola's insecurity. Almost a year had passed since *Le Siècle* had agreed to serialise *The Fortune of the Rougons*, the introductory novel to the *Rougon-Macquart* chronicle. Yet here he was, working away at the second novel while the public had not read a word of the first, still unaware of the unique enterprise he was creating. Publication had been delayed by dissent among the editorial management of the paper, and it wasn't until the end of June 1870, that *The Fortune of the Rougons* finally appeared.

Publication of the initial volume of the *Rougon-Macquart* had for Zola the significance of laying a foundation stone, for his commitment to the undertaking was now public; there was no turning back. In it, of course, he also establishes the origins of his fictional family, although the actual events in the novel occupy only a few days in December 1851, during the *coup d'etat.*

The story opens, ominously, in an old cemetery on the outskirts of Plassans, where a young boy, Silvère Mouret, waits for his girlfriend, Miette. Silvère has a gun, and intends to join the band of Republican insurgents who are assembling in the countryside close by. News has just reached Plassans that Napoleon III has overthrown the government of the Second Republic in a *coup d'état* in Paris, and in many of the provinces the Republicans are gathering in a confused attempt to counter-attack to protect the constitution.

The events of this night have been building up for months. The Republicans, although they had held power since the revolution of 1848, could never count on much support from the rural areas of France and the provincial towns. Plassans is a typical town in which the Republicans are outnumbered ten to one by the combined conservatives – the aristocrats and their supporters, the middle classes, the clerics, liberals and royalists – all of whom have been waiting for the opportunity to extinguish the Republic and to return to the monarchy.

Plassans is also the birthplace of the Rougon-Macquarts, and we are here concerned with Aunt Dide's legitimate son Pierre Rougon and his wife Félicité; and her illegitimate son, Antoine Macquart. Rougon and Félicité are retired trades-people with social ambitions quite beyond their modest nest-egg, but they do have a potentially valuable investment in their son Eugène. Eugène is an up-and-coming politician in Paris who for some time has been secretly scheming with Napoleon's supporters to organise the *coup d'etat.* Rougon, his father, is a minor parish-pump politician in Plassans but when Eugène tells him of the impending take-over the value of this information immediately becomes obvious to his conniving mind. Keeping this knowledge to himself, Rougon begins to hold meetings with the local conservatives so that he will be in a good position, after the *coup*, to claim a well-paid government sinecure, the post of local tax-collector, much to the joy and satisfaction of his wife.

On the night of the *coup* in Paris, Silvère and Miette join the assembled army of Plassans Republicans, armed with scythes, pitchforks, muskets and sticks. They march through the countryside singing the *Marseillaise,* but without any clear idea of where to go or what to do. Initially they disarm the gendarmerie in Plassans – in the fight Silvère accidentally puts out the eye of one of the troopers – but hours later the undisciplined mob is routed by a column of soldiers from Marseilles. Miette is mortally wounded in the attack, and Silvère is taken prisoner. The Republicans are vanquished.

In the meantime, Antoine Macquart, who backed the Republicans because he thought they would win, has taken possession of the town hall with twenty or so other sympathisers. While the soldiers are busy pursuing the fugitive rebels, Rougon, disappointed that it is all over so quickly, looks for a short-cut to glory by leading a posse of royalist townsfolk to the town hall to capture Macquart. In the only farcical episode of the novel – a superbly satiric passage underlining the inherent craziness of violence – Rougon's gun is accidently discharged.

> In the struggle, Rougon's gun, which an insurgent had tried to wrest from him, went off of itself with a frightful explosion, filling the room with smoke; the ball shattered a magnificent mirror that reached from the mantelpiece to the ceiling, and was reputed to be one of the finest mirrors in the town. This shot, fired no one knew why, deafened everybody, and put an end to the battle. (14)

After Macquart is imprisoned, Rougon spends the next couple of days dilating on the episode, making it appear that he alone was fearless enough to arrest Macquart in the face of gunfire. Although he is now looked upon as a hero, however, Rougon decides to aim for greater glory and plots with Macquart to round up the remaining Republicans. In return for his freedom and 1,000 francs in cash, Macquart agrees to lead his followers into an ambush on the town hall steps the following night. It all goes according to plan; the Republicans are shot or captured, Macquart escapes, and Rougon is credited with the victory which leaves Plassans in the hands of the royalists.

The account of the *coup d'état* in Plassans closes with two moving episodes – both symbolic – which foreshadow Zola's great power as a novelist of genius. After the ambush, Macquart hides in Aunt Dide's house where, only a short time before, the old lady had been paralysed by a stroke. When Rougon arrives to pay Macquart the thousand francs, however, Dide struggles from her bed in a delirium and brands the two half-brothers as murderers. The effort costs the old woman her sanity, and she sinks back into mute imbecility, never to talk again for the rest of her life, a cautionary reminder of the family insanity right through to the final novel in the chronicle. One of her grandsons, Pascal, is a doctor, and as soon as he sees her he attributes the stroke to some shocking sight she has recently witnessed.

It is true. When returning to the house a few hours before she had seen Silvère, another of her grandsons, shot in cold blood as a Republican prisoner. For days the loyalist troops had been rounding up the scattered insurgents, and thousands died in the cruel reprisals. Silvère had been captured while still mourning over his lover, Miette, and might have escaped death had he not been recognised by the gendarme whose eye he had blinded. Maddened with pain and hungry for revenge, the gendarme had taken Silvère into the cemetery, the same cemetery the youth and Miette had used as their meeting place, and has blown his skull apart with a ball from his pistol. Silvère's tragic death symbolises the destruction of the first ideal of the Revolution, while Rougon's triumph is as pointedly symbolic of the corrupt foundations on which the Second Empire was to be built.

In transferring the significant events of the 1851 *coup d'état* to the smaller stage of conservative Plassans Zola showed considerable ingenuity, for it allows us to examine the mechanism of a political overthrow under strong magnification.

Plassans is none other than Zola's home town of Aix-en-Provence, and indeed the author's dislike for the upper-crust, pro-monarchy families he knew in his boyhood surfaces at times in the soured portraits of some of the characters, particularly those of Rougon and his wife Félicité. But the overall portrait of the town, its factions and rivalries, reflects memories of observations which have the unspoiled, intuitive clarity of youth.

In Plassans, political power is in the hands of the conservatives, comprising two main groups, the old aristocratic families and the middle classes, both contemptuous and suspicious of each other. The Republicans are not only in the minority but are politically inept, disloyal, uneducated and easily led. Zola has little difficulty in demonstrating how, by exploiting the dissensions and inertia of all the political groups, the Second Empire was largely the creation of a surprisingly small opportunist élite whose first loyalty was to themselves.

Zola's treatment of the conflict is impartial despite his own strong Republican sympathies. In fact neither side emerges with any credit. The novel can be summarised as a satire on man's pretension that an ideal society can result from violence, whatever the political excuse. The heroes in the novel are only heroic because they are deceived or deceive themselves, while the political strong-men are merely selfish individuals. Zola had a healthy distrust for politicians and political parties, not so much because he thought power was inherently corrupt in that it corrupted all who touched it, but that it was simply beyond the capacity of man to control it.

It is a pity in a way that *The Fortune of the Rougons* is the opening book in the *Rougon-Macquart* chronicle for it is not an easy book to read. A substantial part of the novel is taken up with the background of the Rougon-Macquart clan and although much of it is interesting – it is at times a fascinating glimpse into a crowded and colourful family album – it demands patient concentration and thus effectively dislocates the narrative, often at crucial moments. On several occasions the reader is plucked from accounts of the most exciting action to study complicated genealogy and great slabs of history. That Zola was unconscious of this structural defect is illustrated by the fact that he added considerably to his cast of characters – none of whom play any direct part in the plot – in a later edition of the book in 1872. These massive intrusions wreck any semblance of unity in the novel and it is interesting in this regard to compare *The Fortune of the Rougons* with the nineteenth novel in the cycle, *The Debacle*, published in 1892. By then the author's technique had flowered to the extent he could take three or four times as many characters and incidents and weld them into one magnificent whole.

In the late summer of 1870, France experienced one of the great series of convulsive spasms of the kind Zola had planned for the *Rougon-Macquart* – war, defeat, insurrection . . .

Were it not for the frightful casualties inflicted by both sides, the voluminous records of the Franco-Prussian War suggest nothing so much as the libretto of a comic opera. The prelude to the war which both the French and the Prussians regarded as inevitable went on for ten years, during which the French suffered a succession of diplomatic defeats. By the end of the decade, Napoleon III's prestige and credibility were badly on the wane, internationally and at home. The new sphere of French influence he'd hoped to establish in the Americas was dashed with Maximilian's defeat in Mexico. Then in 1866 the Prussians had taken a mere seven weeks to overwhelm Austria, while France stood by, shaken and dumbfounded. National pride took a further knock when the neighbouring north German states were unified under Prussian domination. With the breakdown of talks to establish an alliance with Austria and Italy the entire eastern frontier was either hostile or noncommittal. This was a constant worry to the French so that when, in July of 1870, the Prussian Prince Leopold announced his candidature for the throne of Spain – vacated by Queen Isabella – the threat of encirclement was the final straw. France demanded the withdrawal of the candidature and evened the diplomatic score by getting King William of Prussia to agree. Regrettably, though, she overplayed her hand by insisting on a guarantee that the candidature would not be renewed. At this point the Prussian king's chief minister, Otto von Bismarck, exploded; was the king's word not enough? The insult was sufficient to provoke the two countries, and war was declared on 19 July.

From the outset France was outnumbered and outmanoeuvred by the Prussian military machine, out-generalled by the wily Field-Marshal Moltke and ignominiously defeated by its surfeit of top-brass buffoonery, absence of planning and criminal neglect of opportunity. With mounting dread French citizens read their newspapers; almost daily they announced fresh defeats. Only two weeks after war had been declared, MacMahon's corps was routed at the Battle of Worth; thereafter August was a pattern of French retreat and Prussian advance. The final curtain came down at Sedan, where MacMahon and Napoleon III, the latter distracted by stones in the bladder, commanded the hastily organised remnants of the French army. Tired, their morale shaken and vastly outgunned, the French capitulated in three days, leaving the way clear for the Prussians to advance on Paris.

The shock defeat of the army and the capture of the Emperor spelt the end of the Second Empire, and as the Third Republic was proclaimed in Paris on 4 September, Empress Eugénie fled to England. The bloodless revolution was led by three men, Jules Simon and Jules Favre, both moderate Republicans, and Léon Gambetta, a radical Republican. The Third Republic, although it was to last for seventy years, saw the light of day in the most chaotic conditions, and in a mood of doubt and desperation. The exiled Victor Hugo returned from the Channel Islands the very next day to the delight of a crowd of admirers; backed by veterans of the 1848 Republican government he was chosen as leader of the left-wing opposition party. Edmond Goncourt, however – his younger brother Jules had died a few months before – viewed the celebrations as presumptuous and complained that the Republican supporters were a rowdy rabble, acting more like frivolous holiday-makers than the citizens of a city soon to be put to the sword.

On 19 September the Prussians reached Paris and began the famous siege. Astonishingly, the spirit of unification Napoleon III strove for in vain spread across the invaded country from beleaguered Paris. More tangibly, Gambetta himself floated heroically above the heads of the Prussians in a balloon, escaped, and set up a provincial branch of the government to direct the war.

At first the besieged inhabitants of Paris met the privations and shortages with a commendable stoicism, although Goncourt, disheartened by the lack of real spirit among the people, tartly argued that it was indifference, not bravery. 'All their heroism will have consisted in eating sirloin of horse instead of sirloin of beef,' he wrote, 'but being quite unaware of the difference, the Parisian being far from fussy, even at the best of times, about what he eats'. It was just as well. As Christmas approached the carp were all taken from the pond in the Luxembourg Gardens and the pet population shrank dramatically. Rats sold for a franc apiece and pieces of bread were exchanged for sex on the streets.

Shortly after war was declared Zola, despondent though he was, wrote a rousing Republican anti-war article for *La Cloche* and was immediately summoned for inciting contempt and disobedience of the law. Only the rapid advance of the Prussians and the proclamation of the Republic a month later saved him from certain prosecution. After that, exempt from military duty because of his two dependent women, he stood by, helpless and disconsolate. 'The war', he wrote to Goncourt, 'has struck the pen from my hand.'

A few days after the Third Republic was proclaimed, Zola, Alexandrine and his mother had hastily left Paris for Marseilles, amid confusion and misgivings. Zola's motives for fleeing in face of the Prussian advance are not entirely clear, although it is recorded that Alexandrine was in poor health at the time. Zola's friends Baille and Valabrègue planned to go to their home town to help defend it against the Prussians; Alexandrine, understandably frightened, asked to be allowed to travel with them. Her mounting fear could have led the novelist to take the entire family away from the city but the probable truth is that, with the Prussian army just two weeks' march from Paris anybody with the means to leave and somewhere to go, and with no inclination to shoulder a rifle, would readily do so. In the event the Zola bolthole was Estaque, a small coastal town within sight of Marseilles, where Paul Cézanne lived with his mistress Hortense.

With his income cut off (the serialisation of *The Fortune of the Rougons* had ceased on 10 August) and two women to support, Zola's priorities were economic rather than patriotic, and he quickly decided to leave Alexandrine and his mother in Estaque and go to Marseilles with the intention to start a newspaper to support the new Government of National Defence headed by Gambetta. With the aid of Marius Roux and a local publisher, the newspaper *La Marseillaise* appeared at the end of September 1870. It was not a success. Sales were poor, the paper was hit by shortages of cash and labour, so he then decided to seek some sort of government post. Casting about, he fixed his sights on the Sub-Prefecture of Aix where, he was heartened to learn, all the councillors had been dismissed amid wild scenes on the day the Republic had been proclaimed. After much enquiry, however, Zola found that the post had already been filled. Instead, in December, he was hired as a secretary to a government minister at Bordeaux at 500 francs a month. At about the same time his ill-fated newspaper closed down; strangely, no copies have survived.

From Bordeaux, crowded with well-to-do refugees, bewildered officials and paralysed by the most incredible disorder, the novelist viewed the stricken country with alarm. Although relieved to be receiving a salary again he could not hide his cynicism for the 'comedy' as he described the provisional government at Bordeaux. Although his contempt for politics and politicians wasn't as profound then as in later life, it is odd that he should have so actively sought a position in government. Afterwards, reflecting on the events, he claimed he could see no other way at the time to support his wife and mother. The chaotic war had certainly thrown him into despair and confusion. His friends were scattered everywhere, and out of touch. Renoir, Manet and Degas had joined the army. Flaubert was in Normandy, Monet and Daubigny in England. Pissarro, who had found himself directly in the path of the Prussian advance, had also fled to England; all his paintings were destroyed and his home was used as a slaughterhouse. 'I imagined', Zola said later, 'that the world was coming to an end, and that no more books would ever be written.'

For France, at any rate, the war *was* coming to an end.

Although huge numbers of volunteers were mobilised and had some successes, they were no match for the disciplined Prussians, the haphazard communications, and a particularly severe winter. It is doubtful whether, in the closing weeks, the average foot soldier knew who or what he was fighting for. Yet there were enough examples of outstanding courage to win back for France some of the international respect she had lost under Napoleon III – the tiny fortress at Bitche, for instance, held out for six weeks after the end of the war and even then only surrendered on the orders of the government. But, even with this new respect, France remained alone, without allies. Inevitably, after 131 days and not without honour, besieged Paris gave in, and on 28 January 1871, the government signed an armistice.

The cost was terrible. Of the million and a half men involved in the conflict, some 200,000 had died and a quarter of a million had been injured. Despite the lessons of the Crimean War fifteen years earlier, 17,000 French soldiers had died of disease and lack of medical care. The French agreed to pay the Prussians an indemnity of 5,000 million francs, to give up the provinces of Alsace and Lorraine, to maintain an occupation army and to allow Prussian troops to stage a triumphal parade through the streets of Paris. Although this act of national humiliation set the stage for peace, recovery and unification, the outrage rankled sufficiently to be a key factor leading to the establishment of the Paris Commune within two months. The country began to open its eyes to the shock and horror of its defeat. 'It was as though we were waking from a nightmare,' Zola wrote, '... as though, through a long, cold winter, we had crouched in a muddy ditch, waiting to die.'

But fresh horrors were in store for France.

During the four-month siege of Paris the revolutionaries had been active, especially in the poorer quarters and among the evacuees who had poured in from the overrun countryside. And in the absence from the city of most of its politicians and leading citizens there was little opposition to their cause. The echoes of the Prussian army's victory march along the Champs Elysées had barely died away when the revolutionaries began to stir the feelings of national outrage into open revolt against the authorities, whom they blamed for the defeat.

In the chaotic conditions following the war a hastily organised and limited franchise election in February resulted in a surprise victory for the two royalist parties. The Legitimists (who believed the monarchy should rule by divine right), the Orléanists (who believed the monarchy should rule by the will of the people) and the Republicans (who believed the monarchy should be abolished) each won about an equal number of votes, thus giving the conservatives an overwhelming majority. That thirty representatives of the discredited Bonapartist party should have been elected, even in an assembly of some 600, indicates just how conservative the national electorate was – although, significantly, the situation was dramatically reversed in the more democratic municipal elections two months later. This not unexpected turn of events, plus the fact that the army and the police were controlled by the Orléanists, undoubtedly led to the Communards' 'now or never' decision to form their own revolutionary government in Paris.

The moment arrived when it became known that instead of coming to Paris the National Assembly was to move from Bordeaux to Versailles which, with its royal associations, implied the threat of a restored monarchy. Forthwith the revolutionaries proclaimed Paris a commune on 28 March 1871, abolished conscription, burned the guillotine, closed pawnshops and clamped down on Catholic control of education. As a symbolic gesture the Commune's Central Committee ordered the destruction of the Vendôme Column, erected in 1810 and topped by the statue of Napoleon III made from the brass of captured cannon. In this they were probably acting belatedly on the recommendation of the artist Gustave Courbet, made soon after the proclamation of the Third Republic the previous September. The huge triumphal column was enthusiastically demolished and crashed to the street amid flying dust and masonry and the jeers of the crowd. Poor Courbet who, although he inspired its destruction but was not a member of the Committee when the decision was made, was penalised severely by successive governments; apart from a six-month prison sentence he was banned from the 1872 Salon and billed for some 300,000 francs for the statue's repair and re-erection.

The Commune provoked mixed reactions among the intellectuals. Goncourt, not surprisingly, was its most sardonic critic; the workers, for him, represented 'convulsive agents of dissolution and destruction'. Paradoxically, he blamed the disorder on the newly won freedom of the press, but reserved his greatest loathing for the middle-class Parisians, whom he labelled moral cowards. 'You could rape their womenfolk before their eyes, or worse – you could steal their purse from their pocket without upsetting them in the least.' On the other hand Courbet wrote ecstatically of the absence of police, quarrels and ill-feeling: 'I am enchanted. Paris is a veritable paradise!' The artist, for once, was blind to the deep shadows in the landscape that would soon make Paris a veritable hell.

The reasoning behind the Commune showed considerably more foresight than most of the political thinking of the time. Rightly suspecting that the power vacuum left by the collapsed Second Empire would be filled by autocratic conservatives elected by the restricted provincial and rural vote, the radical leaders had planned to establish Paris as a revolutionary state, with other worker-dominated cities as satellites. The idea was ingenious, and even possible; but the insecure, emotion-charged condition of the country and the near-total breakdown of communications proved to be obstacles impossible to overcome. The revolutionary torch was carried across France but was caught at only a few cities, Lyons and Marseilles among them. At Marseilles, regular army troops, led by a government general and backed by the town authorities, attacked the city and recaptured it in a decisive, bloody assault in which 150 citizens were killed and 500 arrests made.

Zola and his family returned to Paris on 14 March to face a home that had been commandeered as a refugee shelter. The little house meant a great deal to the novelist and he worried constantly about it in his absence, even to the extent of sending Paul Alexis money for the gardener to protect his roses. Alexis seems to have acted as housekeeper during this period and managed to confine the family installed there to the ground floor, having removed Zola's valuables to an upstairs room.

The mood in Paris was electric. When the government infiltrated troops into the working-class suburbs, instead of instilling fear into the population the confrontation between soldier and citizen produced little more than friendly bantering. The frustrated Thiers, who had been appointed chief of the executive of the Republic, then withdrew not only the army from the city but the entire civil service. Paris was under siege again, this time by its own government.

Zola, at this time, must have been somewhat at odds with his conscience. Some of the most dramatic chapters in his country's history were being enacted before his very eyes yet all he had done was to sit on the distant fringe, and taken no part in the drama. It seems that, as with many of the country's intellectuals, he was paralysed into a state of depression and inertia by the succession of sudden and violent events. He must have discovered, too, that he was useless without a pen in his hand, and the ambivalent situation could have given him little joy.

Everything had changed, but nothing had. *Le Siècle* mechanically resumed the interrupted serialisation of *The Fortune of the Rougons* until it concluded on

21 March. On most days Zola commuted by train to Versailles, where he reported, in an increasingly desultory fashion, the doings of the new Assembly. With a sinking heart he watched helplessly as the government blundered from one absurdity to another, and as the radicals fell from reason to riot. The sounds from the army firing squads at Versailles echoed to the very depths of his conscience, for his sympathies lay with the Communards. He could no longer bring himself to sign his dispatches. He wished for the end of the phoney peace, but dreaded it, too, for he knew Thiers and his ministers were preparing for a final, bloody showdown.

During his travelling to and from Paris and Versailles, Zola was evidently so preoccupied with his thoughts that he seemed unaware of the danger he was in. One day he was arrested by the Communards and only released after protesting his Republican sympathies. A few days later he was arrested again, this time by government forces, and only the chance intervention by the son of a prominent politician secured his release. 'My only consolation', he wrote, 'is that there is no third government to arrest me tomorrow.' He remained in the city, stumbling short-sightedly among the barricades, deeply lamenting the stupidity of both sides, disoriented and frustrated until, in the middle of May, because of the growing bombardment – shells sometimes whistled over his house – he took the family to Bonnières until it was over.

Thiers' government was now becoming disturbed by the solid resistance of the Communards. But fear alone did not motivate the bloody reprisals they were planning. It was necessary, after the humiliating defeats of the war, to show a strong arm to the electorate, to expiate the humiliation; and here, against an enemy more feared by the bourgeoisie than the Prussians, was the opportunity. Karl Marx said later that the Third Republic had inherited from the Empire 'not only ruins, but also its dread of the working class.'

The twenty-first of May 1871 was a warm, sunny Sunday. In its owner's absence the big plum tree in Zola's garden dappled the lawn with gently moving patterns of light and shade. Below Montmartre, anglers sat unconcernedly on the banks of the Seine. The restaurants and cafés were crowded with patrons, joking with groups of Communard guardsmen in their ill-fitting uniforms about the occasional, distant explosions. Above Montmartre, fashionable ladies in carriages watched the half-hearted bombardment of the city through opera glasses. From one end of Paris to the other there was a suicidal indifference to the holocaust of vengeance that was only twenty-four hours away.

'Bloody Week,' as it has been called, began on the Monday with cautious, disciplined sniping as the embattled Communards were forced slowly back by government troops into the centre of the city. By Tuesday the desperate defenders were reduced to setting fire to buildings to try and stem the advance of the army regulars, and when, in the process, a powder magazine exploded with terrific force on the Left Bank, hell, as they say, broke loose. The sniping became a fusillade from both sides, indiscriminate and murderous; hostages were rounded up and shot in batches which swelled in numbers as the fighting grew fiercer. Innocent citizens caught in the crossfire and who resisted capture as hostages were roped to the railings in front of the Bourse and shot. The slaughter was so merciless that hardened Prussian soldiers, camped on the outskirts of Paris, allowed hundreds of fugitives to escape, despite orders to the contrary. In the La Moquette prison alone, 2,000 were summarily executed by government troops. Another 25,000 died in the streets among the barricades. When the fighting was over, 13,000 were speedily condemned to prison and another 70,000 were deported and exiled. For many days afterwards the Seine ran blood; decomposing corpses bubbled phosphorescently in the dark water by night. Vast pits were dug ten metres deep to receive thousands of anonymous bodies; in other places corpses were buried superficially wherever there was soil. A shaken *Evening Standard* reporter (8 June 1871) described one chilling incident: 'In the daytime the roar of the busy streets prevented any notice being taken; but in the stillness of the night the inhabitants of the houses in the neighbourhood of St Jacques-la-Boucherie were roused by distant moans, and in the morning a clenched hand was seen protruding through the soil. . .'

Finally, the smoke from the raging fires cleared and the echoes of the executions in the *Père Lachaise* cemetery died away. But the evocation of the sight, the sound, the smell of butchery among the buildings, in the houses and gutted ruins, in chapels even; the knowledge that blood had flowed into countless cracks on friendly footpaths, that savagery had rampaged along the dignified boulevards, all of it just an omnibus ride from his home; that the unspeakable, the *unthinkable*, had been committed each minute of every hour through eight bloody days, was as ghastly a memento for Zola as it was for any combatant. It was all a memento for which he needed no notes, but the horror of it would stay with him for two decades, when it would be regurgitated in *The Debacle*. On his return to Paris Zola wept, as much for the future as for the past.

6

Picking Up
the Threads

While the war and the Communard insurrection raged about him a precious bundle of paper was burning a hole in Zola's baggage. This was the half-completed manuscript for the second *Rougon-Macquart* novel, *The Kill*. But for many weeks after the last explosion was heard, the last shot fired, the final drop of blood shed, the novelist found it impossible to pick up the threads of its narrative. Rather larger problems were ravaging his concentration, problems which had been worrying him for many months.

Although Zola's person, family and property had escaped unscathed during the crisis, his most prized possession, the plans for the *Rougon-Macquart* chronicle, was in shreds. Only a year before, at the beginning of *The Fortune of the Rougons*, he had dramatised the fall of the Second Republic and the bloody birth of the Second Empire. He had publicly announced a commitment, his intention to write ten or so novels, each one a contemporary study of life under the Second Empire. And in doing so, he had intended to predict the eventual collapse of the whole rotten social structure.

Now, no prediction was necessary; the Second Empire had abruptly crumbled into history. The novels he'd intended to write on contemporary life would now be little more than historical romances; instead of drawing from the juices of daily life they would choke in archival dust. The idea of becoming a mere recorder of dead history shrieked against all his inclinations and beliefs. And there was no turning back; somehow a solution would have to be found.

Zola's solution was an ingenious and logical compromise. The setting would have to remain within the time span of the Second Empire; there was no escape from that strait-jacket. But the more he thought about it, the less important the chronological and historical elements seemed to be. Life, he soon observed, was not appreciably different in 1871 than during the two decades of the Empire; nor, considering the right-wing Republican government which had moved into power, was it likely to change much in the next two decades. Even his half-written novel, *The Kill*, and the events it described, would not be out of place. Although the story was woven around the creation of Haussmann's Paris and the scandalous speculation which ravished the city in the 1850s, a brief visit to the Bourse convinced Zola that the speculators, eager to share in the economic boom that was following on the heels of the disastrous war, were just as rapacious and as insatiable as they'd been during the Second Empire. By playing down the chronological and historical aspects of his chronicle, Zola reasoned, he would be able to write books about contemporary life after all, although they would appear between historical covers. Apart from the birth and death of Napoleon III's regime, which was historical fact, he would deliberately write his narratives out of historical context. The physical history of the Empire would clothe his novels with the thinnest of veneers. And the only books affected by this change of plans would be the first and the last. The first had already been serialised and was being set for publication as a book in October; but the last, *The Debacle*, which was to have prophetically described a mythical war which brought down the Empire, would now simply re-create the Franco-Prussian War.

But there would be chronological inconsistencies, especially with the ages of some of his characters. Nana's birth-date, for instance, had been irrevocably fixed on his genealogical tree at 1852, and she was to expire, after a long and sordid career, just as war broke out. Zola had thought that war was inevitable and that it would bring down the curtain on the Empire, but apparently thought it unlikely to happen before 1880. His readers of the future, at least those with any eye for historical accuracy, were going to be surprised, for the old harlot would now have to die at eighteen! Although the novelist was probably unaware at the time, the demise of the Empire did bring some benefits to his great literary enterprise, in freeing him considerably from the restrictions of historical fact, and allowing him to exploit a certain amount of hindsight. That he took advantage of this is fairly obvious by the weighty presentient symbolism which recurs throughout the *Rougon-Macquart* chronicle.

At this point Zola's life began to be ruled completely by a new calendar: the *Rougon-Macquart*. The sands of his days were the words he wrote; the hours his pages, regular and unceasing. For more than twenty years he was to be a captive among the cogs of a chronometer of his own making. The overwhelming presence of this vast chronicle in his life demands its own chronology, to which I intend to accede for the balance of this book. From now on his literary achievements will take precedence over the account of his own everyday life, although it will soon become clear that so much of it is reflected in what he wrote. Rather than see the books through the man we will see, perhaps with greater penetration, the man through his fiction.

The Kill, begun before the Franco-Prussian War and finished soon after, is in some ways a continuation of the story of *The Fortune of the Rougons*, relating how, after the *coup d'etat*, the wolves and sharks poured into Paris for their share of the spoils.

Zola's title – *La Curée* – is extremely apt, referring to the skinned carcass of wild animal which is thrown to the hunting pack, as Paris was to the speculator during the early part of the Second Empire. Although sometimes translated a

The Quarry', *The Kill* is far more emotive and therefore appropriate, especially as 'making a killing' is a common English term in financial speculation.

Zola's imagination was forced to move into top gear. While he had stored away ample hard-won knowledge about the poorer classes he knew nothing about high society when he began to write *The Kill*, which says as much about his courage as his naïvety. What he lacked in first-hand experience of the Parisian season, the receptions and fancy-dress balls, the network of *salons* and mistresses, procurers and procured, he made up with study. With Alexandrine he visited the hot-houses of the Jardin des Plantes in Paris to make long lists of the exotic species which bloomed there, spent days poring over auctioneers' inventories of great mansions, and long evenings turning over the fashion plates in the ladies' journals. For behind-the-scenes information about Haussmann's gigantic planning and building operations in the city he spent laborious days examining the files and cost sheets of contracting firms. For his hero's mansion he chose, after some deliberation, the imposing home of a millionaire chocolate manufacturer, M. Menier, although not having the nerve to ask to inspect its interior he satisfied himself by standing outside, visualising its contents. His imagination leapt over the gaps in his knowledge of a world he had never entered, and he was so successful that critics, condemning the novel for its immoral tone, also assailed him for its realism.

Encouraged by his parents' success in Plassans after the *coup d'état* and emboldened by his brother Eugène's powerful position with the new Second Empire government, Aristide Rougon sweeps down on Paris like a carrion bird scenting spoils. He brings with him his wife Angèle and their daughter, Clotilde, but he has little time for his family. A true Rougon, he loves only intrigue and money, and immediately sees his fortune in the massive rebuilding that is going on in Paris.

'They have begun already', he continued. 'But it is nothing much yet. Look down there, over by the Halles, they have cut Paris into four....'
And with his hand spread out, open and sharp-edged as a cutlass, he made the movement of separating the city into four parts.
'You mean the Rue de Rivoli and the new boulevard they are building?' asked his wife.
'Yes, the great transept of Paris, as they call it. They're clearing away the buildings round the Louvre and the Hôtel de Ville. That's mere child's play! It serves to awaken the public's appetite.... When the first network is finished the fun will begin. The second network will pierce the city in every direction so as to connect the suburbs with the first. The remains will disappear in clouds of plaster.... Look, just follow my hand. From the Boulevard du Temple to the Barrière du Trône, that's one cutting; then on this side another, from the Madeleine to the Plaine Monceau: and a third cutting this way, another that way, a cutting there, one further on, cuttings on every side, Paris slashed with sabre cuts, its veins opened, giving sustenance to a hundred thousand navvies and bricklayers, traversed by splendid military roads which will bring the forts into the very heart of the old quarters of the town'.
Night was falling. His dry, nervous hand kept cutting through space. Angèle shivered slightly before this living knife, those iron fingers mercilessly slicing up the boundless mass of dusky roofs. During the last moment the haze of the horizon had been descending slowly from the heights, and she fancied she could hear, beneath the

gloom that was gathering in the hollows, a distant cracking, as though her husband's hand had really made the cuttings he spoke of, splitting up Paris from one end to the other, severing beams, crushing masonry, leaving behind it long and hideous wounds of crumbling walls. The smallness of this hand, hovering pitilessly over a gigantic prey, ended by becoming disquieting; and as, without effort, it tore asunder the entrails of the enormous city, it seemed to assume a strange reflex of steel in the blue of the twilight.

'There is to be a third network,' continued Rougon after a pause, as though talking to himself; 'that one is too far off yet, I do not see it so distinctly. I have heard only a little about it.... But there will be a sheer orgie, a bacchanal of millions, Paris drunk and overwhelmed!' (17

But it takes money, as they say, to make money, and that is what Rougon lacks; and each day intensifies the rapacity in his blood. Then a disaster paves the way to the fortune he dreams about: Angèle dies. Even in her death throes Rougon is considering a proposition from his conspiratorial sister Sidonie, who has come to him with news of a pregnant nineteen-year-old convent schoolgirl whose parents wish to have married to avoid a scandal. What attracts the distracted husband is the girl's half-million franc dowry. When Angèle finally expires, Clotilde is packed off to her Uncle Pascal, a doctor in Plassans of whom we shall hear a great deal later on in the chronicle. Aristide Rougon changes his name to Saccard, marries the young girl, Renée, and is soon elbow-deep in her dowry, which consists mostly of houses and property in Paris.

Through his brother Eugène's influence in high government circles Rougon – now Saccard – obtains a position which enables him to discover the secret routes of the new boulevards being driven through the centre of the city and of the properties due to be appropriated. Using Renée's money he buys and sells these buildings with his cronies acting as dummy vendors and buyers inflating their value with each sale to get the maximum compensation from the government. In a few years of feverish speculation Saccard is a rich man, and with his young wife moves to a sumptuous great house on the Rue Monceau.

Into the household now enters Maxime, Saccard's son from his first marriage, and who had stayed in Plassans to finish his schooling. Maxime is thirteen and already depraved, and soon finds that Renée's luxurious life of pleasure and idleness, spent among the fashionable salons, dressmakers hairdressers and jewellers, is his natural habitat. By the time the limp-wristed young man is seventeen he is her constant companion, 'a little toy man that kissed, and made love, and had the sweetest vices in the world' and who 'had a way of kissing that heated the skin'. At this time Renée, only twenty-one herself and thoroughly neglected by her older, money-mad husband, is bored and satiated, and searching for 'something different'. She discovers it, one evening in the overpowering atmosphere of her tropically heated conservatory, where she spies on Maxime and his young friend, Louise. Renée finds that she is in love with her elegant, dissolute stepson, and her moment of truth is touched by a note of symbolic bitterness:

> The shrub that half concealed her was a malignant plant, a Madagascar tanghin-tree with broad box-like leaves with whitish stems, whose smallest vein distilled a venomous fluid. And at a moment when Louise and Maxime laughed more

loudly in the yellow refraction, in the sunset of the little boudoir, Renée, her mind wandering, her mouth parched and stung, took between her lips a sprig of the tanghin-tree which came to the level of her teeth, and closed them on one of its bitter leaves. (17)

Meanwhile, although neglecting the bedroom, Saccard has not been idle. By speculating, contracting, demolishing and building, he is amassing a fortune. Renée is his crown jewel and despite his greed he sees her 100,000-franc dress allowance and other extravagances as a good investment. Their dinners and parties in the great house are important for Saccard's financial stature and security, and he uses his beautiful wife to charm secrets from government ministers and business competitors. But his fortune is being built on the already crumbling edifice of the Second Empire, unable to bear the weight of the accumulating rottenness.

The appetites let loose were satisfied at last, in the shamelessness of triumph, amid the sound of crumbling districts and of fortunes built up in six months. The town was become a sheer orgy of gold and women. Vice, coming from on high, flowed through the gutters, spread out over the ornamental waters, shot up in the fountains of the public gardens to fall down again upon the roofs in a fine, penetrating rain. And at night-time, when one crossed the bridges, it seemed as though the Seine drew along with it, through the sleeping city, the refuse of the town, crumbs fallen from the tables, bows of lace left on couches, false hair forgotten in cabs, banknotes slipped out of bodices, all that the brutality of desire and the immediate satisfaction of an instinct fling into the street bruised and sullied. Then, amid the feverish sleep of Paris, and even better than during its breathless quest in broad daylight, one felt the unsettling of the brain, the golden and voluptuous nightmare of a city madly enamoured of its gold and its flesh. The violins sounded till midnight; then the windows became dark, and shadows descended upon the city. It was like a colossal alcove in which the last candle had been blown out, the last remnant of shame extinguished. There was nothing left in the depths of the darkness save a great rattle of furious and wearied love; while the Tuileries, at the waterside, stretched out their arms into the night, as though for a huge embrace. (17)

By now, Renée is virtually estranged from this financial madman. Although brought up in an environment of starched, religious gentility she has little defence against the riotous, licentious atmosphere of the Rue Monceau, and sets out to seduce Saccard's son. Maxime has no defence at all, and the lusts of both are inevitably satisfied in a private room in the Café Riche, the scene of many of Maxime's conquests. Their incestuous love-making at first leaves them both shaken but neither finds the will to resist the forbidden delights of their relationship. It is the 'something different' Renée's loins have been aching for, and as Saccard is rarely in the house they give free play to their passion, favouring the conservatory for their illicit copulating. The young woman begins to relish her dominant role.

One night, in an hour of anguish, Renée sent her lover for one of the black bearskin rugs. Then they lay down on this inky fur, at the edge of a tank, in the large circular pathway. Out of doors it was freezing terribly in the limpid moonlight. Maxime arrived shivering, with frozen ears and fingers. The conservatory was heated to such a point that he swooned away on the bearskin. Coming from the dry, biting cold into so intense a heat, he felt a smarting as though he had been whipped with a birch-rod.

When he came to himself, he saw Renée on her knees, leaning over him, with fixe
eyes and an animal attitude that alarmed him. Her hair down, her shoulders bare, she
leant upon her wrists, with her spine stretched out, like a great cat wit
phosphorescent eyes. The young man, lying on his back, perceived above th
shoulders of this adorable, amorous beast that gazed upon him the marble sphin:
whose thighs gleamed in the moonlight. Renée had the attitude and the smile of th
monster with the woman's head, and, in her loosened petticoats, looked like the whit
sister of this black divinity.

Maxime remained supine. The heat was suffocating, a sultry heat that did not fa
from the sky in a rain of fire, but trailed on the ground like a poisonous effluvium
and its stream ascended like a storm-laden cloud. A warm dampness covered th
lovers with dew, with burning sweat. For a long time they remained motionless an
speechless in this bath of flame, Maxime prostrate and inert, Renée quivering on he
wrists. . .

They passed a night of mad love. Renée was the man, the passionate, active wil
Maxime submitted. Smooth-limbed, slim and graceful as a Roman striplin,
fair-haired and pretty, stricken in his virility since childhood, this epicene bein
became a great girl in Renée's inquisitive arms. He seemed born and bred for
perversion of sensual pleasure. Renée enjoyed her domination, and she bent unde
her passion this creature with the still indeterminate sex. For her it was a continua
astonishment of lasciviousness, a surprise of the senses, a bizarre sensation c
discomfort and of keen enjoyment. She was no longer certain: she felt doubts eac
time she returned to his delicate skin, his soft plump neck, his attitudes c
abandonment, his fainting-fits. She then experienced an hour of repletion. B
revealing to her a new ecstasy, Maxime crowned her mad toilettes, her prodigiou
luxury, her life of excess.   (1

Their ecstatic love-making continues for months, until Saccard, innocent o
his wife's adultery, decides to return to the connubial bed. It is not love tha
draws him to it, however, for although he is a wizard with money he is nervou
and clumsy in the presence of women. The true temptress is the deed of a larg
property which lies in the path of a projected boulevard and which, i
Saccard's speculative hands, could be worth millions. It is the one portion c
her dowry Renée has kept intact, on her father's strict advice. Saccard's weapo
is a great bundle of debts, amounting to a couple of hundred thousand franc
which Renée has run up with her dressmaker. By pretending that a series e
business calamities has brought him near to ruin, while at the same tim
heroically offering to settle his wife's outrageous debts, he thinks he will wi
her undying love and trust – and, in due course, her property.

Renée now experiences the most bitter remorse, and the burden of guilt a
having to make love to both father and son almost crushes her. When Maxim
arrives unexpectedly one night and learns that she has a man in her roon
Renée cannot bring herself to tell him it is his father, and her husband; instea
she confesses to having another lover. The fickle Maxime walks out, no
spiteful and determined to marry the deformed, consumptive Louise, whos
million-franc dowry he had previously scorned.

The dénouement, although a model of restraint, is shattering in i
mounting tension and spectacular in its irony, and is among the best dramat
passages Zola ever wrote. During a fancy-dress ball at the house, Renée 'ear
of her stepson's engagement to Louise, and in a blind fury drags him to he
bedroom. There she implores him not to leave her but to elope to Le Havre an
America that very night. Maxime, powerless against his former lover

70

rocious strength, ridicules her by revealing that his father plans to cheat her her property. Protesting that it doesn't matter any more, Renée crushes him to her and kisses him, just as Saccard enters the room.

The three – husband, wife and son – are profoundly stunned; but only until accard's Rougon blood heats up with the smell of money. On the mantlepiece e the deeds of the property transfer which Renée has just signed in order to alise a quick half-million francs for her intended flight with Maxime. As the ice for his condonation, Saccard coolly puts the deeds in his pocket and, with s arm around Maxime's shoulders, amiably walks from the room.

It is a disastrously retributive moment for Renée, whose frenzied sexuality is cruelly mocked by the indifference of her husband and her lover, his son. lthough this is the climax of the narrative it is followed by a touching, collective coda which brings further anguish and a tragic end to the convent rl brought to ruin by the double dose of evil Rougon blood.

The construction of *The Kill* is one commonly used in modern novels, and cidentally paved with dangers: the setting and the main characters are tablished, followed by a series of flashbacks giving the history of the aracters, and then a resumption of an unbroken narrative. The principal nger in this form of construction is that, having barely begun the narrative, e flashbacks can, in unskilful hands, confuse the reader, freeze the action and ll interest.

At no time in *The Kill*, however, are we aware that these dangers exist, for spite flashbacks which take up three of the seven chapters – almost half the vel – the pace is unflagging and one's interest is not only sustained but grows th every page. Zola also courts disaster by bringing the climax of the rrative forward to the second-last chapter, but by then we are so sympathetic Renée's predicament that we are generously disposed to read on to the end.

While much of the action in the novel revolves around Saccard, and depends on him, he is rarely physically present, and thus as a character he exists only a very sketchy portrait, a cipher almost, whom the author uses as a device to pose the speculative excesses of the Second Empire. Saccard's career as an portunist and financier – his name was composed of two syllables sounding e 'two rakes gathering up gold' – is continued in a later novel, *Money*, in ich his portrait is carried to completion.

Far more interesting is Maxime, who appears fleetingly in *The Fortune of the ugons*; he is one of Zola's rare sexually ambiguous characters.

In him the race of the Rougons had a tendency to refinement and became delicate and vicious. The offspring of too young a mother, constituting a strange, jumbled, and so to say unmingled combination of his father's furious appetites and his mother's self-abandonment and weakness, he was a defective offspring in whom the parental failings were completed and aggravated. This family of the Rougons lived too fast; it was dying out already in the person of this frail creature whose sex must have remained in suspense during formation, and who no longer represented a will, eager for gain and enjoyment like Saccard, but a species of cowardice, devouring

71

fortunes already made; a strange hermaphrodite ushered at the right time into
society that was rottening. (1

By other accounts Parisian society had its fair share of these ambiguou
young men and Zola would have ample opportunity to observe them. But it
doubtful that the novelist was ever friendly with a bisexual, which explains wh
Maxime's portrait is essentially one made from a distant, exterior viewpoin
Nor is it at all compassionate; 'a quaint abortion' is one term Zola uses
describe the elegant fop. In tune with his times, he equated bisexuality an
homosexuality with vice and depravity. When Renée's maid reveals the
Saccard's valet, far from being interested in horse-racing, was really after tl
stable lads, she adds: 'It seems that filthy sort of thing had been going on in th
stable for years...' Nevertheless, within the confines of Zola's morality an
limited understanding of the phenomenon, Maxime's ambivalence
portrayed with no more scorn than is Saccard's preference for money over sex

Although Zola's pen slips occasionally, Renée is the novel's most subt
drawn character and although she is useless and depraved she arouses or
sympathy as her sad story unfolds. Like many of the author's heroines Renée
a beautiful animal caught in a trap, and then kept captive to perform accordin
to her master's whims. Her descent from an upright, convent-trained teenag
to a disillusioned, humiliated woman is told with detachment and understan
ing, although there is an ever-present feeling that she is a type rather than
individual. Zola attempts to sow in her early life a portent of instinctive lust, b
the incident he relates, in which as a young girl she spies on a swimming-pool
catch a glimpse 'of the men in their bathing drawers showing their nak
bellies' is surely only healthy schoolgirl curiosity. Renée, sad to say, is just
mindless pawn, seduced into the boring and easy life of a rich man's plaything
She does, however, have a conscience, if not a will to resist, and among the mc
moving passages in the novel are the descriptions of the visits to her fathe
apartment in the Hotel Béraud which, by comparison with the furnace-li
heat of her own house is gaunt, cold and silent. The spare, arctic chill of h
former home symbolises the conscience she left there years before, and ea
visit fills her with sadness.

There are some similarities between Renée and Flaubert's Emma Bovar
but where, with Emma, we are right inside the woman's head, a second or tv
ahead or behind her own thoughts, the subtler shadings of Renée's though
and feelings are inferred by symbolism. Her entire conflict with her passion
conducted in this way, by sympathetic or contrasting objects and atmosphere
as with her return to the antiseptic serenity of her father's home, and the illi
love-making in the tropically hot conservatory. Zola shows a strange reluctar
to go deeply into the minds of his characters; instead he typically backs aw
and projects their feelings with external imagery.

The taboo of incest has been accepted by most societies since antiqui
certainly since early Christianity when St Paul excommunicated the Cor
thians who committed it. Notable exceptions were ancient Peru, Japan, a
Egypt – where incest was a requirement in the royal families – but in

Western world both law and church have come down very hard on perpetrators of the forbidden union. In Britain, incest between consenting adults earned a penalty of seven years' imprisonment, with a life sentence for incest with a minor; and up until 1887 incest in Scotland was punishable by death.

Not surprisingly this mysterious taboo abounds in folklore, mythology and literature, from the biblical account of Lot and his daughters to Sophocles' classic *Oedipus Rex*. Sophocles' tragedy says most of what there is to say about the taboo but down the centuries writers have been unable to leave the theme alone. Shakespeare's Claudius sleeps with his sister-in-law in *Hamlet* to be the forerunner of modern incestuous themes, in Poe's 'The Fall of the House of Usher', F. Scott Fitzgerald's *Tender is the Night,* Herman Hesse's *Damian* and Iris Murdoch's *A Severed Head* among many others. Zola, in *The Kill,* with its rather incestuously tame relationship, barely manages to join the list. Interestingly, when he adapted the novel for the stage, he rang an ingenious change on the incest theme. The adaptation had been suggested by Sarah Bernhardt who, while seeing it as a vehicle for her talents, possibly requested that the incestuous relationship be toned down in some way. Zola achieved this by having the marriage between Saccard and Renée unconsummated, by agreement. Subsequently Renée falls in love with Maxime, and Saccard discovers a passion for his wife, and wants the agreement revoked. Alas, his son has beaten him to the marital bed, thus creating the paradox that if Saccard insists on his marital rights, the *husband* will be committing incest!

In *The Kill* Zola uses two groups of symbolic images to insinuate his themes of lust and decadence deeper into the reader's subconscious. The most transparent of these – used with impressive effect – is the celebrated hot-house in which grotesque tropical plants grow in monstrous profusion. It is in this conservatory that Renée first conceives her passion for Maxime and, in this over-heated, mind-blowing atmosphere, one can hardly blame her.

> At her feet steamed the tank, the mass of tepid water thickened by the saps from the floating roots enveloping her shoulders with a mantle of heavy vapours; a mist that warmed her skin like the touch of a hand moist with concupiscence. Overhead she could smell the palm-trees whose tall leaves shook down their aroma. And more than the stifling heat of the air, more than the brilliant light, more than the great dazzling flowers, like faces laughing or grimacing between the leaves, it was the odours, above all, that overpowered her. An indescribable perfume, potent, provocative, composed of a thousand perfumes, hung about her; human exudation, the breath of women, the scent of hair; and zephyrs sweet and swooningly faint were blended with zephyrs coarse, pestilential, laden with poison. But, amid this rare music of odours, the dominant melody that constantly returned, stifling the sweetness of the vanilla and the orchids' stridency, was that penetrating, sensual smell of flesh, that smell of love escaping in the morning hour from the close chamber of a bridegroom and bride.
> (17)

But all the time the plants are shrieking their warnings. Tendrils are 'bent and twisted like the limbs of cripples' and tiger plants exhale an 'acrid breath, as from the throats of the convalescent sick'. Death is never far from illicit love, and to drive the point home Renée, in a gesture of self-immolation, bites on the bitter leaf of a Madagascar tanghin tree, 'whose smallest veins distilled a venomous fluid.' One can be in little doubt among these vegetable stop-signs that Renée is about to embark on a dangerously illicit adventure. Zola's intuitive use of lush vegetation to symbolise forbidden desire is interesting, for it pre-dates the Freudian interpretation of luxuriant growth by at least a couple of decades.

Tropical heat also plays an important part in his vegetative imagery; it is always present when Renée and Maxime lust after one another. The incestuous lovers can't get enough of it. Renée seduces her stepson in a stiflingly hot room in the Café Riche. Even the flaring gas jet increases the temperature. In the house they draw the curtains and build up the fire and light candles, shutting out the accusing sun. Even Renée's remorse is made bearable by exposing herself to the scourging, hellish heat:

> In this burning atmosphere, in this bath of flames, she almost ceased to suffer; her pain became as a light dream, a vague oppression, whose very uncertainty ended by becoming voluptuous. Thus she lulled till the evening the remorse of yesterday, in the red glow of the firelight, in front of a terrible fire, that made the furniture crack around her, and that at moments deprived her of the consciousness of her existence. She was able to think of Maxime as of a flaming enjoyment whose rays burnt her; she had a nightmare of strange passions amid flaring logs on white hot beds. (17)

Zola's second-line symbolism in the novel isn't nearly so successful, however, and derives more from his obsessional love–fear regard for female nudity than from his intuition. To Zola, nudity equated with depravity, and evidence of this superficial morality shows up time and time again throughout the *Rougon Macquart* chronicle. In *The Kill* decadence is consistently emphasised by mute displays of nudity. The decor of Saccard's house is a museum of semi-erotic statuary: baskets of plaster flowers are supported by 'great naked women with straining hips' and elsewhere 'great naked women are playing with apples' and satyrs carry off swooning maidens and so on. It was meant to shock, and it probably did excite the Victorian reader, but it hardly evinces even a mild thrill today. All this imagery really does is to strike a false note, for one wonders who was responsible for the tatty décor in the first place. Renée appears to have had no part in it, and decorating wasn't Saccard's scene at all. The truth is that Zola was the designer; the fictional house on the Rue Monceau was a repository for all his erotic bric-a-brac, the stuff he would have liked to have placed in his own home but couldn't. Away from the plaster cupids, though, the nudity motif does contribute to the voluptuous atmosphere the novelist was striving for; the merciless repetition of hot breaths, bare shoulders and musky perfume does, in the end, convey a world of steamy sensuality from which we are allowed to escape, only on a few occasions, to the fresh outside air.

While few modern readers could possibly be shocked, or aroused in the slightest by the goings-on in *The Kill*, it cannot be denied that some of the sensual scenes, for instance the love-making in the Café Riche and on the bearskin in the hot-house, are extraordinarily exciting and memorable. Why? The supporting symbolism we know about, but surely this cannot be the whole answer. Perhaps it is because they are written with a vivid intensity springing from the author's own confused sexuality, a conflict between fear and desire. They are not mere breathless descriptions by a writer peculiarly gifted in the genre, but key-hole glimpses of deep-sourced images rising out of his own mind, darkly varnished with sensual symbolism, tantalising projections that will flash again and again through the pages of the *Rougon-Macquart* and which will cease only when, late in life, their source will be destroyed by a most unexpected event.

The Café Riche seduction scene certainly lingered in the minds of some of the gentlemen in the Public Prosecutor's office in Paris, who called the author in for an interview. The novel had begun serialisation in *La Cloche* at the end of September 1871, and had only run a month when the volume of complaints about it reached such proportions that Zola was warned that a prosecution would follow unless the story was dropped. Disappointed that a change of government had not significantly changed the censorial powers of the police, the novelist no doubt argued that the scene emphasised the decadent morals of the Second Empire. But the Public Prosecutor was apparently a less fervent Republican than Zola who reluctantly abandoned the idea of fighting the case for its publicity value and agreed to the cessation of the serial on 5 November. The novel was published as a book the following January.

The Kill is one of Zola's most sensational novels, with its electric emotional episodes, its mounting tensions and its violent colouring. Interest never flags for a moment, and the book is as enjoyable today as it ever was. The great gulf between this novel and its lumbering predecessor, *The Fortune of the Rougons*, is almost breathtaking, and reveals the great reserves of power and technique waiting in the wings.

Soon after the publication of *The Kill*, Lacroix, who had been under considerable financial pressure for some years, finally went bankrupt. It was a heart-sinking disaster for Zola, for the publisher's creditors seized all the promissory notes he'd signed, amounting to many thousands of francs, and which he was now forced to repay. The hoped-for royalties against which he signed the notes had not eventuated, and from a life of modest comfort he was plunged, overnight, deeply into debt. Apart from small amounts from his newspaper articles he had no publisher and no income, and had his wife and mother to support. In sinking despair he went to one publisher after another, without luck, until, after many weeks, he won the interest of Georges Charpentier, a young man who had just inherited his father's business on the Quai du Louvre.

The young Charpentier was an intelligent and, fortunately for Zola, an adventurous publisher, eager to make his mark. His father had established a conservative back-list of romantic authors; nothing remotely approaching a realist novel had ever issued from his press. But the idea of promoting Emile Zola appealed to Charpentier as a gesture of independence from his father's ideas. It was a little daring, too, for at that time his new author was far from

75

being a successful novelist; so far the public had responded to his genius with the alacrity of snails. Before agreeing on a contract, however, Charpentier sought the advice of Théophile Gautier, who was one of his father's friends. Gautier, it seems, nourished quite an admiration for the novelist – ironically enough, as a romanticist – and advised the publisher to take him on. Charpentier then bought out Zola's contract with Lacroix for 800 francs and continued the agreement on much the same terms, with the author receiving 500 francs a month in advance of royalties from the sales of the books he would write. Although both writer and publisher were to struggle for several years their professional partnership grew into a prodigiously profitable and lasting association. Besides a measure of security, the contract brought another blessing to the earnest author, so naïve in the manners of Parisian society. This was the glamorous patronage of the lionizing Madame Charpentier, in whose *salon* Zola was to meet and observe some of the most famous people of his day. They soon became close friends, and more than once, right up until his death Zola was advised and encouraged by the beautiful young wife of his publisher.

For the present, though, the 500 francs each month brought Zola little relief from his crushing financial burden; the promissory notes had to be renewed until he could settle them, and the interest paid. He also had to make regular payments towards his father's debts. Rent for the house alone was eighty francs a month. But with the knowledge of an assured income, however inadequate he could just manage to keep his head above water, he slowly began to prosper again, and even acquired a pet dog and a hutch of rabbits.

He was now thirty-two and writing for eight solid hours a day, every day driven by a need that was becoming an obsession. His meal-tickets, the daily articles he wrote for newspapers, were a source of great frustration for they took him from the *Rougon-Macquart*. At night his buzzing brain precluded sleep and he would toss, turn and sweat for hours, so that he began each working day in an exhausted state. The strain began to affect his health; his hands shook, and aches and pains were translated by an emerging hypochondria into suspected paralysis and heart disease. He was, by his own confession, the most easily distracted of writers, yet day after day, without fail without regard for his health, he drove himself through his self-imposed eight-hour stint at his desk.

With its interminable, constricted, tortuously winding passageways between the stalls and piles of produce, the ceaseless flow of food through its entrance with the regularity of human meal-times and its evacuation afterwards, the blood, the warmth, the exhalations – immediately the great market of Les Halles suggested to Zola's mind a simile that was to become famous, and also one that grew into an epic metaphor, a novel: *The Belly of Paris.*

Les Halles, between the Palais-Royal and the Boulevard de Sebastopol, was the Covent Garden of Paris. Like London's Covent Garden Les Halles also moved from the centre of the city; to Rungis, near Orly Airport, in 1969. But for 101 years it was as Zola described it, the 'belly of Paris'. In 1873, when he used it for the setting of his novel, its acres of steel and glass swallowed up each day some 50,000 traders, buyers and carters, and 30,000 tons of produce. The place fascinated him and during his field-work he spent many weeks there, sometimes staying overnight, waiting for the dark, echoing caverns to explode with the daily pre-dawn confusion, with the bustling of the sweating porters under their great, mushroom-shaped hats, the screaming *dames des Halles*, ferociously guarding their nests of produce, the equally vociferous fishwives, the dictatorial market officials, the sweepers, the shouting buyers – the flowing, restless tide of produce and people never failed to stimulate both his gastric juices and imagination.

Then there was the satellite world that attached itself to the markets: the stables, agents, merchants, auctioneers, cafés and charcuteries. Zola observed them systematically, methodically taking notes and carefully copying down the market regulations; seeking permission to stand behind the counters and in the kitchens of charcuteries to study the making of black puddings, patés and cooked meats; trying to translate the weird patois of the fish auctions. And the denizens of the *halles*, as fat and white as maggots, who spent their entire lives within its boundaries, eating and sleeping in the place where even the air was so saturated with protein you could grow fat just by breathing it – nothing in the vast market escaped his notice. It was the world's biggest cornucopia and Zola immediately felt at home.

With his hyperesthesia it was to be expected that the novelist, once he had money in his pocket, would quickly become a gourmand. He celebrated the arrival of Charpentier's first cheque by sending for a case of burgundy and before long it became evident that his heightened senses were going to be expensive to maintain in top condition. But it was his nose, above all the other perceptive organs, which became for him what radar is to a bat. In appearance it belied the genius of its function; a small split which divided its upturned tip suggested nothing less than a miniature bum. Goncourt made some amusing notes in his Journal: 'Zola's nose is a most particular nose, a nose which interrogates, which approves, which condemns... a nose that is gay, a nose that is sad... the nose of a true hunting dog whose impressions, sensations and appetites decide the forms of its termination: two lobes, which at certain moments, one could describe to be *fluttering*...' To its owner, everyone and everything exuded an odour: innocence and evil, damnation in particular, priests and prostitutes – and the memory of some smells launched him into lengthy fantasies, as with a fish-seller in the *halles*, who carried with her an 'odour of spawn, one of those heavy odours which rise from slimy cane and nenuphar, when the eggs cause the bellies of fish to swell and burst, to languish from love in the sunlight'.

The markets might seem an odd environment for what Zola planned as a political novel but, reeking with prosperity, repletion and greed they were, on the contrary, ideal. If the novel had a subtitle it would be *The Fat and The Thin*, for the story is about the war between the Fat, the prosperous, well-fed traders and the complacent customers, and the Thin – the poor, the starved human rats, the revolutionaries who want prosperity and justice for all, not for the few. The markets provide both the realistic and symbolic settings for this novel which examines – I find it difficult to resist extending the simile – the guts of the middle-class Parisian living under a regime the majority of the population finds intolerable.

The story opens with Pierre Florent, the Thin man hero, secretly returning to Paris from the penal colony of Devil's Island to which he had been deported with thousands of others after Napoleon III's *coup* in 1851. As it happened, he was innocent of any crime, although his terrible experiences certainly sharpen his naïve socialist ideals. Eventually, however, Florent escapes from Devil's Island and claws his way back to France, ironically making his entrance into Paris on a load of vegetables destined for the Halles.

Assuming a new name but retaining Florent as his Christian name, he is welcomed back by his brother Quenu who, with his stunning wife Lisa and small daughter Pauline, runs a charcuterie opposite the markets. The escaper enters a life vastly different from his cruel years of exile for he finds the Quenus, like all the traders in the Halles, bloated and shiny with prosperity. Everyone seems as fat as barrels, and the women in particular are all curvaceous, with round, comfortable bellies and great quivering breasts which, like the surrounding produce, threaten to burst from their containers. Florent cannot come to terms with the place at all, and it offends his sense of justice that his own family should be profiting from the corrupt government of Napoleon and his henchmen.

Contrasted with Florent's emaciation, Lisa Quenu is plump and radiant, a perfect example of honest, complacent middle-class womanhood. Her honesty, while as spotless as her linen, is also as practical as her corset, and the essence of the novel is to demonstrate the fine dividing line between law-abiding respectability and the true honesty of conscience, especially when a comfortable way of life is threatened.

For the moment, though, Lisa treats Florent as a welcome guest, and she even finds him a job in the markets as a fish inspector. In his exhausted state it is not surprising that at first Florent succumbs to the life of plenty and the cosy delights of the Quenu kitchen. Gradually, however, his socialist ideals reawaken and he joins a group of clandestine Republicans who meet in the back room of a local bar, hatching a plan for a political overthrow so naïve in its conception that it is never likely to eventuate.

Ironically it is Lisa Quenu's glowing goodness that leads to Florent's undoing, for *La Belle Lisa* is the target of the haggling fishwives who are jealous of her starched pride and middle-class virtues. Because she remains aloof and impregnable their hostility is transferred to Florent, her brother-in-law, and they conspire to make his life intolerable. On his rounds as fish inspector he is teased and pelted with fish and his orders are insolently ignored. Matters come to a head when, during an argument between one of the stall-holders and a customer, Florent decides in favour of the latter and suspends the offending rader for a week. The fishwives, united now, see this as a victory for Lisa, and one way or another they intend to have their revenge.

They do not have to wait for long. Soon after, Lisa's daughter Pauline innocently repeats to one of the fishwives a conversation she has heard between her parents, that Florent has escaped from gaol. The story flashes around the market and when it reaches the ears of Lisa she is understandably alarmed. Without warning Florent, however – who is in the greatest danger – she instead searches his room above the charcuterie, finding red flags and arm-bands and scribbled notes containing a childish plan for a *coup de force* against the government. Fearing for her reputation and business she goes immediately to the police; it is an instinctive errand, fulfilling her duty as a proper citizen who accepts the government of the day and who feels it is dishonest to want to overthrow it.

Lisa's betrayal turns out to be unnecessary. At the police station she discovers they are quite aware of Florent's activities, and have been watching him since his return to France. She is shown a voluminous file and as she goes through it she finds anonymous letters of denunciation which she recognises as the work of many of her neighbours. For a moment she is shattered to realise she is no better than the people she despises, but bourgeois justification comes to her rescue: *her* denunciation was frank and open and not anonymous, and her motives were honest and not malicious. In any case, she rationalises, Florent's fate was sealed long before her own intervention, and she returns to her shop with her corseted back ramrod straight and her head held high.

Within hours her brother-in-law is in custody again, along with the dozen or so Republican plotters involved with him. Their destination: Devil's Island, or worse. The Fats have won. And Claude, a young artist whom we'll meet in a later novel, is moved to mutter as he passes the neat, serene and pink-complexioned Lisa standing in the doorway of her charcuterie: 'What swine decent people really are!'

That is the story, partly about politics, substantially about morality, a very simple story, really, but told in an oblique fashion. While we watch the actions of the tiny figures on the stage we are also compelled to watch the gigantic symbolic silhouettes that tower above them on the backdrop behind. When it came to symbolism, Zola's choice was invariably inspired, and the symbolic resources of the markets were overwhelming. The butchered, bleeding, hanging carcasses oozed carnality, and so did the strings of sausages. Piles of butter looked like 'sculptured bellies' and slimy fish suggested primeval organs immediately after copulation. Images of gluttony, rottenness – any of the deadly sins in fact – were lying about for the taking. By the sheer volume of the produce and its tide-like movement it was difficult to escape from an analogy to the sea: 'The flood of cabbages, carrots and turnips was starting afresh. The Halles were overflowing. He tried to escape from the deluge... vegetables which seemed to twine around him, clinging to his legs with their thin tendrils...'

Zola did not invent the technique of symbolic counterpoint but after so successfully deploying it in *The Kill* he set about, in *The Belly of Paris*, to squeeze the maximum effect from the device. Never before or since has symbolic counterpoint been so over-used with such devastating results.

The key is 'fat' and its family of associated words: belly, overflowing, food, eating, cooking, tastes and smells. They are everywhere, and intrude into every human activity – even in death: 'One morning Uncle Gradelle was struck down while preparing a galantine. He fell right across the mincing table.' Even in grief – as when Quenu learns that his brother Florent has been arrested again: 'Quenu was crying, wiping his cheeks with his overall. . . automatically he had sunk his fingers into a heap of sausage meat which lay piled on the chopping board; he was driving holes in it, roughly kneading it with his hands.' Even the Quenus' bed is as bloated as a fat, stuffed turkey: '. . . with its four matresses and four pillows, its thick wad of blankets, its eiderdown, its bellying folds of softness as it stood in the sultry depths of an alcove. . .' A house is not merely dark, but filled with 'intestinal darkness'. And food is not only carried in the belly, but also outside it – or at least the smell of it, as La Belle Normande, one of the fishwives, knows to her annoyance:

> It was a lingering perfume, clinging to the smooth silk of the skin, a sweat of fish flowing from her splendid breasts, her regal arms and supple waist, bringing a sharp tang of something else to her woman's smell. She had tried all the aromatic oils, she washed in running water, but as soon as the freshness of the bathing wore off, her blood conveyed even to the tips of her fingers that insipid presence of salmon, the musk violet of the smelt and the pungency of herring ray.

It is as though Zola had written the narrative with his right hand while his left frantically banged out a steatopygous counterpoint. It is undeniably effective, too, for the fleshy imagery accumulates to leave us in no doubt that this is a world of belly-worship, the world of the Fats.

With the Thins, though, Zola is not nearly so successful, for the imagery here is nowhere near as captivating, nor are the associations so likeable. Florent is a Thin, but, in his threadbare black clothes, in his barely furnished room and with his quiet, gentle manner, he is hardly a scintillating character. Zola's idea of symbolic contrast never really gains any lyrical altitude, for the Thins are buried out of sight in the enormous folds of the Fats.

There are occasions when the symbolic embroidery tends to run away with itself, as in the celebrated passage popularly known as the 'Cheese (or "Lactic") Symphony', perhaps the most-quoted piece of all Zola's prose. I will certainly quote it again for I can never read it without a smile of admiration. The purpose of this virtuoso passage is, however, frequently misunderstood, for which the novelist must accept most of the blame; instead of being integrated with the conversation it counterpoints, it stands out like the Minute Waltz inserted in the middle of a Bach fugue. The passage follows the discovery by the market fishwives that Florent is an escaped political prisoner, and the news is conveyed through the market by the rancorous, gossiping women. It is a model operatic introduction to an aria; the tattle ceases and the theme is taken up by a single descriptive voice, supported by an orchestra of cheeses. . .

Mademoiselle Saget was silent for two whole minutes at least, then, seeing that the other two were burning with curiosity, she said in her shrill little voice, 'You know that Florent? Well, now I can tell you where he comes from.'

And for a moment longer she kept them hanging on her words.

'He comes from prison,' she said at last, lowering and deepening her voice terribly.

All around her the cheeses were stinking. On the two shelves at the back of the shop enormous blocks of butter were lined up; butter from Brittany was overflowing its baskets; Norman butters, wrapped in canvas, looked like sketches of bellies on to which a sculptor had thrown wet rags; other mounds, already in use, cut by large knives into sharp-pointed rocks full of valleys and crevices, had the appearance of summits in collapse, gilded with the pale light of an autumn evening. Under the display counter of red marble veined with grey, baskets of eggs suggested the whiteness of chalk, and in their crates on wicker trays, bung-shaped cheeses from Neufchâtel were placed end to end, and *gournays*, laid flat like medallions, brought expanses of more sombre colour, stained with their greenish tints. But for the most part the cheeses stood in piles on the table. There, next to the one-pound packs of butter, a gigantic *cantal* was spread on leaves of white beet, as though split by the blows of a hatchet; then followed a Cheshire cheese the colour of gold, *gruyère* like a wheel fallen from some barbaric chariot, some Dutch cheeses as round as heads from the block smeared in dried blood, with that hardness of an empty skull which has earned them the nickname of 'dead-head'. A *parmesan* added its aromatic sting to the thick, dull smell of cooked pastry. Three *bries*, on round boards, had the melancholy look of extinguished moons: two, extremely dry, were at the full; the third was in its second quarter, running, creeping out in a white cream which spread into a lake, making havoc of the thin boards which had been put there in a vain attempt to hold it in check. Some *port-saluts*, shaped like the ancient discus, showed the names of their makers inscribed round the perimeter. A *romantour*, dressed in its silver paper, made one think of a bar of nougat, a sugared cheese which had strayed into this realm of bitter fermentations. The *roqueforts*, too, under their crystal bells, were of princely aspect with their fat, marbled faces veined in blue and yellow, as though the victims of some shameful disease common to rich people who have eaten too many truffles; while on a dish, at one side of them, stood the goat's-milk cheese, as big as a child's fist, hard and grey like the pebbles which the rams start rolling at the angles of stony paths as they lead their flock. And then there were the smells: the pale yellow *mont d'ors* exhaled a sweetish odour; the *troyes*, very thick and bruised at the edges, of a harshness already stronger than the others, adding the fetid stench of a damp cellar; the *camemberts* with their scent of game too far gone; the *neufchâtels*, the *limbourgs*, the *marolles*, the *pont-l'évêques*, each one playing its own shrill note in a phrase that was harsh to the point of nausea; the *livarots*, dyed red, as terrible to the throat as the fumes of sulphur; and then, above all the others, were the *olivets*, wrapped in walnut leaves in the fashion of those decaying carcasses which peasants cover with branches on the edge of a field, steaming in the sun. The warm afternoon had turned the cheeses soft; the mould on the rinds was melting and glazing over with the rich colours of red copper and verdigris, like wounds that have badly healed; under the oak leaves, a breeze lifted the skin of the *olivets*, which heaved like a breast, with a slow deep breathing of a man asleep; a flood of life had driven a hole in a *livarot*, which gave birth through this gash to a people of worms. And behind the scales a *gerome* sewn with aniseed in its narrow box spreads such an infection around it that flies had fallen dead by the box on the red marble veined with grey.

This *gérome* was almost under Mademoiselle Saget's nose. She recoiled and leaned her head against the large sheets of yellow and white paper which hung down from a corner at the back of the shop. (21)

The actors then resume, discussing Florent, piling rumour upon rumour until the voice and orchestra return again for the final refrain:

They all looked at one another cautiously. And as they were rather short of breath by this time, it was the *camembert* in particular that they could smell. This cheese, with its odour of venison, had conquered the tamer smells of *marolles* and *limbourg*; it exhaled expansively, stifling the other smells beneath a surprising abundance of stinking breath. Into this striking and vigorous phrase, however, the *parmesan* still from time to time threw its thin shrill note of a shepherd's flute, while the *bries* came into play with the soft dull thudding of a damp tambourine. The *livarot* launched into a suffocating reprise. And this symphony lifted for a moment to the high sharp note of the aniseeded *gérome*, prolonged like the roar of an organ.

As a point of interest, Zola omits from his orchestra an E-flat Limburger, a variety usually accepted as the world's smelliest cheese called *Le Vieux Puant*, 'the old stinker of Lille', which is, or was, discriminated against by a curious by-law which forbids passengers from carrying this cheese in Lille taxicabs.

Elsewhere in the novel there are passages similar to the Cheese Symphony – symphonies of flowers, fruit, poultry and, yes, fish; but while they are not so remarkable they are much more effectively integrated into the narrative. Perhaps the best of these is a passage in which a display of fruit is accorded the voluptuous sensuality of the boudoir.

The Belly of Paris is replete with interesting characters, drawn with tungsten-tipped precision from Zola's acute observations. His insight into the psychology of jealous women and gossipy old ladies like Madame Lecoeur and Mademoiselle Saget is quite extraordinary. There are also the two children of the Halles, Marjolin and Cadine, teenage urchins as shameless as sparrows who feast and love among the produce and on the zinc meadows of the market roofs. But one character dominates this novel and that is Lisa Quenu, although the action revolves around her brother-in-law, Florent. Florent, however, is too gentle, too grey, to ever command our close attention in all the profusion and it is even difficult to summon up anger at the injustice which compels him to be a Thin.

Lisa is a Macquart who fortunately escapes the family taint and instead inherits her mother's capacity and respect for honest hard work. She arrives in Paris expecting nothing but what she can make from her own hands, and works alongside an industrious apprentice named Quenu in a pork-butcher's owned by her uncle. After the uncle dies she discovers his hoard in a cellar, and together she and Quenu tip the coins on to her bed to count them. As they survey the fortune, it becomes a substitute for a seduction, and the foundation for their future lives:

> They stacked the gold coins on the pillow, leaving the silver in the hollow of the blankets. When they had completed the figure, which struck them as fabulous, of eighty-five thousand francs, they began to talk. They talked, naturally enough, of the future; they talked of their marriage, without either of them raising the question of any love existing between them. The money seemed to loosen their tongues. They were still more deeply settled on the bed, leaning back against the street wall of the room under the white muslin curtains, their legs stretched out more comfortably than before; and their hands rummaged amid the money as they talked, their hands met and abandoned themselves to each other in the midst of the hundred-sou pieces. The twilight overtook them, and only then did Lisa blush at finding this boy at her side. They had upset the bed, the sheets were hanging down to the floor and the gold made imprints on the pillow which separated them, as though two heads, hot with passion had rolled and twisted there....
>
> Lisa, adjusting her clothes as though she had been guilty of a crime, went to fetch her ten thousand francs. Quenu wanted her to add them to her uncle's eighty-five

thousand. Laughing, he mixed the two sums up together, saying that the money had to become engaged as well; and it was agreed that Lisa should keep the 'hoard' in her dressing-table. When she had locked it away and remade the bed, they went peacefully downstairs. They were husband and wife. (21)

It is a superb and understated symbolic passage in which Zola is tempting us with the thought that middle-class marriages are founded on a bed of money, rather than love. Only once is Lisa caught unawares out of her corset; it is her armour of respectability, for appearance is everything. Standing in the doorway of the charcuterie she is not only a good advertisement for a food shop but for the good life itself:

> Her linen had never been so white as it was now; never had her pink, refreshed complexion been so neatly framed in smooth waves of hair. She exhibited a calm and splendid repletion, an enormous tranquillity, which nothing could disturb, not even a smile. This was absolute peace and complete felicity, lifeless and unshuddering, as she bathed in the warm air. Her breast within the tightened bodice was still digesting the happiness of the day before; her plump hands, lost in the folds of her apron, were not even outstretched to take the happiness of the present day, for it was certain to fall into them. And just close to her the window display suggested a similar felicity; it too had recovered, and the stuffed tongues lay redder and more healthy, the hams were once more showing their handsome yellow faces, the garlands of sausages no longer wore that expression of despair which had cut Quenu to the heart. A fat laugh rang out from the kitchen at the back, accompanied by the joyful rattle of saucepans. The charcuterie was once again steeped in good health, in rich and fatted well-being. A glimpse of sides of bacon, half-pigs hanging against the marble, brought to the picture the rounded contours of the belly, the belly triumphant, while Lisa, standing motionless in a posture of great dignity, offered the Halles her morning greeting with her large well-fed smile. (21)

This is Lisa just a few days after turning in her brother-in-law to the authorities, to suffer God knows what ghastly punishment. Outwardly, the belly is triumphant, but Lisa knows her insides are spotless, too. Going to confession she tells herself, 'I could finish in ten seconds, if I wanted to!' Yet, mysteriously, this woman still commands our sympathy, which says volumes for Zola's compassionate understanding of his characters.

The Belly of Paris baffled Zola's critics, for it has very little to do with realism and naturalism. The principles are there, surely enough, but the novelist's poetic fancies have drawn it out of the mainstream of naturalism to more lyrical, tranquil waters. With this book Zola must have been conscious of his great power to breathe life into the events he was narrating, unifying man and nature, observed fact and invention, with broad, sweeping masses of words. Napoleon might have claimed that the markets of Paris were the Louvre of the people, but to Zola they were his lexicon.

83

7

Priests and Politics

Far from releasing a wave of radical sympathy, the bloody suppression of the Commune in 1871 had the reverse effect. For most of the following decade, France was ruled by a fiercely reactionary government, Republican in name but not in effect, and a new 'moral order' was established and window-dressed with religious processions, pilgrimages and consecrations; the Sacré Coeur in Montmartre remains to this day a memorial to this outburst of national contrition. The widespread inclination of the country to bury its head in the sands of religion at first angered and then alienated many intellectuals and writers, and Zola, for instance, attempted to redress the balance by exposing, in his next two *Rougon-Macquart* novels, what he saw as the threat to France by the excesses of the Catholic Church.

For two centuries before the French Revolution the Jesuits had been the schoolmasters of Europe, and education was almost exclusively Catholic. But as new nations emerged, the Jesuit ultramonatism – their total allegiance to the Pope – began to stand in the way of nationalistic aspirations. Because they were invariably the confessors of kings and administrators, and patronised by the aristocracy, the suspicion grew that the Jesuits were more involved in politics and commerce than they ought to be, and in a long and involved manoeuvre beginning in 1773 the Society of Jesus was suppressed in most European countries.

The Revolution finally broke the Catholic stranglehold on education. The church and the state were declared separate, and church property was confiscated. But by 1814, with the restoration of the Bourbons in France, the Jesuits were allowed to resume their teaching, although this was no longer a monopoly. Nevertheless, right up until the fall of the Second Empire, tradition and religious coercion still triumphed over free public education, and it wasn't until the more forceful policies of the Third Republic were put into operation that the state made any real progress in this direction. Until then any priest with the scantiest of qualifications could teach and run a school. It is against this background that one must view the intense hatred of intellectuals and writers like Zola for Catholic education and what was termed 'the cretinisation of Europe'.

But the quality of Catholic teaching wasn't the only source of discontent among the French radicals. The church, during the nineteenth century, was a hot-house of political intrigue. In post-Revolution France the church and the Royalists were logical allies; the church pinned its hope of survival in the continuation of the monarchy, while the Royalists needed the support of the church to keep the throne warm. Thus, in time, the clergy and the monarchist tradition became, in the popular belief, one and the same; and almost as widely accepted was the belief that every priest was a politician.

The involvement of the church in commerce and property, when exposed, did nothing for its image either; in Republican eyes the material wealth of the church only underlined its rapacity. Then, as now, it deliberately kept what is called a low profile on its function as a business enterprise; but then, as now, occasional exposures highlighted its roles of landlord, shareholder and custodian of art treasures. Revelations of this kind only served to reinforce the cynicism and contempt men like Zola held for the church, and it is not surprising that, quite early in his chronicle, the novelist should set out to reveal the extent of Catholic power in government and education.

In the decade following the *coup d'état* in 1851, people were hardly aware of the church's political strategy. In any case it was a confused situation with only one thing clear – that the church and the Republicans were deadly enemies. Even before his proclamation as Emperor, Napoleon III realised he would need Catholic support for his regime and it was in the nature of a bargain that he sent a large French force to Italy to ensure the restoration of Pope Pius IX in 1850. The papal tradition of 'the divine right of kings' was too strong, however, to win outright support for Napoleon, and the majority of the French clergy continued to back the Royalist cause. But there was a minority prepared to help the Emperor win over both the members of the church and waverers among the old nobility, which brings us to the opening chapter of Zola's next novel, *The Conquest of Plassans.*

I have sketched in something of the chaotic political and religious background of the time, as some knowledge of it is essential if we are to understand what is going on in *The Conquest of Plassans,* which is as much a political as a clerical novel. Its setting is again Plassans – which, although it has returned a Royalist in the elections is politically divided by three parties: the Bonapartists, who are in power, the Royalists, and the minority Republicans. Into the town rides a fanatical young priest, the Abbé Faujas, who is an agent for the Second Empire government. His job is to subvert the local clergy and their flock to the Empire cause.

The Abbé Faujas becomes a lodger with a local middle-class family, the Mourets. François Mouret is a retired merchant and with his wife Marthe and his three children, Octave, Serge and Désirée, is happy and content. But there is also an omen which threatens the family: both husband and wife are cousins with a common grandmother, the mad Aunt Dide, who is locked up in an asylum at nearby Les Tulettes. The only sign – so far – of hereditary degeneracy in the family is the backwardness of Désirée, who at fifteen has the mind of a child of five.

Marthe is not in favour of taking in a tenant, for she feels their sedate, easy-going life will be interrupted. Mouret insists, however, pointing out that the upper rooms of the house are empty, and might easily earn a few francs for them. The new arrival, with his piercing eyes and secretive manner, is a little disconcerting, especially as his mother unexpectedly comes to live in the house as well. It turns out that they are unobtrusive to the point of invisibility, but it is just this – their silent comings and goings and the interminable whispering – that begins to get on Mouret's nerves. Eventually the priest comes out of his shell and attends political meetings held at the nearby home of Marthe's mother, Félicité Rougon. This is a hornet's nest of intrigue, and it is there that we learn the nature of the priest's task. Félicité advises him that if he wants to win the town over to the Empire and Napoleon III, he must win it through the women.

The scheming priest begins with Marthe, by suggesting that she form a committee to establish a home for delinquent girls in the town. Marthe is thrilled by the idea and from that moment becomes increasingly involved in charitable work, neglecting, in the process, her home and family, to Mouret's great annoyance. The priest also convinces Marthe she will gain extra inspiration and energy for her work if she becomes a penitent, and so long hours on her knees each day in church are added to those she spends away from her family.

The home for girls is a great success, and so is the priest, who is credited with the idea. The project brings him into close contact with the influential women of the town, who now adore him. But at the Mouret home events take a nasty turn, for it is now invaded by the priest's sister and brother-in-law, the Trouches. Both husband and wife are idlers and, we suspect, worse; but Trouche is given the job of accountant at the girl's home. Mouret is quite stunned by this invasion and in his helplessness begins to sulk in an empty, locked room. His health starts to fail, his hair turns grey and he becomes morose. Quarrels, previously unknown in the household, begin to break out between Mouret and his wife.

But Faujas and Marthe, by contrast, are on top of the world. The priest acquires a dashing new cassock while Marthe becomes radiant and youthful; fifteen years of married complacency have melted away in the flame of her devotion. Aglow in her beatitude, she is serenely unconscious of what is going on around her. The Trouches, scenting easy prey, tell her confidentially that the priest is in deep financial trouble, and that they must find money to pay off his debts before his situation is made public. Marthe takes the bait and, because she has no access to ready cash, secretly sells the family belongings and even the furniture. In this way she manages to give the Trouches a couple of thousand francs which they immediately spend on rich food and fine wines. Mouret is apoplectic when he finds the furniture disappearing, but by now Marthe, with her new-found spiritual strength, can stand up to him. He is powerless, even when the evil pair upstairs descend to take over the family kitchen, and then the dining-room. Eventually, at the meal table, Mouret is a forgotten, baffled, intensely frustrated man.

But if this is bad, there are fresh disasters in store. Octave decides to leave, and – horror of horrors – Serge falls under the influence of Faujas and decides to enter a seminary. Désirée, Mouret's only remaining child, is unhappily sent off to a nursing home which leaves him quite alone, for by now his wife is totally subjugated by the priest. There is trouble in store for Marthe, too. The long hours of praying, and the interminable confessions begin to unhinge her mind. She has a series of fits during which she scourges herself by lacerating her body in a most frightening way. As these fits take place at night, with only her husband in the bedroom, poor Mouret is accused of beating her, while in truth the unfortunate man is terrified out of his wits. This persecution compounds his own neurosis and, he too, begins to disintegrate and exhibit a mild form of erratic behaviour. It is enough, though, to kindle the malicious tongues of his neighbours and soon Mouret is a prisoner in his own house, unable to leave it for fear of being ridiculed in the street. Eventually, at the instigation of the Trouches – who see possession of the entire house within their grasp – Mouret is pronounced mad by a doctor and taken away to the asylum at Les Tulettes.

At the elections, all the priest's scheming comes to a successful conclusion, for the Bonapartist candidate is returned. The Abbé Faujas is triumphant; his mission has been accomplished. His intrigues, which have included condoning the Trouches' guilt, have been justified. The Trouches are triumphant, too, and like sharp-toothed rats take over the Mouret household.

Amid this jubilation, Marthe is at her lowest ebb. Confused by hallucinations, disoriented by the loss of her family, she finally realises that she loves Faujas – not the priest, but the man. But Faujas, now that his job is done, has nothing but scorn for the ailing woman, who has now become a burden to him. When her mother tells her this, Marthe goes to the priest and in a most pitiable scene entreats him not to desert her in her hour of need.

The priest's rejection shocks Marthe back to some semblance of sanity. Her first impulse is to drive to Les Tulettes to seek the release of her husband, to try and pick up the pieces of their shattered lives, but – alas – by now Mouret is too far gone. He really *is* mad. Shocked at his condition, Marthe leaves, with nothing to live for, and falls desperately ill. The final chapter is Zola at his melodramatic best and there is little to be gained by revealing the ending except to say that very few of the characters are left standing as the final curtain comes down.

It will be evident, even from this brief synopsis of the story, that *The Conquest of Plassans* has two themes or intentions, both deriving from Zola's anti-clericalism. The first theme is an exposé of church meddling in politics, and the insidious but powerful influence of the clergy at election time. This accounted for much of the conservatism in provincial and rural France where the flock voted like sheep, according to the wishes of the local priest. Zola was also at pains to point out that the clergy themselves could be manipulated; in the novel it takes Faujas just two years to swing the church hierarchy of Plassans around from rock-solid monarchism to supporters of a cardboard Emperor. It might be argued, of course, that Faujas's intriguing is mere fiction, and, historically or sociologically speaking, proves nothing. But Zola was too conscientious to be caught out there; Faujas was a type well-founded on documented evidence.

Where the novel departs from its documentary sources is in the malice which the author freely uses to paint the portrait of the Abbé. Faujas was, in Zola's preliminary notes, intended to be a real villain who seduces Marthe and makes her his mistress. But wisely, I think, the priest was portrayed as a more typical figure whose high-minded dedication, religious and political, does more harm than good. Nevertheless, the finished portrait has many malevolent touches to it, and I think that in writing this book Zola enjoyed unleashing his spite. This personal rancour also overflows into the second anti-clerical theme, which attacks the influence priests have over certain women.

Marthe's unhappy experience, while not unknown in real life, is an extreme case and the author's exploitation of it tends to get a little heavy-handed as her anguish builds to crisis point. While the intrusion of personal malice undoubtedly adds sparkle and drive to the narrative it does, in places, destroy much of the conviction. At the end it is difficult to accept that even a fanatic like Faujas would so cruelly and so scornfully dismiss Marthe at the most desperate moment in her life; or to declare to her mother, 'Your daughter's out of her mind; I'm tired to death of her... I'd pay the man well who took her off my hands.' None of the clergy in the novel are in the least attractive; they are either dull, lazy or plain evil. Even Abbé Surin, at first sight a pleasant character, turns out to be a feeble homosexual.

With the townspeople of Plassans, Zola's venom is applied with deep strokes of an etching needle rather than with dabs from a brush, and the various characters are left to incriminate themselves with their own gossip. The Mouret household, with its tragic burden of ancestral insanity, is the only group in the large cast to be treated sympathetically. Evidence suggests that the Mouret family is modelled on one the author knew in his youth – that of his friend Paul Cézanne. Fanatically religious, Mme Cézanne was the source of much tension in the household, in which there was also political discussion; Paul's father, Louis Auguste, stood as a candidate in the Aix Council elections of 1848. Marthe Mouret was probably distantly based on Zola's youthful recollection of Mme Cézanne, through whom he could project his hostility to the religious conversion of nervous and neurotic women, and awaken the country to the power that priests wielded over female penitents. He had, in fact, written essays on the potential dangers of conversion and confession for *La Cloche* in 1872. He was also known to admire the Goncourts' novel *Madame Gervaisais*, published in 1869; its harrowing story of religious coercion causing a woman's insanity may have provided some inspiration. Whether Balzac's *The Curé of Tours* influenced Zola's narrative is unclear, but there is a close affinity with its plot and main character; Balzac's Abbé Troubert is also an ambitious priest who charms his landlady.

Zola was in some ways becoming quite a literary gymnast, for every new book was different from the others. If he had confounded his critics with the lyrical romanticism of *The Belly of Paris, The Conquest of Plassans* must have bewildered them yet again. In all its twenty-three short chapters there are hardly a dozen pages of descriptive prose. Most of the action and information is conveyed by conversation, mostly gossip, and the narrative moves forward at such a pace that real concentration is needed to catch the lurking subtleties. In its technique it is one of the most modern novels Zola ever wrote, right to its compelling, melodramatic ending.

If *The Conquest of Plassans* has pace it also has its *longueurs*, but specific lapses are minimal. Although Mouret's disintegration into insanity occupies a period of perhaps a couple of years we are barely conscious of this; madness seems to descend upon him with the speed of a raging fever. He is one of the victims of the novel's very large cast of characters; the author juggles them well but, with the exception of Marthe and Faujas, can allot only so much time and space for each, which in Mouret's case is a great pity, and we follow the progress of his illness and eventual madness through what amounts to a series of doctor's bulletins. The Trouches also suffer from acceleration, changing from believable rogues to unlikely villains in the space of a few months. Another deficiency applies to Plassans itself. Zola gives 33,000 electors, indicating a substantial town of perhaps 100,000 people, but the feeling persists throughout the novel that we are reading about the affairs of a small village. Only on a couple of occasions is the reader taken outside the close circle of intriguers and even then is not made aware that Plassans is a sizeable town. Consequently there is some puzzlement as to what the political fuss is all about; why has Plassans been singled out by the government for this subversive operation? In truth Plassans – Aix-en-Provence, the author's model – was an influential centre, with church headquarters, courts, academies, museums and commercial institutions, and whose political support was considered vital to the imperial regime.

The novel was published in May 1874, and because of its theme aroused more interest than Zola's previous novels, although its sales by the end of the year of 1,700 copies did not exactly place it in the bestseller class. Still, it was encouraging.

From the political and domestic conniving of the clergy in *The Conquest of Plassans* Zola proceeds, in the following novel, to deal with the problems of priestly celibacy.

Like the incest theme in *The Kill*, the subject of priestly celibacy has always been a favourite with novelists. It was, even when Zola sat down to write *The Abbé Mouret's Sin*, a thin lode mined to near-exhaustion: Hugo's *Notre-Dame de Paris*, Lamartine's *Jocelyn* and Ernest Daudet's *Le Missionnaire*, published only a few years previously, are three novels on the theme. Despite this, Zola determined to ring a few changes, and at the same time avoid courting too much displeasure from the book-buying public who were by no means as vigorously anti-clerical as he was. In essence, his priest would *unknowingly* break his vow of celibacy.

The link between this novel and the last is perhaps the strongest coupling in the entire *Rougon-Macquart* cycle; in fact the first chapter of *The Abbé Mouret's Sin* could logically follow the last chapter of *The Conquest of Plassans*, the final paragraph of which is in itself a presentiment:

> Marthe was convulsed by a fit of coughing. Her eyes opened wide with surprise, and she sat up and gazed about her. Then she clasped her hands and expired with a fixed look of unspeakable terror. She had just seen Serge's cassock in the crimson light.

Marthe Mouret, as we know, suffered terribly at the hands of the Abbé Faujas, and the shock of realising that her own son would perpetuate the same evil was too much for the poor woman. The follow-on novel assumes a gap of several years, during which Serge completes his seminary training and accepts a curacy at Artaud, a squalid village not far from Plassans, where some 150 poor, ignorant peasants live in wretched hovels, 'poverty black and hunched against their own dunghills'.

Serge Mouret hasn't escaped the family curse of madness, nor has his sister, Désirée, with whom he lives at the vicarage. Désirée, now a beautiful, strapping young woman of twenty-two, still has the mind of a child, but is happy and content in her little farmyard and among her pet animals. But Father Mouret is far from content; his life is a conflict between the exigencies of the flesh and his desire for eternal joy. His exile at Artaud, with its uncouth flock and decrepit church, is according to his own wish, for there he can abandon himself to inner contemplation in a quest to annihilate his masculinity.

He is helped in this by the fearsome, insensitive and cruel Friar Archangais, a real fire and brimstone tyrant for whom all women have perdition in their petticoats, and who sees in Father Mouret a potential backslider. He rarely misses an opportunity to instil into the younger man his own disgust and hatred for women.

The day arrives when, quite by chance, Serge visits a patient of his Uncle Pascal's, who is the local doctor. The patient is a man who lives in a lodge in the neglected and overgrown ruin of a once-great park, established in Louis XV's time. This is *Le Paradou*, a wild, luxuriant garden guarded by nettles and hedges and a high stone wall. During the visit Father Mouret meets the sick man's daughter, a lovely sixteen-year-old named Albine. Immediately her beauty penetrates his defences and he becomes the reluctant prisoner of her sunny laugh which seems to exude all that is good in nature. Back at the vicarage he tries to erase her from his memory, but while he can banish her vision during the daytime with constant praying, at night, in his dreams, she blossoms like a dazzling, seductive flower. Finally though, after weeks of prayer and mortification, he emerges triumphant, but at a terrible physical cost:

'Oh, Mary, Vessel Elect, castrate what is man away from me, make of me a eunuch among men, so that I may without fear be awarded the treasure of your virginity!'

Then, his teeth chattering wildly, overcome at last by his fever, the Vicar of Artaud lost consciousness on the tiled floor of his room.

Serge recovers in a white, brightly lit room in the lodge at *Le Paradou* to where he has been taken to convalesce by his uncle, Dr Pascal. For weeks he is semi-conscious and delirious, and is patiently and lovingly nursed by the beautiful, wild Albine. Gradually his health and strength return, and with them new sensations and a child-like innocence. For Serge has lost not only his priestly garb but also his memory and dogma. His tonsure has grown over, too, and in this remote garden, ablaze with sunshine, he awakens to a new world of green profusion. His illness has been like a second gestation.

Inevitably, he becomes aware of Albine's beauty. Together they explore the great garden; eating its fruit, fishing in its pools and playing games with childish enthusiasm. The splendour of the garden intoxicates them and in the climate of innocence they fall, hesitantly, in love. Many of their excursions are devoted to finding a gigantic tree in whose shade, according to legend, shall be found perfect bliss, and eventually they discover it:

It was a tree in the centre drowned in such dense shade that one could not make out the nature of it. It was a tree of immense height, with a trunk breathing like a thorax, and branches wide-stretched like protecting arms. In appearance it was sound, robust, powerful, fertile. It was the doyen of the garden, the father of the forest, the pride of all the herbage, the friend of the sun which every day rose and set in a flood of light cast over its summit. From its green vaulting, all the delight of creation descended, the scents of flowers, the song of birds, the raindrops of light, dawn's fresh awakenings, the drowsy warmth of twilights. Its sap was of such energy that it oozed and trickled down the bark, bathing it in a drenching of fecundity, making it the very virility of the soil. From it derived all the magic of this glade. The other trees, round it, formed an impenetrable wall which isolated it deep in a tabernacle of silent half-light. There was but one continuous mass of verdure, without a chink of heaven, or glimpse of horizon, solely this rotunda, every inch of which was draped with the loving silk of the leaves, the floor below covered with the satin velvet of the mosses. Entering it was like plunging into the crystal water of a spring, a world of greenish clarity, sheet of silver lulled beneath the reflections of the reeds. Colours, scents, all vibrant sound and quivers of delight preserved a vagueness, a transparency, an anonymity, rapturous with a delight in which all consciousness faded away. The languor of an alcove, the dream of summer nights dying on the naked shoulder of a loving mistress, a scarce distinct murmur of love suddenly sinking to the tremor when all words disappear, all clung to the immobility of those branches, on which not a breath stirred. A nuptial retreat, where all were laced in loving coupling, an empty room in which behind the drawn curtains of a bed, one sensed Nature, in the arms of the sun, satiate in fiery union. At moments the loins of the tree creaked and its limbs stiffened like those of a woman in childbed, and the sweat of life which drained from its bark then poured down more copiously on the greensward all round, breathing out the languor of love's desire, soaking the air with its yielding, till the glade turned pale at sight of such enjoyment. And then the tree with its shade, its grassy carpet, its belt of dense undergrowth, was nothing but the weakness and the sweetness of sex.(27)

In its shade they experience a feeling of supreme serenity, absolute trust and secure contentment; even the air itself tastes like fruit. With the fatality of generation surrounding them, Albine and Serge consummate their love:

He kissed her cheeks, her eyes, her lips, then, with little fluttering kisses, her arms, from fingers to shoulders. He kissed her feet and her knees, bathing them with a rain of kisses, which fell in large warm drops like a summer shower, then watered every part of her, her throat, her breasts, her thighs, her loins. With utter calm, little by little, he took possession of her, conquering the most minute filigree of veins under the rose-tinted skin.   (27)

But their ecstasy is short-lived. There are ominous vibrations. Albine has the feeling they are not alone, that they are being watched. In sudden shame she covers her naked body with leaves. 'Now even the touch of a branch, the fragile collision of an insect's wing, the slightest breath of air, made her tremble as though she had been improperly touched by some unseen hand.' Hastily covered in shame and vegetation the guilty pair run from the tree and become lost in the park's jungle-like growth. In panic they find themselves by the big stone wall of *Le Paradou*. There before them is a gaping hole, which Albine had repaired with stones and branches, years before; now it has been breached again, 'enlarged by infuriated hands'. And there, on the other side, looming like Judgement Day, is the fearsome Friar Archangais.

In tears, Albine watches aghast as her lover, looking through the breach in the wall at the distant village of Artaud, recovers his memory. It all returns – even the recollection of his priestly vows. And his terrible guilt. Friar Archangais is victorious, and Serge is led off meekly to the vicarage.

Both Albine and Father Mouret suffer abominably in their separate ways. The priest, watched closely by the friar, flays himself with exhausting hours of prayer. Albine pines away at *Le Paradou* and falls seriously ill. Dr Pascal, learning this, pleads with his nephew to return with him to the lodge, to care for the sick girl as she did for him. But Serge offers only to pray. 'I am a priest,' he tells Pascal, 'I have only prayers to give.' Even when Albine herself visits the church to entreat her lover to return, he sends her brusquely away.

Her visit, though, provokes a fresh bout of hallucinations, for the priest's mental balance is now precarious, and he becomes convinced he is eternally damned. In this state of confusion he wanders one evening to the breached wall of *Le Paradou* and, stepping over the sleeping figure of Friar Archangais who has mounted guard there, he meets Albine inside. She soon realises she cannot rekindle their former love; Serge is cold and impotent, and lost to her. She knows now that the idyll is over, and drives him from the garden. Alone, she contemplates her death. 'It was beyond doubt that her garden, as a supreme satisfaction, would provide death for her, and it was to her death that it so delicately led her. After love there could be only death, and never had the garden loved her so.'

Albine's death is one among a cluster of ironies with which the novel ends, not the least of which is the incident when, at the graveside of a double burial, the innocent Désirée runs joyously into the cemetery yelling: 'Serge! Serge! The heifer has made a new calf!' Death follows love; life springs out of death.

The plot of *The Abbé Mouret's Sin* is disarmingly simple; biblically simple, even. For from the moment Serge finds himself in *Le Paradou* we find we are reading an exotic and semi-erotic parallel to Genesis. *Le Paradou* is the Garden of Eden. Albine is Eve and Serge is Adam. Their love is an idyll of innocence in a timeless place as yet unvisited by evil. The parallel continues with the consummation of their love under the great tree, and their fall is Adam's fall: 'The moment their flesh touched, they fell to the ground, lips to lips, without a cry. There seemed no end to their fall, as if the rock gave way infinitely beneath them.' And there, by the breach in the wall, is Friar Archangais, holding a stick, a reference to the flaming sword. With consummate skill Zola embroiders the biblical story and while one is enchanted by the poetry of his extended simile, the narrative is perfectly convincing.

But whereas the Garden of Eden story is powerfully explicit, ambiguities abound in Zola's recounting of the interrupted idyll at *Le Paradou*. Neither Serge nor Albine break any law; on the contrary their love and consummation of it does nothing other than fulfil natural law. There is no sin. That is, of course, if we ignore the breach in the wall, through which can be seen the world outside. Once the lovers are conscious of that breach they have sinned in the eyes of the world, and they *feel* they have sinned, even though their act of love was an act of innocence, with the full connivance of Nature herself. And Friar Archangais: does he symbolise God – an angry, prohibitionist, anti-sex God? For Zola, perhaps. Some Zola scholars have made out a case that he might symbolise the author's father, whose personification in the character of the friar reveals the surfacing of childhood guilt. This theory is reinforced if we also consider that Father Mouret was 'reborn' at the age of twenty-five; in other words, to erase the guilt Zola is indulging, through his fiction, in a fairly common dream-wish of rebirth, to regain innocence by returning to a natural, Garden-of-Eden life. Or is Friar Archangais simply a frustrated victim of continence, with his half-mad sexual fantasising and denunciations of fornication, which is what the author set out to demonstrate in this novel?

One would have thought, in line with all his other essays on this theme, that Zola would have let nature emerge as victor, in the form of Albine. But both Serge and Albine suffer the same torments and shame as their biblical counterparts. Is Zola, then, trying to tell us, with abysmal pessimism, that all sex is sinful because it perpetuates the race? This can hardly be, for in this novel more than all the others the theme of regeneration recurs throughout. It is reiterated with every mention of Désirée and her farmyard. It is everywhere, seen, smelled and even heard: 'the sighing of millions of grass stalks, kissed by the sun, the vast cry of countless creatures on heat'. No, what I think Zola is really saying is that man is on a hiding to nothing, that the moment of birth is the beginning of death, and that there is nothing he can do about it. Man is dependent upon the act of copulation to live, but all germination is doomed and all life leads through despair to death. And priestly celibacy is just as helpless in the face of this law as potency, with a measure of misery thrown in.

These, of course, are the implications of what is, on the surface, a charming love story, and we can find other messages by mining the underlying strata of the novel. *The Abbé Mouret's Sin* might have represented for some, even the novelist himself, an effective attack on the church dogma of celibacy, but with deeper analysis this is not the case at all. Celibacy, as a theme, is dwarfed by the age-old conflict experienced by man, torn asunder betwixt heaven and earth, his life in eternal despair because of split loyalties, wanting both grace and earthly bliss and achieving neither. Man is destined to remain unfulfilled. Zola expounds this brilliantly with his convincing account of Father Mouret's experience, attracted alternately by the Virgin Mary and the nature girl, Albine. Both symbolise his, and man's, contradictory desires in life; and each is capable of inducing despair and defeat for man cannot seem to possess both.

Leaving aside Friar Archangais, who is an outright monster, Zola is, through Father Mouret, surprisingly sympathetic to the Catholic Church. Until the final years of his life, when he viewed Catholicism as inherently evil, the novelist allowed that religion did have the power to alleviate the misery of the desperate, the ill and the unbalanced. This is approximately his position at the time of writing *The Abbé Mouret's Sin.* Father Mouret does, on his return from *Le Paradou,* find a kind of peace, an illusory joy, that will sustain him for the rest of his life. Albine, a non-believer, finds her only solace in suicide, yet she is one of the innocents of the earth, and has broken no commandments. As for the anti-religious peasants of the village, whose existence is one of animalistic freedom, their life is but a grim trek from womb to cemetery. Life, then, is whatever you make of it; but every path leads to death. The dark pessimism of these implications in the novel, contrasted with the joyously lyrical prose which expresses it, is profoundly ironic.

With all of this we are inclined to forget Father Mouret's beautiful simple-minded sister, Désirée. Désirée is the only 'pure' character in the novel, remote from life's travails; she is a sort of universal mother and symbolises life itself. When her animals copulate and procreate the union is hers, too; she can achieve orgasm by the mere tickle of a wisp of straw on her face. She can lovingly raise a pig, then just as lovingly have it slaughtered, kissing its back to comfort it as the butcher's knife plunges into its neck. The processes of birth, life and death hold not a single terror for her. But it is clear that this situation can only exist for as long as she remains a child, possessing a child's grace. Suspended in her development, Désirée is the only character free from human contradictions, at one with heaven and earth – but at the cost of her reason. That's the sting.

So, far from being a trite side-swipe at a religious curiosity, *The Abbé Mouret's Sin* is really a poetic essay on the insoluble contradictions of human life and the immutability of the cycle of regeneration. Désirée might have 'sprung from the very compost-heap of her farmyard, drawing its juices as if through roots into her powerful, white-skinned legs, round and firm as young tree trunks'. As her pig is bled in that same farmyard, the chickens gather round to peck at the drops of spilled blood. At times the earth's fertility is almost threatening, symbolised by the giant tree in *Le Paradou,* with its sap 'of such energy that it oozed and trickled down the bark, bathing it in a drenching flood of fecundity'. Whatever else he was, Zola was the propagandist of eternal fertility.

Looked at with one eye, this remarkable novel is all about the sexual act. If it had been written many years later we would probably say that it reeked with Freudian imagery. At any rate I find it difficult to recall any novel which projects sexual imagery on such a sustained scale. It is also difficult to single out particular passages to illustrate this because it saturates the narrative. But there are inevitable highlights, as with this sensual description of flowers: 'exposing beauties hidden in modesty, crevices of the body not usually seen, of silky softness, with tiny capillaries showing faintly through the blue transparency...'; or as when Father Mouret, tortured by his obsession for Albine, contemplates the landscape from his bedroom window one sleepless night:

> By night this land assumed the strange arching spasm of lust. It slept, but with coverlets torn aside, hips naked, limbs contorted, legs straddled, while from its bosom rose heavy, tepid sighs and the pungent odour of women's bodies moist with sweat as they slept. One might have said it was some tremendous Cybele fallen on her back, bosom upthrust, belly bare to the moonlight, intoxicated still from the sunshine of the past day and crazed in expectation of new impregnation. In the far distance, following that vast body, Mouret's eyes followed the Olivette road, thin pale ribbon outstretched like the disengaged cord of a corset. He heard Friar Archangais lifting back the skirts of his little hussies and whipping them till the blood came, he saw him spitting scornfully in the faces of the bigger girls, he felt the man himself stinking goat-like in his person and never to be satisfied in his lust. He saw Rosalie laughing at mother earth, like an animal on heat, while her father flung clods of soil at her loins.
> (27)

The prose style of *The Abbé Mouret's Sin* is an advance and a departure from the more mannered and sometimes self-conscious symbolic counterpoint used in *The Belly of Paris*. Here, the symbolic imagery is superbly unified with the narrative, sometimes muted and at other times as powerful as a tidal wave, completely taking over from the story yet never interrupting its continuity. The unification is so total that it is impossible to tell, once absorbed in the novel, where reality ends and fantasy begins; indeed the myth is so compelling as to project a reality of its own. As this is a not inconsiderable achievement it is interesting to examine how the author managed it.

The novel is divided into three books or parts, and each part is divided into extremely short chapters. Book One contains seventeen chapters; Book Two has seventeen chapters; while, curiously, Book Three has only sixteen chapters. As this offends the kind of constructional symmetry Zola achieved in many of his other novels there could be a good case here for a 'search for the missing chapter' game. Significantly, the hero is referred to as Father Mouret in the first and last parts, while in the middle section only his Christian name, Serge, is used. In a loose sense the three divisions represent Conception, Birth and Death, and within them Zola wisely designed a tight, almost fugal, framework to contain the wilder effusions of his lyrical prose.

There is ample evidence to suggest that, in the actual writing, the novelist was not in the least concerned with naturalism and reality. Customarily, of course, Zola immersed himself in research and documentation for a novel. 'You cannot imagine', he told the Italian journalist de Amicis, 'the trouble the wretched Abbé Mouret cost me.' Although he had ransacked Catholic bookshops, attended several Masses at Notre-Dame and read manuals for the clergy and other religious works, he was still considerably in the dark about the vows of priestly celibacy, and what happened when they were broken. He was eventually enlightened by 'a priest who had abandoned his orders, and who gave me the necessary information'. *Le Paradou* is firmly based on the Domaine de Gallice, an old garden near Aix in which Zola and Paul Cézanne often wandered in their youth. As his memory of it was completely romantic the novelist attempted to anchor it to reality by the assiduous study of seed and plant catalogues, and by visiting horticultural shows. In the event his futile search for reality turned out to be laughable for the result was a soaring, sometimes overblown but amazingly sustained flight of imagination lasting some 200 pages, or a third of the novel, which must leave few readers untouched. The pages and pages of notes on varieties of plants and trees were wholly subjugated by Zola's poetic invention, distorted, reshaped and romanticised; they merely served as inspiration, much as Van Gogh carted his canvas and easel into blazing hot cornfields to create paintings he might conceivably have painted in the comfort of a room, so little did they owe to 'reality'. This intrusive lyricism exasperated Zola, especially when his colleagues referred to him not as a realist, but as a poet. Maupassant called the novel a 'three-part poem' in which he could almost smell the flowers and touch the earth. 'I finished it in a fever of excitement' he told Zola. Taine was also a little put out by the book's lyricism, which reminded him of a fragment of Persian poetry. The truth was that when Zola the realist left his imagination unguarded, Zola the poet robbed the store. It is not surprising that this novel possesses more inaccuracies than one usually finds in Zola's fiction. A baby is born a few months after conception, and a cow accomplishes a similar miracle. Flowers bloom out of season and the geography of the place shifts and changes as though projected on to ephemeral clouds. Albine runs along the top of a wall that surrounds *Le Paradou* during Father Mouret's first visit there; yet weeks later we are told she has never seen the wall. None of this matters much, however, for Zola did not need his customary accuracy to say what he wanted to say in this novel. The mythopoetic visionary triumphed over the naturalist.

As a prose poem, flawed and laboured through it may be in parts, few readers will be less than enthralled by the novel's captivating language and its systematic yet inspired composition. For myself, I marvel at the perfection of its many parts: long, lyrical passages with never a false note; the stunning aptness of the imagery; the imaginative patterns of words choreographed so effortlessly that their source seems bottomless... *The Abbé Mouret's Sin* is a novel you can willingly give yourself up to in return for hours of enchanted pleasure.

From politico-religion and religion, Zola now turned to pure politics, for he had plenty of scores to settle in this quarter. But his malevolence towards politicians, not untypical in creative individuals, served only as a spur, for the hero of his new novel, *His Excellency*, published in 1876, who would be defined as a fascist power-seeker in our age, is treated with insight and sympathy and even cautious admiration. What eventuated is an anecdotal and graceless novel in which this hero, Eugène Rougon, obviously captured the interest of the author at an early stage of the book's development. The rise of a dominant political figure, using all the weapons at his command to achieve personal power, was just as intriguing a phenomenon to Zola as it is today.

With its notoriety for corruption, decadence, repression and political intrigue, how on earth did the Second Empire of Napoleon III manage to last for twenty years? The same question has been asked many times since of similar undemocratic regimes, yet such governments continue to rise in one country as they fall in another. The greed of reactionary interests, public inertia, opportunist coalition, uncoordinated political groups, general unrest . . . all or most of these factors are usually present at the birth of a dictatorship. But invariably there is a personality, a strong man, an iron-willed authoritarian, whose position at the top of the pedestal depends as much on the support of well-placed friends and colleagues as it does on his own abilities.

In *His Excellency* this strong man is Eugène Rougon, the clever son of Félicité Rougon whom we met in *The Fortune of the Rougons* and also in *The Conquest of Plassans*. In the first novel, you may remember, Eugène is in Paris, plotting for the *coup d'état* which in 1851 transformed the infant Second Republic into the Second Empire, with Louis Napoleon as Emperor. As a reward, Eugène is given a senior post in the new government and by 1852 – the year in which *His Excellency* opens – he has been made president of the Legislature.

At sixty-six, Rougon is second only to the Emperor in power; impressively built, handsome, and with a world-weariness which cloaks an intense vitality. Unlike the Emperor, however, Rougon's power is based on a shifting foundation of patronage and intrigue, and even as we meet him in the first pages of the novel, he has been forced to resign.

He accepts this setback philosophically, for to him power politics is akin to a game of tennis; you try to win but all is not lost if you lose a set. There is always the next game. The two years he spends in the political wilderness is mere waiting on the sidelines. His will to reassume power is not in the least dented, for in his blood is the hunting-pack urge of the Rougons.

Rougon's exile is not spent in idleness. He has many influential friends who, for various selfish reasons, want him back in power and who are willing to intrigue and subvert to achieve it. One of his admirers is Clorinde, the daughter of an Italian countess. Clorinde is a beautiful and adorable adventuress with Machiavellian ambitions, and who does not hesitate to use her charms to get what she wants, as she demonstrates by inviting Rougon to her salon:

> 'I thought you asked me to call so that you could show me something.'
> She however was so solemnly engrossed in her posing that she did not answer at once. Indeed, he had to repeat the question:
> 'What is it, then, that you wanted to show me?'

'Myself!' she said.

This declaration she made in a commanding tone, but without moving a limb, rigid on the table in her goddess pose. Her gravity imparted itself to Rougon. Drawing back a pace, he contemplated her. There was no gainsaying it, she was superb, with that pure profile of hers, that supple neck, that graceful sweep from neck to shoulders. Above all, she possessed that most queenly beauty, a lovely bosom. Her rounded limbs, too, had all the gleam of marble. Thrusting forward, her left hip carried her body slightly at an angle, and she held her right arm aloft, so that from arm-pit to heels was one uninterrupted line, powerful and flexible, incurving at the waist, flowing freely out over the buttock. Her other hand was resting on her bow and, indifferent to her nakedness, she radiated all the tranquil strength of the ancient goddess of the hunt, scornful of the love of men, a cold, haughty, immortal goddess indeed.

'Very nice, very nice,' murmured Rougon, not knowing what else he could say.

The truth was that she embarrassed him by her statuesque stillness. She seemed so victorious, so sure of being classically lovely that, had he dared, he would have criticized her as if she really were a thing of marble, some of the salient features of which offended his bourgeois eyes. He would have preferred a smaller waist, haunches less broad, a higher bosom. A moment later he was suddenly overcome by a violent masculine desire – to fondle her calves. He had to draw back from her, not to give way to the impulse.

'Have you seen enough?' Clorinde asked him, still deadly serious and grave.   (31)

Despite his coldness and contempt for women, Rougon is fascinated, and a friendship develops between the calculating young beauty and the older man. Within months, Rougon dreams of making her his mistress, but his first attempt at seduction is a clumsy, humiliating affair in his stables in which he is fought off with a horsewhip. The incident leaves Rougon frustrated and exasperated, but he is just as calculating as Clorinde. She wants nothing less than marriage before she will let Rougon touch her, while his pride will not allow him to give in to this demand. Instead, he proposes that she marry his younger protégé, Delestang, for whom he can promise excellent prospects in the government; it will be a marriage of convenience which will remove the obstacle to her becoming his mistress. In a spirit of adventure Clorinde sees the advantages of this and duly marries Delestang. Then, unexpectedly, Rougon himself marries advantageously, to the daughter of a senior magistrate who is favoured in court circles.

With new and powerful supporters, Rougon effects a *rapprochement* with the Emperor, and bides his time. It comes about in a curious way when a colleague informs him about an assassination plot he's got wind of, aimed at Napoleon III. Instead of alerting the authorities, Rougon sits on the information so that, a few nights later, three bombs explode under the Emperor's carriage outside a theatre. Although several people are killed and many more wounded, the Emperor escapes unhurt. The bombers happen to be Italians but the attempt on the Emperor's life is blamed on the Republicans, and provides a timely excuse to suppress the rising wave of liberalism. For this despotic operation the shaken Emperor obviously needs a mailed fist in charge, and Rougon is recalled – just as he has anticipated. Backed by the Emperor's demand: 'No moderation! People must be made to fear you!' Rougon asserts his renewed authority with round-ups, mass arrests and deportations. Florent, in *The Belly of Paris*, is, incidentally, one of the victims of this reign of terror, which lasts for years.

But a politician like Rougon cannot avoid having enemies. To protect himself he is calculatingly loyal to his friends, for he realises that without them he is nothing. As the years pass, his cronies have priority over government business and nepotism is the order of the day. As these self-seeking people get what they want, however, their loyalty wanes. Even Clorinde now scorns him, especially after a further attempt to make her his mistress. The trouble is that Rougon doesn't know the difference between 'subdue' and 'seduce', and on one occasion his insensitivity earns him a lighted cigarette in his face.

Ironically, the one honest action in his career leads to his downfall, for he offends the Catholic Church. As a non-believer he regards it only as an error of political judgement but he has reckoned without clerical intrigue. Crushed by the burden of his office and troubled by his impending ruin he sees his supporters, like stealthy rats, desert him one by one. In the end he has no alternative but to send the Emperor his resignation.

As his political power disintegrates his personal life crumbles, too. Clorinde has slept with his rival and now shares the bed of his ultimate patron, the Emperor; her victory is the one which stings most, for it is the triumph of a woman scorned. But for Rougon his political downfall is only another beginning. He will wait, and return to conquer, for his Rougon blood wills it; and he does.

His Excellency is of considerable documentary interest, for it gives a faithful picture of the first decade of the Second Empire and shines a light in a corner which in many histories has remained dim. Zola was an observant young man during the period covered in this novel – from about 1856 to 1861 – but as his interests at the time were artistic and literary rather than political he found it necessary to refresh his memory of personalities and events. Much of his research consisted of sifting through the two standard histories of the Second Empire, by Taxile Delord and Ernest Hamel, but of particular value to him were the state papers discovered in the Tuileries after the 1870 downfall. From these he obtained interesting details like the cost of the Imperial Prince's baptismal layette – 100,000 francs, no less – and other Cabinet secrets which helped to give verisimilitude to his descriptions of life in the corridors of imperial power. Perhaps more to the point is the influence of Zola's own political experience. He was, during the Franco-Prussian War, something of a self-seeker himself, and his modest job of ministerial secretary was partly a product of patronage; that is, he knew someone who could pull a political string for him. While at Bordeaux, he had plenty of opportunity to study at first hand the manoeuvrings and stratagems of power-seekers. And for two years before the war he was a regular contributor to the socialist paper *La Tribune*, which had the advantage of bringing him close to the outside offices of power though not into its corridors; as a vociferous opponent of the regime he would have hardly been welcomed as a visitor.

Politics is like an iceberg; it is seven-eighths submerged, and Zola had only observed the tip. It was this lack of intimacy with the centre of government which drove the author into a quest for historical accuracy, and the narrative of *His Excellency* is peppered with little news items. Cabinet discussions are taken from old state papers and most of the speeches are based on verbatim report published in a government newspaper. The assassination attempt is a reconstruction of the Orsini affair when, in 1858, an Italian revolutionary and his accomplices threw three bombs at the Emperor's coach in the cause of Italian independence. In his study of the novel, Richard B. Grant states that of its fourteen chapters only four – chapters 2, 3, 5 and 12 – are pure fiction; all the others are based on various political and social events during the Second Empire. This historical accuracy extends to chronological precision, and one wonders whether *His Excellency* might have been a much better novel had its author sacrificed the tyranny of exactitude in favour of imagination. The opening scene, for example, is an account of the servile legislature voting an extra 400,000 francs of public money for the christening ceremony of Napoleon III's son, the Imperial Prince. This fixes the date at the beginning of 1856. Rougon's recall as Minister for the Interior after the bomb attack on the Emperor has its parallel in the similar appointment of strong-man General Espinasse in January 1858, and his downfall a short time later. The result of Zola's fidelity to historical chronology is that there are strange, unaccountable interludes or vacuums, during which the characters do little else than nervously wait.

Zola might have found the freedom to shuffle and reshape his facts had he not founded his two main characters on real persons; the psychological effect of this was to draw him even deeper into a commitment to historical veracity. Although the novelist vigorously denied that *His Excellency* was a *roman à clef*, this is hard to accept on the evidence. The character Count Marsy is clearly the Duc de Morny, for whom Alphonse Daudet worked as a secretary. But the most glaring case is Eugène Rougon, whose real-life twin was substantially Eugène Rouher (1814–84), one of the most senior statesmen during Napoleon III's regime. He was responsible for the revision of the Constitution; he was Minister of Agriculture, Commerce and Public Works, an immensely powerful position; and eventually the ministerial president. After resigning he returned as Minister of Finance. The similarity of the names, the positions they held even to their manner of speaking and personal habits, like a weakness for games of patience – the parallel is too close to be dismissed as coincidence. There is a theory that Eugène Rougon represented Zola's fantasy of himself as a politician, and it is true that his political stance was ambivalent: on the one hand, contempt, on the other a frustrated desire to experience political action. Indeed, before he got his secretarial job during the war he had tried for political position, and at Médan, where he later bought a country house, he was an energetic municipal councillor for many years. At any rate, if Eugène Rougon was not a photograph of Eugène Rouher, at least he was a romanticised portrait, for Zola reveals considerable admiration for his character, or at least for the power he represented.

Clorinde has a real-life counterpart in Virginia, Contessa di Castiglione, a political animal of marble-like coldness. She was reputed to have earned a million francs for a nocturnal dalliance with an English aristocrat and eventually became Napoleon III's mistress. Whatever she was in real life, though, Clorinde is an insubstantial piece of putty and woefully unconvincing in her role as an imperial ball-breaker. In fact, with the exception of Rougon, the entire cast are a dismal and delible lot; and that he, alone among all the characters, is an individual with some substance can only be ascribed to the infusion of the novelist's own personality into his creation.

In *His Excellency* Zola couldn't resist pecking at two of his pet aversions: religion and censorship. One incident is completely gratuitous, in which the crucifix of Clorinde's rosary is accidentally broken. Rougon laughs at her distress: 'Such are the fruits of superstition,' he jokes, and goes on to deplore the Catholic education of young women and the degradation of priest-ridden Italy. This is a not unfamiliar Zola diatribe, but the author's tilt at book censorship is of greater significance, reflecting his feelings about what he viewed bitterly as the politician's characteristic hatred of literature. Rougon is especially outraged by novels. 'Our novel writers today,' he says in *His Excellency*, 'have adopted a lubricious style, a manner of saying things which brings them to life before your eyes. They call it "art". It is just impropriety, nothing less.' There is also an account of how the government's heavy hand of censorship worked during the Second Empire, which must have come directly from Zola's recollections of his newspaper days; an erring editor is summoned to the office of the Minister of the Interior to explain why the heroine in the serialisation of a novel in his paper displayed no remorse for her misdeeds. The novel could well have been Flaubert's *Madame Bovary* which had been serialised in the *Revue de Paris* during the last three months of 1856. Zola's novel also relates another incident in which the Emperor's ministers try to close down the only remaining Republican newspaper – which, conveniently, happens to be *Le Siècle*, the very paper which had bought the serial rights to *His Excellency!* But the main anti-literature debate is in the form of a Cabinet discussion during which Rougon passionately calls for more stringent censorship of books: 'They constitute a rising flood against which the country cannot be too well protected. Of twelve books published, eleven and a half deserve to be burnt, with their subversive theories and monstrous anti-social ideas...' The Minister of Public Instruction adds that, 'novels in particular are tainted food, served up to satisfy the unhealthy curiosity of the crowd.' The sentiments may sound unsubtle, but they were only too real early in the author's career and, in many countries today, still are. The manner of justifying political censorship of newspapers and books hasn't changed in a century, either. Listen to Rougon's rousing speech:

As for the press, gentlemen, it has never enjoyed a greater freedom under any government determined to have itself respected. Every great question, every major interest has its outlet. The government only opposes the propagation of false doctrines and the dissemination of public poison. But for the honourable press, which is the great voice of public opinion, we have the deepest respect. It assists us in our task; it is the tool of our age. If the government has taken it under control, it was only to keep it from the hands of the government's enemies....

Symbolism is markedly absent in *His Excellency*, although there is some vague counterpoint between Rougon's political graph and his relationship with Clorinde. But there are several effective analogies with animals, for whenever Rougon loses his power over people he dreams of substitutes: a farm, in which he can command his dogs and sheep; an industrial estate, on which he can lord it over the workers, and so on. The imagery is also inverted. Just before his return to power he sees his adversaries as ravening dogs: 'He pictured himself with a whip, keeping their snarling jaws at bay all around him. The insults intoxicated him. In the pride of his isolation he grew in stature.' And he feels the same way about his friends; he needs to reign over them, too. The most powerful imagery, though, is that of the hunting pack, symbolising the voracious appetites of the supporters of Napoleon's corrupt regime. Early in the novel, at the Emperor's hunting resort at Compiègne, Rougon watches a pack of hounds feast on a stag's head, thrown to them by the kennel master.

> Down in the courtyard, the dogs were now finishing off their bones, thrusting wildly in underneath one another, to get at the heart of that pile of offal, till it was one carpet of pulsating canine backs, a confusion of black and white, heaving, stretching, hoarsely breathing, reaching out like a living swamp of voracious flesh. Jaws could not gobble fast enough, in this feverish longing to swallow it all. There were brusque clashes, invariably ending in harsh howls. Suddenly one immense hound, a magnificent animal, enraged at finding itself still on the outer edge, drew back, with one unhesitating leap to charge into the heart of the confusion and thrust his way in, and a second later he was sucking down a long string of the stag's entrails.   (31)

Do you hear the distant refrain to the snarling of the hounds in *The Kill?* What we are watching, really, is Zola's soured vision of the Second Empire in miniature. His character, however, Eugène Rougon, sees it rather differently. What has happened to the stag will happen to him, and surely enough, at the end of the novel, Rougon himself is the cornered, bleeding beast:

> Now he began to recall all that steady work the band had put in, and their sharp jaws, daily taking new toll of his strength. They were all round him. They clambered on to his lap, they reached up to his chest, to his throat, till they strangled him. They had taken possession of every part of him, using his feet to climb with, his hands to steal with, his jaws to tear and devour with. They lived in his flesh, drawing all their pleasure and their health from it, feasting by reason of it, without thought for the morrow.   (31)

Although at times it hints at insights, *His Excellency* ends up as neither a love story nor a political novel of any depth. The sexual element reflects Zola's belief, with which he struggled through most of his life, that love dissipates a man's energy and vitality, especially in the creative sphere. It is essential to know this otherwise the curious relationship between Rougon and Clorinde is likely to amount to a lot of nonsense. It explains Rougon's almost wilful clumsiness in the art of seduction, and also the relief he experiences when he fails. For Rougon, too, believes in his creator's theory, and all his life has chosen to remain aloof from women. He has no love for his wife and only fleeting esire for Clorinde in moments of weakness. So rather than a love story, it is a ontest of two strong wills; and physically Rougon never gets beyond grabbing lorinde's resisting wrists.

His Excellency is a political novel, although not a good one. The true political ovel is a rarity; one calls to mind Edwin O'Connor's *The Last Hurrah* (1956) nd Gore Vidal's *Washington, D.C.* (1967) and even his more recent *Burr* (1974) s late additions to a surprisingly small list. Most novelists, doubtless with ifferent intentions, appear to find themselves preoccupied with more ersonal, non-political themes. That Zola could quite easily have fallen into this ap is illustrated by what happened in *The Kill*; he set out to tell the story of a peculator, only to have his main character upstaged by the intensity of the ersonal relationship between his wife and son. If the same thing had appened in *His Excellency* it might not have been a political novel but it would ave most certainly been a better novel. In 1875, when he was writing *His xcellency*, Zola's grasp of political motivation was still simplistic, and his echniques for orchestrating large casts of characters still undeveloped. The ovel might have benefited immeasurably if it had been written later in the ycle; as it is, its scale is limited and the action is almost all in close-up, isolated om the population affected by political decisions.

Even before he had finished writing *His Excellency* Zola felt it would be the ook to change his fortunes. The newspaper *Le Siècle* had agreed to serialise it thirty-five instalments from January 1876, and Charpentier felt it would be a reat success. Zola needed it badly. His books were selling neither well, nor oorly enough for him to claim that he was misunderstood by the public, which ight have been some consolation. There also seemed to be a conspiracy of lence among the reviewers and critics, and the corrosive thought that he ight be a mediocrity began to haunt him. Charpentier wasn't complaining, ough, and generously awarded his ambitious author a bonus of several ousand francs besides the agreed 500 francs a month. Zola also received nother 500 francs each month from *Le Bien public* as its drama critic. ronically, at this time, he was one of the biggest-selling authors in Moscow and Petersburg; but in France. . .nothing but silence. His friends tried to cheer im up by telling him the country was so immersed in political turmoil that the eople couldn't settle down to read novels. Zola heard all the arguments, all the ationalisations, but he knew the truth; if he was ever to be as famous as his urning ambition demanded, he'd have to smash through the national onsciousness with something really big. . .

It was in this frame of mind, in the summer of 1875, that he began to prepare reliminary notes for his next novel, something completely original, a study of e working classes and of their desperate predicament. It was his own redicament, however, that began to worry his friends. He was suffering from outs of depression and had experienced some frightening hallucinations hich, night after night, denied him sleep. Some months of this had left him rained and empty, physically and mentally, and friends suggested a seaside holiday. 'Do nothing!' boomed Flaubert, who, despite his own troubles, wa deeply concerned. 'And especially, *write* nothing, nothing at all!'

In August Zola could no longer ignore his need for a break, and the famil went to stay in a cottage Paul Alexis found at Saint-Aubin-sur-Mer i Normandy. The vast, open sea stirred him but his southern nature was at odd with the cold, rough Atlantic. The crashing waves disturbed his serenity an the constant wind was irritating. The water was cold, too, and he couldn bathe. The seaweed stank. Alexandrine and his mother quarrelled.

But the most unsatisfactory aspect of the holiday was that the novelist wante to be back in Paris. Despite Flaubert's warning he had sneaked into the baggag a great parcel of books and notes and, once in the cottage, soon set up makeshift desk by a window looking out on to the sea. He would lose himse there for hours at a time, dreaming of the slums of Paris; or he would lie on th beach, sheltering from the wind behind rocks, watching the clouds, or th merging of sky and sea in the hazy distance, with a dictionary of slang on h knees, muttering the words he imagined his characters would use in a domest squabble, or in a drunken brawl, or to a landlord who was throwing the out... He gave up smoking, and breathed deeply, filling his lungs with the se air, walking miles for exercise, begging his health to improve. For now he kne he was going to need every reserve of his strength; he could *feel*, with a sur instinctive knowledge, that the new novel growing and resounding in his brai was going to be a masterpiece.

1. EMILE ZOLA, from the portrait by Manet, 1868, now in the Louvre. *Snark International*

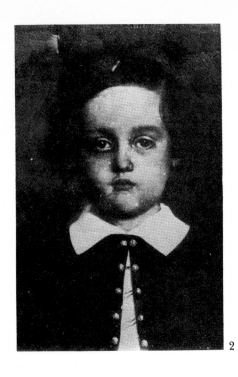

2. ZOLA as a boy, aged five.
3. A TYPICAL illustrated letter from Paul Cezanne to Zola in Paris, October 19, 186‹
4. LOUIS HACHETTE, founder of the famous French publishing house, who employe‹
Zola between 1862 and 1866.
5. ZOLA at twenty-five, from a studio portrait.

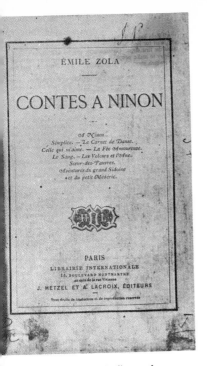

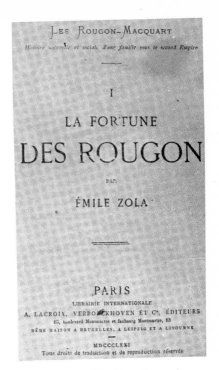

6. TITLE PAGE of Zola's first published book: *Stories for Ninon*, 1864.

7. TITLE PAGE of the first volume of the Rougon-Macquart chronicle, *The Fortune of the Rougons*, 1871.

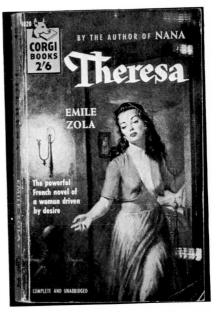

8. EARLY English editions of Zola's novels featured lurid and quite violent wood-engraved illustrations like this one for *Thérèse Raquin*, Vizetelly & Co, London, 1887.

9. BY THE 1950s, Zola's novels were promoted by emphasising their sexual content, as with this Corgi paperback edition of *Thérèse Raquin*, Corgi Books, London, 1952.

8

A Drink to Success

It is many years since I read *L'Assommoir* for the first time but I remember the occasion with crystal clarity. We read perhaps hundreds, even thousands, of books during our lives, and we can recall, years later, most of them. But how many can we remember *reading*?

Every once in a while a book comes along which provides the reader with an extra-literary experience. For me, one such book was *L'Assommoir*. It was winter. Half-way through the novel I wanted the narrative to continue forever, while at the same time I galloped through the pages at an alarming rate. I would find excuses to read only a chapter at a time, to have the pleasurable anticipation of picking it up again next evening, and the next. My life, for a week or so, seemed to be a strategic, self-defeating game: how to get to the end of the story as quickly as possible, and how to make the book last as long as possible. When I did finish, before the echoes had faded, I read it all over again, at one sitting.

Even before its completion, *L'Assommoir* began to acquire the reputation of a bestseller, to the extent that Yves Guyot, the editor of *Le Bien public*, paid the surprisingly high fee of 10,000 francs for the right to serialise it. It was a bold move in the circulation race, but unfortunately the editor was a little out of touch with the tastes of his readers. Serialisation began in April 1876, but by June the volume of complaints which poured in about this crude slice of life so terrorised the management that the story was dropped even before the half-way point had been reached, the paper artfully excusing the abrupt cessation on the grounds that its author needed more time to finish it. The novel was then quickly snapped up by Catulle Mendès, poet editor of *La République des lettres*, and the serialisation of the remainder was resumed in July. Circulation soared, thanks to thousands of disgruntled readers of *Le Bien public* who had been cheated of their serial, and helped by a controversy that began to break out in newspapers all over France. *L'Assommoir* was praised, damned and defended, but mostly damned: '*A mass of gutter filth! A slander on France! A monstrous abortion!*' Even Villemessant in *Le Figaro* turned maliciously on his former employee, denouncing his prose as coarse, obscene and ungrammatical. For Zola, to whom any publicity, even bad publicity, was a

105

thousand times more preferable to indifference, it was a satisfying time, and of course he was well aware that the uproar would pave the way for an enthusiastic reception of the novel in book form.

The novel appeared as a book at the end of February 1877, and Zola's hunch proved to be right. *L'Assommoir* was an instant, runaway success. Before its publication, Zola and Charpentier had agreed that a sale of 5,000 copies might eventually be achieved. But by the end of 1877, 38,000 copies had been sold; by 1880 a sale of 80,000 had been reached, and a year later the hundred-thousandth copy was sold. The bonanza spread to the author's other novels, of which several had sold only a few thousand copies. With this spectacular eruption of publicity all his novels went through between five and ten editions during 1877, all riding on the wave of *L'Assommoir's* incredible popularity.

This great novel had, like the characters in it, the most humble of beginnings. Its origin has been traced to a single sheet of paper with a few notes scribbled on it: Gervaise's feast, with passers-by joining in; some laundry scenes; women looking for their husbands in pubs – the sketchiest of notes, written in about 1871. Yet the grand intention was firmly resolved in Zola's mind: an honest, frontal portrait of a working-class family and its vicissitudes. This may not seem much of a novelty today, but in France a century ago working people were as foreign as savages to most writers in their everyday lives, let alone in literature. Even the encyclopedic Balzac had excluded them. Ironically, the dilettantish Goncourts were the first to set down some of the cruel facts about working-class existence in *Germinie Lacerteux* in the mid-1860s.

Resolving the form of the novel from that single page of notes produced for Zola a whole train of problems. Although, alone among the *Rougon-Macquart* novels, it opened before the *coup d'état* of 1851, it had a contemporary setting; apart from some stray scenes it owes nothing to the Second Empire period. Furthermore Claude had already appeared in *The Belly of Paris* as a youth; now he had to reappear as a young child. For Zola the methodologist the inconsistency must have been difficult to accept, but in the event the anachronism disturbs nothing but a few leaves on the Rougon-Macquart family tree.

Gervaise, his heroine, was also still a hasty sketch. Her fictional biography in Zola's notes has the brevity of a police file:

> Born 1828, has two sons by her lover Lantier, who counts paralytics among his ancestors; is taken to Paris and there deserted by him; is married in 1852 to a workman, Coupeau, who comes of alcoholic stock; has a daughter by him; dies of misery and drink in 1869. Prepotency of her father. Conceived in drunkenness. Is lame. A washerwoman.

And that is all. Interestingly, the importance Zola vests in the manner of Gervaise's conception is as good an illustration as any of his wholesale acceptance of some of the wilder theories of heredity current at the time.

Then there were problems of political discretion. The Communards were still exiled, and the Worker's International was still an illegal organisation. Sympathy for the proletariat was tolerated to a degree, but could the authorities take the lashing Zola was planning to deal out in *L'Assommoir?* Four years passed before he felt it prudent to proceed with the final draft of the novel.

As soon as the novelist arrived back in Paris early in October 1875, he unpacked his notes and walked about the area between the Gare du Nord and Montmartre for several days to fix the location in his mind. If you are ever in Paris you can still visit the setting of the novel by taking the Metro to Barbes-Rochechouart, crossing the Boulevard de la Chapelle, and walking through the streets that run north opposite the Hospital Lariboisière as far as the Rue Marcadet. For one of Gervaise's lodgings he selected a decaying five-storey tenement building, with its rows of windows made crooked by sagging shutters and with four dingy shops at street level. He found a laundry, open to the street, its owner half-hidden by the clouds of steam. He noted the bars and all the narrow streets and the people who lived in the district: workmen and factory girls, tired mothers carrying babies, housewives shopping, children playing, all the time tuning his ear to the local *argot.* He even peeped into windows, memorising details of furniture and decorations. Once he had assimilated all this background detail he translated it on to a canvas as visually memorable as any created by his artist friends.

Zola mulled over the problem of a title for the novel for several months. There were a number of fondly defamatory terms for the grotty wine bars in the poor quarters – 'zinc', 'bouge' and 'bistrot', for example – but none of these suggested the evil power of the kind of den he had in mind: one into which its victims are sucked, stunned and eventually killed. He found it, eventually, in his well-thumbed slang dictionary, a word for the pole-axe used to stun cattle before slaughter in an abbatoir – an *assommoir.* The term had been used in working-class districts to describe the lowest class of drinking den but had fallen out of use, but it was perfect for the novelist's purpose. The title, *L'Assommoir,* is so apt and evocative it is unfortunate that the term defies translation into English.

The story opens, ominously, with Gervaise, unable to sleep, waiting by the open window of a tiny Paris flat for her lover to come home. Only a short time before, Lantier, a hatmaker, has brought her and their two children to the capital to seek work. She suspects, when he fails to show up by morning, that he plans to move in with another woman, but doesn't want to believe it. The reader is left in little doubt, however, that Lantier is something of a playboy and, sure enough, while Gervaise is at the laundry that morning, he skips. She hears about his departure from the children, who come to the laundry with the house-key; and from the other women learns that he has moved in with the sister of Virginie, a malicious virago who is washing at a nearby tub. Virginie taunts the lame Gervaise until a fight ensues, witnessed by her two children. The battle among the suds is the first of many virtuoso set-pieces in the novel.

'Well – yes, it was my sister. Will that satisfy you? They're awfully in love with one another. You should see them kissing and cuddling! And so he has thrown you and your bastards over? Nice kids they are, with their snotty faces! You had one off a

107

policeman, didn't you? and you starved three more, so as not to have too much luggage to bring with you. Your Lantier told us all that. Ah, he says nice things of you; he's had quite enough of your old carcase!'

'You slut! you slut! you slut!' shrieked Gervaise, beside herself, and shaking with fury.

She turned, looked down, and finding only the small tub full of blue, seized it by the legs, and flung the water in Virginie's face.

'The jade! she has spoilt my dress,' cried Virginie. One shoulder was simply soaked, and her left hand all over blue. 'Wait a minute, you dirty whore!'

And she too seized a bucket, and emptied it over her opponent. Then began a regular battle royal. Both ran to the tubs, seized on the full buckets, and dashed the water at one another, accompanying each deluge with a volley of abuse, in which even Gervaise joined.

'Take that, dirty beast! That got you! That'll cool your arse for you!'

'Ah! the drab! There's for your dirt. That'll wash your face for once in your life.'...

Finally they filled the buckets at the taps, and while they waited for them to fill, they still went on hurling abuse at one another. The first few buckets, badly aimed, hardly touched them. But they soon got more expert. Virginie was the first to get one full in the face; the water went in at her neck, streamed down her back and chest, and ran out under her dress. She had not recovered from the shock when another caught her sideways, giving her a sharp slap on the left ear, and soaking her chignon, which unrolled like a cord. Gervaise was hit first in the legs; one bucketful filled her shoes, and squirted half-way up her leg; two others deluged her thighs. And it was soon impossible to tell which strokes took effect. Both were streaming from head to foot, their bodices plastered down on their shoulders, their skirts glued to their waists; they seemed to have shrunk up and stiffened out, they were shivering with cold, and the drops ran out of them on all sides like umbrellas in the rain.   (35)

From black despair at her humiliation, Gervaise bounces back to marry her good-natured neighbour, Coupeau, a tin-smith and roof-mender, although against her better judgement. The couple are married by the mayor and the rambling wedding party that follows, with Zola orchestrating fifteen disparate guests from one tragi-comic situation to the next, is one of the great masterpieces of descriptive prose. From the town hall they walk to the church and from there to a bar for a lunch of bread, ham and wine. From that moment the celebration begins to crumble, and concludes as a riot. Not knowing what to do with themselves until the wedding dinner at six o'clock, Coupeau's friend M. Madinier suggests they visit the Louvre, despite the heavy downpour that has set in. Borrowing umbrellas the party struggles through the wet streets, gets lost, and finally, uncomprehendingly, comes face to face with the alien world of art under the guidance of the unfortunate M. Madinier who, as a cardboard boxmaker, claims an affinity with artistic creation denied to the rest of them. The party blinks at the huge paintings, rubber-necks at the ceiling frescoes but above all is most impressed by the mirror-like shine on the floors which gives them the feeling of walking on water.

Then the wedding party invaded the long gallery occupied by the Italian and Flemish schools. More paintings, always paintings, saints, men and women, with faces which none of them could understand, landscapes that were all black, animals turned yellow, a medley of people and things, the great mixture of the colours of which was beginning to give them all violent headaches. M. Madinier no longer talked as he slowly headed the procession, which followed him in good order, with stretched necks and upcast eyes. Centuries of art passed before their bewildered ignorance, the fine sharpness of the early masters, the splendours of the Venetians, the vigorous life, beautiful with light, of the Dutch painters. But what interested them most were the artists who were copying, with their easels planted amongst the people, painting away unrestrainedly; an old lady, mounted on a pair of high steps, working a big brush over the delicate sky of an immense painting, struck them as something most peculiar. Little by little, however, the news had probably spread that a wedding party was visiting the Louvre; painters, with broad grins on their faces, hastened to the spot; some of the curious secured seats beforehand to witness the procession comfortably; whilst the attendants, repressing their laughter, refrained with difficulty from making some very cutting remarks. And those forming the party, already feeling tired, losing their respect, dragged their hob-nail shoes, and knocked their heels on the sonorous floors, like the stamping of a bewildered drove of cattle let loose in the midst of the cleanliness and quiet of the rooms. (34)

The married couple enjoy four years of modest prosperity. They find a comfortable apartment in the Rue de la Goutte-d'Or, Nana is born, and they establish a neighbourly friendship with the Goujets – Madame Goujet and her handsome, shy blacksmith son, who soon becomes secretly infatuated with the blonde, vivacious laundress. But Gervaise's ambitions lie elsewhere; with the 600 francs she's saved she wants to buy a little shop.

Then – tragedy. Coupeau falls from a high building. For a week he lingers close to death but the only serious damage is a broken leg. Months pass before he is able to walk, and in lavishing all her care on him Gervaise goes through her savings to the last franc. However, her admirer Goujet comes to the rescue with a loan, and her happiness is complete when she leases a shop and establishes her own hand-laundry business. The shop prospers and in no time Gervaise has three women working for her – she, a former washerwoman! All the while, though, Coupeau is convalescing, mainly in the neighbourhood wine bars; his leg has healed but now he is inflicting upon himself injuries of a different kind. One afternoon, when Gervaise and her three assistants are busy in the laundry, Coupeau turns up drunk and mauls his wife in front of the others, with her good-natured consent. Zola adroitly buries the incident in the piles of washing, but the damage has been done; it is the beginning of their descent. Before long, Coupeau is coming home drunk every evening, soaking up his wife's spare cash and playfully molesting her young assistants. But Gervaise, complacent and growing stouter with good living, merely smiles and indulgently lets him have his way. In her easy-going style she goes to any lengths to avoid rocking the boat, but suddenly it hits a reef: accidentally, she sees Lantier, her former lover. He has returned to the district, and for weeks Gervaise is in a state of apprehension, fear and ecstasy until, at her birthday party, Coupeau, spotting him outside, invites him in. During the months that follow Lantier becomes a regular visitor and eventually Coupeau, in a fit of *bonhomie*, suggests he becomes their lodger; after all, two of the children are his, and he will make a good drinking companion to while away Coupeau's days of boredom. In a short time Lantier takes over as man of the house, and it isn't long before the opportunity occurs to take over Gervaise, too. Her seduction is recounted in a passage of brutal sensuality and compelling logic, following her return from a dance and finding her husband dead drunk in the bedroom.

'Oh, the swine! the swine!' Gervaise kept on saying in outraged indignation. 'He has messed everything up.... No, even a dog wouldn't have done that, a dead dog would have been cleaner.'

Neither dared move, not knowing where to tread. He had never come home in such a state and made the room in such a disgusting mess. The sight of it dealt a rude blow to any feeling his wife might still have for him. Before, when he had come home a bit tipsy or fuddled, she had shown herself sympathetic and not at all disgusted. But this was too much, and her stomach was heaving. She couldn't have touched him even with a pair of tongs. The mere thought of this lout's skin coming near hers gave her the horrors, like having to lie beside the corpse of somebody who had died of a foul disease....

She tried to step over the drunken hulk, but had to hold tight to the chest for fear of slipping in the muck. Coupeau barred all access to the bed. Then Lantier, seeing she would never sleep on her own pillow that night, smiled a little smile, took her hand and whispered passionately:

'Gervaise... listen, Gervaise...'

She saw what he meant and snatched her hand away. In her confusion she fell back into the affectionate language of the old days.

'No dear, leave me alone... Please, Auguste, go into your own room. I'll manage somehow. I'll climb in over the foot of the bed.'

'Gervaise, look here, don't be silly. It smells too nasty, you can't stay here... Come along, what are you afraid of? It's not as though he can hear us.'

She went on struggling, shaking her head vehemently. In her distress, as if to prove that she meant to stay where she was, she began undressing and threw her silk dress over a chair, stripping violently down to her chemise and petticoat, showing her bare neck and arms. Her bed was her own, wasn't it? She meant to sleep in her own bed. Twice she tried to find a clean spot where she could get across, but Lantier was persistent, and put his arms round her waist, saying things that set her blood on fire. Oh, what a position to be in, with a useless husband in front preventing her from getting decently between her own sheets, and a dirty-minded man behind whose one idea was to take advantage of her trouble and have her again. As Lantier was beginning to raise his voice she begged him to shut up. She listened, straining her ears towards the slip-room where Nana and Grandma Coupeau slept. By the sound of their heavy breathing they must both be asleep now....

He said no more, but went on smiling. Then he slowly kissed her ear, just like he used to in the old days, to tease her. The strength went out of her and she was conscious of a great buzzing in her head and a great shudder running through her flesh. Yet she took one more step forward. But she had to recoil. She just couldn't, the nausea was too much for her and the smell was getting so awful that she would have been sick herself in the bed....

'Oh, it's no use,' she faltered, 'it's his fault, I just can't... Oh God, he has turned me out of my own bed... I haven't got a bed of my own any more.... No, I can't, it's his fault.'

She was shaking all over and didn't know what she was doing. And as Lantier was guiding her into his room Nana's face appeared behind one of the panes in the glass door of the slip-room. She had just awakened and got quietly out of bed in her nightdress, pale with sleep. She had a look at her father wallowing in his own vomit and then, glueing her face to the glass, she stood there watching for her mother's petticoat to disappear into the other man's room opposite. She concentrated attentively, and the child's vicious eyes, staring wide, were lit up with a lubricious curiosity. (40)

Note that the author, by allowing a presentient glimpse of Nana, is already preparing readers for his future novel; without a doubt, the girl is going to turn out a thoroughly bad lot, and we can hardly wait to read about her.

Little by little, Gervaise lets go. She now uncomplainingly provides for two spongers, the debts pile up, the drunken arguments increase, and she becomes distracted, despairing and dreadfully fatigued by the unequal battle. Her enemy Virginie, mischievously helped by Coupeau, takes over her shop, yet Gervaise cannot find enough resentment in herself even to show annoyance. The family is forced to move to poorer quarters in a dismal, soul-destroying tenement block owned by the despicable landlord Marescot. The environment, as always in Zola's fiction, plays its sinister part:

> In the midst of this existence, soured by poverty, Gervaise suffered too on account of the starving people she found all around her. It was the lousy corner of the house, where three or four households seemed to have agreed not to indulge in a meal every day. The doors might open, it was not often they let out a smell of cooking. All along the corridor, there was a deathly silence, and the walls rang hollow, like empty \
> stomachs. Now and again there was a bit of a row, women crying, hungry brats screaming, families, who went for each other tooth and nail, in default of anything else to use their jaws upon. A sort of general cramp seemed to yawn from all those gaping mouths; and chests grew hollow, merely with breathing the air of the place, an air in which a gnat could hardly live. (35)

On her wedding night, Gervaise had bumped into Old Bazouge, the undertaker. He was drunk, as usual, but the incident terrified the superstitious young bride. Now she is appalled to discover that he is, through the thinnest of partitions, her neighbour; the symbolism being as obvious to the reader as it is terrifying to Gervaise.

> The laundress suffered equally from the nearness of Bazouge, the undertaker's man. A mere partition, quite a thin one, separated the two rooms. He could not put his finger in his mouth without her hearing it. As soon as he came in at night, she listened, despite herself, to every sound that came from his room, the black hat sounding on the chest of drawers like a clod of earth, the black cloak, as it was hung up, scraping against the wall like the sound of some night-bird's wings, all the black things thrown all about the room, like mourning being unpacked.... \
> And she would turn quite pale, wondering what he was up to now; she had the most horrible fancies, would get it into her head that he had brought home a corpse with him and that he was stowing it away under his bed. Why, wasn't there a story in the papers about an undertaker's man who had quite a collection of children's coffins in his house, which he had made to save the trouble of going to the cemetery more than once. Certainly, when Bazouge arrived, he brought with him the scent of death on the other side of that partition. (35)

By now Coupeau is tossing back a pint of brandy a day and this, coupled with a bout of pneumonia, puts him in hospital and then, after an attack of delirium, into the asylum. The experience temporarily chastens him but in a couple of weeks he is back on the bottle as savagely as ever. And worse – Gervaise, her spirit now completely broken, takes to drink too, in yet another sad seduction. One wet evening, fearing that Coupeau is drinking away the last of their almost exhausted resources, she tracks him down to Colombe's Bar. First, she is seduced into the evil establishment.

> The place was flaring, the gas alight, white flames like suns, the jars and bottles illuminating the walls with their coloured glass. She stood there an instant leaning forward, with her face against the glass, between two bottles in the window, peering in at Coupeau, who was sitting with his friends at the other end of the place, at a little zinc-topped table, all vague and misty in the smoke of their pipes.... The rain dripped in her neck; she moved away and went on to the outer boulevard, turning it over in her mind, not venturing to go in.... Twice she went back and stood outside the window, putting her face against the glass again, vexed to see those infernal

drunkards in out of the rain, chatting and drinking. The light of the bar was reflected in the puddles of the pavements, where the rain pattered and bubbled. She stepped back and splashed into it whenever the door opened and shut, creaking on its rusty hinges. After all she was merely coming after her husband; and she had a right to for he had promised to take her to the circus that evening. Well, here goes! she was not going to melt out there on the pavement, like a cake of soap.   (35)

At first she is repelled by the place and its brutalising atmosphere:

Old fat Colombe, reaching out his huge arms, the terror of the establishment, calmly served out drinks. It was very hot, the smoke of pipes went up in the blinding glitter of gaslight, spreading like a cloud of dust, and covering the drinkers with a slowly thickening steam; and out of this cloud there came a deafening, confused hubbub of cracked voices and the clink of glasses, oaths and blows of the fist, like detonations. Gervaise made a wry face, for a sight like that is not a very entertaining one for a woman, especially when she is not used to it; she choked, her eyes burned, her head swam in the alcoholic smell exhaled by the whole place.   (35)

Then, after some teasing by the men, Gervaise is seduced into having a drink.

'I say, mealy-mouth!' cried Coupeau, 'don't makes faces. Wet blankets may go to Jericho! What'll you have to drink?'
'Nothing, certainly,' replied the laundress, 'I haven't had dinner.'
'All the more reason; a drop of something will keep you up.'
But as she still kept a glum visage, Mes-Bottes once more came forward politely.
'The lady surely likes liqueurs,' he murmured.
'I like men who don't get drunk,' she answered surlily. 'Yes. I like people to bring back their pay and keep their word when they have made a promise.'
'Ah! that's what upsets you!' said the tinsmith, still laughing. 'You want your share. Well, you blockhead, why don't you have a drink? You'd better have it, it's all profit.'
She looked straight in his face, very seriously, wrinkling her forehead till a black furrow came out all across. And she answered slowly:
'So be it, you are right, it's a good idea. We'll drink the cash together.'
Bibi-la-Grillade went to get her a glass of anisette. She pulled up her chair to the table. As she sipped her anisette she remembered all at once how she had had a prune with Coupeau, long ago, there near the door, when he was courting her. At that time she left the brandy sauce. And now here she was drinking liqueurs again. Oh! she knew herself now, she had not a halfpennyworth of will. She only wanted a good kick behind to send her headlong in to the drink.   (35)

The still, behind the bar, takes on the threatening appearance of a live monster. When Gervaise switches to the fiery raw brandy, it begins to attract her with a fearful fascination.

'You'll have another, madame?'
No, she had had enough. Still, she hesitated. The anisette was not quite the thing. She would rather have had something a little sharper, to settle her stomach. And she glanced sideways at the drinking machine behind her. The blessed object, round as a publican's belly, with its nose that trailed and twisted, sent a shiver through her, half fear, half desire. It might have been the metallic intestines of some sorceress, distilling, drop by drop, the fire that burnt within her. It was a poisonous thing, a thing that should have been hidden away in a cellar, so shameless and abominable was it! But, all the same, she was drawn to the thing, would fain have sniffed at its odour, tasted its bestiality, even if her tongue had burnt and peeled off like an orange.   (35)

Gervaise's slide down is terrible to behold. When it becomes too harrowing for our faint hearts, and we'd rather not continue, we find Zola has us in an iron

112

grip. Lantier leaves her. Nana, now a coquettish young woman, also quits; the bestial burlesques that are a daily feature of her parents' lives are too much even for her. Coupeau's body, soaked for years in alcohol,

shrivelled up like a foetus in a chemist's jar. When he stood in front of a window, you could see daylight through him, he was so thin. His cheeks were hollow, his eyes ran with rheumy wax, enough to supply a cathedral. Only his flaming nose, fiery and florid, stood out like a carnation on his wasted face. Those who knew his age, just forty, shuddered as he shambled past, bent and shaking, and as old as the streets themselves. The trembling in his hands got worse, especially the right hand, so that on some days he had to hold his glass in both hands to lift it to his lips. Oh! the trembling! it was the one thing that really frightened him. Sometimes he would curse his hands, or sit for hours watching them dance uncontrollably, jumping like frogs...

The portrait was a gift from Heaven to the temperance workers.

If the reader at this point thinks that things simply can't get any worse, there are more shocks in store. Their furniture goes into hock, then their belongings and their clothes. Marescot, the landlord, is waiting to turn them out into the street. Gervaise appeals for just the tiniest scrap of help from her neighbours, but like starved and spiteful dogs they turn her away with snarls and curses. Hungry, stupefied, she totters from one barbaric scene to the next. At Coupeau's suggestion she resorts to prostitution for the few sous with which to buy her next drink.

Few people passed along, only folks in a hurry who swiftly crossed the Boulevards. And on the broad, dark, deserted footway, where the sound of the revelry died away, women were standing and waiting. They remained for long intervals, motionless, patient, and as stiff-looking as the scrubby little plane trees; then they slowly began to move, dragging their slippers over the frozen soil, taking ten steps or so and then waiting again, rooted as it were to the ground. There was one of them with a huge body and insect-like arms and legs, wearing a black silk rag, with a yellow scarf over her head; there was another one, tall and bony, who was bare-headed and wore a servant's apron; and others, too – old ones plastered up, and young ones so dirty that a rag-picker would not have picked them up. However, Gervaise tried to learn the trade by imitating them; girlish-like emotion tightened her throat; she was hardly aware whether she felt ashamed or not – she seemed to be living in a horrible dream. For a quarter of an hour she remained standing erect. Men hurried by without even turning their heads. Then she moved about in her turn, and venturing to accost a man who was whistling with his hands in his pockets, she murmured in a strangled voice:
'Sir, just listen.'
The man gave her a side glance and then went off, whistling all the louder.
Gervaise grew bolder, and, with her stomach empty, she became absorbed in this chase, fiercely rushing after her dinner, which was still running away. She walked about for a long while, without thinking of the flight of time or of the direction she took. Around her the dark mute women went to and fro under the trees like wild beasts in a cage. They stepped out of the shade like apparitions, and passed under the light of a gas lamp with their pale faces fully apparent; then they grew vague again as they went off into the darkness, with a white strip of petticoat swaying to and fro....
'Sir, just listen.'
But the men passed by. She started from the slaughter-houses, which stunk of blood. She glanced on her way at the old Hotel Boncœur, now closed. She passed in front of the Lariboisière hospital, and mechanically counted the number of windows that were illuminated with a pale quiet glimmer, like that of night-lights at the bedside of some agonising sufferers. She crossed the railway bridge as the trains rushed by with a noisy rumble, rending the air with their shrill whistling! Ah! how sad

everything seemed at night-time! Then she turned on her heels again, and filled her eyes with the sight of the same houses, doing this ten and twenty times without pausing, without resting for a minute on a bench. No; no one would have anything to do with her. Her shame seemed to be increased by this contempt. She went down towards the hospital again, and then returned towards the slaughter-houses. It was her last promenade – from the blood-stained courtyards, where animals were stricken low, down to the pale hospital wards, where death stiffened the patients stretched between the sheets. It was between these two establishments that she had passed her life.

'Sir, just listen.'

But suddenly she perceived her shadow on the ground. When she approached a gas-lamp it gradually became less vague, till it stood out at last in full force – an enormous shadow it was, positively grotesque, so portly had she become. Her stomach, breast, and hips, all equally flabby, jostled together as it were. She walked so lame that the shadow bobbed almost topsy-turvy at every step she took; it looked like a real Punch! Then as she left the street lamp behind her, the Punch grew taller, becoming in fact gigantic, filling the whole Boulevard, bobbing to and fro in such style that it seemed fated to smash its nose against the trees or the houses. Good Lord! how frightful she was! She had never realised her disfigurement so thoroughly. And she could not help looking at her shadow; indeed, she waited for the gas lamps, still watching the Punch as it bobbed about. Ah! she had a pretty companion beside her! What a figure! It ought to attract men at once! And at the thought of her unsightliness, she lowered her voice, and only just dared to stammer behind the passers-by:

'Sir, just listen.'   (34)

Gervaise's humiliation is complete when one of the men she accosts in the dark turns out to be her faithful admirer, the blacksmith Goujet. He takes her to his apartment and feeds her.

'Will you have some more bread?' he asked, in a low voice.

She wept, she said no, she said yes, she knew not what she was saying. God in heaven! how good and sad it is to eat when you are starving!

And he, standing in front of her, gazed at her. Now he saw her clearly, under the bright light of the lamp shade. How aged and faded she was! The warmth melted the snow on her hair and her dress, and the water streamed off her. Her poor shaking head was all grey, grey locks all blown about by the wind. Her head was sunk in upon her shoulders, she sat there huddled up, ugly and clumsy enough to make you weep. And he recalled how they had loved each other, when she was all rosy, ironing away and showing the baby-crease that put such a pretty collar round her neck. Then he would gaze at her for hours, content merely to look at her. Later on she had come to the forge, and they had tasted huge delights, while he hammered his iron and she stood there, caught up into the dance of his hammer. Then how many nights he had bitten his pillow, longing to have her and hold her, so, in his room! Oh! he would have broken her in pieces, if he had had her, so ardently had he desired her. And now she was his, he could take her. She finished her bread, she wiped up her tears, big silent tears that fell upon what she was eating.   (35)

But it is not to be. It is annihilation Gervaise wants, for she is past all care, beyond the comforts of love; and she knows also that she will be the ruin of Goujet. Mercifully, for both Gervaise and the reader, only a few pages remain. Reduced to a human animal in an alien environment, helpless, alone, blameless and without hope, even her instinct to survive is blunted and confused. Wishing only to die to be rid of her misery, yet stubbornly clinging to life, she drags herself towards the only lover who can give her what she craves: Old Bazouge the undertaker.

114

By presenting this rather extended synopsis of the narrative of *L'Assommoir* I've given no more than a superficial glimpse – like taking a visitor through the interior of St Paul's in two minutes. Nothing short of reading the novel can give any idea of the profoundly affecting experience it provides; but if by this summary I've encouraged you to read or re-read *L'Assommoir*, then most of my purpose will have been accomplished.

I think you will find it interesting to attend a dissection of this masterpiece which is, above all, a true amalgam of inspired writing, superb craftsmanship, a range of literary devices and a uniquely compassionate view of mankind. Page by page the author captures and drives us into the crucible of a situation so hotly personal that we wonder at times why we don't or can't escape. This is no accident, it is art, for Zola commands the sequence of events, the strategic presentiments, the pervasive symbolism, the ironies and the sheer logic of it all into a single, unified force that is overwhelmingly compulsive. These elements are so effectively hidden, however, that only careful analysis will reveal them all.

The key to the compulsive quality of *L'Assommoir* is its structure. With the exception of *The Abbé Mouret's Sin*, all the *Rougon-Macquart* novels written before *L'Assommoir* are distended by the complexity of several themes and also by the great volume of documentary material Zola crammed into them. While this novel is no less detailed, its single theme has the classic simplicity of a parabola. The entire construction of the novel is based on this powerful and dominating curve which with miraculous economy carries the reader to its zenith and then remorselessly down again.

Our journey upwards is pleasant and carefree, for we are happy to see hardworking, thrifty Gervaise do well after her early setbacks. We are delighted that her marriage to Coupeau turns out better than we might have expected, and that Goujet thinks enough of her to lend her the money to buy a little laundry business. As the years pass we are comforted by the fact that Gervaise is making as much of her life, with its limited horizons, as she possibly can. Even Coupeau's accident, when he falls from the roof, is taken in their stride; in fact it brings husband and wife closer together, for the laundress's warm heart flows over in her efforts to make his convaslescence as pleasant as she can.

But, wait! Aren't we just a little concerned that Gervaise is pampering Coupeau a bit too much? And upset that Coupeau, knowing what ambitious plans she has for her savings, allows his wife to spend the lot on his welfare? If we are, then everything is going according to plan, for Gervaise's excessive indulgence is the first of several presentiments planted by Zola to infect us with a vague disquiet. This feeling crystallises as Coupeau, almost at his wife's insistence, becomes drink-prone and work-shy. The seeds of disaster are beginning to germinate in the warmth of Gervaise's easy-going indulgence. Appropriately enough, it is in the steamy heat of her laundry that these seeds sprout and then flourish, when, one afternoon, Coupeau, amiably drunk, calls in to see his wife.

The sun slanted through the doorway; the shop was a blaze of heat. Coupeau, the heat of the place getting more and more into his head, was seized with a sudden tenderness. He came towards Gervaise with open arms, very moved.

'You're a good wife,' he stuttered. 'I must give you a kiss.'

But he caught his feet in the petticoats which were in the way, and nearly fell.

'What a nuisance you are,' said Gervaise, without showing any annoyance. 'Be quiet, we have finished now.'

No; he must give her a kiss, he must, he loved her dearly. As he stammered out these phrases, he made his way round the heap of petticoats, stumbled against the heap of shirts, and then, still pushing his way on, his foot caught, and he fell flat on the heap of dusters. Gervaise, beginning to get angry, pushed him away, declaring he would get everything mixed up. But Clémence, and even Madame Putois, found fault with her. After all, it was nice of him to want to give her a kiss. She might as well have let him do it. . . .

Gervaise, recovering herself, was already sorry for her impatience. She helped Coupeau up again, and held out her cheek to him with a smile. But the tinsmith, without minding the people about, took hold of her breasts.

'I don't want to say it,' he murmured, 'but your linen is nifty, isn't it? But I love you all the same, you know.'

'Let me go, you are tickling me!' she cried, laughing more than ever. 'You silly thing! How can you be so silly?'

He had seized hold of her, and would not let her go. She gave way, overcome with a sort of dizziness that came to her from the pile of clothes, without minding the liquorish breath of Coupeau. And the great kiss that they exchanged, mouth to mouth, in the midst of the dirty things, was like a first step in the slow, downward course of their life.   (35)

In its context, this kiss is the most exquisitely subtle of premonitions, and the ten most unnecessary words in the novel are those in the final phrase: 'first step in the slow, downward course of their life'. We don't need to be told this, for we can sense that we have reached that heart-stopping, weightless moment which tells us we are at the top of our trajectory. From this point the path of the parabola is downwards.

At first, though, the descent is imperceptible. There is no panic, no dramatic turning-point, and we are still allowed to feel that Gervaise will find some handhold to save herself. But, no, we are bothered by an insinuating pessimism, for the author now seeds his prose with loaded words: fall, tumble, collapse, downfall, failure, ruin – all in their way prescient clues to the disaster which is to come.

Then the slide downwards accelerates. Gervaise begins to drink to ease her burden, the visits to the pawnshop become more frequent, and Coupeau switches from wine to raw spirit. At times, just when the couple might realise their danger and save themselves, some fresh misfortune intrudes. Every chapter, in fact, begins on a note of optimism, with the possibility that Gervaise might escape her fate, only to end with fresh despair. In the happy atmosphere of her birthday party, for instance, who should appear but Lantier, her former lover, like a ghost from the past. Gervaise's character is unequal to the pressures that now crowd in upon her. When she goes to bed with Lantier it is aginst her will, but the circumstances are so stacked against her she seems to have no alternative.

She does, of course. There is the promise of a good life with her steadfastly loyal admirer Goujet, who is ready to give her love and respectability. Or she could abandon Coupeau and Lantier, take the children, and make her own way in the world, for she lacks neither courage nor the capacity for hard work. But poor Gervaise is locked securely in a prison, the walls of which are her inherited character and her circumstantial environment – both, in Zola's view, insurmountable.

Gervaise's fall is as logical as the parabola on which it is based, and inevitably the path of her grim descent steepens. She abandons her ambitions and becomes sloppy. Her laundry business is taken over by the scheming Virginie, for whom she now slaves. The family breaks up and even Lantier leaves her. The hopelessness of her position is aggravated by Coupeau's drunkenness, and then madness; even his death offers no relief for by then Gervaise herself is a mindless sponge, a body cracked and senile before its time. Only at the very base of the great arc does she find peace, on a bed of mouldy straw in a neglected cupboard under some stairs, in circumstances which are as revolting as they are moving.

However harrowing, the laundress's sad end is nothing to the one Zola thankfully abandoned. According to his notes he had toyed with a grotesquely melodramatic finale in which Gervaise found Virginie in bed with Lantier, threw acid over them both, was dragged by the hair into the yard by her lover, now berserk with pain, and kicked to death in an ensuing brawl. But it must have become obvious to the author that it was not in Gervaise's temperament to be violently jealous; and in the end it is her own accommodating nature which brings about her downfall and death. Even in her most wretched moment, when as a prostitute she picks up her admirer Goujet in the street, she is still capable of self-sacrifice. It is the most moving of all Gervaise's relationships, and the scene in which the blacksmith offers to love and care for her is especially touching. Although she loves Goujet and knows that he alone can save her from further degradation, Gervaise also knows she is not the same woman he fell in love with years before. Afraid of dragging him down with her, the laundress's natural warmth and tenderness triumph, and she decides in favour of her own destruction.

In *L'Assommoir*, Zola displayed a mastery of construction and narrative organisation none of his contemporaries could touch, and that he himself would only equal or approach in a couple of subsequent novels. The same can be said of his characterisation, for, if the author's classic construction provides the skeleton to this masterpiece, his compassion supplies the flesh. Despite its gloomy horizon, the very ordinariness of its characters, settings and action, the chill of the novel's logic is warmed by its author's deep-felt sympathy for the working class predicament.

For the most part, Zola's feelings are conveyed through his heroine. Gervaise is the prototype happy-go-lucky soul, charitable, sensual, all heart; and so finely and indelibly is she drawn that we feel we know her with a greater understanding than we know many of our close friends. Had she been born into a comfortably off middle-class family she would have been a most popular woman, delighting her female friends and charming all the men, always happy,

117

always in demand. She would have married well and conscientiously pushed her husband to the top, to success and happiness. Instead, she is caught in the cruel grip of her slum environment; she never had a chance to realise her potential. Gervaise's story is simply the chronicle of millions of deprived people, and while its message rings out awesomely clear, Zola never once succumbs to the temptation to preach. Gervaise *is the novel*, and when we close its covers, notwithstanding our final view of her as a degraded, prematurely aged wreck, we remember her only with sympathy and affection.

Nothing could have been more calculated to arouse Zola's compassion for dispossessed humanity than those two years of poverty and misery in his youth. The scenes he witnessed – drunken wife-beatings, promiscuity, the desperation of the starved, the hopelessness of the breadwinner without work, the vicious squabbles, the battered children, sickness and brutality – were of the kind that would have sent a more fortunate visitor to those districts retreating in horror and righteous repugnance. But Zola had lived among these people, as one of them, and he soon saw that the source of their degradation was largely an accumulation of social and hereditary forces outside their control. The sympathy which grew out of those years, however, is not without a tinge of bitterness which on many occasions darkens his vision. In *L'Assommoir* the intensity of this bitterness is projected through Marescot, the landlord of a big tenement building, and one of the most malignant and detestable characters the novelist ever created. A former poor worker, Marescot uses his savings to become a landlord, and then proceeds unmercifully to screw his own kind, living a life of luxury while his tenants live in fear and misery. In Marescot, Zola is portraying the worst side of human nature.

L'Assommoir is, for most readers, a damning indictment of the evil caused by bad living and working conditions. What comes through with dramatic force is that life in the slums is far from picturesque; it is a drab and depressing incarceration from which the only escape is money – which the inhabitants can only dream about – alcohol and sex. And as they are more or less constantly sozzled few can do more than hope, by some miracle, to climb out of their sad environment. Although there was a strong streak of the reformer in Zola at the time, he resisted the urge to dogmatise; *L'Assommoir* is an exposé, not a sermon, and gains enormous strength from its impartiality. In his preliminary notes for the novel Zola had written, 'Do not flatter the working class nor malign it.' Typically, he rigidly followed his admonition. His poor, ignorant slum-dwellers are neither saints nor sinners. He takes no political sides and there is a total absence of working-class martyrs. In fact the most voluble spokesman for the socialist viewpoint is the layabout and soapbox pundit, Lantier. To even the balance the Royalists are represented by Poisson, an old civil servant bore. Not surprisingly, critics from both sides of the political fence were enraged that their sacrosanct beliefs were made to look faintly ridiculous by mere association with these worthless characters.

That a novel about working-class people should have whipped up such a storm seems odd to us now. But in mid-nineteenth-century France writers of every rank, with one or two exceptions, were preoccupied with the boudoir, the *salons*, and the financial ambitions and crimes of passion among the rich and middle class. Zola was the first novelist to recognise that world-shaking changes were taking place; commercial capitalism was usurping feudal paternalism; craftsmen and small traders were being made redundant by mass-production; vast factories were springing up everywhere, as were new industrial towns. Yet most of his fellow writers, especially those with talent, persisted in burying their heads in the stale and perfumed haunts of fashionable society. The vapid productions of his contemporaries made it look as though Zola was ahead of his time. He wasn't; he was simply in it. What is remarkable, though, is that a middle-class writer should have produced the world's first major novel based on the working class, and which reflected so accurately, and with such genuine sympathy, the underprivileged lives and thwarted aspirations of the proletariat. Yet when it was published Zola was set upon by right, left and centre; the conservatives said, well, didn't we tell you, the working class *are* dirty, illiterate, irresponsible scum, and quite unfit to vote; the Republicans were furious that such a bestial picture had been painted of the working man; the socialists, on the other hand, accused Zola of holding his hand, dodging the issue, of leaving unsaid what should have been written with gallons of revolutionary blood. Too few people, it seems, had the wit to deduce the cause from the effect – Zola must have wished, at times, that he had sermonised the obvious – and ironically the only faction to use the novel's reformist potential were not the campaigners for free education, better housing and fewer working hours, but the prohibitionists.

The moralists turned *L'Assommoir* into a homily against alcohol, and the book became a Bible to the temperance movement which, to advance its cause, thumped its covers unceasingly in Britain and America for two or three decades. With its fearsome symbolism and horrific accounts of alcoholism and its side effects, it is easy to understand how the novel came to be called the world's greatest temperance tract. In recent years, however, thoughtful analysts of the novel have pinpointed morality, not drink, as the true cause of Gervaise's downfall. To some extent this is true, but it is also an over-reaction to the mis-labelling of the novel as an exposé of the evils of cheap drink, for Coupeau's abuse of alcohol, and ultimately alcohol's abuse of Coupeau, are definite and important elements in Gervaise's tragedy. With raw brandy only a franc a litre, alcohol was just as available to poor working-class people as sex, and equally good as an opiate against hardship and despair. Zola was well aware of this and in fact promoted the novel in certain medical and religious quarters as a study of what happens when the more extreme forms of inherited instability are stimulated by excessive drinking. According to the Italian journalist de Amicis, the novelist told him that he'd intended writing a book about alcohol. He'd researched its effects, studied patients in the Sainte-Anne hospital and so forth, and defined his characters. But the plot had given him trouble; he had Lantier abandon Gervaise, who took up with Coupeau, who took up with drink; their sad ends had been plotted but somehow there was something missing in the middle. It was this void that led Zola to have Lantier return to make up the fateful *ménage à trois*. In the end, Zola said, the novel was 'simply a lesson in morality'.

This is, of course, the essence of *L'Assommoir*. It is not alcohol which ruins Gervaise, nor is it promiscuity; like the grog, sex in all its forms is freely available in the slums. The poor were no less randy than the rich, but if sex for the bourgeoisie was an expression of their greed, and for the aristocracy an extravagant distraction, sex for the working classes in Zola's novels was an escape from the cruel reality of their lives. No, what brings down Gervaise is an inherited weakness of character, the cracks in which only appeared under extreme stress to be prised open by factors beyond her control. The laundress was no easy mark; her easy-going nature did not extend to sleeping around. While Lantier's mistress she remained loyal; while married to Coupeau she was virtuous; and who could blame her when, insulted, humiliated and driven from her bedroom by her husband, she hesitantly submitted to the seductive manoeuvres of her former lover? Interestingly, despite Zola's neurotic belief that a former male lover has some physiological hold over his formerly beloved, Lantier's seduction of Gervaise follows a strictly logical progression from familiarity to circumstance and opportunity. Earlier, when Lantier shows up after several years' absence, the laundress is certainly disturbed: 'She always felt, at the name of Lantier, a burning sensation at the pit of the stomach, as if the man had left there, under the skin, something of himself.' This is the classic Zola Lover's Return Syndrome, but thereafter the author makes no further reference to it. When Gervaise finally sees Lantier, she feels 'a chill strike through her, mounting from her legs to her heart'; but this, surely, is not such an unusual emotion in the event of two ex-lovers meeting unexpectedly. Thankfully Zola did not intrude his neurotic obsession into the passage describing poor Gervaise's seduction by her former lover, for it stands as one of the most superbly conceived climaxes in the novel.

From beginning to end *L'Assommoir* is imbued with irony, symbolism and even humour, although for the most part the humour is grim – when, for example, the Lorilleux hang a blanket over their door when they cook rabbit stew to stop the smell reaching their starving neighbours – or bitter-sweet, as with Gervaise's wedding day. After the hurried, off-hand Nuptial Mass – a subtle thrust at the church on the way – the party visits the Louvre, their only escape in the entire novel to a world beyond their own, geographically only half a mile distant but horizons away in every other sense. The Louvre visit is deliberately designed as an ironic set-piece, but mostly the ironies are set like tiny jewels in Zola's prose, becoming more concentrated as Gervaise begins her fall. Vertical incongruities play an important role here. Coupeau could have hurt himself in many ways, but it is significant that he falls. With Gervaise there is a preoccupation with verticality: we have her climbing and descending stairs, looking up, looking down, raising her eyes, tilting her chin, feeling that buildings are about to topple on her. As she descends down the ladders of poverty and morality, she climbs physically. As Zola had discovered in his own days of poverty, the top floors of walk-up tenements were, for the really destitute, a franc a month ahead of damp basements and box-rooms under stairs. The rooms up there were cramped, miserably cold in winter and oppressive in summer. On one occasion Gervaise is in a stifling, fifth-floor room, and looks down to see an apparition of herself in the street below, as a young woman, looking up to examine the house for the first time, and the jump back in time makes her heart jump and awakens her momentarily to her sorry condition. There is also a cruel irony when she visits Coupeau in Sainte-Anne's hospital, the same hospital he helped to build, singing in the sun and shouting down to bystanders like a playful sparrow. But now he is locked in a padded cell in the basement, a madman. The most persistent irony, however, is Gervaise's intermittent relationship with Old Bazouge, the undertaker; with each fall she draws closer and closer to him, moving into the same slum building and finally into the room next to his, so that only the thinnest of partitions separate them. As with many of the characters and objects in *L'Assommoir*, the appearances of Bazouge are symbolic. It is not fortuitous that Gervaise's beat as a first-time prostitute begins by a slaughter-house, to the wailing whistles of nearby trains; nor the feeling in the reader that the buildings she lives in are more like prisons than homes: 'He led the way down a long corridor, turning twice, first to the left, then to the right. The corridor went on further still, going both ways, cramped, dilapidated and unplastered, lit at intervals by tiny gas-jets; and the doors, all of one pattern, like the doors of a prison...' And again: '...one felt the breath of starvation, the walls which resounded like empty stomachs, the doors through which ever came the sound of blows and the whining of starving children...' Even the weather is subtly used to reinforce or suggest a mood. In the courtyard of one of the tenements in which she lives is a gutter carrying the run-off from a dyer's shop; its reflections change colour according to the degree of apprehension Zola wishes to invoke.

But the pre-eminent symbol in *L'Assommoir* is the still in Colombe's Bar, which Zola invests with the properties of some terrible monster, with copper claws, giant jaws and intestinal coils through which pass the poison in which its victims eventually drown:

> Then, suddenly, she had an uncomfortable sensation of something behind her back. She turned, and saw the still, the drinking-machine, working away under the glass of the narrow court, with the quivering motion of its wizard's kitchen. At night the coppers looked duller, they had merely a sort of big red star where they were round; and the whole apparatus flung monstrous shadows on the wall at the back, figures with tails, great beasts opening their jaws as if to swallow up everything. (35)

The sleeping beast at first merely disturbs Gervaise, for it is introduced so casually as the 'distilling apparatus', the 'sozzling machine', that even we can hardly believe the terrifying powers ascribed to it. But the sleeping monster is soon aroused and the tone of Zola's descriptions of it become more violent and touched with hate and anger; it is, after all, the abomination which distils the venom responsible for misery on a vast scale, and the still eventually becomes

121

the author's personal symbol for an evil that, unchecked, will grow until it destroys all mankind.

Zola's absorption with the environmental effects upon his characters led him to introduce a new dimension into the craft of descriptive prose. Read any of his novels and you soon become aware that for their author the place is never separate from the plot; locations are never limp backdrops, quickly painted and then ignored. Again and again they intrude, and sometimes even monopolise the narrative. It is as if, in a stage play, the scenery and props were to come to life and join in with the actors. Zola's environment is always an integral and vital part of the narrative which accounts for much of the memorable, brighter-than-bright quality of his descriptive passages. In *L'Assommoir* the novelist took this welding of place and story an important stage further by infusing his prose with the *argot* of the environment. One of the great achievements of this novel is that it records for all time Zola's solution to the problem of blending the linguistic demands of narrative prose with the crude vocabulary, spoken and thought, of his characters. In this he departed from the tradition that the narrative style sets the tone for the characters' dialogue. In fact he turned it completely about; *L'Assommoir* is the first major novel in which the idiom and the inarticulation of the characters govern the style of the narrative. We take this for granted now, but in 1876 it was positively revolutionary. Not only are the characters convincingly idiomatic in their speech, but the descriptive passages also use a vocabulary Gervaise and her friends would be quite at home with. Of course the narrative abounds with slang – 'pins' for legs, 'saw-bones' for doctor, 'ticker' for watch and so on – and with idiomatic similes, but the significant effect of it all is that we tend not to be visitors to the pages of the novel, loftily watching all the goings-on from some remote vantage point, but intimate observers in the streets, the houses and the rooms in which Gervaise lives. With the exception of the visit to the Louvre we see all the action throughout the book as though through the eyes and *mind* of a working woman, an innovation which adds immeasurably to its superb parabolic unity.

While the intention was inspired, the fact that the overall effect is near-faultless is an accident of time. For all his research into contemporary slang, Zola was apparently wide of the mark in his appreciation of its subtleties. Henry James remembered one Sunday afternoon in the early 1870s at Zola's Paris home, where a group of disciples were passionately discussing their writing plans. Zola told him, 'As for me, I'm engaged on a book, the study of common morals, for which I'm making a collection of the swear-words in the language, those used commonly by the people in their everyday language.' The remark, according to James, was made in passing, just as though an interesting idea had occurred to the novelist, and the American was particularly impressed by the seriousness with which Zola treated the project. It was only some years after that James discovered that he had witnessed the genesis of a masterpiece. Zola had an extraordinary ear for speech patterns and idiosyncrasies that reflected a great range of emotions and human foibles, but he was never master of the working-class patois of the time. Now, a hundred years on, with the niceties blurred by time, the argument about the accuracy of the slang in *L'Assommoir* is academic, and need not concern us, especially as this point is further blurred by the limitations and skill of numerous translators – a discussion of which will be found in Chapter 22. If some of the passages read as though they were composed from Brewer's *Dictionary of Phrase and Fable* or from Eric Partridge's *Dictionary of Slang* by a Roumanian, it is hardly fair to blame Zola.

If Zola's deadpan portrait of the common working man provoked a storm among the politically conscious readers of the novel, so did the author's blunt use – or alleged misuse – of the language. Henry James's view was, as usual, two-sided, complaining of the 'ferociously bad smell which blows through *L'Assommoir* like an emanation from an open drain and makes the perusal of the history of Gervaise and Coupeau very much such an ordeal as a crossing of the Channel in a November gale'; but adding that '*L'Assommoir*, in spite of its fetid atmosphere, is full of magnificent passages and episodes, and the sustained power of the whole thing, the art of carrying a weight, is extraordinary.'

Another critic, after damning the novel as pornography, warned that its author was 'about to follow in the footsteps of the Marquis de Sade'. But the critics were mostly ignored by the public, who loved Gervaise; she became the heroine of a popular song, and her story was pantomimed at a Parisian circus. Nor was Zola without his defenders. An exasperated Huysmans wrote, 'Is it possible there are people who deny this man's priceless talent, his powerful personality, his breadth of understanding, his strength of purpose, unique in this age of weakness and langour?' Huysmans was then, of course, white hot in the cause of naturalism, from which he later defected. But the poet Mallarmé, whose admiration remained constant, wrote to Zola: 'You have endowed literature with something entirely new.'

L'Assommoir had sold well over 100,000 copies in France when it was introduced to English readers with Vizetelly's 1884 translation. It was thought prudent to add a preface by the Italian writer and journalist Edmondo de Amicis. 'After reading Zola's romances,' he wrote, 'it is like finding truth for the first time,' although, he warned, 'sometimes you spring back as if from a sudden whiff of bad air.' The disclaimer went on to suggest that delicate persons should withdraw, because 'Zola does not conceal or embellish anything... he is at once a judicious romancer, a surgeon, a casuist, a physiologist, and an expert chancellor of the exchequer, who thus raises every veil, putting his hands into everything, and calling a spade a spade. Morally he unveils in his characters those deepest feelings which are generally profound secrets, tremblingly whispered through the grating of a confessional. In language he scarcely refrains from those few unspeakable words which naughty boys stealthily seek for in the dictionary. No one has ever gone further in this extreme, and you really do not know whether you ought to admire his talent or his courage.' No wonder this translation sold 162,000 copies over the ensuing twenty-five years; no modern-day cover blurb could more calculating-ly rivet a reader to its contents.

From the reaction to the serialisation of the novel, Zola was ready with his defence by the time the book was published some months later. Commenting on the *brouhaha* in a preface to the first edition, he wrote, '*L'Assommoir* is without doubt the most chaste of all my books. I have often had to point out sores far more frightful. It is the style which has shocked. It is the words that have angered. My crime has been to write a novel using the language of the people.' Also included in the preface is Zola's somewhat chaste view of himself: 'If only it were realised that the blood-thirsty and ferocious novelist is merely a worthy citizen, a man of studious and artistic tastes, living quietly and soberly in his little corner, and whose only ambition is to leave to posterity as great and vital a work of which he is capable!' Zola need hardly have bothered, for epithets like 'pornographer' and 'filthy Frenchman' continued to be thrown at him for the rest of his life, and even afterwards. As for the 'great and vital work', the novelist's ambitions were more extravagantly realised than he can have imagined. *L'Assommoir* is one of the greatest masterpieces of literature, a work which heralded a new era in the craft of fiction, a work in which all the elements of the novelist's art are unified into one magnificent whole. Perhaps more than in any of his other novels it reveals the depth of his compassion for humanity and the breadth of his vision. In it Zola's social conscience was forged into a weapon he was to throw repeatedly into the heart of indifference and injustice. In Gervaise he created one of literature's most unforgettable heroines, richly human, weak and generous. There is a logical inevitability about her life which creates the powerful illusion of reality, an illusion which persists long after the reader has finished the book. Gervaise also pervades four of her creator's other novels, in the sense that her four children are the protagonists of *Nana* (Nana), *Germinal* (Etienne), *The Masterpiece* (Claude) and *The Beast in Man* (Jacques).

Yet only a third of the way through his daunting, self-imposed task of writing the *Rougon-Macquart* chronicle, Zola created an unsurpassed story of courage and despair, tenderness and brutality, humour and sadness which is never likely to go out of print. In it his characters find, at the end of the story, no happiness, no enlightenment, no fulfilment, no reason, no purpose. They are corks in the stream of life. But through this great novel flows a magnificent passion, the quivering vibration of tremendous, purposeless energy, the shockwaves of the primal force by which man expresses his presence on earth.

9

Nana,
The Naughty Novel

Paul Alexis records a story of Zola asking him one day about prostitutes: 'Tell me, Paul, how does one pay a street woman? Does one settle the bill before or after?' When Alexis laughed at the novelist's naivety, Zola confessed that he had never slept with a woman of the streets. Yet at that very moment he was shaping in his mind a character who was to be not only a harlot but a whore who would become the most beautiful, rich and powerful prostitute in Paris, a combination of diamond-hard acumen and destructive whimsy, a perfect mirror-image of the neurotic, hypocritical society which would fashion her. For all Zola's innocence the character he had in his mind would become a legend and perhaps the most famous *femme fatale* in literature. That this character should emerge so frighteningly convincing despite her creator's ignorance suggests a source far more obscure than the results of Zola's formidable powers of observation.

But there is much more to *Nana* the novel than Nana herself. Zola nursed a violent loathing for the middle classes, who to a very great extent held the future of France in their soft, work-shy hands. He was concerned. A warning had to be sounded: unless they changed their ways the working class would be avenged, and the country brought to its knees.

There was a more personal score to settle, too. The theatre, the only public arena in which the author had not yet triumphed over his defeats, provided ample fuel for his hatred of the upper middle classes from which its patrons were drawn. Zola, cringing in the wings at the opening performance of his farce *Le Bouton de rose* at the Palais-Royal in May 1878, had watched the proceedings with a sinking heart, and when the mindless shouting began in the second act, so loud the actors could not be heard, his private humiliation became public. Looking about him from the darkened wings he could be forgiven for despising the elegant dandies who, lemming-like, joined in the swelling chorus of abuse. And afterwards, the critics: Zola wasn't a mere meal on that occasion, he was a feast! But *Nana* was shaping in his mind, and it would provide the opportunity for revenge on these stupid, starch-shirted cuckolds. If some of the portraits in *Nana* are glazed with bitterness, the theatre was one obvious source.

At about this time, too, Zola was increasingly in the company of worldly-wise writers like Turgenev and Flaubert, not to mention sensualists like Maupassant; Zola records that their literary dinner conversations about love and sex made even the waiters' hair curl. True, the experiences and exploits that would make Zola's nose twitch were second-hand; but from *raconteurs* like Flaubert and Maupassant, the latter a master of the intricacies of sexual passion, the telling was probably more exciting and memorable than the real thing.

Whatever the prompting, Zola's writing underwent a sexual revolution during the years immediately before *Nana*, and he wrote about love more openly, with a deeper penetration, if you like, beginning with *A Love Episode*, published in 1878. In his new novel he proposed to explore more profoundly the neurotic potential of the genital urge, to be projected through the career of Nana, the precocious daughter of Gervaise Macquart. Nana, from the proletariat, would rise to the top of society as a fashionable courtesan, where she would revenge her class against the aristocracy by bringing them to financial ruin and suicide.

How *Nana* has maintained its *Fanny Hill* reputation over the years is something of a mystery, for while throughout its considerable length there are numerous erotic passages, they are hardly of the kind literary lecheratti would find the least titillating. The novel is in fact a quite seriously conceived moral lesson in that Zola set out to warn that the hypocrisy and rottenness of upper middle-class society left it vulnerable to destruction by the poorer classes, not by force or political power but by sexual exploitation. Nana would be his symbol of destruction, and at the same time an *instrument* of destruction, for as an individual she has all the usual human, excusable faults: she is greedy, vain, sly and not very bright. She uses people when she can, and in turn is exploited herself. Her most profitable and dangerous asset is her beauty, combined with a magnetic sex appeal. This is her weapon, and the weapon of her class.

Zola was wholly justified in including a story about prostitution in a cycle of novels documenting life under the Second Empire. Prostitution, at every level of French society, was a burgeoning profession, a fact of life. In the years of the Second Empire courtesans had reigned supreme; many were accepted as respectable without question; countless others were folk heroines. To the veteran Paul Saint-Victor they were directly responsible for the loss of the Franco-Prussian War: 'Who can measure how much energy was consumed, strength wasted and spirit enfeebled by the laxity of morals?' he asked. Zola was in agreement with the view that prostitution and sexual excess had played a key role in the collapse of the Empire. The rich and idle ruling classes had fiddled in boudoirs while Paris burned. The courtesans had returned in force to Paris after the war, now to infect the Third Republic. 'Tarts to suit every pocket,' one writer quipped. Nothing had changed. Being weak, being so morally corruptible, so vulnerable to this army of fresh recruits, the upper middle classes were in their turn the greatest threat to France. *Nana*, although set during the Second Empire, would be a timely warning to the young Third Republic.

At the time of *Nana's* publication, prostitution in England was a largely underground occupation; the Contagious Diseases Prevention Acts which had helped regulate the trade were suspended in 1883 and repealed in 1886; and the word 'prostitute' had been bowdlerised from most books since 1860. In America, too, although bawdy and sporting houses flourished wherever there were congregations of men, such as mining and construction camps, most city populations kept well clear of areas where there was the possibility of meeting a prostitute. Thus Nana, who represented, during her life, every sordid aspect of harlotry, had for English readers a mystique about her that was vastly different from her appeal in France, where, until brothels were abolished in 1946, the fame of certain notorious procurers and whores was sufficient to override considerations of respectability.

For a section of society so prominent on the boulevards, prostitutes had been largely ignored in literature. With the exception of Henri Murger's bohemian stories, most books with harlot heroines were dreary affairs and published anonymously, while Huysmans's *Marthe, the Story of a Whore*, and Goncourt's *Elisa the Whore*, both of which appeared just before *Nana*, had poor sales. The theme of the prostitute-avenger was not new – Defoe's *Moll Flanders* for example – but it had not been reworked for some time. Zola revived the theme to exploit it with devastating effect, although many have questioned the justification for the explicit eroticism which he unleashed in the novel.

Whatever eroticism is present in the novel owes its existence to Zola's vivid imagination, for his first-hand knowledge of the *demi-monde* was just about limited to a single lunch he'd arranged with an actress from the *Variétés*. Nevertheless, he begged information where he could. Paul Alexis supplied him with some background about a lesbian establishment, and another acquaintance took him to the theatre to point out some of the city's more notable courtesans, where the novelist's eager eyes raped them of anything that might have contributed to their notoriety. Zola's personal research was restricted to observing street prostitutes from a safe distance, and smartly disappearing when they approached him. For Nana's apartment he was able to inspect the luxurious home of Madame Valtesse de la Bigne, where he saw the bed which was to become Nana's throne, a bulging, sumptuous creation encrusted with gilt cupids and erotic bas-reliefs. At the *Variétés*, Zola struck up a friendship with Offenbach's librettist, who took him backstage for a view of the famed Hortense Schneider's dressing-room – the same dishevelled room in which ten years before she had entertained the Prince of Wales. Zola's nose twitched uncontrollably in the presence of so many voluptuous memories. The briefest visit to the stage doors of several other theatres provided him with any number of models for his male characters, who, by his own account, disgusted him: 'They cling to the skirts of these women... debauched old men, fated to breathe their last in a strange bed... young fools ruining themselves to be fashionable or from senseless infatuation...'

The final chapter gave the novelist a lot of trouble, not the least being his unsuccessful efforts to find out what a smallpox victim's corpse looked like. In three letters written from Médan Zola entreats a friend in Paris to sketch the death-mask of someone who had died of the disease he intended to inflict on Nana. 'Make sure you include details of the state of the eyes, the nose and the mouth', he wrote, 'to give me a precise geographical chart.' Apparently his friend had no luck at the various morgues so Zola went ahead and invented it all as best he could.

When his invention flagged, he adapted. The celebrated scene where the humiliated Count Muffat is made to act like a dog by his mistress was borrowed from an old English stage play, Thomas Otway's *Venice Preserved*, which the novelist had read about. Finally, his documentary sources exhausted, he sat down in his painstaking way and took three whole days to allot names to his sixty or so characters.

For a writer who proclaimed the naturalist ideal of detached reportage and scientific observation, Zola's methods of gathering material for *Nana* were little short of farcical. Not by a long chalk can the observations for *Nana* be considered objective; as we have seen, most of the documentation was second- or even third-hand. Zola's method boiled down to having a quick peep and then bolting to the security of his study to let his imagination fill in the gaps. Whether *Nana* would have been much changed had Zola spent a few francs on prostitutes provides an amusing area for speculation; it is almost certain that Zola would have changed. That he failed to practise what he preached is, in the context of his creative achievement, hardly important; that in the absence of experience his awesome intuition and imagination were almost alone responsible for so many hauntingly authentic sequences in his novels is cause for wonder.

Zola's heroine, who in 1869 was just a tic in the novelist's eye, was to be called Louise Duval, whose life would be ruined by her greed for luxury and sensual pleasure. By 1875 the character had acquired a good deal more flesh, and Nana's course among the beds and boudoirs of the Second Empire must have been roughly charted during the writing of *L'Assommoir*, in which he devotes the best part of a chapter to describe her development as a virgin of fifteen.

> Nana was a great coquette. She did not always wash her feet, but she wore such tight boots that she suffered a perfect martyrdom; and if anyone questioned her, seeing her face grow purple, she answered that she had a stomach-ache, so as not to confess her coquetry. When there was no bread in the house, she found it difficult to trick herself out. But she achieved miracles, carried off ribbons from the work-room, worked up wonderful toilettes, dirty dresses covered with bows and rosettes. It was in summer that she had her triumphs. With a six-franc cotton dress she went out every Sunday, filling the whole quarter of the Goutte-d'Or with her blonde beauty. She was known from the outer boulevards to the fortifications, and from the Chaussée de Clignancourt to the Grande Rue de la Chapelle. They called her 'the chicken', for she had in truth the soft flesh and country freshness of a chicken. (35)

In some detail Zola establishes Nana's startling precocity: we note the eager ear she lends to the amorous experiences of her workmates; the effect of the

128

senseless cruelties inflicted upon her by her father, Coupeau; the countless occasions on which she witnesses drunken scenes and parental brawls. And then there are her disappearances, sometimes for months at a time, when she returns 'so dirty you wouldn't touch her with tongs', scratched, bruised – the reader can only imagine what tricks she's been up to:

> And Gervaise, too, was angry with Nana for her way of sleeping on till noon after one of her escapades, her nightdress all open, her hair undone and still full of hair-pins, so white, and breathing so short, that she seemed dead. She shook her five or six times of a morning, threatening to empty a pail of water over her. The lovely, lazy girl, half naked, buxom with sex, exasperated her, as she lay there sleeping off the lusts that seemed to fill out her flesh, unable even to waken herself. Nana opened one eye, closed it again, and stretched herself out more comfortably than ever. (35)

Zola seems to have concentrated on two models for his composite Nana: Blanche d'Antigny, one of the most powerful courtesans in Paris, and Eliza Crouch, an English actress better known as Cora Pearl. He solemnly inspected both these great ladies from a respectable distance.

Further inspiration came from Edmond de Goncourt who, at the time, frequently dined at the home of a notorious lady called La Païva. Born in Russia of German parents, her real name was Theresa Lachmann. When very young she had married a French tailor in Moscow, then eloped with a pianist to Paris, where for a time she lived as a courtesan. In less than a decade she ruined several French nobles and brought near-ruin to an English duke, capping this performance by marrying, ruining and causing the suicide of a Portuguese diplomat. Despite this frightening reputation she still managed to charm and marry Count Henckel von Donnersmarck, a member of the Bismarck family, with whom she settled down in the luxury to which she had become accustomed. If she had read *Nana* before her death in 1884, La Païva would doubtless have been struck by some curious parallels between her life and Nana's.

All Zola's observations and imaginings finally resulted in a kind of literary identikit, as his notes for the novel reveal: *At seventeen she is big, and looks twenty. Blonde, pink, wide-awake Parisian face, nose slightly retroussé, small mouth, dimpled chin, bright blue eyes with golden lashes. The few light freckles on her forehead look like sprinkled flecks of gold. Tangle of fine hair on the nape of her neck. Light down on her cheeks. Smells very much a woman.*

After describing Nana's precocious life of ups and downs after running away from Gervaise and Coupeau – she lives for a time with an old man, wins a small part in an operetta, lives largely by prostitution – Zola establishes her personality: *Good-natured, easy-going, sympathetic towards unfortunates. Scatter-brained, lives for today. Always happy and laughing. Is superstitious, afraid of God. Is fond of animals and her parents (although they are dead). By nature coarse and slovenly but learns quickly how to be fashionable.*

Finally Zola outlines the part Nana will play in his story:
Without realising it, without meaning to, she comes to regard men as fools to exploit. With her sex and odour she becomes a destructive force, destroying everything she

touches, souring society as menstruating women will turn milk sour. She symbolises the cunt, the power of the cunt, the cunt on the altar, with all the men offering sacrifices to it. Her extravagance will consume every kind of wealth; the waste will be terrible, and only ashes will remain. She is not to be witty, but merely flesh, beautiful flesh.

In his notes, Zola underlined *une bonne fille* – 'good-natured'. It was important that as an instrument of destruction Nana was to be a playful puppy romping in a luxuriant, over-pampered garden, unaware of the damage she is doing.

There is certainly something pathetically child-like about Nana. She is ruinously extravagant, selfish and thoughtless, although never mercenary. She grinds and humiliates men for money and power, yet is capable of throwing it all away on a mere whim. Although she rampages her deadly way through high society like a scourge, Nana is completely insensitive to social conventions. Her screwing knows no class divisions. She screws to maintain her luxurious way of life, as with Count Muffat; she screws out of necessity, for ready cash and pocket-money, with clients hastily procured off the streets; and she screws for sheer indulgence, as with Georges, a penniless, admiring youth who has nothing to offer her except devotion.

Nana's reputation preceded her arrival in Paris. In what amounted to an auction among editors, Jules Lafitte of *Le Voltaire* bought the serial rights to the novel when the manuscript was only half-finished, and commenced publication on 16 October 1879. Parisians were then subjected to a punishing promotional blitz: newspaper advertisements and puffs, posters, outdoor signs, sandwich boards and even street songs. One of Zola's colleagues, Henri Céard, complained that Nana was becoming an obsession, 'a nightmare'. The unrelenting publicity created an uproar, although little of this was Zola's doing. The uproar intensified as the first instalments appeared. As with *L'Assommoir*, public protest soon began to build up a full head of steam and the novelist, facing the threat of having the serial stopped, reluctantly agreed to some modest editing.

When *Nana* appeared in book form on 15 February 1880, a staggering 55,000 copies were sold in a few days. The sales were unprecedented, and so was public reaction. Music hall comedians joked about her; singers composed songs about her; artists – including Manet – painted her; roués toasted her; Paris went wild over *Nana*. Even its author was moved to pay a curious tribute to her; he had 'Nana' lettered on the stern of the little skiff he kept moored on the Seine at Médan. It became almost impossible to live through a day without hearing some reference to the splendid harlot. For weeks she was a favourite topic for discussion among the *salon* crowd; *Nana* was required reading and it was socially essential to know something, at least, of her story.

The novel opens just before curtain-time at the Variety Theatre in Paris, in an atmosphere of intense curiosity: an unknown actress called Nana has been billed to appear in a new operetta.

The lobby is packed, but it gives us an opportunity to meet the main characters – the cynical journalist Fauchery; Nana's fiercely jealous co-star,

Rose Mignon, her husband, and the ugly banker Steiner, who is her lover; Nana's current lover is also in the crowd – Daguenet, who has already demolished most of his fortune pursuing her; and two aristocrats: the racehorse-owner Count Vandeuvres, and Count Muffat de Beuville, a chamberlain at the Imperial Court. The conversation is bitchy; all predict the theatre's new attraction will be an embarrassing failure, for it is rumoured that Nana can neither sing nor act. Bordenave, the theatre's opportunist but perceptive manager is, however, confident:

'A failure! Nana a flop!' shouted the manager, whose face became purple. 'Has a woman any need to know how to act and sing? You're just too silly, my boy, Nana has something else, be sure of that! And it's something which takes the place of everything. I smelt it and it's pretty strong in her or my nose is no better than an idiot's. You'll see, you'll see: she has only to appear and the whole house will hang out its tongue.' (49)

The operetta, *The Blonde Venus*, begins and grinds through scene after idiotic scene until Nana appears as Venus, insolently self-assured despite her tinny voice and child-like clumsiness, disarming the critical audience with her self-mocking laugh. But this is only the beginning. In the next act:

A shiver went round the house. Nana was naked, flaunting her nakedness with a cool audacity, sure of the sovereign power of her flesh. She was wearing nothing but a veil of gauze; and her round shoulders, her Amazon breasts, the rosy points of which stood up as stiff and straight as spears, her broad hips, which swayed to and fro voluptuously, her thighs – the thighs of a buxom blonde – her whole body, in fact, could be divined, indeed clearly discerned, in all its foamlike whiteness, beneath the filmy fabric. This was Venus rising from the waves, with no veil save her tresses. And when Nana raised her arms, the golden hairs in her arm-pits could be seen in the glare of the footlights. There was no applause. Nobody laughed any more. The men's faces were tense and serious, their nostrils narrowed, their mouths prickly and parched. A wind seemed to have passed over the audience, a soft wind laden with hidden menace. All of a sudden, in the good-natured child the woman stood revealed, a disturbing woman with all the impulsive madness of her sex, opening the gates of the unknown world of desire. Nana was still smiling, but with the deadly smile of a man-eater. (51)

A little later, Zola builds the audience response up to a pitch of almost tactile intensity:

A murmur arose, swelling like a growing sigh. There was some hand-clapping and every pair of opera-glasses was fixed on Venus. Little by little Nana had taken possession of the audience, and now every man was under her spell. A wave of lust was flowing from her as from a bitch on heat, and it had spread further and further until it filled the whole house. Now her slightest movements fanned the flame of desire, and with a twitch of her little finger she could stir men's flesh. Backs arched and quivered as if unseen violin-bows had been drawn across their muscles; and on the nape of many a neck the down stirred in the hot, stray breath from some woman's lips. In front of him Fauchery saw the truant schoolboy half lifted out of his seat by passion. Curiosity led him to look at the Comte de Vandeuvres, who was very pale, with his lips pursed; at fat Steiner, whose face was apoplectic; at Labordette, ogling away with the astonished air of a horse-dealer admiring a perfectly proportioned mare; and at Daguenet, whose ears were blood-red and twitching with pleasure. Then a sudden instinct made him glance behind him, and he was astounded at what he saw in the Muffats' box. Behind the Countess, who looked pale and serious, the Count was sitting bolt upright, his mouth agape and his face mottled with red, while beside him, in the shadows, the misty eyes of the Marquis de Chouard had become

131

cat-like, phosphorescent, speckled with gold. The audience were suffocating, their very hair growing heavy on their perspiring heads. In the three hours they had been there, their breath had filled the atmosphere with a hot human scent. In the flickering glare of the gaslight, the cloud of dust in the air had grown denser as it hung motionless beneath the chandelier. The whole house seemed to be swaying, seized by a fit of giddiness in its fatigue and excitement, and possessed by those drowsy midnight urges which fumble between the sheets. And Nana, in front of this fascinated audience, these fifteen hundred human beings crowded together and overwhelmed by the nervous exhaustion which comes towards the end of a performance, remained victorious by virtue of her marble flesh, and that sex of hers which was powerful enough to destroy this whole assembly and remain unaffected in return.   (51)

Nana's dizzy flight to the top has begun, but she is still surrounded by echoes of her past life. The next day, for example, all her regular clients, sent to her by the procuress Madame Tricon, have to be accommodated in different rooms because of the adulatory crush. Three callers in particular have come to pay their respects, leagues apart in age and rank although with intentions in triplicate. One is Georges Hugon, a precocious, handsome boy who has spent all his pocket-money on a huge bouquet for the actress; the second is the banker Steiner, with whom Nana toys with the idea of taking him from her rival Rose Mignon; while the third, an older man of patrician appearance, is Count Muffat, on a spurious mission to collect for charity. Muffat is a top-drawer aristocrat, and is infatuated with Nana although, fearful of being compromised, refuses an invitation to her supper party the next night.

There have been many famous fictional parties but Nana's is one of my favourites, a brilliantly described midnight-to-dawn orgy in all its phases: the occasional chilling lulls which panic the hostess, the rowdy gate-crashers, the arguments that get out of hand, the dismal somnolence that invariably sets in before dawn. The party is a clever literary device which allows us to be flies on the wall, to watch as the guests slander, intrigue and flirt, and to observe the manners and morals of the time – the triangle, for instance, not uncommon then, of Mignon, a willing cuckold to his wife and Steiner's chequebook.

Muffat eventually succumbs to his lust for Nana. During the thirty-fourth performance of *The Blonde Venus*, he and the Prince of Wales, resplendent in his admiral's uniform, visit the actress in her dressing-room – remember Zola, sniffing about in Hortense Schneider's old room for any amatory odours left by the Prince's visit there, years before? He captured some, apparently, and they are reproduced in the novel, as Muffat sweats in a rapture of expectation:

> The same dizzy feeling he had experienced on the occasion of his visit to Nana, in the Boulevard Haussmann, again seized hold of him. He seemed to sink deeper into the thick carpet beneath his feet; the gas-jets burning on either side of the dressing-table and the cheval-glass were like the hissing flames of a furnace surrounding his temples. One minute, fearful of fainting away under the influence of all that feminine odour, full of warmth, and rendered ten times more pronounced by the lowness of the ceiling, which he encountered for the second time, he seated himself on the edge of the well-padded sofa that occupied the space between the two windows. But he rose up again almost immediately, and returned to the dressing-table, no longer to examine anything, but with a vague expression in his eyes, and thinking of a bouquet of tuberoses which had been allowed to fade in his

room a long time ago, their powerful smell having nearly killed him. When tuberoses decay they emit a kind of human odour. (46)

While the Prince is ogling the actresses and eyeing Nana's generously exposed breasts and thighs, Muffat is at the mercy of some exquisite inhibitions. In a single paragraph of striking economy we learn why Muffat has become a fountain of perspiration.

His thoughts had returned willy-nilly to his younger days. His bedroom as a child had been very cold. Later on, at the age of sixteen, after kissing his mother good night every evening, he used to take the icy sensation of that kiss with him into his sleep. One day, passing a half-open door, he had caught sight of a maidservant washing herself; and that was the only memory which had ever disturbed him from puberty until the day he married. After that, he had found his wife punctilious in carrying out her conjugal duties, but had himself felt a pious repugnance for them. He had grown up, and was now growing old, in ignorance of the flesh and in conformity to rigid devotional practices, having always ordered his life according to laws and precepts. And now, all of a sudden, he was thrown into this actress's dressing-room, into the presence of this naked courtesan. He, who had never seen the Comtesse Muffat putting on her garters, was witnessing the intimate details of a woman's toilet, in a chaotic disarray of jars, in the midst of that powerful perfume which he found so sweet. His whole being was in revolt: the way in which Nana had slowly been taking possession of him for some time past terrified him, reminding him of the pious stories of diabolic possession which he had read as a child. He believed in the devil; and, in a confused sort of way, Nana was the devil, with her laughter, her breasts and her rump, which seemed swollen with vice. But he promised himself that he would be strong. He would know how to defend himself. (51)

Later on in the performance Muffat watches the naked Nana through a backstage peep-hole; in his impotence he has become the voyeur, a role he will often play in his desperate struggle to possess her. He climbs again to the dressing-room, his senses assailed by the sights and smells of the theatre.

Despite the sensual assaults on his inhibitions, many months pass before Count Muffat is driven into Nana's bed by his mounting passion. During the summer he and the Countess spend a week at Les Fondettes, the country house of Madame Hugon, mother of Nana's cherubic admirer, Georges. Coincidentally, Steiner the banker has bought Nana a country house nearby, and inevitably she and Muffat meet. Nana, obviously, has not been idle. She has Steiner in her clutches, although, using one pretext or another, she adroitly avoids his. She also has a secret, idyllic affair with young Georges, making love in the surrounding forests and orchards, for the countryside is a refreshing novelty to her. But of all the dogs sniffing around her tail – including Daguenet, her former lover, waiting for the chance to return to the nest, and the Marquis de Chouard, a skinny, rheumy-eyed but active old roué, optimistically measuring the competition – it is Muffat who is finally tormented into action.

Lust, whipped up by Nana's skilful tactics, was at last wreaking terrible havoc in that sanguine, virginal nature. The grave-faced chamberlain, accustomed to crossing the state apartments of the Tuileries with dignified step, now bit on his bolster every night, sobbing with exasperation as he conjured up the same sensual vision. (51)

133

Several slow-paced months as Muffat's mistress are enough to induce boredom and impatience in the fickle courtesan. She has an affair with Fontan, an actor, and speedily strips Steiner of his last few thousand francs. Then from Fauchery, the journalist, she learns that Muffat is in turn being deceived by the Countess, and her maternal concern for her lover knows no bounds – for an hour or two. When she mischievously breaks the news to him the poor Count falls into a passion of rage and despair, and when he returns to Nana after spying on his wife, only to find the Marquis de Chouard in her bed, he is reduced to the depths of desolation.

With Muffat dismissed, Nana devotes all her time to Fontan – for she is really in love with him – but his meagre wages as an actor won't support her escalating debts nor keep her baby son, Louis. Once more she is forced to place her name in Madame Tricorn's catalogue of young ladies, and she even hunts men in the streets for the ready cash of short-time tricks. But this doesn't concern her unduly; what does is the fact that her life with Fontan is becoming one long round of arguments and beatings. More and more she seeks the comfort of Satin, her one-time companion of the gutter. Satin is a bisexual, and takes Nana on nocturnal bargaining forays into the most notorious and squalid sections of the poor districts.

Despite the beatings from Fontan Nana holds on to her lover until he throws her out, humiliated into the bargain by seeing another woman in her own bed. This has a touch of poetic justice, considering it was precisely the taunt Nana had delivered to Count Muffat, months before. Nana turns in despair to Satin until, one night, when they are in bed together, their cheap lodgings are raided by the 'vice squad'. Nana escapes, but the experience is enough to send her scurrying back to the dull life of a good mistress. But Muffat, in the meantime, has been collared by Mignon for his wife Rose, as Steiner's bank account is now exhausted. And worse – Rose has the leading role in a new play at the Variety Theatre. Nana is nevertheless confident: Muffat still lusts after her, and in no time she has her revenge on Rose, plus her role in the play – now financed by Muffat – besides a house of her own on the elegant Avenue de Villiers. And, of course, Count Muffat.

Shifting her course slightly, Nana becomes a woman of fashion, a lady of leisure, and her beauty is the toast of Paris. Her photograph is displayed everywhere. She enchants the entire city. Her house becomes an attraction; packed with costly furnishings and with eight coach-horses in the stables it requires a budget of 300,000 francs a year for its upkeep. In return for another 12,000 francs a month Muffat has the privilege of visiting Nana during certain restricted hours. Although she has sworn utter fidelity to the Count as her part of the bargain, Nana's libidinous body soon begins to itch for more sexual action – and money. The boy Georges Hugon provides the former, and Vandeuvres, fast heading for ruin, the latter. Nana controls this merry-go-round of love, which includes Satin and other sundry lovers, by the clock.

Eventually Muffat discovers that he is sharing Nana's perfidious thighs with others, but he is a captive of his own lust, as the following impressive passage reveals. One can feel sympathy for Muffat's predicament as he contemplates the woman he can never possess, gloating over her own body in a performance infinitely more sensual than any Sin City striptease.

Nana had grown absorbed in her ecstatic self-contemplation. She was bending her neck and was looking attentively in the mirror at a little brown mark above her right haunch. She was touching it with the tip of her finger, and by dint of bending backward was making it stand out more clearly than ever. Situated where it was, it doubtless struck her as both quaint and pretty. After that she studied other parts of her body with an amused expression, and much of the vicious curiosity of a child. The sight of herself always astonished her, and she would look as surprised and ecstatic as a young girl who has discovered her puberty. Slowly, she spread out her arms to set off her figure, to bring out her plump Venus torso. She bent herself this way and that, and examined herself before and behind, stopping to look at the side-view of her bosom and at the sweeping contours of her thighs....

Muffat sat looking at her. She frightened him. The newspaper had dropped from his hand. For a moment he saw her as she was, and he despised himself. Yes, it was just that; she had corrupted his life, he already felt himself tainted to his very marrow by impurities hitherto undreamt of....

And, unable to take his eyes from the sight, he sat looking fixedly at her, striving to inspire himself with loathing for her nakedness.

Nana no longer moved. With an arm behind her neck, one hand clasped in the other, and her elbows far apart, she was throwing back her head, so that he could see a fore-shortened reflection of her half-closed eyes, her parted lips, her face clothed with amorous laughter. Her masses of yellow hair were unknotted behind, and they covered her back with the fell of a lioness.

Bending back thus so that her flanks stood out, she displayed her solid Amazonian waist and firm bosom, where strong muscles moved under the satin texture of the skin. A delicate line, to which the shoulder and the thigh added their slight undulations, ran from one of her elbows to her foot, and Muffat's eyes followed this tender profile, and marked how the outlines of the fair flesh vanished in golden gleams, and how its rounded contours shone like silk in the candle-light. He thought of his old dread of Woman, of the Beast of the Scriptures, at once lewd and wild. Nana was all covered with fine hair, a russet down made her body velvety; whilst the Beast was apparent in the almost equine development of her flanks, in the fleshy exuberances and deep hollows of her body, which lent her sex the mystery and suggestiveness lurking in their shadows....

But Nana was absorbed in herself. A little thrill of tenderness seemed to have traversed her members. Her eyes were moist; she tried, as it were, to make herself small, as though she could feel herself better thus. Then she unclasped her hands and slid them down her body as far as her breasts, and these she crushed in a passionate grasp. After which she threw her head and bosom back, and melting, as it were, in one great bodily caress, she rubbed her cheeks coaxingly first against one shoulder then against the other. Her lustful mouth breathed desire over her limbs. She put out her lips, kissed herself long and long in the neighbourhood of her armpit, and laughed at the other Nana who, also, was kissing herself in the mirror.

Then Muffat gave a long sigh. This solitary indulgence exasperated him. Suddenly all his resolutions were swept away as though by a mighty wind. In a fit of brutal passion he caught Nana to his breast and threw her down on the carpet.

'Leave me alone!' she cried. 'You're hurting me!'

He was conscious of his undoing; he recognised in her stupidity, vileness, and falsehood, and he longed to possess her, poisoned though she was.

'Oh, how stupid!' said she savagely, when he let her get up. (47)

Nana now affects a tremendous style, and perhaps her supreme public moment comes during the Grand Prix of Paris, enthroned in her silver-ornamented landeau and dressed in the colours of the Vandeuvres stable. The infatuated Vandeuvres has a filly in the race named Nana, and in a remarkable passage Zola has the courtesan responding to the crowd's chanting of her name as the horse flies to the finishing post.

But now the poisonous touch of this corrupting Venus begins to infect the men around her. In a holocaust of unsurpassed extravagance she swallows up whole fortunes, several inheritances, a dozen country estates, farms and properties until, one after the other, her lovers are reduced to destitution, misery and even suicide. Yet at the end of the tragic trail, Nana, as splendidly healthy, as radiantly beautiful and as good-natured as ever, alone triumphs over the carnage. When she sets off on a journey to the East – a whim on her part – she looks as fresh and as wholesome as a virgin.

Zola wrote the final chapter of *Nana* in a white heat of creation that disturbed him sufficiently to make him physically ill for several days. It is an unforgettable chapter with a nail-biting narrative that doesn't let the reader relax until the last words. But that makes it sound like a police-chase finish, which it isn't; the novel concludes symbolically but with terrifying logic, and with multi-faceted observations and ironies on the way.

The final scene is set in the sumptuous Grand Hotel, where Nana has been taken after contracting smallpox from her child, Louis, her last action being one of motherly affection when she visited the sick child immediately on her return from her journey. Hearing of her illness, men friends and ex-lovers begin to gather in the lobby downstairs, none of them showing any desire to go up to her room to see her or to join Nana's few women friends at her bedside. Instead, the men linger on, and talk in desultory fashion about various topics including the impending Franco-Prussian War. We, the readers, are with the men, cowardly and safe from infection. It is not until the last few masterly paragraphs that we are allowed to see the harlot, a horrible apparition covered with stinking black pustules. If Zola had created the most famous *femme fatale* in the history of literature, the beautiful, deadly golden fly, then he left nothing to chance in the manner of her destruction. Nana's death takes place in such revolting circumstances – so repellant that her friends and lovers flee in terror from her lifeless body – that I believe it was an act of expiation on the author's part. He had created a symbol which had come to life, wreaked havoc in the 'experimental laboratory' of his fiction and which had escaped to enchant and seduce the world. This voluptuous, carnal fantasy had certainly seduced its creator, or at least the moralist in him, but if a moral warning was what Zola had in mind then it comes through with terrifying effectiveness. Afflicting Nana with a venereal disease might have underlined the moral with greater precision, but the author was more subtle than that, and in any case 'poetic justice' was ruled out by his naturalist beliefs. Nana's fatal disease was entirely accidental, and thus credible. But the extent of her disfigurement in death was of vital importance to him, for it appeased his own fear of the horrifying potential of his creation, and of the unbridled carnality she represented.

Like *L'Assommoir*, the construction of *Nana* is based on a simple parabola but with two significant differences. The zenith of Nana's trajectory through life occurs just before her death; her fall is so sudden she is hardly aware of it

1. NANA, from the painting by Manet. The model was the actress Henriette Hauser.

2. NANA has inspired many illustrators over the years. This engraving of Nana and Count Muffat is one of the earliest graphic interpretations of Zola's harlot heroine.

3. NANA, celebrated in song: sheet music decorated with a drawing of Nana at the Grand Prix of Paris. 1881.

4. CARICATURISTS were fond of Nana, too. A typical cartoon comment by Forain, c1880.

15. THE AUTHOR at the huge table which served as his work-desk, from a wood engraving made in 1893.

16. ZOLA'S country house at Médan, enlarged ten times its original size during the novelist's prosperous years. The tower was built with the profits from *Nana*.

17. THE DINING ROOM at Médan, showing the decorations and furnishings which became notorious for their vulgarity.

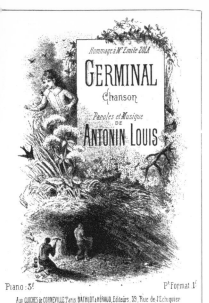

8. GERMINAL. Sheet music with
lithographed pictorial cover, obviously trading on the popularity of
the novel. 1888.

19. THE PUBLICATION of *Earth* was
greeted by the cartoonists with an
outburst of graphic ribaldry. In this
1887 *Journal le Clou* cartoon Zola is
shown imitating a favourite feat of
his windbag character, Jesus-
Christ.

0. LE REVE took the public by
surprise. A Berlin cartoon of 1888
depicts the bête noir of literature as
a humble, virtuous toiler.

21. FOR his documentation of *The
Beast in Man*, the naturalist writer
rode the footplate of a locomotive
from Paris to Mantes in search of
authenticity.

22. A RATHER forbidding study of the novelist at work at Médan. From *Revue illustrée*, 1887.

23. A MANUSCRIPT page from *Doctor Pascal*, 1893, displaying a sureness of approach lacking in his early manuscripts.

24. CARICATURE of Zola by Valotton, 1893. The novelist was mercilessly lampooned throughout his working life.

25. PORTRAIT of Zola by the famous French photographer, Nadar, made in 1898.

And while Gervaise's ascent is sure and secure, Nana's is a kind of nervous suspension, like a misfired artillery shell that is likely to drop out of the sky at any moment. As with its predecessor, *Nana* gains immensely from the simple line narrative which moves to the curve of the Second Empire's fortunes, so that they disintegrate and fall together.

Although the essence of Nana's life is to be found in one or another of her various bedrooms, there is never a sense of claustrophobia in the novel. Throngs of people are always coming and going, bringing with them the sights and sounds and smells of Paris from all levels of society. On several occasions we are taken to the countryside and, on one occasion, to the races. Here, Zola's brilliance at painting crowds is seen at its best; his description of the Grand Prix displays the same carefully positioned groups and incidents as, for example, does W.P. Frith's famous painting, *Derby Day* (1854), but with the enlarging dimension of the reader's own imagination, and with what amounts to cinematic technique: impressionistic glimpses and candid snapshots linked with wide views of the whole colourful panorama. The swirling movements of the crowd, the opulence of the dresses and carriages, the feverish excitement over nothing more than a few tons of horseflesh – all this parallels a materialistic, pleasure-mad, corrupt society dashing madly around a pre-dictable course hell-bent on its own destruction.

None of this, however, matches the painstakingly applied brushstrokes with which Zola builds his portrait of Nana. Of all his triumphs, one of his greatest was to make his symbol entirely credible.

Zola's creation is a subtle blend of images of his heroine reflected from a revolving, multi-faceted mirror: the real Nana – fleshy and sexy, sometimes good-natured, occasionally bad-tempered; the Nana of her own imagination – proud, beautiful, powerful and sophisticated; the Nana created by the society about her – the Marine Venus of her age, the public sex-goddess. And, of course, there is the symbolic, avenging Nana with a destructive destiny and a corrupting quality that contaminates a whole section of Parisian society.

Despite her potency as an agent of subversion, Nana is really a brainless pawn. We see glimpses of this flesh-and-blood woman throughout the novel; at first clumsy and ingenuous, then progressively selfish and capricious, and finally perverse, even vicious. But Zola is always careful to avoid projecting Nana as an inherently evil character. The incident of Muffat's cuckoldom, for instance, is exploited to illustrate Nana's easy-going compassion. Although she despises and unmercifully screws Muffat in every sense of the word, and hardly knows the meaning of the word fidelity, Nana is deeply concerned, briefly, anyway, when she learns that his wife is deceiving him. There is a tragi-comic aspect about the incident, but here is a situation she understands and her maternal concern for the cuckold's bruised feelings is perfectly in accord with her character, from which Zola never wavers.

The fantasy heroine – Nana's own image of herself – is a brilliant device for it shows how with each step to success her self-deception increases; how society is corrupting her. At the race-track, watching Vandeuvres's horse gallop past the winning-post to the roar of the crowd, Nana believes the crowd is cheering her and not her equestrian namesake. It is a marvellous instance of self-parody, marking the extent to which Nana has departed from reality.

With Nana the Sex Goddess, Zola intuitively anticipates the twentieth-century phenomenon of the sex symbol, created by public adulation, the mass expression of sexual fantasising. The pretty, untalented girl is elevated by public hysteria to an erotic throne to assume mystical qualities of beauty and sexuality – lead transmuted into gold by the alchemy of mass escapism: 'Nana became an elegant woman, the marquise of the fashionable streets, kept by the stupidity and the filthiness of the male population... proud, rebellious, planting her foot on the neck of Paris like an all-conquering mistress.' She is crowned as the 'Blonde Venus' and enthroned on a sumptuous gold and silver divan, ordered for her by Count Muffat, on which she flaunts her body before her subjects:'...her sex was exposed and displayed with the religious shamelessness that belongs to an idol feared by men.' But just as Nana appears to shake from her foot the last traces of the dung-heap, Zola brings her – and the reader – back to earth with a thump, for we are never more than a hastily drawn curtain away from the hairpins, the soiled underclothes and the cracked, grime-encrusted wash-basins.

But it is in the role of Nana the Destroyer that Zola's heroine has achieved her enduring fame. Throughout the novel we can observe Nana polluting and infecting with apparent impunity, but in case some readers miss the point Zola resorts to literary trickery by having Muffat read to his mistress a newspaper article about her:

> And letting go her chemise, she stood there naked, waiting for Muffat to finish Fauchery's article. Muffat read it slowly. Entitled *The Golden Fly*, it was the story of a girl descended from four or five generations of drunkards, her blood tainted by an accumulated inheritance of poverty and drink, which in her case had taken the form of a nervous derangement of the sexual instinct. She had grown up in the slums, in the gutters of Paris; and now, tall and beautiful, and as well made as a plant nurtured on a dungheap, she was avenging the paupers and outcasts of whom she was the product. With her the rottenness that was allowed to ferment among the lower classes was rising to the surface and rotting the aristocracy. She had become a force of nature, a ferment of destruction, unwittingly corrupting and disorganizing Paris between her snow-white thighs, and curdling it just as women, every month, curdle milk. It was at the end of the article that the comparison with a fly occurred, a fly the colour of sunshine which had flown up out of the dung, a fly which had sucked death from the carrion left by the roadside and now, buzzing, dancing and glittering like a precious stone, was entering palaces through the windows and poisoning the men inside, simply by settling on them.
> Muffat raised his head and stared into the fire. (51)

Only Nana misses the point of the allusive article, for half-way through she becomes bored and begins instead to contemplate herself in the mirror. The message gets through to Muffat, of course, but he is so sucked down into degradation that he is helpless to escape.

As a Golden Fly, Nana has a highly decomposed heap of rottenness to work on; one which we suspect would decompose itself, given time. But the golden fly hastens the process. The depths of national degradation are reached symbolically, in a scene towards the end of the novel when the outrageous harlot commands the pious royal chamberlain to fall on his hands and knees, and perform like an obedient animal:

> It was as if a blast of lunacy gradually swept through the closed bedroom. A feeling of luxury threw them off their balance; and into the delirious imaginings of the flesh. What used to be the pious dreads of a sleepless night now turned into a bestial craving, a passion to get down on all fours, to growl and bite. Then, one day when he was playing at bears, she pushed him so roughly that he fell against a piece of furniture; and she burst into an involuntary laugh to see him with a bruise on his forehead. From then onwards, given the taste for it by her trial on La Faloise, she treated him as an animal. She whipped him and pursued him with kicks.
> 'Gee up! Gee up now!... You're the horse.... *Hi-up!* Won't you get along, foul nag!'
> Other times he was a dog. She threw her scented handkerchief to the far end of the room for him, and he had to run and pick it up in his teeth, trailing along on hands and knees.
> 'Fetch it, Cæsar!... I'll give you something if you loll about! Well done, Cæsar! Obedient dog! Nice dog! Do it nicely!'
> And he wallowed in his debasement, feeling the joy of being a brute. (49)

Ultimately, we witness the moral nadir of the Second Empire, symbolised by Muffat in his official chamberlain's uniform – the full regalia: knee breeches, cocked hat and sword – being beaten and yelled at by the whore:

> It was her revenge, an instinctive family grudge bequeathed to her with her blood. Next, when the chamberlain was undressed and his coat spread on the floor, she shouted to him to jump, and he jumped; she shouted to him to spit, and he spat; and she shouted to him to trample on the gold, on the eagles, on the decorations; and he trampled on them. *Crash!* There was nothing left; everything was destroyed. She smashed a chamberlain as she smashed a decanter or an empty candy box, reducing him to filth, a heap of mud in the gutter.

The layered symbolism of this magnificent passage – conveying the inevitable revenge of the working classes on the aristocracy, the destructive power of unrestrained promiscuity, and the fatalistic willingness of the ruling classes to destroy themselves and their Empire as well – is only matched at the end of the novel, which is a masterpiece of dramatic skill in itself. As Nana expires in a luxurious bedroom, her face and body already disfigured by the loathsome, evil-smelling smallpox pustules, the consequences of her contaminating power pass on the street below her window. *To Berlin! To Berlin!* A crowd cheers as some soldiers go by on their way to the front, acclaiming an Empire doomed by corrupt leaders, marching to extinction.

There is a decidedly voyeuristic tone in *Nana*, and the extraordinarily detailed eroticism which pervades the narrative suggests more than a professional attempt at verisimilitude by the author. On occasions this eroticism can engage the reader as a vicarious *experience*, for the sights and smells and the reactions of the watchers are conveyed with an uncanny sensibility. For all his puritannical attitudes, Zola was quite likely a latent or practising voyeur.

Take Nana's entrance on stage at the Variety Theatre in the opening chapter, with its delicious sense of anticipation: 'A shiver went round the auditorium.' Six words, and the reader is in a state of expectancy. Then the calculated shock-phrase: 'Nana was naked.' We strain forward to see more. 'She was naked with a calm audacity, certain of the overwhelming power of her flesh... her Amazon's breasts with their pink tips rigid like spears, her broad buttocks which rolled voluptuously...' Even today, with stage nudity *passé*, the passage is not without erotic power, and despite ourselves we join the tense audience in the hot, stuffy theatre. 'She was Venus rising from the waves, veiled only by her long hair. And when she raised her arms the golden hair of her armpits glistened fleetingly in the footlights...' At this stage we sneak a look at the rest of the audience, reassured that it is as intent as we are, dry-mouthed, stiff-necked, hardly breathing.

Did Zola compose this passage from notes taken during a conversation with some Parisian rake? Not very likely; much of it reflects the erotic fantasising of an imaginative voyeur, and similar examples occur throughout the novel as we peep into dressing-rooms, glimpse uncovered flesh and watch as Nana, naked, toasts herself by the fire.

It is not necessary to search too long for the source of this voyeuristic quality in *Nana*. The ample, warm sponge of Alexandrine's body must have been a great comfort to her husband on cold nights but, exuding domesticity, she was hardly the companion to satisfy his libertine desires. Even from the flimsy evidence available it is plain that Zola and his wife at this time suffered the deep personal anguish of childlessness. For a man who had written, 'Men and women are in this world solely to procreate; they become destroyers of human life the moment they retreat from this ordained task,' Zola's attitude to sexual intercourse was inevitably one distorted by guilt. At nights, particularly, the sterile spring of procreation must have erupted in torrents of guilt, a cataract of torment that became, for man and wife, a mocking barrier at their most intimate moments. They would lie on their bed for hours in the dark, sometimes holding hands, but never daring to speak of the sterility that both bound and separated them. Alexandrine, her maternal instincts satisfied in part by mothering Emile, suffered for her husband, but for him there was no solace. For one so proficient in conveying the subtlest drift of transient emotions in his novels, Emile was singularly inarticulate when it came to unburdening his own mind, and the silent space between them came to symbolise the unfruitfulness of their union, a treacherous space that was probably only crossed for the fulfilment of sheer physical need. Ultimately, until exhaustion or sleep overtook him, Emile would turn away and escape to his ascetic refuge to dream the carnal passages of tomorrow's chapter. Like a greyhound off the leash the novelist's sexuality took off into aphrodisiac fantasy; unfortunately for him sex was a tin hare, to be pursued in his fiction, but never caught. One consequence of this unhappy denial, however, was the sharpening of an ability to externalise his erotic fantasies with extraordinary clarity.

Also evident in *Nana* is Zola's preoccupation with nakedness, which I noted in *The Kill*. Nana's nudity exposes the nakedness of Zola's own deep-seated association between the bare flesh of the female, and wickedness, and it is apparent that he is both attracted and repelled by the mysterious implications of feminine nudity. Havelock Ellis commented that, 'On the one hand he over-emphasises what is repulsive in the nutritive side of life, and on the other hand, with the timid obsession of chastity, he over-emphasises the nakedness of the flesh.' Ellis, a psychologist and sexologist, was inclined to think Zola was a victim of coprophilia, an uncontrollable neurotic desire to dwell on obscenity and excrement, but this is obviously going too far. Zola held many beliefs, one of which was that whatever threatened or destroyed good, honest work, was a sin. Sex being the most corrosive agent against work, it was therefore a sin. The sexy people in Zola's novels are invariably lazy, useless and weak and if you happen upon a promiscuous character in one of his books you can be sure he or she will meet a bad end. Zola's mind, so impressively intuitive concerning most human transactions, seems to have lingered in a state of extended adolescence when it came to sex, and so it is not surprising that he should make the equation, *nakedness = promiscuity*. In his fiction, nakedness provided an obvious and exciting symbol for a whole range of carnal activities.

What is more disturbing in *Nana* is that sex is invariably sordid, selfish and destructive. This is an extension of his deep hatred, revealed with even greater force in his next novel, *Piping Hot!,* of the sterility and the sexual charade-playing of the upper and middle classes. In *Nana* the adulteries are less hypocritical in that they are an accepted part of life among the houses of the aristocracy and the rich, but the results are no less appalling. Neither Nana nor her lovers enjoy the satisfactions of love, apart perhaps from fleeting, superficial physical pleasure. Nana's embrace is that of an iron maiden. It is not too difficult to see the novelist's neurosis at work here, for at no time does Nana indulge in sex for its procreative purpose; even her baby Louis is an accident. Whatever *Nana* may promise, the possibility of healthy, gratifying sex won't be found between its covers.

The publication of *Nana* provoked mixed reactions among readers. While the man in the street loved her, *salon* society was horrified by the crude language, and aghast at the accusatory allusions to Catholicism and capitalism it contained.

The critical response was more consistent; it was, with very few exceptions, negative and malicious. One notable dissenter was Flaubert, who called it a beautiful book, fresh and original. To the publisher Charpentier he wrote: 'If I were to note every original and powerful thing in it I would have to make a note on every page. . . Zola is a man of genius!'

But such congratulations were rare. One journal labelled the novel the product of 'a mental abberation of an ambitious, enfeebled mind tormented by sensual fantasies'. Others claimed the book had been tarted up with obscenities to seduce the prurient. Still others took a knowing delight in pointing out that Nana could never have achieved in real life the power and wealth she did in the novel. There were dozens of variations on the same theme: 'He presents us with his decoction of "Nature" in a vessel unfit for the purpose, a receptacle lamentably, fatally in need of scouring, and in which no article intended for intellectual consumption should ever be served up.'

Henry James (1843–1916), immediately the novel was published, wrote in *The Parisian* on 26 February 1880, that the work was 'inconceivably and inordinately dull'. James was sympathetic to realism, but when it came to criticism was a somewhat capricious individualist. Although he later came to admire Zola enough to call him a genius, he gave the novelist a good deal of stick over *Nana*. Whether the fact that he and Zola were transatlantic rivals (*Portrait of a Lady* appeared in 1881; *The Bostonians* in 1886) had anything to do with his initial hostile, irrelevant and often unfounded criticism of the French writer, we can only surmise, but it is glaringly clear that he completely misread both the character of Nana and the author's intentions. 'To say the book is indecent is to make use of a term which M. Zola holds to mean nothing and to prove nothing... Never was such foulness so spontaneous and so complete, and never was it united with qualities so superior to itself and intrinsically so respectable.' This sort of comment makes sense only if we allow that James was including *Nana* in that genre of fiction – and this included almost all the American fiction at that time – which was written and read by unmarried ladies, to whom a good part of life was a sealed book. 'The human note is completely absent,' he wrote, 'the perception of character, of the way people feel and think and act, is helplessly, hopelessly at fault... The figure of the brutal *fille*, without a conscience or a soul, with nothing but devouring appetites and impudences, has become the stalest of the stock properties of French fiction, and M. Zola's treatment has here imparted to her no touch of superior verity.' James could not resist the snipe that, human nature being what it was, had something to do with the fact that *Nana*, in a short time, had reached the thirty-ninth edition.

Even more scathing was the later criticism by W.S. Lilly in the August 1885 issue of *The Fortnightly Review*:

> Blank and crude materialism, the trivial, the foul, the base of animal life, is the staple of the book from beginning to end. The heroine, whose role M. Zola deems to embrace the whole keyboard of human existence, is 'a beast, no more', indeed, rather less. Even her affection for her child is merely the instinct of a beast, and not so pure or touching as the devotion of a bitch to its puppies. A movement of prurient curiosity, a spasm of concupiscence, a thrill of physical horror – these are the highest emotions which the book excites. That such literature can possess the slightest interest for anyone who has not sunk to Nana's spiritual level is inconceivable; and herein is the appalling significance of its popularity.

When he came to promote *Nana* in England, for his translation of 1884, Henry Vizetelly used what he could usefully salvage from James's review, including his enthusiastic estimate of Zola as a novelist, and added other reasons why English readers should buy the book:'...the subject is very interesting, because it raises questions which no one apparently has the energy or the good faith to raise among ourselves. (It is of distinctly serious readers only that I speak, and *Nana* is to be recommended exclusively to such as have a very robust appetite for a moral.)' A novel like *Nana*, Vizetelly went on, was not easily found in England or the United States, 'where the story-teller's art is almost exclusively feminine, and mainly in the hands of timid (even when very accomplished) women, whose acquaintance with life is severely restricted . . .' There could have been few at the time who could teach Vizetelly much about publicising a novel.

Nana, whose career spanned the full spectrum of harlotry from the gutter to the Grand Hotel, has become a legend in literature and a figure of folklore. As the supreme literary cunt she constantly exercises the imaginations of others; *Nana* has been adapted for the cinema and for television on numerous occasions and the potential of the complex symbolism she projects is by no means exhausted.

In some ways it is unfortunate that Nana is such a dominant character, for her powerful presence tends to obscure other outstanding but less strident qualities of this fine novel, which among other things is a monument to Zola's patient craftsmanship. Only upon reflection can one see the extraordinary balance he achieves between the surreal poetry of the dung-heap and the swarming exuberance of the life that springs from it. For with his ubiquitous vegetative imagery Zola stresses once again that all life is ephemeral and cyclic.

10

A Pause on the Way

Although *Nana* was successful, it was *L'Assommoir* that laid the golden egg for Zola and, in doing so, left a lot of egg on the faces of his critics. Because of the intense controversy the novelist had aroused and the acclaim he had attracted, they could no longer ignore him as they had done in the past. Emile Zola was news. Editors, under pressure from their readers, their families and friends – who now began to examine Zola's fictional family with interest – simply had to insist that their critics discuss the most talked-about author of the day, a situation which was to continue for a couple of decades.

Zola had finally arrived, not as a flash-in-the-pan writer of a bestseller, but as a popular author of depth and quality – the sort of writer, like Dickens, a society throws up only once or twice in a generation, a writer about the people, for the people. But having propelled himself to the top, the problem was to stay there.

The booksellers' hottest property in years was no stranger to the value and techniques of publicity. Trained at Hachette's and coached by Villemessant he had an unerring nose for scandal and controversy. For years this instinct had been frustrated by his own unimportance and almost atrophied from the conspiratorial silence of the critics. But publication of *L'Assommoir* had breached the dam, the breach he had been waiting for. Overnight Zola became a public figure, and he intended to stay one, with calculatingly inflammatory articles in the newspapers he wrote for and provocative pronouncements in those he didn't. *Nana* had added an ocean of fuel to the flames, and the fleet of public opinion was constantly under attack from his thunderous broadsides. It was impossible for him at times not to succumb to the showman in his nature. *Le Figaro* offered battle, accusing him of 'betraying French literature', the result of an article he'd written for a Russian newspaper in which he flayed the contemporary romantic writers and reserved praise only for Flaubert, Daudet and Goncourt. Unfortunately the favoured writers were all Charpentier authors, a point picked up eagerly by *Le Figaro*, which implied bribery by the publisher. The argument raged for weeks, to Zola's undisguised delight.

There had been a period when Charpentier must have had serious misgivings about his decision to underwrite his promising but relatively sales-shy author. Zola, in any case, was at least two novels behind in the agreement, which had called for two manuscripts a year. And Charpentier's business was still far from thriving.

L'Assommoir, unexpectedly, pulled a jackpot for both author and publisher. Charpentier's faith in his author was richly vindicated, and this was only the beginning. In a matter of months Zola was a rich man, helped considerably by Charpentier tearing up the old contract in favour of a far more generous royalty arrangement. The author's income in 1877 from book royalties, articles, reviews and serialisation fees must have been at least 30,000 francs.

Zola's new prosperity helped to restore his self-confidence and, cloaking his timidity, a public image began to emerge of a loud-mouthed boor who made love to the reading public with a whip. It was what the public expected, and Zola made no effort to soften it. Indeed, he sprinkled his conversation with 'carefully chosen words and expressions of calculated inelegance, more frequent than agreeable', according to Henry Vizetelly, who met him about this time. If the novelist was reticent about his personal life, no such reserve inhibited his opinions on the controversial topics of the day, which he insisted on delivering with unrestrained force. His passion seemed to renew itself daily. 'There must be passion!' he often told visitors, 'so that one can rise up from the newspaper each morning boiling with indignation over the imbecilities in its pages!' Later, writing in the preface to *Une Campagne* in 1882, he admitted that his passionate feelings might have sometimes led him to unjust views, but he nevertheless affirmed, 'I believe in living in a constant state of rage against pretence and deceit and the mediocrity which surrounds us.'

Not only his reputation but also the novelist's face and figure were becoming familiar to Parisians, for Zola was now a favourite target for the caricaturists. He discouraged newspaper interviews, which led many journalists to fantasise; one reporter exceeded even Zola's gift for linking brief observation to imagination when he noted that the novelist's black hair and beard 'gave him a look of virility and of asceticism which denotes great strength of will and indicates sufficiently clearly his love of solitude, his delight in thought, and the broadest sense of observation'. Perhaps. A less adulatory portrait would have shown Zola with his big frame filled out, a rather sombre figure, rarely smiling and even disdainful, with the pouting mouth of a sulking child. Henry James, when reviewing *Nana* in 1880, said of him, 'M. Zola disapproves greatly of wit; he thinks it is an impertinence in a novel, and he would probably disapprove of humour if he *knew* what it is.'

Privately, away from the public gaze, the author's life ran on a rigidly prescribed course. Vizetelly describes him as 'cold as the grave, living a monotonous and mechanical life, his inspiration regulated by the hands of the clock, leaving nothing to chance.' After a substantial breakfast of fried eggs he would take a short walk, health and weather permitting, and then sit down at a huge table to begin writing. Chillingly methodical, his pen – a J-nib set in a heavy ivory holder – would be laid down immediately he had completed his set daily quota of words, four pages a day, thirty lines to each page of unruled quarto, when he would take a light lunch followed by a nap, 'as prosaically as a retired grocer'. Even when on holiday, his notes and manuscript travelled with him. Work was his narcotic, in strictly regulated doses.

It is easy to make fun of Zola's plodding technique and of his almost destructive urge to mechanise the craft of fiction, and many critics have. It would be a mistake, however, to dismiss what many regard as an amusing idiosyncrasy which had little to do with his finished work. After his death, Alexandrine carefully collected all his original manuscripts, plus the notes, plans and research material used for the novels, some ninety bulky volumes of them, and presented all but a few to the Bibliothèque Nationale in Paris. The completeness of these essentially private notes allows us the unique opportunity to observe the inner workings of a creative intellect of genius, of a man's sometimes agonising journey of exploration into his imagination during which there is a constant struggle between his mind and his pen. Surveying this mountain of documents, one can be forgiven for wondering how Zola's novels ever came to life under their weight. The painstaking methodology, the silly theories, the structural mechanics, the mass of scaffolding – how all this inhibiting procedure failed to prevent him from writing some of the most exciting, lyrical and emotionally charged fiction in literature remains as a tribute to his imaginative gifts.

After he had written the first two *Rougon-Macquart* novels, Zola fell into working habits that hardly changed for the rest of his life. His first thoughts on a book were set down in a draft called an *ébauche*, in which he established the framework, outlined the plot, planned the construction and sketched rough portraits of the characters. He used the *ébauche* to feel his way through the maze of ideas and material he'd accumulated; he would select and develop some and discard others. Then slowly, like a photographic print in a developing tank, the picture would emerge, the fuzzy, grey image would resolve and sharpen, with depths and highlights; and, finally, even the smallest details would show up. The *ébauche*, though, was only a rough working draft.

At this point he would usually return to his characters; all their actions had to be appropriate to the personalities he'd invented for them, even to their speech and personal habits. The information about each character would be put down on separate sheets, like psychologists' file cards: mental and medical history, analysis of temperament and any emotional shocks or experiences that might have relevance. Zola regarded his characters, as we've already seen, with clinical detachment, like laboratory rats.

Finally, like a bricklayer setting down the first row of bricks on a foundation and allowing for all the pillars, openings and corners, he would draft out the plan of the novel in some detail. This was developed in two stages. At the first stage he would organise his chapters and what action was to take place in them, allowing for changes of pace, contrasts of light, shade and colour, the ebb and flow of conflict and tension, the critical placement of climax and anti-climax. In so far as effects were concerned, Zola's novels were composed with all the care of a concerto. Then came the last stage of the plan, in which all the details in

146

each chapter would be rearranged and fitted together, logically and intuitively. After many months of planning, he was ready to write.

In all his years in Paris Zola had never really settled down; biographers can never agree on how many apartments he had during his early years, or even where they were, there were so many. The house on the Rue Condamine had been the nearest thing to a home but it was dreadfully cramped, a fact that became increasingly embarrassing as his circle of friends grew. With the money pouring in from *L'Assommoir* one of his first actions was to move to a far more spacious apartment on two floors of a house in the Rue de Boulogne.

Within a few months it had taken on the appearance of a museum, the result of the spectacular release of the novelist's pent-up craving for possessions. The rooms gave the impression of some medieval tent pitched simultaneously in several countries; everywhere there were sumptuous curtains and ancient tapestries, behind which filtered a dim light through seventeenth-century stained-glass windows, revealing in the gloom an incredible array of Venetian furniture, Turkish divans, Indian sculpture and reproduction Louis XIV chairs. Suits of armour gleamed dully from several niches in the walls and there was an aviary in the dining-room. The pride of the bedroom was a magnificent carved Louis XIII bed, around which billowed hangings of Genoese velvet. But the *pièce de résistance* of the new apartment was Zola's own study on the first floor. The room was so stuffed with plush that despite three large windows it conveyed a mood of eternal dusk. The novelist sat on a huge, carved rosewood chair behind a massive Dutch table some ten feet long, from where he could contemplate an extensive collection of gee-gaws, each of which had its nominated position on the work-table; a china cabinet, two glass-fronted bookcases, a piano, a variety of wall hangings and a collection of Impressionist paintings, including his portrait by Manet. The room was a castle keep in which he could detach himself from the outside world to create a world of his own, that of the *Rougon-Macquart*.

Before long the effect of this orgy of decorating was so claustrophobic that he felt the need to escape to the country, and in August 1878, he purchased a small house near Médan, a quiet village between Poissy and Triel in the Seine valley, about twenty-five miles from Paris, and 'with not a single bourgeois in the area' as he proudly told friends. From its upper windows he could look over his garden and down a steep hill to the broad expanse of meadows and orchards either side of the Seine, lined with poplars and alders, a scene of idyllic peace after the pace and noise of Paris. It was, at the time of purchase, a modest rustic retreat, costing 9,000 francs – 'paid for by literature' as its owner was fond of repeating.

But within a year the modest retreat at Médan began to bulge with an eccentric accumulation of bric-a-brac, much of it the overflow fron his Paris apartment: tapestries, hugh vases, carved Buddhas, chests and medieval furniture as heavy as lead, both genuine and fake. During his visits to the Goncourts he had often admired their home, tastefully and originally decorated with oriental pieces; so now Japanese screens, scrolls and carvings jostled with the European antiques. To house the growing pile he was forced to build a tower – the 'Nana Tower', so named because the novel paid for it – and then another, so that the house became a rambling mansion with half a dozen staircases linking the various levels and rooms. It is not surprising that builders, decorators and antique-dealers loved him, and constantly sought him out. Although one of the themes of his *Rougon-Macquart* chronicle was a running denunciation of the decadent opulence of the Second Empire, he outdid the ostentation with ease, and single-handed.

Zola's patchwork education was the source of much of this naïve and execrable taste, which soon became a legend and a target for his more waspish critics. But Médan was much more than a museum of bad taste, a repository for Zola's irresistible collector's instinct. Sitting alone in his vast, baroque study, thirty feet square, under a ceiling as high as the sky and beneath bookshelves which required a spiral staircase and a gallery to reach the topmost shelves, the novelist at last felt the deep sense of security he'd yearned for, and at every turn he could see and feel the trappings of the success that had eluded him for so long. His knowledge and experience had been hard-won, and he needed these tangible symbols of wealth to fill the void left by his academic failure. Yes, he could admit to himself, he was unquestionably vulgar, but then the Goncourts could never have written *L'Assommoir*.

Midway through the 1870s one of Zola's greatest pleasures was the regular Sunday soirée at Flaubert's house in the Rue Murillo. Here, in the late afternoon, a couple of dozen friends of Flaubert would gather to drink, smoke and talk. For Zola it was heady literary company of the kind he craved. Gradually, his associations with the artist friends of his youth had fallen away, to be replaced by the more conversational Goncourt, Daudet and the Russian Turgenev.

The Sunday afternoons were above all a stage from which Flaubert, gigantic, almost airborne at times by his great yellow moustache, often in oriental costume, could hold court, and by a number of accounts he was loud, opinionated and immensely entertaining. Flaubert had been one of Zola's first heros. This youthful hero-worship, after *Madame Bovary* in 1857 and *Salammbô* in 1862, had progressed to deep professional admiration. At this time, though, the great writer was clearly on the way down, although he would never admit it; after 1870 he began to suffer more and more from a nervous disease with the symptoms of epilepsy. Yet his artistic powers seemed unimpaired; he would still spend a week, if necessary, honing the beauty from a single page, or a night hunting for a single word until he was certain he had the most exact, the most perfect word for his purpose. He was, in some ways, a father-figure to the younger writer, who took no pleasure in seeing his idol age so prematurely.

Zola's friendship with the surviving Goncourt brother, Edmond, was never really close. Goncourt was a neurotic who seemed permanently soured by the fact that on the very day his first book was published in 1851 the entire country could think of nothing else than the *coup d'état*, news of which reached them the

148

same morning. Although it lasted for several years the uncertain friendship between the two writers finally disintegrated after a long series of petty disagreements and misunderstandings. It seems clear now that Edmond, growing more cross-grained and disputatious with the years, became convinced that Zola was pirating passages from his new novels, which he would read to the group from time to time before publication. With his imagination distorted by jealousy – *L'Assommoir* was hailed as a masterpiece while its progenitor, the Goncourts' *Germinie Lacerteux*, was a forgotten novel – he improbably envisaged Zola soaking up his ideas and then running back to his study to incorporate them into his own work. Even when these allegations were proved to be quite unfounded, Goncourt remained exceedingly touchy, especially when Zola's novels containing the disputed passages were published before his, thus implying that *he* was plagiarising Zola!

Less uncertain, though still lacking a certain warmth, was Zola's friendship with Alphonse Daudet. Daudet was the same age as Zola and shared a similar background. Born at Nîmes he experienced a depressing youth, several intolerable years as a schoolteacher, several more years as a bohemian poet and many years of public indifference until, in 1874, his *Fromont jeune et Risler aîné* made him a literary celebritiy. The bond between the two writers was one of respect rather than affection; Zola's conversational denseness irritated Daudet and he could be very spiteful behind his back. When, many years later, he was asked for a statement to be included in a journalist's article about the completion of his friend's *Rougon-Macquart* chronicle, Daudet bluntly offered to 'advise Zola, now that the *Rougon-Macquart* family tree is fully grown, to go and hang himself from its highest branch'.

Of the four, Ivan Turgenev was to remain Zola's closest friend. He was a huge, bearded, archetypal Russian, the eldest in the group and although reserved, a prolific story-teller. His life seemed cursed by sadness. Embittered by the criticism his work had attracted in his own country he found himself an exile in France, spurned by his one great love, the singer Pauline Viardot-Garcia, and permanently scarred by his tyrannical mother. The world-weary, tri-lingual poetically inclined realist admired Zola openly, and was, for several years, his Russian literary adviser, agent and business manager.

But I am racing ahead. In the late 1870s the five writers were close and in some ways even dependent upon one another. They took to having regular monthly dinners at leading restaurants including, curiously, the Café Riche, the scene of Renée's seduction of Maxime in *The Kill*, where they would gourmandise and booze late into the night; the cool, elegant Goncourt needling the conversation with witticisms; Flaubert thumping the table and roaring; Daudet always charming, always the one to smooth ruffled feelings; Turgenev, the best listener, with the ability to top the tallest of tall stories with a quiet, wry comment; and Zola, earnest, enthusiastic, eternally optimistic until, after a glass too many, he would lapse into sentimental self-pity and tearful melancholy. All of them loved food, often eating continuously for three to four hours. Zola's weakness was the sea-food cooking of his Provençal youth.

'Eating is the only pleasure left!' he would often cry in his cups. 'Nothing else exists for me now!' The monthly dinners were an outlet for his real and imagined misery, a release from the disciplined prison of his study, an escape from his ascetic life-style, where, among friends who understood, he could bare his most private and painful feelings which were always kept locked up at home.

Zola drew immense comfort and confidence from the group, for between them they represented the very spearhead of French literature. Their friendship and meetings represented to the novelist a tangible symbol of his own high place in the world of letters, enabling him, for instance, to launch an attack on Victor Hugo, of whom he was once a fanatical admirer, for allowing himself to be acknowledged the leader and figurehead of the romantic school. He was, Zola wrote, 'a sponge, which, by its absorbent qualities, sucks up to its profit all that is near it and, thanks to this, swells out to an enormous size'. Yet, for all that, Zola never lost his great respect for Hugo's genius.

Apart from his regular contact with Flaubert and the others, Zola found himself the centre of two other literary circles. The first of these was the fashionable *salon* of Madame Charpentier, his publisher's charming wife, where he was more or less the permanent guest of honour. Although he was no socialite he found the evenings tolerable and not the kind of trial he'd imagined they would be, for his customary timidity and bluntness were excused by his notoriety and the lionising wasn't entirely unpleasant.

The second circle, which was to have a lasting impact on his own career and on all literature, grew from a single visit by a young admirer. One Sunday in 1876, soon after he'd finished writing *L'Assommoir*, a writer named Henri Céard called at his home unannounced to tell him how much he valued his novels. Up until then Zola had only a single dedicated fan – Paul Alexis – and he was a little disconcerted by the visit until, after telling Flaubert about it later the same day, the great man boomed, 'How touching, Zola! It's the sort of thing that always gives one great pleasure!' Reassured as to how he should feel, Zola encouraged a second visit. This time Céard brought with him another novelist who had just published a book in Brussels, a young man with heavy black brows and a sharp-featured face named Joris Huysmans. In the meantime, Paul Alexis had struck up a friendship with Leon Hennique, an emergent writer with realist inclinations, whom he also introduced to Zola. Then along came a fun-loving, broad-shouldered sportsman whose athletic build and interests seemed oddly out of place in the group, Guy de Maupassant. All six began to meet every Thursday evening at Zola's house and with one or two defections they remained close for many years.

As a literary group, the Naturalists were born, champagne, cigars and all, at a dinner given by the younger writers to their elders, Zola, Flaubert and Goncourt. The date, which was extensively puffed in the newspapers, was 16 April 1877. Thereafter the small group succeeded, like a bawling infant, in attracting perhaps more attention than it merited, with each of its members writing about one another in adulatory terms. As a kind of reward for his loyalty, Zola included a poem by the unknown Paul Alexis in an article he wrote on Baudelaire, who had died the previous year, passing the verse off as the work of the great poet. The bluff was eventually exposed but Alexis couldn't have wished for a better introduction into Parisian literary society. With his fame and output, Zola was unquestionably the leader of the group, and tirelessly encouraged the younger members to the same level of patient industry. Evidence of this is found in the group's only publication *Evenings at Médan*, a collection of six stories published by Charpentier in April 1880. Zola wrote a preface, anticipating attacks from the critics, adding that 'our only concern is to publicly proclaim our solidarity, together with our literary aspirations.' With the exception of one story, none are remarkable, certainly not Zola's 'Attack on the Mill', but the book had a good sale, attracted much publicity, and efficiently launched the five young writers. The exception among the stories was Maupassant's contribution, *Boule-de-Suif*–'Ball of Lard', which was to earn for him a place in literature as one of the world's greatest short-story writers. Rarely has a writer's career been launched with a masterpiece.

The purpose and activities of Zola's group of disciples weren't confined to self-congratulation, however. There was a strong and influential body of literary opinion in France openly at war with realist writing, and especially with Zola and his naturalism, and the group saw that it would be failing in its duty to literature if it did not look to its defences. The inevitable clash had been gathering momentum for several years, with constant sniping from the critics. A typical pot-shot was an essay by Ferdinand Brunetière in the *Revue des deux mondes*, who saw himself as one of the guardians of the ideals of the French Academy:

> If he [Zola] merely paraded his base doctrines and philosophy to conceal a sterile talent, we could be patient. But it is worse! With his crude style, his repulsive and vulgar preoccupations, he has outdone the other realists. Is Humanity composed exclusively of rascals, madmen and clowns? What is to become of the honest purity of our French tongue?

Up until now, Zola's cause had been primarily a personal one; one of reform. He had hoped that realist fiction would lead the nation into an enlightened social epoch. In his defence of *L'Assommoir* he had claimed the novel 'had opened the social sores' of France, and was thus a 'useful' book in that it pointed to the moral for all to see; that his defence was at odds with his fictional achievement, which did not moralise in the least, completely escaped him. But now he had to acknowledge another cause, the defence of the concept of realist writing and of its place in literature. Because of his aggressive, polemical articles he soon found himself at the forefront of the realist defence, leading a counter-charge against the literary establishment. His young followers rallied to his battle-cry, pouring scorn on the critics and firing off rounds of wit at his attackers through a dozen newspapers and journals.

Once the campaign was launched the counter-attackers could not withdraw, and the battle raged for months. It seems remarkable today that an essentially literary argument could monopolise so much press space for so long, but then this was Paris, and at a time when newspaper readerships, although smaller, were vastly more literate (in the literary sense) than those of today. Perhaps also there was the smell of change in the air, of exciting and ominous new ideas, however little understood. One of the ideas, one which Zola little understood, was his concept of the 'experimental novel'. The controversy about realism was running down. Despite his instinctive flair for debate even Zola's invention flagged, and he cast about for some fresh ammunition to prolong the war of words. One of the problems which faced him and his followers was the indefinable nature of the terms *realism* and *naturalism*; what was wanted was a positive theory, a set of definitions backed by unarguable logic. Naturalism was by now a well-publicised term, but what did it mean exactly?

Although the term had been used by a Russian critic many years before, its transformation into the term as we know it began with the historian Taine, who used it to convey with more brevity the clumsy title, 'natural scientist'. Zola, when reviewing Taine's work in 1866, picked up the term and used it in his preface to *Thérèse Raquin*. At that time, you may recall, the novelist was already coming to grips with the marriage of science and literature, and 'naturalist', with its scientific overtones, perfectly described a writer whose sources were real and scientific rather than supernatural and philosophical.

In the ensuing decade Zola's loose notions had begun to develop into something that looked like a system. The idea that a writer could observe nature and mankind with the detachment of an experimental scientist because all life is predetermined seemed to make more sense now than ever before; had he not written a masterpiece, *L'Assommoir*, to prove the logic of it? The only trouble was that Zola was not a scientist, and whatever he said on the subject was inevitably – and justifiably – ignored or ridiculed. Then, in 1877, Céard introduced him to the work of a physiologist named Claude Bernard, and to a book of his published twelve years before, *An Introduction to the Study of Experimental Medicine*. Even a quick browse revealed to Zola that his theories and Bernard's were amazingly parallel. Bernard was no quack, either. He was a respected physician, and the Sorbonne's first professor of physiology. He had been honoured many times and had made significant discoveries on the importance of the pancreas to the digestion, the workings of the liver, and of the existence of the vasomotor nerves. And here he was, saying substantially what Zola had been thinking all these years!

The result of Zola's accelerated theorising was a collection of essays which appeared first, with Turgenev's help, in the St Petersburg newspaper, *The Messenger of Europe*, and subsequently in France in 1880 under the title of *The Experimental Novel*. Together they outlined Zola's definition of a literature determined by scientific principles adapted from Bernard's work, the 'force and marvellous clarity' of which won his unstinting admiration. Difficult though it is to make an understandable summary from sixty pages of mumbo-jumbo, the theory of the experimental novel and the tenets of naturalism can be abridged as follows:

152

— NATURE only must be the subject of art. The writer must face her openly and frankly, and must recognise and document the beast in man.
— THE naturalistic novel is a true scientific experiment which the novelist makes on man, with the support of observation. As we have experimental chemistry and physics, we shall have, eventually, the experimental novel.
— THE naturalist writer must operate with characters, emotions, human and social data just as the chemist and the physicist work on inert bodies and as the physiologist works on living bodies.
— NATURALISM rejects utterly the concept of supernatural Nemesis, the idea that Providence affects the affairs of mankind, recognised by the popular beliefs in 'poetic justice' and 'crime doesn't pay'.
— NATURALISM rejects the concept of absolute morality. Morality is relative, to an age, to a place, to a race. It is wrong to subject people living in the nineteenth century to a moral code created in the Middle Ages; wrong to subject, say, people living in France to a moral code concocted for Romans. Moral laws are a movable feast, for we make many exceptions – the heroic suicide, the sympathy for a starving child who steals, the excuse of self-defence for killing another human.
— NATURALISM rejects utterly the concept of a free will.
— NATURALISM will show the mechanism of the useful and the harmful, and will isolate the determinism of human and social phenomena so that one day we may control and direct these phenomena for the good of mankind.
— NATURALISM repudiates the belief that personality dominates creative writing. Determinism governs everything. By scientific investigation and experimental reasoning, novels of pure imagination will be replaced by novels of pure observation and experiment.

Predictably, the flagrant materialism of *The Experimental Novel* caused a furore. Even those writers and few critics who were otherwise enthusiastic about the movement could not swallow that part of Zola's doctrine which denied the freedom of the human will. It was the bitter pill of determinism, and not unnaturally this fundamental keystone in the naturalist arch drew cries of dismay and disgust from the establishment. The more logical among them argued that, having exposed social injustices and revealed the sores of society, how could naturalism cure them when it denied human incentive, a product of a free will? The critics saw masses of inferior and degenerate humans exploiting the theory to the detriment of law and order. As one cleric put it, 'Indoctrinate the masses with this pestiferous teaching and there will be some of us who shall not taste of death till we seen the reign of moral anarchy and disintegration set in.' But the defenders of the law of free will were saddled with the paradox of the law of causation, to which all but bigots must subscribe, and which implies that every action, event and circumstance results from some previous cause. Moreover, argued the naturalists, considering the harsh punishment meted out to criminals during the past few centuries, why were there still criminals? No amount of time spent in prison could make these men penitent. What they did before and after spells in a prison was invariably beyond correction because the actions were beyond the control of the criminal. Zola emphatically denied that the naturalist movement was descending to fatalism in seeing man as an animal machine acting only by the laws of heredity and environment. 'It is necessary to be accurate,' he wrote, 'We are not fatalists, we are determinists, which is not the same thing.'

Nevertheless, critics of naturalism could see nothing but a black future for humanity in the movement; extinguish the shining light of the individual will and there is no hope for collective man, was their objection. The naturalists, however, saw no inconsistency. Mankind was its own shining light, they argued, with vast energies, love and spirit, and thus with the potential to proliferate and better itself. In a word, Man was Nature.

Objections to naturalist theory, in England and in America, came from two sources, the establishment literary critics and the moralists, but as their attacks were largely emotional reactions to imagined threats of global immorality and bestiality it is often difficult to separate the two. An essay called 'The New Naturalism' by W.S. Lilly in the *Fortnightly Review* of August 1885, is fairly typical of these attacks, from which I give these extracts. 'The Naturalistic Revolution means everywhere the banishment of sentiment, of imagination, of empirical doctrines, of poetic idealism,' he began, before comparing the naturalist with the vivisector. He cut away at the flesh of *The Experimental Novel* to reveal what he saw as the bones of Zola's argument:

> Art must disappear from the novel and the drama. The science of the vivisector is to take its place.
> The theory of the vivisectionist, succinctly stated, amounts to this, that by the observation of symptoms artificially created in sound animal organism, we may arrive at a knowledge of the causes of animal symptoms in unsound human organisms; for example, that by studying the phenomena of death in a rabbit baked alive, we may understand the mechanism of febrile disturbances in a man.
> We live in an era of vivisection. And the voice of reason is as ineffectual against that ghastly shibboleth as it was against the vomiting of the emetic era, the evacuation of the purging era, the depletion of the bleeding era, the poisoning of the mercurial era and of the iodide of potassium era. Certain it is that the whole race of vivisectors, from the first until now, have not discovered one single agent for the cure of any malady nor established any therapeutic fact or theory helpful in the smallest degree for the treatment of disease, nor contributed at all to the advance of scientific surgery.

Lilly, unfortunately, possessed a similar trait to the writer he was criticising he often did not know when to stop. At this point he was unlucky enough to choose as an example a 'vivisector' whom history would remember as one of the great benefactors of mankind:

> ...the vast series of experiments in splenic fever (anthrax) performed by M Pasteur have yielded results which are worse than valueless, so insufficient and so evanescent is the immunity against natural infection conferred by his preventative inoculation, and so grave are the dangers which it develops for man and other non-inoculated animals. And there is not the slightest reason for believing that the new vaccine of rabies, prepared in the laboratory by the same savant, by similar processes, will be one whit more efficacious.

Elsewhere, though, occasional voices of reason were heard. 'What is needed now,' wrote the American critic Hamilton Wright Mabie in 1885 in the *Andover Review*, 'in fiction as in poetry, is a revitalisation of the imagination and a return to implicit and triumphant faith in it.' He concluded,

> Science not only leaves the imagination untouched, but adds indefinitely to the material with which it works. The more intelligent study of facts which it has made possible and inevitable, purifies and enlarges in a corresponding degree the

conceptions which underlie them, and will add in the end immeasurably to the scope and majesty of life.

The first effects of the scientific tendency...must not be mistaken for the final effects; it is this mistake which gives our poetry its elegiac note and our fiction its general confession of the futility of all things. Great works of art never come from hands afflicted with this kind of paralysis.

It often happens that marriage ends a love affair, and so it was with the naturalists after the publication of *The Experimental Novel*. Once launched into an exploration of the possibilities of the naturalist and experimental novel, Zola in due course overreached himself by projecting his theories into the conduct of society itself. He even advocated a Naturalist Republic. Most literary historians agree that had Zola not republished the avalanche of words which made up his theoretical writing, his reputation among intellectuals and academics today would be immeasurably greater. As most of it had originally appeared in a journal published in far-off St. Petersburg, there is a good chance that, like most polemical writing, it would have mouldered, mercifully forgotten, in the seldom-disturbed bowels of some library.

But this speculation doesn't take into account Zola's inborn thirst for publicity – nor his need, in 1880, to fuel the fires lit by his novels with theoretical justification and argument. With the publication in Paris of *The Experimental Novel* he naïvely supervised his own exhumation, and in doing so destroyed much of his credibility with generations of academics and students of French literature who seem unable or unwilling to separate the theoretical chaff from the creative grain. There is evidence that Zola knew his theoretical essays were themselves largely experimental. He was one of those writers who think with their pens; when they begin a sentence they have little idea how it will finish. This explains to some extent why his theoretical writing was so voluminous, and so little in sympathy with his fiction; at the time of his peak theoretical output, between 1876 and 1880, he was also writing *L'Assommoir* and *Nana*. In a sense he used the columns of newspapers as other thinkers would use their minds, but without the benefit of privacy. Zola not only 'thought aloud', but did so through a megaphone. His public utterances, I suspect, were not as ingenuous as they might appear; they provided a means for exploring new ideas, and however illogical they might be proved they certainly challenged the literary *status quo*. Once the real reason for their existence is understood, the significance, or insignificance, of the more absurd of Zola's theories can be seen not as a detracting feature in his work but as yet another element in the man's complex psychological make-up.

One must understand, too, that as a natural and trained publicist, Zola believed that it was not enough to write; what was written had to be propagated and read, or the writer's job was only half done. He was a crusader; he could not open his mouth or put pen to paper without being controversial. Even his name, ZO – LA! sounded, to Maupassant, like successive bugle notes, one to signal the attack, the other to announce victory. It could be said that while half of Zola's time was spent in writing, the other half was devoted to seeking publicity in one form or another, something worth remembering by today's typically retiring author when gloomily contemplating public disinterest in his work.

With their leader in conflict with his own ideas it was inevitable that the younger followers of naturalism should lose their sense of direction. Zola's fictional output simply could not be reconciled with his theories; they knew it and he knew it, and in fact Zola hated himself for being unable to detach his writing completely from the romantic tradition.

'Is it my fault,' he said once, 'if the power of romanticism has been such that even the most resolute of its enemies – such as myself – have had the greatest difficulty in freeing themselves from its pernicious influence?' He maintained, however, that his personal failing did not necessarily invalidate his theories: 'Shall I, as a critic, cease laying down a law which I consider useful and necessary, just because as an author I am not able to follow that law as absolutely as I would wish to do?'

The first defector from the naturalist group was Maupassant. He was, despite a seven-year apprenticeship under Flaubert, little more than a literary dabbler until the publication of *Boule-de-Suif*. With this story, an acknowledged masterpiece, he revealed a brilliance which dazzled his friends and the public alike, and immediately followed this success with a string of great novels including *The House of Madame Tellier* and *Bel Ami*; his books were full of vagabonds and scoundrels, and female readers adored him. He was, above all the supreme non-committed observer, writing nothing that he did not see or experience, never preferring good to evil, and setting it all down with such directness and economy that the best of his work still provides valuable lessons in expression for aspiring writers. He produced some thirty volumes in ten years until, by the self-inflicted punishment of debauchery and drugs on a body already racked by syphilis he broke down and died in 1893.

Maupassant was, by his very nature, hardly in sympathy with the aims of the naturalists, so his leaving caused little surprise. But Joris Huysmans' departure in 1883 affected Zola greatly. Following his conversion to naturalism, Huysmans set out to explore its potential with an urgent dedication, even outdoing Zola in transcribing the details of the sordid side of life into fiction. He was also one of its most spirited defenders, constantly irritating the critics with his gently mocking tone:

> Green pustules or rosy flesh, we touch them both because they both exist, because the boor merits study just as much as the most perfect of men, because fallen women abound in our cities and have a right there just as much as honest women.
> Art cannot confine itself to celebrating the marriage of worthy young men and amiable maidens who timidly lower their eyes and bite the ends of their fingers; art cannot be limited to adopting the role established by Dickens: to bring a tear to the eye of families gathered together in the evening or to lighten the tedium of convalescence. Art has nothing to do with shame or shamelessness. A novel that is dirty is a novel that is badly written, and that is all there is to it.

Within a couple of years, however, Huysmans had touched the four brick walls that enclosed the naturalist philosophy and renounced it with the publication of *À Rebours* in 1884. The novel satirised the decadence of the country's art, literature and language, and although the ideas projected in it are far superior to its qualities as fiction, the novel was tremendously fashionable, striking a particularly responsive chord with the idea that man, individually and collectively, could only look forward to progressive degeneration. It was a belief held by many pessimistic thinkers of the time, and Huysmans provided them with a seductive hymnal. In *The Picture of Dorian Gray*, Oscar Wilde even ascribed Huysmans's novel as being one of the principal influences in the corruption of his hero. Huysmans later became immersed in mysticism, a member of the French literary establishment, a ferocious opponent of naturalism, and died a devout Roman Catholic.

With Maupassant and Huysmans gone, Zola was left with only his loyal but unproductive admirers. At about this time, he, too, came to realise that there was a vast gulf between the extremes of his naturalist theorising and his art, and lost interest in the fight. To be fair, Zola never relished the idea of being the leader of the naturalist 'school'; it was a position that had been thrust upon him. And it hurt him as much as his young followers that they were lampooned by the critics as his mindless slaves. Time and time again he insisted they were merely his friends in harmony with his ideas, and always fought for their recognition as individual writers. He was, I think, greatly relieved when the hot-air balloon of naturalism floated gently down to earth again, without injury to any of the occupants.

The dreams of a theatre crowd, standing and applauding thunderously and crying for *Author! Author!* still persisted in Zola's mind. In a way it was understandable; few things can be so immediately satisfying, so personal and so stimulating as an enraptured audience wanting to pay homage to the playwright who has given them so much delight; by contrast any acclaim a novelist may win is distant in time and place from the actual scene of his labours. So he continued to write for the theatre. Unfortunately, failure followed failure; in this he was to join the distinguished ranks of Balzac, Goncourt, Daudet and even Flaubert. His third play, *Les Héritiers Rabourdin*, had been performed at the Cluny Theatre back in 1874, just after the appearance of *The Conquest of Plassans*. The public stayed away and the critics panned it. Four years later, in May 1878, *Le Bouton de rose*, a three-act farce, drew a similar response, and his efforts to interest the Comédie Française star Sarah Bernhardt in *Renée*, a spin-off from *The Kill*, proved to be abortive on account of its incest theme and an argument between La Bernhardt and the theatre management. Perhaps a little self-satisfied with the success of his novel *L'Assommoir*, the theatrical jolt was just the kind of reverse calculated to speed the stubborn author forward. 'It's made me younger!' he confided to Goncourt after *Le Bouton de rose* had closed at his own request, 'It's given me a new lease of life!'

Although he was as determined as ever to storm the stage, Zola finally got the message after his five successive disappointments; he had little talent for writing original plays. On the other hand friends had suggested that his novels should be adapted for the stage. *L'Assommoir* was a raging success as a novel, so why not as a play? With the help of two collaborating dramatists, the novel was reshaped into a script involving ten tableaux for twenty-nine actors, and it premiered at the Ambigue Theatre in January 1879.

Perhaps anticipating a débâcle of the kind they witnessed at the first night of *Le Bouton de rose*, when the second half of the play was inaudible because of the heckling, the first night of *L'Assommoir* was booked out weeks in advance. Zola was somewhat dazed to see it well received, although the applause was considerably tempered by sheer surprise. The critics, though, were not to be cheated, and roughed up their old enemy in the press; but despite them the play was an undoubted success and continued for 300 performances.

He also had another success with *Nana*, which was adapted for the stage by William Busnach, one of the co-authors of *L'Assommoir*, with Zola collaborating. Although most of the so-called shocking incidents in the narrative were omitted, the play opened at the Ambigue and ran for a hundred performances. In one of the early performances the leading role was played by a statuesque, sensual actress of forty, Léontine Massin. All Paris, apparently, flocked to the theatre to see her, and the success of it all went to Léontine's head to such an extent that she began to play Nana in real life, taking the theatre manager as her lover, causing scenes in public and squandering his money at such a rate that he eventually shot himself. Although the occasion was marred by this tragedy, with *L'Assommoir* and then *Nana* Zola the novelist had finally triumphed at the footlights.

The puffs of wind that in 1880 cracked the foundations of the naturalist group were merely the spent forces of a violent storm which threw three thunderbolts into Zola's life.

In April of that year one of his closest friends died, Edmond Duranty, co-founder of the realist school and an important early influence on the young Zola who was mortified that such a gifted man should die with his work unrecognised by an indifferent public. The second thunderbolt came a month later: a telegram from Maupassant told him that Flaubert had died suddenly of apoplexy. Zola shivered apprehensively in the calm that followed, his own mortality naked to a strange, heart-piercing chill. The wild-eyed Viking giant had been struck down in the middle of a great satire he was composing, and he was not yet sixty. Zola was forty, with enough achievements behind him to satisfy most creative writers, but it was the future that alarmed him. The *Rougon-Macquart* chronicle was still less than half completed, and the mountain towering above him under the threatening skies suddenly looked unscalable. The air was already rarefied; each succeeding movement as he climbed became more difficult, more painful. And now, more hopeless. And there was still that vague threat in the air, of a storm renewing itself for another onslaught, the crackling, highly charged warning of a holocaust. And then it came, six months later, the third thunderbolt: Zola's mother died.

The crisis soon revealed some disquieting aspects of Zola's psychological make-up. He had experienced, from his youth, periodic outbreaks of a nervous kind ranging from mild melancholia to acute depression. From many accounts he also suffered from a variety of psychosomatic complaints which for no apparent organic reason would rack his body with pain and fits of trembling. Although a post-mortem at the end of his life revealed that his heart was perfectly healthy, he was convinced throughout it that he had heart disease, and suffered many of the symptoms. For most of the time these disorders were effectively hidden behind their owner's robust and portly exterior, and his depressions and melancholic periods were easily dismissed by his friends with a not unkindly 'There's Zola grumbling and pitying himself again.' Goncourt, in his journal, describes Zola in 1880 as rather like a child, complaining 'of kidney trouble, of gravel, of palpitations, and then talking of his mother's death and how it had left a great gap in his home, speaking with great emotion and viewing his own future with dread'. As it turned out, though, the novelist was not crying 'wolf' for no reason.

The shock from the successive bereavements produced in Zola a paralysing black despair, and seeing no more foot-holds on his lonely rock-face he let go, abandoning himself to the dark abyss below. Even his only solace, those long hours of writing in his study, proved useless in the face of the mental agonies and nervous fears which tortured him day and night. Hallucinations of his mother's coffin being passed out of an upstairs window at Médan – because the staircase was too narrow – obsessed him, and released memories of his father's coffin in similar circumstances. His fear of death became so powerful that he transmitted his dread to Alexandrine; they would lie awake through endless nights with the lamp lit, silent and ashamed of their terror. He gave up his journalism; his confidence ebbed away and his normal self-assurance crumbled under the intense pressures. His concentration suffered too; time and time again he began work on his next novel, *Joy of Life*, only to abandon the effort after a few days. Finally, unable to resolve his intentions for the book he put it away and started on *Piping Hot!* instead. Then, as winter approached in 1882, the accumulation of disorders which had been tormenting him for two years combined in a single, crushing blow. The crisis sent him to bed, helpless, trembling and physically ill, and there he stayed for several days. Then, at the end of October, he began, in his painstaking way, to resume his climb.

Whenever he was able throughout his illness, he continued to write; but a measure of its seriousness is the two-year gap between the publication of *Nana*, in February 1880, and *Piping Hot!*, published in April 1882. Until now he had turned out a novel every year. Indicating a slow but positive recovery, *The Ladies' Paradise* followed in March 1883, and a month later he opened his long abandoned notes on *Joy of Life*. This novel was to be a therapeutic vehicle for the recuperating novelist. It served as a personal receptacle for the phantasmagoria of his neuroses, and he poured them out into its pages, although if he'd believed this transference would put an end to his black despairs he was to be disappointed. But *Joy of Life* was something else for Zola, too: an inner debating forum for a problem which had increasingly obsessed

159

him – the very elemental question of whether life was worthwhile or not
Perhaps he would discover, like the philosopher Kierkegaard, that though life
might be understood backwards, it must be lived forwards.

11

Middle-class
Life and Love

The middle-class citizens of the Second Empire were never really the equivalent of the middle classes of modern Britain, the group that has, by one political definition, 'foresight, thrift, independence, concern for their families, and a preference for deferred, rather than instant, gratification and reward'. With its twin-set enclaves and cocktail belts the English middle class is sometimes mocked though good-humouredly tolerated by the rest of the population and, with the exception of the orthodox Marxist, not at all the target of hatred. But by many accounts the Second Empire middle classes were an obnoxious lot indeed: dishonest, conniving, mercenary – and promiscuous to a dangerous, self-defeating degree. The former characteristics provided Zola with a theme for *The Ladies' Paradise*; but it was the latter peculiarity that his angry pen was to lash in his next novel, *Piping Hot!*

By exposing the rotten kernel of accepted mid-nineteenth-century middle-class morality, Zola showed considerable insight into a problem which had been exercising his agile mind for some time, and early in 1881 he had written a study, 'Adultery Among the Middle Class' for *Le Figaro*. He saw the problem of promiscuity as largely the result of miseducation; it wasn't so much a matter of children not being told the facts of life, but rather their access to those frightful novels which presented love exclusively in an unreal, romantic light. Little wonder, then, that the wedding night was invariably attended by traumatic shock, and married lives by subsequent adulteries, forced on each partner by sheer physical desperation. In particular the middle-class code insisted that the ideal woman be respectable, chaste and even devoid of all desire. The answer was to give the nod to the practice of married men having mistresses, into whose bodies they might spill their filth, thus sparing chaste wives. From the privilege of our sexually enlightened position, relatively speaking, it is easy to imagine the fearful consequences of such a moral code. In fact, we don't have to imagine, for they are forthrightly and comprehensively documented in this superb novel, *Piping Hot!*

In the previous chapter we saw how Zola, after several attempts, finally abandoned work on *Joy of Life*; its theme was too painfully close to his own predicament. So, in a way, was *Piping Hot!*, the novel he chose to work on

161

instead. But while *Joy of Life* promised a therapeutic outlet for his neuroses – the morbid nightmares and the obsessive fear of dying which followed upon his mother's death, but which he couldn't bring himself to face at the time – *Piping Hot!* offered some release from his marital frustrations.

Although this aspect of the novelist's life has already been mentioned and will be explored more fully in a later chapter, it is clear that the great bed in which Zola and Alexandrine slept was not often warmed by physical love, and this had been the case for many years. True, to the public and even to close friends, their marriage seemed loving and content; and in this they successfully exercised one of the skills of the middle classes, that of putting on a false front. But behind this façade of serenity lay a sterile marriage, a void which drove the novelist to his study each morning to seek the anodyne of his relentless, self-imposed workload to relieve his misery and frustration. For this purpose, *Piping Hot!*, a savage satire on the treacherous emptiness of middle-class marriage, was the ideal punching-bag. Consequently, the novel is not the ruthlessly objective study of middle-class morals and manners it is often made out to be; too much of the author's personal passion intrudes. Remarkably though, there is no vengeance expressed against Alexandrine, nor any masochistic whipping of himself, which we might reasonably expect to detect among his characters and in the narrative; no, society is the culprit again, with its idiotic conventions and destructive hypocrisies controlling the lives of the inhabitants of the apartments on the Rue de Choiseul. The savagery in the book is directed point-blank at the middle-class code; the characters, good and bad, are blameless, and they alone receive the author's pity.

This, however, did not prevent Zola from detesting the middle classes in real life, a dislike which probably stemmed from his provincial boyhood. It was also the contempt of ignorance, because he had very little personal knowledge of them – even though he had admitted in his defensive preface to *L'Assommoir* that he was a *bourgeois* himself. His early bohemian years in Paris, followed by a highly circumscribed life among writers and publishers, had conspired to separate him from the clerks, public servants, businessmen and professional people who made up the Parisian middle class. Yet, in 1881, he set out to write his novel about the morals of this class, knowing that its veracity would depend on his reflecting all the subtle shadings by which a reader might identify the hypocrisy, inanity and weakness he wished to satirise. But lack of knowledge about a subject was never an insurmountable obstacle to the anything but gregarious novelist. In the first place he had as a model the magnificent *L'Éducation sentimentale*, published a dozen or so years before, Flaubert' mid-century portrait of the middle class. Although the novel drove him to professional despair with its unblinking realism, it was undoubtedly his inspiration. For further documentation he turned to his young colleagues, particularly to Joris Huysmans, with his equally sour view of the middle class, and to Henri Céard. According to notes left by Zola, they must have regaled him for hours with tales of bourgeois vanity, infidelity and dishonesty and

ese, supplemented by the novelist's enlarging imagination, provided the
ulk of the documentary material for *Piping Hot!*

To outline the plot of this novel would be to describe the mechanism of a
ck. The point is, for someone who wants to lock a door, it works. *Piping Hot!*
orks through a complex arrangement of interlocking levers; push one and all
e others react in a predetermined way. Having said that, I will confine myself
describing the action of Zola's lock, rather than its mechanism.

The initial impetus is supplied by the introduction of a vain, ambitious,
nooth-talking young stud, Octave Mouret, into a fashionable block of
artments in the Rue de Choiseul, a solidly middle-class district in Paris. It is
rough Octave's restless, roving eyes that we explore the building and its
ccupants, both hiding a fundamental shoddiness beneath a veneer of
spectability.

Octave, in his early twenties, is ambitious for success and sexual conquest,
d several of the idle, sleek matrons are appraised for the roles they might
lay in helping him up the social ladder. Madame Compardon, for instance,
ith her mysterious ailment; Madame Valérie, with her fiery, challenging eyes;
d, above all, the cool, crisply efficient Madame Hédouin, proprietress of a
shion store, the Ladies' Paradise, from whom he obtains employment. Then
ere is Madame Josserand who desperately hawks her daughters Berthe and
ortense around in search of rich and well-bred husbands. Her own husband,
an equally desperate attempt to keep up appearances, is martyred to writing
dresses on wrapper labels for a publisher at three francs a thousand,
orking through every night so that his daughters might have a new dress, or
eir party guests some expensive cake. But however hard they work at it, the
acks beneath the paint show through, as in this delightful passage describing
e of the Josserands' receptions. Berthe, their daughter, is commanded by
er mother to play the piano for the guests.

> The girl attacked the piece without the least sign of nervousness; albeit her mother
> never took her eyes off her, with the air of a sergeant ready to punish with a slap the
> least technical blunder. What mortified her was that the instrument, cracked and
> wheezy after fifteen years of daily scale-playing, had not the sonorous quality of tone
> possessed by the Duveyriers' grand piano. Moreover, as she thought, her daughter
> never would play loud enough.
> After the tenth bar Octave, with a rapt expression, and keeping time with his head
> to the more florid passages, no longer listened. He watched the audience, noting the
> polite efforts on the part of the men to pay attention, and the affected delight of the
> women. He surveyed this collection of human beings left to themselves, quit of their
> daily harassing cares, which had deepened the gloom on their tired faces. The
> mothers, it was plain, cherished fond dreams of marrying their daughters, as they
> stood there with mouths agape and ferocious teeth, unconsciously letting themselves
> go. It was by the weird madness that pervaded this drawing-room – a ravenous
> appetite for sons-in-law - that these middle-class women were devoured, as they
> listened to the piano's asthmatic utterances. (53)

It is soon obvious to Octave that he is living in a hot-house of frustrated
nsuality, but breaking through the conventions is far from being the
ush-over he thought it would be. In five months, after being rebuffed several
mes, his only conquest is the shameful, near-rape of Marie, the young wife of

a clerk, across her kitchen table. Madame Hédouin, nicknamed 'Polar Bear' because she seems always twenty degrees below zero, is as resistant as ever to his charms. When, in a reckless moment, he decides to breathe more hotly on his employer's icy white neck he is no match for her self-possession, and no judge of her fortress-like frigidity, either, for she declines his overture with chilling unconcern.

Confused by this unnatural glaciation of hot blood, Octave feels he has no alternative but to resign from the Ladies' Paradise. Then, at another gathering, he receives a further lesson in middle-class morality.

> At the same moment, Trublot, on the sofa, was leaning over and whispering to Octave.
> 'By the way,' he asked, 'would you like me to get you an invitation from a lady at whose house one has some fun?'
> And, as his companion wished to know what kind of lady, he added, as he pointed to Duveyrier:
> 'His mistress.'
> 'Never!' exclaimed Octave, in amazement.
> Trublot slowly opened and shut his eyes. It was so. When one had married a wife who was not obliging, who appeared disgusted at the idea of having babies, and who thrashed the piano until all the dogs of the neighbourhood fell sick, why, one went elsewhere about town to find consolation.
> 'Let us make marriage moral, gentlemen; let us make it moral,' repeated Duveyrier, stiltedly, with his inflamed visage, in which Octave now noted the traces of disordered blood, the result of secret excesses.   (5)

Note, incidentally, how the final two lines, with their hint of inherited degeneracy, reduce the effect of the hypocritical comment, an example of Zola's unfortunate habit of not knowing when to stop.

Eventually, Madame Josserand's efforts bear fruit and Berthe is married off to a seedy specimen of a man, whose neuralgia and tics are offset by his financial prospects. Madame Josserand is jubilant; Berthe, though, is worse off than before – her husband is a skinflint with both money and ardour. Bored and idle, she indulges her sensuality by flirting with Octave, who, by now maddened with frustration, throws her down and takes her by force. Berthe submits like a mute, compliant doll, but at least she is spared the kitchen table. Although their assignations are impossibly difficult, for not the least breath of scandal can be allowed in the building, they become lovers.

Even so, Octave is forced to buy her continued favours by supplying her with the pocket-money denied by her husband, and it is only for this that Berthe returns to his room. They also use one of the servants' bedrooms on the top floor, and one morning they are trapped there. This is the time when all the servants open their windows to the courtyard to discuss the scandalous goings-on of their employers; and Octave and Berthe, forced to listen, learn that their affair is far from secret.

> 'I say, pot-belly, up there! When you had your first baby, did it come out in front or behind?'
> At such coarse jesting all the kitchens were convulsed with merriment, while Adèle, looking scared, rejoined:
> 'A baby? no, none of that! It's not allowed; and besides, I don't want one.'

'My girl,' said Lisa, gravely, 'everybody may have a baby, and I don't suppose the Lord made you different from anyone else!'

Then they talked of Madame Campardon, who, at any rate, had no fears on that score; it was the only pleasant thing in her existence. Then all the ladies of the house were discussed in succession. Madame Juzeur, who took her own precautions; Madame Duveyrier, who was disgusted with her husband; Madame Valérie, who got her babies made for her out-of-doors, because her precious husband wasn't man enough to make the tail of one even. Then from the fetid hole there came gross bursts of laughter.

Berthe again grew pale. Waiting thus, she was afraid to leave the room. She looked down in confusion, as if outraged in Octave's presence. Indignant with these servants, he felt that their talk was becoming too filthy, and that to embrace her was impossible. His desire ebbed away, leaving him weary and extremely sad. Then Berthe trembled. Lisa had just mentioned her by name.

'Talking of high jinks, I know someone who seems to go it pretty hot! I say, Adèle, isn't it true that your Mademoiselle Berthe was up to all sorts of games when you used to wash her petticoats?'

'And now,' said Victoire, 'she gets her husband's clerk to turn her over, and shake out all the dust.'

'Hush!' cried Hippolyte, gently.

'What for? Her pig of a cook isn't there to-day. Sly devil, she is, that looks as if she'd eat you if you mention her mistress! She's a Jewess, you know, and they say she murdered somebody once at her place. Perhaps the handsome Octave gets her in a quiet corner too. His governor must have engaged him just to make babies for him, the great booby!'

Then Berthe, evidently suffering unutterable anguish, looked at her lover, imploringly, as she stammered out:

'Good God! good God!'

Octave caught hold of her hand and pressed it. He too, was choking with impotent wrath. What was to be done? He dared not show himself and silence those hussies. The foul talk went on, talk such as Berthe had never yet heard, while the cesspool brimmed over, as each morning it had done, close to her, although she had no suspicion of its existence. (53)

By this time the pot, heated by so many adulterous fires, is about to boil over. The nocturnal comings and goings, from apartment to apartment, from bed to bed, leave one breathless; in the hush of the night the loudest sound is not a snore but the collective creaking of adulterous bedsprings. When Octave and Berthe are caught by her distraught husband in the young man's room a storm breaks that shakes the building from basement to attic but, like the well-ordered house it is, no scandal leaks outside its gate. Octave, who had been working for his mistress's husband, returns to the Ladies' Paradise; unexpectedly M. Hédouin dies and the young man is surprised to receive a proposal of marriage from his frigid, widowed employer, although as a partner rather than as a lover. Thus he escapes the worst of the turmoil he caused, for the recriminations continue. Berthe's father, shattered by his daughter's conduct, is brought near to death. Another husband unsuccessfully attempts suicide, shooting off his jaw and losing a good many teeth in the process. But, in the end, the most outrageous behaviour is accommodated by the families who occupy the building, which continues to slumber on, all its spurious dignity intact.

As we read through this remarkable novel we become aware, by degrees, of the interlocked maze of hypocrisy which supplies the creaking foundation for

165

the overlying morality of the place. Its exposé is most naked in the relationship
between the middle-class households and their working-class servants. Thus
while adultery runs rampant up and down the grand staircase, a carpenter, the
building's sole working-class occupant, is refused admission for his wife by the
landlord.

> 'It is scandalous, disgraceful! I won't allow such a thing in my house!' Then
> addressing the workman, who at first seemed somewhat abashed, 'Send that woman
> away at once! At once, do you hear? We don't want any women brought in here.'
> 'But she's my wife!' replied the carpenter, with a scared look. 'She is in service, and
> only comes once a month, when her people let her have a day off. That's the plain
> truth about it. It's not your place to prevent me from sleeping with my wife, I should
> think!'
> Then both porter and landlord lost their heads.
> 'I give you notice to quit,' stuttered old Vabre, 'and, meanwhile, I forbid you to
> make a brothel of my premises! Gourd, turn that person into the street. No, sir, none
> of your nonsense with me. If a man is married, he ought to say so. Hold your tongue
> and let me have no more of your insolence!'   (5?

In another instance a young single woman, apparently respectable, is taken
in as a tenant. Soon, however, it becomes obvious that she is not only pregnant
but worse – she is a working girl! – a fact which outrages the doorkeeper
Although a former servant himself he has now assumed the virtues of the
families who employ him, applying the house rule of 'no dogs and no women'
with the vigour of a martinet. The woman's lease expires on the very day her
labour pains begin, but she is turned out just the same. Zola uses the incident to
dramatise the cruelty of the middle-class double standard.

> At a quarter to twelve the girl appeared, her face as white as wax, looking as sad, as
> despondent as ever. She could hardly walk, and until she got out into the street
> Monsieur Gourd was all in a tremble. Just as she was giving up her key, Duveyrier
> came through the hall, so heated by his night that the red blotches on his brow looked
> as if they were bleeding. He put on a haughty air, an air severely, implacably moral, as
> the poor thing went past him. Shameful and resigned, she bowed her head, and
> walked out after the little truck with the same despairing gait as she had come on the
> day that the black funeral hangings had enveloped her.
> It was then only that Monsieur Gourd had his triumph. As though it was the
> work-girl's belly that had removed all unhealthiness from the house, all those
> shameful things that caused the very walls to blush, he exclaimed to the landlord:
> 'Well, Sir that's a good riddance! We shall be able to breathe now, for, upon my
> word, it was getting positively disgusting! It's like a hundred-weight off my chest. In a
> respectable house like this, you see, sir, there oughtn't to be any women, least of all
> work-women.'   (5?

Nowhere in the narrative, however, are the hypocritical posturings of the
middle-class characters more savagely denounced, nor more dramatically
than when the magistrate Duveyrier proudly announces that he has passed
five-year gaol sentence on a woman who murdered her newborn baby. The
unfortunate woman is, in fact, the same woman who has earlier been turned
out of the apartments and who has passed the magistrate returning from
night of debauchery. Duveyrier speaks with a new authority in his voice, the
strange result of the jaw injury caused by his suicide attempt. And, as he speaks
in his warm parlour, one of the servants of the house, alone in a freezing attic

oom, is herself giving birth to a child, conceived by the man to whom the
nagistrate is speaking.

As I said, the plot of *Piping Hot!* is an exceedingly complicated lock.

Considering Zola's lack of intimate knowledge of the class of people he was
writing about it is not surprising that contemporary reviewers found plenty to
riticise in *Piping Hot!*; the author, for one thing, had failed to capture the
haracteristic nuances of middle-class speech. Not that, a century later, this
natters in the least, and especially to English readers; Zola's portrait of this
ection of nineteenth-century French society is, with its impressionistic
nsights, one of the most vivid we have. If his ear was a little out of tune, his nose
vas not; it could detect hypocrisy a mile away.

Not unnaturally, the novel wasn't liked in certain quarters; Zola was accused
f 'stalking truth between the morgue and the garbage dump' and *Le Figaro*
xploded in exasperation, 'It is about time Paris avenged herself on M. Zola's
utrages!' But these reactions were to be expected and, in any case, the novelist
imself was quite pleased with his achievement. With its seventy diverse
haracters playing their parts in a compact drama *Piping Hot!* was a triumph of
rganisation over detail, an exposé of a high technical order. Many thoughtful
ritics, though, while admitting the novel swarmed with humanity, also
uggested it swarmed with too many ideas and too many characters of
alculated ordinariness; and that in many ways the book was a cliché of
aturalism. Zola was not blind to these faults; to him *Piping Hot!* was a model of
recision and neatness, with no heroic overtones and no lyrical flights. There
re no moments of great tragedy, no depths of despair, no monstrous
xtravagances in the novel, it is true; its encephalograph is a level line disturbed
nly by occasional blips. But what it has is the density of a strong, dangerous
urrent, bearing with it a moving mass of helpless figures. If the author could
e accused of any fault, it would be his failure to discipline his own passions in
he novel. 'But all this', he wrote to Céard, commenting on the criticism, 'is
imply an academic question; for I am very satisfied with *Pot-Bouille*.' Zola's
nstinct was right, for it is his passion that breathes life into what might
therwise have been a brilliant, if arid, technical feat.

In selecting an apartment house as the sole setting for the novel – an idea that
as been used in hundreds of novels, plays and films since – Zola reveals that
nexhaustible ingenuity we have come to expect from him. The building
ecomes a kind of God's Little Doll's House, with the front wall knocked out so
ve can voyeurise to our heart's content. Peering at the puppet-like occupants it
s often difficult to discover exactly what is going on, and to what purpose, like
ome oriental opera. For although there is no lack of intrigues, assignations
nd amatory flurries in its pages *Piping Hot!* has about it a pervasive *ennui*
vhich draws the characters to each other and into bed without love, without
oy, without even any tangible satisfaction. The wonder of dawning love is
educed to a nervous, desperate game in which the players know too many
heoretical moves for their own good. The characters have no more depth than

167

plastic counters and when it comes to action they never leave the bland flatnes of the games table. Promises of emotional blow-ups fizzle to nothing. A suicid attempt inevitably fails. The carnality of the middle class is uniformly grey

A common complaint about *Piping Hot!* is that while on the one hand Zol attempts a grand generalisation by indicting the whole middle-class spectrum his main characters are too extreme as individuals to represent it accuratel Many years later, André Gide made this point in a different way; it was the ver *excess* of the novel that pleased him, he wrote, with its brutality and lack c subtlety. There is no getting away from it, Zola's heavy hand is evident on to many pages to be ignored. Repeatedly he makes a delicate thrust, only to follo with a sabre slash. In a conversation near the end of the novel between a docto and a priest on the subject of human frailty, the doctor's neat comment spoiled by a burst of the author's moralising:

> Both were sharers of the self-same secrets; if the priest heard the ladie confessions, the doctor, for the last thirty years, had attended the mothers in the confinements while prescribing for the daughters.
> 'God had forsaken them,' said the abbé.
> 'No,' replied the doctor; 'don't drag God into it. It's a question of bad health or ba training, that's all.'
> Then, going off at a tangent, he began violently to abuse the Empire; under republic things would surely be better. And amid all this rambling talk, the fligh speech of a man of mediocre intelligence, there came the just remarks of th experienced physician thoroughly cognisant of all his patients' weak points. He d not spare the women, some of whom were brought up as dolls and made eith corrupt or crazy thereby, while others had their sentiments and passions perverted h hereditary neurosis, who, if they sinned, sinned vulgarly, foolishly, without desire without pleasure. Nor was he less merciful to the men – fellows who merely ruine their constitutions whilst hypocritically pretending to lead sober, virtuous, and god lives. And in all this Jacobin frenzy one heard, as it were, the inexorable death-knell a whole class, the collapse and putrefaction of the bourgeoisie, whose rotten pro kept cracking of themselves.   (5

The last paragraph is superfluous, for the characters have amp demonstrated any lesson contained in the sermon. But perhaps this moralisir was more of a defensive mechanism, behind which Zola could shield h considerable ignorance of middle-class life in all its shadings. His guess-wo was undoubtedly inspired, but on one occasion at least the underpinnings his documentation were proved to be somewhat shaky. A court action whi arose out of the serialisation of the novel throws an interesting light on th suspicion. In the serialised version, which began in *Le Gaulois* in January 188 the would-be suicide, the magistrate Duveyrier in the later version, was calle Duverdy. It happened that at the Court of Appeal in Paris there was a lawyer the same name; moreover his description tallied uncomfortably with that Zola's character. Having established that the novelist could have borrowed h name, character and face from some election posters which had been display around Médan, the real Duverdy applied for an injunction to stop serialisatio of the novel on the grounds that it was obscene, and thus use of his name w defamatory. Zola lost the case, and had to change the name of his character Duveyrier. The incident would have blown over had not Zola puffed hims up with rage at the charge that *Piping Hot!* was obscene; as a result the author let loose an impressive barrage of moral reasons to justify the carnal pattern of the narrative. It was another step backwards, begun with his defence of *L'Assommoir*, into the corner of moral justification. Fortunately the moralising spent itself largely in the columns of newspapers rather than in the remaining *Rougon-Macquart* novels.

As a consequence of all this, one must have reservations about the documentary accuracy of *Piping Hot!* but this in no way seriously detracts from its qualities as an outstanding novel. In any case the intrusion of the author's personal enmity towards the middle classes is only too obvious; to him, as a class, they were animals. The sexual encounters in the book are little removed from the compulsive couplings of animals; and, pushing his contempt to the limit, he even extends the bestial simile to childbirth. The servant girl who is later sentenced by Duveyrier for killing her newborn baby simply did what a bitch might instinctively do to a pup if she were unable to feed and rear it.

But this is carping, for *Piping Hot!* is a novel of awesome technical accomplishment, textured with melodrama, intrigue, satire and humour, and, despite the apparent unworthiness of its characters and its author's contempt for a whole class of society, is threaded with an ever-present compassion.

If *Piping Hot!* stripped the middle classes naked, Zola's next novel clothed them again, for its setting is the bustling interior of a huge Parisian store with its rambling fashion departments, seductive displays, fitting rooms and clothing sales.

Ostensibly the story of the establishment and rise of a big retail store, *The Ladies' Paradise* is really the vehicle for Octave Mouret's sexual drive to get into top gear after merely ticking over in the previous novel. But the store itself, made extra-dimensional by Zola's observational powers and vivid imagination, intrudes and captivates. With his book-keeper's instinct Zola very quickly established a rapport with the commercial world, and in this novel he examines, with an insight into the psychology of retailing as valid today as it was a century ago, the world within a world of the department store. The novel is also the first of a series of investigations into the industrial and economic life of France in which the author cautiously explores how socialist principles might alleviate the all too apparent evils of nineteenth-century capitalism. The capitalist ogre in this instance is the retail monolith, with its power to crush and obliterate its weaker rivals. *The Ladies' Paradise* was published in 1883, yet many passages in it could have been written yesterday; in the dynamics of retailing very little has changed in the ensuing century.

Unlike *Piping Hot!* Zola did not rely on his friends for the documentation of *The Ladies' Paradise*. For days at a time he wandered through the big stores already established in Paris: the Bon Marché, the Louvre, the Printemps and the Petit Sainte-Thomas – witnessing the excitement of the sales, talking to the shop-girls, interviewing disgruntled nearby shopkeepers who were struggling against the competition from the retail giants, asking about wages, profits and shoplifting, chatting with the customers – so that, in just two or three weeks of dedicated observation, he walked away with the knowledge and 'feel' of the business that would have taken an average employee years to acquire.

The Ladies' Paradise, you may recall from *Piping Hot!*, was the former small drapery shop owned by the frigid Madame Hédouin, who, at the end of that novel, married Octave, the salesman adventurer from the south. Owing to an unfortunate accident, in between books as it were, Madame Hédouin dies, leaving her young husband as the sole owner of the store and also a millionaire. This novel, although not a sequel to *Piping Hot!*, continues to follow the career of Octave, former stud, now matured lover, possessor and exploiter of women.

Octave shares the spotlight with twenty-year-old Denise Baudu, who, at the beginning of the novel, arrives in Paris from Cherbourg with her two young brothers, all of them orphans, hoping that her Uncle Baudu will take them into his family. It requires all Baudu's family loyalty to do so, however, for he is a small draper in the shadow of the Ladies' Paradise and like dozens of other small traders in the vicinity is already suffering from the competition.

Uncle Baudu is bitterly resentful of the big store's astonishing success and, whitefaced with impotent rage, he stands in front of his little shop for hours watching the crowds pour into the Ladies' Paradise, while hardly a customer comes his way. Denise, on the other hand, is immediately fascinated by the tinselled monster. At this early stage Zola establishes the major conflict which will hold the reader until the end of the novel, the life-and-death struggle between the old-fashioned shops, specialising in one kind of merchandise, and the rising department store, sprawling over half a block and decked out like a circus. We are, in fact, witnessing the development of the modern retail giant of the 1860s, so new in concept that old hands like Baudu simply can't understand the reasons for its success:

> 'And gloves,' added Madame Baudu; 'isn't it monstrous? He has even dared to add a glove department! Yesterday, as I was going along the Rue Neuve-Saint-Augustin, I saw Quinette, the glover, at his door, looking so downcast that I hadn't the heart to ask him how business was going.'
> 'And umbrellas,' resumed Baudu; 'that's the climax! Bourras feels sure that Mouret simply wants to ruin him; for, in short, where's the rhyme between umbrellas and drapery?... You've seen his display, haven't you? He always places his finest made-up goods there, surrounded by a framework of various cloths – a cheapjack parade to tempt the women. Upon my word, I should be ashamed to use such means!'
> (55)

The architect of this new retail philosophy is Octave Mouret, whose store has grown to an enterprise with nineteen departments and 400 employees. But this, to Mouret, is only a start; his ambition is for the store to occupy an entire city block, to pander to the whims and needs of every woman in Paris. As a retail entrepreneur he seems ideally equipped for the task; women are his life, and he is always being carried away by some new love affair: '... his amorous affairs were a kind of advertisement for his sales; it seemed as though he was embracing the whole female sex in the same caress, the better to dazzle it and hold it at his mercy'.

170

Zola's intensive research into the revolutionary new retailing methods is injected in various ways into the novel and, among other things, we soon see that the psychology of selling to women is timeless. At a gathering at the apartment of Madame Desforges, the mistress he shares with the financier Baron Hartmann, Mouret outlines to the banker his sales philosophy:

> At last he came to something more important than all the facts already given, of supreme importance, indeed: he spoke of the exploitation of Woman. Everything else lead up to it, the capital ceaselessly renewed, the system of piling up goods, the low prices which attracted people, the marked prices which reassured them. It was Woman the shops were wrangling over in rivalry, it was Woman they caught in the everlasting snare of their bargains, after they had dazed her with their displays. They had awoken new desires in her weak flesh, they were an immense temptation to which she inevitably yielded, succumbing in the first place to purchases for the house, then won over by coquetry, finally completely enslaved. By increasing sales tenfold, by making luxury democratic, shops were becoming a terrible agency for spending; inspired as they were by the extravagances of fashion, which were growing ever more expensive, they were causing havoc in homes. And if, when she was in the shops, Woman was queen, adulated and humoured in her weaknesses, surrounded with attentions, she reigned there as an amorous queen whose subjects trade on her, and who pays for every whim with a drop of her own blood. Beneath the very charm of his gallantry, Mouret allowed the brutality of a Jew selling Woman by the pound to show through; he was building a temple to Woman, making a legion of shop-assistants burn incense before her, creating the rites of a new cult; he thought only of her, ceaselessly trying to devise even greater enticements; and, behind her back, when he had emptied her pockets and wrecked her nerves, he was full of the secret contempt of a man to whom a mistress has just committed the folly of yielding.
>
> 'Get the women,' he said to the Baron in a low voice, giving an impudent laugh as he did so, 'and you'll sell the world!'   (56)

A little further on Mouret proves his point to Hartmann by hypnotising the women present with some sales talk in his carefully modulated, flute-like salesman's voice.

> 'We have other materials which are amazingly inexpensive and yet sumptuous,' Mouret was continuing in his melodious voice. 'For example, I recommend our Cuir-d'Or to you, a taffeta with an incomparable sheen.... Amongst the fancy silks there are some charming patterns, designs chosen from thousands of others by our buyer; and for velvets, you will find an extremely rich collection of shades.... I warn you that a lot of cloth will be worn this year. You will see our matelassés, our Creviots....'
>
> They were no longer interrupting him, but were drawing in even closer in their circle, their lips slightly parted in a vague smile, their faces close together and craning forward, as if their whole being was yearning towards their temptor. Their eyes were growing dim, a slight shiver was running over the napes of their necks. And, in the midst of the heady scents which were rising from their hair, he maintained the composure of a conqueror. Between each sentence he went on taking little sips of tea, the perfume of which cooled down those other, more pungent scents, in which there was a touch of musk.   (56)

Meanwhile, Denise, unable to find work elsewhere, joins the staff of the Ladies' Paradise, the store so hated by her uncle. A poor provincial, she is cruelly teased by the other shop-girls, cold-shouldered by Madame Aurélie the departmental buyer, constantly worried about money – her low wages being insufficient to keep her two young brothers – and tortured by the demands the long hours make on her half-starved constitution. The ultimate torment is the

171

periodic sale, with the crowds, the impossible customers and the heavy work. Zola brilliantly describes several of these events, but perhaps none so graphically as a description of the chaos left after one of the sales.

> Inside, in the blaze of the gas jets which, burning in the dusk, had illuminated the crowning commotion of the sale, it was like a battlefield still hot from the massacre of materials. The salesmen, worn out with tiredness, were camping amidst the havoc of their cash-desks and counters, which looked as if they had been wrecked by the raging blast of a hurricane. The ground floor galleries were obstructed by a rout of chairs which made it difficult to get round them; in the glove department one had to step over a barricade of boxes, piled up round Mignot; in the wollens it was impossible to get through at all. Liénard was dozing on a sea of materials in which some half-destroyed stacks of cloth were still standing, like ruined houses swamped by an over-flowing river; further along, the white linen had snowed all over the ground, one stumbled against ice-flows of table-napkins, one walked on the soft flakes of handkerchiefs. Upstairs in the mezzanine departments the havoc was the same; furs littered the floor, ready-made clothes were heaped up like the trench-coats of disabled soldiers; the laces and underclothes, unfolded, creased, thrown down at random, looked as if a multitude of women had undressed there haphazard in a wave of desire; while downstairs, in the depths of the shop, the dispatch service, working full blast, was still disgorging the parcels with which it was bursting, and which were being carried away by the delivery vans in a final movement of the superheated machine. (56)

We now follow the workings of this giant machine through two pairs of eyes: through Mouret's, which gives us the management's perspective; and through Denise's, where we are in the midst of all the petty intrigues and love affairs of the staff, and perhaps also sharing their terror of hearing the hated five words *Proceed to the Pay Desk!* during the summer slump.

Denise, along with a hundred others, is sacked, and for many months lives in a squalid room above an old umbrella-maker's shop next to the Ladies' Paradise. Eventually finding work at a nearby silk shop she then shares with all the small shopkeepers their fear of the retail monster which is swallowing them up one by one. The silk shop, in a desperate battle for survival, is forced into a suicidal sales contest with the big store, inevitably to lose. And ruin is just around the corner for those who, like the umbrella-maker, refuse to sell their premises to the all-devouring giant.

Just before Denise is sacked, Mouret is somehow charmed by the skinny shop-girl. For a man with hundreds of beautiful, sophisticated and desirable women a finger-snap away his infatuation for Denise is unaccountable, except as a plot device. At any rate, when Mouret meets her one day in the street he invites her back to the store at a high salary, without really knowing why. 'An idiotic whim,' he muses afterwards. So Denise rejoins the big battalions and goes on to conquer her enemies in the store with stubborn gentleness and smiling persuasion.

Denise's return signals a secondary conflict which effectively revives the reader's interest now that the contest between the store and the small shops is more or less resolved: will she or will she not be seduced by her rich and powerful boss? Promoting her to assistant buyer seems as good a way as any to her heart, but Mouret is to be disappointed. When he invites her to dine with him she declines, for there is no secret among the staff as to the nature of the dessert. Even his sincere protestations of love are rebuffed, so that at his moment of triumph – at the end of a stock-taking day when his worth is calculated at eighty million francs – he is benumbed by the agonies of unrequited love. Denise is the first woman not to yield to him.

Mouret now spends his days in a despondent cloud, distracted during business deals and sublimating his pent-up passion by building vast extensions to the store – just as his creator's sexual frustrations were externalised in frenetic bursts of writing. Whether Zola was conscious of this or not, it was a phenomenon he could write about with considerable feeling, and Mouret's anguish is projected with sufficient conviction to avoid undue sentimentality.

The ending of *The Ladies' Paradise* is its least satisfactory aspect. The shopkeepers are finally obliterated amid pathetic scenes: Denise's aunt and cousin die and her uncle's business is ruined. The umbrella-maker's shop collapses under the strain of all the rebuilding going on about it, reduced to a muddy heap of rubble. Another small trader attempts suicide by hurling himself under an omnibus. Yet, at each calamity, at each cruel victory by the retail monster, Denise's respect and love for its master grows. However moved she is by the devastation she sees that it is a process of life, of progress, for which Mouret is blameless.

> That night, Denise once more could not sleep. She had now plumbed the depths of her impotence. She could do nothing to relieve the distress even of her own family. She had to witness to the bitter end the inexorable workings of life, which must have death in order that it may be continually renewed. She no longer fought against it, she accepted this rule of the struggle; but her woman's heart was filled with compassion, moved to tears and brotherly love for the whole of suffering humanity.... Mouret had invented this mechanism for crushing people, the brutal working of which aroused her indignation; he had strewn the neighbourhood with ruins, he had despoiled some and killed others; yet she loved him in spite of it for the grandeur of his achievement; and each time he committed some fresh excess of power, notwithstanding the flood of tears which overwhelmed her at the thought of the misery of the vanquished, which was sacrosanct, she loved him even more.   (56)

Thus even the driving force of greed, propelling that most artificial of man-made institutions, the department store, shelters under the compassionate canopy of Zola's ubiquitous regenerative theme. Mouret and Denise are at the mercy of the monster; they are no less its victims than the destroyed shopkeepers. Throughout the novel the author presents the store as a huge machine, feeding upon the cascade of bales and crates that tumbles into its basement belly, lubricated by the queues of willing victims who pour daily into its maw. On sale days Mouret stands on a staircase, his senses attuned to the components of its mechanism, the murmur of the sparse morning crowd as the machine cranks up, the shrill roar at top gear in the afternoon, the rattle of money at the cash desks. Even at night, when the clanking has ceased, it becomes an immense, dark belly, its metabolism suspended, its innards temporarily at rest, its interior shadows evoking the terror of a Piranesi prison.

Often, though, the mechanical symbolism gives way to vegetative imagery. The polished floors of the Ladies' Paradise may be a long way from the fields but this doesn't deter Zola from introducing his beloved fertility symbolism on to the counters and in the display windows of the store: 'The counters, symmetrically arranged, seemed like flower beds, changing the place into a garden where rows of flowers bloomed...' The store is at times heady with erotic symbolism, too; frothy lace peeps seductively from the narrative at unexpected moments: the fleshy odours of the crowd, the climactic hysteria of sale days, the licentious disorder of the underwear department where the garments 'conjured up visions of the lazy mornings that follow nights of love'.

But what of our hero and heroine? I find them both disappointing as characters. Having painstakingly constructed Mouret over the span of two novels as a man who, as an exploiter of women, can never be successful with them – 'Don't be silly!' Octave exclaims to a colleague on one occasion, 'The woman who can catch me hasn't been born yet, old man!' – there is inevitable disappointment and disbelief when he falls to his knees, vanquished by the virginal goodness of diminutive Denise. I know of a case in real life in which the owner of a large department store fell in love with and married one of the salesgirls, so I can't censure Zola for departing from realism. But the Octave Mouret from *Piping Hot!* is a character presented with steel-tipped detachment, with an arrogant belief in himself and an almost total disregard for others. Even allowing that his love was a genuine, mad product of the heart, or that he simply became obsessed with Denise because she was the only woman he couldn't have on his own terms – after the death of his first wife, Madame Hédouin, he vowed never to marry again – Mouret tends to turn into a sand sculpture towards the end of *The Ladies' Paradise*. As for Denise, she also suffers from an unaccountable breakdown of character in the closing stages of the novel. On several occasions she unhesitatingly places her moral principles ahead of opportunity; in fact Zola makes it clear that she is incapable of evil. At no point in the narrative does she ever yield to temptation. Her courage, her fortitude, honesty and gentleness, is inspiring, and her virginity is reserved exclusively for a loving relationship. Yet in the final pages she seems prepared to sell it for something considerably less. When it becomes obvious to her that Mouret is really suffering because of her indifference, she concludes that his torment is the price of his contempt for women; and thus he is redeemed, a much nobler man than he was before. But at the same time she realises her virginity is a powerful weapon, and using it she extracts from Mouret generous compensation for some of the ruined shopkeepers, and unheard-of amenities for the store's staff. Her love for Mouret comes up like thunder, and it is all a bit of a cheap trick. The truth is, I think, that Zola wanted Mouret's adventure to end on an optimistic note, and the successful conclusion of a love match always exudes a warm feeling. And we can see how Denise's compassion is already at work on Mouret's ruthless, exploitative nature; a workers' cooperative is just over the horizon. We can hardly condemn Zola for wanting to suggest, in the novel, that humanity and enlightenment might be a better basis for better business, but it is a pity he had to destroy the integrity of his characters to do it.

These weaknesses, however, hardly dilute the entertainment value of this exceptional novel. The descriptive passages, springing from Zola's astonishing gift for imaginatively enlarging his observation, are at times breathtaking in their effect. The complex workings of a department store, involving as they do an understanding of the art of seducing women, are eternally fascinating. And the duels between the store and its rivals, and between Mouret and Denise, give the reader a keen sense of involvement. If *The Ladies' Paradise* shares a resemblance to the institution it describes in that its shallowness and untidy corners are hidden behind an imposing façade, it also displays a diverting and varied charm and, on occasions, the ridiculous excitement of a great sale.

12

The Pitiless Pit:
Capital v. Humanity

Germinal was the novel that introduced me to Emile Zola. The *Everyman's* *Library* translation by Havelock Ellis came into my hands quite by accident in a Northern Australian mining camp in the late 1940s. In more than one sense I discovered Zola rather late in the day, or rather by several days, for the book, with its War Economy Standard paper and octavo format – ideal for recycling – had been requisitioned as lavatory paper. By the time I had occasion to use it, thirty pages – most of Part Six in fact – had been torn from the binding by the horny-handed philistines who made up most of the camp's population. I remember replacing it with another book from the canteen library, a Rider Haggard I think it was, and then completely losing myself for a day and a half in what to me, at eighteen, was nothing short of a revelation. Years later I managed to find another copy with all the pages intact, and since then have read it many times, in several translations, with increasing enjoyment.

It seems, from letters that Zola wrote about *L'Assommoir* in 1877, that during its composition he had realised that being mostly confined to family parlour, bedroom and corner bistro, the novel would not be the complete portrait of working-class life he'd intended it to be. It certainly exposed the crushing load borne by the exploited workers, but what it did not do was explore the political and social roles of the class, and its hopes and aspirations. This omission concerned him and eventually led to the concept of *Germinal* in which the workers would use the ladder of socialism to try and scale the economic walls that imprisoned them.

At the time he began to plan *Germinal*, socialism was emerging as a political force; at least, through strikes and agitation, it had brought about some humanitarian legislation. The regulation of the employment of women in mines was one advance; it was forbidden in 1874, although children over the age of twelve were still expected to work the twelve-hour day which was universal even into the 1890s. Unions were legalised, but only after a two-year struggle, in 1884. But although these movements were rumbling across the country, the middle-class managers of the economic life of France were obstinately blind to the warnings and heedless of their implications. A half-column grey, close-set type in a newspaper about some distant strike was too easily ignored... but, thought Zola, what if the arguments and warnings were to be dramatised in a novel?

By the beginning of 1884 Zola was clear about the kind of book he wanted to write, but where would this life-and-death conflict between labour and capital take place? Bitter strikes in textile factories were frequent, but somehow they lacked the portentous quality he was searching for. He finally decided on a mine, a coal mine, but apart from a few books he'd read which touched on the mining industry he knew almost nothing about it. Quite possibly his choice reflected a sympathy for the miner's lot which today, now that some of the facts about coal mining are known, is more widespread. Miners' strikes seem to involve more hardship, injustice and bloodshed than those in any other industry.

Subconscious reasons could also have been at work in influencing Zola's choice of a coal mine for the setting of *Germinal*. The very idea of a mine – with its tortuous dark passages and ever-present dangers – exercises a fascination on imaginative minds. So many fantasies can be realised down there in the secret dark; it is an ideal womb for fictional gestation. But more significant, perhaps, is the analogy between a mine and the mind, for so many things can be hidden there, and also discovered, and this is the aspect which may have appealed to Zola, who could safely release his dark apparitions and nightmares in its subterranean depths. A mention might also be made of the influence of the novelist's memories of his father, for Zola senior was an engineer of the earth; and the drama of rock drilling, of bringing down great cliffs of earth, must have stayed in the imaginative child's mind.

Germinal's eventual setting wasn't resolved until 19 February 1884, when a strike broke out in a coal-field some 120 miles north-east of Paris, a few miles from the Belgian border. The novelist lost no time getting there to witness the event at first hand.

The coal-field was at Anzin, a black and dreary mining community on the outskirts of Valenciennes, where coal had been mined since 1717 and which had been racked by industrial unrest for several years. By a fortunate coincidence Zola had met a university lecturer, Alfred Giard, during his holiday the previous summer. Giard was also a left-wing deputy for the Valenciennes constituency, and, posing as his secretary, Zola was able to attend strike meetings, tour the mines and interview the miners and their families. Walking through the mean, monotonous streets of the town, crowded on either side with cramped, hastily built cottages, he soon sensed what it was like to be a coal miner. Most of the families knew no other life and if ever there was a flicker of ambition to move on they had neither the money, nor the energy, nor the wits to do more than just talk about their dreams in one of the endless pubs provided by the managements to keep them permanently stupefied. Nor would they have been able to adapt to any other form of work: generations of exploitation, starvation and animal toil underground had transformed them into a race of crippled pygmies, ignorant and potentially violent. Violence was their only weapon, but even that weapon was largely ineffective in their ignorant hands. Their only fulfilment in life, and a questionable one at that, was the instinct and ability to breed more slaves like themselves, which they did with promiscuous abandon.

Zola stayed a week or more at Anzin, absorbing the atmosphere like a sponge, having technicalities explained and asking, as one of his guides recalled years later, 'more questions than a magistrate'. As a result, life in the coal mines is evoked in *Germinal* with almost choking authenticity, and if there are more gripping accounts of life underground, I have yet to read them. Nevertheless, a week spent in and around a colliery was hopelessly inadequate to master all the details and lore of the mining industry, so for many weeks after his return, Zola's study was packed with reference books: on mining technology, on economics, socialism, nihilism, and even on the illnesses peculiar to miners – so that if we learn in *Germinal* that mining families changed their bed linen only once a month and suffered from scrofula, asthma, chlorosis and ephemeral fever, we can take it as absolutely authentic.

Zola's next step was to plan the framework of his novel, which was only roughed out when he had left for Anzin. What he had seen stimulated his imagination into a frenzy, and the remarkable feat of composition which followed can be traced, thought by thought almost, in his working notes that have been preserved. Not to lean too hard on the analogy, you can see the novel actually *germinating* as his writing races across the pages, jotting down ideas, incidents, details of character; then the random thoughts are disciplined and marshalled into chapters, finally to give full expression to the fierce eloquence which leaps from every page of the finished manuscript. Many of these hasty notes are addressed to himself, typically admonitory:

> To achieve a broad effect I must have my two opposing sides as clearly contrasted as possible, and carried to the extreme of intensity. I must therefore begin with all the troubles and fatalities which weigh down the miners. Facts, not emotional pleas. The miner must be shown crushed, starving, a victim of ignorance, suffering with his children in a hell on earth though not persecuted, for the masters are not purposely vindictive – he is simply overwhelmed by the existing social condition. On the contrary, I must make the masters humane while their personal interests are not threatened; there is no point in getting on a soap-box. The worker is the victim of the facts of life – capital, competition and industrial pressures.

The title of the novel, *Germinal,* has a strange, compelling mystique about it – even in English – and it cost Zola a long search. Although it evokes to the English reader visions of the germinating, avenging army referred to in the final paragraph of the novel, it symbolises, ironically, a spring-time of revolution, for Germinal was the seventh month of the calendar adopted by the Revolutionaries in 1793, the period covered by April and May. Choosing the title was the novelist's final task; he wrote the first words of *Germinal* on 2 April 1884, and the last on 23 January the following year. It appeared as a serialisation in *Le Gil Blas* from November 1884 and was published in book form in March 1885.

Germinal is a delightfully easy book to read, perhaps because the dense body of its text is fractured into so many short, impressionistic sequences. There are forty chapters grouped into seven parts, yet the author achieves a page-turning continuity that is quite astonishing. It is well worth looking at the method of construction to see how this is done. The first eleven chapters encompass a time-scale of a single day only. With this complex and extended prologue we are absorbed into the mining community of Montsou; we meet a multitude of characters, miners and managers; we go down into the black bowels of the pit with them, sweating in the intense heat and straining every muscle to dig and move enough coal to keep them in bread for another day; we go into their homes to see them washing, eating, boozing and sleeping; we share with them their terrors and suffering, and sympathise with their desperate fight for survival. By the time we reach Part Three, when the monotonous weeks and months begin to pass in quick succession, we are on familiar terms with Montsou and its inhabitants. This was Zola's specific intention.

There is another aspect of this prologue worth mentioning too: most of what we see is seen through the eyes and experiences of Etienne Lantier who, like us, is a stranger not only in the town but also to coal mining. Thus his impressions and reactions are very likely what ours might be in the same situation; we might ask the same questions, and display the same curiosity about things which would be taken for granted by one of the inhabitants. This extraordinary feeling of 'being there' which is remarked on by many readers of *Germinal*, is one of the novel's great strengths, and we have little alternative but to be involved, often disturbingly so, in the events that follow. After the prologue the construction of the narrative follows a course analogous to the mine itself: a course of continuous descent into darkness, becoming more close and constricted, and interrupted at intervals by violent explosions. It takes us inexorably down, past the point where we'd believed there could be no survival, from which there could be no return. Yet the author avoids giving the reader a feeling of utter hopelessness; it is *uncertainty* he strove for, and achieved, for even as we read the last paragraph there is a faint glimmer of hope in all the blackness.

The action of the novel takes place between 1866 and 1869 and begins with the arrival of Etienne Lantier at Montsou, late one night, to be confronted by the frightening silhouette of the monster which dominates the town: the towering pit-head above the Voreaux, one of the big coal mines of the district. Next day Etienne finds lodgings with one of the mining families, the Mahéus, who persuade the mine foreman to take on the young man as a temporary labourer.

At home among the miners Etienne is soon made uncomfortably aware of their plight; they are permanently hungry and overcrowded, often diseased and constantly haunted by debt; other than alcohol and sex there are no diversions, and even the church has deserted them. Like all the miners the Mahéus are desperately poor and, to get a little money to buy food the wife takes her two youngest children to the house of the Grégoires, a kindly but complacent couple who live on the proceeds of their investment in the mine but who have little knowledge of the appalling living conditions of the miners who work for them. The truth is, as the following interview illustrates, that the Grégoires simply prefer not to know:

The servants also looked at the wretched trio with the degree of pity and concern of the domestic whom the prospect of meal times inspires with no uneasiness. While the housemaid went upstairs, the cook, lost in contemplation, had put back the remainder of the milk cake on the table to leave her arms dangling idly by her sides.

'I have just two nice little woollen dresses and scarves left,' continued the young lady; 'you will see they will keep them beautifully warm.'

La Maheude recovered her speech at last. 'Thank you very much, mademoiselle,' she stammered. 'You are all very kind.'

Tears had started to her eyes; she made sure of her five francs; she was only debating with herself as to the manner of asking for them, in case they did not offer them. The housemaid was a long while coming back; there was a moment of awkward silence. To the right and left, hanging on to and half hidden by their mother's skirts, the little ones were staring with wondering eyes at the cake on the table.

'You have only these two?' asked Madame Grégoire, feeling the silence becoming irksome.

'Oh! madame, I have seven.'

Monsieur Grégoire, who had taken up his paper again, started indignantly.

'Seven!' he exclaimed, 'seven children! But whatever for, in the name of all that's good?'

'It is very imprudent,' purred the old lady.

La Maheude made a vague gesture of excuse. Children came when one least expected them. And, besides, when they grew up, they brought money in. They would have been right enough at home, if they had not had the grandfather, who was becoming stiff and unfit for work, and if the others, besides the two lads and the girl, had been old enough to go down. The little ones must have food, though they couldn't work. (61)

Maheude leaves with the cast-off clothes, but without her five francs; it is not the custom of the Grégoires to give money. The views of the Grégoires on the fecundity and improvidence of working-class people were probably typical of middle-class attitudes of the time. Why poor Maheude has seven children she can't afford to keep is made evident a little later on when she helps dry her husband after his bath:

Now she began to wipe him, plugging with a towel the parts that would not dry. Feeling happy, he burst out laughing and took her in his arms.

'Leave me alone, stupid! You are damp, and wetting me.'

He took her in his arms again, and this time did not let her go. The bath always finished in this way: she enlivened him by the hard rubbing, and then by the towels which tickled the hairs of his arms and chest. Besides, among all his mates of the settlement it was the hour for stupidities, when more children were planted than were wanted. At night all the family were about. He pushed her towards the table, jesting like a worthy man who was enjoying the only good moment of the day, calling that taking his dessert, and a dessert which cost him nothing. She, with her loose figure and breast, struggled a little for fun.

'You are stupid! My Lord! you are stupid! And there's Estelle looking at us. Wait till I turn her head.'

'Oh, bosh! at three months; as if she understood!' (62)

Soon Etienne joins the stream of victims who line up each morning by the shafts to be devoured by the malevolent monster. Down below, in the fetid, black heat, men and women work side by side, some naked; the men, lying on their backs and sides hewing at the narrow seams of coal, the women and children loading it into baskets and skips and hauling it through cruelly narrow and steep passageways, often toiling in a dripping rain with noxious fumes of firedamp fogging their eyes like clammy cobwebs. The deepest levels were the worst, for there the heat was fiercest. The following passage describes a day in the life of Catherine, Maheu's teenage daughter.

Painfully, Catherine had managed to fill her cart; now she pushed it off. The gallery was too wide for her to be able to brace herself against the timbers on both sides, and her bare feet were twisting between the rails; searching for a point of purchase: she was moving ahead slowly, her arms held out stiffly in front of her, her body bent double. And as soon as she came alongside the *corroi* the fire torture began again, and the sweat ran from every pore, like a rainstorm.

Before she had gone a third of the way to the relay point she was drenched, blinded, as caked with black mud as the men were. Her tight shift seemed soaked in ink, and it stuck to her skin and worked its way up her back with every movement of her legs, restricting her so painfully that she had to stop again.

What was the matter with her today? She'd never felt her bones turned to water like this before. The air must be bad. There was no ventilation here in this far-off gallery. You breathed in all kinds of vapors that came bubbling out of the coal – sometimes they were so heavy that the lamps wouldn't burn – to say nothing of the firedamp, which nobody paid any attention to anymore because they sniffed up so much of it from one end of the week to the other. She knew it well, this bad air – 'dead air,' the miners called it – with the heavy asphyxiating gases down at the bottom, and up above, the light gases that catch fire and can destroy all the workings of a mine, hundreds of men, in a single clap of thunder. She had swallowed down so much of it from childhood on that she was surprised to find it bothering her so, making her ears buzz and her throat burn.

She couldn't stand it anymore – she would have to take off her shift too. It was torture, this cloth whose every wrinkle cut into her, burned her. She tried to resist, tried to go on with the hauling, but she had to stop and straighten up. Then suddenly, telling herself she would put it on again at the relay point, she took it all off, the cord, the shift, everything; she was so feverish that she would have torn her skin off if she had been able to. And now, naked, pitiful, reduced to the level of an animal hunting for food in the filth of the roads, she struggled on, her haunches smeared with soot, her belly caked with mud, like a mare pulling a carriage. Down on all fours, she kept pushing. (65)

But if conditions at the mine are bad, they deteriorate even more with the introduction of a new pay system which reduces the miners' earning power. The miners, who 'buy' their seams at auction, are paid only for the coal they dig, and as the payment is so pitifully small they begrudge every wasted minute, which includes the time they have to spend timbering the mine. As a result, many tunnels are badly propped and cave-ins are frequent and often fatal. Fearing a general collapse of the mine the company introduces a new system so that the miners will be paid separately for the timbering and the coal they dig. The men, however, correctly suspect that the move is a trick to reduce their overall pay, and a strike erupts.

There are three ways out. Rasseneur, the moderate miners' leader, wants to avoid the strike by negotiating with the management, through the manager, Hennebeau. Etienne, who has in the meantime been elected a leader, wants to adopt a more radical course, believing they will get better conditions by prolonging the strike and causing great financial loss to the company. Souvarine, an anarchist, wants to destroy everything so that a better system can replace it.

Not all the action in *Germinal* is toil and misery, however. Zola relieves this at

181

a strategic point in the narrative by describing a miners' picnic, so that we can see the characters in a lighter, more genial mood. The scene is in violent contrast to the mine, 'too, with the breath and freshness of an impressionist painting, exuding light and air, gaiety and enjoyment. But it is, unfortunately, too brief a respite.

As the miners' bellies contract the tension increases, the strike spreads as the pits close down, and the miners' families prepare to endure the inevitable misery and starvation. Etienne is now the leader of all the miners, who attempt to close down one of the pits still working, owned by Deneulin. The damage resulting from sabotaged machinery ruins him and he is forced to sell out to the monopolistic Montsou company. As the people sink deeper and deeper into despair the violence increases, giving the company the excuse to call in the military.

The echoes of the bugle call are clearly premonitory and presage death, so we are aware, as a mob of several hundred miners and their families gathers before the soldiers, that a tragic clash is imminent. To the background of shouts, *Kill the blacklegs!* Etienne tries to reason with the captain of the soldiers, without success; and he returns to the mob to shout insults with the rest. The sixty soldiers are now faced by the angry, yelling mob, which begins to press forward. Even bayonets are useless; Maheu, in an act of defiance, bares his coal-grimed chest and presses it against a bayonet, so that it draws blood. In a helpless gesture the captain orders the soldiers to load their rifles, but still the mob refuses to be cowed. Led by one of the miner's widows, old Mother Brûlé, the strikers begin throwing bricks and finally, just as the captain is about to order his men to fire over their heads, the guns go off.

The crowd is frozen, stupefied, unable to comprehend what has happened. All around the strikers are falling: children, women, men. Then, amid frightful scenes, there is panic and retreat as the miners scramble over the corpses in the mud. The courageous captain suffers too: 'he preserved his pallid stiffness in face of the disaster of his life, while his men reloaded with mute faces.' This unforgettable chapter, which propels the reader's eye, brain and emotions with the force of a hurricane, owes its haunting power to the most painstaking construction and interlocking detail; it is an intricate device which flares and flashes and then blows up in the hand.

In the wake of this disaster the starved miners, to survive at all, have no alternative except to return to the pits. Then comes a culminating catastrophe: the anarchist Souvarine sabotages the mine one night by wrecking the water-tight timbering of the main shaft.

The monster, mortally wounded, is spectacular in its death throes. In the ensuing flooding and collapse, many miners are trapped deep underground, including Etienne and Catherine and Chaval, the girl's brutal lover, who manage to escape the rising waters by huddling at the end of a dry tunnel. A fight breaks out between Etienne and the jealous Chaval, and in a fit of blind passion Etienne kills his rival. Then, in one of the starkest love scenes in literature, in the presence of the floating corpse of the dead man, in the darkness and with the consuming water lapping only inches away, the two exhausted survivors spend their remaining strength in an instinctive, doomed act of procreation.

> With a sudden impulse she clung to him, seeking his mouth and pressing her own passionately to it. The darkness lighted up, she saw the sun again, and she laughed a quiet laugh of love. He shuddered to feel her thus against his flesh, half naked beneath the tattered jacket and trousers, and he seized her with a reawakening of his virility. It was at length their wedding night, at the bottom of this tomb, on this bed of mud, the longing not to die before they had had their happiness, the obstinate longing to live and make life one last time. They loved each other in despair of everything, in death.
>
> After that there was nothing more. Étienne was seated on the ground, always in the same corner, and Catherine was lying motionless on his knees. Hours and hours passed by. For a long time he thought she was sleeping; then he touched her; she was very cold, she was dead. He did not move, however, for fear of arousing her. The idea that he was the first who had possessed her as a woman, and that she might be pregnant, filled him with tenderness. Other ideas, the desire to go away with her, joy at what they would both do later on, came to him at moments, but so vaguely that it seemed only as though his forehead had been touched by a breath of sleep. He grew weaker, he only had strength to make a little gesture, a slow movement of the hand, to assure himself that she was certainly there, like a sleeping child in her frozen stiffness. Everything was being annihilated; the night itself had disappeared, and he was nowhere, out of space, out of time. (62)

Étienne, close to death, is eventually rescued, and when he regains his health leaves Montsou for Paris, defeated, alone, an outsider, just as he arrived.

Although too detached to offer or recommend solutions, *Germinal* is nevertheless a revolutionary novel in the way it so ruthlessly exposes one of the most terrible social injustices of the time: the criminal exploitation of labour by the excesses of the capitalist system. It is at the same time an enthralling and inspiring account of the struggle between the oppressed victims and the lucky legatees of capitalism.

At the time of the book's publication there were many who believed Zola had overstated his case. On the contrary, the fictional incident at Montsou has been repeated, with real privation, real savagery and real spilled blood countless times during the century since. Zola saw the dangers of unrestrained capitalism only too clearly, though his prophetic warnings that the system has a built-in suicidal capacity to devour itself and everyone with it continues to echo emptily from the façades of larger and larger corporations.

Just how carefully the novelist balanced the conflict in *Germinal* is illustrated by the teams he chose to fight the class struggle in his story. For the workers' side he has Étienne Lantier, the self-educated socialist who becomes, for a brief time, the miners' leader during a strike; Rassaneur, a true representative of his class, a moderate trade-unionist; and Souvarine, an extremist anarchist. Against these three Zola pits a capitalist captain of industry: Deneulin, who owns a small mine; Hennebeau, the manager of a big colliery in Montsou, owned by a public company headquartered in faraway Paris; and Grégoire, a non-working shareholder of the company. There are many others involved in the struggle, of course, but these two teams of three, with their different backgrounds, beliefs and life-styles, and so perfectly opposed, represent them all.

In his original genealogical tree Zola described Étienne as taking after his mother, Gervaise, and inheriting her alcoholism which, in time, develops into homicidal insanity. Eventually, according to his notes, he would become a criminal. Happily for Etienne, Zola changed his mind when he came to write *Germinal,* although on one occasion when the character is drunk he does reveal an ancestral streak of violence:

> A demoniacal voice within him drowned all other thoughts. It ascended from his very entrails, kept beating his brain like a sledge hammer; it was the sudden thirst for blood, the need to kill. Never before had the attack shaken him so violently as now. He was not drunk, though. And he struggled against his hereditary evil, with the shudder of despair of the man, maddened by passion, about to commit a rape. At last he obtained the victory over himself. He flung the knife behind him, and gasped in a hoarse voice: 'Get up and go!'   (61)

Much later, he kills Catherine's former lover, Chaval, down the mine. Again, there is an irresistible need to kill: 'It rose and broke out beyond his will, beneath the pressure of the hereditary disease.' But Zola makes it clear that Etienne, normally a sober, industrious and even gentle man, has to be taken to breaking-point before the violent genes are activated.

Politically, Etienne is impressionable, his education consisting, in the main, of the hasty digestion of whatever political tracts he can come by. Marxists, not surprisingly, pick holes in Zola's presentation of the young man's radicalism, but that is hardly the point; he was a true product of the times, a combination of idealist and self-seeker yet sincere in his beliefs; weak at times, strong at others, and no better or worse than anyone forced to fight for their very survival.

When Etienne becomes the miners' leader, Zola, perhaps for the first time in a novel, reveals what we can take to be the political education of a typical labour leader of the time. From his notes it seems that Zola intended to use an official of the International Workmen's Association (*l'Internationale*) as the agitator to lead the miners' strike, but decided to use Étienne instead, a young, uneducated, out-of-work labourer who could be shown undergoing the process of realising his ideals through political action. In doing so the novelist isolated a 'type' of political man who is still very much with us today and, indeed, whom we must thank for innumerable improvements to our social condition. So in *Germinal* we see Étienne reading blindly through acres of political dogma and idealism; it is hard-won knowledge, and perhaps more dangerous than none at all, but it does give him the veneer of authority which wins for a time the respect of the miners. But as his power over the ignorant miners grows, certain changes – observable in the same species today – take place in his personality. From among the miners he emerges to be above them, and from his vantage point sees them in a new, contemptuous perspective, as whipped mongrels. Humility is replaced by arrogance. He becomes vain and self-important, and ambitious for more power. Every time he earns their admiration his contempt for them increases, and inevitably he removes himself from his class.

Rasseneur, our second agitator, is a miner who after being dismissed for his part in a strike establishes a little bistro which becomes a popular meeting place for the miners of Montsou. In today's political terms he is a moderate, seeing conciliation rather than radical action as the way to advance and win better conditions. This character is almost certainly modelled on a union organiser named Basly, whom Zola met during his visit to the Anzin mines.

Finally, there is the extremist Souvarine, the Russian aristocrat and medical student turned anarchist who, after the strike, sabotages the timber lining of the mineshaft so that it collapses under the pressure of the surrounding water and reduces the colliery to one vast crater. Following this catastrophe, Souvarine stubs his cigarette and walks out of the novel cloaked in a mystique which unaccountably earned for him the stature of a Ché Guevara. He solves nothing; on the contrary, his action brings even greater misery to the miners by taking away their livelihood. Why then is this relatively minor character the only one in *Germinal* to break free of his fictional bonds? Nana and Gervaise achieve this, but it must be remembered that they are transcendent creations of a vastly higher order than Souvarine. It's worth looking into, because there are many intriguing aspects about this character. While Etienne and Rasseneur were recognisable political types in the late nineteenth century, political terrorists or anarchists were then unknown in France. They were, though, active in Russia, and Zola must have received the idea of Souvarine from Turgenev, his Russian agent and friend. A Russian *emigre* anarchist working down a mine in northern France was about the most improbable single element in *Germinal* so there must have been a strong reason for Souvarine's inclusion in one of the most realist of Zola's novels. And I think there was, for the author's intuition must have warned him that radical political activity, in the face of entrenched capitalism, must eventually grow an anarchistic arm which, as we know today, it has. Political terrorism is now a fact of life. So Zola must be credited with isolating yet another political type, in addition to that represented by Etienne, before it became a reality. Critics of the novel, however, saw Souvarine as an anachronism rather than an innovation; although there had been a bombing attempt on Napoleon III's life (which Zola recounted in *His Excellency*) in the 1860s, the anarchist using sabotage as a political weapon during the Second Empire was, historically speaking, out of place. But the critics misunderstood; with the creation of Souvarine Zola held up for all to see the logical three-pronged spear of conciliation, radical agitation and anarchism which would become the weapon of the class struggle. It was above all a warning to his middle-class readers, who substantially represented economic and industrial management at all levels, that unless there were reforms society was in danger of sinking into a hellish pit of anarchy and violence. Interestingly, soon after the publication of *Germinal*, fiction did become fact, and Souvarine's philosophy, 'Any reasoning about the future is criminal, for it prevents pure destruction and holds up the march of the

185

revolution' became the catchcry of a new breed of terrorists. Indeed, the very words from the novel were quoted in court by one of the anarchists accused of a terrorist bombing in Paris during 1893-4, and Zola himself was blamed for a strike at Décazeville in 1887. Souvarine became something of a Frankenstein creation, a symbol of terror and destruction, which was obviously far from the author's intention; but the power of the character over the imagination of the public certainly illustrates Zola's remarkable ability to crystallise diffuse elements into a single, striking symbol. When Henri de Montherlant wrote, half a century later, that although all the characters in *Germinal* had an authentic ring with the exception of Souvarine, who 'smacks of the stereotype', he was unaware, apparently, that before Zola's anarchist character there was no stereotype. It was Souvarine, in fact, who became one, to be eventually caricatured as a furtive Russian clutching a plum-pudding bomb under a black cloak.

For reasons of balance Zola tried hard to present the opposing side, representing Capital, as faithfully and as sympathetically as possible. In this he was undeniably successful but his efforts are diminished to a large extent because we – and the author too – are almost completely concerned with the fate of the oppressed miners and not terribly interested in the private lives of the owners. Realising this, Zola resorted to inventing a couple of sub-plots designed to heighten our compassion for the privileged members of his cast, but they are not entirely convincing.

The Grégoires in *Germinal* are a fortunate family, having inherited shares in the Montsou colliery bought by the grandfather years before for 10,000 francs. These shares now provide an annual income of 50,000 francs which, while providing a comfortable living for the Grégoires is patently unjust to the workers who make it possible, the original capital having been repaid hundreds of times over. But this is not the Grégoires' fault; so long as the system prevails it is their right. As individuals they are charming, kindly and charitable, if a little tiresome, and are only vaguely aware of the plight of the miners in the village nearby. This awareness, however, never interferes with their self-righteous, indolent, worry-free way of life, and all their love and kindness is lavished on their daughter, Cécile. This idle life-style of the Grégoires, who are the Montsou representatives of thousands of families like them in Paris, is used by the author to provide flashes of sharp irony with which the novel abounds. Ultimately, the family is drawn into the miners' struggle and punished in the most terrible way.

The character Deneulin is an example of the paternalist, the owner-operator class, who is the proprietor of a small mine. Zola seems to have great respect for the individual entrepreneur, and Deneulin emerges as such a forceful, admirable character that we are really sorry to see him defeated at the end, his business devoured by the distant monolith, himself a victim of the system as much as his workers. Here again one marvels at Zola's extraordinary insight, this time at his concern for the survival of the small company in the face of corporate gluttony. I am reminded of the recent case of a huge American publishing conglomerate which, between 1967 and 1969, took over ninety small companies in an orgy of acquisition, ran up a debt of seventy-one million dollars, and miscalculated economic trends so badly that, in 1975, a third of its staff had to be dismissed and many of its newly acquired subsidiaries, some of which had been in existence for over half a century, closed down. Deneulin's mining company and what happens to it is a forerunner of a common modern phenomenon.

The final member of the capitalist team is Hennebeau, who manages the Montsou colliery for the public company which owns it. A former worker, he has crawled out of the pit and reached his position by hard work and intelligence; nevertheless he is a paid servant and protector of the system, and thus the miners' enemy. To breathe life into his group of little capitalists, Zola contrasts Hennebeau's fading sexuality with the bawdy fecundity of the miners. Unlike the complacently comfortable Léon Grégoire, his unhappy domestic life is racked by an impotent desire for his spoiled, unfaithful wife. His agonising dilemma is dramatically projected in an incident during which, searching for something in his nephew's bedroom, he discovers that his over-sexed wife has spent the night in his bed. At this very moment a mob of starving miners gathers outside the house, shouting for bread.

> Beneath the window the shouting burst out with renewed violence:
> 'We want bread! We want bread!'
> 'Imbeciles!' hissed Monsieur Hennebeau through his teeth.
> He heard them insulting him because of his big salary, calling him a pot-bellied good-for-nothing, a dirty swine who stuffed himself sick with good things while the workers were dying of hunger. The women had seen the kitchen, and there was an outburst of invective directed at the pheasant roasting there and the greasy-smelling sauces which tortured their empty stomachs. Oh these bleeding bourgeois! They should be stuffed with champagne and truffles till their innards burst!
> 'We want bread! We want bread!'
> 'Imbeciles!' repeated Monsieur Hennebeau. 'Do you think I'm happy?'
> His anger boiled up against these people who would not understand. How gladly would he have made them a present of his fat salary if he could have had their tough hide and could have copulated like them, easy come, easy go! Why couldn't he sit them at his table and stuff them with his pheasant, while he went off fornicating behind the hedges, laying girls without bothering about who had done so before. He would have given up everything – education, comfort, luxurious life and his powerful position as manager – if just for one day he could have been the humblest of these poor devils under him and be free with his own body and be oafish enough to beat his wife and take his pleasure with the wives of his neighbours. He found himself wishing he were dying of starvation too, and that his empty belly were twisted with pains that made his brain reel, for perhaps that might deaden this relentless grief! Oh to live like a brute, possessing nothing but freedom to roam in the cornfields with the ugliest and the most revolting haulage girl and possess her! (63)

It's laid on a bit thick. We may scrape up some sympathy for the poor man at this moment, but his sexual dilemma in no way matches the prolonged and seemingly hopeless predicament of the miners and their families, many of whom are dying from starvation. Although his intentions were honest, the author's compassion for the Hennebeaus of his time clearly falters in his portrait of the mine manager, whose sexual frustrations are nothing more than an ingenious ironic device.

Except for Etienne Lantier, Zola seems to have developed his characters as he worked on the manuscript of the novel; there are indications that as the narrative unfolded he was forced to rub out a portrait and sketch it again. The behaviour of many of his characters in the novel show a wide variance from that indicated in his notes, perhaps more than in any other of his books. An immense amount of work, for instance, went into the creation of the oppressed, hard-working Maheu family which takes Etienne in as a lodger; the intimate details of their domestic life, their unity and relationships with each other are presented with uncanny credibility.

The rest of the miners, beaten and brutalised, are not entirely without human virtues; Chaval, for example, unexpectedly cares for Catherine when she faints from the underground heat one day; and her brother, Zacharie, works like a demon to free her when she is trapped in the flooded mine. But although, miraculously under the circumstances, the miners and their families never lose their link with compassion, it is inevitable they should throw up, once in a while, a sport without a single human virtue whatsoever. Maheu's son Jeanlin seems to be one of these, a degenerate creature without a conscience, who can knife an innocent man just for the thrill of it.

Much has been said about Zola's mastery at portraying crowd scenes. 'The Crowd was his hero!' almost became his epitaph, but the statement is too narrow to be the truth. Certainly, he revelled in mob scenes, projecting their violence or gaiety with startling vividness. The psychology of crowds fascinated him and he applied the results of his observations with tremendous effect in *The Ladies' Paradise*, during the great sales; and at the Grand Prix races in *Nana*. But even these brilliant, crowded canvases are eclipsed by the insights he displays when directing the crowd sequence in *Germinal*. 'Directing' is an apt description of Zola in this role, for the impressions, with broad sweeps intercut with close-ups, panoramas irising into cameos, have a powerful cinematic effect that antedates Eisenstein. But a deeper intensity that the cinema finds difficult to convey underlies Zola's crowd scenes. This springs from the novelist's instinctive understanding of crowd chemistry, of the changes that take place among individuals when they become part of a mass, the admixture of ferocity and cowardice that can turn a crowd into a blunt instrument of hate and destruction. In *Germinal* the author paints the mob in several moods, from the happy frivolity of a miners' holiday to the ugly savagery of the strikers as they storm towards Montsou:

> The women had appeared, nearly a thousand of them, with outspread hair dishevelled by running, the naked skin appearing through their rags, the nakedness of females weary with giving birth to starvelings. A few held their little ones in their arms, raising them and shaking them like banners of mourning and vengeance. Others, who were younger with the swollen breasts of amazons, brandished sticks; while frightful old women were yelling so loudly that the cords of their fleshless necks seemed to be breaking. And then the men came up, two thousand madmen – trammers, pikemen, menders – a compact mass which rolled along like a single block in confused serried rank so that it was impossible to distinguish their faded trousers or ragged woollen jackets, all effaced in the same earthy uniformity. Their eyes were burning, and one only distinguished the holes of black mouths singing the

Marseillaise; the stanzas were lost in a confused roar, accompanied by the clang of sabots over the hard earth. Above their heads, amid the bristling iron bars, an axe passed by, carried erect; and this single axe, which seemed to be the standard of the band, showed in the clear air the sharp profile of a guillotine-blade.   (62)

Zola also observed another crowd phenomenon; although it can be swayed and directed by demagoguery, a mob also has the treacherous capacity, like a squeezed sponge, to revert to its original form, to bite the hand that feeds it. Etienne learns this from bitter experience when he becomes first an agitator, and then the miners' leader. He manages to form the miners into a single-minded, disciplined army, only to see them revert, twenty-four hours later, into a maddened rabble of saboteurs. Finally, when the strike is broken by the military, Etienne is stoned by the very same mob that willingly followed him before.

If, in *Germinal*, the miners are treated as, and act like, animals, so are animals given the qualities of humans. It is easy to get sentimental about pit ponies and mine horses, but Zola, during his tour of Anzin, was genuinely moved by their plight. While the animals are well cared for, and even loved, by the grooms and the miners, theirs is an unnatural life down there in the claustrophobic dark, and one that can make an animal lover's flesh prickle with pure pity. Some of the novelist's most moving passages describe the mute suffering of animals, and such passages occur in *Germinal* with disturbing frequency. The extent to which he touchingly personifies the feelings of dumb beasts is revealed in his account of the arrival down the mine of a new horse, Trompette, to be greeted by one of the veteran pit ponies, Bataille.

Trompette was soon placed on the metal floor in a mass. Still he did not move: he seemed in a nightmare in this obscure infinite hole, this deep hall echoing with tumult. They were beginning to unfasten him when Bataille, who had just been unharnessed, approached and stretched out his neck to smell this companion who lay on the earth. The workmen jokingly enlarged the circle. Well! what pleasant odour did he find in him? But Bataille, deaf to mockery, became animated. He probably found in him the good odour of the open air, the forgotten odour of the sun on the grass. And he suddenly broke out into a sonorous neigh, full of musical gladness, in which there seemed to be the emotion of a sob. It was a greeting, the joy of those ancient things of which a gust had reached him, the melancholy of one more prisoner who would not ascend again until death.   (62)

It is only too true. Trompette pines in his underground cell and dies after a few months, the unfortunate fate of many mine horses unable to adapt themselves to the appalling conditions.

At the stable they were neighbours at the manger, and lived with lowered heads, breathing in each other's nostrils, exchanging a constant dream of daylight, visions of green grass, of white roads, of infinite yellow light. Then, when Trompette, bathed in sweat, lay in agony in his litter, Bataille had smelled at him despairingly with short sniffs like sobs. He felt that he was growing cold, the mine was taking from him his last joy, that friend fallen from above, fresh with good odours, who recalled to him his youth in the open air. And he had broken his tether, neighing with fear, when he perceived that the other no longer stirred.

They harnessed Bataille to bring him to the shaft. The old horse slowly pulled, dragging his dead comrade through so narrow a gallery that he could only shake himself at the risk of taking the skin off. And he tossed his head, listening to the grazing sound of the carcass as it went to the knacker's yard. At the pit-eye, when he was unharnessed, he followed with his melancholy eye the preparations for the ascent – the body pushed on to the cross-bars over the sump, the net fastened beneath a cage. At last the porters rang meat; he lifted his neck to see it go up, at first softly, then at once lost in the darkness, flown up for ever to the top of that black hole. And he remained with neck stretched out, his vague beast's memory perhaps recalling the things of the earth. But it was all over; he would never see his comrade again, and he himself would thus be tied up in a pitiful bundle on the day when he would ascend up there. His legs began to tremble, the fresh air which came from the distant country choked him, and he seemed intoxicated when he went heavily back to the stable. (62)

So *Germinal*, far from being a 'novel of the crowd' as it is sometimes called, is rather a mass of strands, woven together by a common conflict. One could say that, ultimately, it is a novel about the forces of life itself in conflict. This could be one reason why *Germinal*, with its teeming cast of characters, endures so indelibly in the memory. And this cast is not limited to those mentioned, by any means. There are a dozen other memorable portraits: La Mouquette, vast-arsed and promiscuous; Chaval, the handsome, brutish lover of Catherine; Negrel, the engineer; Bonnemort, the old miner stupefied by toil; Maigrat, the evil grocer; the witch-like Mother Brûlé – even the mine itself, Le Voreaux.

Although Etienne Lantier enters *Germinal* in the first paragraph and leaves it in the last, it would be wrong to say that he plays the key role in the novel. The same goes for any of the individual characters, the mine and even the miners themselves, as a group. The main 'character' in *Germinal* is the *community*; we see it develop and merge into a single collective conscience before disintegrating into the mob of individuals it was before. It is this profound mass upheaval, this single groan of humanity, and not the intricately interwoven activities of the main characters, which gives the novel its stirring unity. This early account of the stirring and fusing of a collective conscience also makes *Germinal* a key work in the history of social change.

With so much stark injustice, so much pointless hardship in the novel, one's first impulse is to look for the villains. If they are difficult to find among the characters it is because there are none. It is no use pointing to the well-stuffed, shareholding Grégoires, for they have no reason to see themselves as anything but the honest, provident, charitable persons they are, and patrons of industry besides! Should they make a present of all their money to the miners to be pissed against the wall in a few days? The mine-owner Deneulin is doing the best he can; competition precludes him paying his workmen a better wage although he would if he could. Hennebeau, of course, is merely a paid employee doing his duty, as unpleasant as it may seem at times. What else would he do – join the miners down below? And the miners, for all their brutal, improvident and promiscuous habits – anyone can see they would be better citizens if they had half the chance, even though their ambitions might not extend beyond a few immediate and selfish comforts. Not even the monopolistic coal-mining company is the villain, for somehow it too is entitled to try to survive in the face of competition and falling prices. The common enemy to every character in the novel is unquestionably the excesses inherent in the capitalist system.

Germinal demonstrates the cause and effect of this as convincingly as any real or fictional account of the phenomenon before or since: the misery, hopelessness and frustration, the seeking of solutions, the reaction of the helpless masters and middlemen, the conflict and violence, the solidarity, the defeat. Every man, woman and child in the novel is the helpless victim of the tyranny of Capital. We never actually meet the tyrant but we become familiar with the terrible effects of its cruel despotism.

Even the church is shown to be an unwitting agent in the massive conspiracy. After the strikers are fired upon by the soldiers, it seems as though the clergy has at last given some priority to the plight of the poverty-stricken workers. But, no! Later it becomes obvious that the clergy is exploiting the strike and is as bad as the rest of them, indifferent to the misery of its flock and dreaming only of the final triumph of the church.

If Zola went to such great lengths to achieve impartiality in *Germinal*, and to report with such moving prose the suffering of the miners, what, then, was he trying to say? That conditions would always be like this? That there was no way out? He gives no answers, nor does he make any suggestions; all purpose seems to be obscured. Everyone in the novel appears to be on a disaster course. Every effort to alleviate injustice results in some fresh catastrophe. Was Zola, ambiguously perhaps, suggesting that only some cataclysmic social upheaval could solve the social dilemma he so convincingly portrays?

I think not. Zola, in any case, and right through his life, shrank from thoughts of violence as a means to an end; all his work shrieks with his belief that violence gets nobody anywhere. Zola viewed the profligacy of French society with much the same feelings of despair and horror as those recorded by Karl Marx. But the similarity ends there for where Marx saw a mass solution Zola found it impossible to quantify human suffering; to him every man's millstone was complex and unique. If *Germinal* departs from this view it does so only momentarily, under the stress of the harrowing situation he is describing, perhaps; but by the end of the novel his view remains unchanged.

This is why *Germinal* never became the Bible of the Marxists, despite the timeless and powerful message it transmits, for if we consider the thought-provoking ending to the novel – 'Men were springing forth, a black avenging army, germinating slowly in the furrows, growing towards the harvests of the next century, and their germination would soon overturn the earth' – it is obvious Zola believed not in the superiority of a socialist system over capitalism but rather in the ability of humanity to survive by means of a social process parallel in a way to Darwin's theory of natural selection. *Germinal*, far from being a book favoured by the Marxists, is frequently accused by them of being weak and passive, and lacking in true revolutionary spirit. This is hardly surprising, for its author was no revolutionary. Although he sympathised with many socialist objectives and held radical views, he was a passenger rather than a driver. But Zola *was* a reformer. He had bitter, first-hand experience of poverty; he had fought many adversaries for his freedom as a writer. He was a humane man, kind and sympathetic to the underdog, and these qualities pervade all his writing. The value of *Germinal* as a force for social reform is in its capacity to involve readers in the injustices of the system. This is probably one of the principal reasons why it has survived and germinated while a thousand political tracts written at the time are now dead and forgotten husks.

Two years or so before he began to write *Germinal*, Zola had praised the work of a talented author and journalist, Jules Vallès, at the same time rebuking him for wasting so much of his time in political agitation; Vallès had fought in the Commune and had been forced, as a result, to spend some time in England. Replying later in *Le Reveil*, Vallès accused Zola of being a pseudo-socialist, dramatically exposing the most outrageous injustices yet allowing them to continue. This accusation stung the novelist and affected him deeply, and doubtless led, many years later, to his active espousal of a utopian kind of socialism. But for the present his art took precedence over political involvement, and his purpose in writing *Germinal* was made clear in the preface he wrote for a later edition of the novel, which was 'a story of compassion, not a revolutionary work'. In writing it, his intention was to warn those in positions of power and wealth to take heed – 'I descended into that underground hell, and if I concealed nothing, not even the degradation of human beings, it was because I wished the picture to be complete with all its abominations, so as to draw tears from every eye. . . a cry of pity, an appeal for justice, I ask no more.'

Many writers will agree that they sweat more over the opening few paragraphs of a novel than over any of the thousands that follow. For those first lines are not merely a baited trap for the reader; in various ways they can influence a reader's attitude to the entire work – like the first sip of a vintage wine, the first impression of a stranger, a room – and even his memory of the book long after he puts it down. Of course there are any number of rules about this aspect of the novelist's craft, but whether they mean anything or not is arguable. What is indisputable, though, is that the opening chapter of *Germinal*, and particularly the vital opening paragraph, are masterly in their effect, triumphs of imaginative, extra-dimensional description:

> On the flat plain, under a starless sky as thick and black as ink, a lone man was following the route from Marchiennes to Montsou – six miles of paved road cutting straight across the beet fields. He was unable to see the dark ground in front of him, and it was only the March wind, coming in sea bursts and chilled by its sweep over miles of marshes and bare land, that made him aware of the immense, flat horizon. Not one tree was silhouetted against the sky, and the road spread before him as straight as a jetty through the blinding darkness of the shadows. (65)

There are dark premonitions lurking about. We may be comfortable in our armchair or bed, but surely those lines evoke a mental shiver? In a few seconds we have experienced the oppressive dread of the place endured by the inhabitants of Montsou all their lives – yet, like the solitary stranger, we have no idea, in a descriptive sense, of what the place is really like. Like him, we'll find out in due course, but in the meantime we have taken the first steps into a symbolic hell. Zola is aiming at the hairs on our neck, not our intellect.

Yet an examination of the complete first chapter reveals the prose is not concerned solely with atmosphere and symbolism; it is packed with information, too: about Etienne's past; about Bonnemort, the old, cracked and brutalised worker he meets at the mine that night; and the wheezing mine, the insatiable instrument of a distant god called Capitalism, the tyrannical ruler of Montsou and all who live there. John Steinbeck, following in the naturalist tradition many years later, was to use the same opening device with similar effect in *The Grapes of Wrath*; the outsider returning, the scenes of hardship, the butchering of a pig at night... a sequence of described scenes and observations magnified, brilliantly lit and made hauntingly memorable by symbolic suggestion.

In a letter to Henri Céard, discussing *Germinal*, Zola wrote, 'I have an obsession for capturing true detail on its flight from the springboard of exact observation. The flash on Truth's wings is often symbolic.' This statement supplies an important key to the appreciation of the novelist's blending of symbolism, consciously and intuitively, into his descriptive prose. Take the opening chapter: is it descriptive poetry or poetic description? There is metamorphism everywhere – the black plain surrounding Montsou isolates it like an island in a dark, stormy sea. The shrieking wind, the fires, the smoky moons, the gaunt silhouettes and shifting shadows – all these presage some kind of hell. Throughout the novel shafts, tunnels, machinery, even men and animals, dissolve eerily into forbidding shapes dictated by the hellish environment.

As long as we are in Montsou, every moment we are reading *Germinal*, we cannot escape from the mine, the novel's ultimate symbol as the master, exploiter and devourer of everyone in the coal-mining community. All the evils of the class conflict of the time could have been demonstrated just as objectively in a brickworks or a hat factory, but the mine, by its very nature a frightening and alien place, and with wide scope for dark symbolism, was an inspired choice. It was the one place on earth where man and beast were equals. The horses worked alongside the miners in their black prison, sharing the same torments and wretchedness, the same fear and danger. Only the capacity to complain and rebel separated man from his work-horse, but if there was nobody to listen and nothing to gain from revolt, they *were* equals.

It is also deep in the mine that symbolic echoes of a more personal kind may be heard in the darkness – echoes of a neurosis to be found in two of the author's earlier works, a short story and *Thérèse Raquin* – the guilt imagery of a body, floating in a rising sea of blood and which not only won't go away but persists in bumping against the guilty one. Zola externalises the nightmare in his description of the experiences of Catherine and Etienne, trapped in the bottom reaches of the flooded mine, and haunted by the presence of Chaval's corpse. They can't escape from its ghastly presence and neither, it seems, can Zola.

> On the seventh day Catherine was leaning forward to drink when her hand touched an object floating in front of her.
>
> 'Look here, what's this?' she said.
>
> Etienne felt in the darkness.
>
> 'I don't understand. It feels like the cover of a ventilator door.'
>
> She drank the water, but as she was taking up some more the object touched her hand again, and she uttered a terrible shriek.
>
> 'It's him! Oh God!'
>
> 'Who?'
>
> 'Him. You know. I felt his moustache.'
>
> It was Chaval's body, which the rising water had borne up the incline and washed up to them. Etienne put out his hand and felt the moustache and smashed nose, and shook with horror and disgust. Seized with a terrible nausea Catherine spewed out the water still in her mouth. She felt she had been drinking blood, that all this deep water in front of her was that man's blood.
>
> 'Wait a minute,' said Etienne. 'I'll push it away.'
>
> He gave the corpse a kick and it floated off. But soon it was hitting their legs again.
>
> 'Go away, for Christ's sake!'
>
> But after a third time Etienne had to let it stay, for some current kept bringing it back. Chaval would not go; he was determined to stay with them, right up against them. This gruesome companion added his foul stench to the vitiated air. All through that day they did not drink, but fought down their thirst, preferring death, but the next day their sufferings won, and they moved the body aside for each mouthful. What had been the use of killing him if he was still to come between them with his obstinate jealousy? He would always be there to prevent their coming together, even in death, even to the end. (63)

Zola's symbolism isn't, however, exclusively morbid, although you may think twice about this when you read the following excerpt which describes what happens to the hated shopkeeper Maigrat at the hands of a mob of avenging miners' wives. For years Maigrat has allowed the impoverished housewives credit at his shop in return for sex with their daughters; in trying to escape from their fury he falls and is killed, whereupon the women shout obscenities at his corpse.

> They surrounded the still warm body. They insulted it with laughter, abusing his shattered head, the dirty-chops, vociferating in the face of death the long-stored rancour of their starved lives.
>
> 'I owed you sixty francs, now you're paid, thief!' said Maheude, enraged like the others. 'You won't refuse me credit any more. Wait! wait! I must fatten you once more!'
>
> With her fingers she scratched up some earth, took two handfuls and stuffed it violently into his mouth.
>
> 'There! eat that! There! eat! eat! you used to eat us!'
>
> The abuse increased, while the dead man, stretched on his back, gazed motionless with his large fixed eyes at the immense sky from which the night was falling. This earth heaped in his mouth was the bread he had refused to give. And henceforth he would eat of no other bread. It had not brought him luck to starve poor people.
>
> But the women had another revenge to wreak on him. They moved round, smelling him like she-wolves. They were all seeking for some outrage, some savagery that would relieve them.
>
> Mother Brûlé's shrill voice was heard: 'Cut him like a tom-cat!'
>
> 'Yes, yes, after the cat! after the cat! He's done too much, the dirty beast!'

Mouquette was already unfastening and drawing off the trousers, while the Levaque woman raised the legs. And Mother Brûlé with her dry old hands separated the naked thighs and seized this dead virility. She took hold of everything, tearing with an effort which bent her lean spine and made her long arms crack. The soft skin resisted; she had to try again, and at last carried away the fragment, a lump of hairy and bleeding flesh, which she brandished with a laugh of triumph.

'I've got it! I've got it!'
Shrill voices saluted with curses the abominable trophy.
'Ah! swine! you won't fill our daughters any more!'
'Yes! we've done with paying on your beastly body; we shan't any more have to offer a backside in return for a loaf.'

'Here, I owe you six francs; would you like to settle it? I'm quite willing, if you can do it still!' . . .   (62)

Frightful though the scene is, it can be understood to symbolise the great wonder of sex, the primal source of man's energy. Maigrat suffers a primitive and symbolic form of posthumous punishment – but not only for his own sins, for the mutilation ceremony is an angry but sterile protest to Life itself. The incident provides just one of many examples of sexual symbolism in the novel, sometimes veiled, sometimes bold; and ranging from the Freudian kind – the mine chimney, proud and erect while the mine is productive, topples when it is flooded and can produce no more, to be replaced by a single, dangling cable, limp in the winding shaft – to more joyous imagery symbolising fertility – the screwing of the miners in the cornfields, the instinctive copulating, the miner's only means of survival.

Germinal, more than any of the other novels since *L'Assommoir*, broke down all but the most bitter opposition to Zola's genius. There were, not surprisingly, still the vociferous critics who claimed Zola soiled everything he touched; others who censured him for defaming working people; still others who couldn't stomach the novelist's blunt vocabulary. But the concensus of several dozen reviews was praise, admiration and enthusiasm, even though one critic qualified his approval with the condescending comment, 'Zola has finally learned how to write.' Maupassant, Huysmans, Pissarro and Monet, among many other prominent writers and artists, were sufficiently moved by the book to send the author personal letters of praise. The novel went unnoticed in England but did attract the attention of an American journal, *The Nation*, which deplored the morals of the miners, and maintained that, 'Neither in England nor in France could there be found a community so depraved, so utterly God-forsaken as that of M. Zola's miners.' As for the public at that time, it was not greatly impressed by Zola's latest, greatest masterpiece. In the ensuing eight years it only sold half as many copies as *Nana* and considerably less than *L'Assommoir*.

From the point of view of a history-minded critic at the time of publication, many of the incidents related in *Germinal* could have been – and were – construed as anachronisms. It is true that the novelist had transposed accounts of actual strikes in the years between 1876 and 1884 back to the period of his novel, which was about 1866 to 1869. It is also true that some of the more barbarous practices inflicted on the miners twenty years previously had been ameliorated by the time of the book's publication in 1885. But in the larger sense, assuming we are not going to consult a history book at every page of *Germinal*, none of this is really important; facts do not by themselves make truth. Stung by one critic who had accused him of historical inaccuracy Zola soon realised that argument over niceties was simply a ploy to avoid accepting the facts about the conditions of the working classes, and instead poured out his feelings to a friend. 'Alas! My description of life in the mines is toned down. The alleviation of misery will only be possible when people are prepared to see the suffering themselves, and to be ashamed. I am accused of inventing filth and deliberately lying about these poor people who brought tears to my eyes. But I can answer each accusation with documented proof.'

It seems impossible for any reader not to be touched, and even haunted, by the powerful narrative of *Germinal*, which instantly invites deep involvement. From discussions with many readers of the book it seems to have a special appeal to youth, or to the adolescent in the adult, but it also appears to be a common experience among readers of all ages to be swept along by the passions released at Montsou.

This emotional involvement with a work of fiction comes not, I think, from its chilling descriptions of suffering, injustice and human degradation – we can still read this every day in our newspapers – but from the sheer force of the writing itself, which at times has the primeval power of a storm, erupting without warning, sweeping over us in great gusts of words and truths from which there is no shelter, no escape. It is a powerful and human study of the conflict between opposing social forces, but it is also a desperate hymn to the belief that man will survive. If there is any hero in *Germinal* it is Humanity, its diversity reflected by the entire cast of characters, often shining brightly when we least expect it.

If you remember the intentions of Zola set down in his notes before writing a single word of *Germinal*, and if I have held your interest sufficiently since, you should have the clear impression that they were carried out to the letter: the broad effect, the two sides of the struggle contrasted; the miserable life of the miners, based on fact; the unsentimental impartiality, showing both workers and bosses as victims of the system; the absence of the soap-box ... yet the amazing thing is that at no time does the novelist merely fill in his outlines. From the first word to the last the progress of the novel is a sustained feat of artistic creation, an epic flight of imagined reality. Perhaps it was ordained that a coal pit should have been the source and the setting of one of the world's masterpieces of black poetry, an eloquent, enduring poem of shocked anger, compassion and, in the final hundred words, hope.

13

Zola and the Artists

n the last hundred years or so I find it difficult to name any movement in any
of the arts which has had such a widespread effect on modern life as that of the
French Impressionists during the 1860s and 1870s. In music one could
perhaps use the comparison of the birth of jazz, which in turn developed a host
of hybrids including pop and rock music which now animates everybody's life
almost everywhere. The birth of jazz was the essential spark which has
scorched most musical sound since, like it or not. Similarly, those humble
canvases of the Impressionists, now million-pound masterpieces, broke a new
dawn in a sunburst of bright colour, gaiety and originality which to me has lost
none of its excitement and romance in the intervening century.

With hindsight, we can see that the way was more or less cleared for the
historic breakthrough. There was photography; there were Turner and
Courbet; there was the discovery of the colour spectrum – that white light was
really composed of all the colours of the rainbow. There was also the
depressing black corner into which academic art had painted itself, crying for
light and air. And finally there was a mood of revolt against the tyranny of the
official Salon in France, for acceptance by the Salon jury was then a necessary
requisite for a career in painting.

Impressionism has many beginnings but the most significant point of
departure from the academic mainstream can be traced to the exhibition of
Manet's painting *Déjeuner sur l'herbe* ('Lunch on the Grass') at the Salon of
Artists Refused by the Jury in 1863. Cézanne, Pissarro, Jongkind, Whistler and
Guillaumin also exhibited but Manet was the most accomplished of them and
became, however reluctantly, the standard-bearer of the Impressionists. The
most important result of the exhibition was the formation of a close association
and friendship between several painters: Monet, Renoir, Pissarro, Cézanne,
Sisley and Bazille – all, with the exception of Pissarro, in their twenties. The
interesting thing about this group is that its members had widely differing
backgrounds and temperaments and, to some extent, divergent aims. But they
were united in their search for representational truth: to capture that 'flight of
truth from the point of observation' which Zola strove for in his writing. They
painted not what they *knew* was there, with the aid of foreknowledge and

197

experience, but what appeared to them at a given moment. Some delve deeper into the effects of light, and the play of light upon form. Others, like Seurat, separated the colours in light and used them to model new forms in brilliant, static mosaics. In doing so, these artists broke the chains of convention to release a new wave of visual innovators, the post-Impressionists. But it was a long and painful path from Manet's *Déjeuner sur l'herbe* of 1863 to eventual success. How slow and painful, in Cézanne's case, is revealed in this scornful remark by a critic ten years later, in 1874: 'Take all the Salon juries and you won't find one imagining, even in a dream, the possibility of accepting a work by this painter, who used to come to the Salons carrying his canvases on his back like Jesus carried his cross.'

Even in 1875, commenting on an unsuccessful auction of paintings by Monet, Renoir, Sisley, Pissarro and Morisot at the Hôtel Drouot, a critic wrote in *Le Figaro*: 'The impression made by the Impressionists is that of a cat walking along the keyboard of a piano, or of a monkey playing with a paintbox.' Two years later, at an exhibition by the Impressionists in which many now-famous works were shown, the public, encouraged by the newspapers, thronged the gallery to abuse and mock the paintings. Typical was the judgement of one art critic: 'It is impossible to stand for more than ten minutes in front of some of the more outrageous canvases without feeling seasick.' But fifteen years had now passed, and there were intimations of success. Manet was beginning to find wider acceptance and Renoir, Monet and Pissarro were selling paintings now and again. But not Cézanne; he was still denounced as a monster and a madman.

What entrances me about the birth of Impressionism is its human side, for it wasn't a flash discovery. The seed could so easily have withered in such adverse conditions but instead it was nourished by the unique dedication of this small group of men, whose vision and tireless devotion saw it through the long and difficult process of labour and birth and eventually to maturity. Thus the story of the Impressionist pioneers is an inspiring example of the triumph of man's inherent genius and love of creation and beauty. Perhaps their example is overquoted, but I think the story lives on with such freshness because it is a clear instance of individuals in creative harmony, helping and inspiring one another for the common good.

Zola, as it happened, was midwife at this protracted event. Although only twenty-six, he was the first critic to champion Manet, and became the publicist for the Impressionists, a role he relinquished only when he felt his judgements inadequate for the task, and because of his intense involvement with his own creative problems. But his impressions of this historic event are first-hand and as memorable as an electric shock, and this is why he was able to incorporate them into his next novel with such force and vividness. We owe it to Zola that the struggles of the Impressionists have been passed on to us as an idealised but inspiriting story. He was deeply affected by their collective genius, their dedication, their patience and their suffering, more so because he experienced everything they did in his own task of writing. It was, therefore, the most natural thing in the world to use the world of the Impressionists as the background for his new novel, *The Masterpiece*, and it is fortunate for us that he did.

Right from the initial concept of the *Rougon-Macquart* chronicle it was Zola's intention to include a novel about art and creative genius, and Claude Lantier, the hero, appears in the cycle as a young man in *The Belly of Paris*, published in 1873.

Twelve years later, when he began to write *The Masterpiece*, Zola's views on Impressionism had considerably matured; in both his notes and the novel he reveals a remarkable insight into the actual and theoretical course of post-Impressionist painting and in particular the conflict between the art of the Impressionists and that of Cézanne. The lack of success among the Impressionists frustrated Zola and he began to wonder if all the blame lay with the public. Like the Impressionists, he was a realist too, yet he was phenomenally successful. Although Monet and Renoir had paintings hung in the 1880 Salon, none had been successful, least of all Cézanne. Zola wasn't without sympathy for their plight, however; in one of his reviews of the Salon he wrote: 'What the public forgets is that most of these mocked martyrs are poor men who will expire of starvation, weariness or disillusionment if they are not soon appreciated.' But then his growing doubts about their abilities emerge too: 'It is unfortunate that not a single member of the group has definitely and effectively succeeded to apply to their work the doctrines they believe in,' and that they are 'still unequal to the task they have set themselves; they stutter, unable to find the right word'. This was not an insult to the Impressionists, but an exhortation to an even greater vision than they could realise on canvas, for it seemed to Zola that preoccupation with technique and indifference to subject matter was drawing them away from the rich potential of emotional experience and the complexities of the human condition. He expressed this rather more tersely at a party given to celebrate the publication of the novel: 'I cannot accept', he said, 'that a man who shuts himself away all his life to draw ballet girls ranks equally in dignity and power with Flaubert, Daudet or Goncourt.'

More than any of his other *Rougon-Macquart* novels, *The Masterpiece* is an instrument of propaganda for Zola's ideas and fears. It is, in parts, intensely autobiographical – to the extent that after his death Alexandrine was often moved to tears when she took the book from the shelf – and in others, biographical, for it contains the thinly disguised portraits and sketches of many friends and acquaintances. *The Masterpiece* is, I think, the only *Rougon-Macquart* novel for which Zola did not journey forth on an information trip, or stack his study high with reference books. It wasn't necessary, for what isn't pure fiction in this novel is personal memoir.

While the sources for the models of many of the minor characters are pretty much of an academic matter, those for the two major figures – Claude Lantier the artist, and Pierre Sandoz the writer – are of considerable interest to those who would like to see the novel in a wider perspective.

First the painter, Claude Lantier. He is the illegitimate son of Gervaise and her lover and you would have met him in *L'Assommoir* with his brother Étienne and sister Nana, in the agonies of a spectacularly deprived childhood; and also in passing, in *The Belly of Paris*. On the Rougon-Macquart genealogical tree Zola describes his personality as a 'blending of natures, with the moral and physical characteristics of the mother predominating. The ancestral nervous affliction develops into genius'. Well, at least some good has come of the tainted Macquart blood. In between books, Claude is rescued from the slums and educated in Plassans (Aix) by a benefactor, and then returns to Paris as an art student with ambitions to take the city by storm with his revolutionary new ideas.

Claude is an imaginative composite of Zola's friend Paul Cézanne, and to much lesser extent, the novelist himself. Zola's contribution is his own knowledge of the processes and toils of creation, and in Claude's struggle with his art we can be sure the agonies are squeezed directly from his own experience. As for Cézanne's contribution, novelists have been sued for less. Upon receiving a copy of the book from the author and acknowledging its receipt with a brief, cool note, Cézanne never wrote or spoke to Zola again.

The bald facts about the similarities between the character Claude in the novel and Cézanne are these: they both had Provençal childhoods; they were abnormally timid about women and sex; they eventually established themselves with models who became their mistresses by whom each had a child then married; they were both struggling vainly to express their visions on canvas while suffering indifference from the public, the critics, and from their own self-doubt. The portrait in the book is muddy and ultimately depressing but recognisable throughout – at least until the catastrophe at the end of the novel.

With such a stark example of the struggling creative genius living, as it were, right on his doorstep, Zola could hardly avoid using Paul Cézanne as his principal model for Claude, and any doubts about the source of his inspiration must be dispelled by a passage in his notes for the novel in which there is momentary but revealing slip: the author substitutes the name Paul for Claude. Also surviving in these notes is a mirror-image sketch of Cézanne: 'A fine nose lost in a bristly moustache; eyes narrowed but clear and tender; a strong voice, rough speech, deliberately coarse... happy in the mornings, low in the evenings...' In the novel itself there is a description of Cézanne's studio: ' stove almost buried in dead ashes; a bed, divan, small washstand, a battered oak wardrobe and a vast deal table littered with tubes of paint, brushes and unwashed dishes... disorder everywhere: old chairs, broken easels, model addresses scribbled on the walls with chalk...' Also in the novel are detailed descriptions of their youth in Aix, evoked memories of their schooldays together and of their escapades in the countryside. With his knowledge of the artist's life from boyhood onwards it was easy for Zola to analyse and set down the most intimate details of Cézanne's ideas and ambitions, self-doubts and personal anguish, and to project what he saw as inevitable failure and disillusionment.

But Zola's portrait of Claude is by no means a duplicate photograph of Paul Cézanne; for here and there the ghostly outlines of the author himself appear. This double image is sometimes difficult to separate, because both men shared common characteristics to an extraordinary degree. Both possessed a deep fear of women and sex; and for both, work was an escape from their frustrations. Consequently it is not surprising that Zola could call upon a deep intuitive understanding of Cézanne's complex nature: 'always unsatisfied, tormented because his genius will not flower. . . a creative artist with too vast an ambition, the ambition to put all nature on to one canvas'.

While Claude Lantier is a fascinating composite, the writer Pierre Sandoz in the novel is a straightforward projection of Zola, who fits himself into the skin of the character so frankly that his motives are puzzling, to say the least. 'My own portrait modified,' he wrote in his notes, 'a friend of Claude, with my own ambitions, disappointments and failures, and eventual success. . . while he continues to struggle.' Much of the detail that connects Zola to Sandoz could have been altered without difficulty or omitted altogether. In Sandoz not only is Zola's earlier life accurately documented, but also his origins: his father is a foreign citizen in France who dies when Pierre is still a child, leaving the family penniless. The boy grows up and is forced to become a clerk to support his mother. His literary beginnings are the same as Zola's; so are the literary evenings, so is the scandal touched off by the publication of his novels; so is his courtship and marriage to Henriette, even to their honeymoon which is a re-creation of the holiday Zola and Alexandrine took with Cézanne at Bennecourt in 1866. Henriette is, of course, Alexandrine, and in a passage where Sandoz is describing his conjugal needs it might well be Zola reflecting upon his own marriage:

> He himself felt the need of an affection to safeguard his peace of mind and a sympathetic home into which he could live cloistered and give up his whole life to the vast work he had so long dreamed of. Everything, he added, depended on the wife one chose, and he thought he had found what he was looking for: a simple girl, the orphan of small business people without a penny to her name, but good-looking and intelligent. . .   (70)

After Sandoz becomes a journalist he begins work on an epic cycle of novels, of between fifteen and twenty volumes, concerned with the lives and fortunes of a family. . . familiar? To those critics who accuse Zola of an almost total lack of imagination, the character of Sandoz is heaven-sent evidence!

We haven't yet, however, seen the last of Zola in *The Masterpiece*. Admittedly the sketch is fugitive, but an important aspect of Zola's troubled creative life shows up in the character Bongrand, who also shares similarities with Manet. With a single masterpiece painted years before, Bongrand becomes the leader of a new art movement, and the responsibility weighs heavily upon him. Every time he approaches a blank canvas he is paralysed by the thought that it might be his first failure, that he will not live up to his reputation. Thereafter, as any creative artist knows, lies certain depression, and worse. Through Bongrand,

Zola is expressing his own morbid fear of failure which, to judge from his letters and records of conversations on the subject, haunted him constantly. This resulted in frequent black depressions; on some days he sat at his desk without a thought in his head, without a single line written, conquered temporarily by what seemed to be an unassailable mountain of self-doubt. For Zola, despair was always just around the corner and he was, throughout most of his creative life, a very unhappy man. The writing of each novel, he recalled in his later years, was like conceiving and giving birth, but with a lot of pain and little pleasure, and this feeling is supported by the notes he sometimes wrote to his publisher, invariably profuse with expressions of enormous relief that a book was at last finished.

So there are really three manifestations of the author in *The Masterpiece*: Zola himself, as Sandoz the journalist and writer, somewhat idealised; Zola the artist, as Bongrand, suffering the agonies of artistic creation; and, in Claude Lantier, Zola the explorer into his own subconscious – three peep-holes, in a sense, revealing three different views of the novelist, naked.

Most of the other characters in the novel can be identified. Dubuche in the story is Zola's youthful friend Baille; Mahoudeau the sculptor is Solari; Champbouvard is Courbet; Fagerolles is Guillemet, while the unscrupulous Jory is a most unflattering portrait of the faithful Paul Alexis. The Café Baudequin, the meeting place of the painters, is the Café Guerbois. I expose these bones in the cupboard only as a matter of interest, however, for it is a mistake to become too obsessed with this aspect of *The Masterpiece*. Zola used real-life models, to some degree or other, for the majority of his characters in all his books, and, in any case, they were always projected 'through a temperament'.

The theme of *L'Oeuvre* – strictly, 'Work of Art' although usually known in English as *The Masterpiece* – is the account of a triangular conflict within the tormented personality of Claude Lantier: the struggle of an inadequate genius with his inherited nature; the contest between a woman's love and a man's art; and the fatal battle between Claude's lust for his art and his lust for a woman. The agonising quality of this conflict is reflected in the titles Zola considered for the novel but later rejected: *The Blood of my Work; The Anguish of Creating Living Work* and *This is my Flesh*. No hint of this emotional tempest is found in the opening chapters of the novel, however; instead the story begins with a thunderstorm that might have come straight from the pages of some romantic novelette.

Returning from a nocturnal ramble late one night, Claude meets a young girl in the doorway to his studio, where she is sheltering from the violent storm. Although he is shy with women he invites her in, and so we meet Christine, who is to figure largely in the pattern of conflicts that follow. Trapped by the storm she stays the night in Claude's studio, sleeping alone in his bed behind the security of a screen. In the morning, when he goes to wake her, Claude sees that the sheets have slipped off and there she is, asleep and half-naked. An instant kindling of carnal desire is just as quickly quenched by Claude's artist's eye, and he grabs his sketch-pad and starts to draw the beautiful girl who, when she wakes, pulls the sheets around her, her modesty so shocked that 'the blood rushed to her cheeks and her blush flowed, in a rosy tide, to the very tips of her breasts'.

Claude incorporates the sketch into a huge painting he is working on which, from the description, is a composition similar to Manet's famous *Lunch on the Grass*: a group of people in a forest clearing at lunch, with a man and three naked women. Claude calls the painting *Open Air*. The painting isn't going at all well, and the naked figure in the foreground is giving him a lot of trouble. With Christine's delicate head painted in, all the professional models in the Latin Quarter are too Rubenesque to provide a matching body, and Claude despairs. Eventually, after a burst of tearful pleading, Christine consents to pose nude for the entire figure.

The huge painting is refused by the Salon and is hung instead in the *Salon des Refusés* where it becomes the joke of the exhibition. In describing both Claude's and the public's reaction, Zola is re-creating a historic incident he witnessed at first hand in 1863 when Manet's *Déjeuner sur l'herbe* was first displayed to the world's disbelieving eyes. Claude, after a long search, finds his painting at last...

The disappointment seemed to have stopped even the beating of his heart. All he could do was stare at his picture, his wide eyes fixed as if by some invincible force. He stared at it in astonishment. Here in this exhibition room he scarcely recognized it: this was not the same piece of work it had been in his studio; it had turned yellow under the sallow light that filtered through the canvas shades; it seemed also somehow less effective, at once more rude and more laborious; and, either through the juxtaposition of the other pictures or simply because of the new surroundings, he saw at first glance all the faults to which he had been blind during the months he had been living close beside it....

He turned to Sandoz.

'They are right to laugh,' he said, simply. 'It isn't finished. But the woman is good, so never mind! Bongrand didn't make fun of me....'

His friend tried to draw him away, but he refused to go. On the contrary, he insisted on going up closer to the picture and – now that he had passed his own judgment on his work – watching and listening to the crowd. The tumult showed no abatement; indeed it was increasing, in a rising scale of senseless guffaws. He could see the visitors' mouths gaping, their eyes narrowing, from the moment they passed the door; across the room, a group of young people were staggering back against the archway as if someone had been tickling them in the ribs; a lady had just dropped on a sofa, out of breath with laughing. The report of this excruciatingly comic picture had been spreading everywhere, and people were stamping in from the four corners of the Salon, pushing up with shouts of 'Where is it?' and then, 'Oh, what a sight!' Witticisms rained down thicker and faster here than elsewhere, for the subject of the picture lent itself to buffoonery: no one understood it; it seemed to them absurd; its ludicrousness, as they saw it, made them laugh themselves sick. 'Look, the lady is too hot, and the gentleman has had to put on his coat for fear of taking cold.' 'No, you're wrong. She's blue already; the gentleman has pulled her out of some pond.' 'It's a girls' boarding school; look at the two playing leapfrog.' 'No, it's a wash-day. The bodies are blue, the trees are blue – he's given everything a good bluing.'

Those who were not laughing were almost beside themselves with rage. They felt insulted by these bluish tones, this new notation of the light. Should anyone be allowed to outrage art in such a fashion? (69)

203

Claude is crushed. Hours later, exhausted and feverish, he returns alone in a daze to his studio. There, waiting for him, is Christine, already aware of the disaster. What follows is one of the most touching passages in the novel:

'Don't take it so much to heart,' she said. 'I had to come and see you and tell you I think they're just jealous, and that I think it's a wonderful picture, and that I am so proud and so happy I was able to help you and have my little share in it too.'

He never stirred as he listened to her warm, kind words, her faltering voice. Then suddenly he collapsed in front of her, with his head on her knees, and burst into tears. All the excitement of the afternoon, his dauntless courage before the hisses of the crowd, his gaiety, all his violence broke down in a burst of choking sobs. From the moment when the laughter of the crowd had struck him, like a slap in the face, he had felt it pursuing him like a pack of hounds in full cry, down the Champs-Élysées, all along the embankment, and still now, at his heels in his own studio. His strength gave way in the end, leaving him helpless as a child, and he kept on saying, in a weary, toneless voice as he rolled his head on her knees:

'Oh God, how it hurts!'

Then, in a sweep of passion, she took hold of him with both hands, raised him up to her lips and kissed him.

'Don't cry,' she said, 'Don't cry, my dearest. I love you.'

And her warm breath carried her words to his very heart.

They were both in love, and it seemed fitting that their love should be consummated there in the studio as part of the story of the picture that had gradually drawn them together. Night closed in around them, and they lay in each other's arms, weeping tears of joy in the first outpourings of their passion. Near them, on the table, the lilacs she had sent that morning filled the evening air with their perfume, and on the floor flecks of gilt from the picture-frame caught the last of the daylight and shone out like a galaxy of stars. (70)

Soon the two lovers cannot bear to be apart and they flee to a romantic derelict cottage by the Seine at Bennecourt, two hours from Paris. Claude is entranced by his mistress; weeks and months pass as they explore the countryside, making love constantly, indoors and out. As for his painting, 'she enveloped him in a searing flame that shrivelled his artistic ambitions to nothing... and having killed his painting, delighted to be rid of her rival, she was determined to prolong the nuptials. Her plump arms and smooth legs made him linger in bed in the mornings, binding him with chains of happiness and lassitude.'

The honeymoon lasts three years, during which a child, Jacques, is born. Claude begins to paint again, with a refreshed vision: landscapes and still-life and, commissioning Christine's body once again, figure studies. But as he loses himself in his renewed struggle with artistic problems the black despairs return and Paris beckons. And as they leave their paradise at Bennecourt, both sense that the idyll is over.

Back in Paris Claude is seized with a new urgency and he paints like a man possessed. Three years pass. Now all his canvases are painted outdoors, an innovation that was not without its discomforts.

The first year, in December, when the snow was on the ground, he went and stood for four hours a day down behind Montmartre on the corner of a patch of waste land and painted: in the background, poverty, dismal hovels dominated by great factory chimneys; in the foreground a couple of ragged urchins, a boy and a girl, devouring stolen apples in the snow. His insistence on painting from life complicated his task

204

beyond description, involved him in almost insurmountable difficulties. Nevertheless, he finished his picture out of doors and limited his work in the studio to cleaning up. When he saw it in the cold, dead light of the studio, the picture amazed even Claude by its brutality; it was like a door flung open on the street revealing the blinding snow against which two pitiful figures stood out in dirty grey. He knew at once that a picture like that would never be accepted, but he made no attempt to tone it down and sent it to the Salon as it was.   (70)

More years pass, each marked by successive rejections at the annual Salons. Then Claude has an idea for what he hopes will be his greatest masterpiece, a single painting into which he will pour all his ambitions, passions and knowledge – an immense cityscape, a view of the Seine with female bathers in the foreground. The concept and the composition are revolutionary and even Claude's closest friend and supporter, Sandoz, is shocked, especially by the artist's insistence on a nude bather in the very middle of Paris. Although it outrages logic and realism the nude figure, to Claude, symbolises Paris as a city of passion and beauty.

He and Christine are married and, their small capital exhausted, they move to a draughty studio in the slums. Claude works week after week on the painting, using his wife as the model for the central figure. But he cannot get it right; his brushes and palette knife merely grope after his clouded vision. Christine suffers terribly from the long hours of posing in the freezing studio – and worse – Claude now sees her only as an object.

> And, as he had to come down to get another tube of paint, he went up to her and, with rising passion, went over every detail of her beauty, touching with his fingers the parts he desired to emphasise. 'There, you see, under the left breast, there's a beautiful bit where those little blue veins bring out the delicacy of the skin.... And there, on that curve of the hip, that dimple where the shadow looks golden, a feast for the eye.... And there now, under the good, stout modelling of the belly, the pure lines of the groin and the tiniest point of carmine showing through pale gold.... That's the part that's always thrilled me more than all the rest, the belly. The very sight of one makes me want to do impossible things. It's so lovely to paint, like a sun!'
>   The sitting seemed likely to go on for ever. Hours and hours went by, and still she stood there, offering herself like a diver ready to meet the water, while Claude on his ladder, leagues removed, burned with passion for the woman he was painting. He even stopped talking to her, and she became merely an object, perfectly coloured. He had been looking at her ever since morning, but she knew it was not her image she would find in his eyes, she was a stranger to him now, an outcast.   (70)

As their circumstances become increasingly desperate, only Christine's devotion to Claude keeps her going until, one evening, after posing all day, he descends from the ladder without offering her his usual kiss. In his total absorption with the painting she has almost ceased to exist for him, and 'she put on her chemise, struggled with her petticoats and only half-fastened her bodice as if wanting to escape from the shame of her impotent nudity, good now for nothing except to wither out of sight beneath a covering of clothes.'

But Claude and Christine aren't the only victims of his obsession; Jacques, now nearly ten, is suffering from neglect and hydrocephalus, and one morning Christine finds him dead in his cot. Claude is grief-stricken but, within minutes, finds himself fascinated by his dead son's glassy, staring eyes, and instinctively reaches for his paints and a canvas. At first the artist's eyes are misted with tears, the hands trembling, but only momentarily; and Claude beings to paint with inspired energy. Possession is now complete.

By a complicated strategy his friends contrive to have the painting, *Dead Child*, accepted by the Salon. It is Claude's first triumph, but it is to be a hollow triumph. Claude finds his painting hung above several other vast, dark monstrosities, so high and in such bad light that few visitors notice it, and those who do ignore it. This callous indifference cuts to Claude's heart; it is far worse than being laughed at. Yet, while his latest painting counts for nothing, the combined efforts of the modern painters have brought a breath of the blue sky and sunlight into the Salon. Its former grim and sepulchral tone is giving way to vibrant colour. The dawn of a new day for painting is breaking at last.

But for poor Claude the sun is setting. Although he persists with his unfinished, flawed masterpiece, he realises he is waiting in vain for his vision to clear so that his frustrated creative urge, as powerful in him as his heartbeat, can be satisfied. The novel ends in the finest tradition of romantic tragedy, but not before Christine extracts a brief revenge from the hated painting, the source of all her misery. Surprising Claude at his painting late one night, and tormented by nine months of loveless nights, she rips off her nightgown to challenge the impotent figure on his canvas with her frenzied sensuality. Little by little her husband is awakened by her writhing body entwined in his, and she tears him away from the picture to hours of victorious and rapturous delight in their bed. But her fleshy triumph is short-lived. In the morning she awakes to the horrifying sight of Claude hanging by his neck in front of the painting. And, in the end, the vast canvas becomes her shroud, too.

This synopsis of the narrative of *The Masterpiece* rather too readily suggests a highly melodramatic account of an artist in travail, painted in violent tones of purple. To some extent this is true, but the novel is scorched by deeply personal intrusions that give its many moving passages an unexpected enigmatic power. Perhaps alone of all his novels, Zola enjoyed writing *The Masterpiece*. Soured, morbid, enshrined in the dark, carved bleakness of his study, setting down the romantic memories of his schooldays and youth with Cézanne and Baille, ablaze with the light from the Provençal sun, filled him with a temporary joy. It was a novel, he recalled afterwards, into which 'my memories and my heart have overflowed'.

This autobiographical frankness is perhaps most remarkable in the glimpses it gives us of its author's paradoxical sexuality. On the one hand, Zola, as Sandoz, expresses the idea that for artists the married state is indispensable: 'It was the essential condition, he said, for the good, solid, regular work required of anyone who meant to produce anything worthwhile today.' He pours scorn on the romantic notion that women destroy artists and artistic creation, and wholeheartedly recommends to Claude that he finds himself a wife. Zola is of course describing his own situation in the novel: 'Since he gave up his office job six months ago, he had made some headway in journalism and found it more remunerative, too. He had just settled his mother into a little house in the Batignolles where he was looking forward to having the two women cherish him...' Everything seems to be fairly cosy. But in his notes for the novel, Claude's attitudes to women, love and sex more accurately reflect what we know to be Zola's *real* beliefs at about this time; that copulation lessens creative power. To Zola the orgasm, the need, the desire for it, and the act itself, was somehow shameful. Claude's actions in the novel tend to bear this out. Soon after his pent-up passions are appeased with Christine, he turns away from sexual contact. And again, towards the end of the book, Christine reacts violently to his self-imposed chastity:

> She continued boldly, she now spoke out freely – she, so strangely compounded of sensuality and modesty, so ardent in love, and so discreet afterwards, who would never speak of all those things, but turned her head away with a confused smile. Now, however, passion excited her, and her husband's continence seemed like an outrage. And she was not mistaken in her jealousy when she accused his art, for all his virility was reserved for it, and was bestowed by him upon her preferred rival. She knew very well why he neglected her like that. At first, he had said that he needed rest so as to do a good day's work on the morrow, and the habit once acquired, the intervals had become more and more prolonged, until at last there had been nothing more in common between them. And at the bottom of it all, there was the theory which he had repeated a hundred times in her presence: genius should be chaste, a man's only mistress, only wife, should be his work. (67)

Genius should be chaste. A few pages further on, Claude's punishment for surrendering to the carnal entreaties of his loving wife – one of Zola's great tragic heroines, incidentally – is death. Zola's duality can, however, be explained: he *knows* that a loving partner can be a valuable and even indispensable asset to an artist, but he *feels* otherwise. Claude's unfortunate life is, I think, an exteriorisation of this conflict, a fictional exploration of it to the bitter end.

But it is not entirely a fictional exploration, for Claude's reactions to women and sex in the novel almost parallel those of Paul Cézanne in real life, which oscillated between passionate desire and fear of possession. The fantasy and the chase were more necessary to Cézanne than fulfilment. He abandoned his mistress and wife Hortense and his child with a small allowance; and at least one other known love affair – with a servant called Fanny – was chaste. It is difficult to know, therefore, how much of Claude's continence is due to Zola's beliefs and how much is owed to his observation of Cézanne.

The same confusion of autobiographical and biographical elements confronts us when we consider Claude's attitude to nudity: '... chaste as he was, he had a passion for the physical beauty of women, an insane love for nudity desired but never possessed, but he was powerless to satisfy himself or to create the beauty that he dreamed of enfolding in an ecstatic embrace'. Cézanne, we know, was hampered in his work by a neurotic reluctance to draw from nude models; and the struggle between carnality and creative compulsion which reduced Cézanne to a bundle of raw nerve-ends and ultimate despair is perceptively re-created in the novel. But Zola goes further, and throughout the novel spends several dozen pages undressing Christine, which, even allowing for the novelty of nudity as a writer's device, is hardly justified. In the incident where she reluctantly poses for Claude for the first time, what is revealed is not so much Claude's – or Cézanne's – ambivalence towards the nude model, but, as with *Nana*, the trembling pen of the voyeur gloating sensually over the voluptuous details:

> And Christine, head held high and pale with emotion, heard every word and was moved by the force of the prayer in his burning look. With slow, deliberate fingers she took off her hat and her pelisse, then, without more ado, continued the same calm gesture, undid and removed her dress and her corsets, slipped off her petticoats unbuttoned the shoulder-straps and let her chemise slip down over her hips. She did all this without saying a word, as if she were elsewhere, or in her own room undressing herself without thinking while her mind wandered off in pursuit of a dream. Why should she let a rival give him her body when she herself had already given him her face? She wanted it to be *her* picture, hers entirely, the token of her affection, and as she realised that, she realised also that she had been jealous all along of that strange nondescript monster on the canvas. And so, still silent, virgin in her nudity, she lay on the divan and took up the pose, eyes closed, one arm beneath her head.   (70)

Despite the element of prurience in the build-up, the passage moves to a powerful and touching climax, with the two lovers, when the pose is over and the spell broken, saddened and ashamed at the violation that has taken place Only Claude has violated Christine's body not for love nor from physica passion, but for art – a betrayal that remains, even after the physica consummation of their love three weeks later, a wedge which eventually split them apart.

The Masterpiece also acted as a wedge which abruptly broke up the long and close friendship between Cézanne and Zola. A couple of weeks after the publication of the novel, the artist sent the following dignified but tart note to Zola: *Gardonne, 4 April 1886*

> My dear Émile,
>   I have just received *L'Oeuvre* which you were kind enough to send me. I thank the author of *Les Rougon-Macquart* for this token of remembrance, and I ask him to permit me to send him a greeting as an acknowledgement of past friendship.
> All yours, in memory of past times, Paul Cézanne

It was a farewell note. Although the artist might have basked pleasantly in the warm memories evoked by the passages in the early chapters of the novel describing his youth – Henri Gasquet relates that he was 'profoundly moved by them – he must have been shocked at seeing himself reflected in the dark and cruelly distorted mirror of the final chapters.

Zola could have pointed out, of course, that Claude's neurosis and suicide were merely the results of the ancestral Rougon-Macquart curse. *The Masterpiece* was, I'm sure, meant to be a tribute to Cézanne, whose beliefs and passions Zola had shared over many years. Zola planned to reveal to the world the terrors confronting a creative artist of genius, perpetually dissatisfied continually rejected, tormented by a visionary ambition beyond his powers, an explorer who knows he has passed the point of no return in his fruitless search fot the unknown, the unseen. But the intended tribute got lost on the way. The exact extent to which Zola fictionalised Cézanne's personal dilemma and externalised his own fears for the artist's personality will never by known – it may have been obscure even to the novelist himself – but the emotional effect on poor Cézanne, subject at this time to morbid bouts of self-doubt, can be imagined.

Claude's suicide, which must have distressed Cézanne most of all, was not so much Zola's prognosis of his friend's personality conflict as the symbolic end of an artist who abandons artistic creation for sexual love. Nor was it simply a melodramatic device intended to shock Cézanne; at least a couple of artists had suicided before their canvases in the years prior to the writing of *The Masterpiece*. One young man, who had shot himself in the head, was the subject of a newspaper article by Zola in 1866. Another may be seen in Manet's painting *L'Enfant aux cerises*; he was apprenticed to the great artist and hanged himself shortly after his perpetuation in paint. Manet, overcome by the horror of the event, moved to another studio.

While it is understandable that Cézanne must have cringed when he wondered what his friends might think after reading the novel, *The Masterpiece* wasn't the sole factor in the break-up between the artist and the novelist. For one thing, Cézanne had become financially independent just before the publication of the book. Over the years, Zola had frequently helped Cézanne with small amounts of money while the artist waited for his father to grant an allowance, often sending sums of sixty francs to Paul's mistress, Hortense, in Marseilles. It was an anxious time for the artist, in debt for painting materials and with Hortense and his child to keep. That he was in extreme financial difficulties is revealed in a letter to Zola in which he complains about the novelist's heavy notepaper: 'At the post office I had to pay 25 centimes for insufficient stamping... when you write, please only enclose a single sheet...'

Cézanne's penury was abruptly removed on the death of his father in 1885, when he received as his share of the will some 400,000 francs, a fortune to the desperately poor artist. But while this relieved one anxiety it could not remove another – Cézanne's fears of imminent death. The hard years had left him, at forty-seven, an old man in deteriorating health. His final years were to be a race against time, and he studied and painted with a renewed and ceaseless energy that he hoped would take him beyond the furthermost frontiers of art. It was with this new-found feeling of impatience and independence that he had visited Zola at Médan when the novelist was deep into *The Masterpiece*. It was to be their last meeting. Cézanne said later that during his stay there he had felt disturbed and uncomfortable, and 'no longer at ease, with all those carpets and servants and that great carved desk. I felt I was paying a visit to the Minister of State.'

There are several conflicting reports of Cézanne's feelings towards the novelist after the break, but unquestionably the distance between them grew with the years. One friend of the artist recorded that Cézanne was always moved by re-reading the early chapters of *The Masterpiece*, and came to realise that at a certain point in the novel Zola had switched from memoir to fiction. But Emile Bernard, writing in 1904, recounts that during the Dreyfus Affair Cézanne had reflected that Zola was a detestable friend, and that the novel was a horrible distortion aimed at increasing the author's own glory. The book was bad, he said, and was completely false. Vollard recalled, too, that the mere mention of *The Masterpiece* was enough to stir Cézanne into such a frenzy that he once tore a canvas to pieces.

The broken friendship was a sad climax to a long and fruitful relationship. Without Zola's persistence, patience and encouragement during his early years it is quite possible Cézanne might have given up the struggle to express his vision in paint, thus changing the whole course of contemporary art. For more than a decade the artist owed what reputation he had to Zola, and this early struggle for recognition was a vital factor in his development. There is also the school of thought that has advanced the theory that the suicidal fate of Claude Lantier in the novel was a salutary lesson for Cézanne. Heeding the warning, and with the sympathetic advice of Pissarro, he withdrew to an absorbed study of nature, emerging eventually with new energies and fresh inspiration to tackle his original goal.

Zola, who had lost faith in the ultimate triumph of his friend's genius at a crucial time, formed a deeper appreciation of Cézanne's intentions later in life. Although he lost interest in the work of the modern artists he told a reporter in 1896 that Cézanne was one of the greatest painters who ever lived, and he always admired his work when he saw it.

The Impressionists followed the serialisation of *The Masterpiece*, which began in *Le Gil Blas* on 23 December 1885, with great interest. Their reactions were mixed. Renoir was incensed. 'Zola', he said, 'never gave a damn about portraying his friends accurately or to their advantage.' Pissarro was noncommittal and unruffled, but Degas remarked at a party that Zola only wrote the book to demonstrate the superiority of literature over art. Two artists failed to see the resemblance between Claude and Cézanne. One was Monet, who, because the novel appeared to equate Impressionism with failure, feared that it played into the hands of their enemies. The other was Antoine Guillemet, the pupil of Corot who appears in the novel as Fagerolles. He wrote, protesting, to Zola, that although it was a fascinating book, and that he was deeply moved by the passages recalling their youthful wanderings, its overall tone was depressing. Almost all the artists in *The Masterpiece*, he wrote, were frustrated, unhappy failures, while in real life so many of them – Daumier, Millet, Courbet and Corot for example – had eventually achieved happiness and success. 'In your latest work', he concluded, 'I find only sadness or impotence.'

What the ordinary Englishman of the time thought of the lives and ideas of the artists in *The Masterpiece* can only be imagined, for 'impressionism' was then, for most, an esoteric word cloaked in confusion. Even Vizetelly, who frequently visited Paris, was confused, as he reveals in the preface to his English translation of 1886. The idea of the novel, he wrote, came from

> ...M. Edouard Manet, who, in his efforts to introduce what he considered to be a truly realistic style of painting, only succeeded in founding what is nowadays known in France as the 'impressionist' school. Claude Lantier, M. Zola's hero, must not,

however, be regarded as a close portrait of the late M. Manet; for the latter was almost a wealthy man...moreover M. Manet's married life was a happy one, and in nowise resembled the pitiful existence led by Claude and his helpmate, Christine.'

Further on he writes that with the exception of Sandoz, 'no other personage in the story can be identified with any individual prototype.' In his role of Zola's English translator and publisher, Henry Vizetelly was on regular speaking terms with the author, from whom he must have acquired the information given in the preface. While it is not strange that Vizetelly would not have known of Cézanne's connection with the character Claude – it is likely that he had never heard of Cézanne at all – what is curious is that Zola did not attempt to correct his interpretation. But from all accounts the novelist held his cards very close to his chest for some time, and it was not until many years later that Cézanne's contribution to the story became known. Vizetelly's ignorance is corrected in his son's preface to the 1902 English edition of the novel.

It must not be thought that *The Masterpiece* is encrusted with heavy discourses on art and philosophy and that its appeal is exclusive to artists. It isn't. Certainly it records those heady and colourful days when a new direction was being shaped for the future history of art, and in this respect it is unique, for Zola was closer in person and in spirit to the early Impressionists than any other contemporary writer. Their struggles, conversations, theorising and habits are incidentally captured in this novel with vivid authenticity, preserving those first uncertain, luminous dabs which were to eventually illuminate a large corner of the world.

The Masterpiece has none of the vulgarity, violence or sustained tragedy of many of the other *Rougon-Macquart* novels, nor the epic grandeur of *Germinal*. And it narrowly escapes the consequences of a near-mortal wound at the start, for the first chapter is disarmingly sentimental with a waif-like young lady on a doorstep, sheltering from a thunderstorm. But what this novel does have is unrelieved conflict, the very stuff of drama, and the tensions of a suspension bridge in a gale, and to produce them Zola bared his deepest fears and beliefs to our gaze.

14

'He Shunned
Not Even Ordure!'

The peasants of mid-nineteenth-century France were the exhausted survivors of a 2,000-year campaign of exploitation and extermination which began with their enslavement by the Romans and continued through centuries of serfdom, injustice and misrule by rapacious aristocrats. Although the Revolution of 1793 didn't pass the peasants by, its benefits did, for when their serfdom was exchanged for land rights they inherited a harsher master and mistress: money, and the land itself. Like the miners in *Germinal* the peasants became grist for the mills of distant, city-based capitalism, victims of supply and demand, increasing taxes and falling prices. But while money was a ferocious taskmaster, the new mistress was even crueller, and more capricious. The land was so impoverished that no amount of work could make it yield one extra ear of grain. A single hailstorm could destroy a year's hard labour. Rain rotted the seed and drought shrivelled the growing corn. The wasted body of the land was prone to all kinds of disease; weeds poisoned the soil and cattle were wiped out overnight by any one of a hundred disorders. Yet, somehow, the peasant survived, and the key to his survival was his blind devotion to his land. With it, he could just hold on to life; without it, he was dead.

Zola wrote *Earth* not so much to expose the misery of the peasant as to explode the middle-class myth that farming was some sort of bucolic pastime, incidental to the enjoyment of the countryside. In an early chapter, Jean Macquart – who fulfils the same role in this novel as Etienne Lantier did in *Germinal* – reads to the peasants from a Bonapartist propaganda leaflet, written no doubt by a politician who has never crumbled a lump of earth nor trodden on a cow-flop, extolling the rustic bliss which most city folk believed was the life of the peasant:

> 'Happy husbandman, forsake not the village for the town, where everything – milk, meat, vegetables – must be bought, and where you would always spend more than necessary, because of the opportunities offered. Have you not fresh air and sunshine, healthy toil, and honest joys in the village? Rural life is peerless; far from gilded pomp, you enjoy true happiness; in proof thereof, do not the town artisans go for jaunts into the country, just as the tradesman's one dream is to seek retirement near you, culling flowers, eating fruit off the tree, and gambolling on the sward. Be sure,

Jacques Bonhomme, that money is but a chimera. If your bosom be at peace, your fortune is made.' (72)

The words, intoned to a bunch of overworked, destitute farmers, are savagely ironic. The fact was that the peasant had no future, for most of the social architects of the time, including Karl Marx, saw that small-scale farming was futile, even idiotic. Yet the blood in the veins of every peasant ran contrary to this theory; if only he had a bit more land and a change of luck, he would prosper.

Zola was country-bred, but he knew little of farming. His interest in farm economics quickened, however, after the acquired Médan in 1878, for there he came into contact with local proprietors and peasants and even kept horses and farm animals of his own. The notion of setting one of the *Rougon-Macquart* novels deep in the country, though, wasn't decided until about two years later. Then, in the spring of 1886, immediately he'd finished *The Masterpiece*, Zola set about scouting a location.

I can remember first reading *Earth* with that marvellous feeling of stepping out on to a country railway platform after a long, stuffy journey from the city, blinking in the bright light, lungs alive to the clean, crisp air, slightly bemused by the soft sounds and voices of the countryside. For me it was an experience loaded with pleasant expectations, and I imagine that Zola was similarly refreshed when he arrived at Châteaudun, then a small market town in the great, grain-growing plain of Beauce, the centre of which is the famous cathedral town of Chartres – a vast plain of nearly 3,000 square miles, treeless and with its flatness interrupted only by windmills and occasional villages. The naturalist was finally confronted with nature at its most primitive, and it is no surprise that from the experience grew what many regard as Zola's greatest masterpiece.

For a week Zola and his wife clopped ceaselessly along the country roads, usually in a two-horse landau, alighting now and then to talk to a solitary farmer, to makes notes on a decrepit cottage, or to hastily explore a village. During the visit they methodically inspected farms, solemnly watched sheep being shorn and cattle being sold. Then, satisfied, they returned to Médan by train. This manner of exploration later prompted a quip from Paul Valéry that Zola's research for *Earth* had amounted to a 'quick drive through La Beauce in a trap'.

Zola's intention, which he had set down in his notes, was to write a 'living poem of the soil: the cycle of the seasons, the labour in the fields, the farmers, the animals, the entire countryside'. As a poem it was also to be as rude and as earthy as a farmyard, as readers were to discover after the first few pages.

The immense, broad plain of the Beauce presented Zola with a new horizon for his descriptive lyricism. Until now, his settings had been confined by walls, coal dumps, city buildings or forest trees. The panoramic landscape of the Beauce widened his vision and must surely have inspired him, because *Earth* abounds with descriptive passages that drift like snow, shimmer with the brilliance of sun-struck quartz or move majestically and rhythmically with the primitive movements of the peasants. Unfortunately the economy of his lyricism tends to be lost in translation, but here is what Zola saw, projected through the eyes of one of his characters:

> La Beauce spread out her greenery before him from November to July, from the moment when the green tips first sprouted to the moment when the tall stalks turned golden. He wanted the great plain under his eyes even when he was still in the house. He had taken down the bars of the kitchen window, the one at the back which looked out over La Beauce; and he would stand there staring over the ten leagues of plain, a huge expanse, that stretched out quite bare under the dome of the sky. Not a single tree, nothing except the telegraph poles on the Châteaudun-Orléans road running in one long straight line till they faded in the distance. First, in the big squares of brown soil, low on the earth there appeared a greenish shade, barely visible. Then, the tender green deepened into carpets of green velvet almost uniform in hue. Then the stalks grew and thickened, and each plant took on its own tinge, so that the watcher could tell at a distance the yellow-green of the wheat, the blue-green of the oats, the grey-green of the barley, the strips stretching indefinitely in every direction with red patches of clover gleaming between. Now was the time when La Beauce was lovely in her youth, clad in the spring, smooth and fresh to the eye in her universal growth. The stalks grew stronger and she became the sea, a sea of corn, rolling, deep, limitless. On mornings of fine weather a fleeting rose mist swathed her. As the sun rose in the limpid air, a breeze blew in big steady puffs, furrowing the fields with a swell that started from the horizon, lengthened and then ebbed away at the outer edge. The hues fluttered and paled, and moiré-lights of old gold rippled through the wheat, the oats were brushed with bluish tints and the trembling rye turned up violet reflections. Endlessly one wave succeeded another, the ceaseless swell went on under the wind from the great spaces. When evening came, the distant buildings, brightly lit up, looked like white sails and church steeples rose up like masts out of dips in the earth. The air turned cold, the deep shadows increased the cool sensation of a murmurous open sea. A distant wood faded from sight like the lost outline of a continent. (74)

The hero, Jean Macquart, is, according to the genealogical tree, a brother of Liza Quenu of *The Belly of Paris* and also of Gervaise of *L'Assommoir,* and thus an uncle of Nana, Etienne, and Claude, whom we have just buried. But the family link is a paper connection only, for *Earth* owes nothing to the heredity of the unfortunate family, and Zola ascribes no outstanding personality defects to Jean. He is, in fact, the only rational character in the novel. He is a carpenter and an ex-soldier, that is all, an outsider entering the life of an isolated farming community. The success of the character Etienne in *Germinal* must have influenced the novelist, perhaps unconsciously, in developing Jean, for they possess many similarities. The most important of these is that Jean is a 'fresh eye' through which we are introduced to a way of life quite foreign to us. Like Etienne, Jean also aspires to better the miserable lives of those around him; and like Etienne he ends up detesting their ignorance and brutishness.

As with *Germinal,* the reader spends much of his time with a single family; in *Earth* it is with the Fouan clan, headed by Old Fouan and his wife who, with their children Buteau, Hyacinthe and Fanny, monopolise the cast. It is Buteau, however, who engages our interest most, for he is one of the most coarse, brutal and unfeeling characters Zola ever created. With lust and greed as the principal forces that motivate him, there is a feeling of inevitability about his destiny, and even though at the close of the novel he manages to escape the consequences of a rape and two murders, we know instinctively that he's bound to come to a sticky end.

Although the Grégoires in *Germinal* were comical figures, they performed on a stage of bitter irony and it is unlikely they provoked many laughs from readers. The Charles's in *Earth*, however, really *are* light relief. For a start, they make their money from a brothel in a distant town, and not from a shareholding as they pretend and – despite their airs of respectability – everyone knows it. They perform on a stage deep in slippery muck, affecting not to notice it; one false step and they could fall on their faces. This is a literary form of music-hall slapstick, and it is at times uproariously effective.

The comic cast of *Earth* also includes Gédéon the drinking donkey and old Mother Caca, whose vegetable garden doubles as an earth closet; but Zola's most ribald creation is Hyacinthe Fouan – nicknamed Jésus-Christ – who is Buteau's elder brother, a happy-go-lucky, heavy-drinking spendthrift with a loud mouth and an even louder sphincter. Hyacinthe could have emerged with an explosive report from the pages of Rabelais, for he is continually demonstrating the audible evidence of a truly Gargantuan flatulence. At the time *Earth* was published, the English had been deprived of the word describing this function for at least half a century. Dr Johnson's *Dictionary of the English Language* (1755) had not only defined the word, but had also illustrated its literary use from Swift: 'So from my lord his passion broke,/He farted first, and then he spoke.'

The word, of course, has ancient roots; an early recorded usage, for example, occurs in the well-known thirteenth-century Saxon song, *Sumer is icumen in*: 'Bulluc sterteth, bucke verteth' - or, bullock leapeth, buck farteth. By the nineteenth century, however, most versions had 'buck departeth'. This gradual but relentless erasure of the word was applied to all classical literature; in Herrick's *Hesperides* the line 'Let me feed full till that I fart, says Jill,' was quietly omitted so as not to disturb the Victorian image of Herrick as a spinner of exclusively dainty verse. So it is hardly surprising that Hyacinthe was greeted with stony Anglo-Saxon disapproval until relatively recently. But even when literary ribaldry became generally fashionable after the Second World War, farting could not claim to be among the top ten funny functions of the human body. The French, on the other hand, do not have the same aversion for farting; indeed, the greatest farter in recorded history, *Le Pétomane*, a music-hall performer of the 1890s who somehow extruded tunes and could blow out candles with ease, was elevated to the status of a popular hero and was also the subject of several serious scientific studies. Although Joseph Pujol (*Le Pétomane's* real name) didn't star at the Moulin Rouge until 1892, his fame had been in the air for many years and it is possible that Zola's legendary nose, getting wind of his unique talent, used him as the model for Hyacinthe. I have doubts that the novelist invented this incredible character and, in any case, he always showed a preference for basing or building his characters on real people. One can imagine Zola, in later years, defending his windy hero by flourishing a copy of the Bordeaux *Gazette hebdomadaire des sciences médicales*, which had published a thesis on Pujol, in the faces of his anti-naturalist critics. But to return from this interesting digression, Hyacinthe is a wholly successful character because his feats are exaggerated beyond what most people recognise as the limits of reality and although there are many instances of this, one should suffice: the episode in which Hyacinthe repels a bailiff's man by letting off a fusillade of what sounds like gun shots.

> Vimeux saw that he'd have to submit. He turned sadly round and presented to view his poor little bottom as thin as a starving cat's. The poacher sprang forward vigorously and planted the toe of his boot just in the right spot with such force that the little man went flat on his face fully four yards away. He rose painfully to his feet and bolted in abject terror as he heard a further shout.
> 'Look out, I'm going to fire!'
> Jésus-Christ's gun was at his shoulder. But he contented himself with raising his leg – and bang! he released a blurt with such a resounding crack that Vimeux, terrified at the detonation, once again fell flat. This time his black hat fell off and rolled away among the stones. He ran after it, snatched it up, then went dodging off faster than before. Behind him the shots continued – bang! bang! bang! without a pause: a perfect fusillade accompanied by shouts of laughter which completed his bewilderment. Bounding down the slope like a grasshopper, he was already a hundred yards distant, but Jésus-Christ's cannonade still echoed through the valley. Indeed the whole countryside reverberated and there was one last formidable blast as the bailiff, who from the distance now looked about the size of an ant, disappeared into Rognes. (74)

It wasn't farting that outraged literary Paris, but the gross exaggeration, for in this Zola had, they argued, destroyed his credibility as a realist writer. The performances of Hyacinthe, however, are no more than comic indulgences on Zola's part, to compensate for some of the grimmer aspects of the novel, and there are endless instances of extravagant overstatement in this work. Seemingly unimportant incidents are magnified for effect: he works on the interior of a room until the atmosphere becomes overpowering; innocent utensils are transformed into monstrous, menacing instruments; shadows become alive, and so forth. Zola rarely used a palette of sombre colours. Repetition, too, is a characteristic of his writing, always for cumulative effect. None of this proves, though, that Zola wasn't a realist; the truth is that the artist in him could never be entirely strait-jacketed in documented reality.

In a nutshell, *Earth* takes its theme from Shakespeare's *King Lear*: it is the story of an old man who, forced to divide his property among his children, is cruelly harrassed by them for what little else remains, until he is dead. The theme, as simple yet as complex as the earth itself, hums with the intrigue of subplots carefully dovetailed into the narrative and constantly arrests the reader with fascinating insights into the motivations of the characters.

Following the pastorale of the opening chapter, in which we meet Jean Macquart, we are immediately plunged into an atmosphere of bitterness and bestiality that sticks like Beauce mud until the very end. The cause of this is the division of Old Fouan's land between his daughter Fanny and his two sons, Buteau and Hyacinthe – or Jésus-Christ.

The old man, at seventy, is now unable to work the land, and hopes that by splitting it between his children while he is alive they will pay him a regular agreed allowance until his death. After a protracted argument an agreement is reached, and the land is surveyed into handkerchief-size parcels, but not before the parents' allowance is reduced by their children's avarice from 800 francs to a bare 550 francs a year. Their greed, in fact, is the source of endless discord; Buteau accuses the others of cheating him and refuses to accept his portion.

Meanwhile Jean, who works as a labourer at a nearby farm, befriends two sisters who have recently been orphaned: Françoise, who is just fourteen, and Lise, older and pregnant by Buteau. Jean helps them work the smallholding they have inherited, and eventually falls in love with the gentler, prettier Françoise. As she is too young for marriage, however, Jean instead proposes to Lise, so as to be near her younger sister. But then Buteau returns; now that Lise is a landowner she is a much more attractive proposition to him than before, and he marries her – to Jean's secret relief, even though he is now odd man out.

Now that he is a married man, Buteau accepts his share of the land he'd sulkily refused two years before, and he is ecstatic in his possession with a near-carnal passion. It is not long, though, before arguments break out over money. Of the three Fouan children, only Fanny and her husband pay their share of the parents' allowance on the dot; Buteau is always short and Hyacinthe scornfully pays them nothing at all. On the contrary, he wheedles more money from his impoverished parents on one pretext or another. Buteau, when he hears of this, can't stand the thought of a single sou of his hard-earned money being given to his wastrel brother so he stops payments, too. The bitter squabbling helps kill off their mother, and old Fouan, now helpless on his own, is forced to sell their house and goes to live with Fanny.

The seasons roll by and Lise has Buteau's child, and then another. Jean is still patiently waiting for Françoise but one day in the fields his lust overcomes him and he forcefully seduces her. The near-rape, however, has the effect of an engagement; the couple come to an understanding that if he will wait, she will marry him as soon as she comes of age. This conspiracy enrages Buteau – who also has his eyes on Françoise – and as she lives in the same house she is an easy target for a series of brutal assaults by her brother-in-law.

Then Françoise and Lise, goaded by Buteau, fall out. They were once inseperable and loving sisters, but now they hate each other. Only the threat of having the joint property subdivided stops Lise from throwing her sister out of the house; for her part, Françoise is trapped, and although she is little more than a slave to Lise and Buteau, and receives no income from the property, grimly hangs on to protect her legal rights. Finally, on the very day she comes of age, she marries Jean.

The union brings about the inevitable division of the property. It is a degrading, drag-down, knockout affair which, though it ends in victory for Françoise and Jean, who manage to buy the cottage at auction, also results in the sisters parting forever.

Françoise and Jean settle down and, although it is as they soon discover a loveless marriage, they are content enough. Françoise also becomes pregnant.

217

Meanwhile, poor old Fouan is hunted by his children like an animal for the small amount of cash he is known to have secreted somewhere, and, starved by Fanny he moves from his daughter's house to live with his son, Hyacinthe. While equally rapacious, Jésus-Christ is at least a little more fun to live with. But the Buteaus, in addition to hounding Fouan, now hunger for the land and cottage belonging to the newly married couple, and their anger and greed know no bounds. In the fields one day, when Jean is absent, Buteau provokes an argument with Françoise, and with the help of his wife rapes his pregnant sister-in-law. Astonishingly, in the middle of this act of lust and brutality Françoise discovers that she loves Buteau, and clings to him with all the passion in her.

> He had managed to bring her up against the rick. Seizing her by the shoulder, he threw her on her back. But at that moment she began to struggle, distracted returning without thought to her old ways of resistance. He held on and tried to avoid her kicks.
> 'You're pregnant already, you damned fool, what difference can it make? I won' give you another one, you can be sure of that!'
> She burst out weeping and had a sort of fit. She made no further attempt to defend herself, but her arms twisted about and her legs jerked in nervous convulsions Buteau found it impossible to take her; he was continually thrown to one side or other whenever he tried. His anger made him callous and he turned towards his wife.
> 'You damned lazy slut, what are you standing there for? Come and help me, hold her legs if you want me to do it.'
> Lise had remained standing motionless about ten yards away, scanning the countryside, then looking back at the other two, without the least change of expression. At her husband's call she didn't hesitate a moment, but went forward grasped her sister's left leg, pulled it to one side and sat on it as if she wanted to crush it. Françoise, pinned to the ground, went suddenly limp, with deadened nerves and closed eyelids. But she remained conscious all the while; and when Buteau took her she was carried away by such a spasm of keen ecstasy that she clung smotheringly to him with both arms and let out a long cry. The crows flying above were frightened Behind the rick Old Fouan's white face appeared; he had been sheltering there from the cold. He had seen everything and was doubtless terror-stricken, for he immediately dropped down in the straw again.
> Buteau rose to his feet and Lise stared sharply at him. She had had only one interest: to see that everything was done properly. But in his excitement he had forgotten their whole plan, the signs of the cross and the *Ave* repeated backwards. She was struck dumb with fury. So it was for his own pleasure that he had done it!
> Françoise gave her no time for explanations. For an instant she remained lying on the ground, as if she had fainted under the stress of a rapture which she had never before experienced. She had suddenly learned the truth: she loved Buteau, she never had and never would love anyone else. The discovery filled her with shame; and she was infuriated with herself, as her sense of justice flared up. A man who didn't belong to her, a man belonging to a sister whom she loathed, the one man whom she could never have without being a whore! She had just now let herself be fully possessed; she had embraced him so madly that he must know! (74

Lise, beside herself with anger at this unexpected turn of events, then attacks her sister and pushes her so that she stumbles backwards on to the point of a sickle. After lingering for a week, Françoise dies, but without ever revealing her secret to Jean.

The Buteaus are overjoyed. Not only does their crime escape detection, but because Françoise never made a will all the land reverts to them. Jean, the

218

hated outsider, who arrived at the village with only the clothes he stood up in, now leaves with no more and no less.

There is one remaining snag, however, and that is old Fouan. Although, following an earlier stroke, he is reduced to near-imbecility, he has witnessed the murder of Françoise in the fields. The final shocking episode in this wretched family feud provides the last chilling climax of the novel.

'I should like to do for the peasant in *Earth* what I did for the working man in *Germinal*,' said Zola in a letter written during 1886.

There are many similarities between *Earth* and *Germinal*: the land is just as demanding a tyrant as the mine; Beauce is just as isolated as Montsou; the peasants struggle just as the miners struggled against an old and unjust order for an existence and a future; and there is distressing misery and violence in both novels.

But there are also critical differences. In *Germinal* there is a relentless build-up of the most excruciating tensions, which contribute to the novel's unputdownable quality. In *Earth*, although it begins promisingly and powerfully, the climaxes seem to roll by like the furrows in the fields, and the narrative undeniably flags towards the end. The climaxes are also always violent – arguments, fights, murders and rapes – so that before the end of the novel we are almost immune from any outrage Zola chooses to throw at us. There is little of the accumulating, horrifying inevitability in *Earth* that gives the violence in *Germinal* that particularly jagged, disturbing edge.

Zola also faced another problem. *Germinal* had the advantage of its setting to induce feelings of apprehension in the reader: the black, hellish bowels of a coal mine, and the ever-present dangers lurking there. But in *Earth* the wide, open countryside is far from sinister, and all the action takes place in the blazing light. This difference is conveyed dramatically at the very beginning of each of the novels; in *Germinal*, Etienne arrives at Montsou on a dark, storm-swept night, to be greeted by the menacing apparition of the Voreaux; whereas *Earth* begins with the most peaceful and pastoral of all scenes, that of a peasant scattering seed on a freshly-ploughed, sun-baked field.

But if Zola's intentions for *Earth* were unrealised in some respects, the novel possesses enough magnificent qualities to permanently ensure its reputation as a masterpiece. One of its more remarkable features is its haunting sexual symbolism, which is attached to the narrative like bark to a tree. Zola somehow intuitively understood the peasant's insane, indecent love for the soil, which was sympathetically revealed in *The Abbé Mouret's Sin* thirteen years before. The passions reserved by the city-dwellers for their women are spent, by the peasants, on their land; what passes for human love between the peasants and their women is intermittent lust, prompted by the call of nature. If the earth is the womb of life then the plough's furrow is the vulva into which the peasant pours his labour and his seed in the hope of returned love. As a man might pleasure his lover with his hands and mouth Buteau, in one instance, takes a fistful of earth and holds it to his face, deeply breathing in its odour and enjoying the feel of it as it crumbles through his fingers. It is a sensual gesture of possession, but it does not necessarily make him any less impotent:

> A year went by, and that first year of possession was sheer bliss for Buteau. In all his time as a hired labourer he never ploughed so deep, the earth he now turned was his earth, he wanted to penetrate right in, fertilise it in the very bowels. Each evening he came home exhausted, with the ploughshare gleaming silver. In March he harrowed his wheat, in April his oats, unstinting in his care and giving every ounce of his strength. When the strips had no need of more work, he still went to look at them like a lover. He walked round, bent down and with his habitual gesture took up a fistful of earth, a rich clod which he loved to crumble and let run through his fingers supremely happy when he felt it neither too dry nor too humid and smelt in it the good smell of growing bread. (74)

The point that the land is mistress, lover and possessor is made on almost every page of the novel with allusive, erotic imagery. But there is no guarantee that the peasant's devotion will be returned, for this earthy mistress is fickle, a quality which breeds jealousy and covetousness in her lovers. Even ownership the most exalted dream of every peasant, doesn't ensure fidelity, for with a single hailstorm or a drought she can ruin him. Yet he still pursues this perfidious lover, driven by lust and blind faith. In one droll but extraordinarily perceptive passage, Zola shows how a farmer's young wife confidently counts on her husband's preoccupation with the harvest while she is seducing one of his farm labourers:

> She had got him to follow her like a dog; she took him into the barns, into the hay-loft, even into the sheep-fold now that the shepherd, whose prying eyes she feared, slept out of doors with his sheep. At night especially she banqueted on his virility, and rose from it slim and supple, and overflowing with energy. Hourdequin observed nothing, knew nothing. He had the harvest fever, his particular fever, the great annual crisis of his passion for the soil. He shivered inwardly, his head on fire his heart palpitating; his flesh quivered as the ripe ears fell. (73)

Images of fertility, which run through most of Zola's novels like spring sap predictably abound in *Earth*: 'It was the thrust of approaching spring which flowed in the fermentation of the liquid manure; matter which had decomposed was returning to the common womb; death was about to recreate life; and, from one end of the countryside to the other a smell was rising, the powerful fumes of the manure which provides the bread of men.' Whenever there is death there is always the promise of replacement with life. When Jean rapes Françoise behind a haystack, and withdraws at her pleading, his seed spurts into the ripe corn. When Palmyre, the semi-imbecile farmhand, dies in the field from sunstroke, she breathes her last amid the fruitful yield of the harvest. Even when her body is borne away on a stretcher covered with sheaves of corn, like some sacrificial victim, Zola redresses the balance in a masterly passage:

> As the sun was setting and putting an end to work, two men came to carry the stretcher away. The weight was not a great one and there was scarcely need to change bearers. Still, other men walked with them and there was quite a procession. They cut across the fields to avoid the bend in the road. On the sheaves the body was stiffening and some corn-ears, hanging down behind the head, swung to and fro at each jolt in the measured pace of the bearers.

220

Now there remained nothing in the sky but the day's accumulated heat – a reddish heat that weighted the blue air. On the horizon, on the further side of the Loire valley, the sun, blurred in a haze, now spread over La Beauce a layer of yellow rays level with the earth. Everything was turned yellow, golden in the lovely harvest evening. The corn that still stood was plumed with rosy fires; the stubble lifted tips of glistening red; and in every direction, on and on, jutting up out of the golden sea, the stacks seemed to grow grotesquely large, islands of sparkling flame on one side while on the other they were dark, with lengthening shadows that stretched on into the lost distances of the plain. (74)

The gauze-like curtain of imagery that Zola has spun throughout the novel suddenly drops down in the final three paragraphs, designed to capture us in case we have somehow escaped entanglement in its threads. It is a quite justifiable device, for a theme as universal as the life force itself can stand plenty of reiteration. Despite his grief at the tragic death of his wife, his despair and disappointment and his loathing of the brutalised peasants, Jean leaves the land on which he's laboured for more than a decade with a feeling of inner serenity and a knowledge that life will triumph; a departure not unlike that of Etienne in *Germinal*:

For a long time this confused reverie, hardly formulated as it was, floated in Jean's brain. But a trumpet sounded in the distance, the trumpet of the fire-brigade of Bazoches-le-Doyen, which came up at a gallop, too late. And at that sound he drew himself suddenly up. It was war coming through the mist – war, with its horses, its cannons, its clamour of slaughter. A sudden emotion choked him. Ah, Lord help him! Since he had no longer the heart to work for her, he would defend her, the old soil of France. He was leaving, when, for the last time, he let his gaze stray from the two graves, bare of grass, to the endless tilth-land of Beauce, which the sowers, with their monotonous gesture, were fertilizing. There was death, and seed-time, and the earth brought forth her fruits. (73)

The passage, which echoes the sowing theme with which the novel begins, is Zola's poetic refrain on the indestructibility of life.

Although the smell of the earth undoubtedly intoxicated the poet in Zola it doesn't explain the plethora of horrors the author conjured up for this novel. The pages of *Earth* are bloody with tragedy: ironic, accidental, horrific and barbaric – the incestuous rape of the gentle, pregnant Françoise followed by her death on the point of a sickle takes the prize for bestial invention – and there is a bountiful harvest of the seven deadly sins. Perhaps the instincts of the peasants seemed to Zola so basic and so crude that he believed any crime, no matter how outrageous, was possible among these people. It is hard to say. I find it difficult to imagine the novelist's state of mind when he wrote *Earth*. The fantasies of a profoundly frustrated man, denied the potential of his sexuality, had surely been given release in his three previous novels. But in this novel Zola seems to be reaching into the very bottom of the barrel for here there is an animality and a brutality that many, even his admirers, found gratuitous. As ever, Zola's deeper secrets are locked in paradox.

From the point of view of a modern reader I doubt if many would find *Earth* gratuitously brutish, for the author achieves a remarkable balance between the repugnant and the poetic. The countryside itself, the open vistas, the seasons and all the processes of nature have the effect of a cleansing breeze on the more fetid incidents with which he confronts us, and also account for the unexpected serenity to be found in the novel. More than anything else he attempted, *Earth* stretched Zola's considerable gifts to the limit, and on this occasion at least he knew 'how far to go too far'.

Another important compensating element is humour, for Zola sows the narrative with a ribald wit that lies somewhere between Rabelais and Brueghel. Despite the rapes, murders and ever-present avarice there are some superbly comic scenes in *Earth*. Many of them are obviously the result of sharp observation, like the long haggle at the market over the price of a cow, or La Grande's country remedies – she judges the state of Old Fouan's health by his eyes, 'just as she did with eels'. Then there is the episode in the cowshed with a race between the pregnant Lise and Coliche her cow to see who is first to give birth; it is as earthy as anything Zola ever wrote. In the hands of a lesser writer it could have been stomach-turning, but here the flying shit and flowing blood seem as natural as the straw on the earth floor. But while incidents like these are isolated (and I realise I am in danger of giving a wrong impression of the novel by dwelling on its bawdy aspect) they are linked from the first word to the last by a stream of rich, loamy invective. This bucolic profanity could well have disturbed Zola's bourgeois nature, but his artistic intuition obviously directed him to an 'all or nothing at all' stance, and this undoubtedly contributes to the novel's beautiful unity. Constructed as it is around a compelling but very simple theme, *Earth* could have easily degenerated into a loose collection of rustic incidents, but at no time is there the slightest danger of this.

But to ascribe the humour in this novel to the ironic transposition of mere observation is to short-change Zola's genius, because there is much comic invention, too. Perhaps Freud's dictum that laughter is energy released when fears are appeased applied to the novelist when the black poetry was spun from his soul, for the ribaldry in *Earth* is terribly funny. I have already mentioned the windbag Hyacinthe, but perhaps even funnier is an episode in which Gédéon the donkey drinks himself into a stupor.

Earth may have won an ingrained reputation for coarseness, ugliness and brutality, but contrarily it contains visions and passages of unsurpassed beauty. Zola laboured painstakingly on the construction of his prose in this novel, and in the measured cadences of his sentences and paragraphs he brilliantly captures the ever-changing moods of the countryside. It is difficult to demonstrate this in translation but I have tried, as an example, to render the opening paragraph in the same lazy rhythms of the original:

> All that morning, Jean was in the fields, his left hand holding open the blue canvas bag of seed tied around his waist, his right hand scooping fistfuls of corn from it, which at every three paces, with a sweep and a flick of the wrist, he'd scatter wide. As he swung along, his clogs sank deep into the rich soil, picking it up in heavy cakes, while at every throw, through the golden shower of flying grain, gleamed the two red stripes on the sleeve of the army tunic he was wearing out. He walked on, like a solitary giant, followed behind by two horses hauling a harrow, and then a man, driving them forward with long, lazy regular cracks from his whip.

If I have been successful, you'll note how the rolling rhythm is in keeping with the movements of the sower and the harrow which follows him, only departing from the mood at the mention of whipcracks. You may also have noted the peculiar construction of the first long sentence, in which the verb 'scatter' is held to the very end. It could have been written:

> All that morning Jean was in the fields, his left hand holding open the blue canvas bag of seed tied around his waist, his right hand scooping it up and scattering it wide at every three spaces.

But what Zola intended was to simulate in prose the natural movement of the sower, in which the scattering of the grain is the very last action: scoop, walk, sweep, flick, *scatter*. More, I think, than in any other novel, Zola is consistently successful with harmony of style and meaning, which adds immeasurably to the overall mood conveyed to the reader.

This paragraph is followed by others, in which the great plain of Beauce is described in a deliberately flat style incorporating muted rhythms as subtle as the hum emerging from the earth, returning again and again to Jean in the fields to strengthen the tempo:

> Jean swung around, and started back again, now heading south, still holding the seedbag with his left hand, and still spreading an unceasing hail of grain with his right... He turned again, at the same slow pace, and resumed his march, this time northward, then south again, always with the same slow cast of his arm, wrapped in a living cloud of grain; and still behind the harrow followed, driven by the cracking whip, turning the earth upon the seeds, at the same, slow, dreamy pace.

There is a sluggishness about the repetitious, measured beat of the words, but here it bestows an extra dimension to the meaning the words convey, and the total effect is extraordinary in its visual power. It is a pity that too often this impressive harmony between grammatic construction and subject has been ignored by the novelist's translators, and the extent to which the original has suffered in this respect is discussed in Chapter 22.

It seems obvious that, perhaps without him realising it initially, certain characteristics of the countryside impressed themselves on Zola during his week of rural research, for they recur constantly throughout the novel. After the closed-in cityscape of Paris it is easy to see how the indolent sweep of the Beauce plain, with its quilted fields broken only by great, flattened mounds barely high enough to hide a church steeple, suggested to him the analogy of the sea, and thus the rhythmic movement of the waves. But there is a secondary recurring motif, and that is the *action* of the sower, the sweep of the raised arm. It is a movement that is lost nowadays with farm mechanisation, but in the nineteenth century it would have impressed itself on an observer as acute as Zola: tossing hay, reaping, threshing, whipping horses and bullocks, herding sheep, shooing chickens in the farmyard. It is significant that even when Françoise helps the bull complete his impregnation of her cow, 'she raised her arm with a sweeping gesture'. It became implanted in the novelist's mind as a movement universal to the countryside, and one essential to the processes of life and fertility. This elemental movement and the patient rhythms of the farmlands are essential to the unity of the novel, for it almost overwhelms with the profusion and variety of its characters, incidents and subplots. But even in this, *Earth* is harmonious with the prodigality of nature, fecund and frightening. Its themes and images swell and germinate, decay and die; the lightning storms of violence are followed by the rustle of healthy growth, the mewling of new life. Always, as with nature, Zola achieves a purifying counterpoise to the dark themes of greed and lust, so that even at moments of defeat and death we are never allowed to doubt the constancy of the life force.

Because of the controversy it aroused, *Earth* could not help but be successful but nevertheless, many readers shuddered, and wondered. Some of them including most critics, were moved to horrified indignation. Anatole France came close to frothing at the mouth in one of the strongest denunciations ever delivered to a writer. 'No man before him has raised so lofty a pile of ordure, he wrote. 'That is his monument, and its greatness is not disputed. Never before has man made such an effort to debase humanity, to insult its images of beauty and love, to deny all that is good and all that is noble.' He concluded. 'There exist some men whom one could wish never to have been born!' Later however, Anatole France confided to Zola that he had loved and read ten time over some of the less harrowing passages in *L'Assommoir*.

Leo Tolstoy (1828–1910) accused Zola of 'a total failure to understand the life and hopes of the workers, while depicting them as repulsive animals moved only by lust, anger and greed is a basic defect in French writers generally. And so I do not believe the pictures of them in novels like *La Terre*.' Moving further afield, the Paris correspondent of the *New York Times* (21 August 1887 described the novel as 'particularly obnoxious' adding that, 'Unhappily, the controversy would only increase the sale for the stupid, unrelieved sewage of the work in question.' In England, the *Saturday Review* (21 April 1888 condemned the book as 'inartistic garbage' and concluded: 'In the French original the sins were glaring enough in all conscience, but the English version needs but a chapter's perusal to make one sigh for something to take the nasty taste away.'

In a later (November 1902) rather condescending commentary on Zola in *The Fortnightly Review*, a critic, Francis Gribble, knowingly claimed that

> all the horrors recorded in *Earth* have happened... one would only have to search the files of the *Petit Journal*; and one has a very shrewd suspicion that this is just what Zola has done. All the crimes, obscenities and miseries of fifty villages in all parts of France have been located in a single village of La Beauce. It is, in fact, as if Zola had emptied the contents of all the cesspools in France into a single farmyard, in order to prove that French farmyards consisted of cesspools.

Zola must have expected *Earth* to incite a barrage of violent criticism, but what apparently took him by surprise was the literary controversy it provoked Critics who felt that Zola was progressively abandoning realism, truth and decency, yet who had been bound to give grudging praise to *L'Assommoir* and *Germinal*, finally found a battlefield on which they could win, for never had an enemy trained so many guns on his own ranks. As the instalments of *Earth* appeared in *Le Gil Blas* from the end of May 1887, these critics massed and prepared for a decisive battle, aimed at destroying naturalism forever. Ironically, however, they were to be forestalled.

Beginning with the appearance of *L'Assommoir* in 1877, and ending with the appearance of *Earth*, Zola had completed a decade during which he had dominated the literary world of France. It had been a period of naturalist supremacy. But under its hard crust boiled a rich stew of literary talent, yearly growing more jealous of the tyranny of realism and of Zola's pre-eminence, which they felt denied them opportunity and fame. Zola was, of course, accustomed to attacks of all kinds, from the public, from critics, from academics. He was, as we know, rarely indifferent to them, but they served only to goad him on to even greater triumphs, always a frustrating result for his adversaries. But even a literary Goliath is not immune from pen-pushing Davids.

Busy with his work and comfortable in his success, Zola may well have been unaware of his stifling effect on the literary growth around him. He was always at odds with his old friends Goncourt and Daudet, but this was nothing new. What he probably failed to perceive was that both men, Goncourt in particular, had attracted a retinue of younger writers to them, while his own naturalist 'school' had shrunk to two or three loyal disciples. If Zola's novels after *L'Assommoir* had been undistinguished productions instead of masterpieces or near-masterpieces, then his disconcerted opponents would have had little to complain about; but with every new work he drew the spotlight of public and critical attention to himself with some kind of deadly magnetism. And now it was *Earth*, which threatened to excite more attention and controversy than anything he'd ever written! But Zola's enemies soon saw that the new novel carried the seeds of its author's destruction: filth, depravity, exaggeration and brutality. Accordingly, among the young followers of Goncourt, a campaign plan was devised to rescue French literature from the mire into which Zola had plunged it. As it turned out, it wasn't the declaration of war, or the reasons for the battle, that astonished everyone at the time, but the manner in which the attack was launched.

Imagine sitting at your breakfast table and opening your morning newspaper to see – screaming from its pages – a vicious personal attack on the things most important in your life: your beliefs, your work, your integrity – even your sexuality. That is what confronted Zola when he spread open his copy of *Le Figaro* on 18 August 1887.

The article was headlined THE MANIFESTO OF FIVE AGAINST *LA TERRE*, and was signed by five young writers. It began:

Until recently it was still possible for Emile Zola to claim, without raising serious objections, that the young writers were on his side. Too few years had passed since the appearance of *L'Assommoir*, since the birth of naturalism, for the rising generation to think of revolt. Even those who were particularly weary of his irritating repetition of clichés remembered too clearly the impetuous breach made by the great novelist in his rout of the romantics.

But after *L'Assommoir*, the manifesto went on, the great writer had betrayed his own beliefs, basking in the applause and collapsing into turgidity and repetition. It had also become evident that the entire *Rougon-Macquart* enterprise was a childish invention based on ignorance. Even so, nobody had wanted to hurt Zola, so nobody had spoken up; but now, with his increasing preoccupation with dirt and obscenity, the writers speculated that

> while some attributed this to an illness of the novelist's lower organs, to the manias of a solitary monk, others preferred to believe it was an *unconscious* development of an insatiable appetite for sales, an *instinctive* cleverness on the part of the novelist in realising that his great success depended upon the fact that 'imbeciles buy the *Rougon-Macquart* not so much for their literary quality as for their reputation for pornography.'
>
> Now it is true that Zola seems excessively concerned with sales (and those of us who have heard him talk are well aware of this); but it is also well known that he spent the early years of his life in isolation and in exaggerated continence, first through necessity and later because of principle. As a young man he was poor and also shy with women, whom he did not experience at the age he should have and who now haunt him with a vision that is false. The difficulty in maintaining a balance which results from this illness of his loins is doubtless the cause of his being preoccupied with certain functions and impels him to magnify their importance. Perhaps the doctors of the Salpêtrière Hospital might be able to discover the symptoms of his illness. And to these morbid motives should we not add the anxiety so often observed among misogynists and also among young men who question their own competence in love-making?

But people were still indulgent towards Zola, the article continued, believing that with his new novel, *La Terre*, the great writer would produce another masterpiece like *L'Assommoir*. But, alas...

> *La Terre* appeared. The disappointment has been profound and painful. Not only is the observation superficial, the devices old-fashioned, the narration flat and characterless, but the foulness is extended and extends to such depths at times to make one think he is reading a scatalogical work! The Master has descended to the very depths of dirt and degradation.

For several paragraphs the document continued with regrets that the writers found it necessary to hurt the one they loved. They had not been moved to indict Zola on account of his decline as a writer, they said, but because of his impotent doctrine of naturalism, and concluded:

> For our part, full of admiration for the great talent which the man has so often displayed, we deny any accusations of disrespect. But is it any fault of ours if the famous formula: 'A corner of nature seen through a temperament', has been distorted in Zola's case into 'a corner of nature seen through morbid sensory organs' and if it falls to us to denounce his works? It is vital that the judgement of the public i aimed directly at *La Terre*, lest the sincere books of the future be tarred with the same foul brush.
>
> It is necessary that with all the force of our hard-working youth, with all the loyalty to our artistic consciences, we take a firm and dignified stand against ignoble literature, that in the name of healthy and virile ambition, in the name of our dedication, we protest our profound love, our supreme respect for Art!
>
> > Paul Bonnetain, J.-H. Rosny,
> > Lucien Descarves, Paul Margueritte
> > Gustave Guiches.

You are unlikely to recognise any of the signatures, for the immortality of the five writers rests not on their talents but solely on their connection with this astonishing attack, which, remembering that it saw the light of day in a major newspaper and not in some esoteric journal, is unique in its ferocity. Bonnetain was on the staff of *Le Figaro* and it was he who arranged publication of the letter, while Rosny was its principal author. Interestingly, Bonnetain, using the naturalist technique, had written a cheap and nasty little volume on the subject of masturbation called *Charlot s'amuse* four years previously; it had earned him prosecution for outraging public morality. But even more ironically, Descarves wrote a novel ten years later about the seamy side of army life which was similarly prosecuted; and Zola was one of the writers who signed a petition demanding that his rights as an artist be respected by the government. In the event, Descarves was acquitted. It should be recorded that, later in their lives, each of the 'Five' expressed their regrets and contrition for the letter.

Zola was, of course, dumbfounded by the attack. Protestations from Goncourt and Daudet eased his mind that they might have played some part in the plot, but it is likely that a shadow of doubt always remained in Zola's memory of the event. The newspapers and literary journals were full of it for months, and more than one critic leapt in to try and administer the long-awaited *coup de grâce*. There is no question that naturalism withered under the onslaught. With *Earth* Zola had himself soared to the apogee of naturalism, although he didn't know it at the time. And it was *Earth* and the earthquake of reaction it caused that tumbled down the remaining moss-covered pillars of naturalism as a living, influential literary doctrine in France.

Whatever the novelist's private feelings about the letter, he chose to hide them behind the kind of amused tone that is a feature of an interview he gave the journalist Fernand Xau:

> I do not know these young men . . . they have never sat at my table, they are not my friends . . . and if they are disciples of mine as they say – and remember I do not seek disciples – then they are without my knowledge. Why then do they repudiate me? The situation is unique. It is as if a woman with whom a man never had any intercourse were to tell him: 'I have had enough of you; let's separate!' The man would obviously reply: 'So what!' Well, this situation is very similar.

But the controversy did generate a rather curious reaction from the persecuted author. Some years previously Zola had been offered the Legion of Honour, which he had bluntly refused. Oddly enough, on the eve of publication of *Earth*, the cherished accolade had been proffered again. It seems that although the novelist had made up his mind to refuse it once more, the Manifesto affair produced a change of heart. Perhaps his bruised vanity demanded some sort of compensation for, to the surprise of his friends, he not only announced his acceptance but also his intention to apply for admission into the French Academy. Zola, yet again a paradox, was to depart just as he had arrived.

227

15

Scandal!

'He is an author very little read in Melford, Wilts,' said Lady Molyneux haughtily, from a page of W.J. Locke's *The Beloved Vagabond*, an English bestseller published in 1906. She was referring to Emile Zola. Although now consigned to literary history as an ephemeral curiosity, *The Beloved Vagabond* was read by the hundred thousand before World War I, and Lady Molyneux's pronouncement reflected and endorsed the current English middle-class attitude to the French author. 'Not to be handled, my dear, even with a pair of tongs!'

To discover why Zola was so very little read in Melford, Wilts, in 1906 requires a step back in time, to 1823, when Dr. Thomas Bowdler, the world's first champion of pasteboard prudery, gave utterance to the principle on which he based his life's work: 'If any word or expression is of such a nature, that the first impression which it excites is an impression of obscenity, that word ought not to be spoken, or written, or printed; and if printed, it ought to be erased.'

Dr Bowdler had earlier floated into prominence on the rising tide of literary delicacy by editing, in 1818, *The Family Shakspeare*. He tore the bard to bits and contributed a new family of words to the language, possibly one of the worst bargains in the history of literature. The words – *bowdlerise, bowdlerism*, etc. – remain; Dr Bowdler's expurgated editions, fortunately, have expired. For the latter part of the nineteenth century, though, Bowdler left a legacy of castrated literature which, at this distance, is little short of comical. In the 1890s, publishers were offering forty different bowdlerised editions of Shakespeare. Add to this the works of most classical authors, all dictionaries and even the Bible, and you will get some idea of the desolation wrought by the grim-faced reapers of ribaldry.

Few authors escaped. Swift's vulgar honesty in *Gulliver's Travels* came in for a thorough scrubbing. Victorian readers simply weren't up to reading about the sixteen-foot tits of the Brobdignagian women nor about the bald buttocks of the hairy yahoos. Bibles were published without a single word of the Song of Solomon, except for the title. Many fairy tales also fell victims to bowdlerism and some never completely recovered. The original Cinderella plotted to murder her stepmother; the Frog Prince originally was quite a horny toad, and

228

Tom Thumb didn't merely sit in the cow's mouth but journeyed all the way down the alimentary canal, to emerge as a cow turd.

England had its Dr Bowdler, while America had Noah Webster. Posthumously his name suggests *dictionary, words, learning* and *scholarship*, but in fact Webster was one of the most ferocious expurgators in history. He began, incredibly, with the Bible. To him, the King James Version then in common use was quite unsuitable for young girls to read in Sunday School, and in 1830 he began to do something about it.

Webster's Bible went to press with thousands of changes. The Nile may have stank, but to Webster it was 'offensive in smell'. The heathen did not make a stink in the nostrils' but an 'odious scent'. Onan's visit to his sister-in-law becomes totally obscure, and, in Leviticus where no man can be a priest who 'hath his stones broken' (i.e. crushed testicles), the qualification became whose peculiar members' are defective. Bellies were banned, too. Webster undoubtedly laid the foundations for euphemistic literature in America and they were so solid that, in 1885, even the clean-as-a-cornfield *Huckleberry Finn* was expurgated of words like 'hogwash' and 'sweat' apparently without protest. Whitman's *Leaves of Grass* was banned by bookstores in New York and Philadelphia in the 1870s, and was also subject to a legal ban in Boston in the 1880s. In 1871, Noah Porter, then president of Yale University, said: 'A generation cannot be entirely pure which tolerates writers who, like Walt Whitman, commit, in writing, an offense like that indictable at common law of walking naked through the streets' – to which Whitman replied, many years later, in 1888: 'Damn the expurgated books! I say damn 'em! The dirtiest book in all the world is an expurgated book.'

With Shakespeare in shambles and the tyranny of cloth-bound bowdlerism almost total by the time Victoria came to the throne, it is not surprising that among subsequent generations the experience of coming across a crude word or expression in a book had the same effect as treading on a dog turd. This excessive prudery soon spread to everyday life, and although Sir Thomas Browne's lament is extreme it undoubtedly served as a Victorian model: 'I could be content that we might procreate like trees, without conjunction, or that there were any way to perpetuate the world without this trivial and vulgar way of coition.' Other bodily functions were also banished; the sight or even the mere mention of them could induce quite serious consequences, particularly in well-bred ladies:

> There was once a young lady named Muir
> Whose mind was so frightfully pure
>> That she fainted away
>> At a friend's house one day
> When she saw some canary manure.

To some extent the prevailing prudery of nineteenth-century middle-class life was a 'chicken and egg' situation; authors and publishers were at the mercy of their readers, while readers and authors were in turn dictated to by the

229

publishers and the critics. The publishers, to be fair, had their economic interests to protect, but there is little defence for the critics, whose reaction to honest literary expression was uniformly pusillanimous.

It is little wonder, then, that outspokenness in literature, where it survived at all, pursued an underground course, sharing the subterranean channels with the more established streams of erotica and pornography. For the most part pornography was the preserve of the intellectual and, in any case, was invariably woefully crude or frustratingly coy, as the following typical example, with its circumlocutory legal phraseology, illustrates:

> Before many minutes had passed the coy lady was spread
> upon the heath couch, and Capias was duly 'entering an
> appearance' in a court in which he had not practiced before;
> but which, as there was no 'bar' to his 'pleadings', he
> contrived to make a sensible impression. His few 'motions'
> were rewarded with a verdict of approval, etc, etc.

(*The Boudoir*, 1860)

Plain writing and honest expression in Victorian times had two other ferocious enemies. One was the Index of the Roman Catholic Church which, until 1966, provided a form of unofficial censorship in England and America. Books in the Index – some 5,000 in all – included all the works of Balzac, Zola and Stendhal, and even Gibbon's *Decline and Fall of the Roman Empire*.

The other enemy was the English library system which, largely in the hands of the twin ogres Charles Edward Mudie and W.H. Smith, contrived to reduce English fiction to the disgraceful level of what the novelist George Moore colourfully described as 'a motley and monstrous progeny, a callow, a whining, a puking brood of bastard bantlings'.

Mudie opened his Select Library in London in 1842 and by 1850 had established, with some help from Dr Bowdler, of course, a new era in English literature. Its cornerstone was the three-volume novel, a Mudie invention which ensured that readers could not afford to buy books, but only borrow them. For almost half a century Mudie, and later W.H. Smith, paid publishers ten times the amount for a novel that a popular edition might reasonably have cost an ordinary buyer, or roughly a guinea and a half. As his circulating library system spread across England – it stocked about 7,500,000 volumes by 1890 – so Mudie's power grew among publishers and authors.

By 1860 few publishers could afford to upset Mudie; they willingly published their novels in three volumes in small editions, of which all but a few were purchased by the libraries on the condition that cheap reprints would be withheld until borrowers had thinned to a trickle, sometimes a period of several years. The system was tolerated because published authors received a fair return for their labours, publishers relished the insurance of certain sales, often established in advance, and borrowers, if they were industrious, could read a couple of hundred novels a year for a guinea. Disraeli, for example, was aid £10,000 by Longmans in 1880 for *Endymion* (about £100,000 today!) of which Mudie bought 3,000 copies. Although he was reputed to have lost on this particular novel, Mudie and the other circulating libraries grew fat on the system. They had what amounted to a country-wide monopoly on the distribution and sale of almost every English work of fiction produced between 850 and 1890. The only way to read the latest novel by Anthony Trollope or George Eliot was to pay out the preposterously inflated sum of 31s 6d. (say £15 today), or join a library.

The drawback, obviously, was that if Mudie and Smith – who perhaps controlled three-quarters of all the lending libraries – didn't like a novel, it wasn't stocked, and usually wasn't published, for many publishers sent their authors' manuscripts to the libraries for an advance opinion. The library system was therefore an effective form of censorship. Mudie's style of censorship was enforced on books which in his opinion violated the Victorian moral code, on the grounds that his borrowers desired 'to have a barrier of some kind between themselves and the lower floods of literature'. It was, after all, a 'Select Library' and it meant what it implied; every book on the Mudie shelves was selected for its suitability to be seen on the drawing-room table and to be read aloud in the company of young girls.

Although he was by no means the sole victim of lending library censorship, George Moore seems to have been treated more roughly than most authors, and objected strongly to the fact that English literature was not permitted to offend the lowest common denominator of the reading public, namely the sensibilities of ignorant young girls. He concluded that 'it is a fact that literature and young girls are irreconcilable elements' but reserved the full force of his invective for the authors who accepted the tyranny of the libraries: 'What a wheezing, drivelling lot they are! They have not a virtue amongst them, and their pinafore pages are sticky with childish sensualities!' Moore paid for his outspokenness by having his novels banned by most of the libraries. W.H. Smith's refused his *Esther Waters* in 1894 because of 'about twenty lines of pre-Raphaelite nastiness'. On this occasion Moore won the round; *Esther Waters* was praised by Prime Minister Gladstone, Mudie's decided to stock the novel, and Smith's rebuked their library manager for his action. Nevertheless, the principle of selective censorship survives today; W.H. Smith's is still alive and prosperous and still exercises its right to decide what and what not to stock.

English prudery was at its zenith and the pulse of English fiction at its lowest at about the time Zola's reputation began to cross the Channel. From the opposite direction, from America, an increasing flow of pirated and mutilated translations of Zola's novels poured into England during the early 1880s, to be sold in the bookstalls of the back streets. As we have seen, no Zola novel could ever have got into the circulating libraries and thus, as an author, he presented a risk few English publishers could contemplate. Moreover his works required laborious translation, and his single-volume economy was out of step with the prolix, 900-page three-decker formula then fashionable. But there was one publisher who, observing that the shoddy, cheap pulp versions of French novels were selling as fast as they could be imported, saw Zola's potential Henry Vizetelly.

The Vizetellys – Henry, and his sons Edward and Ernest – who loom so large in the early history of Zola translation, were a family of Italian origins who had set up as printers in England during the late eighteenth century. The French connection was established when Henry (born 1820), after a short career as a publisher of illustrated books and journals, became the Paris correspondent of the *Illustrated London News*. The great French novelist had been pointed out to him at Versailles, just after the 1870 Franco-Prussian War, when he had been covering the early days of the new Republic. Zola, he remembered, was 'a silent, pale, shabby man, an unobtrusive figure whose most distinctive feature was a misshapen, slightly cleft nose...'

Although he was now a journalist, Vizetelly's burning ambition was to be successful as a publisher. Inspired by the realist fiction then flowering in Paris he returned in 1880 to London where, although neither his talent nor his capital were equal to the task, he began, with almost blind courage, to translate and issue French novels in English. He began with translations of Daudet George Sand and Sala for which, unfortunately, there was little demand. The tiny business faltered and Henry, searching for something a little more sensational with which to revive it, and remembering the furore which had greeted the publication of Zola's *L'Assommoir* in Paris at the beginning of 1877 promptly bought the English translation rights of the novel and also those of *Nana*. He rushed both into print in 1884 in unabridged, single-volume editions, and both were so unexpectedly successful that he very quickly came to an agreement with Zola to purchase the English copyright to all his published and projected work. It is a matter of interest that by publishing the novels in single volumes – at six shillings illustrated and five shillings without illustrations – Vizetelly was one of the first to insert a wedge into the despotic hold of the three-decker novel, which finally expired a decade later.

Vizetelly worked hard to sell his author as a French Dickens, a stern unflagging moral satirist with 'the same love as Charles Dickens had for little children and dumb animals'. Whatever his faults as a translator, Vizetelly displayed an intuitive knowledge of the sentimental underbelly of the book-buying public. He also kept a sensitive finger on the tremulous pulse of Victorian taste, and invariably attempted to de-obscenitise the novels by contributing apologetic prefaces. In *L'Assommoir* he affirmed that Zola was a moral writer:

> He is one of the most moral novelists of France, and it is really astonishing how any one can doubt this. He makes us note the smell of vice, not its perfume; his nude figures are those of the anatomical table, which do not inspire the slightest immoral thought; there is not one of his books, not even the crudest, that does not leave in the soul, pure, firm, and immutable aversion or scorn for the base passions of which he treats. Brutally, pitilessly, and without hypocrisy, he strips vice naked, and holds it up to ridicule, standing so far off from it that he does not graze it with his garments. Forced by his hand, it is Vice itself that says, 'Detest me and pass by!' His novels, he himself says, are really 'morals in action.' The scandal which comes from them is only

for the eyes and ears. And as he holds back, as a man, from the mire in which his pen is dipped, so does he, as a writer, keep completely aloof from the characters which he has created. Herein lies his greatest merit. He has flung into the air with one kick all the toilet articles of literature, and has washed with a dish-cloth the bedizened face of Truth.

Vizetelly's prudence was well-advised, for, as Zola's popularity grew, so did he volume of outraged protest, a surprising amount of it from the English iterary establishment. Tennyson, for instance, in his *Locksley Hall, sixty years after* (1886) coined a new, contemptuous term:

> Rip your brothers' vices open, strip your own foul passion bare;
>> Down with Reticence, down with Reverence – forward – naked –
>> let them stare...
> Set the maiden fancies wallowing in the troughs of Zolaism,
>> Forward, forward, ay and backward, downward too into the abysm.*

As a result, Vizetelly proceeded warily, and began to abridge the novels in an attempt to forestall criticism. In the translation for *Germinal* (1886) there are no details of the evil shop-keeper's emasculation by the old women of the village, nor any mention of the very moving circumstances of the onset of Catherine's menstruation.

Zola was, as is crystal clear today, condemned as a pornographer quite unfairly and for quite the wrong reasons. In a society so anxious to banish anything that might increase promiscuity it was a wonder the moralists didn't attempt to abolish the sale of beds, the fear of the consequences of unbridled depravity degenerated into fear of sex, and an avoidance of anything that touched on the unpleasant realities of life. In the 1880s the influences considered likely to deprave and corrupt occupied an area as wide as an ocean. Only in this context can we appreciate why Zola – a realist – was singled out for special censure by the prudes.

With few exceptions sex in Zola's novels is ugly, squalid and disagreeable. Even in the bedrooms of enlightened society it is presented as sterile and furtive. It is difficult to imagine anything less pornographic. Yet, curiously, the arbiters of Victorian propriety ignored the erotic element in Zola's novels, which they might logically have taken to task; they appear to have read passages from *The Kill* and *The Abbé Mouret's Sin,* positively steaming with sensuality, with no other emotions than excitement and pleasure. Zola's sin against the Victorians was simply to write frankly about life.

What were the motivations behind the remarkable frankness of Zola's writing? There was an audacious streak in Zola, but he was also careful and calculating when it came to his career as a novelist. He certainly wasn't foolhardy, but, considering the times, it took more than nerve or a spirit of rebellion to have so bruised the sensibilities of France with such a barrage of

*The first two lines also exist in an alternative version: 'Feed the budding rose of boyhood with the drainage of your sewer;/Send the drain into a fountain, lest the stream should issue pure...'

taboo language and ideas. And with premeditation, too. He had written to Flaubert about his plans for *Nana*: 'I fear it will appear to be rather crude. I intend to leave nothing out, although some things are extremely coarse.' Knowing full well the wrath – and publicity – *Nana* would bring down on his head, was this the fearless artist, the scheming pornographer, or the serious, ingenuous, faintly moralistic Zola?

I think the ball, after a lot of bouncing around, has to land in the final court. Too often was Zola to be genuinely upset and disturbed at being labelled a pornographer. By the time he came to write *Earth* he was a well-established, best-selling novelist, and if injecting shots of pornography into his books had been the formula for early success – and of course there are doubts about that – he would have surely realised in later years that it was no longer necessary, and that it could retard sales rather than increase them. But *Earth* appeared with scenes and language stronger than anything he had perpetrated before.

By the summer of 1887 the London offices of Vizetelly & Co. were like an assembly line, with the French proofs of Zola's novels going in through the front door and issuing, a couple of months later, as bound volumes from the warehouse at the back. It was a happy and successful period and even when Henry received a letter from the novelist outlining the plot of a new book about the French peasantry it was assumed that it would be yet another bestseller.

The first indications of trouble ahead occurred when one of the translators objected to the frank language in the new novel, *La Terre*, towards the end of 1887. The work was transferred to another translator but he, too, encountered the same difficulty. At this stage Henry's son Ernest was asked to read the entire text, which, until then, had been received each week as packets of proofs from the serialisation in *Gil Blas*. Ernest was 'immediately struck by the boldness of the story, which seemed to surpass in outspokenness any of the novelist's previous works'. He immediately advised excisions and alterations.

Ernest recalled later that 'he found one of the characters, Hyacinthe Fouan called by the nickname of 'Jésus-Christ', afflicted with a nasty infirmity.' The sobriquet didn't upset him, for it was not uncommon in France, and was frequently applied to young men with long hair and beards. Nevertheless, Ernest felt, correctly, that the nickname would offend English readers, as would Hyacinthe's 'nasty infirmity' – particularly to people 'who no longer read Sterne, and who knew little or nothing of Rabelais.' When the last of the proofs were received, so was news of the outcry from Paris that had greeted publication of *La Terre* as a book. In English, the novel threatened to be an even hotter potato and only after a lot of vacillation did Henry finally decide to publish and be damned. By March 1888, after Ernest had attempted to rub as much dirt off the text as he could, *La Terre* – now retitled *The Soil* – was set in type ready for the presses, and it seemed that all would be well. Unfortunately the Vizetellys were unaware of the advance of a hastily formed army at the head of which marched the influential Pecksniffian moralist, W.T. Stead.

Stead, if little else, was a colourful figure. From humble journalistic beginnings he had inherited the editorship of the *Pall Mall Gazette* and had immediately set about refining a new kind of campaigning journalism that still persists today in some of our Sunday newspapers. Ostensibly reformist, Stead specialised in exposing the seamy layers of English life in great and lurid detail, and is most remembered for proving that child prostitutes could be bought in England. Stead broke the sensational story in the *Pall Mall Gazette* with crowd-stopping headlines: THE VIOLATION OF VIRGINS, and CONFESSIONS OF A BROTHEL KEEPER! The success of the story as a circulation builder was so phenomenal that he kept it going, week after week, inventing sordid details when he'd exhausted the facts. As a result of the disclosures the age of consent was raised to sixteen, but they also brought the whole weight of Victorian hypocrisy down on Stead's head; as Zola had discovered across the Channel, one earned no thanks from society for exposing distress and injustice.

On the surface it would appear that Stead would have been the last person to persecute a writer in whose works ran a strong stream of reformism. But it seems clear that the editor of the *Pall Mall Gazette* was nothing more than a megalomaniac with no less a fascination for pornography than his eager readers. When, in 1888, he was visited by officers of the National Vigilance Association asking for help in their campaign to suppress Zola's novels, he immediately jumped at this new opportunity to inject fresh life into the flagging sales of his newspaper. The campaign opened with an article by Stead claiming that the English publishers had made no effort to expurgate this pernicious literature from France, and that because sales of the novels 'ran into millions' they were growing rich from the sale of filth. Vizetelly loudly denied the translations were unmutilated; instead he was proud to announce that 'none of them was an exact replica of the original.'

If Vizetelly had used the covers of *The Soil* to shovel real ordure on the delicate scales of public prudery he couldn't have tipped them more effectively against him. The novel had more bawdiness than Shakespeare's collected works in their original form. It plumbed unthinkable depths of bestiality and depravity. No person of any sensibility could fail to be shocked by its coarse language. Moreover, its author was French. The moralists knew, as they savoured each page, that they held a winning hand; indeed, it was such a gift that they could be forgiven for suspecting some kind of trap.

The pickings were so amazingly rich that it must have been difficult to know where to start – but Zola had made it easy. Even in the first few pages there was a passage that made them suck in their breath, when Françoise, a young girl of fourteen, takes her cow to the bull:

> When Cæsar was ready, he got upon La Coliche with a jerk, and with such weighty force as to shake the ground. She had not given way, and he compressed her flanks with his two feet. But she, a strapping animal from the Cotentin, was so tall, so broad for him, who was of a smaller breed, that he could not reach her. He was conscious of it, and made a vain effort to raise himself and to bring her nearer.
> 'He is too small,' said Françoise.
> 'Yes, a little,' said Jean. 'But that don't matter; he'll do it all the same.'

She shook her head in doubt; and, as Cæsar still fumbled about, and seemed to be getting exhausted, she came to a resolution.

'No, he must be helped,' she said. 'If he goes wrong, it'll be waste of time.'

Calmly and carefully, as if bent on a serious piece of work, she had drawn near. Her intentness made the pupils of her eyes retreat, left her red lips half open, and kept her features motionless. Raising her arm with a sweep she aided the animal in his efforts, and he, gathering up his strength, speedily accomplished his purpose. It was done. Firmly, with the impassive fertility of land which is sown with seed the cow had unflinchingly received the fruitful stream of the male. Indeed, she had not even trembled at the shock; and he had already dropped again to the ground, shaking the earth once more.   (72)*

This was how Vizetelly translated the passage, carefully avoiding Zola's casual bluntness. Nevertheless it left little to the average imagination.

Then there was this ghastly fellow Hyacinthe, perversely nicknamed Jesus-Christ, performing the unmentionable at almost every step he took, with neither shame nor remorse. And again, while Vizetelly took care not to use the word 'fart' he could not, without dropping the chapter altogether, avoid the implications of terms like 'explosions', 'detonations' and 'discharges' when applied to the human body. Of course, when we read about Hyacinthe's peculiar talent today it is all jolly good fun, but imagine a dour, muttonchop-whiskered moralist with three teenage daughters, *circa* 1888, face to face with this diverting bit of ribaldry:

> Hyacinthe was a very windy individual, and he was constantly going off in explosions, which kept the house in a lively state, for he never allowed one of these reports to pass without indulging in some facetious jest. He had a contempt for your timid little reports, suppressed as much as possible, and sounding as though they were ashamed of themselves. He himself never let off aught but loud detonations, crisp and crackling, like gun shots; and every time, as he raised his leg with a gesture of self-satisfied complacency, he summoned his daughter in a tone of urgent command and with an air of serious gravity.
>
> 'Come here, you troll, come here at once!'
>
> As soon as the girl hurried forward, the explosion was allowed to take place, going off with such a sharp vibrating report that La Trouille quite started at the noise it made.
>
> 'Quick, run after it and catch it, and see if it's come out straight!'
>
> At other times when she approached him, he would give her his hand.
>
> 'Pull hard, now, you jade! Make it go off with a good crack!'
>
> Then, when the explosion took place with all the sputter and row of a tightly jammed charge, he exclaimed:
>
> 'Ah, that's a hard one! but I'm much obliged to you all the same.'   (72)

Hyacinthe's daughter La Trouille was no better, either, and a disgraceful example of young womanhood – not only doing 'it' at every opportunity, but doing it for money! Depravity seems to follow her father like a bad smell. Here he is again, in a cafe with the drunken Bécu and his wife, anticipating multi-sexual partnerships by a hundred years:

> 'I say, La Bécu,' he repeated a dozen times over while he was eating, 'if Bécu don't mind, we'll sleep together? What do you say?'
>
> She was very dirty, not having known, she said, that she should stop at the fête; and

*As with all the excerpts in this chapter I am using the *original* emasculated Vizetelly translation, published in 1888 as *The Soil*. The extent to which such passages were bowdlerised is examined in Chapter 22.

236

she laughed, did this dark pole-cat of a woman, wiry and rusty like an old needle; while Hyacinthe, without further delay, grabbed hold of her legs under the table. Meantime the husband, blind drunk, dribbled and chuckled, shouting out that two men would be none too many for the hussy. (72)

And so on. Lewdness on every page. Even poor Palmyre was not spared. The most unfortunate of individuals, she is an orphan, ugly, feeble-minded, ageing and desperately poor. Her only comfort, the only contribution she can make to mankind, is to love her equally helpless brother Hilarion, which she does, between the sheets. One day, to her shame and dumb horror, she is questioned by Jean. Zola's sensitive and compassionate handling of this moment is lost in Vizetelly's expurgatory translation, but the purpose here is to confront the reader with exactly those words that so stirred up the novelist's English persecutors:

'Then it's all lies what they say about you and Hilarion?' he asked.
Palmyre's face suddenly turned from white to crimson, the rush of blood momentarily restoring her the aspect of her lost youth. She stammered with surprise and vexation, at a loss for the disclaimer she desired.
'Oh, the backbiters! Only to think of it!'
Françoise and Jean, with a resumption of noisy mirth, spoke both at once, pressed her hard, and flurried her. Why, in the ruined cow-shed, where Palmyre and Hilarion lodged, there was hardly any room to move about. Their mattresses lay touching on the floor; how easy it was to make a mistake in the dark!
'Come, it's true; confess it's true! Besides, it's well known.'
Drawing herself up, Palmyre, quite bewildered, gave vent to her passion and pain:
'Well, and supposing that it were true,' she exclaimed, 'what the devil is it to you? The poor boy hasn't so happy a life as it is.'
A couple of tears rolled down her cheeks, so wrung was she by her feeling of motherhood for the cripple. After earning him his bread, supposing she did accord him what others refused him, why it cost them nothing! With the darkened intellect of clod-like beings, these pariahs and outcasts of love would have been at a loss to relate how the thing had been brought about. An instinctive approach without deliberate consent, he stung by desire, she passively yielding to his purpose; thus it had begun. Then, too, there was the happiness of their feeling warmer, in that miserable hovel where they both shivered with the cold.
'She is right, what is it to us?' resumed Jean, in his grave, kindly way, touched to see her in such agitation. 'It's their own concern and nobody else's.' (72)

Incest in rural regions was not, apparently, uncommon, but to be reminded of it was something the Victorians found difficult to forgive. What was worse, the author seemed to be condoning this wretched relationship. In fact the novel not only ran counter to every Christian ideal but even held them up to scorn! At one point Palmyre, old and sick and thoroughly worn out, begs a menial job at one and a half francs a day from Buteau: 'Even to secure this piecework she had to implore him; and he had taken advantage of her position, assuming the resigned air of a Christian performing a work of charity.' Was this not bordering on blasphemy?

The publication of *The Soil* gave Stead and the National Vigilance Association just the ammunition they were waiting for. The Association had clearly planned to prosecute for it had already appealed to the public for information about pernicious literature so that it might bring legal proceedings against the offenders.

The peculiar and special nature of the work done by this Association [it announced in its prospectus] affords exceptional opportunities of ascertaining the enormous amount of evil which is wrought by the circulation of immoral literature and obscene pictures, and the matter is one of such urgent and vital importance as to leave no doubt that as soon as the nation realises the dreadful havoc which is being caused by the dissemination of this vile stuff, it will rise as one man, and demand such a strengthening of the law as shall simplify the process of legally laying by the heels the scoundrels who live by its production.

The Soil seemed to possess all the qualities of what the Association defined as 'vile stuff' and, armed with a bundle of Vizetelly translations its officers had little difficulty in persuading Mr Samuel Smith, the M.P. for Flintshire, to carry the campaign into the House of Commons.

To a desultory House consisting of only about forty Members, Mr Smith opened the debate on 8 May 1888, speaking in a high, quiet voice which, according to a contemporary observer, 'was peculiarly suited to the expression of lamentation'.

The motion submitted by the Member for Flintshire was 'That this House deplores the rapid spread of demoralising literature in this country and is of the opinion that the law against obscene publications and indecent pictures and prints should be vigorously enforced and, if necessary, strengthened.'

In Mr Smith's view this literature was working terrible effects upon the morals of the young and he looked upon it as a gigantic national danger, more dangerous than strong drink.

'There is nothing that so corrodes the human character,' he went on, 'or so saps the vitality of a nation, as the spread of this noxious and licentious literature, which is at the bottom of the shocking state of many of the streets here in London.'

Encouraged by the murmurs and nods and an increasing state of attentiveness, Mr Smith warmed up.

If the House should want proof of the development of this evil in recent years, it will be found in the confession of Mr Vizetelly, a publisher of French novels, who, in the *Pall Mall Gazette* a short time ago, boasted that his firm had translated and sold a million copies of these French novels, some of them, I might add, in the worst class. And at the present time this Mr Vizetelly is selling a thousand copies of the writings of Zola each week!

Of these, Mr Smith added that in his view nothing more diabolical had ever been written by the pen of man; they were fit only for swine, and their constant perusal would turn the mind into a sty.

Quoting from *The Saturday Review*, Mr Smith went on to educate the House about the Realist movement, of which

Zola is its Prophet. Realism, according to latter-day French lights, means nothing short of sheer beastliness; it means going out of the way to dig up foul expressions to embody filthy ideas; it means not only the insinuation of petty intrigue, but the laying bare of social sores in their most loathsome forms. In a word, it is dirt and horror pure and simple; and the good-humoured Englishman, who might smilingly characterise the French novel as 'rather thick', will be disgusted and tired with the inartistic garbage which is to be found in Zola's *La Terre*. Yet Messrs Vizetelly, of Catherine

Street, Strand, are allowed with impunity to publish an almost word for word translation of Zola's bestial *chef d'oeuvre*.

Mr Smith then quoted from *The Sentinel*, which reported an incident in which a boy of fourteen was seen to peruse an opened copy of a Zola novel placed in a well-known bookseller's window. 'The matter was of such a leprous character that it would be impossible for any young man who had not learned the Divine secret of self-control to have read it without committing some form of outward sin within twenty-four hours after!'

'Now,' he asked the House,

> are we to stand still while the country is corrupted by literature of this kind? Are we to wait until the moral fibre of the English race is eaten out, as has almost happened to the French? Look what such literature has done for France – it overspread that country like a torrent, and its poison is destroying the whole national life. Indeed, France today is rapidly approaching the condition of Rome at the time of the Caesars!

Mr Smith, as is often the case with moralists, had done his homework with heavy-breathing enthusiasm. For half an hour he gave the House the benefit of his considerable knowledge of this kind of literature. Zola's books were forbidden to be sold in Germany; the children were protected there but not in England where Penny Dreadfuls were sold by the hundred-ton weight and were the staple diet of the poor and even the respectable artisanry. Men were employed as agents to push this vile literature into the hands of schoolchildren. Young girls were invited into low shops to read indecent literature for a deposit of sixpence, and when their minds were sufficiently polluted and depraved were consigned to brothels. In one London street alone, ten shops were carrying on this abominable trade. The law did nothing. The much-travelled Mr Smith had also inspected bookstalls in India, their racks groaning with English translations of French novels, passing as samples of European civilisation. But dirty books weren't necessarily cheap. He referred to a London society devoted to the publication of lascivious literature; one book had recently been published at ten guineas. 'Many Members will know of the book I refer to,' he said. It was so popular it was now fetching twenty-six guineas a copy. He then congratulated the Home Secretary for prosecuting an issue of a paper called *Town Talk* and seventeen of its vendors, although the publisher had escaped. 'Somehow,' he complained sadly, 'our laws touch the weak, not the strong. They always strike the agent, and not the author.'

When the Member for Flintshire finally resumed his seat, his recommendations for the law against obscene publications to be vigorously enforced and strengthened met with loud vocal approval.

The Home Secretary, to whom Mr Smith's motion was addressed, then stood up. A Roman Catholic lawyer and subsequently a peer, Mr Henry Matthews had some strange views of his own about literature. 'When comparing modern French writing with classical works,' he suggested to the House, 'it should be borne in mind that while the latter had been written with no evil purpose in mind, the former was produced with the object of drawing attention to the foullest passions of which human nature was capable, and to present them in the most attractive forms.' He was bound, of course, to explain why the deplorable situation outlined by Mr Smith was tolerated. The existing laws were sufficient, he said, only the difficulty lay in getting juries to draw a hard-and-fast line and to convict those cases that crossed the line. He should deprecate, he went on, handing over to the Public Prosecutor or anyone else the task of deciding what was punishable, criminal and obscene within the meaning of the law, and what was merely indelicate and coarse. He sensibly relied on the public's judgement, and if the general moral sense of the community did not compel individuals to prosecute, then no good would be done by trying to create an artificial moral sense by the action of the Public Prosecutor. The Home Secretary also warned of the dangers in attempting to prosecute obscure publications where the resulting publicity could outweigh the benefits of a conviction, but nevertheless he would urge prosecutions where appropriate.

The debate was widely reported and the Hon. Member for Flintshire's views found enthusiastic allies in the British press. Following this public success the National Vigilance Association pressed home its advantage by applying at the Bow Street police court for a summons against Henry Vizetelly for having published three obscene works: *Piping Hot!* (*Pot-Bouille*), *The Soil* (*La Terre*) and *Nana*. The summons was granted and Vizetelly appeared at Bow Street to answer it with the argument that because the French originals were allowed to circulate freely throughout Britain the same privilege should logically extend to their translations. The magistrate considered that this point should be tested by a jury and accordingly committed the defendant for trial at the Central Criminal Court.

At this juncture one has to admire Henry's nerve. As an answer to the National Vigilance Association, which was proclaiming victory in advance, Vizetelly circulated the trade with a notice advising that there were no legal restrictions on the sale of the books in question, and until a jury decided otherwise he would continue to supply them. Unfortunately the plucky shot – admittedly ill-timed – backfired, and enraged press opinion was influential in deciding the government to pursue the prosecution itself.

But still Vizetelly fought back gamely. Working day and night, he produced a booklet containing excerpts from the works of English classic authors, including Shakespeare, Dryden, Congreve, Defoe, Swift, Sterne, Fielding and Byron, demanding to know if, in the event Zola's novels were found to be obscene, publishers would be allowed to continue issuing the works quoted from. While the case had remained a private prosecution, brought by a group of people who might be proved to be a bunch of fanatics, Henry felt he had little to fear, but he was now somewhat apprehensive at the intervention by the Crown. So the booklet, together with Henry's plea, was sent to the Solicitor to the Treasury, who was to conduct the prosecution, to members of the government and also to the leading newspapers which, despite it being *sub judice*, were flagrantly and adversely commenting on the case.

The trial took place on 31 October 1888, at the Old Bailey. Henry Vizetelly was sixty-eight years old and a sick man, and although he had decided to contest the case he must have known in his bones that he had little chance of success. He was also aware of the disastrous effect that losing the case would have on his business.

The prosecution was conducted by the Solicitor-General, Sir Edward Clarke, stern and forbidding and one of the most astute cross-examiners of his day, although not without a certain naïvety. When, years later, he was approached to defend Oscar Wilde, he told the playwright, 'I can only accept this brief, Mr Wilde, if you can assure me on your honour as an English gentleman that there is not and never has been any foundation for the charges that are made against you.' Wilde solemnly did so, and Sir Edward accepted the brief. The Solicitor-General also displayed a profound ignorance of French pronunciation, for when he began to read extracts from *The Soil* he persisted in referring to Jean as 'Jeen'.

But first Sir Edward dealt with what was likely to be the defence argument, that outspokenness in contemporary literature had to be allowed on logical grounds because of equal frankness of language in works of literature recognised as classics.

> In our own literature and the literature of other countries [he began], there are works whose authors are recognised as kings in the world of letters, but which contain certain immoral and indecent passages. Two or three centuries ago, especially, men used and wrote expressions which very sharply conflict with the modern judgement of what ought to be printed and circulated, but that is entirely out of the question here. 'It is perfectly clear,' said Lord Chief Justice Cockburn, many years ago, 'that there are a great many publications of high repute in the literary productions of this country the tendency of which is immodest, and, if you please, immoral, and possibly they might have been the subject-matter of indictment; but it is not because there are in many standard and established works objectionable passages that the law is not to protect the public from books of an immoral, debauching and depraving nature.' This argument was accordingly dismissed [Sir Edward continued] as an excuse for the publication of obscene matter. In the case you are now investigating it is not a question of an isolated passage, and such a plea would not be applicable to the filthy book – *The Soil* – which I hold in my hand at this moment. I shall have to lay before you twenty-one extracts taken from different parts of the work, some of them extending over two or three pages, and all of them of the most immoral and degrading nature. There is no question here of a book written by a distinguished author for the wholesome purpose of teaching or of innocently amusing. This book is filth from beginning to end. I do not believe there was ever collected together between the covers of a bound volume so much bestial obscenity as is to be found in almost every page of this work, and I am sure you will be of the same opinion when I read to you even a few of the passages. I have also to say that there is not a passage in this work that I can find, that contains any display of literary genius or the expression of any elevated thought. There is not a single scene described which is free from vicious suggestion and obscene expressions. Nay, more – I challenge my learned friend who appears for the defence to point out to me among the female characters which appear in the book, one who is represented to be a decent woman. I am desirous of impressing this upon you to show you that the case is not a prosecution for an isolated passage, but is a prosecution against a book which is filthy from beginning to end, and which has been published and sold in this country by those who, for the sake of money, pander to the worst tastes of those who gloat over obscenity.

Sir Edward then began to read extracts from *The Soil*. He did not get very far into the first extract, which recounted how Françoise assisted the bull to mate her cow, before there was a buzz from the public gallery and murmurs of shocked protest from the jury. Nevertheless he persisted until, at the ninth extract, the jury foreman stood up.

> FOREMAN OF THE JURY: I am requested to ask whether it is necessary to read all these passages?
> SIR THOMAS CHAMBERS (the Judge): They are charged in the indictment. They are revolting to the last degree, no doubt, but they are in the indictment.
> THE FOREMAN: Is it necessary to prove them all? We think we have heard enough of them.
> SIR THOMAS CHAMBERS: The Solicitor-General will no doubt exercise his judgement as to how much he will read.
> SIR EDWARD CLARKE: I can assure you, gentlemen, it is as unpleasant to me to read these passages as it is for you to have to listen to them. If you think the passages I have read are obscene of course I will stop.
> SEVERAL JURYMEN: We think so.

Vizetelly's counsel – who must have been asleep during this exchange – soon saw, however, that the jury's mind had been made up and advised his client to change his plea to one of guilty. Sir Edward had given notice that he intended to read twenty-one excerpts; here he was, less than half-way through, and the verdict was already clear. To let him continue would have weakened any plea for leniency on Vizetelly's behalf, so his counsel's decision was the proper one. After a brief consultation the issue was decided, but not before there was a heated exchange about the status of Zola as an author. Vizetelly's lawyer asked the prosecution to take into account Zola's esteemed place in French literature.

> MR WILLIAMS: I need hardly remind your lordships, for you know perfectly well, that these works are the works of a great French writer.
> SIR EDWARD CLARKE: Oh, no. A great French writer? Oh, dear, no! A voluminous French writer.
> SIR THOMAS CHAMBERS: Say, a popular French writer?
> MR WILLIAMS: I will put it, a writer that stands high among the novelists of France.
> SIR EDWARD CLARKE: No, no! Do not malign the literature of France in that way.

Sir Edward, to his credit, did not press for imprisonment; instead Henry was admonished by the Recorder, fined £100, and entered into a good behaviour bond for twelve months.

As with all proceedings of this kind, the prosecution depended upon the ruling applied in the 1868 case, *The Queen* v. *Hicklin*, when, in upholding a magistrate's order for the destruction of an allegedly obscene tract, Lord Chief Justice Cockburn had said: 'The test of obscenity is this: whether the tendency of the matter charged as obscenity is to deprave and corrupt those whose minds are open to such immoral influences and into whose hands a publication of this sort may fall.'

This classic ruling has always been a sore point with writers and publishers, yet is curiously immune. Almost a century later, at the Old Bailey in 1954, the Judge, Sir Gerald Dodson, presented the following view to the jury:

> A book which would not influence the mind of an Archbishop might influence the minds of a callow youth or girl just budding into womanhood... It is a very

comforting thought that juries from time to time take a very solid stand against this sort of thing and realise how important it is for the youth of this country to be protected and that the fountain of our national blood should not be polluted at its source.

The book in question was *September in Quinze*, published by Hutchinson, and the overawed jury convicted; yet, only three months before, in a similar case, Secker & Warburg were found 'Not Guilty' for publishing *The Philanderer*.

The problem was that Lord Chief Justice Cockburn's imprecise definition left a legacy of confusion and ambiguity. In the Hicklin case he went on to say that he believed the work in question would suggest to the mind of a reader thoughts 'of a most impure and libidinous character'. This clue to what he meant by his definition only complicated matters. When is a thought impure and libidinous? When it arouses sexual desire? If so, is the resultant sexual desire impure also? We know now that there are only complex answers to questions like these. After many serious studies on the subject, like those of the American Presidential Commission on Obscenity and Pornography (which reported that it found no evidence that exposure to explicit erotic material plays a significant role in the causation of criminal and delinquent behaviour among youth and adults, despite the finding of another study that fifty-seven per cent of a sample of rapists and eighty-seven per cent of pedophiles admitted to imitating sexual behaviour witnessed during adolescent exposure to pornography) we only know that it is still impossible to measure the effect of an allegedly obscene book on the sexual behaviour of an individual.

Yet as recently as 1966 in England, even after various moves to reform the Obscene Publications Act (1959 and 1964), the publishers of *Last Exit to Brooklyn* were convicted, although they later won at the Court of Appeal. If the appeal had been dismissed there should have been, by inference, some 13,000 depraved and corrupted citizens at large, because 13,000 copies of the book were sold before proceedings began. I mention all this because if books like *Last Exit to Brooklyn* can be prosecuted in relatively enlightened times, Henry Vizetelly had no chance in the obsessively prudish climate of the 1880s.

How would Vizetelly have fared today? In several important respects Zola's novels would have been more fairly treated. The 1959 Act provides that the book must be considered as a whole; there were to be no more carefully selected snippets read to the jury by the prosecution. The jurors in the famous *Lady Chatterley's Lover* trial, for example, had to read every word of Lawrence's novel. Also the would-be readers of the book were not to be taken as fourteen-year-old girls or callow youths, but persons who might be likely readers under the circumstances. Further, if it is proved that publication of the book is justified as 'being for the public good on the ground that it is in the interests of science, literature, art or learning, or other objects of general concern', then no offence has been committed. Faced with these safeguards of the 1959 Act and assisted by competent counsel, Vizetelly's conviction today would be most unlikely.

In the event, however, Vizetelly was not only convicted by the court but also by almost every newspaper in England. *The Times* cheerfully agreed with the outcome of the trial, and was pleased that Vizetelly would incur a considerable commercial loss by the enforced withdrawal of the convicted books. The paper also made the curious point that because the translations were cheap editions implying that they were available to the working classes, the offence was that much greater. 'If the line is not to be drawn so as to exclude translations of such works as *La Terre* and *Pot-Bouille*', it editorialised, 'it is plain that it cannot be drawn at all.'

'If dirty fiction is to be suppressed, why should we not take one step further and check the sensational histories of actual crimes?' asked the *St James's Gazette* in a rather muddled article on morality, while the *Whitehall Review* roundly congratulated the National Vigilance Association on its success. With a touch of world-weariness, however, it observed that *The Soil* was not really in the top rank of pernicious literature, but merely 'an appetiser to make men and women create a demand for more seasoned matter . . .'

Further congratulations were offered by *The Star*, this time to Mr Vizetelly for getting off so lightly. The paper recognised that Rabelais was obscene, that Chaucer was coarse, that Boccaccio's ladies and gentlemen were all too frank but that Zola's *La Terre* had none of their charm, humour or style, just unrelieved and morbid filth. It went on to make one of the few judgements on the case with any insight: 'Indifferent translations are not literature, and there is an end of the matter from the standpoint of art.'

The *Liverpool Mercury* was gratified that the law was strong enough to prevent the dissemination of demoralising literature, but discovered an inconsistency: 'If the English versions are offensive to the law, it is hard to understand why the far more revolting French versions are allowed to circulate. A man is not a superior person morally because he can read French and there is no logical reason why he should be privileged on this account to touch and look upon rank fruits which are wisely forbidden to the exclusively English reader.'

From among the vultures of the press flew forth an eagle, in *The Globe*: 'It is idle to argue that great men have ere now written books which have been far from free from the taint of the obscene. The eagles have, it is true, sometimes stooped to carrion, but it has not been their normal food.'

'If there is such a thing as improper literature, M. Zola has produced it,' puffed the *Morning Advertiser* a trifle obscurely, while the *Western Morning News* managed to introduce a note of racialism into its editorial: 'Zola is filthy in the extreme . . . more unclean, and realistically so, than any other writer, not an Oriental, whose name we can recall.' And, summing up, the *Methodist Times* sermonised: 'Zolaism is a disease. It is the study of the putrid. No one can read Zola without moral contamination, and the only plea that can be made is that the disgust inspired destroys the fascination of the evil.'

But to return to the events of 31 October 1888, poor Henry Vizetelly was not only convicted, but further subjected to the unfortunate result of a quite astonishing misunderstanding.

To secure leniency, Henry gave an undertaking to the court to withdraw the three offending novels from circulation and to refrain from being party to the circulation of any other of Zola's works the contents of which – in Sir Edward Clarke's words – 'are at least as objectionable as those which are indicted before your Lordship today.' The ambiguity of this definition is appalling and not surprisingly it led Vizetelly to believe that he could continue to publish translations of works by Zola providing they were rendered less objectionable than those before the court.

At this time Vizetelly's business was in a sorry mess, and his warehouse was glutted with stocks of eighteen different novels by Zola at various stages of production, representing an investment of many thousands of pounds. With creditors pressing and with public demand for the novels whetted by the court proceedings, Vizetelly decided to continue selling those novels to which no objection had been made, and to modify certain others by judicious editing. A start had barely been made on this project when, early in 1889, W.T. Stead and the National Vigilance Association returned to the fray by issuing another summons.

This time Henry had to answer for almost every Zola translation he had in print: *The Fortune of the Rougons, The Kill, The Belly of Paris, The Abbé Mouret's Sin, Joy of Life, His Excellency, L'Assommoir* and *Germinal* – with Flaubert's *Madame Bovary* and Maupassant's *Bel Ami* thrown in as well. The case was again heard at Bow Street and Vizetelly was committed for trial with respect to five of the Zola translations and *Bel Ami*; objections to *Germinal, L'Assommoir* and *Madame Bovary* were withdrawn. The charge against Henry was now a serious one, for while there was enormous confusion as to what constituted a translation 'at least as objectionable' as those titles previously prosecuted, the publisher was in considerable danger if it were proved he had broken his bond. Although he was in financial difficulties and in constant pain from an agonising bladder complaint there was no alternative but to fight, and a Mr Cock, Q.C., was retained to lead his defence.

The second trial opened at the Central Criminal Court on 30 May 1889, and if it were not for the tragic consequences the entire affair could be considered one of the law's more comical performances. The case began disastrously for Vizetelly, for Mr Cock's only briefing consisted of a hurried meeting half an hour before the trial was due to begin. At this meeting Cock peremptorily advised Henry not to argue but to throw himself on the mercy of the court. The publisher and his friends had prepared themselves for a lengthy duel and the advice left them shaken and stunned. Meanwhile Cock disappeared for a few minutes to ascertain the consequences of a Guilty plea, returning to say that although the Solicitor-General was in no mood to grant clemency on account of Henry breaking his bond, he saw no other course than the one he'd advised.

The proceedings were brief. Vizetelly, dazed by the bewildering turn of events and in great pain, stood at the foot of the solicitors' table and, when challenged, pleaded guilty to the charge. Very little argument was offered by the defence; even Cock admitted to the court that whatever further expurgation had been undertaken on the translations, it had 'not gone sufficiently far'.

The Recorder then passed sentence and, recognising that because of his financial position the defendant was not able to pay a fine, sent him to prison for three months. By now quite distressed, Henry was immediately taken from the court to Holloway Prison, where he stayed the full term. The series of misfortunes adversely affected his health and following his release he lived in retirement in Surrey until his death, at Churt, four years later.

If the court proceedings were bewildering to Vizetelly they are just as baffling today. There seemed ample room within Sir Edward Clarke's confusing definition of what he deemed objectionable to allow the publisher to print and sell, say, a novel as innocuous as *His Excellency* – or any other, for that matter – until proved objectionable by further court proceedings. Remember that Vizetelly did not reissue *The Soil, Nana* or *Piping Hot!* The second committal was clearly based on an understanding that Vizetelly had been forbidden to circulate *any* translations of Zola's novels in *any* form, an understanding which, according to the surviving shorthand notes of the first trial, had no substance whatsoever. One cannot escape the feeling that the prosecution had stretched the law beyond reasonable limits, and it was lucky to get away with it through what can only be described as sheer legal incompetence on the part of the defence. In the event, the National Vigilance Association, the government and the puritans were satisfied with the result, and so apparently were the newspapers which, while they had brayed so vociferously after the first trial, were strangely silent after the second, perhaps chastened and not a little ashamed.

Interestingly, Zola was more amused than distressed by this *cause célèbre*, holding that the English were making themselves ridiculous by creating a puritannical standard of morality when their own literature often achieved a frankness far beyond anything that had issued from his own pen. While not unsympathetic to his publisher's plight he remained quite remote from the historic issues that were being fought across the Channel; he had been ground by the puritan millstones himself, and perhaps enough was enough.

Henry Vizetelly's imprisonment produced a delayed and lasting shockwave rather than an immediate blast for, as I have mentioned, not a lot of published comment followed his second trial. This has led to many accounts of his prosecution which, while mentioning his first conviction and fine, completely neglect the second, the implications of which are of far greater significance, not to mention the tragic effect on his health. As far as translations of Zola's novels are concerned, the consequences are only too evident, as will be seen in a later chapter. Even Ernest Dowson's privately printed translation of *La Terre*, commissioned by the Lutetian Society in 1895 and published confidentially in an edition of only 300 copies, reveals evidence of caution. For the popular editions of the translations, however, the outcome was catastrophic.

After the trials, the firm of Chatto & Windus bought the English translation rights to Zola's novels and Ernest Vizetelly was given the task of editing fifteen of the novels to avoid further complaints. *La Terre, Nana* and *Pot-Bouille* were the exceptions because possession of an English translation of any of them was now an offence in Great Britain and all her dominions. Vizetelly's translation of *La Terre* never saw the light of day again, not even as a thoroughly expurgated edition. Even in 1912, little hope was held for a faithful popular translation of *La Terre*. J.G. Patterson, in his *A Zola Dictionary*, wrote that certain incidents and expressions 'must always render it impossible to submit the book in its entirety to the general English reader', and added, a trifle waspishly, 'It is to be regretted that the author, in leaving nothing to the imagination, has produced a work suitable only for the serious student of sociology.'

How Ernest Vizetelly went about his task of editing those translations considered 'respectable' is worth recording. Many of the novels, after being set in type and paginated, had been cast into metal plates, which were stored for further reprinting. To drop a word or to alter a sentence meant resetting not only the page affected, but often the following pages, right to the end of the chapter. This was obviously out of the question because the cost would have been prohibitive. Vizetelly's solution was to make his cuts and changes and then to *rewrite* the affected page to fill out the exact space; the new page was then set in type and dropped into the forme along with the other unaffected pages. Vizetelly deleted or modified no less than 325 pages in the fifteen volumes which entitled him, in the case of several novels at least, to claim a dubious co-authorship.

The enfeebling effect of the court judgement is evident in most of the translations reissued from about 1895 onwards by Chatto & Windus. *Germinal* is a typical case. Readers were warned by Ernest Vizetelly in a preface that 'The present version is practically a new one, but as I have used here and there some amended passages from previous translations after acquiring the copyright thereof, I have preferred to describe myself on the title page as editor rather than translator.' The effects of some of Ernest's editing borders on the burlesque. In the scene where the miner Maheu has his Sunday bath, assisted by Maheude, his wife now doesn't dare touch him, either with soap or towel. And when he leaps, all frisky, from the tub to embrace her – as a preliminary to intercourse across the kitchen table – Maheude now modestly retreats, with the added admonition: 'That'll do, you big stupid! You're soaking, and you'll make me all wet!'

Some of the novels, like *The Ladies' Paradise*, reissued in 1895, escaped severe mutilation but were dispatched to the public with honourable mentions: 'It is a book with a good, sound moral, fit for any thoughtful woman to peruse.' *L'Assommoir*, however, was an obvious candidate for Ernest Vizetelly's blunt scalpel. Although it had been one of Zola's best-selling works in English, and its republication could be justified by its strong moral message, its sordid background and frank language posed a tricky editing problem. The result was that the already debilitated prose of the 1884 translation was not only completely emasculated but also forced into a corset of moralism: 'This translation has not been made for philological reasons,' Vizetelly explained disarmingly in a snivelling preface to the new 1897 Chatto & Windus edition, 'but chiefly to diffuse the wholesome lessons against drink, sloth and ignorance with which the work abounds.' Nevertheless, he added, he had tried to give 'the words and thoughts of the various characters in more or less slangy form, while seeking milder expletives and less coarseness of expression generally.' Finally, he concluded with some pride, he had made 'such a vast number of corrections and modifications in the former text that the translation has become almost my own'.

It is worth looking at the mechanics of how this was achieved, keeping in mind that the original English edition was itself a disconcerting example of preciosity. Here is part of the laundry scene where Virginie picks a quarrel with Gervaise, as it was rendered in the first edition:

> 'Well, yes! it's my sister. There now, does that satisfy you? They adore each other. You should just see them bill and coo! and he's left you with your bastards. Those pretty kids with scabs all over their faces! One of 'em's by a gendarme, isn't he? and you had three others made away with because you didn't want to have to pay for extra luggage on your journey. It's your Lantier who told us that. Ah! he's been telling some fine things; he'd had enough of you!'
> 'You dirty jade! you dirty jade! you dirty jade!' yelled Gervaise, beside herself, and again seized with a furious trembling. She turned round, looking once more about the ground; and only observing the little tub, she seized hold of it by the legs, and flung the whole of the blue water at Virginie's face.
> 'The cow! she's spoilt my dress!' cried the latter, whose shoulder was sopping wet and whose left hand was dyed blue. 'Wait a minute, you walking dungheap!'   (34)

If you compare this with the more faithful, modern translation, quoted in the chapter on *L'Assommoir*, you'll see how Vizetelly's tame invective hardly does credit to a voluble Parisian laundress. But now read the same passage as it appeared in the super-expurgated edition of 1897:

> 'Well, yes! it's my sister. There now, does that satisfy you? They adore each other. You should just see them! And he's left you with those ugly brats of yours! One of 'em's by a gendarme, isn't he? and you made away with three others because you didn't want to have to pay for extra luggage on your journey. It's your Lantier who told us that. Ah! he's been telling some fine things; he'd had quite enough of you!'
> 'You filthy wretch! you wretch! you wretch!' yelled Gervaise, quite beside herself, and again seized with a passionate trembling. She turned round, once more searching on the ground; and only finding the little three-legged tub near her, she caught hold of it and flung the whole of the blue water it contained at Virginie's face.
> 'The cow! she's spoilt my dress!' cried the latter, one of whose shoulders was sopping wet, and whose left hand was dyed blue. 'Wait a minute you muckheap!'   (36)

The changes are interesting; Gervaise's children are no longer bastards with scabs on their faces, and the taunt, 'dungheap' is now 'muckheap'.

Any passages suggesting sensuality were dampened down, too. At one point in the narrative Zola gives us a glimpse of Nana who, at fifteen, is already exhibiting signs of the precocity and waywardness that were to make her the *femme fatale* of the later novel. Vizetelly's original 1884 rendering is, for once, a fairly faithful translation:

Nana was growing up and becoming wayward. At fifteen years old she had expanded like a calf, white skinned and very fat, so plump indeed, you might have called her a ball. Yes, such she was – fifteen years old, with all her teeth and no stays. A hussy's phiz, dipped in milk, a skin as soft as peach rind, a funny nose, pink lips and eyes sparkling like tapers, which men would have liked to light their pipes at. Her pile of fair hair, the colour of fresh oats, seemed to have scattered gold dust over her temples, freckle-like, as it were, giving her brow a sunny crown. Ah! a pretty doll, as the Lorilleux said, a dirty nose that needed wiping, with fat shoulders which were as fully rounded and as ripe in smell as those of a full grown woman.

Nana no longer put balls of paper into her bodice. A couple of titties had come to her, a pair of bran new titties too, in white satin. They did not inconvenience her, far from it; she would have liked to have had an armful, and dreamt, in fact, of growing a wet nurse's bubbies, so gluttonous and inconsiderate indeed is youth. What made her particularly tempting was a nasty habit she had of protruding the tip of her tongue between her white teeth. No doubt on seeing herself in the looking-glasses she had thought she was pretty like this; and so all day long she poked her tongue out of her mouth in view of improving her appearance. (34)

In the later version, Nana's emerging 'titties' disappear, along with the nose that needed wiping; and while the girl is allowed the maturing, rounded shoulders, their ripe smell is considered far too exhilarating for the Victorian readers:

Nana was growing up and becoming wayward. At fifteen years old she had expanded like a calf, white skinned and very fat, so plump indeed that you might have called her a ball. Yes, such she was – fifteen years old, with all her teeth and no need of stays. And she had a hussy's phiz, dipped in milk, a skin as soft as peach rind, a funny nose, pink lips and eyes sparkling like tapers. Her pile of fair hair, the colour of fresh oats, seemed to have scattered gold dust, freckle-like, over her temples, giving her brow a sunny crown. Ah! she was a pretty doll, as the Lorilleux said, childish still in some respects, but with shoulders as rounded as those of a full-grown woman. One bad habit which she had acquired was that of protruding the tip of her tongue between her white teeth. No doubt on seeing herself in looking-glasses she had fancied that she was pretty like this; and so all day long she would poke her tongue out of her mouth in view of improving her appearance. (36)

These are just two examples of dozens of de-sensualised passages in the revised edition of *L'Assommoir* that was to be read by millions of English readers over the next quarter of a century.

Even more amusing are the changes wrought by Ernest Vizetelly for the new Chatto & Windus edition of *His Masterpiece* published in 1902. With its fascinating background of art and artists this novel had a latent respectability and good sales potential. The only problem was that rather too many passages were bound to produce heated blood in the reader – even in the original translation that appeared just before the trial of Vizetelly senior in 1888. I have selected four short passages for comparison to show the Victorian expurgator at work.

You may remember from the synopsis of *The Masterpiece* in Chapter 13 that Claude, finding Christine on his doorstep one stormy night, invites her to sleep in his studio. She does so, and the next morning he peeps around the screen to see the girl, still asleep, revealed half-naked on the bed. In a fit of inspiration Claude begins to sketch her, but she soon wakes:

Suddenly a shiver ran like a ripple over the satin-like skin. The girl had perhaps felt this man's look mentally dissecting her. She opened her eyes very wide and uttered a cry.

'Ah! great heavens!'

A sudden terror paralysed her, as it were, at the sight of this strange room, of this young man in his shirt-sleeves crouching in front of her and devouring her with his eyes. With the impulse of despair she pulled up the counterpane, and kept it tight over her bosom with both arms; her blood sent coursing so violently by the anguish of outraged modesty that the burning flush on her cheeks spread to her neck and breasts in a rosy flow.

'Well, what's the matter?' cried Claude, angrily, his pencil suspended in mid-air: 'what wasp has stung you now?' (67)

Now compare the 1902 edited version of the same passage:

But suddenly a shiver rippled over the girl's satiny skin. Perhaps she had felt the weight of that gaze thus mentally dissecting her. She opened her eyes very wide and uttered a cry.

'Ah! great heavens!'

Sudden terror paralysed her at the sight of that strange room, and that young man crouching in his shirt-sleeves in front of her and devouring her with his eyes. Flushing hotly, she impulsively pulled up the counterpane.

'Well, what's the matter?' cried Claude, angrily, his crayon suspended in mid-air; 'what wasp has stung you now?' (68)

It seems that a hot flush was considered right and proper for a young lady surprised in this way, but not one that produced a discolouration of the breasts. The same denial of sensuality occurs again and again in Ernest's edited version of his father's translation. Even a passing reference to the act of undressing was considered too arousing. When, as the result of Claude's pleading, Christine finally agrees to pose naked for him, she disrobes in a state of self-induced mental numbness in order to quell her shame. The original rendering is quoted in Chapter 22 in a discussion on the various translations of this novel, but the 1902 version is notable for the lack of *any* reference to undressing and reproduced none of Christine's small terrors as each garment drops to the floor; as an example of circumlocution it is something of a minor masterpiece itself! What is clear in this is that explicit language was not necessarily the expurgator's sole target; it was the *idea* that had to be expunged – in this case the very idea of undressing. Mention undressing to anyone and it is likely to release a flood of mental images, and this is what the Victorians obviously feared. This is even better illustrated in another passage further on, when Claude and Christine consummate their new-found love on the studio couch. In the original, Zola merely alluded to the act in phrases that might be translated, '... The night closed around them, and they embraced each other, weeping tears of joy in the first ecstasies of their passion.' In the pre-trial edition of *The Masterpiece* Vizetelly's translation is reasonably faithful:

They adored each other; their comradeship was bound to result in this fashion, amid the adventures of that picture which had gradually united them. The dusk enveloped them; they remained in each other's arms, overcome, in tears, amid this first transport of love. Near them, in the middle of the table, the lilac she had sent that morning embalmed the night air, and – alone shiny with lingering light – the scattered particles of gold leaf, wafted from the frame, twinkled like a swarming of stars.

At first sight there seems to be nothing in this passage to inflame even the most prudish sensibility. But despite the periphrasis, the *idea* of physical sex persists, however dim. In the 1902 edition it is extinguished altogether:

> They adored each other; it was inevitable. Near them, on the centre of the table, the lilac she had sent him that morning embalmed the night air, and, alone shiny with lingering light, the scattered particles of gold leaf, wafted from the frame of the big picture, twinkled like a swarming of stars. (68)

The quite unexpected and moving climax in this novel occurs, as we saw in Chapter 13, when Christine surprises Claude late one night when he is feverishly working on his doomed masterpiece. Here is the original Vizetelly translation in which he captures quite well Christine's frenzied desperation to win the heart and mind of her husband from his art:

> She felt that he was giving way, and she caught him in her arms:
> 'But why all this folly, why think of anything else but me, I who love you? You took me for your model, you made copies of my body. What was the use, say? Are these copies worth me? They are frightful, they are stiff and cold like corpses – But I am alive, and I love you. One must tell you everything, you don't understand one; but when I loiter near you, when I offer to pose, when I am there brushing against you, beneath your breath, it means that I love you – do you hear? It means that I am alive, and that you must be mine –'
> Quite distracted, she wound her limbs around him. Her swelling bosom had bounded from her torn chemise, and was pressed convulsively against him, in this last battle of passion. And she was passion itself, unbridled passion, with disorder and flame, without aught of the chaste reserve of yore, but maddened to say everything, to do everything, so that she might only conquer. Her face had become swollen, her soft eyes and limpid forehead were hidden by the twisted locks of her hair; she only showed her salient jaw, her square, determined chin, her ruddy lips.
> 'Perhaps you think that I am old. Yes, you told me that my figure was getting spoilt, and I myself believed it. I examined myself, I looked for the wrinkles while I was posing. But all that wasn't true! I feel it well enough; I have not grown old. I am still young, still strong –'
> Then, as he continued struggling: 'Look!' she cried.
> And indeed in the pale light she looked radiant with youth. In this great transport of love, her limbs looked charmingly slender, her hips spread out their silky roundness, her firm bosom heaved excitedly.
> She had already caught hold of him and pressed against him; and her hands wandered over him, as if she were seeking for his heart in this groping caress. She took possession of him, as if she wished to' make him her own; and she kissed him roughly, with an unsatiated mouth, on his skin, on his beard, on his sleeves, everything. Her voice died away, she now spoke with panting breath, mingled with sighs:
> 'Oh! come, oh, let us love one another! Have you no blood in your veins then, that shadows suffice you – Come and you will see how sweet it is to live – Ah! to live on one another's necks like that, always and always –'
> He quivered, and little by little he returned her caress, in the fright which the other one, the idol, had caused him, and she increased her efforts of seduction; she was softening him and conquering him.
> And she dragged him from the execrated painting, she carried him into her room, triumphantly. The candle, now nearly burnt, flared up for a minute behind them on the steps and then went out. Five o'clock struck on the cuckoo clock, not a gleam as yet illumined the hazy November sky. And everything subsided once more into chilly darkness.
> Christine and Claude, after groping their way, seated themselves on the bed. All the past rose up again to their hearts, intoxicating them with delicious transports. Darkness reigned all around, and they ascended higher, higher above the world,

251

borne upwards on wings of fire. Far away from his misery, forgetting it, Claude seemed to be born anew to a life of perfect felicity.

And then she pressed close to him, almost stifling him, and they started off again in vertigo, careering through the stars. Their transports began anew, and thrice it seemed to them that they flew upwards from the earth to the uttermost limits of heaven. What felicity was theirs! And how was it that he had not previously thought of curing himself by this certain happiness? Surely he would live, happy, saved, eh? now that this supreme pleasure was his.

Daylight was about to break when Christine fell asleep in Claude's arms. She twined herself around him, as if to make sure that he would not escape from her; and, with her head lying on his chest which served her as a warm pillow, she breathed softly, a smile upon her lips. (67)

In the later version, however, Ernest Vizetelly throws a bucket of cold water on Christine, and she shivers, rather than steams. Believe it or not, here is the equivalent passage, and you are excused if you fail to recognise it:

She felt that he was giving way, and she caught him in her arms:
'But why all this folly? – why think of anyone but me – I who love you? You took me for your model, but what was the use, say? Are those paintings of yours worth me? They are frightful, they are as stiff, as cold as corpses. But I am alive, and I love you!'

She seemed to be at that moment the very incarnation of passionate love. He turned and looked at her, and little by little he returned her embrace; she was softening him and conquering him.

And she dragged him from the execrated painting, she carried him off triumphantly. The candle, now nearly consumed, flared up for a minute behind them on the steps, before the big painting, and then went out. It was victory, yes, but could it last?

Daylight was about to break, and Christine lay asleep beside Claude. She was breathing softly, and a smile played upon her lips. (68)

This final, fatal struggle is the culminating tragedy in the conflict that has relentlessly pursued Claude and Christine throughout the novel, and in the French original – also captured in modern translation – it has the searing effect on the reader of being too close to an explosion. But in tampering with the intensity of the language with which Zola described it, Ernest Vizetelly reduces a brutal, primal confrontation to an effete, romanticised incident.

The effects of Henry Vizetelly's trial and conviction in 1888–9 strengthened the tradition of dishonest literature which had grown up in England since the early years of the nineteenth century and which, had it not been for the furious reaction that followed the trial, might have fizzled out within a decade. As we have seen, the insidious effects were still actively at work with his son's editing of Zola translations in 1902, producing counterfeits to be reprinted and sold for a further twenty years.

What must be remembered is that during these years Zola was quite alone in his fight against literary deceit and public prudery; although there were occasional tentative tugs, no writer in England or America in this period had dared to wrench so purposefully at the closed velvet drapes of Victorian hypocrisy.

When the affair had cooled a little, towards the end of Zola's life, Havelock Ellis made some useful observations in his *Affirmations* (1898) on the French novelist's attempts to enlarge the sphere of language by the inclusion of robust and forceful common words dealing with the functions of life. Zola's novels, he wrote, displayed none of the customary circumlocution when it came to the central sexual and digestive functions of man – to Zola the fundament was fundamental to life. Deploring the uproar over Zola's brazen ride through the barriers of polite paraphrase, Ellis pointed out that in contemporary literature 'we take the pubes as a centre, and we thence describe a circle with a radius of some eighteen inches – in America the radius is rather longer – and we forbid any reference to any organ within the circle, save that maid-of-all-work, the stomach.' The fault was, Ellis continued, what the French recognise as *le cant britannique*, the inclination to call a spade a spade on one day of the week but on no other – the ability to label a promiscuous neighbour a scoundrel but the Prince of Wales a gay blade. 'If the discovery of the Bible had been left to us to make,' he wrote, 'any English translation would have to be issued at a high price by some esoteric society, for fear lest it should fall into the hands of the British matron.'

This whole sorry episode in the history of Zola translation cannot be said to have ended, for the effects of the prosecution and persecution are still in evidence today. We can, however, leave this chapter on a note of light irony. In September 1893, Zola visited London with a group of eminent French journalists to address English scribes at a Press Congress held in the Guildhall. The novelist had just completed the *Rougon-Macquart* chronicle and his reputation had to some extent been rehabilitated by the awesome success of *The Debacle*. Zola and Alexandrine were greeted at Victoria Station and well looked after during their stay, with tours of the capital and its slums, a launch trip to Greenwich with George Moore, and endless dinners; he was even made an honorary member of the Athenaeum Club. At the Guildhall he addressed the gathered journalists on the subject of 'anonymity in journalism' and although there must have been present many who had so virulently attacked him a few years previously – and anonymously at that – the novelist was given a typical British ovation by the crowd of four thousand.

The moment he departed, however, the attacks were renewed at a dangerously influential level. At a Church Congress in Birmingham two months later, the Bishop of Worcester declared that Zola 'had spent his life corrupting the minds and souls not only of thousands of his fellow-countrymen... but also, by the translation of his works, thousands and hundreds of thousands of young souls everywhere'. Zola was denounced by the headmaster of Harrow as 'infamous', and at another church gathering the Bishop of Truro complained that Zola's 'horrible books' were sold at railway station bookstalls, something 'that would never have happened in the lifetime of that good man, Mr W.H. Smith.' At that time the only Zola novels on the Smith stalls were the laundered translations of *The Dream*, *The Debacle* and *Doctor Pascal*. Angered by these attacks, Vizetelly sought legal advice on the prospect of suing, only to be told that 'it is useless to proceed against an English bishop; there is so much cant in this country that you would never obtain a verdict against him, however complete your evidence.'

At this point Zola found a new champion in Arthur Quiller-Couch, future professor of English Literature at Cambridge. Writing a series of anonymous articles under the pseudonym 'A.T.', he defended Zola and Vizetelly and concluded that the public conscience would never permit a repetition of the proceedings that had landed the publisher in gaol. If this was a suggestion that Vizetelly could now issue all of Zola's works without risk, Henry wisely ignored it. In any case, the embittered old publisher, who had followed Zola's London welcome by his former tormentors through newspaper reports brought to his bedside, died a few months later, on New Year's Day 1894.

16

Four Faces of Love

Within days of completing the manuscript for *Earth* in August 1887, Zola went into Paris and made what was for him a most unusual purchase: a medieval missal, the sacred book which contains the liturgy of the Roman Catholic Church. Although it cost him several thousand francs it was bought not as an investment, nor for his notorious collection of antiquities, but as an item of research for his next novel.

It was to be an idyll of love and filmy-eyed devotion, a symphony in white, a poem vibrating with the sanctity of innocence -- a novel, Zola slyly realised, that would confound his critics once again. The novel was *The Dream*, but it was not the author's first book with love as its theme. In 1878 he had written *A Love Episode*, a story of frustrated passion; and the ironically titled *Joy of Life* had followed in 1884, a story of love denied. Now, to complete the trio, Zola's imagination soared to ethereal heights, to the realms of pure love. I have grouped these three novels together partly for convenience but also because they collectively played a part in a most astonishing event that occurred in the middle-aged author's life.

To begin the train of events which concluded with Zola's real-life idyll, it is necessary to return to 1877, to the writing of *A Love Episode*. This novel preceded *Nana* and was the first *Rougon-Macquart* story to have exclusively as its theme the destructive power of the passions released by love, although in previous novels he had dealt with aspects of it: Eugène Rougon 'uses' it, for example, in *His Excellency*; and Maxime and Renée illuminate its incestuous side in *The Kill*.

A Love Episode was composed during the months the novelist spent with his family at L'Estaque, Cézanne's Provençal painting retreat, in the latter half of 1877. There, although the sun burned down on the arid countryside as hotly and brightly as ever, what came forth was in utter contrast to *L'Assommoir* and *Nana*, the novels which preceded and followed it: a novel which on the surface was like a deep, dark, tranquil pool, only revealing signs of life when disturbed. Perhaps it was Zola's intention to seek relief from the strident passions unleashed in *L'Assommoir* and the eroticism he had in mind for *Nana*, for curiously the same pattern occurred later when he sandwiched *The Dream* between the lyrical, intense *Earth* and the fast-paced *The Beast in Man*, a homicidal thriller.

The plot of *A Love Episode* revolves around an eternal triangle – though not the usual kind – and a moral conflict between two of the protagonists. The heroine is Hélène Mouret, attractive, virtuous and respectable. On the geneological tree she is a descendant on the middle-of-the-road Mouret branch, a balanced personality although her grandmother, Adélaïde Fouque, is mad in an asylum. But while Hélène may be temperamentally normal it soon becomes apparent that she has passed the family curse on to her unstable daughter, Jeanne.

When we meet her in the novel, Hélène is a widow, living in Paris. Her late husband, father of Jeanne, died in 1853. Outwardly, the short-lived marriage was a happy one, and M. Grandjean admired his young wife. But for Hélène it was a union without passion, and she faces her widowhood with no great sexual hunger to satisfy. What love she has is devoted to her sickly but precocious daughter.

Little Jeanne possesses the bad seed, and it is her inherited organic feebleness that is the snowflake which causes the avalanche. When she suddenly becomes ill, her mother sends for the physician, Dr Deberlé. The illness is prolonged, the visits multiply, and Hélène and the doctor soon find they are attracted to each other.

Their emerging love faces considerable obstacles. Hélène is a virtuous woman with a deep respect for convention; and, never having known it, has no pressing need for sexual love. Dr Deberlé is married, but it is not Juliette, his wife, who becomes the third member of the triangle – it is young Jeanne who, jealous and alarmed by the transfer of her mother's affection to another, attempts to wreck the blossoming love affair by inducing a psychosomatic condition.

Eventually, Hélène succumbs, partly to Deberlé's patient insistence and partly to exciting and receptive stirrings mounting within her. The long seduction and its climax is tangled with symbolism, the most effective of which is a view of Paris seen from an upper window of Hélène's apartment on the heights of Passy. The way in which this is integrated into the novel is peculiarly mathematical. We are treated to five separate descriptions of the view, each under different atmospheric conditions and each linked to Hélène's moods and each occurs in the fifth chapter in each of the five parts of the novel.

It is, finally, the seductiveness of spring which unlocks the latent passion in Hélène, sensual feelings and desires she never knew she had, and Dr Deberlé willingly satisfies them. At this point, though, the reader has a fair idea that this is not the way to solve a moral conflict and that, naturalist novel or not, retribution will surely follow. It does. The couple have reckoned without Jeanne, the 'delicate and neurotic creature' according to the cover blurb on a modern translation, 'who fights to separate the lovers with all the weapons in her power, and succeeds at the cost of her life'.

A Love Episode is by no means as dull as many critics have made out. True, it not a book in the style for which its author is most admired, but the thoughtful, poignant story has plenty in it to hold interest. One of its most remarkable features is the penetrating study of Jeanne, and the novelist's observations – full of insight, considering Zola had no children – on juvenile jealousy and possessiveness. Although at times Zola hesitated, with the feeling that he might be writing a book for schoolgirls, and that readers might criticise him for waxing sentimental, the lyricism of the novel never drifts free from its anchor of irony and realism. The emergence and maturing of a woman's love is analysed with the same devotion to truth and detail accorded the examination of alcoholism in preparation for *L'Assommoir,* with the result that Hélène's love affair is a psychological study of some depth.

One of Zola's favourite themes runs through *A Love Episode* – that the inevitable consequence of loveless, middle-class marriages is promiscuity or adultery – and was explored thoroughly in *Piping Hot!* In this novel, however, the author is rather sympathetic to the plight of two healthy and attractive but lonely people in their search for idyllic love. Zola's thoughts on sex were, as we have seen, somewhat ambivalent. On the one hand love other than for the purpose of procreation led to personal degradation. But in *A Love Episode* he seems, in his descriptions of Hélène's sexual awakening, to be seeking a justification for sex purely as an expression of love, happy and guilt-free. Unfortunately the idyll abruptly ends and the exercise is clouded by infidelity on Deberlé's part, Zola's punishment for which is, as we know, frustration and tragedy.

I have mentioned the so-called *Five Pictures of Paris* which Zola composed into the novel, and of which he was not a little proud. The idea behind the five views is ingenious, for they not only serve as symbolic counterpoint to the states of Hélène's mind at various stages of the narrative, but also to offer a welcome break from the claustrophobic confines of Jeanne's sickroom, in which Hélène is virtually a prisoner. Each view is a virtuoso word-picture, and the pentateuch can be compared with Monet's celebrated impressionistic murals of a lily pond, seen under different atmospheric and lighting conditions. The descriptions were very dear to Zola who apparently went to enormous trouble to compose them.

> Since my twentieth year [he wrote], it had been one of my dreams to write a novel in which Paris, with its ocean of roofs, should enact a character, somewhat after the style of the Chorus of the ancients. In my poverty-stricken youth I lodged in an attic in the suburbs from which I could view its wide expanse. Paris, like a huge Titan, motionless and indifferent, lay always beneath my window, a grim confidant in my joys and sorrows. I suffered the pangs of hunger, I wept in its presence; and in its presence I first knew love and my greatest happiness.

Zola was aware of accusations that he had yielded to the temptation to show off. 'In my mind,' he replied, 'the views have a consistent and human connection with the action... and in striving to make these descriptions an integral part of the work, I have thought of the story as a bridge in which they served as a key-stone.' His defence carries a blush of apology, but none is needed, for the views are legitimate and effective devices, the broad vistas of the city reflecting Hélène's own contorted emotional landscape, an orchestral accompaniment to her inner conflicts, joys and moods. The five views begin with the great city glistening in the spring sunlight while Hélène experiences the first stirrings of love; then we see Paris at sunset; at night; then lashed by a violent storm, and finally, as Hélène stands penitent by her daughter's grave, Paris suitably enveloped in a shroud of snow. Paul Cézanne immediately grasped Zola's intention, and after reading the book wrote to him: 'The locations, by the way you've painted them, are suffused with the passion that agitates the characters, and are thus not backgrounds but an essential part of the whole. They seem to be alive, sharing in the sufferings of the characters.'

Not all critics saw the views with Cézanne's painter's eye, however, claiming that they were self-conscious and intrusive, but I disagree. It is difficult to choose a single example to illustrate the skill with which Zola integrated these grand canvases into his story, but one particularly memorable passage occurs when Hélène leaves her child in the house while she goes to meet her lover. Jealous and resentful, Jeanne contemplates the storm from her window, while trying to understand the nature of her morbid passions.

> She got up and looked out, pressing her forehead against a window-pane. The rain had ceased, and the last batch of storm-clouds, driven by a squall, were sailing away towards the distant heights of Père-Lachaise, shaded with grey; and Paris, against this stormy background, bathed in a flat light, assumed a mournful, lonely grandeur. It seemed uninhabited, like some nightmare city glimpsed by the light of a dead sun. It certainly wasn't nice to look at; and Jeanne started vaguely dreaming about all the people she had loved, since she had first come into the world. Her oldest, dearest friend in Marseilles had been a huge, heavy ginger cat; she used to pick it up with both her arms clutched round its stomach, and carry it thus from chair to chair, and it never got cross; then it had disappeared, and that was the first cruel thing she could remember. Then she had had a sparrow, and that had died; she had picked it up one morning on the floor of its cage; and that made two. And then there were her toys, that got broken on purpose to make her unhappy; it was all most unfair, and she was such a silly that it upset her dreadfully. One doll in particular, no bigger than her hand, had driven her to despair by getting its head smashed; indeed, she was so devoted to it that she had buried it secretly, in a corner of the yard; later on, seized with a longing to see it again, she had dug it up, and the sight of it had made her sick with terror, it was so black and hideous. It was always the same; other people gave up loving before she did. They got spoilt, or else they went away; in any case, they were partly to blame. Why did it happen so? She herself never changed; when she loved anyone, it was for life. She could not understand desertion; it was something so huge, so monstrous that the notion of it made her little heart break. The slow dawning of confused awareness in her mind sent a shiver through her. So, one day, people parted; they went their separate ways, they stopped seeing one another, they stopped loving one another. And she sat gazing out over the huge and melancholy city, horribly depressed by these glimpses of life's cruelty revealed to her passionate twelve-year-old heart.
>
> Meanwhile her breath had clouded the pane again. She wiped away with her hand the haze that prevented her from seeing out. In the distance, rain-washed buildings shimmered like tarnished mirrors. Rows of houses, clear and clean with their pale façades amongst all the roof-tops, looked like countless pieces of linen spread out to dry on sun-baked fields. The light grew whiter, the tail of the cloud that still hung mistily over the city let milky gleams of sunlight through; and over certain districts a hesitant gaiety seemed to hover, as though the sky were on the verge of laughter. Jeanne looked down and saw the streets coming to life again, along the quay and on

the Trocadéro slopes, after the sudden showers of heavy rain. Cabs started jolting slowly along, while the rattle of passing omnibuses echoed more loudly in the silence of the still deserted streets. People shut up umbrellas; pedestrians sheltering under trees ventured from one pavement to the other, through the streams that flowed from puddles to gutters. (45)

The integration of external atmosphere and Jeanne's interior monologue is arresting, and this beautifully wrought passage – only a small portion of one of the views – also reveals clearly Zola's psychological insight into a child's obsessive and selfish state of mind.

The novel was greeted with a mixed reception. The poet Mallarmé spoke of as an interrupted poem, displaying 'profound and lucid vision'. George Moore, one of Zola's first foreign converts to naturalism, called it 'that most beautiful of beautiful books' and thought Turner might have been proud of the Paris views. André Gide's view was as blunt as his comment: 'Written with a blunt pencil,' he snapped.

Joy of Life is bitterly and ironically titled, for it is a novel touched with a haunting, melancholy sadness of an intensity that cannot fail to affect most readers. Maupassant admired its simple majesty, and understood only too well the obsessional sources from which it sprang: 'Over the whole book there hovers a black bird, its wings outstretched: the bird of death.' And one of the most perceptive of modern Zola scholars, Angus Wilson, called *Joy of Life* 'Zola's wasted glory', a magnificent failure in which only the overflow of the author's personal misery and the accompanying undercurrent of self-pity prevented it from being his greatest novel. Why was the novel such a near miss if indeed it was?

Joy of Life was unquestionably a therapeutic novel in that it provided a reservoir for the storms of unhappiness and despair that fell into Zola's life around 1880: the deaths of Duranty and Flaubert, both close friends, and then that of his mother. During the mental breakdown which followed he began work on *Joy of Life*, but its theme – that of a man's failure to realise his destiny in the face of scepticism and doubt – was so painfully close to his own condition that he abandoned it and wrote *Piping Hot!* instead. It wasn't until he had completed *The Ladies' Paradise* that he felt able, in the spring and summer of 1883, to pick up the threads of *Joy of Life*. By then there were fresh watersheds of obsessive despair – Alexandrine's childlessness was one; his own despondency at the increasing intellectual pessimism and decadence of the time was another – and both found their way to the desolate tide of melancholy from which Zola drew the sources for his novel. Because of the intensity with which it reflects memories of the blackest depression he'd experienced, you are not advised to read this book for laughs.

Pauline Quenu, ten years old and suddenly orphaned, arrives at Bonneville, desolate fishing village, to live with her uncle and aunt, the Chanteaus. It is a new world for her, living in a house perched half-way up a cliff like the nest of a

259

seabird, with ocean from one end of the horizon to the other, while below cluster fishermen's hovels which threaten to disappear at every storm.

It is not a happy household, however. Madame Chanteau, the daughter of destitute but noble family, married her husband when he was a partner in thriving business, but since he retired because of gout they barely manage to live on the proceeds of a small investment. Now, all they have is the seaside cottage, to Madame Chanteau's bitter regret. Still, they have put their only son Lazare through college and have high hopes for his future; moreover Pauline' arrival also helps the family income for she pays for her board from the 150,000 francs inherited from the proceeds of the sale of her parents' poor butcher shop in Paris.

Pauline brings a ray of sunshine into the gloomy house and her happy honest nature endears her to everyone, and particularly to Lazare, who several years her senior. The years pass pleasantly, punctuated by Lazare absences in Paris, studying first music, then chemistry. One year he returns with enthusiastic plans to extract chemicals from the tons of seaweed that pile up on the beach. Pauline, in her desire to make the young man happy, willingly lends him half her fortune to build the extraction plant. But the project is failure, Lazare despairs, and the money is lost.

Fearing a family scrutiny of Pauline's bank accounts, which she supervise Madame Chanteau conceives the idea of marrying her to Lazare, for it obvious the two have a deep affection for each other. Both she and her gout husband feel guilty at having exploited their niece, for it was at their suggestion that she lent their son the money. But instead of trying to make good the loss they feel resentful that the young girl should have this humiliating power over them simply because she possesses money. Pauline's natural generosity however, allows her to sacrifice her savings cheerfully to indulge the Chanteaus, and, undismayed, she takes up charity work among the poor villagers. She is appalled every time a storm demolishes one of the village hovels, and is immediately attracted by Lazare's scheme to construct a system of breakwaters to stop the destruction. Bang goes another 12,000 francs. Her money is now used to pay the household bills, too, and every time an account settled the Chanteaus grow more embittered. 'She'll end up thinking herself indispensable!' Madame Chanteau says unreasonably on one of these occasions.

A series of illnesses descends upon the unhappy family. First, Chanteau racked by more frequent and more painful attacks of gout, and while Pauline virtually chained to her uncle's bedside, Lazare is seeing more and more of Louise, a childhood friend who is now a pretty young woman. Madame Chanteau also finds Louise attractive because of her 200,000-franc dowry, and encourages a romance between the girl and her son by having her stay at the house for several weeks. When it dawns on Pauline what is going on she breaks down with a serious illness and comes very close to death before she recover But no sooner is she about again when, on a tip from Véronique the servant she storms to an upstairs room to find Louise swooning in her fiancé's arms

260

he reader, at this juncture, can be excused for wanting to cheer, for at last the
laster saint in Pauline cracks apart to reveal a full-blooded, possessive woman:

> Upstairs, when Pauline reached Lazare's door, she hurled herself against it. The
> key was twisted and the door burst open, banging the wall. And what she saw within
> drove her even more frantic. Lazare was holding Louise pressed back against the
> cupboard and devouring her chin and throat with kisses, while she, almost swooning
> in sudden sexual panic, offered no resistance. They had begun in fun, no doubt, but
> the game was ending badly.
> There was a moment's stupor. All three stared at one another. At last Pauline cried:
> 'Oh, you slut, you slut!'
> It was the woman's treachery that maddened her most. With a gesture of contempt
> she had dismissed Lazare, as a child whose weakness she knew of old. But this woman,
> who spoke to her with intimate affection, this woman who was stealing her husband
> from her while she was downstairs nursing a sick man! She seized her by the
> shoulders, she shook her, she felt an urge to strike her.
> 'Tell me, why did you do that?... It was a vile thing to do, d'you hear?'
> Louise, desperate and wild-eyed, stammered: 'He got hold of me, he nearly broke
> my bones.'
> 'He? Nonsense! He'd have burst into tears if you'd so much as pushed him away.'
> The sight of the room whipped up her resentment still further; Lazare's room,
> where they had loved one another, where she too had felt the young man's passionate
> breath, turned her blood to fire. How could she be revenged on this woman? Lazare,
> dazed with shame, was about to intervene at last when she let go of Louise so abruptly
> that the girl's shoulders were flung back against the cupboard.
> 'I tell you I don't trust myself!... Go away.' (59)

Ablaze with indignation, Pauline insists that Louise leaves the house
mmediately, or she will. This places Madame Chanteau in a quandary, for the
ousehold cannot now exist without Pauline's money, so Louise goes. Then,
oon afterwards, the old lady herself dies from dropsy, followed by Mathieu
le ageing pet dog; and, at the height of a storm, Lazare's breakwater is
estroyed. Depressed by the sequence of events, Lazare's despondency sinks to
new low.

Weeks pass with monotonous regularity when it becomes obvious to Pauline
at Lazare is neither bored nor lonely but pining for Louise. After nights of
rment she decides to bring them together again, risking her own future and
appiness so that Lazare might choose freely. Inevitably Pauline loses out and
er cousin marries Louise, with the intention of living in Paris. The passage
escribing Pauline's return to the empty house on the cliff is one of the most
loving Zola ever wrote. Even her own room seems alien, and the memories
lat crowd in on her now seem distant, remote...

> Although her life seemed shattered, her sense of method still prevailed. She
> carefully put away her hat and made sure that her boots had come to no harm. Her
> dress already hung folded on the back of a chair and she was wearing only a petticoat
> and chemise, when her glance fell on her own young bosom. Gradually a hot flush
> overspread her cheeks. In her troubled brain there rose up a vivid picture of the other
> pair in their own room, over there, a room she knew, in which she had herself set
> flowers that very morning. The bride was lying in bed and he came up to her,
> laughing tenderly. With a violent gesture she let fall her petticoat, tore off her
> chemise; and, naked now, gazed at herself. Would she, then, never reap love's
> harvest? Was her own wedding never to be? Her eyes roamed over her breasts, firm as
> buds bursting with sap, to her broad hips, her belly within which lay dormant a
> promise of powerful motherhood. She became aware of her own ripeness, of the

abundant life that filled her rounded limbs and made the black fleece grow in th
secret folds of her body; she could breathe her own female odour, like a blossomin
bough awaiting fertilisation. And it was not she but that other, in the distant room sh
pictured so vividly, who lay in ecstasy in the arms of that husband for whom sh
herself had waited so many years.

But she leaned further forward, surprised to see along her thigh the red trail of
drop of blood. Suddenly she understood; her chemise, lying on the ground, wa
splashed with blood as though from a knife-thrust. So that was why, ever since leavin
Caen, she had felt such a faintness pervading her whole body? She had not expected
so soon; it was as though the loss of her love had wounded her there, at the very four
of life. And the sight of that life flowing uselessly away completed her despair. Sh
remembered how she had shrieked with terror that morning when she had firs
found herself stained with blood. Later, before blowing out her candle that evenin
she had yielded to a childish whim and examined herself with a furtive glance, prou
like a fool, of attaining physical and sexual maturity, relishing the delight of being
woman. Alas, today the red rain of her puberty was falling there, like the futil
weeping of her virginity within her. Henceforward every month would bring bac
that stream as from a ripe grape pressed at the vine-harvest; and she would never be
wife, and she would grow old in barrenness!

Then jealousy stirred once more in the depths of her being, as her hecti
imagination called up fresh pictures before her. She wanted to live, and live fully, an
to give life, she who loved life! What was the good of existing, if you couldn't giv
youself? She visualised the other two, and an urge to mutilate her own naked forr
made her look round for her scissors. Why not slash that bosom, break those thigh
rip open that belly and make that blood flow out to the last drop? She was mor
beautiful and stronger than that puny blonde, and yet he had chosen her. She woul
never know him, no part of her body could expect him henceforward – neither he
arms, nor her thighs, nor her lips. It could all be cast away like a discarded rag. Was
possible that they should be together, while she was alone, shivering with fever, in th
cold house?   (5!

Pauline's quixotic sacrifice brings no happiness to Lazare, after all. As wea
and vacillating as ever he returns to the house for a short visit which, i
Pauline's spirited company, stretches into weeks. But Louise is pregnant, an
soon joins them, though not before Lazare realises his great error and tries t
seduce Pauline.

The final chapter in this powerful and moving novel is a series of juxtapose
and related ironies, the uniting force of which also unites the new household
Chanteau, gradually being consumed by gout; Lazare, his will corroding awa
with pessimism; Louise and her baby; and, destined to spinsterhood, the nobl
Pauline. And even to the last line, at its final breath, the novel manages t
proclaim the triumph of life over death, the victory of mankind's bette
qualities over its worst.

If we examine the construction of *Joy of Life* it is difficult not to be impresse
by the novel's astonishing unity, for despite the fact that the story ramble
through a period of twelve years or so in the lives of people whose commo
characteristic is inertia, the narrative is propelled forward with incredibl
drive. This unity derives from Zola's single-minded adherence to his them
which is man's will to live out his life even in the most discouraging an
distressing circumstances. The flame is lit in Pauline's eyes early in the firs
chapter and we breathlessly follow its threatened, hesitant flickering righ
through to the end. There are no really weak links, either, to endanger th
unity, although some sections benefit more from the author's insight tha

others. The deaths of Madame Chanteau (which almost certainly borrows from Zola's observations on the death of his mother) and of Mathieu the dog are masterpieces of moving description, only surpassed by the amalgam of detachment and symbolism with which he describes the birth of Louise's baby. The novelist's astonishing insight is also evident during the vague stirrings of Pauline's puberty, and in recounting the young girl's shock and fear when she menstruates for the first time, Zola stuck a particularly savage knife into the hypocritical idea of keeping adolescent females ignorant of the reproductive processes:

> One morning Madame Chanteau was just leaving her room when she heard cries from Pauline's, and she hurried upstairs in great anxiety. The girl was sitting up in bed, with her covers thrown back, white with terror, and screaming continuously for her aunt; her bare, parted legs were stained with blood, and she was staring at what had come out of her, all her habitual courage driven away by the shock.
> 'Oh, auntie, auntie!'
> Madame Chanteau, at a glance, had understood. 'It's nothing, darling. Don't worry.' (59)

Later, after secretly studying Lazare's medical textbooks, the young girl discovers the reasons for the discharge that frightened her.

> And Pauline knew, now, why that red stream, the sign of her puberty, had poured from her as from a ripe grape crushed at the vine-harvest. Her enlightenment set her pondering gravely, in the midst of that full tide of life that she felt surging within her. She was puzzled and resentful of her aunt's silence, at the complete ignorance in which the latter tried to keep her. Why should she have been left to suffer such terror? It was unfair, for there was no harm in knowing. (59)

Pauline is one of Zola's most attractive heroines. She positively radiates kindliness and to her the world and all the beings in it are a source of wonder and delight. She is a compulsive giver of whom others take advantage; her gout-ridden uncle squanders her time, while Lazare and Madame Chanteau squander her money. Her saintliness – which at times hovers on the border of credibility – is not solely the product of an inherited good nature, however; it involves great self-sacrifice. Almost as an afterthought Zola endowed Pauline with a terrible temper and a streak of jealousy, but when she discovers them within her they are ruthlessly suppressed. Her sexuality suffers the same fate. Only a saint could find real happiness and contentment in the face of such self-denial.

Pauline is a saint but Zola deliberately makes her a non-believer. On her saintly journey through life, helping the poor, the diseased and the dissipated among the fishermen's families of the village, without reward and often without the satisfaction of success, she has no need to sink to her knees at the end of the day to seek revitalisation from religion. Her philosophy, deriving from a radiant inner joy that she is alive and healthy, is to devote herself to making others as happy as she is; thinking that if every human on earth who was able did the same it would be a paradise. Zola no doubt intended that Pauline's very existence should not only be a taunting object lesson to the venal priesthood, but also demonstrate that there was an alternative to orthodox religion.

The character of Lazare was most likely conceived during the darkest moments of Zola's period of self-doubt, when he wondered if life was at all worthwhile because he could be struck down, like Flaubert, before the completion of his work. Zola of course recovered, but Lazare is the complete sceptic; although he has endless ambitions and dreams of great projects he abandons them half-way through, paralysed into inaction by the fear he may never finish them. This characteristic of Lazare's hints at the novel's broader theme, the purpose or pointlessness of life; whether, in the end, one can say life is worth living or not. This question is the subject of a running debate throughout the novel. Zola seems to have digested a portion of Schopenhauer's pessimistic philosophy – although dead for twenty years his works were popular in France in the 1880s – and some of his ideas are worked into the novel. The debate is not one-sided. While Lazare represents the belief that life and striving are pointless, Pauline epitomises the belief that for man, life is the greatest gift, and he should make of it what he can.

In a way, *Joy of Life* comes close to what Zola envisaged as an 'experimental novel' although it is the author, not his characters, who is the laboratory rat reacting to a flux of influences and ideas with the object of arriving at a single philosophical formula for life. Throughout the novel we witness the lives and beliefs of the two protagonists, the debaters, and with the novelist's summing-up we are invited to make our own judgement at the end. But right at the very end of the novel Zola plants an incident designed to unduly influence the reader, who is left in no doubt about the author's final belief in the potential of mankind. Of all the book's characters, the one with the least to live for is Chanteau; every minute of his day is filled with ceaseless, excruciating pain and the disease is getting worse. All he can look forward to is the most agonising of slow deaths. Yet when he receives the news that their old servant Véronique has hung herself from the pear tree in the garden he exclaims, with furious indignation: 'How can anyone be so stupid as to kill themselves?'

It has been suggested that *The Dream*, its pages so pure and uplifting, was written with an eye to Zola's election to the French Academy. Where *Earth* had resounded to the oaths of the ribald peasants and stank of the manure heap, *The Dream* enfolds the reader in a sanctified hush, exhaling the breath of incense and damp flagstones.

The truth was that the critics could find no explanation for the unexpected appearance of a pious fairy story from the pen of literature's *bête noire*. 'M. Zola has sought in this charming story to prove that he too can write for the virgin', said *The Speaker*; 'An idyll so exquisite, so pure and dainty, that one wonders involuntarily how it can have emanated from the mind that produced *La Terre*,' announced the puzzled *Morning Leader*; while the *Review of Reviews* echoed much the same sentiments: 'It is most difficult to believe it was written

EMILE ZOLA, from the etching by E. Boucourt and C. Mauigaud, Paris, 1892.

The Belly of Paris

L'Assommoir

Germinal

Piping Hot!

27. EXAMPLES of wood-engraved illustrations to Zola's novels published during the 1880s. Seen here are incidents from *The Belly of Paris, L'Assommoir, Germinal* and *Piping Hot!*

28. THE NOVELIST's second family: his children Denise and Jacques, Zola, and Jeanne Rozerot, photographed during his exile in England, 1898.

29. ZOLA in what he called his 'working dress', about 1892.

30. OVER many years cartoonists poked fun at Zola's vain efforts to gain entrance to the French Academy. This Gilbert Martin cartoon of 1892 suggests that Zola was writing *Lourdes*, a novel with a religious background, simply to win his nomination.

31. MAJOR Marie-Charles Ferdinand Walsin Esterhazy, the real culprit in the Dreyfus scandal. Zola sits behind him with hands clasped. *Collection Viollet*

32. THE FAMOUS '*J'Accuse...!*' letter, as it appeared on the front page of *L'Aurore* on January 13, 1898.

by the same uncompromising realist who gave us *Nana*.' Was Zola sprouting angels' wings with which to pursue some heavenly vision, many wondered?

The novelist was doing nothing of the kind, of course. Superficially, the whole plot and its rhapsodic, high-key treatment, the pious environment – we're never more than a hundred yards from a church – and the transcendental quality of the novel are almost comically incongruous in the company of *Earth* which precedes it and *The Beast in Man* which follows it. But on closer examination the heroine of *The Dream*, Angélique, is a true fruit of the Rougon side of the genealogical tree and thus the novel is firmly rooted in the *Rougon-Macquart* chronicle. That Angélique successfully suppresses her temperamental inheritance of lust for power and greed for riches is but an accident of fate; with perhaps a different upbringing she might have turned out to be a female financial whiz-kid like her Uncle Saccard, or a political animal in the mould of her Uncle Eugène.

The plot of *The Dream* is one of the simplest Zola ever devised, for the narrative is exclusively concerned with the angelic heroine, Angélique. She arrives one night in the country town of Beaumont as a runaway foundling, nine years old, a waif sheltering from her cruel foster parents and the driving snow. Fortunately she is taken in and adopted by the Huberts, a kindly couple who embroider sacred vestments.

Angélique becomes an apprentice in the craft and as several God-fearing years pass she becomes an expert. She is also entranced by the atmosphere of sanctity from the great cathedral that adjoins the Huberts' house, which vibrates and shakes every time someone plays the organ.

The girl, whose history is eventually discovered by her guardians, is a Rougon, and her temperament is marked by excessive passion. She goes into fevers of ecstasy before pictures of the saints, and one evening the Huberts find her 'in a half-fainting state, with her head upon the table, and her lips pressed to those of the images'. But a dark side emerges, too. There are occasional outbreaks of greed and stealing and moments of blind anger, at which the dismayed Huberts would 'draw away from her, for she was like a little monster ruled by an evil spirit within her'. Under the kind and gentle influence of the childless couple, however, Angélique conquers her hereditary afflictions and grows into a beautiful and virtuous young woman.

In her whitewashed room in the shadow of the cathedral, Angélique dreams of what, to her, is the ultimate happiness: to fall in love and be loved by a rich, handsome prince. She explains her naïve fantasy to the Huberts:

'Happiness is a very simple thing. We are happy, are we not? All three of us? And why? Simply because we love each other. Then, after all, it is no more difficult than that; it is only necessary to love and to be loved. So, you see, when the one I expect really comes, we shall recognise each other immediately. It is true I have not yet seen him, but I know exactly what he ought to be. He will enter here and will say: "I have come in search of you." And I shall reply: "I expected you, and will go with you." He will take me with him, and our future will be at once decided upon. He will go into a palace, where all the furniture will be of gold, encrusted in diamonds. Oh, it is all very simple!' (77)

Soon afterwards, the dream begins to assume reality, for an admirer appears persistently below her balcony at night. Angélique has no doubts that the young man is her prince, resembling 'either a Saint George or a superb picture of Christ, with his curly hair, his thin beard, his straight nose, rather large, and his proudly-smiling black eyes'. The admirer turns out to be Félicien VII d'Hautecoeur, the last descendant of one of the oldest and richest families in France. Notwithstanding she is a nameless, penniless embroiderer, Angélique is sure she will marry him, to live happily ever after.

Félicien's father, Monseigneur the Bishop, has other ideas though, and betroths his son to a young lady from an equally noble family. The Huberts, seeing the love-match between Félicien and Angélique as hopeless, and wishing her to be spared unnecessary suffering, secretly contrive to break up the romance by telling Félicien she does not love him. For her part, Angélique is told that the Bishop is implacably against their marriage, but although she is bitterly disappointed and crushed to a state of humiliation and resignation, she still has faith that her dream will somehow come true.

But the extent of her grief at Félicien's approaching marriage is too much for her delicate constitution and she falls ill. Death advances on Angélique but before she lapses into unconsciousness she requests Extreme Unction, 'that celestial remedy, instituted for the cure of both the soul and the body'. The Bishop, after a violent argument with his son and days of prayer and struggle, finally agrees to administer the rite to the dying girl.

> He made no haste. It was true that death was there, hovering near the old, faded chintz curtains, but he knew that it was patient, and that it would wait. And although in her state of utter prostration the child could not hear him, he addressed her as he asked her:
> 'Is there nothing upon your conscience which distresses you? Confess all your doubts and fears, my daughter; relieve your mind.'
> She was still in the same position, and she was always silent. When, in vain, he had given time for a reply, he commenced the exhortation with the same full voice, without appearing to notice that none of his words reached her ear.
> 'Collect your thoughts, meditate, demand from the depths of your soul pardon from God. The Sacrament will purify you, and will strengthen you anew. Your eyes will become clear, your ears chaste, your nostrils fresh, your mouth pure, your hands innocent.'
> With eyes fixed upon her, he continued reading to the end all that was necessary for him to say; while she scarcely breathed, nor did one of her closed eyelids move.   (77)

After the ceremony of applying the holy oils the Bishop's indifference crumbles before the innocent, fragile beauty of the young woman; his human, paternal feelings are aroused and he prays for a miracle that Angélique should live. 'If God wishes, I also wish it.' At this moment the girl's eyes open, and the way is clear for the realisation of her dream.

The marriage ceremony in the great cathedral several months later is magnificent. At the end of the long, solemn service, when the couple pause at the cathedral's entrance just before leaving, Angélique, her heart overflowing with happiness, raises herself on her toes and with her last remaining strength kisses her husband. Then, as the bells of the church chime joyously and the crowds outside cheer and shout good wishes to the couple, she falls down, dead.

> Everything is only a dream.
> And so, at the moment of supreme earthly happiness,
> Angélique had disappeared in the slight breath of a loving kiss.

One of the few notable qualities of this book is that it is short, for at times the reader's eye is inclined to glaze over, his mind wanders, and he distinctly feels the author is addressing him through several cubic metres of cottonwool. One real disappointment is the dream itself. For all her humility and piety Angélique's illusion is pretty much the stuff of common mankind: to love and be loved by a rich, handsome, respected and powerful partner. At one point she admits frankly to Félicien's father that the young man's money is an important consideration: 'Ah! to become rich by him and with him, to owe all my happiness to him, to live in the sweetness and splendour of luxury and to have no more sorrow, no misery around us. That is my ideal!' Is Zola trying to tell us that all ideals are basically materialistic if we are absolutely honest with ourselves?

But this is only one striking ambiguity. One of the interesting qualities of the novel is that, far from reflecting the author's own mordant views on religion, the religious beliefs of the various characters are treated with sensitive respect. This is not, of course, to suggest that Zola fell under the spell of religion before and during the writing of *The Dream*; his research was, as usual, the result of intense observation and detached study. What it does indicate, I think, is that the novelist was prepared to make some concessions to the value of religion. His view of Christianity was simple: if you believed in Christ you believed in miracles. Religious faith, to Zola's thinking, could not be countenanced by any balanced adult, but he did not deny, as we noted in the discussion of his earlier clerical novels, its therapeutic value to the sick, the aged and the mentally ill. In *The Dream* he explores another aspect, that of the inspirational benefits of the Christian faith to extraordinarily imaginative individuals.

It is said that Zola's inspiration for *The Dream* arose from his first view of the magnificent stained-glass windows in the cathedral at Chartres, where he went to research the background for *Earth*. Little of this inspiration filters through to the novel, however, and few would dispute that *The Dream* is not one of his best books. There is no biting irony, no adventurous ideas, no humour, no gripping dramatic moments and no passages of special brilliance. Moreover, some of the writing is downright bad. The characters are paper cut-outs. Angélique is a manufactured article, and not a very well made one, either. Perhaps the reason for all this is that, unlike his approach to any other novel, Zola was confused about what he wanted to say. Zola, in fact, wasn't writing so much as building romantic castles in the air.

As short as it was, composing *The Dream* was a long and exacting task. Without violence and conflict to spur his imagination, the protracted rapturous passages acted like a sedative on Zola's methodical way of working, and the flights of a young girl's fancies led him into hours of non-productive daydreaming. Angélique's dreams worked upon his own romantic nature; if she could dream, why not he? If his heroine's dreams could come true, why not his? Only there would be no miracles. If his dreams were to become reality only he could make it possible.

But, at forty-seven, Zola was the fat prince of Médan, battling, like many writers, with the enlarging effects of a sedentary occupation. With computer-like precision he rose at eight, dressed in a brown corduroy suit and heavy boots to walk the dogs, and returned to the house at 8.45 sharp for a snap breakfast of eggs. At nine he went to his study from which he punctually emerged at one o'clock for lunch. He fell asleep at two, was awakened at three to attend to his correspondence, and at four o'clock precisely left the house again for a long walk or to row on the river. Occasionally he would ride on his new safety bicycle he'd purchased in an effort to slim. None of this determined exercise, however, had any noticeable effect on his corpulence.

The novelist's personal unhappiness had flowed like a swollen river into his stomach which now had the dimensions of a tree trunk. He weighed nearly sixteen stone and the bulge around his waist measured forty-four inches. Profuse sweating and breathlessness accompanied any exertion and where, once, he would write without pause throughout a morning, he now punctuated his days with dozing. The anxieties which oppressed him were revealed in his face, too. Not yet fifty, he looked ten years older. His forehead was bald and creased; his shortsighted eyes struggled to view the world over puffy cheeks and his mouth was a tense slit half-hidden in an undergrowth of beard.

A remarkable transformation – which was to become a talking-point in Parisian literary circles – began at the end of 1887. By restricting himself to a low-liquid, wine-less diet, Zola dropped a stone in a few months and by autumn the following year had reduced his weight to twelve stone. At the same time he began to take an interest in his appearance, perhaps in an effort to recapture the image Manet had preserved of him many years before. He brushed his hair front to back, trimmed his beard goatee-style and invested in a wardrobe of impeccably cut suits. At the end of this regime he was photographed, and the change was little short of a metamorphosis. Now he looked ten years younger, with an alertness and humour to match, and his friends were amazed. Goncourt recounted that after an interval of several months he had quite failed to recognise him. What was behind it all?

Zola had fallen in love. The lady of his desire was a twenty-year-old maid, Jeanne-Sophie-Adèle Rozerot, who had been employed some months before by Alexandrine to care for the household linen. She was tall, statuesque even, with sensual lips and strikingly large, dark eyes. Her happy nature had endeared her to Alexandrine, and she accompanied the Zolas on their summer holiday to Royan. The urge to realise his long-suppressed fantasies when the opportunity presented itself must have been for Zola overwhelmingly compulsive, for he had not only observed to the letter the sanctity of marriage but had extolled it far and wide. He was the antithesis of the philanderer: shy, nervous and almost certainly beset with obsessive doubts about his potency. The woman he admired was twenty-seven years younger, a gulf that even his great fame and stature might not be sufficient to bridge in such an intensely personal undertaking.

How the relationship came about and blossomed is not known, for not a single love letter survives. Perhaps Zola was reticent about writing to Jeanne because of the danger of discovery, but against this must be weighed the fact that the novelist expressed his deepest emotions with his pen rather than with long-unpractised murmurings in the ear. More likely Madame Zola, after her husband's death, destroyed anything to do with the romance, for significantly the outline for the last of the *Rougon-Macquart* novels, *Doctor Pascal*, which dramatises the love of an older man for a young woman, was the only outline missing from the otherwise complete collection of Zola's manuscript material his widow presented to the Bibliothèque Nationale.

During the holiday at Royan in October 1888, Zola's ubiquitous environmental influences set to work on the novelist himself. Alexandrine arrived ailing and proceeded to spend a good part of the holiday in bed. Free from many of her usual household chores, Jeanne had time on her hands, which she used to explore the countryside and beaches, often on a bicycle. Zola began to take an interest in bicycles too, and decided to give up his siestas. Surprised at his unaccustomed cheerfulness, and thinking all the outdoor exercise had something to do with it, Alexandrine even encouraged him to go out riding with Jeanne. At the same time, the novelist developed a passion for photography, and there are no prizes for successfully guessing who became his favourite model.

The six weeks at Royan brought the couple close together; so close, in fact, that on their return Jeanne left the household and Zola installed her in a small apartment in the Rue St Lazare, not far from his own house in Paris. From there, out of the mists of supposition, comes the first evidence of consummation, although the world had to wait a decade for it. In 1898, during his exile in England, Zola sent a touching greeting to his mistress, 'in memory of 11 December 1888, with my gratitude for ten happy years. . .'

There have been many attempts to establish a valid connection between Zola's sexuality and its expression in his fiction, beginning with the vindictive suggestion in the *Manifesto of the Five against La Terre* (1887) that he was afflicted with an 'illness of the loins' and that he had lived a life of exaggerated continency. Perversely, when reviewing all the available facts, there does seem to be more useful evidence – albeit treacherous – contained in the autobiographical elements of his fictional output than from the documentation of his private life, which might lead an investigator to some reasonable conclusions.

Until its recent challenge by Zola's premier English biographer-critic, Professor F.W.J. Hemmings, the popular simplistic view was that the eroticism of his novels acted as a safety valve to a contrained sexual appetite, and his sheer output to its sublimation. Hemmings, however, sees no worthwhile evidence of continency during Zola's major creative years: 'for nearly the whole of his literary career, Zola was living what would surely be called a normal sexual life. . .' But the kind of evidence – reliable or factual – that suggests Zola had what could be called a normal sexual relationship with Alexandrine is no stronger than the evidence which suggests that he hadn't. Zola would not have been the first celebrity to have, for professional reasons, cleverly hidden a desolate and unfulfilled marriage behind an image of contentment. That the novelist possessed a repressed sexuality of considerable potential is illustrated only too well, I think, by the intensity with which Zola threw himself into the liaison with Jeanne Rozerot, by the dedication with which he pursued it, and with the prompt arrival of two children – all involving behaviour contrary to a morality and way of life to which he had unwillingly subscribed for twenty years.

The freakishness of the novelist's work-load, which would have crippled most writers, and his output of brilliant prose which was sustained over two decades, does not necessarily require an explanation, least of all one suggesting that its source was domestic unhappiness. After all, Johann Sebastian Bach, whose creative output was vastly more prolific, led a life so domestically fulfilled he had twenty children by two wives. One is, however, led into believing that marital discontent and sexual frustration was to some extent sublimated in his writing by Zola's own admissions. Unlike John Ruskin, his art critic counterpart the other side of the Channel, the compulsive effects of whose unhappy and unrequited love affairs were not exactly unpublicised, very little is really known about the marital problems of Zola and Alexandrine. But there were occasional leaks. At about the time of his mother's death Zola was known to have referred to the state of marriage in the most derogatory terms. A German naturalist writer, Michael Conrad, recorded in a posthumous biography that the novelist had told him marriage was a 'sick man in pain, tossing about in a bed trying to find a comfortable position' and also that 'living together is basically disagreeable.' Hemmings, in his biography, admits that Zola's difficulties with the plans for *Joy of Life* might have stemmed from conjugal misery; Pauline, his heroine, was to be an attractive, self-sacrificing, noble-minded *married* woman but after months of wrangling he changed her to an *unmarried* woman, perhaps unable to reconcile the saintly, generous nature of Pauline with that of a woman in the married state. Then he abandoned the manuscript altogether and wrote *Piping Hot!* instead, with its biting portrayal of the torments and deceits of married life.

Zola's marital distress quite likely began on the day he married Alexandrine. In *The Masterpiece* he reveals an extraordinarily perceptive understanding of the phenomenon that marriage to one's mistress can often kill love:

He claimed her body and she gave it to him, but it was an empty embrace, for the

270

passion that had once been theirs was now dead. They knew, as they released each other and lay side by side again, that from that moment they were strangers, that some obstacle now existed between them, another body whose chill breath had touched them more than once even in the passionate early days of their love. Never again would they be everything to each other; the rift between them would never be healed. The wife had despoiled the mistress, and marriage seemed to have extinguished love.

As *The Masterpiece*, from which this passage is quoted, is one of the most autobiographical of all his novels, the comment is not without significance.

The attitude of Zola's mother, too, undoubtedly had a negative effect on the relationship. She was a strong, single-minded and possessive woman who might well have seen in the humble Alexandrine someone less than the ideal wife for her gifted son. Her eternal presence in the household must have been equally trying for the younger woman, and a source of constant conflict, having to share her husband's affections with the cantankerous old lady; and Zola must have resented his wife at times for having failed to win his mother's goodwill. A story persists that, during her death throes, the old woman imagined that Alexandrine was stabbing her with a pair of scissors, a final explosion of hostility which had built up over many years. As social workers can readily testify, a tense triangular situation like the one that appears to have existed in the Zola household is rarely conducive to a serene and happy sex life between husband and wife.

The family triangle was destroyed with his mother's death in 1880, but the novelist's subsequent nervous collapse and drawn-out recovery must have imposed unbearable strains on their relationship. With her husband perpetually in the grip of some form of melancholia and frequently physically ill, Alexandrine's role, one imagines, would have been that of a comforting mother, inevitably relinquishing, perhaps over a period of years, her sexual role. If we add up all the accounts of Alexandrine at this time a confusing picture emerges, but it can be said with assurance that Madame Zola had become something of a battle-axe; big, solid, physically unexciting and invariably complaining. She suffered from a variety of real and imagined illnesses, for the Zolas undertook many journeys to spas and health resorts in search of remedies. Not a little of Alexandrine's trouble can reasonably be blamed on her husband, for with all his phobias he must have been a most difficult person to live with. At any rate, he was paying for it now, and increasingly becoming a recluse in his study. And again, corroboration of sorts may be found in *The Masterpiece* – the novel in which Zola most painfully revealed his creative and sexual torments; the author has Claude's wife Christine contemplating her ageing body and wondering why her husband has ceased to love her, preferring instead to squander his passion on his painting.

In respect of Zola's married life, *The Masterpiece* is an interesting and vital document, for it contains a debate on the benefits and threats married life offers the creative artist. Through the character Sandoz, Zola reflects that marriage 'is the essential condition for good work, the solid, carefully-planned work required of any writer who wants to produce anything worthwhile'. And he adds, 'Woman who seeks to destroy, Woman who kills the artist, who crushes his heart and devours his mind, is a romantic myth which ignores the facts.' The novel soon reveals, though, that while this might be a sound, commonsense argument, it fails to take account of the artist's sexual passion. Sandoz is happily married to Henriette, but she is utterly dwarfed by the projection of Christine, Claude's model-mistress, an almost tactile fantasy flaunting herself while escaping briefly from the cell of Zola's sexual longings. Later in the novel, Sandoz/Zola, after reviewing the painful course of his life, exclaims, 'Oh, for another life! Who'll give me a second life...!' This was written in 1885, indicating that at least from that date Zola must have been aware of his craving for an alternative to the comfortable but sterile days and nights in the company of Alexandrine.

One must also consider the effects of Zola's childlessness, which was to the novelist nothing less than a tragedy. The reason for the absence of children is perplexing. A few years after Alexandrine's death in 1925, Louis de Robert recalled a conversation with the novelist's widow in which she said, 'Why didn't he want children by me when I could have given them to him?' – inferring that Zola put off having a family until it was too late. But just as men will go to great lengths to hide the humiliation of impotence, so women find barrenness a fault difficult to admit. One could argue, of course, that Zola, like many dedicated artists, would have been self-centred enough not to want the distraction of young children during his most creative years; or that, as a bourgeois, and having been a child in a poor family himself, with some knowledge of raising a family on a low income, he would have chosen to wait until he was financially able to give his children the privileged kind of upbringing denied to him as a child. If this were so, Alexandrine would have been forty at the time the couple were financially secure, and perhaps incapable of childbearing.

But there is no tangible evidence to support these speculations. Zola at various times professed a great love for children, so why not for his own? With his methodical routine they would never have been allowed to distract him. As for the family finances, while his income was modest in the years after the 1870 war, there was ample to accommodate a couple of children. The cost of some of Zola's famous feasts during that period would have fed, clothed and educated a child for a month. His intense desire for fatherhood is accurately transcribed, I suspect, in Dr Pascal's outburst in the last novel of the *Rougon-Macquart* cycle. Although written some three years after he had consummated his love for Jeanne, Zola would have had little difficulty in recalling his neurotic fears of dying without heirs, which had been a particular source of misery for a long time.

> He had never lived! Some nights he even went so far as to curse science, which he accused of having deprived him of the best years of his manhood. He had allowed himself to be swallowed up by his work, which had consumed his brain, his heart and his muscles. And all this solitary, unremitting labour had produced was books, black marks on paper, which would be blown away by the wind. The pages felt icy cold when he touched them. And no living breast to press against his own, no silky child's hair to kiss! He had lived alone in the cold and bloodless fastnesses of science, selfish and alone, and he would die alone. Was it really true, was that to be his fate? Would he die

without experiencing the simple happiness of ordinary men, yes, even street-porters and the carters, whose whips cracked under his windows? He became frantic at the thought that he would have to hurry, it would soon be too late. All his youth wasted, he felt all his repressed desires reviving and sweeping through him in a tumultuous flood. He swore to himself that he would not let himself be extinguished without having loved.   (91)

As the novelist proved his potency late in life I think we have to accept that either Alexandrine was physically incapable of having children, or that her childlessness was the result of continency. If we believe her claim that earlier in her life – that is, during the 1870s – she could have given her husband children, then we are left with the clear probability that, apart perhaps from its earlier years, Zola's marriage to Alexandrine was agonisingly chaste. That the union should have ground to a barren halt, however, cannot be ascribed solely to her, for her husband's complex ambiguity with regard to the sexual act itself has already been made clear, and must loom as a principal factor in the tragedy.

While, to his friends, Zola attached little importance to the attack made upon him by the Manifesto Five, it is highly likely that he suffered in private. Few men can shrug off the indignity of public doubts about their virility. Did he have an 'illness of the loins' as they had charged? Until he could prove otherwise he had no alternative but to continue to suffer in silence. Still, he must have gained some comfort from his own feelings. Goncourt relates a conversation with Zola in which the novelist confessed to 'experiencing a renewal of life, a youthfulness, a desire for physical enjoyment', and later exclaiming, '"As my wife's not here, I can tell you – I can't pass a young girl, like that one over there, without wondering: Isn't that worth much more than a book?"'

It is significant that when he did finally take the plunge it was with a very young girl and not with a woman nearer his own age. There are many markers in his novels indicating – by sheer repetition alone – his fascination for small-breasted girls. In *The Masterpiece*, Claude ogles Christine's 'firm little breasts tipped with palest rose-colour, thrust upwards with all the freshness of spring'; and, later, 'as frail as a child, but so supple, so youthful! And yet her breasts were fully formed!' There is a long, voyeuristic passage in *Germinal* where Etienne and Catherine undress in easy familiarity, a common enough masculine fantasy. After the preliminaries come the breasts: 'then her bosom with little rigid breasts as she leant over the bowl in the morning'. In *Earth*, almost the first thing we learn about the young heroine Françoise is that she has 'small firm breasts'. Jean, the hero, is thirty; Françoise is sixteen. Jean is a little tremulous about the age-gap but when it comes to firm, young flesh he can't help himself:

> The sharp feminine smell mingled with the scent of beaten hay in the open air intoxicated him and stiffened every muscle in his body in a sudden harsh fury of desire. Then still another feeling awoke, an unrealised passion for this youngster; he was abruptly gripped by a tenderness of flesh and spirit . . .

The obsessive preoccupation with small, young breasts persists in *Joy of Life* when the strap of Pauline's swimming costume breaks, and a whole page is spent as Zola teases the reader as to whether a breast will pop out or not. And again, in *Doctor Pascal*; Clotilde is described several times as having 'small, rounded breasts', and even when she is nursing her baby Zola refuses to depart from this description. This is curious because one would expect Zola to be describing Jeanne who, from the few photographs which exist, appears to have been a well-built young lady.

Conversely, there is a consistent repugnance to female fat and old age in Zola's novels. In *Germinal*, Zola almost cruelly draws attention to Maheude's sorry dugs, and scorn is heaped on Berthe's hairless, wrinkled body in *Earth*.

As one might imagine, Zola's autumnal romance was a clandestine affair, for Alexandrine possessed a pretty horrific temper and discovery would have spelled disaster for all concerned. Zola's happiness soared to heights he'd only dreamed of, but his literary output suffered. He began work on *The Beast in Man* but his mind was in a constant ferment. In March 1889, he wrote to Van Santen-Kolff, his closest correspondent at the time: '... I am undergoing a kind of crisis, possibly to do with my being fifty. But I hope in the future it will contribute to the profit and honour of literature. Pardon my long silence, for there are weeks, months, when a storm rages within me, the storm of desires and regrets...' There is little doubt that Zola is not only alluding to the raptures of his new-found love, but also to the pangs of guilt and remorse he felt at setting up, with premeditated care, a second home. And his principles? How different was he from one of the adulterous characters in the rabbit warren of sensuality he created in *Piping Hot!*?

It says a lot when one considers that Zola not only kept his love affair a secret from his wife for three years, but that two children were born in that time as well. Alexandrine's bed was probably no more loveless in those three years than it had been for some considerable time, but what did she make of his long and frequent absences, the inevitable growing distance between them? Zola's state of mind, though, was faring rather better, progressing from the guilty anguish of his first sexual encounters to something approaching self-congratulation on the birth of the children: Denise Henriette on 20 September 1889, and a son, Jacques Emile, two years later, on 25 September 1891. Jacques was born while he and Alexandrine were staying at Lourdes. While there he read *Le Figaro* with mounting anxiety every day, because before his departure from Paris he had arranged with Henri Céard to pass on news of the birth by inserting a coded message in the paper's personal column.

The arrival of the two children meant everything to the novelist. Procreation as an end to some extent justified the means; the desire for adulterous paternity, and the realisation of it, was to Zola infinitely less guilt-inducing than mere desire for a young woman's sexual affection. Moreover Zola, little by little, was able to unburden himself to his friends and the couple were, it seems, frequently to be seen walking openly about Paris, an indication that perhaps there was a fatalistic instinct in the erring husband to seek a confrontation, and to be rid of all the deviousness.

He did not have to wait for long. Whether it was an anonymous letter or the discovery of some love letters in his desk, Alexandrine was apprised of the situation a couple of months after the birth of Jacques. Predictably furious, she stormed around to the love-nest, but not before Zola was able to telegraph Céard to go immediately to the apartment to warn Jeanne and remove her and the children. He added, with a touch of pathetic desperation: '*My wife is behaving like a lunatic. Forgive me.*'

The discovery of her husband's infidelity was a bitter blow to Alexandrine who, whatever her faults, loved and admired him. For three years she had been cruelly deceived and publicly shamed. Not only had she been rejected as a lover, but as a mother, too. A storm of terrific proportions broke over the novelist's head, but at least he was prepared for it. Alexandrine's despair can only be imagined, but fortunately for them both it largely spent itself in a brief but spectacular display of fury. Thereafter one can only admire the woman's generosity, for she not only managed to live with the situation, sharing her husband with another, younger woman and their family, but eventually recognised the children as legally best she could.

Jeanne remained discreetly in the quiet backwaters of Zola's life, for although intelligent she was uneducated and there was a large part of her lover's life she could never share. As for Zola, despite the comforts he derived from his young family, he could never escape completely from the guilt and unease into which the liaison thrust him. Alexandrine applied a certain amount of domestic blackmail, winning a large and luxurious apartment on the Rue de Bruxelles as a form of compensation, and also a long holiday. This, she knew, was especially painful for her husband, who would have dearly loved to have his children with him.

The facts about Zola's extra-marital family were known to few outside his friends and literary acquaintances, although there was a good deal of uninformed rumour. This is strange, for whatever the novelist wrote, said or did was news, and the French newspapers of the time were both hungry and scurrilous. Even in 1893, after the children were born, Zola's first English biographer Sherard revealed his profound ignorance of his subject's private life:

> Nobody ever heard the breath of a story about or against his conduct as a husband. In Paris that sort of thing is differently considered from what it is in England, which is only all the more to Zola's credit. Often, when friends, chaffing him, have asked whether he has not in town some *petite amie*, he has always answered with the greatest seriousness, and not without surprise, 'Another woman! But I am married. I live happily with my wife. Why should I run after anybody else?' Zola... is most certainly clean-lived, exceptionally clean-lived, a fact which gives him all the more right to sit in judgement on the rotten immoralities of the present age.

Written five years after his subject had taken up with Jeanne Rozerot, and two years after Mme Zola knew of the affair, the passage offers a cautionary tale for biographers of the living! Vizetelly probably knew about it, but he certainly wasn't going to give anything away even though, at times, the information was almost consuming him. In the preface to *The Belly of Paris*, published in 1896, he hinted that the novelist might be more worldly than people thought: 'Both French and English critics have contended that although M. Zola is a married man, he knows very little of women, as there has virtually never been any feminine romance in his life. There are those who are aware of the contrary, but whose tongues are stayed by considerations of delicacy and respect.'

Towards the end of his life, when the children travelled about with the novelist and Alexandrine, it was of course difficult to hide the fact of some irregular relationship, but surprisingly it was not until about 1898 that the story finally found its way into several newspapers. It remained for Ernest Vizetelly, in his biography of 1904, to reveal that the two children were born when their father was 'carried away from the path of strict duty', but his account, while heavy on apologies on behalf of his departed master, is light on facts. The apologia runs for some eight pages in which Vizetelly names every erring author and statesman he can think of: Nelson, Wellington, Lord Melbourne, Benjamin Franklin, Daniel Webster, Victor Hugo... 'If the world were to reject all the great men who have erred,' he pleaded, 'would not the pantheons of the nations be well-nigh empty?'

17

Rails, Money and Guns

The sheer magnitude of *Germinal, The Masterpiece* and *Earth*, all undertaken and completed within the span of three years, had left Zola severely drained. *The Dream*, for all its uplifting qualities, was a swamp which dragged his creative spirit to its lowest level, and still four novels remained to be written before he could close the covers on the *Rougon-Macquart* chronicle. But falling in love with Jeanne Rozerot, while obviously an interruption to the steady beat of his working habits, was the very stimulus the novelist needed. The exhilarating liaison restored his tired mind, opened it up to optimism and eventually to a vigorous ferment, and it was in this mood that he began to tackle the tail-end of his monumental undertaking. The first three of these last novels would introduce his readers to three pillars of the burgeoning industrial age: rails, money and guns – the railways, the stock exchange, and the army.

The arrival of the railway train in the nineteenth century introduced a new dimension to terror and murder. It is difficult to convey today the effect these belching iron monsters had on the population a century ago; they steamed and roared like angry serpents, achieving speeds unattainable by any other form of transport, shrieking through the night, disappearing into long, black tunnels, and occasionally destroying themselves and their passengers in spectacular accidents.

As with other novelists of the time the railway exercised a powerful effect on Zola's imagination, and he had already used its haunting, plaintive aura – intuitively, I suspect – in *L'Assommoir* and *The Masterpiece*. When Gervaise, in her last, sad days, walks the night streets of Paris as a prostitute, she is accompanied by wails of pain from the passing trains, 'tearing the air with the desperate cry of their whistles'. A train also lends a heart-rending dirge to the burial of Claude; the cemetery is so close to the railway line that the priest's voice is drowned by the mechanical lament from a passing shunter.

Zola had long contemplated a novel on the theme of homicide, a murder mystery if you like, and the railway obviously appealed to his dramatic sense as an ideal environment for the dark deeds he had in mind. A murder in a back alley, in deserted dockland, in a tenement or at an isolated farm was nothing out of the ordinary, but death on a speeding express was still a sensational novelty. There were all kinds of exciting possibilities, too: the victim could be shot, stabbed, strangled, poisoned or pushed out the window, his cries unheeded in the roaring din. The murderer could escape and evade detection in various ways – and in fact Zola was aware of two contemporary cases of homicide on the rails in which neither murderer had been caught. This was 1888, and Zola's mind, feverish and excited no doubt from his passion for Jeanne Rozerot, was unusually receptive to a whole 'grab-bag' of horrific influences. Dostoevsky's *Crime and Punishment* and *The Brothers Karamazov* had just appeared in French editions and Zola read them avidly; as keenly, perhaps, as he followed the appalling killings of Jack the Ripper, then on his nightly rampages through the East End of London. Possibly the novelist was even inspired to name the homicidal maniac of his story – Jacques – after the Ripper. What is a little more certain is that the Ripper's victims, always young prostitutes, suggested to Zola that Jacques's obsession should be similarly exclusive: to kill young women by stabbing. Throughout all his documentation for his books the novelist invariably chose to borrow, adapt and expand real-life incidents rather than invent them.

Zola's house at Médan was quite close to the tracks of the Western Railway Company and as their trains often rattled his windows he no doubt felt they owed him some assistance in his research. He set about getting his material in his usual patient way, talking to the employees, exploring stations and marshalling yards, and even – at the invitation of the chairman of the Western Railway Co. – riding on the footplate of a locomotive, in overcoat and topper, from Paris to Mantes and back again. He finally chose the railway yards at Le Havre for one of his settings, and he took Jeanne with him there in March 1889, to complete his documentation. When it became known that the novelist was spending some time on Western Railway premises, one jokester put it around that the naturalist writer had demanded the Company stage an accident, so he could study it at first hand! At this point in Zola's career he could be almost overwhelmed with advice. In preparation for *The Beast in Man* he had read a newly published work on the railways, *Les Chemins de fer*, by Cerbelaud and Lefèvre; when he wrote to one of the authors for further information on some details, the request resulted in a mass of correspondence, notes, maps, and even blueprints for stations and goods yards.

The railway, then, is the immediate backcloth for the terrifying events that approach, take shape and flash by in the careering narrative, but beyond this there is another, grander backdrop - that of the final, convulsive moments of the crumbling Second Empire.

The Beast in Man has its genesis in tangled threads. Right from the start Zola had projected a story around a homicidal maniac, who would represent the most rotten fruit of the Rougon-Macquart genealogical tree. Originally this role was reserved for Etienne Lantier, but Zola developed him for *Germinal* instead and had to invent a new character for the later novel. Thus Jacques Lantier becomes an eleventh-hour addition to Gervaise's family of Nana,

Etienne and Claude, afflicted with the most horrible of all the gifts bestowed by Adélaïde Fouqué on her descendants.

Zola began writing the final manuscript of the novel in May 1889 and finished the following January. Serialisation commenced in *La Vie populaire* on 14 November 1889 to the accompaniment of a spirited publicity campaign, using hundreds of posters slapped up on walls around Paris. This caused a furore, not to mention brisk sales. The poster illustrated the first instalment of the story with an engraving of Roubard beating up Séverine, his wife. Unfortunately, because of poor reproduction, it looked as though the station-master was raping the poor woman. A newspaper reporter rushed a copy of the poster to Zola for his comments. The novelist professed to be aghast; as he was at that time a candidate for that most virtuous of institutions, the French Academy, he doubtless genuinely was.

The Beast in Man is one of the most gripping of all Zola's novels, combining the best elements of a murder mystery with an intensive study of homicidal obsession and jealousy. Roubard is the assistant station-master at Le Havre, and is married to Séverine, a pretty girl very much younger than himself. An orphan, Séverine was brought up by Judge Grandmorin, a rich and influential Royalist dignitary, and it has always been a mystery to Roubard how readily her guardian gave her hand in marriage to him, a poor working-man. His suspicions begin to crystallise, however, after several revealing incidents, and finally he extracts from his wife that she has not only slept with the senile judge but, as a young girl, indulged with him in certain unnamed perversions. Although Roubard still loves Séverine he cannot tolerate the triangular situation; moreover he is humiliated to discover that his position with the railway company – of which Grandmorin is chairman – and even his wife's dowry, are simply ploys so that the old man can retain some influence over Séverine, the woman he has corrupted. Roubard then resolves to murder Grandmorin, and forces Séverine to be his accomplice. The murder is duly carried out one night on the Paris–Le Havre express, but it precipitates a chain of interconnected homicides and disasters.

At this point we meet Jacques, a decent, handsome young man who, because of a psychopathic condition, is a loner. By an odd circumstance he is a witness to Grandmorin's murder and is drawn into the investigation. But, charmed and fascinated by Séverine, he withholds information that would certainly incriminate the guilty pair, and as a kind of reward becomes her lover.

It promises to be a fatal liaison, for the one thing Jacques fears most is that his congenital obsession might break out and force him to kill someone he loves. Only weeks before, during a passionate embrace with his stepcousin Flore, he tried to strangle the girl and only tore himself away in time. The incident brings back a flood of painful memories of his fight against madness:

> The memory was clear as day, he was barely sixteen when this ill first took possession of him. It was one evening, when he was playing with a young girl, the daughter of a relation of his, two years his junior. She had fallen down. In a flash he saw her legs revealed to the thigh, and he had flung himself at her. The following year

he recalled honing a knife to thrust into another girl's throat. That was a fair-haired little thing whom he saw pass his door every morning. She was very plump-bosomed and very pink, and he had actually selected the spot, a mole directly under her ear. Then came others and yet others, a succession of nightmares, so many women whose flesh he had touched, to be possessed with that sudden lust for murder, women he happened to jostle in the street, women he did not even know... Did it mean that this was all of such very ancient origin, springing from some evil that womenkind had done to men, born of rancour accumulated in the male through the generations since a first act of deception deep in prehistoric caves? For in those fits he also felt a need to give battle, to master the female, to conquer her, a perverse need to sling her dead body on his back as if an animal killed for food, snatched from all other males, in lust for eternal killing.   (82)

In Séverine, however, Jacques finds a partner who can satisfy his sexual and blood lusts without the desire to actually kill. She *has* killed; Jacques knows it, and she knows he knows, and their ecstasies ride on the tide of the murdered man's spilled blood.

He knew that her only reason for seeking absorption in him was to ease herself of that which she kept stifled within her. From her loins would suddenly rise a profound shudder, stiffening her lustful nipples, and emerging on her lips in a confused tangle of whispers.   (82)

After a while, however, knowing isn't enough; Séverine has to repeat over and over again the details of the victim's death, and this ultimately becomes the prelude to all their love making:

'The knife, tell me, did you actually feel it go in?'
'Yes, a sort of thud.'
'I see.... A sort of thud.... No feeling of cutting? Sure?'
'Oh no! Only a sort of thud.'
'Then he heaved back, you said, didn't you?'
'Yes, three times. *Ugh!* From one end of his body to the other, such drawn-out heaves I could follow them through, down to his feet.'
'And those heaves stiffened him, did they?'
'Yes, the first very strong, the others feebler.'
'And then he was dead. Now what exactly did you get out of that, I mean, feeling him dead like that, by a knife blow?'
'Me? I... I don't really know.'
'You don't really know? Why lie about it? Do tell me what you got out of it, everything, come on.... Did it hurt?'
'Oh, no, it didn't hurt.'
'Pleasure?'
'Pleasure? Why, darling, no, of course not, not pleasure.'
'Then what, my love? Do tell me! Everything! I beg you! If you only knew.... Tell me what anybody feels when they do it!'
'Good heavens, can such things be told? It is terrible. You feel, oh, you feel so far away! I went through more in that minute than in all my life before.'
Only now, teeth tight closed, able only to stammer incoherently, Jacques took her and she him too, and again they possessed one another, finding love in the depths of death, in a spasm of accomplishment as fraught with agony as that of those creatures to whom copulation spells evisceration.   (82)

Zola's insight into Séverine's need to confess and also into Jacques' inherited aberration is astounding. Séverine's account of the killing, an act which Jacques fears but finds irresistible, is delivered as one might recite the details of a sexual conquest; and at the end, under his excited questioning, she is almost on the verge of describing what in another context would be an orgasm. And that is just what Jacques is hearing, for he is a voyeur of death. The details of the murder arouse Jacques and drive them both into further frenzies of love-making among the haunting symbolism of their surroundings: 'The blood-like glow on the ceiling had now vanished. The stove was going out. The room grew chill in harmony with the bitter frost outside. From snow-muffled Paris not a voice was to be heard.' Intuitively, Zola always invests his dramatic scenes with that electric charge of irony and symbolism which makes them so memorable.

The density of the narrative of *The Beast in Man* is breathtaking, for several murders are perpetrated in the span of little more than a year, all linked through the characters and by a plot as complex yet as logical as the Walschaert's valve-gear on Jacques's locomotive. But while the novel may be read with easy satisfaction as a thriller, only a near-illiterate can leave this book without an awareness of some of its deeper values and implications. Zola's penetrating study of jealousy and possessiveness is as disturbing as it is thought-provoking, for it chips away at our faith in romantic love as the proper foundation for marriage. The novelist shines a light into those dark corners we pretend aren't there, but from which crawl the motivations for murder under the cloak of passion. To this end he also strips bare man at his most elemental, naked and alone on the ecstatic heights of physical love-making, to reveal the breeding grounds of lust and murder.

Of the seven murders in the novel, the two that are investigated are each vastly different in character and motivation. Although premeditated, Roubard's and Séverine's murder of Grandmorin is clearly a crime of passion, inspired by jealousy and vengeance. This serves as a stark contrast to Jacques's murder of Séverine. Without his inherited mania, it is difficult to guess what kind of a man Jacques might have been. On the one hand he is gentle, even sensitive, and certainly repelled by the idea of killing. This is demonstrated on one occasion when, goaded by Séverine to rid themselves of her husband, Jacques has the murder all set up but at the last moment simply cannot go through with it. But then his love affair with Séverine is based on a dreadful complicity – his withholding information about Grandmorin's murder in return for her favours – and twice he is so easily influenced by her evil pleas that he is willing and ready to murder, despite his revulsion for the act. Whether he would have succeeded in a second attempt to kill Roubard is conjectural, for in the few minutes before the deed is to be done he is sexually aroused by Séverine, his mania takes possession of him, and she is unlucky enough to be within his reach. The mindless compulsion behind his knife thrusts is exactly that which precedes orgasm and ejaculation.

Sexual symbolism and imagery isn't confined to humans in *The Beast in Man*; it is extended to the pulsing locomotives themselves, and there, perhaps, the sexual element is seen at its most lyrical and pure. Before he falls in love with Séverine, Jacques's tender affection is reserved for *Lison*, his engine; it is a sublimated love, and therefore safe from murderous impulses: 'She was gentle, she was responsive... easy on the pull-off... broad-bosomed, long and powerful in the loin...' Jacques treats her with all the consideration a lover might accord a beautiful, sensuous woman. He 'loved her for her quick get-away', but 'He had only one thing to reproach her with – she was greedy on lubrication... she was always hungry for oil, her lust never sated.' Throughout their relationship he 'never forced her violently' although as Séverine comes more and more into his life he becomes increasingly demanding on his engine: 'He possessed her, he rode her in his own way with absolute will, as her master, yet never relaxing his severity, treating her like a wild animal he had tamed, but whom he could never quite trust.'

Even if you've never cared about steam trains you'll find it difficult not to be aroused by several of the passages in this novel describing journeys on the footplate, in the hot glare from the fire-box, eyes creased against the freezing wind, nerves taut at every junction. Although the prose is lyrical it is rarely overdone; nor does the author dwell on obtuse technicalities. On one occasion Jacques is driving the Paris–Le Havre Express through a heavy snowstorm; they have struggled all night but now they encounter deep snow that seems impassable:

> He and Pecqueux resumed their stations, and when the two guards had reached their vans, he opened the steam cocks, and a jet of super-heated steam gushed almost soundlessly into the snow, and finished clearing what still stuck to the rails. Then, hand on control, he reversed her. Slowly, they ran back about three hundred yards, to get a good run. Then, with the fire well stoked and pressure up above the limit, he drove *Lison* hard at the wall of snow which barred them, and crashed her into it, head-on, with all the weight of the train behind her. There was a tremendous grunt, like that one hears when a timber-feller brings down his heavy axe into the heartwood, and *Lison's* powerful frame groaned. But still she could not get through, still she was halted, belching smoke, quivering from the strain. Twice more he tried the trick, drew back, rushed at the snow, to carry through it. Each time, loins straining, *Lison* forced her broad bosom against the mass, her breath angrily hissing, then seemed to get second wind, gathered her steel muscles in a supreme effort and got through. Slowly, the train lumbered behind her between the two walls of snow into which she had carved her way. And she was free.   (82)

This scene, of an expanse of countryside under a purifying blanket of snow, is rare in the book, which, from the environmental point of view, is the most claustrophobic of all Zola's novels. That a feeling of 'dark corners' persists in *The Beast in Man* is no accident. Secrecy, conspiracy and concealment are deliberate symbolic elements in the novel's construction, and while from time to time we experience the exhilaration of thundering across desolate countryside in a locomotive, the significant action takes place in confined places, in curtained rooms, behind closed doors, in dark sheds, in the tiny cottage of the level-crossing keeper – even in the private chambers of the magistrate Denizet. Throughout the story everyone is looking furtively over his shoulder, as it were; each has some secret to hide. Even the Minister of Justice is no exception, for he suppresses and finally destroys the one piece of evidence which could convict the real murderers of Grandmorin.

The symbolism, however, stops here, although some scholars see in *The Beast in Man* an overall symbolic indictment of corruption in high places, with the railway – with its timetables, signals and discipline – representing order in society, and the final catastrophe representing the inevitable result of debasing and breaking the laws that govern good society. It is certainly true that readers who doubt that the judiciary are motivated solely by the principle of impartiality have their worst suspicions confirmed by the very convincing account of *political expediency* v *the murderers of Judge Grandmorin*. And it is equally clear that the disaster at the end of the novel symbolises the ultimate breakdown of the Second Empire. But these are only isolated analogous messages in what finished up as a compulsively exciting murder story.

With the enormous shifts of power and commerce across the Atlantic during the twentieth century, one needs a reminder to appreciate the size of the European industrial beehive in the 1890s. To take 1890 as an example, Britain was producing more coal than any other country in the world – 184 million tons of it. Britain and Germany between them produced half as much steel again as the United States. Roughly one third of all sea-going ships were British. Two European exports, in particular, reached their peak – people and money. Between 1881 and 1890, one and half million emigrants left Britain and Ireland for America, but this was nothing compared to the movement of money, for the major European countries had their fingers in just about every development going, laying the foundations for colossal investment empires in Africa, Asia and both the Americas, capturing vast sources of raw materials, building ports and railways, providing banks. Money was needed more than ever before, from the labourer who was paid in coins to the speculator who dealt in thousands but never saw it. Money made everything possible; money was power.

The stuff was also a commodity which broke the social barriers; good breeding was not a necessary qualification for its ownership and exploitation. And while the laws were strict and explicit for theft, highway robbery and piracy, those covering fraudulent financial speculation were woefully unsophisticated. For the schemer there were as many ways of making a quick fortune as there were dates in the perpetual calendar. Financial bubbles were pricked with alarming regularity; as one crash was being tidied up, busy speculators were at work inflating another balloon to lift more money from pockets and purses. The process continues; even today there are loopholes wide enough to allow prominent citizens to emerge from unethical and unprincipled financial *coups* with hardly a blemish on their reputations; the corporate sector of a capitalist economy has its own morality. But the public investor these days is positively cosseted compared with his counterpart in the last century when little thought was given to the humble contributors of their life savings. Just after Zola's next novel, *Money*, was published, a British institution called the Liberator Society crashed – a disaster in which, according to Ernest Vizetelly, 'more people were absolutely ruined than by all the betting on English racecourses over a period of many years.' In a society nervously balanced on the twin pillars of money and matrimony it is not surprising that *Money*, published in March 1891, proved to be a bestseller; in France alone, 90,000 copies were sold in less than a decade.

Researching *Money* proved to be an onerous task for Zola. He knew very little about the intricacies of speculative finance and in his anxiety to be accurate modelled most of his characters and set-pieces on real people and events. Saccard, the financial brigand from *The Kill*, who is the hero in the new novel, is a composite portrait of a Jewish financier named Jules-Isaac Mirès, and Bontoux, the founder of the Union Générale bank. Indeed, Saccard's bank in the novel, the Universal Bank, is a barely disguised twin of this same institution. They were both solemnly blessed by the Pope, and their common purpose was to undermine the financial power of the Jews. Saccard's fictional opponent is Gundermann; the Union Générale's was the de Rothschild family. At first both banks prosper and grow at a meteor-like rate, heavily supported by the Roman Catholic Church and its parishioners, until (for the Union Générale it was 1881) the Jewish side scores a win by secretly buying up shares and then flooding the market with them at reduced prices. Blessed by the Pope or not, what the investors want is their money back immediately, thus causing a run of disastrous proportions. The story, as retold by Zola, is quite fascinating, but it has to be faced that the narrative bogs down continually in knee-deep pelf; at times it has all the excitement of the Stock Exchange on a Sunday. Goncourt heard the novelist complain one day to his publisher, Charpentier, '... there's altogether too much money!' The richness of the material proved, in the end, to be Zola's undoing.

The best thing than can be said for this novel is that it preserves for us an accurate and often perceptive documentary account of a financial scandal that ranks with the best – or the worst - of them. If a modern translation is ever published (the novel was first translated and published in England in 1894; nobody has touched it since), share punters would be well advised to read it. In its day, of course, the novel did embody a cautionary tale for investors, which Ernest Vizetelly stressed in a rather plaintive preface to the English edition, appealing for contributions to aid destitute investors burned in the Liberator crash: '*I would ask all who read* Money *and who have money to spare, to send some little of their store to the Rev. J. Stockwell Watts, at the office of the Fund, 16 Farringdon Street, E.C.*'

Money allows us to pick up the continuing fortunes and misfortunes of Aristide Saccard, the buccaneering speculator of *The Kill*. Although a disaster of epic proportions has reduced him to financial impotence, the predator's instinct survives intact. While he cannot enter, he contemplates the Paris Bourse 'like a lover driven from the presence of a mistress he still desires', convinced that he will again rise from the ashes of his lost millions.

Fortune at first favours him with a chance meeting with Hamelin, a brilliant engineer with dreams of adventurous schemes in the Middle East. Saccard immediately sees the potential of forming a syndicate to finance these projects, and with consuming enthusiasm begins to tap his former associates for the financial backing for a bank. Whatever they may think of Saccard they are in no doubt about his ability to create wealth, and the money readily flows in.

The middle-aged financier prepares an almost irresistible scheme. In the first place, Hamelin's projects appear to be extraordinarily sound: the development of a rich silver mine; the amalgamation of several steamship companies to capture a monopoly in the Mediterranean; and the establishment of a Turkish bank. But the second string to Saccard's bow has even greater appeal – the creation of a Catholic institution with the power to challenge the financial might of the Jews, and to protect the threatened Pope. France had recently signed a treaty with Italy under which its troops would withdraw from Rome, and many French Catholics saw this as the abandonment of the Pope, in danger of being driven from country to country like a beggar seeking alms. A Catholic bank which had as one of its aims the installation of the Pope as King of Jerusalem would attract every loyal parishioner, who would consider it an honour to become a shareholder. At the same time the new bank would reap wide support for its frankly stated anti-Jew policy. This element in the bank's charter shows Saccard at his shrewdest, but also at his weakest, for the detachment of the cool banker evaporates in the emotional heat of his detestation of the Jew. Saccard's hatred for Gundermann, the most powerful financier of the time, was fairly typical of the French businessman:

> Ah! the Jew! Against the Jew he harboured all the old racial resentment, to be found especially in the South of France; and it was something like a revolt of his very flesh, a repugnance of the skin, which, at the idea of the slightest contact, filled him with disgust and anger, a sensation which no reasoning could allay, which he was quite unable to overcome.... He indicted the whole Hebrew race, the cursed race without a country, without a prince, which lives as a parasite upon the nations, pretending to recognise their laws, but in reality only obeying its Jehovah – its God of robbery, blood, and wrath; and he pointed to it fulfilling on all sides the mission of ferocious conquest which this God has assigned to it, establishing itself among every people, like a spider in the centre of its web, in order to watch its prey, to suck the blood of one and all, to fatten itself by devouring others. 'Did anyone ever see a Jew working with his fingers?' he would ask. Were there any Jewish peasants and working men? 'No,' he would say; 'labour disgraces, their religion almost forbids it, exalting only the exploitation of the labour of others. Ah! the rogues!' Saccard's rage was all the greater because he admired them, envied their prodigious financial faculties, that innate knowledge of arithmetic, that natural facility evinced by them in the most complicated operations, that scent and that luck which assure triumph in everything they undertake. 'Christians,' he would say, 'make sorry financial rogues, they always end by coming to grief; but take a Jew who does not even understand book-keeping, throw him into the troubled waters of any shady affair, and he will not only save himself, but bring out all the profit on his back.' It was the gift of the race, the reason why it ever subsisted among all the other nationalities that start up and disappear. And he would passionately predict the final conquest of every nation by the Jews, when they should at last have secured possession of the entire fortune of the globe, a feat which it would not take them long to accomplish, since they were allowed every day to freely extend their kingdom, and one could already see in Paris a Gundermann reigning on a firmer and more respected throne than the Emperor's.   (83)

Saccard's Universal Bank is established on modest lines and is an instant success, and nothing seems to stop his progress. By a brilliant, off-the-cuff speculation he makes a killing on the Bourse, relieving Gundermann and the other Jewish bankers of several million francs. Stung at being so craftily outmanoeuvred, Gundermann plans revenge. Saccard, however, is now in a strong position. The enterprises flourish, shares rise spectacularly, and the shareholders are delighted with the enormous dividends. Saccard is also personally happy and content, for he finds a measure of love and affection in Hamelin's sister, Caroline, who becomes his mistress.

All this should have satisfied Saccard but the rapacious Rougon blood begins to overheat his imagination. Fired with the idea of a new Crusade and the economic conquest of Asia, he increases the bank's capital with a wave of share issues, at the same time pushing up their prices on the Bourse. This brings on a fever of greed among both shareholders and speculators and Universal shares rocket to undreamed-of heights, to 1,000 francs, to 2,000, and finally to their peak of 3,050 francs. Saccard's triumph is complete; he is the creator and manager of the most successful, most powerful bank in France.

It is the moment Gundermann has been waiting for. Over the years he has been quietly buying up millions of francs worth of Universal stock, which he begins to sell at ever-decreasing prices, while still making substantial profits. The Jewish financier has discovered that the shares are really worth barely their issue price, and that a large proportion of Universal's funds has been expended in inflating the price of the shares. Millions of shares are, in fact, locked away in Universal's own safe. Gundermann's action provokes panic and, in the daily deluge of selling, Saccard vainly tries to check the fall by buying the shares himself, using dummy purchasers. In this way he buys 200 million francs' worth, all with Universal's own funds. Finally, he can no longer sustain the defence, and the shares tumble disastrously, from 3,000 francs to 430 in a single day. After a few weeks the rout is complete, and jobbers are buying the discredited, worthless stock at one centime a share. Gundermann, with a profit of fifty million francs, emerges victorious. Saccard and Hamelin are arrested and imprisoned.

The substance of the novel is essentially the story of the rise and fall of a financial speculation of the kind that has become depressingly familiar since Zola wrote it, and as a documentary the book is undeniably interesting. But he attempted to flesh the narrative with a number of minor plots and side issues which achieve nothing except to add to the book's length. There is the discovery of Saccard's illegitimate son Victor, who eventually escapes from Caroline's care after attacking and robbing a young girl, 'like a beast frothing with heredity virus, fated to spread the evil at every bite'. Victor contributes little except to remind us of the hereditary Rougon taint. Then there is Caroline, a person of noble honesty; she could have been forged into a combative foil for Saccard's insane greed but she never comes to life. And the same goes for the dozen or so other characters, potentially interesting but utterly swamped by the flood of francs that compels our fascination.

Readers familiar with the workings of a stock exchange may well be more at home with *Money* than those who aren't. Inhibited by a basic mental block about the stuff, I find parts of the novel hard going, for, unlike *Germinal* and *Earth*, where the technicalities of mining and farming are observed and described through the fresh eyes of a newcomer to the scene, *Money* is four years in the life of a seasoned financier with no time to explain the finer points of his calling. When explanations are attempted, Zola uses direct description or the conversations of old ladies, all of which comes over with the convincing ring of a lead penny. And when, through his Marxist character Sigismond, Zola attempts to enlighten us about monetary theory, the episodes are too contrived to be in the least persuasive.

This is not to say the novelist's ideas about money are simplistic, for they are not. They emerge symbolically, mostly, entwined in Zola's beloved fertility imagery, as when Caroline, disillusioned by Saccard's perfidy, sees that while money may be the root of all evil it can also be a source of good works.

> Then Madame Caroline acquired the sudden conviction that money was the dungheap in which grew the humanity of tomorrow. Some of Saccard's remarks, scraps of his theories respecting speculation, came back to her mind. She recalled that idea of his that without speculation there would be no great fruitful enterprises, just in the same way as without love, though love may have its horrid aspects, there would be no life. If life is to continue in the world, there *must* be passion. If her brother over yonder in the East was in such high spirits, shouting victory amidst the workshops and yards which were being got in order, and the buildings which were springing from the soil, it was because the passion for gambling was making money rain down and rot everything in Paris. Poisonous and destructive money became the ferment of all social vegetation, served as the necessary compost for the execution of the great works which would draw the nations nearer together and pacify the earth.
>
> She had cursed money, and now she fell in awe-stricken admiration before it; for was not money the sole force that can level a mountain, fill up an arm of the sea – briefly, render the earth inhabitable by men, who, once relieved of labour, would become but the conductors of machines. From this force, which was the root of all evil, there also sprang everything that was good.   (83)

This vegetative symbolism – *dungheap, compost, fruitful* – recurs, often with intriguing aptness. Money, necessary and fascinating, arousing disgust and ecstasy, causing disaster and happiness, is so like sex. Of Saccard's deeds in the bedroom with Caroline, Zola writes not a word; speculation is the sexual act to the financier, and of this we are told a good deal. In the end it seems that Caroline comes to terms with Saccard's bisexuality just as she comes to terms with the essential innocence of money: 'Why then should money be blamed for all the dirt and crime it causes? For is love less filthy – love which creates life?' These are the last words in the novel, not so much ending a laborious lesson as justifying the author's own recent amorous speculation. For although Zola had come a long way on his journey of sexual discovery, he had never strayed far, in the twenty-two novels he'd written, from the view that physical love was the rather revolting expression of the carnal instinct. We know now that Zola was, with Jeanne Rozerot's willing help, doing all his sums over again. Copulation was a life force, like breathing, instinctive and essential. But though the novelist is not yet entirely endorsing this view it undoubtedly led him to a new optimism. Thus *Money* closes on a hopeful note, as will *The Debacle*, his next novel.

THE END IS AT HAND! Zola had hawked this notice about for twenty years through many of the *Rougon-Macquart* novels. At the end of *Nana* the soldiers march past her corpse to the battlefields; in *The Beast in Man* troops hurtle to the front in a runaway train; in *Earth* Jean leaves the Beauce to resume his old calling; in *Money* the corrupting effects of speculation act like a fifth column in advance of the Prussian shells. In *The Debacle*, the penultimate novel in the chronicle, the long-awaited military disaster arrives to demolish what remains of the tottering Second Empire.

The Debacle is, by its huge sales, by the multiplicity of its translations and by common critical consent, one of the great war novels of literature. Like most war novels it is a real doorstopper, some 200,000 words long; unlike most war novels it is not a rambling, impressionistic documentary but a brilliantly unified, painstakingly detailed and deliberately purposeful creation whose moving indictment of the horror and futility of war is almost as powerful today as it was in 1892, the year it was published.

The French defeat in the Franco-Prussian War of 1870 was a cataclysmic event, for it brought about the collapse of Napoleon III's Second Empire and the deflation of French arrogance which had kept much of Europe in a state of tension for a century and a half. True, the Empire was a shaky and corrupt regime, but without the Franco-Prussian War it might have staggered on for another couple of decades. Many thinkers thought so; even Zola thought so, and designed his *Rougon-K. .cquart* chronicle accordingly. After the first novel appeared, however, the contemporary chronology of the cycle became past history, forcing the novelist to modify his plan. *The Debacle* was the book most affected, for Zola had intended to finish the Empire with a fictional war based on a previous campaign between Italy and France. Suddenly there was no point, and twenty years later found the novelist writing instead an historical account of the war he'd prophesied in 1868.

With *The Debacle*, Zola returned to the practice of studying everything that had been published on the subject which was to supply the background of a projected novel. The material on the Franco-Prussian War was voluminous: newspaper reports, maps, the memoirs of countless generals – invariably in conflict with one another – tomes by military historians and politicians, and even personal letters from foot soldiers who had fought in the battles. Sorting through it all took up most of 1891, and gave him violent indigestion. 'I am working furiously', he wrote in July, 'to begin on my terrible book; I have almost digested all the documents and hope to set about writing it in a few days.' That Zola managed, in the end, to breathe life into this tremendous pile of facts and incidents is a measure of his genius, even though the pulse falters at times.

In April 1891, Zola spent less than two weeks in the Sedan locality visiting the field of the battle which had broken the French army. *The Spectator's* reviewer, incidentally, marvelled at this, adding that 'after twenty-two years' acquaintance with the ground, and after perusing almost every work in French, German or English which has appeared on the subject, we have been unable to detect a single important error in M. Zola's topography or facts.' It was just as well that the author's skill at documentation was as fabulous as it was reputed to be, for the novel was subjected to microscopic examination. A controversy raged for some time in England, for example, about the execution of captured communists during the Commune, who, according to Zola, were 'shot down almost at point-blank range'. After 1894 all English editions of the book carried the explanation that the intention was to convey the impression of a distance of about seven or eight feet from the rifle barrel to the victim's chest; the exasperated translator added, with a note of finality: 'I may add that I personally witnessed some of these executions.' Such was the demand for precision. Zola's account of Napoleon's rouged and powdered face on the morning of a battle also caused a furore, and disputes about this and other alleged inaccuracies rumbled on for years.

Zola had left little to chance. Although his trip to Rheims and Sedan had been short – the intense public curiosity his visits aroused was beginning to tire him of on-the-spot investigations – he observed and wrote notes from daybreak to dusk. The novel was already in draft form, and his head was 'teeming with the shadows of my marionettes, and of all the things they were to do and to explain'. At first he drove through and around the area and then, on foot, retraced the marches of the ill-fated Seventh Army Corps which was to be the regiment through which the reader would follow most of the action. He spent hours taking down the recollections of peasants and townspeople who lived near the battlefield. He also visited the hotel room in which the Emperor had spent the night of the surrender. With touching irony, two large engravings were hung on the walls – one of Rouget de Lisle singing his famous hymn 'La Marseillaise', and another of *The Last Judgement.* Zola was moved by his visit to the extent that it provoked an hallucination, as he drove from the hotel by moonlight, of an immense cemetery, with all the dead waking up.

Although overburdened with the sheer weight of the documentary material, the novelist took great care not to lose sight of the individual in the vast panorama. Conscious of the danger of having the two armies emerge as his heroes, he constructed the novel in such a way as to protect the individuality of several dozen characters through whose eyes the action would be seen, while at the same time adding further force to the book's ultimate message. He did this by ascribing to each of these characters a different national trait: the pleasure-seeking France, the despairing France, France the volatile enthusiast, France doomed to disaster. These characters would thus symbolise types who, by their thoughts and actions, would reveal the roles played by the various national characteristics in the debacle. This, Zola thought, was also a genuinely scientific way in which to study the causes of the French collapse and the destruction of the Second Empire – an interesting theory, but open to debate. What his method did achieve, however, was a clarity notoriously difficult to accomplish in accounts of complex and confused action, and the Battle of Sedan was exactly that. If this innovation was inspired, some other aspects of the novel's construction are contrived. The narrative is logically divided into

289

three sections, but by subdividing each section into eight chapters Zola aimed for a symmetry quite out of harmony with the haphazardous events he describes. More in keeping with the epic subject matter is his deployment of the ever-roving eye, the constantly changing point of view and the diversity of opinion and reaction – devices aimed at imparting a totality of understanding of an incredibly confused engagement.

Here is the skeleton of the story:

Part One opens with the Seventh Army Corps, 30,000 strong, camped near the Rhine in August 1870. Jean Macquart and Maurice Levasseur, the two heroes, are among them, as infantrymen. The war has not been going well for the French and when the corps receives news of fresh disasters, it retreats in panic back towards Paris. Almost immediately the travel-worn soldiers are moved to Rheims, marched from there to Vouziers, from where they advance and then retreat, then wait, then march north again, this time towards Sedan and the Prussian trap that will annihilate 17,000 soldiers of the French army. The whole lamentable episode is riddled with inefficiency and confusion. Rifles and cannon are delivered to one camp, ammunition to another; food is sent to one location and the fuel to cook it with is dispatched somewhere else; fodder arrives where there are no horses, while elsewhere hundreds of animals starve. The troops are marched this way and that without reason; in place of orders there are only rumours. They are weary, hungry, angry and disillusioned – at one stage dozens abandon or hide their rifles. Finally, they tramp into Sedan, the stage for the battle that will humble France.

Part Two is a masterpiece of military reporting of an action which lasts little more than twenty-four hours, from the morning of 1 September to dawn the following day. While the French armies assemble in the valley around the old fortress town of Sedan, the Prussians build their strength on the surrounding heights. From their position across the River Meuse their artillery poses a lethal threat to the French, but first a ground attack is needed to drive them into a tighter trap. On the morning of 1 September, under cover of fog, the Bavarians throw a pontoon across the Meuse and take Bazeilles, only a couple of miles from Sedan. Although the French counter-attack with their cavalry, the heroic horsemen are no match for the accurate Prussian artillery and inevitably the entire French army is forced to retreat into the town of Sedan amid the most monstrous chaos and with ghastly casualties. With the incessant shelling, further manoeuvre by the French is impossible, so that when a line of Prussian infantry almost two miles wide advances, surrender is the only alternative to pointless bloodshed.

The title of Part Three is *Woe To The Vanquished!*, and indeed the French pay dearly for their defeat. The shattered and beleaguered French army of some 100,000 men is trapped in a loop of the River Meuse about a mile wide and two miles long, encircled by Prussian artillery and infantry. There they are held captive for a week, without food, shelter or adequate medical attention. The river water is polluted with corpses, the stench is unbearable, dysentry rages, and crazed horses, many of them shockingly injured, stampede within the enclosure.

Jean and Maurice manage to escape from this hell, and hide at a nearby farm owned by Maurice's uncle. Jean is seriously wounded but Maurice, who is anxious to rejoin the fighting, leaves for Paris. Jean, meanwhile, is cared for by Maurice's twin sister, Henriette, whose husband has been killed by the Prussians; and as his health returns, they fall in love. Eventually Jean decides to rejoin the army, and leaves for Paris where the final, fateful meeting between the two friends takes place. Unbeknown to Jean, Maurice has joined the Communards, and one day, at the height of the insurrection, Jean is sent into the city with a detachment of soldiers to storm the barricades. In the haze of battle he sees a Communard about to raise a rifle, and bayonets him. It is Maurice.

As Paris burns, Jean drags his friend to safety, for he would be shot on sight by government troops if discovered. This time Henriette, who is now also in Paris, tends her brother, but the wound is mortal. Just before Maurice dies, Jean admits to the woman he intends to marry that it is he who has fatally wounded her brother. They both realise that happiness together is now beyond them, and Jean departs, weighed down with personal anguish yet hopeful that out of all the bloodshed a new France can be built.

The two heroes in *The Debacle*, Jean Macquart, who was the outsider in *Earth*, and Maurice Levasseur, symbolise the contradictory qualities of France itself. Jean is conservative and sensible, courageous and industrious, while Maurice is intelligent, egoistic, volatile and frivolous. When the two men establish a profound and unbreakable friendship, the symbolism is complete.

Jean, as we noted in the chapter on *Earth*, has been subjected to the most horrific experience, having lost his wife and home and the fruits of ten years' hard work in a series of personal tragedies. He emerged from *Earth* as one of the most likeable and certainly the most balanced member of the entire Rougon-Macquart clan, and he adds to his stature in *The Debacle*. As Corporal Macquart in the Seventh Army Corps, one of the recruits in his platoon is Maurice, a headstrong, spoiled trainee lawyer. At first Maurice displays the mistrust of an intellectual towards an uneducated man in a position of authority, but before long Jean's honesty, common sense and warmth win him over and a deep friendship develops. The symbolism personified in Jean and Maurice continues through to the end of the novel. While the disparate qualities of the French character are welded together for the common good, all goes well. But when the intellectual, reckless Maurice escapes from Jean's steadying influence, the parting is disastrous. Maurice joins the rebellious Communards, thus threatening the nation with overthrow and ultimate destruction, and it is Jean's fate to be his executioner. Whatever the rights or wrongs of the Commune, Zola saw conservatism, not revolution, as the answer to France's problems at that time. The killing of Maurice by Jean was the final, symbolic act in the drama of national survival.

The Debacle is a war novel, as distinct from a wartime romance, so the absence of women among the major characters is not surprising. Passion, in this seven-week conflict, is reserved for killing and self-survival. Even the civilian women have their softness temporarily frozen, as with Sylvine, who lures a spy to his death. The spy is Goliath, her former lover and the father of her child but fond memories and old loyalties now have no place in her heart. The local guerrillas seize Goliath in her home and after a mock trial bleed him to death while they all watch. Sylvine's child watches, too.

'I'm sorry to bother you, Sylvine, but I wonder if you could let me have a bucket.'

Throughout the trial, Sylvine had not stirred. She had simply stood there waiting, her face rigid, her thoughts elsewhere, preoccupied with the obsession, which, for the past two days, had completely dominated her. And now that she was asked for a bucket she merely obeyed, disappearing for a minute into the cellar and returning with the big one she used for washing Charlot's clothes.

'Good, put it under the table, near the edge.'

She put it down, and, as she straightened her back again, her eyes once more met Goliath's. In the wretched man's gaze was a last entreaty, the expression of a man who does not want to die. But she felt no trace of womanly pity; at that moment, all she desired was his death, which for her meant freedom. She retreated once more towards the dresser, and there she stood.

Sambuc had opened the table drawer, and now produced a large kitchen knife.

'As you've behaved like a pig, I'm going to bleed you like a pig.'

Apparently in no hurry, he discussed with Cabasse and Ducat the best way to perform the operation. They even began arguing, Cabasse maintaining that, in Provence, they hung the pigs up to bleed them, Ducat indignantly insisting that this was a clumsy and barbarous method.

'Pull him to the side of the table, over the bucket, so that everything doesn't get splashed.'

They did as they were told, and Sambuc set about his task, calmly and skilfully.

With a single stroke he opened up the side of the throat, and immediately the blood began to flow from the severed carotid into the bucket, making a faint sound, like water falling from a fountain. He had made the incision as small as possible, so that only a few drops of blood, under the pressure of the heartbeats, missed the bucket. Though death was slower this way, there was no sign of convulsions, for the rope was strong, preventing the slightest movement of the body. Not a spasm, no sound of the death rattle. All the anguish was concentrated in the face, a mask etched with terror from which the blood drained, drop by drop, leaving the discoloured skin white as a sheet. And slowly the eyes, too, emptied; then clouded over, and went out. (87)

Only at the end does the enormity of the outrage penetrate to Sylvine's consciousness, and she becomes woman and mother again. In the most terrifying way the scene symbolises the bestial madness which grips otherwise sane and compassionate nations in conflict.

One of the striking differences between *The Debacle* and the other novels is its lecturing tone, for while Zola exposed many social sores he had never previously attempted to put forward ideas for healing them. This is far from the case in *The Debacle*, for at times it assumes the weight of a military manual in its dissection of the French defeat. The reasons for the easy Prussian victory had for twenty years been the subject of intense discussion and any intelligent comment on the rout was bound to excite public interest. There was also the ever-present layman's suspicion about the way the army was run, for although was protected from public scrutiny by the usual brass-bound secrecy, scandals emerged from time to time to give plenty of cause for alarm.

That novels about a war do so amazingly well ten, twenty and even thirty years after the event is a phenomenon that still has publishers scratching their heads. At any rate, *The Debacle* found an immediate and eager readership and its publication was greeted with almost universal acclaim, controversy and prodigious sales. It was translated into half a dozen languages within months. With its appearance in England, Zola's reputation, smeared by the Vizetelly trial several years before, was miraculously restored and even enhanced. Its accuracy and documentary flavour appealed to the military mind: *The Army and Navy Gazette* complimented the author on his 'stern grasp of the psychology of the battlefield'. War correspondents, having only a minor skirmish in Dahomey to report at the time, wrote at great and glowing length about the book. *The Spectator* called it 'the most wonderfully faithful reproduction of an historical drama ever committed to writing... a literally true Inferno' in which any reader bold enough to traverse this lacerating jungle must be prepared to have his flesh morally torn to ribbons...' *The People* praised it, too, as 'the most instructive and fearfully fascinating book that has been written, or possibly could be written, on the Franco-German War' and even Zola's old enemy, the *Pall Mall Gazette*, which had so actively campaigned against *Earth*, was moved to pronounce the novel a 'brilliant success'. And, to reassure the timid, *The Athenaeum* announced that 'from cover to cover it does not contain three needlessly repellant sentences'.

Although Zola could not have been completely unconscious of this international hunger for an analysis of the most important war of the second half of the nineteenth century, it does not wholly explain the remarkable departure from his previous reticence to prescribe remedies for social disorders. The Franco-Prussian War was not lost on the battlefield; France's entire social fabric – ill-designed, rotten, and torn by greed, corruption and ineptitude – was at fault. Zola's patient analysis often takes on the tone of a concerned parent, and here lies an interesting clue – for the author was by now the father of two children. Before their birth, though doubtless his concern for the state of France was no less sincere, his studies on the French way of life were detached enough to conclude on a logically pessimistic note. If the country ignored his warnings it would go to the dogs, but so what? He would be dead. But now, if his children were to have a future in the land of their birth, his responsibility was somewhat more personal. And as a man with a powerful influence over French life he must have been aware that his opinions could have a profound effect on the destinies of his fellow-countrymen. As the Dreyfus Affair was to prove a few years later, this turned out to be correct.

Even with today's advanced military technology it is peculiarly easy for citizens to teach the army its business, and what is depressing is that they are so often right. Case histories abound of governmental blunders being thwarted by mere tax-payers, but this private intervention was something of a novelty in nineteenth-century France. Military primacy was sacrosanct. A French machine-gun, the deadly 25-barrelled *mitrailleuse*, which might have changed the course of the Franco-Prussian War, was never used because it had been kept so secret no soldiers had been trained to use it properly. While Zola was not the first citizen military critic he was undoubtedly one of the best informed and publicised, and of the first 100,000 copies of *The Debacle* sold perhaps half were read as an analysis of the French war machine rather than as a novel about war. Certainly Zola had picked an easy target, for French military unpreparedness was legendary. In the 1870 conflict French muzzle-loading brass cannon duelled unequally with Prussian breech-loading guns which fired percussion shells with unheard-of accuracy. The army Intelligence services would have been more at home in the comedy theatre. Regimental rivalry obscured the national interest, but the French soon discovered that the fear induced by a superbly uniformed lancer at full charge went for nothing in the face of Prussian discipline, strategy and rifled field-pieces. One of a hundred illustrations of top-brass incompetence and arrogance was the issue to officers, on the eve of the war, of detailed maps of Germany, but not of maps showing the French terrain they were expected to fight on. Once confusion reigns at the top it inevitably filters down the line. One of the reasons for the defeat of the army at Sedan was that the French failed to blow up three bridges that spanned the Meuse; the party of engineers sent to do the job were left stranded on the first bridge when the train that took them there inadvertently steamed off with their tools and explosives. The consequences of this and countless other blunders were tragic, yet in the twenty-year period following the defeat few of the lessons had penetrated into the thick heads of the military authorities. Soon after the publication of *The Debacle* a storm of controversy broke over Zola's unrepentant head. After nit-picking trivialities, his French critics combined in a single, unreasonable howl of 'Unpatriotic!' One influential commentator damned the work as 'demoralising, perfidious, false and misleading'. A prominent Catholic priest condemned it as 'unhealthy, a hideous nightmare', and a large section of the Establishment had no hesitation in denouncing Zola as a traitor to his country. At a dinner party given in the novelist's honour by his publishers, one of the speakers was General Jung, who had been the personal assistant of the former War Minister, General Boulanger. 'I hope with all my heart', he said, 'that after *The Debacle*, our illustrious guest will give us *The Triumph*.' Zola immediately replied, 'That, General, depends on you.' It was, according to one Zola scholar, the only witty remark the novelist made in all his life.

It is difficult to avoid comparing *The Debacle* with Tolstoy's monumental *War and Peace*. Henry James, for instance, thought in 1903 that Zola's novel took its place 'with Tolstoy's very much more universal but very much less composed and condensed epic as an incomparably human picture of war'. *War and Peace* had been published in a French edition in 1879 and it is likely that Zola read it but the two novels are vastly dissimilar. Zola's is a war novel, confined solely to a short conflagration in which a decaying Empire expires in the flames; its only connection with other aspects of life is symbolic. Tolstoy's great classic, with its

everal themes and five hundred or so characters, is a far grander epic of life
self, gifted with the author's insight into the human condition and, as a bonus,
ome of the most unforgettable characters in fiction. As a novel, *The Debacle* is a
wasp compared with this leviathan, but as a war novel, *War and Peace* cannot
compare with Zola's bloody assault on militarism. With many of its themes and
characters deployed away from the battlefields, with its action so often
obscured by the smokescreen of interior monologue, Tolstoy's narrative
inevitably induces tedium, which is not what a war novel is about at all. On the
other hand, *War and Peace* has escaped the fate of war novels, which is that
much of their power fades with time. The monumental quality of *The Debacle*,
o impressive and heroic to a nineteenth-century reader, has been somewhat
overshadowed by two far more terrible and grislier memorials to militarism
that make the debacle of 1870 seem like a quaint and unimportant territorial
engagement.

Zola's account of the Franco-Prussian War is about as fair as it could possibly
be, despite his well-advertised dislike for Napoleon III's regime. The
emperor, in fact, is surprisingly well treated and emerges in a much more
favourable light than in many other accounts. Zola displays an admirable
impartiality throughout his fiction, preferring, with few exceptions, to present
the facts and leave judgements to others. It must have been difficult to resist
leaning to one side or another in the chapters on the Communard uprising, but
here again the novelist has no illusions. The Communards were composed of
idealists and men of great qualities, but their ranks were so shot through with
self-seeking freebooters and cynical troublemakers that their cause was in
jeopardy from the start. Zola reported all this, for that is what he had observed
himself. The novelist's primary emotion during those final, hysterical, bloody
days of the Commune was one of profound sadness at all the bestial violence,
regardless of the side responsible. The sadness remained locked away for
twenty years, to emerge with such riveting recall in *The Debacle*.

Zola did not set out specifically to write a novel on the horror and imbecility
of war. Its purpose was to be revelatory: 'I should be quite satisfied if people in
France and Germany recognised the great lengths to which I have gone to tell
the truth.' The simple truth about the Franco-Prussian War should have been
sufficient to indict all war.

With *The Debacle* Zola had reached the shattering climax of his tremendous
undertaking, but despite his careful plans he was faced with a dilemma. One
more novel in the chronicle remained to be written. From the novelist's point of
view it was to serve as a logical corollary: a mopping-up operation in which all
the loose ends would be neatly tied and tucked away; an apologia, if you like,
for the very existence of the nineteen novels which preceded it. But while this
concept fitted in with Zola's desire for formal completeness, there was no
guarantee it would fascinate his readers. It would be disastrous for the whole

enterprise to stumble at the finishing line. An idea, however, had been growing in the novelist's mind over several years, to tell the intimate story of how an old man found love and renascence with a young girl. It was now resolved: Zola would reveal, in the guise of fiction, the story of the happiest event in his own life.

34

36

33. ERNEST VIZETELLY, son of Zola's first English publisher and his champion in later years. 1899.

34. ZOLA in a Surrey garden, taken during his exile in England in 1898.

35. BILL OF SALE for the contents of Zola's house in Paris, seized by the Department of Justice to be auctioned to pay the 30,000 franc fine imposed on the novelist for libel during the Dreyfus Affair.

36. THE DREYFUS TRIALS. An 1898 Berlin cartoon depicts the prosecution and jury as a menagerie.

37. ZOLA was reviled by dozens of newspapers and journals for defending Dreyfus. This 1898 cartoon is not untypical of the savage attacks made upon the novelist.

38. PUBLIC reaction to Zola's intervention on behalf of Dreyfus was often violent, as this contemporary cartoon indicates.

39. IN 1893 Zola was invited to address three thousand English journalists at a Press Congress held in the Guildhall, London.

41. EVEN immediately after
his burial Zola was vilified.
The caption to this 1902
Italian cartoon reads: 'Take
that, you beast! You pornographer! Corruptor! Traitor!
Foreigner! Damned scum!'

. TAKEN in September,
02, this is the last photo-
aph of Zola during his life.
ne Dreyfus Affair and the
blic attacks have clearly
en their toll.

. ZOLA: a sketch made of the novelist on his deathbed in 1902.

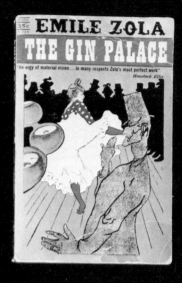

43. L'ASSOMMOIR. Four different paperback treatments of the same novel:
The Dram Shop, London, 1913; *The Gin Palace*, New York, 1952; *Drunkard*,
London, 1958; *L'Assommoir*, London, 1970.

18

The River of Ink
Dries Up

From the day it first appeared in 1893, every single published copy of *Doctor Pascal* has carried the following printed dedication: *To the memory of MY MOTHER and to MY DEAR WIFE I dedicate this novel which sums up and concludes my whole work.* A unique copy, however, carries an additional and a rather more personal dedication, and that is the one Zola sent to Jeanne Rozerot. On the title page he wrote: 'To my darling Jeanne – to my Clotilde, who gave me the royal banquet of her youth, and made me thirty years young again...' Clotilde is the youthful heroine of the novel, and Dr Pascal, more than forty years her senior, is her lover. Less equivocally than in any other novel in which the author's own personality intrudes as a character, Dr Pascal is Emile Zola; and Clotilde is Jeanne. But it wasn't always so.

The preliminary notes for this novel, the only important manuscript missing from the collection given by Madame Zola to the Bibliothèque Nationale, and which has given rise to so much speculation, do exist in private hands. Its history is uncertain. Perhaps the manuscript was mislaid by the author or Alexandrine, or given to Jeanne Rozerot and later sold, but the significant point is that it was detached from the main body of the novelist's papers. Disappointingly, it offers no sensational disclosures, but it does prove that Zola's decision to use himself and Jeanne as the central figures in the story came very late. Originally the love affair was to develop between the doctor and a friend of Clotilde's, and there was also a great deal of hesitation in having the older man consummate his love with the much younger woman. In the end, however, Zola decided in favour of consummation resulting in pregnancy, but on logical and symbolic grounds. With Clotilde giving birth to Pascal's child the saga of the five generations of the Rougon-Macquart family could not be said to have ended, except with a question mark. It seemed an ideal solution; readers would have to think for themselves, as Clotilde does when feeding the child after Pascal's death: 'She looked at him intently. Did he resemble anyone? There were his father's eyes, the forehead, and the same massively-shaped and elongated head. The small mouth and delicate chin were definitely hers. But then, with a shiver of apprehension, she realised she was searching for traces of the others, those abominable forerunners, each of whose lives was a leaf on the genealogical tree...'

The birth of his first child Denise in 1889 must have been one of the most profoundly affecting events in Zola's life – sufficient, at any rate, to encourage him to spill his happiness into some literary creation. *Money* was the first novel to receive some of this overflow which, by the end of *The Debacle*, had swelled to a flood of optimism for the future. But it remained for *Doctor Pascal* to receive in full the contents of Zola's cup of new-found bliss with Jeanne Rozerot. Whatever plans the novelist had for his original heroine they were scrapped, for with every line he writes about Clotilde in *Doctor Pascal* Zola cannot get Jeanne out of his mind. The details of her pregnancy, and of the mother suckling her child in the last chapter, are all set down with a glowing intensity. Even trivialities, as when Clotilde mends and folds the baby's linen (Jeanne had been a linen-maid in the Zola household) are described with a fond acuteness which very likely has its source in personal memory. Not since the far-distant *Claude's Confessions* had Zola set down a love affair in such an autobiographical way, nor left such a trail of clues. When the dying Dr Pascal receives a letter from Clotilde telling him she is two months pregnant, he muses: '... she must have conceived at the end of August, most likely on that delirious night when she had served him the royal banquet of her youth...' These were the very words Zola used in his handwritten dedication to Jeanne Rozerot.

That Zola is the character Dr Pascal in terms of their common philosophy of life there can be no doubt. Just before he finished the novel he admitted, during an interview with a biographer, Robert Sherard, that it

> amuses me because in it I am able to defend myself against all the accusations that have been brought against me... It is a scientific work, the logical conclusion of all my preceding volumes; and, at the same time, it is my speech for the defence before the court of public opinion of all that I have done... But perhaps my greatest pleasure in the book consists of the fact that, with Dr Pascal for a mouthpiece, I am able to vindicate myself and to justify myself... People, especially abroad, have accused me of being a pornographer. This I shall refute through Pascal... And the conclusion of it all will be the philosophical one, which I have sought ever since the day on which I first took pen in hand to write the series, that we should have faith in life and confidence in Nature; that good will come out of all that is bad; that justice will emerge from the slough of injustice; that a day of beauty will dawn after a night of hideous darkness... Thus, the last scene in the book is a mother nursing a baby at her breast...

So we have the novelist's word that the philosophies of Dr Pascal are the author's, although this does not necessarily mean the identities are common. It is reasonably clear that the Pascal–Clotilde affair, from the first kiss to the last rapturous night on which, her long limbs intertwined with his, strands of her hair caught in his beard, is the Zola–Jeanne affair. But there is one intriguing piece of evidence which deserves consideration, and that is Zola's use of the name *Pascal* as a pseudonym. When the novelist arrived in London in July 1898 to escape imprisonment for libel over the Dreyfus case, he signed the register of the Grosvenor Hotel with the name, 'M. Pascal, Paris'. He might just as usefully have signed 'M. Zola', for the fictional name, coupled with his appearance, would have tipped off anyone with the least acquaintance with his books. What it indicates, though, is the extent to which Zola was steeped in his *alter ego*.

Once he had decided on the novel's confessional tone, Zola was impatient to begin. For years he had been dreaming of the moment when he would embark on the novel that would complete his stupendous enterprise, begun half a lifetime before. Its uneven composition is an indication of the haste with which he undoubtedly wrote it. Although the eye of the storm in his life had passed – Alexandrine had learned about Jeanne and the children at the end of 1891 – he still tossed in a very stormy sea when he sat down to transpose the cause of it all in the spring of 1892. *Doctor Pascal* was published as a serial in *La Revue hebdomadaire* between March and June 1893, but after protests from indignant subscribers the journal was printed in two editions: one containing *Doctor Pascal*, the other with an innocuous serial substituted which was sent to the offended subscribers.

Dr Pascal Rougon is an elderly physician who has devoted his life to research on heredity. He uses his own family as guinea-pigs and he has detailed files on every one of them, through five generations. He lives in an old house called Souleiade on the outskirts of Plassans with a servant, Martine, and his niece, Clotilde, who acts as his secretary. Clotilde, a beautiful, delicately featured girl in her early twenties, is the daughter of Saccard the banker, by his first marriage, brought up by her Uncle Pascal since the age of seven. A frequent visitor to the house is Pascal's mother, Félicité Rougon, who hates her son's work and the files containing the inglorious history of her family.

Pascal's choice of his family as the subjects for his research is inspired, for there is no shortage of defects which have been transmitted down the line; moreover both the original ancestor Adélaïde Fouqué, or Aunt Dide, and the youngest, Charles Rougon, are still alive and living nearby. Aunt Dide, in fact, is 103 years old and locked up in a local asylum. On one of his visits to the asylum with several other relatives, Pascal suddenly realises he is confronted by the Rougon-Macquart family skeleton:

> Then an extraordinary emotion took possession of Pascal. He had caught hold of Clotilde's arm, and was pressing it tightly, but without being able to convey his meaning to her. The fact was it had suddenly dawned upon him that there, before his eyes, was the whole race, both the legitimate branch and the bastard branch that had sprung from that one trunk when it was already impaired by neurosis. The five generations were there face to face, the Rougons and the Macquarts – Adélaïde Fouqué, at the root, then the old bandit uncle, then himself, then Clotilde and Maxime, and finally Charles. Félicité filled the place of her dead husband. There was no gap, the chain of logical, implacable heredity spread out complete. And what a century it was that he thus evoked, in the tragic depths of that madhouse, where the atmosphere reeked of far-descending human woe, amid such a seizure, too, of fright and awe that every one of them stood there shivering, in spite of the oppressive heat!
> (89)

Life in Pascal's house is peaceful and disturbed only by the conflict between the scientist and his religious niece. Clotilde cannot accept her uncle's theories of heredity and evolution and she frequently pleads with him to abandon his work and destroy his files. Félicité also believes her son is in the grip of the devil and encourages Clotilde to steal and burn all his papers. One night Pascal surprises her in the middle of this task and a frightful scene follows, leading to the first great emotional climax in the novel. Right through that night the doctor forces his niece to read the contents of his files and to recognise the scientific value of his work; in the end Clotilde is not only converted to science but is also possessed by a more earthly sensation, the emerging love for her elderly uncle. The scene ends on a superb symbolic note:

> She went up to the table and started helping him; she was subjugated, broken by such a brutal embrace which had seemed to penetrate her whole body. The candle, flaming steadily in the heavy night, threw a bright light over them both; the distant rumbling of thunder had not stopped and the window, open to the storm, seemed to be on fire.

Then Pascal falls ill, and while he is tortured by hallucinations of madness and death he is nursed by Clotilde, who is now devoted to him. As the doctor convalesces he, too, falls in love, and after their passion for each other is consummated they lead a life of complete bliss, with Clotilde accompanying Pascal on his medical rounds and assisting him in his research. But although sixty-year-old Pascal is rejuvenated by Clotilde's youthful love it is too late, for he is a victim of heredity too, of degenerative cardio-sclerosis. Clotilde, for her part, is the victim of cruel gossip in the town for which Pascal feels he is the cause, and to alleviate his guilt sends her to Paris on the pretext that he cannot finish his work with her distracting presence in the house. Clotilde leaves him with misgivings which prove to be justified, for his health rapidly declines while she is away.

Only when he learns that Clotilde is pregnant does Pascal ask her to return, but the journey back is a race between life and death. When Clotilde arrives at the house her uncle has been dead for some hours. With this tragedy the novel moves to a touching climax. Pascal's mother Félicité seizes the opportunity to make a bonfire of her son's life-work which goes up in flames as Clotilde sleeps by the death-bed of her lover in a room above. But although Pascal's research is lost, Clotilde holds the key to it all, in her belly, a fifth-generation Rougon to be born in 1874.

Zola's naturalist philosophy and theories permeate the narrative and are personalised in Clotilde, who is a convert from religious mysticism. After Pascal's death she ponders on this, in a long reverie in which she reiterates Pascal's credo, which is Zola's: life has to be a communal undertaking on behalf of all mankind, which can only be achieved by self-denial – even the rejection, if necessary, of one's beliefs, knowledge, understanding and happiness. The progress of human reason is through science; and the sum of all the truths so painfully earned would endow man with incalculable power and serenity. In a phrase, man must acquire a passionate faith in life itself.

Doctor Pascal is the first novel to reflect the sexual revolution in Zola's life wrought by Jeanne Rozerot. In reality a passionate love affair between a man of sixty and a much younger woman cannot be without its practical difficulties, yet while the liaison between Pascal and Clotilde is projected on an idealistic screen it comes over with astonishing believability, and there is none of the disgust for sex evident in earlier novels. At the same time the author cannot abandon his deep-felt belief that love has a singular purpose, which is not simply to make love. Listen to him speak through Clotilde:

> ...her studies in natural history had taught her that nature was solely concerned with the fruit. It alone was important, it was the sole objective, every precaution was taken to make sure that the seed was not lost and that the mother gave birth. And man, on the contrary, by civilizing and emasculating love, had discarded the very thought of the fruit. The hero's sex drive, in refined novels, was merely a lust-machine. They worshipped each other, took each other, left each other, endured a thousand deaths, embraced, unleashed a tempest of social evils, all just for a few moments of pleasure, violating all natural laws, without even seeming to realize that making love was a preliminary to begetting children. It was indecent and utterly stupid.   (91)

Clotilde's sentiments are those of Zola's, who, in his preliminary notes for the novel had written, 'The natural end of love is child-bearing. Underline that any departure from this is selfish, frivolous and unnatural.'

One of the most delightfully outlandish episodes in all of Zola's fiction occurs in *Doctor Pascal*: the death of old Uncle Antoine Macquart by spontaneous combustion. Zola had dug the case out of a very old textbook and although he was advised by medical experts that such a phenomenon was physiologically impossible he insisted, with a stubborn disregard for scientific detachment, on including it in the narrative. It is a credit to Zola's skill that Macquart's bizarre death is presented so convincingly, but it rather explodes his pretensions as a realist writer.

Not without interest, too, are the postscripts on various members of the *Rougon-Macquart* characters who appeared in other novels. From his defeats in *Earth* and *The Debacle* Jean starts a new life on a farm, marries, and has two healthy children. Etienne, after walking out of the last page of *Germinal*, has his career in politics cut short by a term of imprisonment in Noumea, where he marries and fathers a child. Maxime, who drifts through *The Kill* and *Money*, finally succumbs to ataxia. Saccard, whom we recently left in *Money*, ruined and on the run, is now managing director of a newspaper; while Octave Mouret is still waxing fat from the profits of *The Ladies' Paradise*. It's a little like looking at an album of photographs, taken many years before: 'And what happened to her...?' we're bound to ask. *Doctor Pascal* relieves our curiosity.

As a novel, *Doctor Pascal* has all the deficiencies of a personal journal and many of its attractions. Viewed out of the context of the *Rougon-Macquart* cycle it is a sermon woven around questionable doctrines and wrapped in a sentimental narrative. It has none of the objectivity shown in *L'Assommoir*, none of the irony of *Piping Hot!*, nor the stark detachment which marks the pages of *Germinal* and *Earth*. All the qualities that help make a novel great are missing in *Doctor Pascal*. But there is an element of unfairness in this kind of judgement, for *Doctor Pascal* was conceived not so much as a novel but as an epilogue to a vast chronicle, an authorial indulgence, even, to the novelist's sense of completeness. It is difficult to see how Zola might have concluded the

Rougon-Macquart in any other way. To begin reading Zola by picking up *Doctor Pascal* would be as inadvisable as beginning any novel at the final chapter.

There need be no apologetic note, though, when considering *Doctor Pascal* as a coda, for which purpose it was designed, reminding us that, rather like the pages of the *News of the World*, 'All Human Life is There'. The book is more than an ingenious recapitulation, however, for the narrative does advance us to the closing of the chronicle, adding new ironies to the history of the family. There are fresh departures: the evil ancestor Antoine Macquart dies, as does the tainted, insane Adélaïde Fouqué and the sickly Charles, the only fifth-generation representative of their progeny. A haemophiliac, Charles was doomed, but a new bud emerges to take his place: Clotilde's unnamed child. Call it a hasty tying together of loose ends or whatever you like, the retrospective view of the Rougon-Macquarts we have in *Doctor Pascal* adds considerably to the reader's understanding of the tribe, perhaps the whole human tribe if we manage to dodge Pascal's theorising and do some thinking for ourselves. In this sense the novel is thought-provoking, which can't be bad. While we should not ignore the novel's faults – which are glaring enough – neither should we ignore its merits. Zola's ability to write lyrical prose is undiminished, and Pascal's autumnal love affair with his niece, while it has its sentimental moments, is a touching idyll nevertheless.

With *Doctor Pascal*, the chronicle closes. Almost a quarter of a century had passed since the day Zola began to tell his epic story of the Rougon-Macquart family. People who were not even born when *The Fortune of the Rougons* appeared in 1870 probably represented the biggest section of his readers for *Doctor Pascal* in 1893. Counting all editions published in France Zola had reached into every corner of the country, to every level of society, with a phenomenal two million published volumes. The *Rougon-Macquart* chronicle was a document of 10,000 pages, 1,200 characters, nearly five million words. The march of science over those twenty-three years seemed to vindicate the novelist's faith: X-rays had been discovered; the gramophone and the cinematograph had been invented. The use of anaesthetics was removing some of the pain and terror from illness and injury. Many of the social sores exposed in his novels were being cured: new divorce laws had been passed in 1884; more children were being educated in non-clerical schools. And the working people were flexing rejuvenated muscles. Trade unions had been legalised in 1884 and had used the strike weapon so effectively that, in 1893, over three million man-days were lost in strikes and stoppages in the desperate fight for improved conditions.

There was one casualty at this time: naturalism. As the later *Rougon-Macquart* novels spun from Zola's pen, the naturalist doctrines with which he had so determinedly launched the enterprise became obscured in lyricism and romanticism, culminating in the mythic idealism of *Doctor Pascal*. With one or two exceptions his naturalist supporters had all departed. Huysmans, perhaps his most talented lieutenant, had added insult to injury by becoming a devout

Roman Catholic. The symbolists and the 'psychological' novelists were the new darlings of literature.

I find it difficult to believe that what Zola finally saw when he contemplated the twenty volumes which sprang from his family tree was anything like the vision he had when he started. Only a few of the novels have any real allegiance to the Rougon-Macquart genealogy, although it is doubtful whether he could ever have begun the chronicle without its disciplinary framework. With the exception of the first and last novels, all of them may be enjoyed by readers with little or no knowledge of the family connections.

Another element, important in Zola's original concept but which was dropped by the wayside as the series proceeded, was his desire for revenge on the burghers of Aix-en-Provence, the scene of his family's humiliations. Plassans, as he renamed the town, virtually ceases to exist after *The Abbé Mouret's Sin*, and Zola can manage only a flicker of vindictiveness against its residents by the time he has reached *Doctor Pascal*.

From the care with which Zola went about planning the *Rougon-Macquart* chronicle and his genealogical tree, he envisaged an interlocking and unified series of novels. The key characters are all related and upon them the author superimposed a unity of historical time and clothed them in a common social fabric, the Second Empire. From this point of view the *Rougon-Macquart* novels represent a sustained and single-minded achievement which has no equal in modern literature.

But one can also view the chronicle from another standpoint, and from there it is difficult to see the twenty novels as a single, unified work. Instead of a panoramic mural what we see are twenty pictures by the same artist, violently differing in subject matter and displaying extremes of technique and intention from the pale pastel tones of *A Love Episode* to the bold impasto of *The Debacle*; from the evanescent lyricism of *The Abbé Mouret's Sin* to the frontal assault of *Germinal*. We should not squabble about this matter of discarded or lost intentions, for instead of leaving us with twenty weak, unified novels, Zola endowed the world with a dozen great works of fiction, two or three of them masterpieces.

The novelist was not a cheerful man, if we can judge from the painted and photographed portraits of him. Robert Louis Stevenson described him as 'fundamentally at enmity with joy', and although this is not quite true Zola was a serious man indeed. He took rather a grim view of life, and this is reflected in his novels. Although his view towards the end is slightly rosier, the twenty volumes of the *Rougon-Macquart* add up to a depressingly bleak picture of mankind. Yet this quality of seriousness was ideal for the task, for Zola painted a very accurate picture of an age which was excessively vulgar, unequal and unjust; of a kill-or-be-killed society in which the weak soon went to the wall. One required compassion rather than a sense of humour to document the terrible sufferings of the workers, the miners and the peasants of that time.

Although he carried a blazing reformist torch, the author's compassion always saves his characters from appearing as mere propagandist puppets.

Zola saw man invariably as a prisoner of his environment; the peasants of the Beauce plain, where hardly a wall can be seen, are just as much prisoners as Octave Mouret, hemmed in by the counters of *The Ladies' Paradise* by the forces of capitalist competition. Interestingly, it is in the area of reform that the only significant shift in direction occurs in the entire chronicle. While the tremors of the change taking place may be detected in *Piping Hot!* their effects can only really be seen by looking at the twenty novels in perspective. Looking down the rank, the early novels are almost a rabble, some wanting to go one way and some another, so that one gets the feeling they've been paraded in a line against their will. But the ten or so novels in the line nearest us have an alert, scrubbed look, a row of shining crusaders, their bindings gleaming with a sense of purpose.

This is not an illusion; if we examine the individual books in this light we discover that the later novels – say, from *Nana* or *Piping Hot!* onwards – reveal a distinct change in design aimed to make them more efficient vehicles in the cause of social reform. This is not to say that *L'Assommoir* was any less potent a weapon of reform than *Germinal*, but where *L'Assommoir* was a ship equipped with powerful guns, *Germinal* was designed and launched as a battleship. In other words, the social evils exposed in the earlier novels – poverty and alcoholism in *L'Assommoir*, political corruption in *His Excellency*, debased religion in *The Conquest of Plassans* – seem to some extent incidental to the plot, while those exposed and explored in the later works – capitalism in *Germinal*, the banking system in *Money*, middle-class morals in *Piping Hot!* – are unequivocally elements in their very foundations.

If we now place the line of books beside the calendar, a likely reason for this shift of emphasis can be seen. The hazy demarcation line falls opposite 1880, which was the year Zola lost two of his closest friends, Duranty and Flaubert, and his mother. It was the year he worked on and abandoned *Joy of Life* and began a long slide down into an acute depression, frozen in panic as the years of his future flashed by and paralysed by his fear of death. None of this resulted, of course, in any kind of instant transformation, but it did bring about in the novelist the obsession that time was running out, and a more urgent awareness of the social ills that beset France. He tended to look at society's machinery more carefully, and with a renewed purpose.

In looking at the ills of mankind, Zola displayed a breadth of vision that is not, I feel, justly appreciated. His examination of the various social inequalities were never piecemeal but linked to the search for a basic system by which man could plan a sure future and live a life which had real purpose. Like many other nineteenth-century writers and thinkers he wanted answers, but being more impatient and less profound than many, proceeded to create his own ideal world according to his beliefs. In this he had very little help from established philosophies and none from religion, both of which were inadequate to the challenge of the vast technological and social changes which characterised the period. The result, as we have seen, was that Zola's vision was improvised upon the unsure foundations of science, with its undeniable promise and potential or mankind. To Zola science wasn't merely useful, but omnipotent. 'I do not believe', he wrote in 1885, 'that thought is anything but a function of matter.' Such was the extent of his materialism.

The scientific revolution which was under way in the nineteenth century has led the world not into the Utopia imagined by Zola but into our own counter-productive technological age, with its global pressures for faster and faster growth, its socially divisive exploitation techniques, its wholesale rape of resources. Science, in the hands of man, has so far dismally failed as the universal panacea for mankind's troubles; people are still at war, still poor, still starving. The technological leaps have surpassed anything Zola ever imagined, but they have been of the kind that now allow India to transmit satellite pictures of her starving millions to the television sets of the affluent world. Zola's mistake was that he confused science with alchemy; his failing that he was a materialist and an optimist. We are no less the prisoners of our environment than was society under his Second Empire; on minor counts like the alleviation of toothache, package holidays and spun beef we can claim to be ahead on points; but against that we are far, far closer to global disaster than Second Empire citizens were. Did the novelist ever envisage that his new religion would lead to a world where a few international monopolistic corporations can practically control the economy of an entire country? In which the imbalance of wealth is so outrageous that the cost of two days in a private American nursing home is equal to the median annual cash income of the world's population? In which masses of its inhabitants are manipulated, conditioned technical animals? When teenage British school-children were recently invited to submit essays on the theme, 'If scientists ruled the world...' the response was uniformly despondent. One winner concluded sadly that technology had wrecked not only nature but the experience of being alive'.

So much for the scientific props of Zola's philosophy, which when kicked away reveal no logical foundations for his theories whatsoever. And his view that man must have a 'passionate faith in life' is so abstract as to be ungraspable in a practical sense when applied to daily life. It sounds such an attractive proposition, too, but as a philosophy it has as many holes as a sieve. Worse: it is self-defeating, for what Zola was asking was what a priest asks of his parishioners, what a charlatan healer asks of his patients – blind faith. But regardless of all this, what Zola wrote in his novels was invariably true in terms of human experience, sometimes profoundly so; that men and societies are more often than not at the mercy of events and pressures beyond their control is as true today as it was in his time.

Understandably there is a sureness of touch in the last novels that is missing in the early books, graphic evidence of which can be found in Zola's manuscripts. A typical written page of *The Fortune of the Rougons* is scored and disfigured by a dozen or more revisions, some of them substantial. Even midway through the cycle he tortured his printers with alterations. 'Scarcely a line is exempted from the hieroglyphics of the master', wrote the Paris

correspondent of the *New York Times* in 1886. 'Zola saw in his proofs
thousand things he missed before – semi-colons for commas, substantives f
pronouns; redundant adverbs are struck out, phrases remodelled, sentenc
condensed, sometimes whole half-columns consigned to the type bin.' For Zo
literary composition was a painful and tormenting activity from which he on
escaped later in life.

Considering the dedication with which Zola wrote his prose it is strange th
in the great paperchase of critical literature on the novelist very litt
consideration is given to his style, and even then most of it is depreciatory. Eve
a critic as enlightened as Martin Turnell, in *The Art of French Fiction,* doesn
think too much of it: 'I cannot recall a single instance in which the pleasu
was derived from the formal beauty of the style. Zola's prose is almost devoid
rhythm or music; it has no magic and no grace. There is a heaviness and
monotony which often becomes downright dullness'

This is harsh judgement indeed, and I would think considerably off tl
mark for there is a persistence of excellence in Zola's composition that cann
be written off like this. Turnell's view likens the novelist to the proverbi
roomful of monkeys with typewriters, mindful of the mathematical probabili
that one will eventually write the works of Shakespeare: 'He (Zola) w.
convinced that if he flung words together with all his might, multiplied acts
violence and heaped one catastrophe on top of another, something was bour
to emerge in the end. His vindication is that it sometimes did.'

This view rather ignores the fact that Zola laboured desperately hard ov
his composition, sometimes succeeding and sometimes not, but rarely could l
be called guilty of flinging words together. Nor does it take into account h
virtuoso performance with the language in *L'Assommoir* in which Zola could l
said to have developed an original style in which the low-life speech of tl
characters is unified with the sophisticated requirements of the narrative l
means of an enveloping colloquial tone.

In twenty volumes there are bound to be occasional founderings and errat
departures, and there would have been more had not Zola developed a sty
that ran on like a river, with a 'wide, monotonous flow, steady and stron
Nothing could have been better suited to the epic quality of his intentions, b
even so he rarely remained waterbound, sometimes soaring above its surfa
with extended prose poems, of which I've given some examples; sometim
sinking into the dark depths beneath to contemplate and explore; and at tim
whipping the flow into angry waves to pound the banks that contained it.

Zola had a 'literary' personality no less interesting and complex than his ow
and indeed much of his nature is projected into the form of his writing. On tl
debit side he is often obvious, naïve and irritatingly heavy-handed. His passic
for detail and acute observation led him too frequently into dreary lecturing,
in *Money* when he is trying to explain the operations of the Bourse. Too oft
his choice of metaphors betrays laboured logic rather than artistic feeling. B
there is a credit side, too. Only a remarkable imagination and rare inspiration
gifts could have created the many deliriously lyrical passages that show up li

patterns of gold in the mosaic of his writing. If Zola tended to be a bricklayer with words, he also created many beautiful vaulted arches and flying buttresses in his constructions, all functional to his purpose. There is no delicate tracery in Zola's style and only disappointment will result if we search for it. Zola's pen, like Cézanne's brush, was an instrument for commanding masses, for stirring up impastos of violence, for launching the reader on some wild, soaring flight. In this respect he is superb, and all the elements of his style can be seen in play when he is dealing with people *en masse:* the sometimes rhythmic, sometimes staccato repetitions, the breathless impressions and glimpsed cameos, the relentless accumulation of detail, the symbolic echoes, the massed adjectives, the rush of substantives, the fleeting appearance of motif-words – all as painstakingly worked out as an orchestration, all striving for the ultimate effect.

Zola's use of single adjectives is commonplace but he was an expert in the use of multiple adjectives to indicate complex action, ambiguity or to convey mood. In an analysis of the novelist's style, Martin Turnell quotes some interesting examples which typify Zola's handling of massed adjectives. 'And the battle continued, *furious, treacherous* with bonnets torn off, flesh bruised, each of them searching with her fingers for the place where she could get at the life of the other.' Note the placement of 'furious, treacherous'; the pairing of adjectives near the beginning of a sentence was a device Zola often used to stretch out the action, to give the reader an impression before following up with details. To take another example: 'He sent him *shivering, stumbling, falling* over backwards' conveys a wealth of action with just a few words. 'All five went into the office, *stiff, silent*' not only describes the action of the characters but infers an ominous mood emphasised, this time, by placing the adjectives at the end of the sentence. Zola's style also reveals a heavy dependence on substantives to convey immediacy, impact and excitement; in his prose we are constantly confronted by a '*rush* of legs', the '*rattling, jangling* of machinery', the '*rustling* of petticoats' and the '*heaving* of bodies'.

Other characteristics of his style include the use of repetition, especially in his more lyrical novels. For the effect he wants he repeats single words, phrases and even sentences. In *The Beast in Man* he has Roubard screaming at his wife, 'Did you sleep with him?' which is repeated word for word three times as the quarrel intensifies. The closing paragraph of *Nana* ends with the soldiers shouting, 'To Berlin! To Berlin! To Berlin!' A symbolic tocsin or mere mindless shouting? Either way, the repetitious cry carries just the right note of doom. Then there are Zola's verbal idiosyncrasies, groups of words which recur throughout his work with almost obsessive frequency and which offer clues to his major preoccupations:

weak/feeble/failure/collapse/fall/downfall/ruin/disaster/disorder
tainted/damaged/spoiled/refuse/muck/excrement/rottenness
outburst/flood/fury/rage/violence/devour/consume/destroy

heaving/swelling/upheaval/revolt/mob/crowd/throng/stampede
lust/rut/stir/swarm/multiply/germinate/fecundate

You might note a common factor in these words: they all have to do with mass of humanity in ferment, restless, frustrated, angry and self-destructive but also regenerative, because from beginning to end the fertility motif run like a renewing spring through the *Rougon-Macquart* novels. Until towards th end, though, there is a grim pessimism about the process – there is nothin joyful about the regeneration of the miners in *Germinal* for instance – but b the time Zola has reached *Doctor Pascal*, thanks to a linen-maid and tw children, the phenomenon is elevated to the most inspiriting experience in th universe.

The effect of the author's love affair with Jeanne Rozerot on th *Rougon-Macquart* chronicle is only one of many instances in which incidents i his life intrude directly into his fiction. The undercurrent of person bitterness which swirls through *Joy of Life* was largely brought about by h mother's death. A period in his life when marital relations with Alexandrin were strained intolerably contributed to the biting satire in *Piping Hot!* Th unforeseen Franco-Prussian War led him to recast his plans for *The Debacl The Masterpiece* might have been a completely different book had not its autho felt so frustrated at what he saw as his friend's failure as an artist.

It is not uncommon for an author, working for long periods with intens absorption, to part company with reality occasionally. A common lapse is on where an author identifies with his own fiction during a momentary loss c control. Less common, perhaps, are those instances when identificatio becomes addictive, offering an escape from problems and frustrations. world of one's own creation in which one is omnipotent, untouched and neve threatened, is a seductive world to a troubled personality. In the twenty-thre years it took to write the *Rougon-Macquart* novels Zola had his share of trouble emotional and physical, professional and domestic, so it is not surprising t find them intruding into the world of his imaginary family. The evidenc suggests that, sometimes for long periods, the novelist lived in a comfortin twilight between reality and fantasy in the security of his baroque stud Outside that study Zola could put on his bourgeois face, and that is how th world saw the physical man: mild, gentle and self-effacing. But with a pen in h hand an ogre could emerge. The pick and shovel labour of the *Rougon Macquart* would bring to the surface a rich haul of angry indictments again injustice, inequality and human weaknesses of all kinds. Deeply burie resentments would burst out to add white-hot savagery to mob scenes; carn frustration would flower into exotic imagery. At times the novels would absor his whole being, all his energies, his hopes and ambitions, every last drop of h talent. With all his powers, his drive and abilities he could have been Eugèn Rougon in real life, a master politician; or Octave Mouret, creating a gia department store, or even a real scientist, like his character Dr Pascal. Instea he spurted out a river of words; his life fell flat on the pages of th

Rougon-Macquart. No wonder, soon after his death, Henry James perceptively observed that Zola seemed to be devastated at the 'betrayal that nothing whatever had happened to him in life but to write the *Rougon-Macquart*'.

Any attempt to grade the *Rougon-Macquart* novels must be a highly subjective exercise; I've never been able to get into *His Excellency* but I know several people who are entranced by it; I've read *The Ladies' Paradise* two or three times with great pleasure but this novel has bored the pants off other readers. Nevertheless, I do find general agreement that among the twenty novels there are three resounding failures, three masterpieces, and fourteen novels which occupy a wide area of middle-ground as brilliant, interesting or readable.

The three misses are undoubtedly *The Fortune of the Rougons*, which sinks under its heavy load of introductory matter; *The Dream*, with its sentimental colouring so fugitive it has faded from sight; and *Money*, throttled by laboured situations, long, boring explanatory passages and annoying repetitions.

At the bottom end of the middle group must be placed the wildly melodramatic though suspenseful *The Conquest of Plassans*; *His Excellency*, Zola's far from successful union of love and politics; and *Doctor Pascal* which for all its melodramatic ingenuity does require for its full enjoyment and understanding some knowledge of the other novels.

Now we are in a disputatious area, for all the following novels are outstanding for one reason or another but at the same time vastly different in style, subject and treatment. It is difficult to imagine, at times, that *The Beast in Man*, with its compelling narrative, and *The Abbé Mouret's Sin*, are by the same hand; the latter is a beautifully spun exotic fantasy and perhaps Zola's best – certainly his most lyrical – love story. The *Belly of Paris* rarely flags in interest, although the novelist's epic sweep tends to exhaust itself by dwelling too long among the market stalls; and *The Ladies' Paradise* suffers in that its superb impressionism has much of the life knocked out of it by too much varnishing of detail. *The Kill*, with its pervasive smell of decadence and its vivid re-creation of a world obsessed with sex, money and social ambition, is compulsive reading, yet no more so than Zola's most poignant novel, *A Love Episode*, dense and introspective, a blend of soft pastel and harsh strokes of charcoal. *The Masterpiece* is as charged with high-octane passion as *A Love Episode* is restrained, but its appeal does to a large extent depend on whether or not you are interested in artists and the story of Impressionism.

This leaves us with a group of seven novels, all great and all entitled to an important niche in literature, but of which four miss out, by an eye-wincing hair's breadth, from inclusion in that category reserved for the greatest masterpieces of fiction. *The Debacle* is one of the finest, most moving war novels ever written, epically conveying the chaotic stupidity and waste of war. Middle-class hypocrisy has rarely been assailed with such satirical finesse as it is in *Piping Hot!* with its deadly mixture of observation and farce. The same deftness is applied further up the social scale in *Nana*, a withering comment on women's mindless exploitation of sex in a decadent society. Lastly, in this group, it is a sad duty to include *Joy of Life*, for it is the nearest of near-misses, a magnificently sustained conflict between despair and faith.

Finally, the great masterpieces: *L'Assommoir, Germinal* and *Earth*. *L'Assommoir* was Zola's stupendous leap to greatness, the first indication of his genius, displaying the full range of his technique and powers of characterisation, yet a simple, intensely moving, compassionately human story. This is hardly true of *Earth*, however, which wins its accolade as a prose-poem as black as the soil the peasants covet, as a novel of violent contrasts from sweet lyricism to bestiality. *Germinal*, if such a fine distinction can be made, is Zola's all-encompassing creation, written with fierce anger barely suppressed by its unnerving detachment: a novel of the crowd, of the ironies of human motivations, of enlightenment, of mass action and emotions – and one with which it is impossible not to be involved.

I do not, obviously, expect universal agreement with this evaluation, but there can be little argument that the twenty novels of the *Rougon-Macquart* chronicle constitute one of the most remarkable, certainly the most breathtaking, literary achievements of modern times. As Henry James put it, 'No finer act of courage or confidence, I think, is recorded in the history of letters.'

19

The Mortal Messiah

By 1893 Zola was the tubby, bespectacled 'Buddha of Letters' in France, a title he inherited from his old opponent Victor Hugo, who had died in 1885. The resemblances between the two men are striking to an extent that would have appalled Zola. Both were writers of genius with visions that extended far beyond the societies of their time. Both had a love for work, a sympathy for the oppressed and a hatred of the church. And both had mistresses: Hugo had his Juliette Drouet, the former courtesan who had been his loyal companion for half a century; and Zola had his Jeanne, still in her twenties.

As the great man sat at his splendid carved desk, even the thought of his annual income – then reckoned to be about 300,000 francs per annum – could not change his thoughtful frown to a satisfied smile. But he was a very contented man, and also a vindicated prophet. The violent storms that had swept through his private life over the affair with Jeanne were safely past, thanks to the tolerance of Alexandrine, and he doubtless drew great strength from the luxury of having a successful public life and a gratifying private one.

The novelist was also something of a national exhibit, such was his fame. In October 1895, he submitted his body and brain to an exhaustive examination by a group of doctors and specialists headed by Dr Edouard Toulouse, in the cause of science. The results of this examination, reputedly the most thorough ever made of a live human being, were subsequently published in France and in America with Zola's approval: 'This study of me is about one who has given his life to work and who has dedicated to this work all his physical, mental and moral forces.' Thus we learn that the length of the writer's right ear was 69mm; the length of his left foot 262mm – 7mm shorter than his right foot; that he suffered from a congenital neurotic condition; that between twenty and forty he suffered intestinal pain, and had cystitis between the age of forty-five and fifty. The assembled specialists also noted his extraordinary sensitivity. He could, blindfolded, easily detect different kinds of fish from their smell, and the pain from a small pinprick could persist for hours afterwards. He was fingerprinted, sphygmographed, plethismographed, pneumographed and dynamometred. Emile Zola had become a unique specimen in the human zoo.

For more than a decade the publication of a new Zola novel was an event that quickened the boulevards, with the bookstalls stacked high with the volumes in their traditional yellow wrappers. Watching the people queue to buy them was the nearest Zola got to a standing ovation from a theatre crowd.

The theatre, which had been for him since 1865 a battlefield of frustration and disappointment, preoccupied him occasionally. The success of the play *Nana* in 1881 was followed two years later with the resounding flop of *Pot-Bouille*, with its unfortunate blend of humour and bitterness, so he could not claim to have taken the stage by storm. *The Fat and the Thin*, adapted by the competent William Busnach, opened in 1887 and although it was a weak play it was far more popular than Zola's original drama, *Renée*, which was performed the same year, surviving for only thirty-eight nights. *Germinal*, written in 1885 but not produced until 1888 because it had been banned earlier, was yet another flop, finding few patrons willing to sit through what one critic condemned as 'five boring hours'. After this, the novelist lost interest in the naturalist theatre, preferring to explore new paths in lyric drama. Collaborating with the composer Alfred Bruneau and the dramatist Louis Gallet, Zola saw his novel *The Dream* transformed into a stage success. It opened at the *Opéra-Comique* in Paris in June 1891, ran for a whole season, and was subsequently revived several times. The success was repeated with *Attack on the Mill* in November 1893, which played in Paris, Brussels and London. The giant strides Zola was taking away from naturalism is reflected in his new interest in writing operatic librettos.

There remained, however, one particular irritation. The novelist had conquered the literary world of France by sheer force of will, the world even, but one last bastion resolutely kept its doors closed to him. Zola was becoming the most famous unsuccessful candidate for the most exclusive club in France, the French Academy. By 1890 he had already been passed over several times in favour of men of pronounced mediocre talent, and Zola was well aware that the annual lock-out was a calculated snub. Yet each year he renewed his candidacy and altogether applied thirteen times. Many writers have deduced from this the presence of still another monstrous growth on Zola's ego, but this is to misunderstand his intentions. Certainly he frankly admitted that membership in the Academy would consecrate his personal contribution to literature, and that he was no different to most other men in desiring an official acknowledgement to fame. Wearing the sacred sword of this hallowed institution would, he said to the biographer Robert Sherard in 1890, give him immense enjoyment. But there were more profound and less egotistical reasons behind Zola's patient lobbying. Literature had been notoriously ill-represented in the Academy; only the election of Pierre Loti in 1891 saved its members from appearing to conspire against the novel. In the past Balzac and Daudet had been refused, and even Hugo had been forced to apply four times before he was admitted. Zola felt he had a duty to see that the novel which after all had flowered during the late nineteenth century into one of the most popular art-forms, was more fairly represented. He was also anxious that the naturalist novel should be recognised, too. As its creator his election, he thought, would confer on naturalism a special kind of acknowledgement that would ensure its permanent place in the history of French literature.

None of this argument, however, impressed the Academicians, who at each election plotted and jockeyed among themselves to keep Zola out. The contest took on the proportions of a huge national joke, though not entirely at the Academy's expense. Each year the newspapers carried cartoohs of the novelist knocking hopefully at the Academy's doors. One writer offered to print a standard application to save Zola having to write them. His persistence attracted a mixture of admiration and scorn, although most of his friends realised the quest was hopeless, such was the intransigent attitude of the Academicians. Typical was the view of one of them, the dramatist Victorien Sardou, who told a correspondent of the *New York Times* (5 August 1888) that 'Zola's literary baggage of indecent works and three or four unsuccessful dramatic attempts are quite insufficient to secure his election.' Sardou went on to advise Zola 'not only to write a healthy work to earn election, but one in good French'. It was enough to make one want to give up writing!

Half-way through the *Rougon-Macquart* saga Zola had in fact envisaged retirement on its completion although, as he mentioned to Goncourt, he might tackle a history of French literature to fill in time. He even imagined he might leave France for the South Seas, to contemplate nothing in particular in the warm sun. Unfortunately this was not to be, for as he plucked the last fruits from his genealogical tree, fresh projects crowded into his fertile mind. He had only begun to write *Doctor Pascal* when he started to research the background for *Lourdes*, the first novel in a trilogy to be called *The Three Cities*. After the magnificent triumph of the *Rougon-Macquart*, however, his was to be the sad spectacle of the famous but ageing actor making comeback after comeback to the disappointment of his fans, for the tumultuous river of Zola's genius was to lose itself in what Henry James called 'deep desert sand' – a wearisome desert which now attracts few travellers. Of the six novels Zola wrote between the completion of the *Rougon-Macquart* chronicle and the end of his life none, to my knowledge, are now available in popular editions in any language.

That *Lourdes* came to be written at all was something of an accident. In September 1891, Zola and Alexandrine were travelling in the Basque country in south-west France and among the resorts of the Pyrenees slopes, near the Spanish border. A visit to Lourdes was included in the tour and the couple arrived there late one night, during a fierce storm. They had difficulty finding a room, which didn't improve the novelist's temper, and he resolved to leave first thing in the morning. But, after breakfast, while taking a brief stroll before departing, he was so moved by the spectacle of thousands of invalids and sick children, all drawn to the image of the Virgin in a mass profession of blind faith, that he spent the following two nights writing down his impressions.

Lourdes is, of course, famous as a place of pilgrimage, to which three million pilgrims still trek every year to visit the Grotto, with its miraculous spring, discovered in 1858 through the visions of a shepherdess named Bernadette

Soubirous. At the time of Zola's visit the country was in the grip of a religious revival, and the concentration of thousands of credulous faces, the emotional prayer meetings and torchlight processions, not to mention the bargain-basement activity in holy water and statuettes, made a profound impression upon him. If ever a book was asking to be written, it was a novel about the pilgrimage to Lourdes.

Zola, however, had missed the great national pilgrimage, which takes place in August each year, so he decided to return in 1892. During the interim he drew up plans for what, on the basis of the material, promised to be one of his best novels, despite the fact that he was still at work writing *The Debacle*, attending to his mistress and two children and suffering from the most dire kind of domestic strife. Alexandrine had by now discovered that her husband had been running a second home.

The philosophical theme for the new novel was ready-made; in fact it would carry on where *Doctor Pascal* left off. In that novel Clotilde undergoes a conversion in reverse, from religious mysticism to agnosticism, though not without doubts and not without regret for the comforts of her former faith. Her plight mirrors, in many ways, the conflict between religion and science which was raging on a national scale in late-nineteenth-century France. Rational thinking had long dominated intellectual discussion, which had made the creation and acceptance of naturalism possible. But now the Christian faith, shorn of dogma and corrupting associations, began to have some appeal, even to intellectuals. Pope Leo XIII was making increasingly successful overtures to France to lessen anti-Catholic bias, especially in government quarters. The strategy was to unite the monarchical and right-wing political groups, which was viewed as a disastrous prospect by the rationalist- and socialist-thinking sections of the population. By 1890 even the diverse groups of symbolists and mystics had added their voices to the pro-religious faction, and altogether they presented a persuasive and influential front against those who believed in the omnipotence of science. Notwithstanding that naturalism was fast expiring as a doctrine of some consequence, Zola decided to fight a rear-guard battle with *Lourdes*.

It had been many years since the novelist had engaged in public combat and now all his fighting instincts returned. The following August he went down to Lourdes again, this time accompanying the pilgrims during the five-day event, and staying a further two weeks to complete his notes. He was sceptical, of course, but seems to have gone to great trouble to try and locate genuine miracles and cures. After interviewing dozens of pilgrims he failed to discover any miracles, but did find people who claimed to have been cured by the waters of the shrine. For the most part, however, these cured people turned out to be cases of mistaken diagnosis; a person with the symptoms of heart trouble, but who in fact merely had acute nervous indigestion, could conceivably be cured by a combination of faith, relaxation and a change of diet. Swellings which had been diagnosed as suspected tumours, and which had driven their owners into a state of mortal terror, often cleared up of their own accord; and, profoundly relieved, the patients were bound to attribute their cures to the miracle water rather than admit they weren't really ill in the first place. It is possible that Zola had been to some extent carried away by the emotionalism he had witnessed during his first visit to Lourdes; indeed, a story got around that he had returned to be converted. In the event he resisted the extremes of scepticism and blind acceptance and during his second stay appears to have been the detached observer. This is reflected in the novel, which is anything but unfair to the church. All the pilgrim sufferers in *Lourdes* were actual cases examined by the author, with only the names changed to protect the injured. There is no evidence that the emotional climate of the town had any effect on Zola's dogged atheism, but one of the first things he did after his arrival there was to send a bottle of water from the Grotto to Paul Alexis, whose eyesight was failing.

'Lourdes, the Grotto, the cures, the miracles, are, indeed, the creation of that need of the Lie [Zola wrote in 1894]. When little Bernadette came with her strange story of what she had witnessed, everybody was against her... but Lourdes grew up in spite of all opposition, just as the Christian religion did, because suffering humanity in its despair must cling to something, must have some hope; and, on the other hand, because humanity thirsts after illusions. In a word, it is the story of the foundation of all religions.'

Lourdes is also a story of how the gullible are exploited. Religious technology then wasn't up to bleeding Christs in 3-D but the profits made by the Fathers of the Grotto from the sale of devotional gimcrackery was almost a miracle in itself:

But the rows of shops began again in the Avenue de la Grotte. They swarmed on both sides; and among them here were jewellers, drapers, and umbrella-makers, who also dealt in religious articles. There was even a confectioner who sold boxes of pastilles *à l'eau de Lourdes*, with a figure of the Virgin on the cover. A photographer's windows were crammed with views of the Grotto and the Basilica, and portraits of Bishops and reverend Fathers of all Orders, mixed up with views of famous sites in the neighbouring mountains.... And it seemed as if there would never be a finish to the statuettes, the medals, and the chaplets; one display followed another; and, indeed, there were miles of them running through the streets of the entire town, which was ever the same bazaar selling the same articles.   (92)

The hero of *Lourdes* is a young priest, Pierre Froment, in whose mind the conflict between reason and faith tries to resolve itself. Pierre is a priest only because his devout widowed mother wished it. It is not until after her death that Pierre discovers the kind of man his father was – not the God-fearing chemist who was killed by an explosion in his laboratory, but a real seeker after truth. Reading through his books and papers, Pierre is struck by the logical order of science, based on a pyramid of proven facts:

Truth was bubbling up and overflowing in such an irresible stream that he realised he would never succeed in lodging error in his brain again. It was the total and irreparable ruin of faith. Although he had been able to kill his flesh by renouncing the romance of his youth, although he felt he had totally mastered carnal passion, he knew now that it would be impossible for him to make the sacrifice of his intelligence.

315

It is this revelatory experience that drives him to Lourdes, a priest who is no longer a believer. There he hopes to find the truth about Bernadette, and to be convinced that the cures effected at the Grotto are truly supernatural; it is the only way in which he can restore his lost faith.

The theme of a priest's search for faith and truth, and hoping to find both, draws its source from the central plot of the novel which is all but buried in documentary material. Pierre's friend from childhood, Marie de Guersaint, is also a pilgrim in Lourdes. Injured by a fall from a horse when fifteen, Marie is an invalid, unable to walk, and is convinced she will be cured by praying at the sacred Grotto. Pierre, however, hears a medical opinion from a doctor he respects, that Marie's paralysis of the legs is a neurotic condition and not organic, and predicts that some shock, some change of mental state – of the kind she might experience at Lourdes – will be sufficient to relax the cramped muscles to enable her to walk. Sure enough, after a night at the Grotto, Marie staggers cured from her wheelchair, convinced it is the result of a miracle. Pierre, of course, is aware of a less supernatural explanation, and his faith remains as wobbly as ever. And worse: Pierre loves Marie but now, in gratitude for the miracle, she vows she belongs to God and will never give herself to any mortal man. Pierre loses out on both counts.

The national pilgrimage to Lourdes occupies five days, and Zola divides the novel into five parts, one for each day. Each of these parts is also divided into five chapters, which was exactly the form of construction used in *A Love Episode*. The similarity extends to each fifth chapter, too; in the earlier novel these are given over to different descriptive views of Paris, while in *Lourdes* the fifth chapters deal with episodes in the life of the visionary, Bernadette Soubirous.

To infuse life into the documentary content of the novel, Zola introduces a number of sub-plots, each dealing with a group of pilgrims who all have different reasons for coming to Lourdes. Many are ill and dying and hope to be cured but others seek a quite different kind of relief, like childless Mme Désagneux who desires fertility; like Mme de Jonquière, who comes to pray for a suitable husband for her daughter; like the Vignerons, a family which includes a dying son and a rich aunt with heart disease. Their request to Our Lady of Lourdes is that the aunt should die first so that her fortune will go to their son and thus, on his imminent death, to them. And then there is Mme Volmar, who arrives each August to spend her entire stay in a hotel room ostensibly because of fatigue; the truth is that the pilgrimage is an annual opportunity to spend three days and nights in devotional seclusion with her lover. Altogether there are some ninety characters weaving in and out of the dense narrative, a density that is heightened by Zola's frequent descriptions of the crowds assembled in the town. His mastery over mass movement and emotion is as undiminished as ever, whether he is describing the haunting misery of the 'white trains' that bring the sick and dying to Lourdes, or the scalp-tingling thrill of the torchlight processions. The so-called 'procession of ailments' stands with the symphony of the cheeses in *The Belly of Paris* as a *tour*

316

de force of lyrical description, despite the nightmarish subject. Zola uses every trick he knows to make it an interesting novel. To add zip to the interminable explanatory passages he uses the 'interview' technique, enabling Pierre (and the reader) to listen as a journalist quizzes a doctor at the Bureau of Verifications, where all the cures are registered. Then there is the horror – and Zola knows how to pile it on. A sick boy watches as priests dip a corpse into the Grotto pond in the hope it will come to life. He attempts to outdo the spontaneously combustible Antoine Macquart in *Doctor Pascal* by inventing a woman whose body is slowly liquefying.

Lourdes was an immensely popular book when it came out in August 1894, after being serialised in *Le Gil Blas,* and some 200,000 copies were sold within a few years. Critical acclaim poured over it like treacle. 'A great and notable book!' said the London *National Observer.* 'The glory of the book is the inexhaustible, overflowing human sympathy which transfuses it from end to end.' The London *Graphic* noted that '*Lourdes* marks a breaking away from orthodox Zolaism and is at the same time the most perfect specimen of literary art yet produced by M. Zola. . . a model of powerful and poetic narrative.' With the newspapers saying things like that the novelist must have begun to be alarmed, although his doubts were mollified to some extent when the novel was smartly placed in the Index of prohibited books by the ecclesiastical authorities in the Vatican. Although he could hardly expect to be surprised at this – also prohibited were all his other books – Zola made a great fuss and spoke of his intention, in September 1894, of seeking an audience with the Pope to resolve the misunderstanding.

Why, then, isn't *Lourdes* read today? With its potentially explosive ingredients, it should be ticking away like a time bomb, even after all these years. The trouble is that despite the proliferation of characters, the swirling, nervous crowds and the fascinating conflict between the sacred and secular activities, the narrative has lead boots, with one foot anchored firmly in a single location, Lourdes, and the other, equally immobile, in Pierre Froment's mind. It is a little like being confined to a dreary little holiday hotel for days on end because of bad weather; even though we are in the company of a raconteur who desperately tries to entertain us, it isn't what we came for. This static feeling might have been relieved by the doubting priest, but his interior monologues lack conviction. Perhaps some of this is due to our knowing too well the author's beliefs and intentions in advance; however subtle his methods in *Lourdes,* however detached his documentation, we are well aware that Zola uses the novel form as an instrument to preach against established religion, often in the most artful, most telling way – the rushed and garbled Nuptial Mass in *L'Assommoir* for instance, or the sorry, deserted church in *Germinal,* or the burial service in *The Masterpiece,* rendered inaudible, and presumably ineffective, by a passing railway train. Zola generally let his priests discredit themselves, and the indifference of the population discredit the church. So, at last, in *Lourdes,* the master meets his match; we refuse to be tricked again, and at no time do we really believe that the doubting Pierre will find his lost faith.

And, as it turns out, he remains a doubter, his conflict destined to be resolved in Zola's next novel.

Soon after he had begun to write *Lourdes*, Zola's instinctive need for a large framework in which to express himself began to manifest itself through his hero, the Abbé Pierre Froment. *Lourdes* came to be written by sheer chance, and Froment was created exclusively for that novel. But Zola very quickly saw all kinds of possibilities with a priest as his fictional puppet, only one of which was explored in *Lourdes*. Froment was henceforth to become the novelist's mouthpiece through two more novels which would make up *Les Trois Villes* – the *Three Cities* trilogy; reason would triumph over religious mysticism, and Froment would marry to have four sons, who would be the central characters of four more novels, way into the future. Zola seemed unable to exist without a view of some distant, visionary horizon, or without creating for himself some vast and crushing burden.

The burden seemed bearable, however, as Zola and Alexandrine lightheartedly left Médan for Rome on a six-week working holiday at the end of October 1894. Although of Italian descent Zola had visited the country of his forbears only once, two years previously, when on the spur of the moment he had taken a two-day excursion from Monte Carlo to Genoa. As a famous figure he had expected to be recognised but was not quite prepared for the flattering attentions of the press and the enthusiastic welcome he'd received from the city dignitaries. The occasion convinced him that he should plan a longer visit in the near future.

Now, the visit had a specific purpose: to provide material for his new novel, *Rome*, the draft for which he carried in his baggage. He also carried with him a letter from Goncourt, whose cousin was Count de Béhaine, the French ambassador to the Vatican. Zola had already made public his intention to seek an audience with the Pope, but as the date of his departure drew near he grew increasingly hesitant; after all, he had already drafted the outline of the novel in which the church was painted as an anachronistic, unyielding institution. If, by the remotest chance it yielded to him, a writer who over many years had attacked it and whose works it banned, he was certainly bound to make extensive revisions, not only to the novel but in his own thinking. As it turned out, neither novelist nor Pope was embarrassed. One audience which did eventuate, though, was the one with Zola's cousin, Carlo Zola, in Venice, where his father was born. This was the only contact the novelist ever had with his father's family.

Interestingly, while in Rome, Zola was a frequent visitor at the French Embassy, and one day arrived to find the staff in a state of excitement over what was to become one of the biggest political hot potatoes of all time. On 15 October, two weeks before Zola had left France, a Captain Dreyfus had been arrested on a charge of high treason, news of which broke on 1 November in the *Libre Parole*. Zola had never heard of the man, and ironically evinced no interest. Instead he left the Embassy with the single-minded purpose of making as many notes and observations on the city as he could in the few weeks that remained of his holiday; 400 closely-written pages of them.

> Sometimes there are masses of blood-red clouds, battles of giants hurling mountains at one another and dying, crushed beneath the ruins of flaming cities. Sometimes only crimson streaks and fissures shimmer on the surface of a sombre lake, as though a net of light had been flung to fish the drowning orb from the threatening ethereal seaweed. Sometimes, too, there is a rosy mist, a kind of delicate dust which falls, streaked with pearls by a distant shower, drawn like a curtain across the mystery of the horizon. And sometimes there is a triumph, a cortège of gold and purple chariots of cloud rolling along a highway of fire, galleys floating on an azure sea, fantastic and extravagant pomps slowly sinking into the darkening abyss of twilight.

That was how Pierre Froment, in the novel, sees the sun setting behind St Peter's, and there are many more descriptive passages like it, perhaps too many, perhaps too purple. With some accuracy, Huysmans described the novel as 'a living encyclopaedia of Rome'; on the other hand Henry James called it a novel of 'inflated hollowness'.

Rome is a long, wide-ranging and complex novel with more merits, I think, than deficiencies. The problem for the modern reader is that it suffers from a marked loss of topicality, a fate that awaits many excellent novels written today. Its historical background, vital then, is irrelevant now: Pope Leo XIII's emerging social conscience, which brought about the establishment of Catholic trade unions. This encourages Pierre Froment, our hero of Lourdes, to publish a book suggesting that the Pope leads the emerging social movements in Europe. Pierre, since we last saw him, has been exposed to the deprivation and vice of the Paris slum districts, and from his experiences has evolved a new, humanitarian-orientated Christianity. Nevertheless he is branded a heretic and his book is threatened with supression by the Vatican authorities. To defend his cause he journeys to Rome to appeal personally to the Pope and, more fortunate than his author, Pierre is granted an audience, although he fails to win papal support.

What is remarkable is Zola's whole account of this papal audience, considering that he neither managed to see the Pope nor penetrate the inner sanctums of the Vatican. But there it is, in super, living detail: Pierre's mysterious, nocturnal confrontation with the Pope in his bedroom, all re-created with stunning verisimilitude and entirely convincing. It is also dramatically successful, for it comes at the end of Pierre's long, Kafka-like mission through the convoluted layers of the Vatican hierarchy. It also follows the climax of the highly melodramatic and improbable sub-plot of the novel, an allegory loosely based on the Pyramus and Thisbe myth, in which two lovers, Benedetta and her cousin Dario, expire together. Benedetta has been the victim of an arranged marriage, but wins her freedom by having the marriage dissolved on the grounds of non-consummation. Unfortunately, before she can marry her lover Dario, he is accidentally poisoned; and just as he dies Benedetta flings herself into his arms in a kind of symbolic consummation. It is

319

worth reading if only because it must be the most un-naturalist passage Zola ever wrote:

> She stepped back to the dying man, and touched him: 'Here I am, my Dario, here I am!'
> Then came the apogee. Amidst growing exaltation, buoyed up by a blaze of love, careless of glances, candid like a lily, she divested herself of her garments and stood forth so white, that neither marble statue, nor dove, nor snow itself was ever whiter. 'Here I am, my Dario, here I am!'
> Recoiling almost to the ground as at sight of an apparition, the glorious flash of a holy vision, Pierre and Victorine gazed at her with dazzled eyes. The servant had not stirred to prevent this extraordinary action, seized as she was with that shrinking reverential terror which comes upon one in presence of the wild, mad deeds of faith and passion. And the priest whose limbs were paralysed felt that something so sublime was passing that he could only quiver in distraction. And no thought of impurity came to him on beholding that lily, snowy whiteness. All candour and all nobility as she was, that virgin shocked him no more than some sculptured masterpiece of genius.
> 'Here I am, my Dario, here I am.'
> She had lain herself down beside the spouse whom she had chosen, she had clasped the dying man whose arms only had enough strength left to fold themselves around her. Death was stealing him from her, but she would go with him; and again she murmured: 'My Dario, here I am.'
> For a second, which seemed an eternity, they clasped one another, she neither repelled nor terrified by the disorder which made him so unrecognisable, but displaying a delirious passion, a holy frenzy as if to pass beyond life, to penetrate with him into the black Unknown. And beneath the shock of the felicity at last offered to him he expired, with his arms yet convulsively wound around her as though indeed to carry her off. Then, whether from grief or from bliss amidst that embrace of death, there came such a rush of blood to her heart that the organ burst: she died on her lover's neck, both tightly and for ever clasped in one another's arms.
> There was a faint sigh. Victorine understood and drew near, while Pierre, also erect, remained quivering with the tearful admiration of one who has beheld the sublime.
> 'Look, look!' whispered the servant, 'she no longer moves, she no longer breathes. Ah! my poor child, my poor child, she is dead!'
> Then the priest murmured: 'Oh! God, how beautiful they are.' (93)

It's amazing how Zola's death-kiss syndrome persists, even after his liberating affair with Jeanne. This fantasy that love must prove fatal is a frequent theme of his novels: Serge's passion for Albine in *The Abbé Mouret's Sin* results in her death; in *Germinal* Catherine dies in the arms of Etienne after consummating their love; and, more dramatically, in *The Dream*, when Angélique dies suddenly as she emerges from the church after the marriage ceremony. But in *Rome*, Benedetta's final flourish is little more than an unconvincing incident, a melodramatic anecdote in a work with far wider horizons. The Roman Catholic Church is thrashed unmercifully in the novel, and not surprisingly it sparked off spirited controversies wherever it was published. It was serialised in Paris, in *Le Journal*, from December 1895, and also in Rome, where it met with a cool reception from almost every section of Italian society. The cause of this was because of the novel's anti-church bias certainly, but few readers could have enjoyed Zola's acute and sometimes stinging observations on Italian life. Predictably, within weeks, *Rome* joined the novelist's other books on the Catholic Index.

Victor Hugo came within an ace of predicting the European Economic Community when he wrote: 'In the twentieth century there will be an extraordinary nation... illustrious, wealthy, thoughtful, pacific, cordial to the rest of mankind... and the capital of this nation will be Paris, but its country will not be known as France.' This was also Zola's dream, a utopian dream of Paris as the universal city of enlightenment, achieved through science and humanitarian socialism.

If the last novel in the *Three Cities* trilogy had appeared, less its characters and without its dramatic and idealistic elements, *Paris* could be alive and well today as a memoir of a great city written by a man who loved it and knew it perhaps more than any other single Frenchman. Only Zola could have attempted the task of portraying the epic immensity of Paris and its people, its beauties and its foibles, its moods, its kaleidoscopic variety, with any chance of succeeding. As a portrait of Paris the book is a triumph; as a novel it is a failure.

At the outset, however, Zola was enthusiastic about the prospects for the novel, for it would chronicle Pierre Froment's final escape from the irrational dogma of the church to the more enlightened haven of compassionate socialism. His researching for the novel took the form of happy outings with Jeanne and the children, during which he made his usual notes and, for the first time, took photographs. This is an indication of the journalistic path his fiction was taking, for *Paris* is full of reportage of contemporary events and the unaltered portraits of prominent people. While this technique is not inadmissible there is, in this case, the suspicion that Zola's imaginative resources are running dry, for the novel also resounds with the dulled echoes of many characters and incidents featured in previous books. Even the construction repeats the five-part, five-chapter format of *A Love Episode* and *Lourdes* which can only be put down to idiosyncrasy or sheer lack of invention.

For those of Zola's readers who were following the massive instalments of the trilogy – and they must have numbered millions at this time – Pierre Froment is ultimately expelled from the church to pursue his humanitarian path to salvation alone; although not quite alone, for he marries his childhood sweetheart Marie, the cured cripple in *Lourdes*. *The Times* saw the novel as a 'scathing satire'; the *Daily Graphic* saw it as 'the work of a rigid moralist'; but most reviewers tended to brush aside the message and melodrama to praise the novel's quality as a panorama of Paris, of which the notice in the *Liverpool Mercury* is typical: 'He paints with relentless realism the darkest shades of life in Paris, corrupt in its politics, venal in its journalism, vicious in its higher ranks, savage and suffering in its lower strata.'

The novels in the *Three Cities* trilogy clearly display their author's departure from creative writing to a preoccupation with social and political problems and their solutions. Breaking a four-year rule, he had returned to journalism, writing regular articles for *Le Figaro* on every topic except literature. Zola had never been unaware of social injustice but from *Lourdes* onwards he is a committed writer. Some of the blame for this can be traced back to *L'Assommoir*, his great masterpiece of sympathetic detachment, for it was this novel that first aroused the international interest and criticism of socialists and Marxists. However thoroughly Zola had researched the various aspects of government, industry, commerce and the other social institutions his novels dealt with, he had a blind spot when it came to the theories and programmes of the Left, and even the trade union movement. In *Money*, for example, he had set out to create in the character Sigismond an orthodox Marxist without, it appears, any understanding of dialectical materialism, a weakness that was pointed out in a review of the novel by none other than Marx's son-in-law, Paul Lafargue. Zola's muddled thinking about socialist solutions is even more murky in the trilogy. One can understand his impatience to see some progress made towards social justice for the workers and the dispossessed; it was twenty years since *L'Assommoir* and ten years since *Germinal* appeared, and France in Zola's eyes was still stubbornly resisting the way to his utopian dream. The answer, as he saw it, was to explore economic and social remedies and to confront his hundreds of thousands of readers with them in an attempt to produce action. Despite the loss to literature this might have been beneficial to the nation and perhaps to the world had his ideas been less confused. At the base of this confusion was the novelist's unyielding belief in the revolutionary potential of science. 'Human happiness can only spring from the furnace of the scientist,' he wrote in *Paris*. This was as illogical as the Cargo Cult of New Guinea, where, after watching aircraft landing at airports to discharge their cargoes, the natives returned to their mountain villages with the conviction that all they had to do was to build crude runways to attract these creatures, loaded with goodies, down from the skies. Commenting on *Paris*, the socialist leader Auguste Jaurès wrote that Zola was misled: 'Science makes possible new shapes for society, but does no more.' The brilliant young critic Léon Blum agreed with Zola that the ideal was to be found in life itself and not outside it, but saw dangers in a philosophy that complacently waited for science to renovate society: 'We must love and respect science, and look to it for everything,' he wrote, 'but not to it alone... if we do not refashion the traditional order of society, the very advance of science will serve to promote injustice and propagate iniquity.' They were prophetic words indeed.

As for Zola's hoped-for audience with Pope Leo XIII, it never did eventuate, although his existence was acknowledged. 'Zola was an enemy of the church,' Leo commented years later, 'but he was a frank and honest adversary. May his soul repose in Heaven...'

Our exploration of *Les Quatre Evangiles* – or *The Four Gospels* – will be done at speed for fear of being bogged down, because we are now indeed in Henry James's 'deep desert sand'. Even Zola himself recognised that this group of novels had little to do with literature when he wrote in 1901 to Ernest Vizetelly that

> I am writing these books with a certain purpose before me, a purpose in which the question of form is of secondary importance. I have no intention of trying to amuse people or thrill them with excitement. I am merely placing certain problems before

them, and suggesting in some respects certain solutions, showing what I hold to be wrong and what I think would be right.

On another occasion he answered a critic by pleading: 'Have I not the right, after forty years of analysis, to end with a little synthesis?'

The themes of the *Three Cities* trilogy novels had been Faith, Hope and Charity, so it is not surprising to find an evangelical element in the construction of his tetralogy. The themes of the four books were to be *Fécondité*, or *Fruitfulness*; *Travail*, or *Labour*; *Verité*, or *Truth*; and *Justice*; and the four character-heroes who would do the preaching and redeeming were to be Pierre Froment's four sons, named after the Gospel evangelists: Matthieu, Marc, Luc and Jean. Zola's intention was to write 'a poem in four volumes, in four chants, in which I shall endeavour to sum up the philosophy of all my work'. While writing them Zola must have imagined himself as a poetic tetramorph, a saviour of the twentieth century, for more than a few passages are intentionally couched in biblical language. At about the same time, too, the novelist took to wearing a velvet coat which, when buttoned to the neck, as it often was, gave him the solemnity of a monk.

Fruitfulness, the first book in this series, has its deepest sources in Zola's guilt-feeling about the purpose of the sexual act which was expressed earlier in *Doctor Pascal*: that sex for any reason other than procreation is inadmissible. This guilt was miraculously removed, however, when Jeanne Rozerot became pregnant, as we have seen.

Nevertheless, this personal experience was not the only inspiration for *Fruitfulness*, for the novelist had for many years pondered over the falling birth-rate in France, and in May 1896, wrote an article on the subject for *Le Figaro*. In it he examined all the causes and influences which in his view had brought about the practice of limiting the size of families, from economic necessity and contraception to the idealisation of virginity. Significantly, he began the article on a personal note: 'For some ten years now I have been haunted by the idea of a novel, although I doubt I will ever write the first page... that novel would have been called *Waste*.' Zola's meditations on the nobility of fertility seem to have been unbroken between *Doctor Pascal* and *Fruitfulness*, for several months of 1896 were taken up with composing the libretto for a lyric drama, *Messidor* – which is also the name of the tenth, or harvest month, in the Revolutionary calendar. Collaborating with Alfred Bruneau the play leaned heavily on symbolism to praise the glories of fertility, and opened successfully at *l'Opéra* in Paris on 19 February 1897. And again, in the *Three Cities* trilogy, Zola's choice of surname for his hero surely has significance, for Froment means 'wheat', a common symbol for harvest and fertility.

Then there was the related bogey of promiscuity. For many years Zola had been obsessed with the idea that a society given to promiscuity and loose morals would inevitably destroy itself, and the theory provided the themes for two of the *Rougon-Macquart* novels, *Nana* and *Piping Hot!* The impulse behind this theory sprang then from vague moralistic notions, in turn a product of Zola's own sexual ambivalence and his personal distaste for promiscuity. He could never arrive at an acceptable dividing-line between valid sexual freedom and indiscriminate sexual activity. In *Fruitfulness*, however, he props the theory up with material evidence, but of a quite different kind: that there existed a correlation between promiscuity and families with few children or none at all. If this was so, Zola reasoned, a promiscuous society would breed – or not breed – itself out of existence.

Rome is the only one of Zola's novels to be set in a country other than France; *Fruitfulness* is the only one written in a foreign country. Before his flight from Paris to England and the threat of imprisonment over the Dreyfus trial, the novelist had made preparatory notes for the new book; and in August 1898, with Ernest Vizetelly's help, established himself in a house in Surrey, between Esher and Chertsey, to begin writing. Later he moved to an apartment in the Queen's Hotel at Norwood, finishing the work ten months later, at the end of May 1899, just before his return to France.

The English weather has been blamed for many things but to hold it responsible, as Angus Wilson does – along with Victorian Sundays, the Sydenham Salvation Army Band and suet puddings – for the 'dreariness' of *Fruitfulness*, is perhaps going too far. Even so, the difficulties under which Zola laboured can be imagined. Away from his wife, Jeanne and his children, severed from familiar surroundings, and particularly his desk, always laid out with the precision of a cemetery, and with the shadows of crushing legal expenses constantly with him, one can only wonder at the tone of joyous optimism which flows through the pages of *Fruitfulness*.

None of this, however, can excuse Zola's debasement of the novel form, for if the temperance moralisers had edited and rewritten *L'Assommoir* as a tract for the times, he saved the anti-contraception lobby the trouble with *Fruitfulness*. It is a sermon with the trappings of realism, but even the novel's tenuous grip on reality loosens as the narrative proceeds. The hero is Mathieu Froment who lives in the country with his wife, Marthe, and their twelve children. They are a robust, honest couple, deriving their happiness from their prolific progeny which multiplies in such biblical proportions that at the end of the novel, when Mathieu is ninety, there are some 200 direct descendants living, scattered far and wide, and breeding as a patriotic duty to France. If there are occasional visitations of disaster and death it doesn't matter in the quantitative sense, for big families like Mathieu's can easily sustain misfortune. On the other hand the half-dozen families in the novel who limit their offspring are subjected to the most dire punishments. One couple, the Beauchênes, are careful to have only one child, so that their prosperous business can be passed on to him intact; ominously, the child dies first, leaving them heirless. A relative with nymphomaniac tendencies has herself sterilised to avoid pregnancy, and goes mad in a spectacular manner. Another couple put off having a child until it is too late; the resultant frustration and distress cause the husband to go blind. Two women who have pregnancies terminated die at the hands of the abortionists. And so on. God knows what sort of punishment Zola would have meted out to a childless masturbator.

At the time, Zola believed it was his solemn duty to drive home to the people of France his message, *Copulate to Populate – or Perish*! With the benefit of hindsight we can now see, of course, that he was barking up the wrong tree. That French influence is still important in the world owes everything to the country's unique contributions in the fields of art and literature, digestion and science, and nothing to the theory of global conquest by mere numbers. Curiously, though, the novel was a critical hit in 1899; almost without exception the reviews, especially in England, were extravagant with praise, even adulatory. *L'Aurore* found it 'difficult to conceive of a more reassuring, more inspiring, more elevating poem' – although it must be admitted that the paper was owned by Zola's close friend, Georges Clemenceau. *The Times* found in the book passages 'among the most eloquent he has ever penned', while the reviewer for the *Sunday Sun* fell on his knees to proclaim, 'I am glad and proud of the privilege of publicly thanking a man of lofty genius for a great and living book.' Ironically, however, the critical praise did nothing for the sales of Zola's books, which had slumped alarmingly, the direct result of his unpopular stand in the Dreyfus Affair. And he must have known, privately, that critical acceptance, for him, was a sure indication of mediocrity. The only common ground the novelist ever found with the Roman Catholic Church was a literary wasteland.

When Zola was preparing his notes for *Earth* in 1886 he interviewed one of the leading socialists of the time, Jules Guesde, in order to brush up on Marxist theories on agrarian reform. One of the socialist's predictions persisted in his mind: that of a society in which science and mechanisation would practically remove the need for human labour. The utopian aspects of socialism were the ones which appealed to the novelist, who abhorred the idea of revolutionary violence and who could not, or would not, grasp the significance of the class struggle in modern socialist thinking. One can therefore understand the attractions of Fourierism to Zola, which, hinted at in *The Ladies' Paradise*, becomes the ideological basis for the second novel in the *Four Gospels* tetralogy, *Labour*, published in 1901.

Zola's kind of Utopia had been elaborately devised at the beginning the century by François Fourier who envisaged a society living in harmony with its environment, its needs and its passions, by means of the principle of cooperation. Of prime importance in Fourier's plan was the removal of unnatural restraints on the human passions, for only in this way could the full and free development of human nature take place. Economically, the community would be divided into *phalanges* of 1,600 people who would be as self-supporting as possible, and contribute labour and talent for communal benefit. Unworkable as they sound, Fourier's ideas did attract a following and a number of communities were actually set up according to his principles; one of them, Brook Farm in Massachusetts, provided the background to Nathaniel

Hawthorne's novel, *The Blithedale Romance*. At the close of the century in France, Fourier's theories were still kept alive by a hard-core group of disciples, but it should have been clear to anyone of Zola's intelligence that they were, at best, utopian dreams with no place in the development of a modern socialist society. This blind spot in the novelist's understanding of the realities of social reform was possibly due not so much to ignorance and stubbornness but, as with many of his beliefs, to deeply personal considerations. For one thing Fourierism justified work, which Zola held sacred. At a publisher's party to celebrate the conclusion of the *Rougon-Macquart* chronicle, to which the famous and the fashionable came to toast the novelist, Zola could think of nothing to toast in reply, except 'work'. 'To work!' he announced. 'To true happiness, which lies in Work!' Fourierism also justified his relationship with Jeanne; and in *Labour* the inhabitants of Zola's idealised city all indulge in free love. The hero, Luc Froment, has *three* women, Josine, Sœurette and Suzanne. The book in fact, is an absolute orgy of joyous love, and Zola was enthusiastically preaching the message *All You Need Is Love* more than half a century before the Beatles.

For those who manage to swim through the treacly lagoon of Zola's idealism *Labour* has a few rewarding aspects, not the least of which is that it provides an imaginative exploration of the utopian dream. Luc Froment arrives at the ghastly steel manufacturing town of Beauclair, which is paralysed by a bitter strike. Inspired by the doctrines of Fourier, Luc wins the cooperation of the workers and establishes a new factory, and after many tribulations, a new city, La Crècherie – a veritable paradise of two hours' work a day, free love, sweetness and health, serene old age and death without sorrow. Some of the writing and characterisation manages to free itself from the bog to which the novelist is committed, and the early chapters in particular, describing the grim lives of the townsfolk, are reminiscent of the finest passages in *Germinal*.

Also interesting is the predictive element in *Labour*. Forgetting that, like a mule, human nature is just as likely to stand still or even regress as fast as technology marches forward, Zola's idyll of cooperation closes optimistically in the mid-twentieth century. Alas, we look around in vain about us to find anything like La Crècherie; and today, his dream, projected from the pages of the novel in 1901, tends to arouse only cynicism. On the other hand, through the memory of Josine in old age, Zola does predict with considerable insight the revolution in a 'great republic' (which he doesn't name, however) and its aftermath: the confiscation of private property, the collectivisation of labour the bloody repression, and the creation of an even less efficient bureaucracy than before. He also predicts World War I with similar accuracy, although in the most important respect he was sadly wrong:

> No nation had been able to resist the impulse; they were drawn into it by others, they drew up in line, two great armies burning with race hatreds, resolved to annihilate each other, as if in their empty and uncultivated fields where there were two men at work there was one too many. And two great armies of brothers turned to foes met somewhere in the centre of Europe upon vast plains where millions o

human beings conveniently could slay each other. The troops spread out over miles and miles, followed by their reserves, such a torrent of men that the fighting lasted for a month. Every day more human flesh was food for bullets and bombs. They even did not have time to carry off the dead. Heaps of bodies served as walls, behind which fresh regiments fought and were killed. Night did not stay the carnage; they killed each other in the darkness. The sun, as it rose each day, shone upon pools of blood, on a field of carnage covered with stacks of dead. There was a roar like thunder everywhere, and whole regiments seemed to disappear in a flash. The men who fought had no need to draw near each other, since cannon threw their shells for miles, and each of such shells swept bare an acre of the earth, poisoning and asphyxiating the very heavens. Balloons, too, sent down balls and bombs to set fire to the cities. Science had invented fresh explosives, murderous engines able to carry death to enormous distances, or to swallow many people at once, like an earthquake. And what a monstrous massacre took place on the last night of that tremendous battle! Never had such a human sacrifice smoked under heaven. More than a million men lay there in the great devastated fields, beside the rivers, and scattered over the meadows. A man could have walked for hours, seeing everywhere a harvest of dead bodies, lying with staring eyes and open mouths, seeming to reproach men for their madness. This was the world's last battle, so completely had its horrors impressed mankind. People woke up from their mad intoxication, and all felt the certainty that war was no longer possible, for science that was meant to make life prosperous was not to be employed in the work of death. (96)

After the completion of *Labour*, two books remained to be written to complete the *Four Gospels* tetralogy: *Truth* and *Justice*. Unfortunately, of *Justice*, only Zola's intentions exist, for he died just six weeks after completing the manuscript for the third novel. The theme of *Justice* was to have been the prevention of war, and it would have been enlightening to have had Zola's fictionalised ideas on the subject, adding flesh and life to the background of the Hague Peace Convention that had taken place in 1899. The Convention, which was organised by Czar Nicholas II of Russia, and attended by representatives from twenty-six countries, attempted to create the machinery for the peaceful settlement of international disputes, and called for the abolition of bombing from the air, poisonous gas and dum-dum bullets. Although partially successful it failed to bring about agreement on a reduction of armaments among European powers; ominously the subject was abandoned at the objections of the German military delegate. Zola had saved his greatest theme – international peace, based not on force but on universal justice – until too late. Unfortunately he was more mortal than messiah.

Truth, then, published posthumously in 1903, is Zola's last novel; an interesting though over-long recapitulation of the Dreyfus Affair tangled up with a ferocious attack on the Roman Catholic Church and the Christian religion. He began work on the book in July 1901, and appears to have written in some haste; Vizetelly, his English translator, complained that he had great difficulty in deciphering the last part: '...the proofs from which my translation was made contain some scarcely intelligible passages as well as various errors in names and facts.' By this time it is evident that the novelist is writing to formula. *Truth* again reveals a symmetrical construction – four parts, each divided into four chapters – while *Labour* had five chapters in each of its three parts. One feature of the book is, however, different from anything Zola had written before; there are many occasions in the narrative when you need to remind yourself you are not reading a pre-war detective pulp.

Throughout the years of the Dreyfus scandal, Zola steadfastly resisted the temptation to make any profit from his involvement with it. Nevertheless he was haunted by the national implications of the conspiracy and it was inevitable that his pen would not be stilled forever. The solution, he found, was to take all the elements of the case and transpose them into another setting: a Catholic school. Dreyfus is fictionalised as Simon, a Jewish schoolmaster who is wrongly accused of the pederastic murder of a young schoolboy, his nephew Zéphirin. From that point the action almost exactly parallels the succession of deceits and injustices of the famous Affair. Zola's part is played by Pierre Froment's third son, Marc, who eventually uncovers the evidence which proves Simon' innocence; the bestial killer, he discovers, is one of the teaching monks at the boy's school.

The murdering monk symbolises everything that Zola was trying to say in this novel: that the church fosters ignorance, hinders the development of freedom and justice, and will stoop to anything, any crime, when its interest are threatened. In a word, the enemy of the Catholic Church is *Truth*.

That the novelist should be so vituperative towards the church in this, his final novel, has two key sources. He had long been a voluble critic of Catholic influence in French life, but his particular *bête noire* was Catholic education. This had been under attack by the government since 1870, but in the 1890s helped along by Pope Leo XIII's conciliatory attitude, Catholic schools were again making quiet progress. This came to an abrupt halt as the result of public reaction to the disclosure of the extent of Catholic power during the Dreyfus trials; among other revelations it became evident that the army was more loyal to Rome than to France. In a series of government measures between 1901 and 1904, 'unauthorised' (i.e. most Catholic) congregations were dissolved and their right to teach withdrawn, involving the closure of some 13,000 school and the transfer of a million and a half children to the state education system Zola had, in his last years, become increasingly interested in the role of education – Denise and Jacques were then going to school – and his views are expressed freely in the pages of *Truth*.

For the other sources of the violent anti-clerical tone of the novel we need look no further than the Dreyfus conspiracy itself. As the Affair grew into a national controversy, the guilt or innocence of the Jewish captain was more and more buried in a wider conflict between Republicans and Socialists on one side and the various right-wing groups on the other: the Catholics, the army and the Nationalists. Although there were enough exceptions to disprove the rule, the former tended to be pro-Dreyfus while the latter judged him guilty. Boiled down further, the anti-Catholics tended to believe Dreyfus was innocent, while the Catholics *tended* to believe he should stay on Devil's Island. In *Truth* Zola took this reduction a stage further; while the free-thinkers believe the Jewish schoolmaster is the victim of a conspiracy, the Catholics – as a body – insist he is guilty and deny him justice.

328

Few people picked up *Truth* at the time without associating the novel with the Dreyfus scandal, and no doubt Zola intended this for he makes little attempt to disguise characters and incidents; but identifying this classic miscarriage of justice as a purely Catholic conspiracy was nothing short of heavy-handed. That the church was responsible for grave abuses of its responsibility to educate children there can be no argument, but the target would have been deflated far more effectively by a few well-aimed arrows than by the indiscriminate mud-slinging in *Truth*.

The real extent of Zola's anti-clerical sentiments is indicated, I think, by the nature of the crime he invents for the murdering monk, Gorgias: the bestial rape and killing of a delicate, deformed young boy. It was obviously the worst crime the novelist could dream up, possibly with the help of distant echoes of the incident in which he was himself assaulted as a child. The technique of 'guilt by association' is, of course, the weapon of the demagogue and how effective it was is indicated in Vizetelly's preface to the English version of the novel: 'The horrible crime on which he bases part of his narrative... is one of the crimes springing from the unnatural lives led by those who have taken vows in the Roman Church...' It is sad to note that in his last book Zola reverted to a form of injustice he fought against for most of his life.

It is a great pity that Zola mixed polemic and fiction in these last two series of novels, for their themes are timeless and fundamental. There is evidence, too, that the craftsmanship and compassion are still there, but only in occasional flashes, for by now the author is committed to the view that his skills exist only to propagate his personal doctrines. Even at the end it cannot be claimed that Zola was deceiving himself, for he was, by his own admissions, fired with a self-imposed patriotic duty to France that pre-empted writing novels for mere art or entertainment. His time was short, and the world had to be instructed for survival.

So this marks the end of Emile Zola's career as a writer, and of a decade as a writer in sad decline. Even his autumnal career as the philosopher of optimism was to be revealed as having foundations of sand, for as he wrote the concluding lines of *Paris* towards the end of 1897 – '... *And Paris flared – Paris which the divine sun had sown with light, and where in glory waved the great future harvest of Truth and Justice...*', an event was taking place the outcome of which was to mock not only this ringing phrase, but to shatter the distorted mirror of his own illusions and make possible the uncharacteristic prejudice and hatred which stain some of the pages of *Truth*. This was the celebrated Dreyfus Affair to which many references have already been made. No account of Emile Zola's life is complete without an examination of this extraordinary and often misunderstood event, for as Professor F.W.J. Hemmings has said, 'The impact of the Dreyfus Affair on Zola was several times more powerful than the impact Zola made on the Affair.'

20

J'Accuse . . !

The Dreyfus Affair is such a well-known story, told and retold, the subject of a thousand articles and books, dramatised on the cinema and television screens, recycled as propaganda and still the cause of heated argument – that despite its deep relevance to Zola's life I hesitate to introduce a single word about it. Yet, paradoxically, ask a hundred people in the street what the Dreyfus case was really about and disappointingly few will be able to tell you. Even those familiar with the outline of the Affair, to whom Dreyfus is not a complete stranger, are often ignorant of its essence and lessons. In all this confusion, however, one echo emerges with greater clarity than any other: the link between Dreyfus and Emile Zola. But that is all. Again, the part played by the French author in the drama is shrouded in mist and myth. What I hope to accomplish in this chapter, then, is not a documentation of the incredible, complex and unprecedented legal and nationalistic battles which raged about Dreyfus (which may be read in Professor Guy Chapman's excellent *The Dreyfus Trials*) but an account of Zola's brave contribution to *L'Affaire* and the considerable effect it exercised on the novelist himself.

To make sense of the Dreyfus Affair at all, let alone understand its significance, then and now, it is necessary to examine the background events which precipitated this shattering, infamous miscarriage of justice.

Following its inglorious defeat in 1870 at the hands of the Prussians the morale of the French army was understandably at a low ebb, and one of the efforts it made to restore its wounded pride, and that of the nation, was to encourage the spirit of *Revanche*: a movement which looked forward to a day of revenge and the restoration to France of its lost border territories, Alsace and Lorraine. The German–Italian alliance was, even in peacetime, considered by the army as its active enemy; patriotism was reduced to 'hate thy neighbours'. By the 1890s the policy could have been considered a success. Alone among French institutions the army displayed a consistent, if blinkered, stability that stood inviolate in the face of economic disasters, changing governments, unemployment, revolutionary movements and threatened anarchy. The army represented authority.

In its efforts to reform itself into a modern fighting force, competition for the military secrets of Germany and Italy reached dizzy heights. This was the era of new developments in weaponry and fortification and the French army, which had suffered from the fatal lesson of 1870, established a network of spies and agents with the aim of keeping a concealed eye on the plans of its hostile neighbours. The other European powers did likewise, of course, so that, by the 1890s, a web of esponiage and counter-esponiage had been created that would have been beyond the belief of the most imaginative writer of spy stories. Because of the nature of the evidence which first convicted Captain Dreyfus and then brought about his release, it is important to know something of the methods of the various Military Intelligence sections. Leaks of information were not uncommon, nor were thefts of documents and plans from army offices. To confound one another it was the practice to manufacture false documents and arrange for them to be planted in such a way that they might be mistaken for the genuine article; inevitably confusion arose so that even genuine documents were regarded with suspicion. This forging was part and parcel of the activities of all the Intelligence sections.

The French army's Intelligence branch was known as the 'Second Bureau', but there was also another unit, a kind of M.I.6 with the cover name of 'Statistical Section', which maintained contact with civilian agents. This outfit was responsible only to the army Chief of Staff and its operations were never less than farcical. So much amateurism prevailed that it is dubious whether the Section had any idea which information was secret and vital and which was not, and which was the enemy's and which was their own. When photographic copies were made of a document no record was ever kept of the number, or to whom they were distributed; there was no proper registry of documents, nor was any record kept when a document was removed from the Section or returned. The only secret kept inviolate was whether the Statistical Section ever at any time performed any useful service. The head of this department was Colonel Sandherr, an Alsatian anti-Semite, who had joined it in 1886. Among his half-dozen assistants was Major Hubert-Joseph Henry, a veteran of the Algerian and Indo-China campaigns, audacious, ambitious, cunning and obstinate. Henry was to play one of the leading roles in the persecution of Dreyfus.

The army, at this time, was all-powerful, symbolising, as it did, the national aspirations of every patriotic Frenchman. To criticise the army – as Zola was accused of doing in *The Debacle* – was considered treason. Despite this, or because of it, the army was not short of enemies. As we have seen, the army was largely a creature of the Roman Catholics and surviving elements of the old aristocracy, which was a constant thorn in the side of the republican and leftist parties. That national security should be entrusted to members of a hierarchy who had been enemies of the Republic and who were devoted to the cause of returning the country to a monarchy, was the source of intense frustration to the government. So while the army was for the moment firmly in the saddle it was also conscious that its position could be undermined and rendered precarious. Sensitive to government and public criticism the army found its best defence in closing ranks; and from this fierce protective instinct to preserve its traditional autonomy arose one of the most disgraceful aspects of the whole Affair.

That anti-Semitism played a part in the arrest and persecution of Captain Dreyfus there is not the slightest doubt, although historians still argue the toss about its degree of importance. Prior to 1880 the Jewish community in France was small and self-effacing; outbreaks of anti-Semitism were rare. The Jewish inhabitants of Alsace and Lorraine, the provinces annexed by the Prussians in 1871, were indeed welcomed as new settlers to the rest of the country. Their families, after all, had been French nationals for many generations. The Dreyfus family was typical. They owned a prosperous cotton mill at Mulhouse in Alsace and were as patriotic as any Frenchman. After the war, of the four brothers and three sisters, all except two chose French citizenship rather than German. Two brothers, Mathieu and Jacques, stayed to run the mill, while the other two, Léon and Alfred, accompanied their sisters across the border to begin a new life in France. Alfred, then only thirteen years old, confirmed his patriotism ten years later by joining the army artillery, studying at the various officers' schools and emerging as a captain in the War Office in 1890.

By then, however, the forces of anti-Semitism had strengthened alarmingly – and vociferously. After the assassination of Czar Alexander II in 1881, anti-Semitism became state policy in Russia, and an endless wave of Jewish refugees poured out over Europe. Many of them settled in France, where their bedraggled appearance, and eventually their vast numbers, gave rise to disquiet and suspicion. With nothing but the rags on their backs and a few possessions, and without government assistance, their integration into French communities was not as speedy as it might have been, which made their presence all the more apparent. Many citizens saw these refugees as an evil, threatening horde.

They could hardly be blamed for this, for violent propagandists were at work. Characteristically, a country with more than its share of troubles tends to look outside, rather than inside, for their source, and the Jews had been, since the defeat of 1871, under a cloud of suspicion. In a series of financial scandals during the 1880s it became customary to look for the Jew, who was frequently found to be implicated. One exposure concerned the Panama Canal company, in which two Jewish financiers were bribing members of the Chamber of Deputies. The biggest scandal, however, was the victory of the Rothschild family over L'Union Générale, or the Christian Bank, established to counter the power of the Jewish-backed banks. By a combination of internal corruption and Rothschild manipulation it crashed, to the epic thunder of thousands of outraged and penniless investors. The story, thinly disguised, was told in Zola's novel, Money. These scandals fuelled the fires of anti-Semitism and ensured the staggering success of a Jew-baiting book by an opportunistic journalist named Edouard Drumont. Encouraged by the sight of copies being ordered in such quantities that the presses could barely keep up with the demand, Drumont founded, in 1892, the Libre Parole (Free Speech), a pro-Catholic newspaper in which all the threads of bigotry and jingoism were drawn together in a single, influential, raucous organ. It flourished from the first issue, and found just the sensational story it was looking for in the arrest of Captain Dreyfus.

If it were not for the tragic elements of the Affair I would be tempted, at this point, to suggest a little light relief, for we have to return to the Statistical Section and Major Henry. One of the major's duties was to monitor the communications to and from the German military attaché in Paris, Colonel Max von Schwartzkoppen. For some time it had been known that the German, and his Italian counterpart, Colonel Alessandro Panizzardi, had been buying military information from a senior French officer, identity unknown. Major Henry's agent was the char at the German Embassy, Marie Bastian, who each night emptied the contents of Schwartzkoppen's wastepaper basket into her bag for later delivery to the Statistical Section. For this she was paid 150 francs a month. Methodically piecing the bits together at home on his kitchen table during the evenings, Henry had discovered little more than diverting insights into the attaché's private life although in 1892 one letter did confirm what they already suspected. It was signed 'Alexandrine' – both attachés, true to Holmesian romanticism, signed their Christian names in the feminine form – and began: 'Enclosed twelve large-scale plans of Nice, which that scum D. has handed to me for you.'

Nothing of any consequence happened until the evening of 26 September 1894, when, on his way home, Major Henry collected two bags of German Embassy rubbish from Marie Bastian. After a couple of hours' sorting he realised, with mounting excitement, that at long last he had hooked a really big fish. The object of his joy was a sheet of onion-skin writing paper only partly torn up, upon which was written a memorandum of documents, obviously passed to Colonel Schwartzhoppen by a French officer:

> Although without news as to whether you wish to see me, I am nevertheless sending you, Sir, some interesting information:
>
> 1. A note on the hydraulic buffer of the 120, and the way in which it behaves.
> 2. A note on covering troops (some changes will be brought in by a new plan).
> 3. A note on a modification in artillery formations.
> 4. A note on the Madagascar expedition.
> 5. The preliminary Firing Manual of the Field Artillery (14 March 1894).
>
> This last document is extremely difficult to procure and I can only have it at my disposal for a very few days. The War Office has sent only a limited number to the corps, and the corps are responsible for them. Each office holding one must return his copy after manoeuvres.
>
> So if you wish to take from it what interests you and then leave it for me, I will come for it. Unless you would like me to have it copied *in extenso* and send you the copy.
>
> I am about to leave for manoeuvres.

The letter was unsigned and undated but Henry repaired it and first thing the following morning took it to Sandherr, the commanding officer of the Statistical Section. The letter was circulated among the chiefs of the War Office for their opinions and to see if any of them recognised the handwriting. After a week no progress had been made as to the identity of the writer but opinion narrowed it down to a staff trainee who had served in all four War Office bureaux (because of the varied information it offered) and who was a gunnery expert (because of the three artillery items). Only a handful of officers fitted into this category, and of these one was, according to all the reports, the most disliked: Captain Dreyfus, the only Jew. A specimen of his handwriting was secretly acquired, examined, and found to resemble the writing on the memorandum. The moment Dreyfus's name was mentioned, Sandherr, the secret service chief, cried out: 'Dreyfus! Of course! Why didn't I think of him before!'

The events of the next few days reveal the disgracefully blind haste with which enquiries were conducted. An analysis of the memorandum would have clearly indicated that Dreyfus could not have been its author; the terms used were not those of an artillery officer, and he could not have been on manoeuvres at the time the memo suggested. Much of the material listed was not confidential, anyway, and could easily have been acquired by hundreds of officers. Nobody looked for a motive, and if they had they would have been baffled. Dreyfus was a rich man, with a private income of almost 30,000 francs a year. He had a wife, Lucie, the daughter of a diamond dealer, and two children. Privately, there was not a stain on his record. In the army he had an unblemished record, too, although dislike for the captain was universal: he was vain, nosey and 'talked too much'. The investigators were further disappointed when a bank handwriting expert pronounced the two samples of handwriting to be from different hands. In desperation the team sought a more agreeable opinion, and called in Alphonse Bertillon, a man of profound stupidity who headed a police department devoted to identifying criminals and proving their guilt by means of cranial measurements. What he lacked in intelligence he made up for with instant opinions, one of which was that the handwriting *was* by the same person. 'But', he added guardedly, 'the memorandum might be a forgery.'

Treason is not a light charge. The War Minister at that time, General Auguste Mercier, knew this. One wrong move and public passions could be aroused. Mercier, moreover, after several blunders, was not in favour with the government, and he realised he must tread warily. Although uneasy about the slim evidence he authorised a staff officer, Major du Paty de Clam, to conduct a handwriting test with the suspected man and to arrest him if the result proved incriminatory. Accordingly, at 9 a.m. on 15 October 1894, Captain Dreyfus presented himself in civilian clothing, as instructed, at the War Office. His escort, Major Henry, ushered him into a room in which were seated a number of officers, including Major Picquart and du Paty. True to his comic opera name, du Paty proceeded to conduct the interview along the lines of a stage farce. He had his arm in a sling and his hand bandaged and suggested that, 'while they waited for General Boisdeffre', the Chief of Staff, Dreyfus take down a letter for the General's signature. The unsuspecting captain found pen and paper ready on a desk and sat down to write. Watching closely, du Paty dictated a letter based on the wording of the memorandum and, half-way through, suddenly shouted: 'What's wrong, captain? Your hands are trembling!' Dreyfus raised his head, adjusted his pince-nez, and calmly replied, 'No, it's just that my fingers are cold.' Undiscouraged, du Paty continued to dictate, watching for any reaction at the mention of the sinister words in the memorandum. Dreyfus, however, displayed no emotion other than patience at having to complete this strange task. When the letter was finished, du Paty nevertheless walked over to the captain, theatrically placed a hand on his shoulder, and said, 'Captain Dreyfus, in the name of the law I arrest you. You are accused of high treason.'

The mad farce continued despite the captain's eye-popping amazement. Du Paty then deliberately reached for a volume of military law lying on the desk, exposing a loaded revolver in the process. The investigating team were so sure of Dreyfus's guilt they even provided him with the means of committing suicide in his shame. To the accused man's protests du Paty read the articles of espionage. Dreyfus pushed the revolver away. 'But I am innocent, I swear! Kill me, if you want, but I am innocent!' Asked what the specific charges were, du Paty remained silent. 'Take my keys!' exclaimed Dreyfus. 'Open everything in my house. I am innocent!' Du Paty ignored his pleas and began an interrogation which, if anything, only corroborated the accused man's ignorance of the memorandum. At the end of it, Major Henry was detailed to escort Dreyfus to the military prison in the Rue de Cherche-Midi. On the way the unfortunate victim was convinced he was going mad.

The next two months were a nightmare for Dreyfus and his family. Without explanation his home was raided the following day and twenty-two bundles of papers were removed. The prisoner was kept in solitary confinement for days at a time. His wife Lucie was forbidden to telegraph his brother Mathieu for help. Their house was ransacked for possible evidence and his bank balance examined to the last centime. Now dangerously close to a mental breakdown, du Paty's merciless grillings each day drove him from despair to desperation, from anger to incredulity.

Little progress was being made on the handwriting, still a worrying piece of ambiguous evidence. Even the ass Bertillon now wasn't sure and to explain away the dozens of dissimilarities finally arrived at the view that when writing the memorandum, Dreyfus had *forged his own handwriting*! None of the other experts were positive and only hesitantly supported Bertillon under pressure. The amateur prosecutors were bogged down through sheer lack of evidence and at this stage there was just a chance that Dreyfus might have escaped his tormentors.

But also at this stage came a sudden, dramatic turn of events. The arrest of Dreyfus was leaked to the *Libre Parole*. The leak, and the manner of its publication, was patently a conspiracy to harden opinion against the accused man. On 29 October the following item appeared:

Is it true that a highly important arrest has been made under orders from the military authorities? The person under arrest appears to be accused of espionage. If our information is true, why do the military authorities maintain silence?

The following day the newspapers of Paris erupted with wild scare stories with no basis of fact whatsoever, but a Jew guilty of treason was, journalistically speaking, in the 'man bites dog' class. In the face of the outcry the Cabinet panicked and General Mercier suddenly decided that without a doubt Dreyfus was guilty. In this he was in sympathy with a large proportion of the population; it took less than a week for Dreyfus to be condemned by public opinion.

Two of the most surprised men in Paris were the two military attachés, Colonel Schwartzkoppen and Colonel Panizzardi. They were relieved, however, when, on 1 November, *Libre Parole* ran the headline:

HIGH TREASON. ARREST OF JEWISH OFFICER, A. DREYFUS

Perhaps, they wondered, Dreyfus had bypassed them and dealt directly with their respective War Offices in Berlin and Rome. Panizzardi telegraphed a coded message to his superiors: 'If Dreyfus had no dealings with you, advisable order Ambassador to publish official denial in order to avoid press comment.' The telegram was intercepted by the French Foreign Office; unfortunately the cipher was new and was imperfectly and only partially decoded to read: 'Dreyfus... our messenger warned.' The message was rushed to the General Staff as another piece of evidence to incriminate the accused captain. The telegram was properly decoded a week or so later, but by then the damage had been done; the first version had stiffened the resolve of the generals as to Dreyfus's guilt at a time when they might conceivably have weakened.

Now that it was decided to proceed with the charge of treason the file on Dreyfus looked pitifully thin. There must be no question of Dreyfus being found innocent through lack of evidence – the War Minister had now publicly stated that there existed 'overwhelming' proofs against the accused man. Accordingly, du Paty and Sandherr attempted to fatten the file with other fragments gathered from Schwartzkoppen's wastepaper basket but making no reference to Dreyfus – with the exception of the note that referred to 'that scum D.'. Then, with the aid of the police, former fellow-officers, and commanders who had known Dreyfus, du Paty concocted a 'biography' which detailed the accused man's career as a spy. With this done, the War Office set the trial for 19 December 1894.

Predictably, all evidence at the trial was heard *in camera*, and few had any illusions about the outcome. Mathieu Dreyfus had approached a prominent lawyer, Edgar Demange, to defend his brother. Although aware of the odium he would incur by defending a so-called Jewish traitor, Demange was soon convinced of his innocence and courageously took the case. The farce of the arrest and the interrogation was repeated. At one stage, seeing the judges were not convinced, Major Henry asked to be recalled to the witness stand. He stated that an informer of honour and repute had named Dreyfus as the spy in the War Office. Asked by Demange to name him, Henry was outraged. 'Sir! There are secrets in an officer's head which even his cap must not know!' The court accepted this evidence on Major Henry's word of honour, and Captain Dreyfus was pronounced guilty by each of the judges. In the absence of the death penalty, abolished in 1848, the condemned man was sentenced to forfeiture of rank, degradation, and imprisonment for life on Devil's Island. Demange broke down and embraced Dreyfus in tears. In his cell that night Dreyfus asked his guard for a revolver so that he might blow his brains out. None of this tragedy touched the press, which generally welcomed the verdict by braying its triumph in an orgy of anti-Semitic justification. Of Dreyfus's guilt they entertained no doubt; the illegality of the trial they did not question. Newspaper after newspaper filled its pages with vitriolic ravings aimed at Dreyfus and Jews in general. The socialists joined in common chorus with the Catholics. General Mercier was proclaimed a hero for saving France and, on the day before Christmas, exercising his unexpected popularity, he tabled a bill to bring back the death penalty for treason and spying.

Three thousand miles away, on Devil's Island, Alfred Dreyfus must have wished at times that he had been born later to benefit from Mercier's patriotic legislation. When he stepped ashore on that blistering, God-forsaken former leper colony, he had hope, but little reason, to believe he would not be doomed to die there. Preparations had been made as though he were a violent psychopathic criminal. As if the two miles long, quarter-mile wide island wasn't prison enough, a stone cell had been built within a wooden enclosure. In this cage he lived, half-crazed by the heat, tortured by insects, numbed by the desolation. He was closely guarded and a light burned in his room all night. The few letters he was allowed were censored. He had to prepare his own food. When, later in 1895, his brother circulated false reports to newspapers that he had escaped – in a desperate effort to revive public interest in the forgotten man – the government's response was to rebuild the walls of his prison higher, fetter him in irons each night, and to send out a new commandant notorious for his sadistic brutality. That under such circumstances Dreyfus continued to have faith in proving his innocence is a profound statement on the human spirit. All he had was this faith and the knowledge that his wife and family believed him innocent. He was a naked man, stripped of his home, his loved ones, his name, his honour and his career. The degradation ceremony that preceded his deportation was a degrading spectacle in itself. On 5 January, the day after he had been allowed to see Lucie for the first time since his imprisonment, he was taken under guard to the main court of the Ecole Militaire. A large parade of soldiers stood to attention while the drums rolled, and every button, stripe and badge was stripped from his uniform. His sword was withdrawn from its scabbard and snapped across an officer's knee. Then, as the grim-faced soldiers looked rigidly ahead and the crowd outside the walls howled insults, he was marched right around the courtyard. His shouted protest – 'Soldiers of France! An innocent man is being degraded!' – went unheard. A further six weeks of imprisonment followed before he was taken on board the *La Ville de Saint-Nazaire* on the night of 21 February 1895, bound for Cayenne the next morning.

While the condemned man languished on Devil's Island, unseen and unheard, all memories of him were quietly erased away in the offices of the Statistical Section. Contrary to orders that certain of the evidence in the infamous dossier should be burned, Sandherr, the Section chief, had Major Henry seal the documents in an envelope which was then locked in a safe. Sandherr, who like the others had private although not public misgivings about Dreyfus's guilt, thought in some vague way that the documents might one day afford him some protection should there be a subsequent enquiry into the case. On one count, he was right.

But while the Statistical Section were tidying their desks of Dreyfus, the condemned man's brother and his wife were tirelessly active. Changes of government always offered hope, but their appeals were turned down. Slowly one by one, Mathieu gathered together a band of influential believers including the editors of several newspapers. But they had to move cautiously because anti-Semitism still raged throughout France; it looked as though the task of rallying enough support to have the case reopened would take decades.

A year or so after the trial, however, a light was being shone in a most unexpected quarter – the Statistical Section itself. This was now commanded by Major Marie-Georges Picquart, who took over in July 1895. On assuming his new command Picquart was asked by the Chief of Staff to look once more into the Dreyfus case; military documents were *still* being stolen and hawked around and there was the likelihood that Dreyfus had been part of a spy network. In any case, Picquart was told, further investigation might uncover more evidence to stiffen the case against Dreyfus, about which the Chief of Staff was obviously still uneasy.

Months of nosing around revealed nothing until – in mid-March 1896 – two bags of rubbish arrived from Colonel Schwartzkoppen's office at the German Embassy. This was examined during Major Henry's absence and found to contain the tiny shreds of a *petit bleu* – a letterform of thin, blue paper used for express local delivery in Paris. When the pieces were painstakingly assembled Picquart and his assistant read the note:

> Sir,
>   I await a more detailed explanation than the one you gave me the other day on the question under consideration. I beg you, therefore, to let me have it in writing so that I might decide whether to continue my relations with the firm R or not.
>   C.

The letter was addressed to M. le Commandant Esterhazy, 27 Rue de la Bienfaisance, Paris.

Here was a French army officer conducting a highly suspicious correspondence with the German military attaché, but there were doubts. It wasn't Schwartzkoppen's handwriting and the letter could be a 'plant' for it hadn't been posted. Nevertheless, Picquart decided to make some enquiries about Esterhazy through a major he knew in the same regiment. The reply was damning: Esterhazy was an habitual gambler, a debauched womaniser and an incompetent officer. Moreover he had on one occasion gone to artillery demonstrations at his own expense and brazenly used soldiers to copy documents. Further enquiries revealed that the man was a descendant of an ancient though illegitimate French branch of a Hungarian ducal family. He was wild, unprincipled and, to some, half-mad. In Paris he shared an apartment with a prostitute, Marguérite Pays, fondly known to the police as Four-fingered Marguérite'.

Picquart had Esterhazy shadowed, and also received an indication from one of the Section's agents in Germany that he could be the spy. The investigation ground on until 27 August when, after considerable vacillation, Picquart was authorised to secure two letters of Esterhazy's for comparison with the letter in the file alleged to have been written by Dreyfus. The handwriting matched, perfectly. Incredibly, Picquart still remained in some doubt, and called in the expert, Bertillon. Examining photographs of the two specimens, with the names and dates masked out, Bertillon readily recognised they were by the same hand. 'Interesting,' he concluded. 'The Jews have trained someone to imitate the writing on the Dreyfus memorandum!'

By now, of course, even Picquart's own undisguised anti-Semitism could not restrain his professional judgement. He was also most curious to know just what evidence it was that had convicted Dreyfus, and asked for the secret file. On opening the envelope, which had remained untouched for more than a year, he discovered that nothing in it remotely resembled the 'overwhelming' proofs claimed by the prosecution witnesses and the War Minister. Shaken, he wrote a full report, together with a request for an enquiry, and took it to the Chief of Staff. At the War Office the generals, from Boisdeffre down, viewed his discovery with great interest, shrugged, and told him to separate the two cases, Dreyfus's and Esterhazy's. Picquart was only too uncomfortably aware of the implications of this crazy, black logic.

Matters drifted along until September, when the case was put before the Chief of Staff and the new War Minister, Billot. While the new evidence raised doubts in their minds about Dreyfus's innocence, Picquart's request for an enquiry was refused. The honour of the senior officers concerned with the conviction had to take precedence over justice. Picquart was staggered, then angry. On being asked to keep silent, he left the meeting with the retort: 'This is one secret I shall not carry to my grave!'

Picquart's fixation about the innocence of Dreyfus now began to gnaw at Major Henry, and he decided to 'improve' the original evidence and at the same time incriminate his superior. On one of the letters that had passed between Schwartzkoppen and Panizzardi, but which had nothing to do with the case, Henry substituted the initial D for Panizzardi's, and took it to the Assistant Chief of Staff, General Gonse, together with the story that Picquart was neglecting his duties. Gonse was impressed. Pleased with this deception, Henry then graduated to clipping the tops and tails from two notes between the German and Italian attachés and forging letters for insertion between the dates and signatures. When torn up and reassembled it was almost – almost – impossible to detect the forgeries. These two fabricated letters were later to be of vital importance; for the moment, however, they completely convinced Henry's superiors that Dreyfus was guilty. The first letter was dated September 1896, in Panizzardi's handwriting. Imitating his style, Henry wrote a short note in which Dreyfus was actually named, followed by 'I will say I have never had any relations with this Jew'. This would indicate that the Italian attaché was panicking about the disclosures being made in the press. The second letter was a trivial one, dated 14 June 1894; this was merely to demonstrate that the handwriting was the same.

But Major Henry was working against a fast incoming tide. Rumours were flying about. In November, a pamphlet appeared by Bernard Lazare, a journalist and one of Dreyfus's supporters, which convincingly pointed out some of the contradictions in the case. *Le Matin*, on 10 November, reproduced a facsimile of the original memorandum, leaked in some way from the amazing Statistical Section. Schwartzkoppen recognised the handwriting immediately and prepared to pack his bags for Berlin. Then, a few days later, Henry's efforts to stab Picquart in the back, combined with the public revelations, succeeded, and Picquart was dismissed from the Statistical Section on 14 November 1896.

Picquart was a good soldier and matters of conscience took second place to what he saw as his duty, which was – for the moment at any rate – to remain silent. Just the same, he foresaw threats to his career and he made a long deposition about everything that had transpired to a close friend, a lawyer named Leblois, at the same time swearing him to silence. He also left with Leblois a bundle of correspondence he'd had with General Gonse, leaving little doubt that the Chief of Staff was uncertain about Dreyfus's guilt but was prepared to do nothing about it.

Leblois would have remained silent had it not been for a chance meeting with a nephew of the vice-president of the Chamber of Deputies, Scheurer-Kestner, one of the most respected politicians of the day. Scheurer-Kestner had been won over by Mathieu Dreyfus and had quietly tried, among the Cabinet, to secure an enquiry, though without result. Leblois arranged to meet Scheurer-Kestner, told him what he knew, and showed him the Gonse letters. Armed with this positive proof the old senator redoubled his efforts to have the case reopened. Unfortunately, in promising not to mention Picquart he could not produce the actual evidence that would incriminate Esterhazy, nor the letters, and his hands remained distressingly tied.

Billot, the War Minister, pushed in exactly the opposite direction. Now thoroughly alarmed that a scandal might break out he ordered a hurried repairing of fences. Partly the result of a misunderstanding, du Paty de Clam was ordered to warn Esterhazy to keep quiet, and to secure his cooperation for a cover-up. Typically, anything du Paty had a hand in took on a decided comic tone. Disguised with a beard he met Esterhazy by appointment in a park. Esterhazy protested that he was the victim of some frightful conspiracy and demanded War Office protection. To ensure this, the madman fabricated a series of letters containing wild accusations compromising prominent

340

diplomats. He then wrote a preposterous letter to President Félix Faure in which he claimed a woman knew of a plot against him devised by Dreyfus and Picquart; in fact she had stolen from Picquart a document which, if published, would be embarrassing and diplomatically disastrous for the government. 'If I am denied justice', he wrote, 'or if my name is made public, this photograph, which at present is safely kept abroad, will be published at once.' It seems unbelievable that this piece of nonsense was taken seriously by the President and the top members of the Cabinet, but it was. Perhaps they each had guilty secrets. But by degrees, not only the War Office but senior government ministers were being drawn into the same insidious net that for two years had cruelly enmeshed an innocent man.

Just as it looked as though the government might succeed with a cover-up operation that could have provided inspiration for the Watergate conspirators, Mathieu Dreyfus's tireless campaign on behalf of his brother at last bore fruit. He had had a facsimile of the original memorandum reprinted as a pamphlet and widely circulated in the hope that someone might recognise the handwriting. Someone eventually did; a banking official told Mathieu the handwriting belonged to one of his clients, 'Count' Ferdinand Walsin-Esterhazy. Armed with this proof, Mathieu publicly denounced Esterhazy as a traitor.

Despite this sensational denunciation, the government still dithered. The ministers were split on the decision of what to do. Esterhazy was distraught and buttonholed every anti-Dreyfus editor in Paris, selling them stories he concocted on the spot. He found that many newspapers were prepared to print anything, any lie, to prevent the Jew being freed. It was a plot, they claimed, by the Jewish 'Syndicate' to besmirch the honour of the French army and of the officers who had condemned him. Picquart was denounced as a traitor, and a diversionary enquiry was ordered into the manner in which official documents were exposed to the lawyer, Leblois. But while he was being examined, the pro-Dreyfus side scored again. A bundle of letters was passed on to Senator Scheurer-Kestner, written by Esterhazy to a mistress he'd left in the lurch many years before. Their contents demolished any claim that Esterhazy was a loyal officer; both the French and the French army were denounced with violent invective. He would like to see, he wrote, 'Paris taken by assault and pillaged by a hundred thousand drunken soldiers'. Members of the government would 'go to populate German prisons' and nothing would please him more than to be at the head of a German regiment, 'sabring the French'. It seems to be stretching human credulity too far to suggest that, after this, Esterhazy still had friends, but he did, and their number increased daily as the battle raged through the French press.

At about this time, towards the end of October 1897 – after Dreyfus had been on Devil's Island for nearly three years – Zola was approached to lend his active support to press for Esterhazy's court-martial and the release of the wrongly condemned man. Apart from once or twice commenting on the terrible drama of it all, the novelist had not become in the least involved. He had been in Rome when Dreyfus was arrested and tried in 1894, and had only just completed his latest novel, *Paris,* currently being serialised in *Le Journal.* Although he had begun to research his next book, *Fruitfulness,* he was much less preoccupied with his fiction than was usual, and agreed to a meeting with Scheurer-Kestner. It took him only a few minutes to be convinced that the Jewish captain was the victim of a shocking and unprecedented conspiracy, the epic proportions of which immediately stirred his imagination.

Zola was no stranger to the corrosive dangers of anti-Semitism. In 1896 he had written an article for *Le Figaro,* 'On Behalf of Jews', in which he warned of anarchy and revolution if the lust to exterminate Jewish citizens did not abate. The editor of *Le Figaro* invited him to write on the subject again, in view of the Dreyfus controversy. Beginning on a subdued note, Zola wrote the first of three articles on the case, stating that he was convinced of Dreyfus's 'absolute and unshakeable' innocence. In the second, a week later, his colourful rhetoric was introduced: 'Truth is on the march,' he concluded, 'and nothing will stop her!' In his last article, which appeared on 5 December, all his linguistic hackles were up. Unfortunately, too many readers began to object, and there were threats to boycott the paper. Regretfully, the management declined further articles on the case.

But the fighter in Zola was now awake. Although nearing sixty, he suddenly felt young again. He hadn't been involved in a public duel for over two decades. The fierce reaction to his articles aroused an instinct in him that could hardly be contained. The pages of *Le Figaro* being closed, he wrote his next tirades in the form of pamphlets, at his own expense. They were wordy, sentimental and pompous, but his was a loud and influential voice.

Early in January 1898, the government, under all this pressure, decided that its safest course was to order a court-martial for Esterhazy – who, in any case, had himself demanded a trial on army advice. Sooner or later it was inevitable that he would be the subject of a civil action in which the government and the army would have no power to suppress evidence. With a court-martial assembled to consider the broadest possible charge – treason – all evidence would be strictly confined to matters concerning only Esterhazy; any evidence having any connection with Dreyfus would not be permitted. Under these circumstances it was a certainty that Esterhazy would be acquitted, and once acquitted he could not be retried in any court on the same charge. Thus, the War Office reasoned, the entire embarrassing mess could at last be buried out of sight.

The trial was set for 10 January 1898, and from the beginning it followed the farcical procedure of the Dreyfus trial – except that this time the court was rigged in the accused's favour. Military evidence was heard *in camera.* Although the evidence was much stronger than that which had condemned Dreyfus it was, under these conditions, insufficient to convict Esterhazy. The similarity of the handwriting in Esterhazy's letters to that on the original memorandum was explained away by Major Henry: 'But isn't it fair to suppose that the traitor Dreyfus disguised his hand to make it look like Esterhazy's?'

This was dutifully accepted by the court of seven officers. The letters Esterhazy had written to his mistress were denounced as forgeries by several hard-pressed experts. The War Minister had already proclaimed Dreyfus as a traitor and the court, while perhaps entertaining deep doubts about the wild-eyed, arrogant Esterhazy, did not wish to differ. The seven officers had their careers to think about. It was a unanimous decision: Esterhazy was effortlessly exonerated. A crowd of several hundred outside the court made him an instant martyr, and carried him on their shoulders to a waiting coach. The next day Major Picquart was arrested on a charge of removing official documents and communicating them to civilians. It was the darkest hour for Dreyfus and his supporters.

To Émile Zola, though, the dark hour was his natural element; he breathed in its crackling ozone with relish. And equally at home in the dusk of hopelessness was Georges Clemenceau, already a political veteran and the owner of a radical newspaper, *L'Aurore*. His fighting qualities in the face of extreme odds were to be glorified twenty years later when he rallied France in the closing year of World War I. Clemenceau opened the pages of his paper to Zola; both men had worked together, briefly, many years before, on the newspaper *Le Travail*. Entering the battle at this late stage enabled the novelist to see the situation with an almost naïve clarity. The legal machinery of the army was incapable of delivering justice; that had been demonstrated. What was needed now was something unconventional, something revolutionary. Zola decided to smash through the impasse by audaciously breaking the laws of libel and defamation in the most public, most spectacular way possible, thus forcing legal action. Let them prosecute him! In this way the facts would come out into the open.

Immediately after Esterhazy's acquittal he went to work, using his previous pamphlet as the basis for a public letter to President Faure. For two days and nights be sweated over the letter which he took to *L'Aurore*'s offices on the evening of 12 January. He stayed all night, checking the galley proofs as the type was set. The staff gathered around the composing stone, reading the galleys with a mixture of disquiet and admiration at the boldness of the letter. It ran for column after blazing column, direct yet eloquent, factual yet intuitive, a holocaust of accusing words written with all the indignation and faith in ultimate justice of which its author was capable. The last galleys were locked up on the front page leaving a large space for a banner headline below the masthead. Zola's title for the letter was 'Letter to the President, M. Félix Faure'. Clemenceau demurred; a missile of such range and power needed a lethal warhead. At the conclusion of the long letter Zola had pointblank accused two dozen individuals with complicity in the dreadful conspiracy, without mincing words. To Clemenceau these accusations were the essence; the word *accuse* was as potent as a swordthrust. The headline, set in the biggest type in the foundry, finally screamed: **J'ACCUSE**...! and one of the most famous documents in history went to press just before dawn on 13 January 1898.

The presses at *L'Aurore* ran without stopping until late in the following afternoon, by which time something like a quarter of a million copies had been sold.

While Zola's critics still argue over his motivations – self-glorification is a frequent charge – the effect of his public letter on the outcome of the case cannot be underestimated. It began diplomatically:

> M. President,
>   I beg to be permitted, in return for the favours you once accorded me, to be concerned for your just fame and to warn you that your record, so fair and fortunate to date, is now threatened with the most scandalous, the most ineffaceable blot.

The letter then went on to point out that this conspiracy was a stain on the President's administration, while at the same time exculpating him on the grounds of ignorance:

> I shall tell the truth because I am pledged to tell it if all the powers of justice fail to do so, completely and without qualification. My duty is to speak; I do not wish to be an accomplice. My nights would be haunted by the ghost of the innocent man suffering the most frightful torture for a crime he did not commit.
>   And it is to you, M. President, that I shall direct this truth, with all the force of my revulsion as an honest man. To your honour, I am convinced that you are ignorant of this crime. To whom shall I denounce this malignant rabble of real culprits if not to you, the supreme magistrate in the country?... I declare simply that Major du Paty de Clam, appointed as prosecuting officer, is the one who is first and most of all guilty of this frightening miscarriage of justice.

For the next few hundred words Zola proceeded to outline the history of the Dreyfus case with frank references to all the culprits. Typical is his biting denunciation of the former War Minister and his two army chiefs:

> Also at work is the Minister of War, General Mercier, whose intellect appears mediocre; there is also the chief-of-staff, General Boisdeffre, whose loyalty is to his clerical passions; and there is the under-chief of the General Staff, General Gonse, whose conscience readily adjusts itself to different situations...

Further along there are veiled suggestions of the Inquisition:

> Ah! The beginning of the affair is a nightmare to those who know the details... And so all the charges were drawn up, as in some story from the fifteenth century, in an atmosphere of secrecy, brutality, expedients – all based on a single, stupid accusation, that of having written the idiotic memorandum, for the so-called secrets delivered were found to be virtually valueless.

For the court-martial of Captain Dreyfus, Zola reserved his most stinging satire. His intuition told him that the alleged 'secret' evidence which the army swore 'overwhelmingly' proved Dreyfus's guilt, simply did not exist:

> Now we have Dreyfus before the court-martial. The utmost secrecy is preserved. A traitor might have opened the frontier to the enemy and led the German emperor right to Nôtre Dame cathedral and no greater measures of silence and secrecy would have been imposed... Is there any truth in all that whispered, unmentionable evidence, supposedly capable of setting all Europe aflame, that it must be buried in the deep secrecy of star-chamber proceedings? No. Behind those doors you will find only the extravagant imaginings of Major du Paty de Clam.

The letter then devoted itself to a detailed analysis of the falsity of the evidence, the lack of motive, Esterhazy's guilt, and the despicable complicity of the War Office, concluding with the scandal of Esterhazy's acquittal:

> Here, then, M. President, is the Esterhazy affair: a guilty man who has had to be exculpated for 'reasons of state'. For the past two months we have been forced to witness this mad spectacle, hour by hour... and we have seen General Pellieux, then Major Ravary, conduct a dishonourable investigation from which criminals emerged purified and honest men besmirched... And, when, at length, they convened the court-martial... they delivered an unjust verdict, one that will forever weigh upon our courts-martial, and which from now on will cast a cloud of suspicion upon all the decisions of military courts. The first court-martial might have been stupid, but the second was patently criminal.

Zola now arrived at the root of the problem, that 'reasons of state' had demanded that an innocent man should remain condemned for the sins of another:

> Dreyfus cannot be vindicated unless the entire General Staff is indicted. So the War Office, using every available expedient, through campaigns in the press, through pressure and influence, has tried to protect Esterhazy in order to convict Dreyfus once more. What a clean-up the republican government must institute in that house of Jesuits... What a nest of low intrigue, corruption and dissipation that sacred precinct – the War Office – has become, to whom supreme command of the national security is entrusted, where the fate of the nation is decided! Ah, what abominable tricks have been resorted to in this affair of witless folly, smacking of the worst police practices, of violent nightmares, of Spanish inquisition – all for the vain pleasure of a few uniformed and decorated individuals who grind their heel into the nation, who hurl back into its throat the cry for truth and justice, under the false guise of 'reasons of state'.

For the novelist, the letter would not have been complete without a scathing indictment of the popular press:

> It is an even greater crime to have used the yellow press, to have allowed all the muckrakers of Paris to come to their aid, so that now we have the scoundrels triumphing insolently in the defeat of right and honesty... It is a crime to misdirect public opinion and to pervert it to the extent it becomes demented. It is a crime to poison small and empty minds, to arouse intolerance and reaction through the exhaltation of that miserable anti-Semitism of which great and liberal France with her rights of man will soon expire if she is not soon cured. It is a crime to exploit patriotism for motives of hatred, and it is a crime, finally, to make of the sword the god of today when all human science is striving to create a future of truth and justice.

Finally, realising that President Faure was to some extent the prisoner of government machinery, Zola appealed to him as a man:

> This then, M. President, is the simple truth. It is the frightening truth. It will persist as a terrible stain upon your administration. I suspect you have no power in this matter, that you are a captive of the Constitution and of your situation. But you still have your duty as a man, on which you will surely reflect and which you will fulfil.

In the 'Wild West' era of the French press, while the letter was sensational it wasn't exactly earth-shattering. The real poison, however, was in the tail, and I quote it in full:

345

I ACCUSE COLONEL DU PATY DE CLAM of having been the author of the judicial blunder, I prefer to believe unconsciously, but of having persisted in defending this deadly error during the past three years by the most absurd and outrageous expedients.

I ACCUSE GENERAL MERCIER of having served as an accomplice in one of the greatest crimes in history, probably through sheer weak-mindedness.

I ACCUSE GENERAL BILLOT of having possessed the positive proofs of the innocence of Dreyfus and of having concealed them, and of having rendered himself guilty of violating the laws of humanity and justice from political motives and to preserve the honour of the General Staff.

I ACCUSE GENERAL BOISDEFFRE AND GENERAL GONSE of being accomplices in the same crime, the former doubtless through religious prejudice, the latter out of esprit de corps.

I ACCUSE GENERAL DE PELLIEUX AND MAJOR RAVARY of having conducted an iniquitous enquiry, an inquest of the most outrageous partiality, the report of which preserves for us a monument of naïve effrontery.

I ACCUSE THE THREE HANDWRITING EXPERTS, MM. Belhomme, Varinard and Couard of having tendered lying and false reports, unless a medical examination certifies them to be deficient of sight and judgement.

I ACCUSE THE WAR OFFICE of having inspired a vile campaign in the press, especially in *l'Eclair* and *l'Echo de Paris*, for the purpose of misdirecting public opinion to cover up its sins.

I ACCUSE, LASTLY, THE FIRST COURT-MARTIAL of having violated all human rights in condemning a prisoner on testimony kept secret from him, and

I ACCUSE THE SECOND COURT-MARTIAL of having concealed this illegality under instructions, committing in turn the judicial crime of acquitting a guilty man with full knowledge of his guilt.

In making these allegations I am aware that I render myself liable to articles 30 and 31 of the Libel Laws of 29 July 1881, which punish acts of defamation. I expose myself voluntarily.

As for those whom I accuse, I do not know them, have never seen them, feel neither resentment nor hatred for them. To me they are only figures, symbols of social corruption. The action I am taking here is simply a revolutionary step intended to hasten the explosion of truth and justice.

I have one passion only, for light, in the name of humanity which has suffered so much and has a right to happiness. My consuming protest is but the cry from my soul. Let them dare to take me to the courts of appeal, and let there be an enquiry in the full light of day!

I am waiting.

M. President, I beg you to accept the declaration of my deepest respect.

Émile Zola

It needs little imagination to appreciate the impact of this massive indictment, by the most-read writer in the country, and blasted over the entire front page of a respectable newspaper. This edition of *L'Aurore* acted like a gigantic cleaver across the length and breadth of France, dividing cities and towns, political parties, friends and families - even husbands and wives.

The letter caught the government completely by surprise. The following session in the Chamber of Deputies concluded with a wild melée during which members were slapped and kicked. While the air was hot with accusations and counter-charges, President Faure, furious at having been railroaded into a civil law-suit, sat through the explosive session silent and apprehensive. Billot, the new War Minister, argued that the army was above such slanders and preferred soldierly silence, but the persuasive right-wing leaders demanded the immediate issue of a writ for defamation.

Outside, mobs burned piles of *L'Aurore* in the streets, while the anti-Dreyfus newspapers howled like injured dogs. The most violent wave of anti-Semitism ever experienced in the country erupted with maniacal ferocity. Even in Algeria there were dozens of attacks on Jews in a four-day blood-bath in which the police were powerless. Jewish cemeteries were pillaged. Anyone unfortunate enough to have the surname Dreyfus was cruelly tormented and at Mantes a mob demanded the removal of a postal official of the same name. For several weeks following the *L'Aurore* letter, not a day passed in Paris and the main provincial towns without a demonstration of one kind or another.

Throughout his life Zola had known ridicule, slander, public insults and unpopularity. But the storm that thundered over his head from 13 January onwards was a hurricane of frenzied hatred. The *Libre Parole* screamed for his assassination. His effigy was burned in the streets and ugly crowds menaced him outside his home in the Rue de Bruxelles. Stones were hurled through his windows, and police had to guard him night and day. A torrent of telegrams and letters, many from abroad, poured in hour after hour, and a policeman was detailed to examine them. The most wounding missive received, however, was a well-packed parcel of human excrement.

In the midst of all this turmoil Zola was almost impossibly calm. Séverine, a feminist journalist, visited him at this time and noted that 'he wasn't at all violent, nor filled with hate... on the contrary, he was serenity itself.' He had, she thought, the tranquillity that accompanies the accomplishment of an important duty, 'the peace of his conscience'. Another journalist, Charles Péguy, also met him, early in February 1898: 'I had never seen him before. It was a thrilling moment, for I wanted to meet the man who had made the Dreyfus case his personal concern. I found no bourgeois, but a peasant, lined and grey... who looked tired... yet had an astonishingly unspoiled manner of registering surprise at the ugliness of events...' Péguy added that Zola's chief disappointment was the sell-out by the socialists, whom he had counted on for support, particularly the leaders and the socialist newspapers.

Nevertheless, Zola's stand seduced a lot of previously silent sympathisers out of the woodwork. These included many prominent poets, painters and politicians – Claude Monet, Octave Mirbeau, André Gide, Léon Blum, Eugène Carrière, Paul Signac, Marcel Prévost and James Ensor. Marcel Proust started a petition in support of Zola's accusations and quickly obtained 3,000 signatures. Even Zola's most vehement critic, Anatole France, applauded his demand for a revision of the verdict against Dreyfus.

On 20 January, Zola received a summons. To a great extent his ruse to force a legal showdown misfired, for the charge was a strategic one, limited to only a few lines of the indictment published in *L'Aurore*. This dealt with the accusation least likely to be proved: that the court-martial of Esterhazy knowingly acquitted a guilty man under instructions. It was a cunning move, to say the least, for it meant that, like the court-martial, Zola's defence would be unable to introduce testimony that had any bearing on the Dreyfus case.

347

The trial was set for 7 February. In the Esterhazy court-martial a young lawyer named Fernand Labori had acted for Picquart with considerable skill under insuperable difficulties, and he was recommended to Zola. Temperamental rather than intellectual, Labori was a voluble volcano in the courtroom, and he was delighted to accept the brief for what could turn out to be the trial of the century. *L'Aurore* was represented by Georges Clemenceau while his brother Albert acted for the newspaper's manager, who was also charged. Although Zola and his advisers realised the outcome of the trial was a foregone conclusion, they felt sure there would be many ways in which they could force the truth out into the open. To ensure this they proposed to call some 200 witnesses, including all the officers who had sat in judgement at the two courts-martial, and the two War Ministers involved. Within the first few minutes of the trial, however, it became obvious that this plan was destined for failure.

On 7 February 1898, the trial at the Court of Assizes in Paris opened in the atmosphere of a big film première. Guarded by friends, including the huge, bearded bulk of Claude Monet, Zola was led through the huge crowd with some difficulty. Most of the spectators outside the Palace of Justice were hostile, and continuously shouted anti-Semitic slogans. One group gathered around a bonfire, singing:

> Zola, Zola is a dirty, fat pig,
> The older he gets the sillier he grows;
> We'll catch you, Zola, dirty fat pig,
> And roast you from your head to your toes.

The court was packed with journalists, lawyers, politicians and whoever else had sufficient influence to secure a seat. The corridors were crowded with witnesses, waiting to be called. The jury was empanelled, all of them tradespeople and small businessmen. The presiding judge was M. Delegorgue a florid, portly man with flaring white sidewhiskers, who for reasons that will become apparent became known as the 'strangling judge'.

Those expecting sensations were to be disappointed on the first day for it consisted of hour after hour of sterile debate and legal preliminaries. On the second day, though, the session began in a lively way. Lucie Dreyfus was called by Labori to the stand as a defence witness, but the judge refused to put any questions to her on the grounds that she had nothing to contribute concerning the present charge. The procedure in French courts differs from that in England in that the accused or his counsel may only put questions to witnesses through the judge, who can of course stop them or put them in a different way. In this instance Delegorgue no doubt felt justified in refusing to put even a single question to Lucie Dreyfus – she had nothing to do with the Esterhazy trial, which was the sole subject of the charge – so she stepped down without even lifting her veil. At this point Zola jumped up indignantly to demand 'the right accorded to murderers and thieves to call witnesses to defend himself'. The judge stopped him and asked the novelist whether he was aware of the

Article which justified his ruling. 'I do not know your law,' shouted Zola, 'and I do not want to know it!' The outburst caused an uproar from among the spectators. Trying to make himself heard, Zola explained that he did not place himself above the law but was protesting about the hypocritical rules which prevented the witnesses being heard.

The protest was in vain, for the order: *The question shall not be put* came from Delegorgue with monotonous regularity. Scheurer-Kestner was not allowed to read the incriminating letters from General Gonse to Picquart. The Chief of Staff, Boisdeffre, was allowed the right to answer only those questions which suited him, on the grounds that some would endanger the national security. The same hedge was followed by the other senior military witnesses. In the absence of tangible evidence the officers were permitted to 'swear on their honour', and this was accepted. General Mercier was taken to the brink of some interesting revelations but slipped from Labori's grasp in the nick of time. Then came Henry's turn; Labori was waiting for him. Henry, with peasant cunning, told the court he was ill, and answered each question only after a great deal of thought. Even so, Labori trapped him into stating that the file on the Dreyfus case had been sealed in an envelope since 1895. This was of course untrue, and it had been demonstrated in this court and at another enquiry that both Picquart and Leblois had seen its contents; indeed Major Henry had informed on them. Henry then became very ill, and Gonse obtained the judge's permission for him to step down.

There was one army witness friendly to the defence, and that was Picquart. Youthful, meditative, and with his career in danger, Picquart emerges from the Affair with considerable credit. Prior to his appearance in court he had been under great pressure to reveal nothing, but in the witness box he resolved to follow the thorny path between his duty as a soldier and his responsibility as a witness. Although Picquart was discredited in army eyes, the court listened to his story with close interest, for he was the star witness for the defence. He recounted in detail his discovery of the *petit bleu* addressed to Esterhazy from the German attaché, and also described the contents of the Dreyfus file, which, contrary to the claim made at the trial which had convicted Dreyfus, contained no proof of his guilt whatsoever. But at this point, Picquart stopped. That was all he was prepared to tell; his duty as a soldier, presumably, preventing him from revealing his conversations with Gonse and Boisdeffre.

On 12 February, Henry was recalled to be confronted by Picquart. His evidence had been contradictory; on the one hand Henry had said that Picquart had communicated the contents of the Dreyfus file to a civilian, while on the other he had claimed the file had been sealed and never opened. To explain this, Henry revealed there was a *second* file, an ultra-secret file; the *real* file, he said, in which there were absolute proofs of Dreyfus's guilt. These, of course, were the two letters fabricated by Henry and which Picquart had not seen – nor had the judges at Dreyfus's court-martial. The story confused both the defence lawyers, Labori and Clemenceau, and Henry was allowed to step down.

Although he had prevented Lucie Dreyfus from speaking, Judge Delegorgue had on numerous occasions permitted testimony concerned with the Dreyfus case to be heard; this all happened to be in the prosecution's favour. However, Clemenceau did catch the judge out once when he extracted from Demange, who had defended Dreyfus in 1894, the fact that one of the judges at that trial had admitted the conviction was illegal.

The trial creaked on with few revelations until 17 February when Pellieux, the prosecuting counsel, was goaded into admitting the existence of the incriminating letter – the one forged by Henry – in the so-called ultra-secret file. Believing the letter to be genuine, and puzzled as to why the War Office witnesses did not table it as evidence to confirm Dreyfus's guilt once and for all, Pellieux then described its contents from memory: 'There is going to be an enquiry into the Dreyfus case. Say nothing about the relations we have had with this Jew.' Labori pounced and demanded that the letter be brought into the court, whereupon Gonse immediately stood up and insisted that it was a military secret and could not be shown in public.

Zola and his counsel were understandably angry and frustrated at the latitude extended to the army witnesses; on several occasions they had been, despite the colossal obstructions, close to toppling the prosecution's case. The best they could do was to recall Picquart to make the very good point that it was convenient for the new letter mentioning Dreyfus's name to turn up just when the case against him needed to be strengthened; and that in all likelihood it was a forgery. Picquart's opinion, however, hardly scored against General Boisdeffre, who returned to the stand to make a statement about Henry's (forged) letter. He confirmed that it existed, that it was authentic and that it contained absolute confirmation of Dreyfus's culpability. Then he turned to the jury. 'If the country has no confidence in its army leaders,' he told them, 'in those officers responsible for the nation's defence, then they are ready to leave this task for others.' It was the old army trick of offering honour in lieu of evidence, with blackmail added. The jury visibly withered under his commanding eye. Their names and addresses had been printed in all the anti-Dreyfus newspapers and they were in no doubt of their fate should they return a 'Not Guilty' verdict on Zola. It was no small thing to bear the responsibility of a mass walk-out by the country's top-ranking army officers.

The final witness was Esterhazy. Waiting about in the corridors had been something of a trial for him as he now had no friends and was icily snubbed by the other officers. On the third day of the trial, in a fit of pique, he actually told several bystanders that he had written the famous memorandum. 'And I am thoroughly bored by it all!,' he exclaimed. Before his appearance in court he had been ordered to say nothing, and that is what he did. At the rate of about two a minute Clemenceau bombarded Esterhazy with a stream of questions for more than half an hour, while the witness, with a straight face, remained mute. On this farcical note the examinations ended. Zola made a speech which, by several accounts, confirmed the opinions of critics who claimed his actions were prompted by self-glorification rather than a compassionate desire for justice.

Labori followed, and spoke for two days. The jury was out for only forty minutes and returned to find Zola guilty by a majority of seven to five. The novelist was condemned under the Press Law of 1881 and given the maximum sentence: a 3,000 francs' fine and twelve months' imprisonment.

The verdict was cheered by the crowd outside. Zola's only comment, as he left the court by the side door, was a single, deeply-felt word: 'Cannibals!'

The two weeks of continual tension had drained Zola, although he was by no means a beaten man. Some light had been let into the terrible conspiracy, and the pro-Dreyfus faction realised that the Zola trial was just a painful beginning. The case was now an international *cause célèbre* and France stood alone among nations in generally welcoming the verdict, which provoked an eruption of glee in most of the newspapers. One called Zola 'a burst bladder and an empty pumpkin, fit only to be ground beneath the heel of the nation's boot'. Many army garrisons swept their mess library shelves clean of Zola's novels. Several duels were fought, notably one between Clemenceau and Drumont, the editor of the *Libre Parole*; both men fired three times and missed. Picquart, who had been called a liar in court by Henry, was more accurate; Henry received a flesh wound in the arm.

But new sympathetic voices were also heard. The poet Mallarmé saw Zola's intervention as 'the heroism of a man who found the strength to emerge so courageously after a lifetime of activity that would have contented, or exhausted, anyone else'. From Russia, Tolstoy championed his fellow-writer, and in America Mark Twain added his support. In England, Ernest Vizetelly followed his master's troubles through reports in *The Times* and on the day after his conviction was moved to write:

> Light, Truth and Justice all denied,
>   He struggled on 'mid threat and blow –
> A brave Voice battling by his side –
>   Till Error's minions struck him low.

In April, Zola's advisers won an appeal and the verdict was set aside on technical grounds. A new hearing was ordered for late May. Successive ministries were falling as soon as they were formed, and the strategy was to buy time. Sooner or later, Clemenceau hoped, a Cabinet would emerge which would be more disposed to open an enquiry into the scandal. The trial had also stirred up mutinous views among the army chiefs and there was always the chance of fresh revelations dropping out of the furious orgy of back-stabbing that was going on.

This turned out to be the case. Picquart was dismissed from the army, which had the effect of allowing him more freedom to follow up his own enquiries. This he did with the cooperation of an examining magistrate named Bertulus, who had assisted at the Zola trial. Bertulus, who had been asked by the War Office to look into certain aspects of the trial, began to play a cat-and-mouse game with several of the witnesses, with surprising results. One was the discovery that Esterhazy's mistress, Four-fingered Marguérite Pays, had forged some incriminating documents, and she was promptly arrested.

Meanwhile, following the elections in May, a new ministry was formed which included a new War Minister, Cavaignac. Almost as soon as he took office, Picquart, on 9 July, sent an open letter to the Prime Minister, alleging that the 'ultra-secret' letter which was supposed to provide overwhelming proof of Dreyfus's guilt was in fact a forgery, and that he was prepared to substantiate this in an open court. The Minister of War acted immediately by ordering all the files in the case – now some 400 documents – to be handed over to him for a fresh internal enquiry. Between them, Cavaignac and Bertulus at last began to unravel the tangled threads of the conspiracy. Esterhazy's quarters were searched and there they found more than enough evidence to arrest him on a charge of uttering false documents. At about this time Gonse and Boisdeffre reported sick, and retreated to nursing homes well behind the firing line. Finally, the trail led to Henry. Working late at night by the light of a lamp, one of the new recruits in the Statistical Section examined one of the 'ultra-secret' letters – the one purportedly sent by Panizzardi to Schwartzkoppen. He noticed that the faint ruled lines on the top and bottom of the sheet were in pale red, while those in the middle were grey. There was no question about it: the letter *was* a forgery. This information was immediately communicated to the Minister of War, and Henry's number was up.

This discovery, however, was made on 13 August 1898, too late to have any beneficial effect on Zola's troubles. On 23 May he was re-indicted for trial at Versailles, where a conservative jury was almost guaranteed. Labori, still playing for time, challenged the jurisdiction of the court, but was overruled. Yet another appeal to the Court of Cassation, the French equivalent of the High Court in England, was unsuccessful and a resumption of the trial was fixed at the Court of Assizes in Versailles on 18 July.

Labori had by now run out of delaying tactics, and both he and Zola were distracted by the incessant snapping of dogs around their legs. On the day of the 23 May appeal, *Le Petit Journal* ran a headlined story about Zola's father being a thief while in the army in Algiers, obviously based on an old report leaked from army archives. Zola replied to the accusation in *L'Aurore* a few days later and sued the paper for libel. Then the three handwriting experts, whom Zola had roundly denounced in his *J'Accuse. . . !* letter, sued the novelist for 300,000 francs, alleging libel.

On the morning of 18 July, Zola arrived at the court in Versailles accompanied by Desmoulin the engraver, Labori and the Clemenceau brothers, and with a police escort for protection. Labori's request for the two cases – Dreyfus's and Esterhazy's – to be considered together, was refused. So was his request for a postponement. No other move being possible, and unwilling to subject his client to a further trial, Labori declined to present the defence case at all and the party abruptly departed. In default the judges confirmed the conviction and the sentence, against which there was no further appeal.

During the journey back to Paris the passengers held a council of war. Zola was resigned to spending a year in prison, and he would certainly be arrested within the next twenty-four hours. Labori and Clemenceau, however, had conceived the idea that Zola should avoid imprisonment by leaving France. The novelist was revolted by the idea; his flight would be denounced as cowardly, even by his mildest critics, and do the cause much harm. In any case, he argued, would he not be a martyr, a symbol, in prison?

The discussion continued with greater urgency when the party arrived at Charpentier's house. Labori persisted with the idea that in exile Zola would constitute a constant threat to their opponents, while in prison he would be helpless – and voiceless. In exile he could even write another *J'Accuse...!* Zola was torn apart, and no doubt confused by the united argument of the other four men. He recalled afterwards, '18 July will always remain a terrible day in my life, the one on which all my blood ebbed away. It was on that day I yielded to tactics, I listened to those who were fighting with me for the honour of France, I departed from all my cherished beliefs of heart and mind.'

But there was little time to consider the situation properly; within hours, perhaps, they would be unable to make any decisions at all. A messenger was dispatched to inform Zola's wife and in an hour Alexandrine arrived with a newspaper parcel containing a nightshirt, his shaving gear and a few toilet articles. She had brought no clothing because she was afraid of being followed, and a large suitcase might have aroused suspicions. Charpentier lent him whatever loose cash there was in the house, and that evening Zola caught the train from the Gare du Nord, bound for Calais and London. As his little knot of friends on the platform disappeared into the dusk he realised, with tears in his eyes, that he had not said goodbye to Jeanne and the children.

21

Temporary and Final
Exile

At a little after five o'clock on the following morning, 19 July 1898, Zola
alighted from the Dover train at Victoria Station. Exhausted and confused, he
managed to find the Grosvenor Hotel nearby, which had been recommended
to him by Clemenceau, and there, in the lobby completely deserted except for
the night porter he changed a 100-franc note and took a room in the name of
M. Pascal. His last act before falling asleep fully clothed on the bed was to
scribble a note to Ernest Vizetelly on a visiting card:

> My dear colleague – Tell nobody in the world, and particularly no newspaper, that
> am in London. And oblige me by coming to see me tomorrow, Wednesday, at eleven
> o'clock, at the Grosvenor Hotel. You will ask for M. Pascal. Above all, absolute silence
> for the most serious interests are at stake. Cordially,
>
> Émile Zola

At the appointed hour the next day Vizetelly arrived to find the novelist
struggling into a shirt he'd purchased the previous afternoon, along with some
other clothing. He had been taken completely by surprise at receiving Zola's
card. The note of secrecy appealed to his imagination, and he immediately
bestowed upon the situation a touch of comic absurdity that belied the gravity
of the meeting. Furtively wandering about the massive, smoke-blackened
masonry of the Grosvenor, and then along Buckingham Palace Road, the two
men didn't exactly melt into the landscape. Zola, his light-coloured suit and
white billy-cock hat stamping him as a Frenchman, was still wearing the red
rosette of the Legion of Honour. He made no attempt to disguise his
well-publicised appearance – his goatee and pince-nez had made him a
favourite with cartoonists – and he persisted in talking loudly in French. Within
minutes he succeeded in being recognised, although fortunately by the wife of
one of the partners of his English publishers, Chatto & Windus, who had the
good sense to restrict her secret to only a few friends. Vizetelly, too, was hardly
forgettable, with piercing eyes gleaming from under a boater, a great, straggly
moustache and a strange wisp of beard hanging from his chin. Nevertheless the
two men felt their identities were safely concealed and anxiously proceeded to
discuss the possibility of the novelist being extradited to France by pursuing
process-servers.

To ascertain Zola's legal position in England, Vizetelly went that afternoon to seek the advice of his solicitor, F.W. Wareham, who not only proved helpful but also offered the novelist rooms at his home in Wimbledon until he found a permanent retreat. This news, and the arrival of two of his countrymen, Desmoulin and Bernard Lazare, drew Zola out of a developing depression and he was overjoyed to leave his gloomy room at the Grosvenor for the Surrey countryside. In his account of the journey, Vizetelly took considerable pains to demonstrate that he was no stranger to the techniques of the undercover agent.

I ordered a hansom to be called to the hotel... then the porter asked me, 'Where to, sir?'
'Charing Cross Station,' I replied, and the next moment we were bowling along Buckingham Palace Road.
Perhaps a minute elapsed before I tapped the cab-roof with my walking stick. On the cabby looking down at me, I said, 'Did I tell you Charing Cross just now, driver? Ah! well, I made a mistake. I meant Waterloo.'
'Right, sir,' rejoined the cabby; and on we went.
It was a paltry device, perhaps, this trick of giving one direction in the hearing of the hotel servants, and then another when the hotel was out of sight. But, as the reader must know, this kind of thing is always done in novels – particularly in detective stories... it might be that the renowned Monsieur Lecoq or his successor, or perchance some English *confrère* like Mr Sherlock Holmes, would presently be after us, and so it was just as well to play the game according to the orthodox rules...

After passing through the shabby slums of Lambeth, the open spaces and tree-lined streets of Wimbledon made a favourable impression on the fleeing author, but after several days of fruitless house-hunting he was prevailed upon to look elsewhere. By now, Wareham had advised that libel was not covered by the Extradition Act between England and France and so, for the time being, Zola was safe on legal grounds. There was, however, the constant threat of some crazy anti-Dreyfusard attack should his whereabouts become known, and therefore his advisers suggested a hideout further south. A good many European newspapers were now asking, 'Where is Zola?' and published a variety of guesses ranging from Norway to Switzerland. One paper reported that he had been recognised in Brussels but a few of the English papers were sniffing uncomfortably close to the truth. So for several weeks the novelist stayed quietly at the Oatlands Park Hotel in Surrey, ironically only a few lanes away from Claremont Park where Louis Philippe spent his final exiled days in 1850. Then, seeing a vacant house at Oatlands Chase that he liked, he leased it under an assumed name and settled in with Vizetelly's daughter Violette as interpreter and housekeeper.

Fernand Desmoulin, his artist friend, smuggled over Zola's research material for his new novel *Fruitfulness*, and he soon fell into his familiar work pattern. In the mornings he would write a measured number of words; the afternoons were set aside for reading or walking along the shaded lanes between Esher, Walton, Weybridge and Chertsey; while the evenings were taken up with reading and correspondence. The summer of 1898 was untypically hot, and the days passed pleasantly enough, except, perhaps, at mealtimes, for the novelist found himself quite unable to come to terms with

English cooking, which he viewed with a mixture of wonder and repulsion. After dining one evening on mutton, boiled potatoes, watery greens and apple pudding, he commented to Vizetelly, 'God sent us food, but the devil invented English cooking.'

Every day Zola anxiously scanned his mail and the papers for news about developments in the Dreyfus fight, but little happened for a month to excite his hopes. Then, on 31 August, came some momentous news: Henry had been arrested following the discovery that two of the letters supposedly confirming Dreyfus's guilt had been forged; and in his cell the same night he had committed suicide by cutting his throat with a razor. The conspiracy was beginning to crack apart at last! But if Zola expected a speedy dénouement and the quashing of Dreyfus's sentence he was to be disappointed. Boisdeffre, the Chief of Staff, resigned, and Esterhazy, minus his spectacular moustache, departed for England, via Brussels. The War Minister, Cavaignac, also resigned. But these were to be merely superficial reactions, for in the face of entrenched bigotry the discovery of the forged letters in no way indicated Dreyfus's innocence of the original charge.

In September the clouds lifted when Jeanne and the children joined him for a few weeks, and together they moved to a new house, Summerfield, near Addlestone. But when they returned to Paris a succession of personal tragedies dragged him deep into a persistent depression. Having won their libel case, the three discredited handwriting experts from the first court-martial were awarded damages of 30,000 francs, and the author's house was seized in default of payment. A public auction was held to sell off his furniture to raise the amount of the damages, but it turned out to be a mercifully brief affair. Fasquelle, now Zola's publisher, bid by arrangement the full amount of 30,000 francs for the first lot offered, and the sale was over – to the disappointment of hundreds of thrill-seekers who had come to gloat. At the same time Zola won the libel action against the newspaper which had defamed his father, and was awarded 5,000 francs damages. The ledger, though, remained resolutely on the debit side; he was vindictively suspended as an officer of the Legion of Honour, and shortly afterwards his favourite dog died. This incident, conveyed to him by letter, invoked in the exiled author a profound sadness. Winter was approaching and as the leaves fell an alien, lonely landscape revealed itself which tugged deeply at the sentimental chords in his nature. Progress on the Dreyfus Affair had stalled to a lamentable halt, and his return to France seemed further away than ever. Vizetelly arranged for him to move into an apartment in the Queen's Hotel at Upper Norwood, near the Crystal Palace, in more populous, less melancholy surroundings. There, in a large sitting-room with five tables, and an adjoining bedroom, Zola continued writing *Fruitfulness* through a bitterly cold winter.

The turning point in the Dreyfus case occurred on the evening of February 1899, in President Faure's private chambers, when the old reprobate died from a cerebral haemorrhage with a terrified mistress locked in his arms. For months Dreyfus had been a political football, the subject of Cabinet treachery, bigotry and petty opportunism. Lucie Dreyfus's petition for a revision of her husband's case had been treated with all the inertia of which the government was capable. It had finally landed in the Court of Criminal Appeal which decided to 'further investigate' the matter. Then, in December, her appeal was moved to the United Appeal Courts. It was here that the patient Dreyfus family were to experience their first glimmer of eventual victory.

President Faure's successor was Emile Loubet, who was known to be in favour of reopening the Dreyfus case. Although in effect he wielded a new broom, Loubet did not sweep away the opposition with impunity. Enough impediments, however, were removed to allow the United Appeal Courts to examine the affair with a judicial freedom which had been denied for five years. For the very first time the secret file was examined in open court, to disclose the shattering news that it contained absolutely nothing to incriminate Dreyfus. The case could have, and would have ended there, had not Dreyfus insisted on a retrial and a verdict of 'Not Guilty', rather than an annulment of his conviction on a technicality. The Courts now had to find reasons for a retrial, which meant the disclosure of some new evidence. On 29 May 1899, the world witnessed the irony of forty-six judges, assembled in their red and ermine robes in a single court, pondering the question of how to remove an innocent man's guilt while the real culprit, Esterhazy, was admitting to newspapers in London that he was the real author of the forged memorandum that had convicted Dreyfus. It was, however, a moving occasion, and as the verdict was read, several of the judges broke down and wept. Captain Dreyfus was to be brought back to France from Devil's Island for a new trial. The anti-Semitic press erupted with a display of pent-up vehemence, but now their arguments were demonstrably empty; the evidence against the army was damning, and they could hardly claim that all forty-six judges were in the pockets of the Jews.

The same evening, in Upper Norwood, Zola received a telegram of only two words: CHEQUE POSTPONED. It was a code message which meant that the courts had granted revision of the Dreyfus conviction, and a new court-martial. Only two days before he had written the final paragraphs of *Fruitfulness* and, elated at the double triumph, prepared for his own return to France. During the spring months he had managed to extricate himself from his depression, helped by the visits of Madame Zola and several friends. Fasquelle and his wife travelled over to London to escort the novelist back to Paris, and on Sunday evening 4 June, they boarded the Dover train at Victoria, bound for the Gare Saint-Lazare. Despite promises to return soon under less harrowing circumstances, Zola left England forever. Early the following morning he slipped unobstrusively into his house on the Rue de Bruxelles. Almost a year had passed since he had left it for his retrial at Versailles; now the silent, grey streets seemed strangely like an abandoned stage, deserted of its players.

The welcomings lasted for several weeks, after which Zola escaped to the tranquillity of Médan, among his familiar possessions. From there, with hardly

357

a break, he began his research for *Labour*, the second novel in the *Four Gospels* tetralogy. *Fruitfulness* was currently being serialised in Clemenceau's paper, *L'Aurore* but, apart from that, there was little interest in his books. The sales picture was quite alarming; his income in 1898 was only a third of what it had been the year before, and the serial rights to *Fruitfulness* had to be sold for only half the amount fetched by his other books. Although now his name was a household name in many countries of the world, and certainly in France, it was for something other than as a writer of novels. Half the population of France expressed its disapproval of his intervention in the Dreyfus case by avoiding his novels on the bookstalls.

Zola's involvement in the Affair was by no means finished; nor, indeed, was the Affair. A few days after the novelist's departure from London, Captain Dreyfus was taken aboard the French warship *Sfax* at Cayenne, still technically a prisoner. Three weeks later, fearing demonstrations, the government ordered the cruiser to stand off Quiberon, in Lower Britanny; where, at nightfall on 30 June, Dreyfus was transferred to a launch and taken in secrecy by railway train to Rennes. There, in the prison, he saw his wife Lucie for the first time in nearly five years. It was as emotional a homecoming as it is possible to imagine.

Poor Lucie was faced with an apparition. The five terrible years on the bare South American rock had aged and transformed her husband. Although only thirty-nine his hair was quite white and his shrunken, hunched frame gave him the appearance of a man twenty years older. Because of his solitary confinement – the guards were forbidden ever to talk to the prisoner – he had nearly lost the facility of speech. Mentally, he was a shell, a confused spectre from some distant, hellish region.

The new court-martial opened in August 1899, and was anything but an official formality to clear the captain's name. The trial was conducted at Rennes, away from the hostile crowds of Paris, but the authorities had failed to take into account the strong local anti-Semitic sentiment. Rennes was, in fact, a notoriously unsympathetic environment for justice to triumph, for it was solidly middle-class, predominantly Catholic, and had a large army establishment.

On 7 August, Dreyfus appeared in the uniform of an officer of the artillery to face his peers, a hundred witnesses and masses of files. Nothing was introduced or considered that hadn't been sifted, examined and argued over before. Witnesses were dragged in whose only contribution was evidence of monumental irrelevance. For a week the court was treated to a farrago of fact and fiction, truths and half-truths, theories, rumours and contradictions. The only dramatic note was introduced from outside the court when Labori, now acting for Dreyfus, was shot in the back at close range and wounded.

The trial dragged on for five weeks, and it was apparent that, once again, the machinery of the law, especially military law, had only the remotest connection with justice. It was a case of Dreyfus versus the Army Command. Nothing had changed. What Dreyfus thought of the masquerade can be imagined; he sat in e court day after day, silent and bewildered, distressed and often feverish. When the verdict was announced on 8 September it stunned all but the most cynical. By five votes to two Captain Dreyfus was declared guilty of treason, with 'extenuating circumstances', the confusing verdict in itself an indication of judicial dilemma. The accused man was sentenced to ten years' imprisonment.

The verdict drove the Dreyfus supporters into volcanic fury, and Zola into writing one last public appeal. Titled *Act V*, the article appeared in *L'Aurore* on 12 September. Understandably, it was even more emotional than his other articles on the issue; and prophetic, too:

> A grotesque Ministry has gone beyond the limits of idiocy to give historians of the future the task of explaining a case so stupid, bewildering and murderous, so blatantly and obstinately vindictive, that it must appear to be unwitting... It is no longer a question of anger, of revenge or indignation, or even of the need to protest aloud against a crime... This is sheer horror, and the profound terror of one who sees the impossible become possible, rivers run backwards and the earth turn upside down.

The Rennes court-martial, Zola concluded, would never be eclipsed as an 'execrable monument to human infamy'.

The Cabinet was also in despair over the verdict, and it was painfully clear that the army was incapable of ever administering justice in this case. Within days it was proposed to take the matter out of army control entirely and on 19 September Dreyfus was officially pardoned by President Loubet. The balance of his sentence was cancelled.

Even this enlightened move was rejected by most Dreyfusards, who wanted to go all the way to prove the accused man's innocence and to indict the army instead. They were further enraged when it was announced that the government, as a sop to the army, proposed an amnesty for all concerned, regardless of guilt and complicity in the conspiracy. This amnesty also included Zola, who still technically faced a prison sentence and a further charge for absconding.

Through all this lamentable affair one has to admire the quiet courage of Captain Dreyfus. Despite the intense pressure from his loyal supporters, and to their undisguised chagrin, Dreyfus decided to accept the pardon but only on the condition that he could continue to try and prove his innocence by whatever legal means were available. This decision was to be roundly vindicated. Notwithstanding violent criticism from the Dreyfusards, the government eventually passed the Amnesty Bill in December 1900, and, for the public at any rate, the affair was finished.

Zola was now slowing down, and there were unmistakable signs that his great powers were fading. *Labour* appeared as a serial in *L'Aurore* from December 1900, and resignedly he set about writing the third novel in the series, *Truth*, based on the Dreyfus case. Firmly bolted down to documentary fact, the novel was not the ideal vehicle for even his languishing imagination, and he turne increasingly to his old battleground, the stage.

The modest success of his opera *Messidor* – although it had to close dow because of anti-Dreyfus demonstrations outside the theatre – encouraged Zo to explore further into the writing of lyric drama. *The Storm*, again with a scor by Alfred Bruneau, was completed late in 1900 and performed at th *Opéra-Comique* in April 1901. Although he wrote the librettos for four othe operas, this was the last their author would see produced.

Zola's frustrations about his relative failure in the theatre can be imagine for he had made an original and far-reaching contribution by introducin realism to the stage. From his early years as a theatre critic to his last years as lyrical interpreter of life, Zola's role had always been that of a reforme Unfortunately his revolutionary ideas fell foul of the Parisian critical cliqu and, more than most, his essays into the theatre, from the 1865 three-a production of *Madeleine* onwards, met with uniform hostility. As the result so many humiliations, while at the same time enjoying such a marked succe with his novels, he was never inspired to fully develop his theatrical ideas. On with the sympathetic collaboration of Alfred Bruneau, with whom he ha worked so successfully in 1896 and 1897 on *Messidor*, did he feel secure enoug to allow his creative imagination full play. Immediately following th completion of *The Storm*, he set about adapting the theme of *Fruitfulness* to lyr drama in an opera called *l'Enfant-Roi*. At the same time he conceived a plan fe a vast cycle of dramas, a theatrical parallel to the Rougon-Macquart chronicl which apparently he intended to begin as soon as he had completed the fin novel in the *Four Gospels* tetralogy.

It will be seen, then, that after 1900 Zola's preoccupation with fiction was o the wane. After completing the *Rougon-Macquart* books the scale of his fiction imagination had shrunk. The *Three Cities* trilogy was the result of sheer chanc and the *Four Gospels* novels were pale shadows in the gargantuan shade cast k his major literary achievement. During the two years of his involvement wit the Dreyfus case his eminence had expanded, nationally and internationally, that of a famous pundit; letters did actually arrive at his house simp addressed to *Emile Zola, France* – just as he'd dreamed at the outset of h career. While it is true that he dignified the dreadful battlefield of the Dreyf Affair with his art it is also true that, because of it, he frequently saw himself nothing less than the conscience of France. Any fictional framework, no matt how ambitious, now seemed restrictive, and there is evidence that after 190 novels were assigned only a minor role in his creative future. After th completion of *Labour* early in 1901 he wrote to Ernest Vizetelly: 'When I hav finished these *Evangiles*. . . it is quite possible I shall write shorter and livelie books. Personally I should have everything to gain by doing so, but for th present I am fulfilling a duty which the state of my country imposes upon me That, of course, is the mortal messiah speaking, with a tricolour mantle acro his shoulders. In this mood he plugged away at *Truth* while dreaming grandiose dramas for the stage. The Dreyfus Affair, as Zola admitted to th journalist Gabriel Trarieux, might have 'made him a better man' but it had also taken an enormous toll on his energies. Trarieux interviewed the novelist in his study in the Rue de Bruxelles, where he found him hunched behind his desk with a rug over his knees. He was balding and his beard was white. A tired, lined face emphasised his characteristic expression of melancholy, and his eyes 'were very sad'.

Truth was a long book – almost a quarter of a million words – and writing it took nearly fourteen months, from July 1901, to August the following year. The summer of 1902 was spent at Médan, with Jeanne and the children, as usual, occupying a cottage at nearby Verneuil-sur-Seine. Zola's relations with Alexandrine were now in calm, although far from blissful waters. Six years or so previously Alexandrine had seriously considered obtaining a legal separation, and to advise her she had dragged in their devoted friend, Henri Céard. Although Céard had done what he could to bring about a reconciliation, Zola angrily resented what he saw as interference and the younger writer departed from their circle, for good. The Dreyfus Affair, however, had the effect of bringing husband and wife close together again, for their dependence upon one another was considerable. Domestically, the summer of 1902 was one of the happier and more fulfilled periods of the novelist's life.

On 8 August, Zola put the finishing touches to *Truth*, which was due to begin as a serial in *L'Aurore* on 10 September. Serialisation rights in England had been sold to *Reynold's News* and Vizetelly had begun translating from the galley proofs of the early chapters. The novelist now commenced preparations for the final book in the *Four Gospels* series, to be called *Justice*, another utopian step in his search for the path to universal love. At the same time his mind wandered to other projects, of which a novel about Zionism was one. The Dreyfus tragedy had opened a new world to him, the world of the Jew, and he was impressed by the fatal role into which they were cast.

Most of September was taken up with the completion of *l'Enfant-Roi*, and on the 25th Zola wrote to Bruneau to tell him it was finished and had been accepted by the *Opéra-Comique* for the 1903 season. Then, although the weather at Médan was still fine and warm, he proposed – against Alexandrine's wishes, for with her recurring bronchial complaint she detested the colder temperatures of Paris – to return to their house in the Rue de Bruxelles.

They arrived there early in the evening of Sunday, 28 September, in the chilling wake of a sudden thunderstorm. Finding the house unbearably cold, Alexandrine asked the housekeeper to light a fire in their bedroom, for the central-heating system, which was fed from a furnace in the basement, had not been turned on because of their unexpected arrival. At about ten o'clock, after their supper, the Zolas retired.

The house at 21 Rue de Bruxelles consisted of the two lower floors of a large building. The ground floor included a reception room, a large dining-room and the kitchens, while on the first floor were two drawing-rooms, two large bedrooms, a bathroom and the novelist's study. Above them lived other tenants, who entered by means of a separate adjoining staircase. On entering their bedroom that evening, Alexandrine noticed that the coal fire was not burning, but smouldering, and that the air in the room was uncomfortably stuffy. The fireplace shared a common chimney with several other apartments in the building, and the tenant of one of these had recently swept the upper section. Assuming that during the process some masonry and soot had fallen down and blocked the chimney, Alexandrine asked her husband whether she should extinguish the struggling fire before they went to bed. Zola thought not; it would most likely burn itself out. Then, according to his custom, he double-locked the door and the window and climbed into the vast, canopied Louis XIII bed.

At about three in the morning Alexandrine awoke feeling faint, nauseous and with a tightness across her throat. Thinking it was another of her bronchial attacks she made her way with some difficulty to the bathroom where, to her surprise, she was violently sick. After about three-quarters of an hour she returned, scolded their pet dog which in her absence had jumped on to the bed and, still feeling weak and exhausted, once more climbed between the sheets. In doing so, she woke her husband, who also complained of dizziness and nausea.

'Should we wake the servants?' she asked him.
'No, it's not worth the bother,' he grumbled. 'It's probably only indigestion.'

Zola then struggled from the bed with the intention of opening a window but before he had taken a couple of steps he fell to the floor with a moan. Anxiously, Alexandrine called him, and, receiving no answer, attempted to rise and go to help him. But now she was helpless with the dead weight of a strange paralysis which was creeping over her limbs; she couldn't even manage to press the electric bell to summon the servants. Finally, gasping for breath, she fell back unconscious on to the bed.

It was after nine o'clock the next morning when the servants, M. and Madame Monnier, became aware of the absence of activity in the Zolas bedroom, and it was well after their usual hour of rising. When repeated knocking failed to arouse any response the door was broken down by a couple of workmen. The servants viewed the scene with horror and shock. The novelist was lifeless on the floor in his nightshirt, with one of his feet on the bedside rug. Madame Zola was on the bed, unconscious and barely breathing. While one of the men rushed off to find a doctor, the other helped the two servants to open the window and carry Zola's body to another smaller bed in the room.

A doctor, who happened to be in a chemist's shop nearby, was in the room within minutes. The novelist had been dead for at least an hour but after some twenty minutes' resuscitation Madame Zola regained consciousness, although she was still very weak. Efforts to revive her husband, however, despite artificial respiration, injections, friction and electric shock, were in vain. Late in the day Alexandrine was taken to a hospital at Neuilly to recover.

362

An urgent post-mortem was, under the circumstances, thought necessary, and the cause of death was soon found. The body exhibited all the signs of carbon monoxide poisoning, and the characteristic cherry-red colour of a blood sample confirmed it. Having fallen on the floor, Zola had inhaled heavy concentrations of the odourless but lethal gas, while Alexandrine, several feet higher on the bed, had escaped the worst. The pet dog had also been seriously affected, while another dog, which had slept outside the room, was perfectly healthy.

An enquiry was opened the same day by the district Commissary of Police, who found that the chimney leading from the bedroom fireplace had been blocked. During the inquest, two weeks later, further tests were made by lighting fires on two nights, 8 and 11 October. Caged guinea-pigs left in the bedroom were examined in the mornings, and samples of the air were taken. The results were puzzling, for the guinea-pigs were alive and the air samples contained only minute proportions of carbon monoxide. A thorough examination of the chimney system in the building revealed some accumulations of soot, but insufficient to block a draught. Despite the absence of an explanation for the presence of the toxic gas on the night of the tragedy, the coroner returned a verdict of accidental death.

The novelist's death caused a sensation. For a week the house in the Rue de Bruxelles was crowded with the comings and goings of Zola's shocked friends. Letters and telegrams flowed in from all over France and from a dozen other countries. Typical was a cable from 'The French residents of San Francisco'. Alfred Dreyfus paid his respects by mounting vigil at the coffin throughout one night. Plans were made for a spectacular public funeral and a subscription list was started for a monument in the novelist's honour. The news of her husband's death had been kept from Alexandrine for several days while she recovered from her ordeal. Two days before the funeral she was brought back to the house by closed carriage to kiss her husband for the last time. On another day, Jeanne Rozerot came, with the two children. Ironically, one of the mourners there was a young writer, Maurice Le Blond, who was later to marry Denise Emile-Zola. Paul Cézanne, unable to travel to Paris, locked himself in his studio for a whole day and night, alone in his grief. But in all the sorrow, one lament stands out as the most fitting for the realist's epitaph; that of Madame Charpentier, who walked numbed and distracted from room to room repeating a helpless cry – 'It's too stupid! How could he die like that? All he had to do was open a single window! How stupid!'

Although Zola had been suspended as an officer of the Legion of Honour the military governor of Paris sensibly ordered that the novelist's funeral was to be accompanied by full military honours, while at the same time arranging for extra detachments of police to be on hand in case of trouble. The funeral took place the following Sunday, 5 October 1902. By noon a crowd of 2,000 people thronged the Rue de Bruxelles to watch the cortège depart for Montmartre Cemetery, the hearse flanked by a detachment from the 28th Infantry and followed by two chariots of wreaths and flowers. At the graveside there were scenes of genuine emotion and detestable hypocrisy. The government, represented by the Minister for Public Instruction, officially interred the novelist but the true tribute came from a man who had been one of Zola's most bitter literary enemies, Anatole France.

In an astonishing and memorable oration delivered on behalf of Zola's friends, punctuated by applause from a crowd that stretched beyond the gates of the cemetery, Anatole France roundly denounced a system of government which could have allowed a conspiracy of injustice on the scale of the Dreyfus Affair. Zola, he proclaimed, had saved France from corruption through his courage. 'His courageous words awoke the country! the consequences of his deeds are incalculable! They unroll themselves today in power and majesty, they spread out to infinity, they have determined a movement of social equality which cannot be stopped.' Anatole France concluded:

'Let us envy him. He honoured his country and the world by an immense literary work and a great deed. Let us envy him! His destiny and his heart won for him the greatest fate – he was, for one moment, the conscience of mankind!'

Montmartre Cemetery shook with unprecedented, tumultuous cheering as the tiny, white-bearded figure of the venerable novelist stepped down from the rostrum. But there were ugly scenes, too, for Zola had more enemies than most. The occasion of his funeral was chosen for a number of demonstrations, mainly by the anti-Dreyfusards, who made no secret of their joy at his death. On 29 September the *Libre Parole* declared that the name of Zola 'inspired horror to all who possessed French hearts' under a banner headline: A PIECE OF REALISTIC NEWS – ZOLA ASPHYXIATED. The *Peuple Français*, by contrast, was lyrical with its headline: ANGEL OF DEATH STRANGLES ZOLA DURING NIGHT, inferring just punishment from God. *L'Intransigeant* ran up a defamatory balloon, alleging that the novelist had committed suicide because he had discovered that Dreyfus was really guilty.

The truth was that, despite the coroner's finding of accidental death, the circumstances remained suspicious and gave rise to obvious speculations. Some did not deny the possibility of suicide, although not because of Dreyfus; the relentless load of writing, the failing powers, the double domestic life – all these factors had driven the novelist's weary mind and body to desperation and suicide. This theory, however, takes no account of Zola's deep attachment to his wife, nor his natural aversion to cause pain and hurt to others, and can be readily discounted.

A far more valid belief, though, and one that persists to this day, is that Zola was murdered, probably by the anti-Dreyfusards; at the time the investigators had their suspicions but because of public feeling the authorities hushed the matter up. This theory gained fresh credence when, in October 1953, the newspaper *La Libération* published a series of articles reviewing the circumstances of Zola's death. The articles drew a letter from one of the paper's readers, a 68-year-old man named Hacquin, who felt the need to unburden himself of a secret he'd kept for over twenty years. Hacquin recounted how he had made the acquaintance years before of a heating

364

engineer who, for many years of his life, had managed a chimney-sweeping business. They had become firm friends. One day, in April 1927, the name of Zola came up in conversation, and the engineer confided to Hacquin that he had deliberately stopped up Zola's chimney in 1902. With some other workmen he had been repairing the roof of an adjoining building on the day the Zolas had returned from Médan. It took only a few moments to block the chimney, which was cleared the following morning. The engineer, Hacquin wrote, had died shortly after telling him this.

As a result of this confession, the editor of *La Libération* investigated further, and discovered in the court records that the facts according to his correspondent fitted closely with the unexplained aspects of the tragedy. Hacquin, by the way, could not have known of the contents of the court reports, which lent further credibility to his story. An inspection of the roofs of the buildings along the Rue de Bruxelles revealed traces of repairs which also tallied with his account, although being fifty years old this could only be regarded as evidence of the most doubtful kind. More important was the information that the engineer had been a rabid nationalist, and thus almost certainly an anti-Dreyfusard. From 1898 onwards, threats to assassinate Zola were not uncommon; the issue had provoked a lot of violence, several duels, and the attempted murder of Labori, the defence lawyer.

Hacquin's account has to be taken seriously, and the event can easily be reconstructed. In the first place, it is not a premeditated political murder, for the Zolas' return was unexpected. A team of workmen is repairing the roof of one of the houses in the Rue de Bruxelles when it is noticed, late in the afternoon, that Zola and his wife have arrived at the house next door. The engineer, still resentful of the victory of Zola and Dreyfus's other supporters, decides in a fit of pique to stop up the chimneys of his house. It is, at that stage, a spontaneous, half-hearted act of aggression, executed with a couple of slates in as many minutes. Back on the job next day – this would be at least two hours before the tragedy was discovered – the engineer has second thoughts, and removes the slates. The workmen complete their task on the roof, and depart. By the time the police find their way to the roof – probably later in the day – the workmen have long since disappeared. This reconstruction provides an explanation for all the puzzling elements in the case, even the curious discovery that there were two distinct types of soot in the chimney. Soot from a stifled coal-fire would be of a different composition from that produced by a free-burning fire.

Whether Zola's death was due to an accident or to murder we cannot be sure, for no other evidence has surfaced since 1954 and the existing evidence pointing to political assassination is inconclusive. But in the absence of explanations for a number of strange irregularities, the assassination theory must be favoured.

If Zola did die because of his audacious, courageous fight for truth and justice, he did not die in vain. The author of *J'Accuse. . .!*, just as much as the author of *Germinal*, had steered the conscience of France towards a more honourable horizon, and irrevocably changed the course of French life. In death he had won the admiration and respect from many who had denied it to him during his lifetime, but this as with other posthumous triumphs and humiliations, could not touch him.

Twenty-five years before his death, Zola wrote the following premonitory passage in *A Love Episode*, describing Hélène's final surrender to her passion:

> ...she experienced a feeling of inner peace; only the sensations and memories of her childhood filled her mind. On a similar winter's day, when she was a girl, living in the Rue des Petites-Maries, she had almost died in a small, stifling room, in front of a huge coal fire that had been lit to dry the linen. On another day, in summer, the windows were open, and in flew a finch from the shaded street. Why should she now think of death? Why should she remember the stray bird's flight? She felt overwhelmed with melancholy and childhood dreams, in the slow, delicious annihilation of her whole being...

This was the ecstatic annihilation Zola might have secretly dreamed of; not the pallid substance of glorious ceremony, but the slipping away, the sweet decay of a minute fragment of matter, dissolving into the earth's dungpile from whence it came.

POSTSCRIPTS

EMILE ZOLA was apotheosised by the transfer of his ashes to the Panthéon on 4 and 5 June 1908, an occasion that was not without its share of disaster and tragedy. The hearse conveying the coffin from Montmartre cemetery to the Panthéon was forced by hostile mobs and demonstrations to detour through a maze of back streets. At one stage, near the rear entrance to the great mausoleum, the hearse was in danger of being overturned by a crowd of students, who were only held off by several energetic squads of armed police. During the ceremony the following day, a spectacular event attended by the President of the Republic, hundreds of notables and great columns of *cuirassiers* in gleaming helmets and breast-plates, Alfred Dreyfus was shot twice and wounded by an assassin, an indication of the high feelings that still prevailed years after the Affair was officially closed. After the ceremony there were more demonstrations and dozens of arrests.

MADAME ALEXANDRINE ZOLA died on 26 April 1925, aged eighty-six. The last twenty years of her life were devoted to the enhancement of her husband's reputation. Shortly after his death she disposed of many of his possessions, including his library of 2,600 volumes. Among the books was a valuable collection of hundreds of presentation copies of novels by Flaubert, Daudet, Maupassant, the Goncourts and many others, and also the fourteenth-century breviary Zola used in writing *The Dream*. Madame Zola donated Manet's famous portrait of her husband to the Louvre, but ten canvases by Cézanne were sold, at prices which left Establishment critics aghast. The prices in fact, were the highest ever achieved for Cézanne's work, ranging from 600 francs for *Portrait de femme* to 4,200 francs for *L'Événement*. A Pissarro sold for 900 francs and a Monet for 2,805 francs. The money was used to establish Médan as an orphanage and to provide for her husband's children. Zola's own manuscripts for his novels, with the exception of the *Three Cities* trilogy, were donated to the Bibliothèque Nationale in Paris, where they still reside. The *Three Cities* manuscripts were acquired by the City of Aix-en-Provence. Madame Zola's final task on behalf of her husband was to oversee the completion of a public monument to his memory, subscribed by members of the Society of the Friends of Emile Zola, and its erection in Grenelle, Paris, in June 1924.

JEANNE ROZEROT AND THE CHILDREN were accepted into the family by Madame Zola after her husband's death. From about the time of the Dreyfus Affair, the novelist's own affair with Jeanne Rozerot was publicly revealed, and she was a member of the family group at the Panthéon ceremony in 1908. Before then she was on regular speaking terms with Madame Zola, who customarily had the children each Thursday. Jeanne died during an operation at a nursing home in May 1914.

In December 1906, the two children, Denise and Jacques, were officially declared the legal descendants of the novelist, taking the surname Emile-Zola. Madame Zola supervised their education and later, with her, the two children devoted much of their lives to perpetuating the memory and works of their father. Denise married the writer Maurice Le Blond, and in 1931 recorded her recollections of her father in *Émile Zola raconté par sa fille* (Fasquelle, Paris) while her husband contributed many research articles on the novelist to various learned journals.

CAPTAIN ALFRED DREYFUS was finally vindicated on 12 July 1906. Yet another investigation into the case was undertaken in 1903 which caused a long-overdue search to be made through the entire files of the Statistical Section. The search unearthed enough evidence – previously suppressed – to positively establish Dreyfus's innocence and Esterhazy's guilt. This new material was submitted to the Court of Criminal Appeal which agreed there was nothing in existence that could reasonably have convicted the persecuted captain. Having allowed the appeal, the court did not return the case to a further court-martial, which would have produced yet another 'Guilty' verdict, but instead annulled the findings of the Rennes trial and declared the matter closed. As for the public's staying powers, the affair was far from forgotten, however; at the trial of Gregori, the assassin who shot Dreyfus during the Panthéon ceremony, a crowded court cheered when he was acquitted. The same court went out of its way to declare that it disassociated itself with the findings of the Court of Criminal Appeal which had vindicated Dreyfus.

In July 1906, Pope Leo XIII pronounced Captain Dreyfus absolved from all suspicion, provoking anti-Dreyfus Catholics in France to hold special Masses for the purpose of asking God to open the Pope's eyes. Even the posthumous publication of Colonel von Schwartzkoppen's diaries in 1930, which described in detail his dealings with Esterhazy, did little to convince the bigoted extremists of Dreyfus's innocence; as recently as 1964 the daughter of the War Minister Cavaignac published a book attempting to prove his guilt.

Ironically, Captain Picquart became Clemenceau's War Minister during the last years of World War I. Esterhazy lived in England until 1923, posing first as an Irishman and then as a French aristocrat. As for Dreyfus, he remained steadfastly loyal to the army, taking no part in the activities of his supporters.

e was reinstated with the rank of major, and was awarded the Legion of onour, Fourth Class. He fought in the 1914–18 war and thereafter lived in tirement until his death in 1935. There is a closing note of deep sadness oncerning the fate of his granddaughter, Madeleine. One of the Jewish ctims of a Gestapo pogrom in the early 1940s, she was dispatched to uschwitz, never to be seen again.

22

The Perils of an English Reader

'If English was good enough for Jesus, it's good enough for you' —
An Arkansas School Superintendent, on refusing permission for foreign languages to be taught at a high school.

The Italian philosopher Benedetto Croce held that translation was impossibl
and after reviewing just under a hundred different English translations o
Zola's novels, spanning almost a century, it is tempting to agree with him. C
about 300 recorded translations into English, perhaps less than a quarter ca
be considered readable by today's standards, and only a handful can claim t
have faithfully and successfully transposed the range of intentions, style ar
language of the original. It could also be said that the vast majority of th
millions of English readers who have read a Zola novel have, over the year
read only the bad and bowdlerised translations. In these circumstances it
hardly surprising that Zola's reputation in the English-speaking world shou
have taken a hiding.

Emile Zola is one of the most translated authors in modern literatur
although the bulk of translation activity took place in the nineteenth centur
By 1890 his novels had been translated into all the main languages, besid
Hebrew, Bohemian, Hungarian and Portuguese, amounting, by the turn of th
century, to several hundred separate translations. After his death in 1902 the
was, however, a marked decline of interest in his work which lasted fifty yea
Today, of his thirty novels, English translations of nineteen are still in prin

The Americans were first off the mark to exploit Zola in the Engli
language, although the reason for this was not so much a thirst for literature
the absence of copyright safeguards. Any early Zola novel was free for th
taking, and it was these cheap pirated versions which poured into England
the 1880s that inspired Henry Vizetelly to begin his own publishing enterpris
But there were other reasons for the American interest too. Translations cou
be doctored to suit all shades of readers, from the pure to the pruries
although all but a few of these versions were extensively bowdlerised. Publici
was plentiful, and free, typical of which was the watershed article by Hen
James in the *New York Tribune* in 1876: '...the real for him (Zola) mea
exclusively the unclean, and he utters his crudities with an air of bravado whi
makes them doubly intolerable.' Comments like this were manna to t
publishers. For the last quarter of the nineteenth century, Zola enjoyed

opularity in America exceeded only on occasions by leading native authors. ome publishers even put his name to novels he never wrote to stimulate sales. *he Two Duchesses* (Brookside Library, 1884) and *Emile Zola's First Love Story* Chicago, 1895) are two examples. There were, during this period, eight ifferent translations each of *L'Assommoir, La Fortune des Rougon* and *Une Page 'amour,* and multiple versions of the other titles. According to Malcolm S. Jones *Translations of Zola in the United States prior to 1900, Modern Language Notes,* altimore, 1940) over 200 French authors were in print in English between 370 and 1900, with Zola by far the most published of them. From the first anslation of *Une Page d'amour* brought out by Peterson & Brothers in 1878, to e turn of the century, thirty-one American publishers issued some 200 ifferent editions of his works. Characteristically, these appeared with lurid tles of which the following represent a small selection: *Driven to her Doom; or, he Finger of Fate* (*Madeleine Férat*); *Wedded in Death* and *The Girl in Scarlet* (*La ortune des Rougon*); *A Stray Leaf from the Book of Love* (*Une Page d'amour*); *A Mad ove* and *A Fatal Conquest; or, Buried in the Ashes of a Ruined Home!* (*La Conquête Plassans*); *Christine The Model; or, Studies in Love* (*L'Oeuvre*).

This sensationalist approach still survives, especially with modern paperback prints. 'DEVOTED WIFE...OR UNREDEEMED WANTON?' describes *adeleine Férat* on the cover of a post-war pulp version. Readers of *Pot-Bouille* e warned that it is the book 'that made all Paris gasp! More daring than *Nana*, ore sizzling than a dozen of the great French romances...'

The story of Zola translation in England could also be called the story of the se and fall of the Vizetelly family, who began to publish English texts of Zola ovels from 1884. They were not the first, however; Tinsley Brothers had put it *Au Bonheur des dames* in 1883. But Vizetelly & Co. bought the translation ghts to this novel a year or so later and from 1885 established a Zola monopoly hich lasted until Henry's imprisonment for pornography in 1889 when it was lit between Chatto & Windus and Hutchinson & Co.

The Vizetellys were an idealistic family with an almost fanatical admiration r Zola's work. The extent of Ernest Vizetelly's devotion to the novelist is uchingly revealed in his preface to *Vérité* (1903), 'the longest as well as the st of my dear master's writings'. The translations had been, he wrote, sentially a labour of love, which may have had something to do with the poor tes of pay he received from the publishers but which also reflects his vareness of the responsibility of his 'self-chosen task of placing the great bulk Emile Zola's writings within the reach of those Anglo-Saxons who, nfortunately, are unable to read French'.

Although their loyalty is commendable, I'm afraid the Vizetellys, father and n, come in for a good deal of punishment in the course of this chapter, for in me ways Zola's novels could not have fallen into less eligible hands. Between em they translated or published almost every one of Zola's novels and for venty years they were the novelist's principal spokesmen to the nglish-speaking world. While they were modestly conscious of their ortcomings they seemed oblivious to their inability to write simple, readable prose, for all their translations are identified by a cataleptic style which has th vivacity of concrete.

The Vizetellys cannot be excused on the grounds that they were victims the circumlocution fashionable in the Victorian era; the Lutetian Socie editions prove with half a dozen Zola novels that outstanding writers cou produce faithful yet stylish translations. If nineteenth-century translation Zola had remained exclusively in the hands of the Vizetellys and Chatto Windus this would be a sorry chapter indeed. Fortunately, in 1894 and 189 the Lutetian Society (*Lutetia* was the ancient name for Paris) in Londo introduced some scholarship into the range by commissioning translations six novels:

La Curée, translated by A. Teixeira de Mattos
L'Assommoir, translated by Arthur Symons
Nana, translated by Victor Plarr
Pot-Bouille, translated by Percy Pinkerton
Germinal, translated by Havelock Ellis
La Terre, translated by Ernest Dowson

In every case the translator was a writer of some literary distinction, with th result that these texts are uniformly excellent. Two of the translations bel Croce's philosophy that translation is impossible, for they are masterpieces their kind: Symons's *L'Assommoir* and Ellis's *Germinal*. Ernest Dowson's te for *La Terre* is also outstanding. It is interesting to note that both Symons ar Dowson were poets of some stature, adding support to the view that poets mal the best translators. The Lutetian texts were the first *unabridged* versions Zola's novels in English, made possible by the fact that they were private printed and sold only to subscribers from editions limited to 300 numbere copies. The books were printed on hand-made paper and each w handsomely bound in two volumes.

But we must be fair to the Vizetellys because without their courageo enterprise Zola's English admirers might have suffered from a drought. Fe publishers in the 1880s could have been anxious to jump on the naturali bandwaggon for Zola and his followers were criticised in the most vitriol terms. 'Naturalism', wrote W.S. Lilly in *The Fortnightly Review*, 'eliminates fro men all but the ape... it is a victory of fact over principle, of mechanism ov imagination, of appetites dignified as rights over duties, of sensation ov intellect.'

One must also admire the Vizetellys' loyalty to their author after th persecution which led to Henry's imprisonment in 1889. After the trials ar book by Zola had become too hot to handle in England. Vizetelly & Co. held th translation rights to both past and future novels but understandably the fir was in no position to publish them. Ernest spent two years trying to find publisher to take over the work but time and time again the manuscripts wou be returned, often unopened. It took *The Debacle* to get the wheels turni again, for its reputation preceded it to England in the form of glowi

estimonials from famous war correspondents and highly respected army
rass. Ernest Vizetelly managed to sell the serialisation rights of the new novel
o the *Weekly Times and Echo*, and sent the proofs, with faint hopes, to Chatto &
Vindus. At that time this firm published a diverse list of authors from Mrs
Alexander (*Valerie's Fate* and *Maid, Wife or Widow?*) to Artemus Ward, and
adventurously decided to add Zola to it. *The Debacle* was published in October
892, and was so successful that the firm was encouraged to republish Zola's
other books — or at least a portion of them, such was the extent of the
mutilation they suffered.

The 1950s revival of Zola's novels is recounted elsewhere in this book. All the
Lutetian Society translations are still in print with the exception of Dowson's *La
Terre*, and the modern reader can choose from at least two translations of the
most important novels; altogether twenty-two different translations are
currently available in Britain but only half a dozen or so in America. One
incidental advantage a translation has over its original is that it can be
'brought up to date', especially with regard to idiomatic expressions which tend
to have a literary life of only a generation or two. 'Heavens!' might have been a
reasonable if prudent substitution for 'Merde!' in a popular translation during
the 1930s, but a translator today would almost certainly use 'Shit!', thus
recapturing the intended force of the original. Descriptive passages can also
gain in contemporary readability from translational revision. As a broad
generalisation, today's descriptive prose is much less prolix and cumbersome
than that of a century, or even half a century ago. An ideal translation will take
cognisance of this while at the same time attempting to retain the author's
idiosyncrasies of style. In the hands of a skilled and sensitive translator, a work
written originally in a previous age can be given an attractive new suit of clothes
without materially affecting its qualities as popular literature, an advantage
denied indigenous writing, which must be read by subsequent generations with
all its verbal warts and antique wrinkles.

The rest of this chapter is taken up with a comparative study of as many
English translations of Zola's novels as I have been able to locate over the past
decade, which I hope will help as a guide for English readers. Quite obviously
the list must acknowledge a large number of omissions, but as these are mostly
confined to early American translations, all but a few of which have sunk
without trace, I hope the default will not too seriously affect its usefulness.

Every translation has been given a key number which identifies each excerpt
quoted in the text of this book. Also given in the list is the original French title of
each novel, date of serialisation and book publication (with one or two
exceptions, book publication followed within a month of the concluding date of
the serialisation), published title in English, translator, date of translation, and
the name of the publisher. Although I have attempted to make this list as
usefully complete and as accurate as possible, I apologise in advance
inevitable errors and inexplicable omissions.

NOVELS

La Confession de Claude

Published 1865

(1) *Claude's Confession*	George D. Cox	1888	Temple Co	London
(2) *Claude's Confession*	—	1892	Crawford & Co	Phila- delphia

Of historical rather than literary interest, Zola's first novel found publisher for an English translation solely because of the author's bestselling name; b 1890, *anything* written by Zola would find readers. Undeterred by the less tha sparkling narrative style, the American publisher blurbed it enthusiastically '...a dark drama of blasted youth and dissipation...the description of th public ball is a bit of lurid word-painting which Zola never su passed...*Claude's Confession* is one of the strongest books imaginable, an will certainly fascinate all who take it up.'

Le Voeu d'une morte

Part-serialised in *L'Evénement* during 1886; published same year.

(3) *A Dead Woman's Wish**	Count C. S. de Soissons	1902	Greening & Co	Londor

Another literary curiosity, this, introduced by a quaint disclaimer: 'Readers o Emile Zola during the last three decades will not find this work in the least lik those which practically made his name as a realist (i.e. pornographer). Many o the "studies", however much we admire the craftsmanship, were revolting i the extreme and exposed the most abominable and debasing side of the base part of human nature – French – and detailed immorality and worse in thei blackest aspects.'

Les Mysteres de Marseille

Serialised in *Le Messager de Provence* from March to December 1867

(4) *The Mysteries of Marseilles†*	Edward Vizetelly	1895	Hutchinson & Co	London

It wasn't until twenty-five years after its publication in France that Zola wa approached for the English translation rights to this dreary work, and the ga

---

* Republished by Stanley Paul & Co, London (1928); and in the U.S. by David McKa Co, Philadelphia (1928).
† Republished by Walter J. Black Inc, New York (1928)† Fertig Howard Inc, New York. (1976 reprint).

says a lot about its magnetism. It also says something about the author for allowing a novel he regretted to be republished in English.

This version does, however, allow us to sample the translatory skills of Edward Vizetelly; his style is as simple and straightforward as his brother Ernest's is prolix and flowery.

Thérèse Raquin

Serialised as *Une Mariage d'amour* in *L'Artiste* from August to October 1867

(5)	*Thérèse Raquin**	Edward Vizetelly	1887	Vizetelly London & Co
(6)	*Theresa*	—	1952	Corgi Books London
(7)	*Thérèse Raquin*	Philip G. Downs	1955	William London Heinemann
(8)	*Thérèse Raquin†*	Lee Marcourt	1956	Ace Books, New York Inc.
(9)	*Thérèse Raquin*	Willard R. Trask	1960	Bantam New York Books Inc.
10)	*Thérèse Raquin*	L. W. Tancock	1962	Penguin London & Books Baltimore Ltd

That there should exist at least six different English translations of this relatively minor novel is an indication of its standing as a popular drama. The narrative moves along at satisfying clip, and with its economy of language and absence of lyrical descriptive passages, few demands confront the translator.

The Vizetelly text, by Edward Vizetelly, is about the best Zola translation issued by the firm and one of the few which can be read today without wincing. The volume, incidentally, is typical of the time with its quite bloodthirsty illustrations in the finest tradition of the penny bloods.

Of the modern translations, the 1955 text by Philip G. Downs has the smoothly urgent style ideally suited to this novel. His craftsman-like command of simple English and direct expression is a feature sadly missing in so many Zola translations. Tancock's version is excellent, too, and bears the fruits of some judicious editing of what the translator considered to be meaningless repetitions, while still retaining the novelist's linguistic mannerisms of that time.

The remaining texts are wanting in various ways although they serve to tell the story with a minimum of fuss. The Marcourt text is the most corrupt, for it compresses the original 85,000 words or so into a raunchy, pulp-style meller of about 35,000 words.

* Republished by Grant Richards, London (1902).
† Republished in Britain by World Distributors, London (1958).

Madeleine Férat

Serialised but discontinued in *L'Evénement Illustré* during 1868
and published the same year

(11)	*Madeleine Férat*	for H. Vizetelly	1888	Vizetelly & Co. Londo
(12)	*Shame**	Lee Marcourt	1954	Ace Books, New York Inc.
(13)	*Madeleine Férat*†	Alec Brown	1957	Elek Books Ltd Londo

Alec Brown's is the only translation that manages to put over Zola's far-fetche
'indissoluble tie' theory – which is the very theme of the novel – with
enthusiasm and conviction. Vizetelly succeeds only in rendering the
physiological explanations even more ludicrous, while Marcourt, perhap
sensibly, discards the relevant passages altogether.

Vizetelly anglicises Guillaume to William and Jacques to James, while
Marcourt has William but retains Jacques; puzzling, that. The Marcour
version reduces the text to less than two-thirds its original length.

Brown's translation, the most recent and still in print, is the best of the three
his easy, anecdotal style ideally suited to the narrative with its relentless twist
and coincidental turns. The translator admits in an introduction to some
editing: smoothing out 'roughnesses in the original' and 'minor blemishes' a
he puts it, although the colour of Madeleine's hair still runs through the
spectrum from golden to titian and finally to blood red. The overall result
though, is a narrative that is consistently readable, despite rather too many
unfortunate phrases as when Guillaume 'fastened worshipping eyes on her
and 'his hand was on her bowels'.

La Fortune des Rougon

Serialised in *Le Siècle* from 28 June to 10 August 1870;
interrupted by Franco-Prussian War, and concluded between
18-21 March 1871. Published as a book in October 1871

(14)	*The Fortune of the Rougons*	for H. Vizetelly	1886	Vizetelly & Co. London
(15)	*The Fortune of the Rougons*	Ed. E. Vizetelly	1898	Chatto & Windus London

The anonymous translation made for Henry Vizetelly in 1886 only adds, by its
glutinous prolixity, to the still-life quality of what should have been an exciting
account of the 1851 *coup d'état*. Although this version was extensively edited by
Ernest Vizetelly for Chatto & Windus in 1898 – he claimed to have altered one
sentence out of every three – substitutions like 'he laid his head upon her

* Published in Britain by Digit Books (Brown, Watson Ltd), London, (1958).
† Published in the U.S. by Citadel Press, New York (1957).

bosom, and watered it with his tears' for 'he laid his head upon her bare breast and bathed her flesh with his tears' hardly amount to an improvement on the original.

A fair case exists for the publication of a modern translation, if only for its historical value and to supply readers of the other *Rougon-Macquart* books with this key opening novel.

La Curée

Serialised in *La Cloche* from 29 September to 5 November 1871, when publication was stopped on advice from the censorship authorities. Book published January 1872.

(16)	*The Rush for the Spoil*	for H. Vizetelly	1886	Vizetelly & Co.	London
(17)	*The Kill**	A. Teixeira de Mattos	1895	Lutetian Society	London

By 1886 the Vizetelly enterprise was in fine fettle, with no hint of storms ahead. The big sales of *Nana* and *L'Assommoir* indicated a substantial market for racy, sensational French novels and with *La Curée* Vizetelly began to issue Zola's earlier *Rougon-Macquart* books. *La Curée* appeared with an embossed cover depicting Renée on Maxime's lap, and with its contents relatively undefiled by one of the smallest crops of bowdlerisms in any Vizetelly translation. This, in 1886, was something of an achievement, for the theme of incest must have represented a formidable hurdle for the enterprising publisher to clear. But clear it he did, with a minimum of circumlocution. In due time the novel suffered not from mutilation, but banishment, for it was one of the translations not republished by Chatto & Windus at the turn of the century.

The Vizetelly version is an intelligent translation although its readability today is marred by the ever-present Victorian archaisms like 'They partook deeply of voluptuousness.' The best thing in the Vizetelly edition is the preface contributed by George Moore, full of remarkable insights into the novel and expressed with a flow of such lyrical language that had the translating been entrusted to him, the only other English version, made for the Lutetian Society in 1895, might not have been necessary.

The Lutetian Society-commissioned translation by A. Teixeira de Mattos, is still in print under the Elek imprint, and remains the standard English text for this novel; its remarkably timeless tone no doubt acts as a deterrent to a more modern competitor.

The Lutetian translation has real style and occasional flashes of wit, as when Renée walks across a crowded ballroom, 'leaving in her wake a trail of

* Republished in England by Weidenfeld & Nicolson Ltd, London (1954), Paul Elek Ltd, London (1958) and Arrow Books Ltd, London (1967); in America by Boni & Liveright, New York (1924) and Citadel Press, New York (1957).

dresscoats astounded and charmed at the transparency of her muslin blouse'. The conservatory sequences, too, are projected as though the change of language were no barrier, with descriptive prose as luxuriant as the vegetation which thrives there: the leaves of water lilies are 'leprous, like the backs of monstrous, blistered toads'; deformed cactuses are covered with 'loathly excrescences, oozing with poison' and quisqualias 'twined and intertwined like slim adders'. No wonder Zola gave the Lutetian Society editions his unqualified approval.

Le Ventre de Paris

Serialised in *L'Etat* from 12 January to 17 March 1873

(18)	*La Belle Lisa: or The Paris Market Girls*	Mary Neal Sherwood for H. Vizetelly	1882	T.B. Peterson Phila-Bros. delphia
(19)	*The Fat and the Thin*	for H. Vizetelly	1888	Vizetelly London & Co.
(20)	*The Fat and the Thin*	Ed. E. Vizetelly	1896	Chatto & London Windus
(21)	*Savage Paris**	David Hughes and Marie-Jacqueline Mason	1955	Elek Books London Ltd

There isn't much I can usefully say about the early translations except that they are tedious, dated and unfaithful. The extent to which the original 1888 Vizetelly version missed the point is illustrated in the 'Cheese Symphony', from which I quote its rendering of the final, dying notes:

> At the mention of Gavard's name there was a pause in the conversation. The three women looked at each other with a circumspect air. The reek of the camemberts made them puff. Their strong odour of high venison had overpowered the less penetrating emanations of the marolles and the limbourgs; and they were choking the other smells with the copious exhalations of their foul breath. Every now and then a slight whiff from the parmesan made itself felt in the midst of the fetid atmosphere, and the Bries added a musty flavour of damp sheep-skin; while at intervals the livarots spouted out a gust of overpowering stench, and the aniseed cheese kept dominating in its turn everything else, by its prolonged and penetrating emissions.

Nowhere does the translator include Zola's orchestral analogies. In 1896 the rights of the translation were bought by Chatto & Windus and the original text was extensively edited by Ernest Vizetelly. By then the passage had achieved some critical notoriety and Vizetelly retranslated it as follows:

> At the mention of Gavard there came a pause. The gossips looked at each other with a circumspect air. And then, as they drew breath, they inhaled the odour of the Camemberts, whose gamy scent had overpowered the less penetrating emanations of the Marolles and the Limbourgs, and spread around with remarkable power. Every now and then, however, a slight whiff, a flutelike note, came from the Parmesan,

* Published in America by the Citadel Press, New York (1955).

while the Bries contributed a soft, musty scent, the gentle, insipid sound, as it were, of damp tambourines. Next followed an overpowering refrain from the Livarots, and afterwards the Géromé, flavoured with aniseed, kept up the symphony with a high prolonged note, like that of a vocalist during a pause in the accompaniment.

The passage is now more faithful to the original but hardly an improvement otherwise; you can compare it with a modern translation excerpted in Chapter 6. In many ways the Chatto & Windus version is less readable than the 1888 version which retained, at least, some of the rather robust language of the fishwives. In his editing Ernest Vizetelly gave this a thorough hosing down, as he confesses in his preface: 'I have frequently chastened their language in deference to English susceptibilities, so that the story, whilst retaining every essential feature, contains nothing to which exception can reasonably be taken.' On that point, to be sure, Vizetelly was an expert.

The translation by David Hughes and Marie-Jacqueline Mason is in quite a different class, as accomplished as the earlier versions are sloppy. The translators have cleverly captured the lyrical flow of the various prose poems in the narrative, and although there are some crazy conversational abberations – they have, for instance, Florent using words like 'pullulating' and 'malodorous' – the text is a faithful version of its French original.

La Conquête de Plassans

Serialised in *Le Siècle* from 24 February to 25 April 1874

(22)	*The Conquest of Plassans*	for H. Vizetelly	1887	Vizetelly & Co.	London
(23)	*A Priest in the House**	Brian Rhys	1957	Elek Books Ltd	London

Perhaps the anti-clerical tone of this novel enthused the radical Vizetelly for there is an element of vivacity in this English text missing from most of the other Vizetelly translations. It was later reprinted, with very few changes, by Chatto & Windus. The only currently available English version is the excellent translation by Brian Rhys who, with a fine nose for intrigue and a well-tuned ear for dialogue effortlessly captures the gossipy flavour of the narrative.

La Faute de l'abbé Mouret

Serialised in Vestnik Evropy, St Petersburg, January–March 1875

(24)	*Abbé Mouret's Transgression*	for H. Vizetelly	1886	Vizetelly & Co.	London
(25)	*Abbé Mouret's Transgression*	Ed. E. Vizetelly	1900	Chatto & Windus	London

* Also published in America by Citadel Press, New York (1957).

(26)	*The Sin of the Abbé Mouret*	M. Smyth	1904	McLaren & Co.	London
(27)	*The Abbé Mouret's Sin**	Alec Brown	1957	Elek Books Ltd	London
(28)	*The Sin of Father Mouret*	Sandy Petrey	1969	Prentice-Hall, Inc	New Jersey

I am not surprised that this novel has attracted at least four major English versions, for in it Zola's linguistic skills are revealed at their peak. Indeed, Sandy Petrey admits in an afterword to his version that the novel 'displays a stunning control of the French language, and it should be stated. . .that no translation can completely capture this compelling quality'.

Alec Brown is just as candid although a shade less modest when he declares that, 'even supposing, as of course I do, that in the main this English version, made with loving and admiring care, does Zola justice', he is at the same time well aware of the immensity of the challenge. He says in his introduction,

> Such prose calls for great elasticity in translation. At one moment, bald word for word English would fail to convey all the aroma of the original and one has to seek an approximating evocative paraphrase, while at others one is obliged to avoid the literal word in English for the very opposite reason, in case, lacking its French precision of emotive tone, it should prove too evocative. In such cases one has to seek safety in understatement.

There is a basic reason for this difficulty. While English may in many ways be superior to French for the logical construction of sentences, it is less precise when it comes to the expression of meaning. Where our dictionaries record the meanings of words, with little attempt to suggest priorities, the French prescribe them. Thus, even with his lyrical, emotive prose Zola is choosing his words with greater intellectual consideration than would his counterpart in English. This is something the translator must keep in mind if he is not to diffuse and corrupt the original intention and effect.

In the present example, however, I am not too sure about the 'understatement' in Alec Brown's version, although it captures the essence and variegated bouquets of Zola's prose with greater success than any of the others. It must be remembered that, despite Brown's reservations, we are reading with English, not French eyes; we are accustomed to the imprecision of our language and while interpretations may be at variance it is this very possibility of variety in our language which can offer an enlarging experience to the reader. At any rate, Brown's language tends to be suitably extravagant, and I think it is all to the good. Petrey's American translation (one is brought up short when a peasant girl 'felt her fanny being pinched', a timeless Anglo-American joke) on the other hand is more literal and considerably less ornate in its language. Perhaps this reflects, to some extent, Petrey's academic background; at the time he was Assistant Professor of Romance Languages at the New York

* Republished in Elek's *Bestseller Library* as *The sinful Priest* in 1960 and by Arrow Books, London (1967).

State University, specialising in translating from the French, and in French literary criticism. His text is spare and neat, but certainly not that of a poet.

A comparison of the two approaches is interesting, and for this exercise I have selected a virtuoso passage which is a kind of floral counterpoint to Serge's declaration of love to Albine in the garden of *Le Paradou*. Here, first, is Brown's rendition:

> All round them the rose-bushes flowered, with crazy profusion, lover's profusion, all scarlet laughter, pink laughter, white laughter. The living blooms revealed their petals as when corsages reveal the naked riches of the bosom. There were yellow roses brushing the golden skins of barbarian maidens, straw roses, lemon roses, sunshine roses, every shade possible of blossoms bronzed by blazing skies. Then the flesh grew more tender still, the tea roses assumed lovely moistness, exposing beauties which modesty had hid, crevices of the body not usually shown, of silken softness, with faint blue transparency of minute capillaries. The laughing rose life expanded to the full, pink whiteness with subtle tinge of the fine red brush, the snow of a virgin foot trying the waters of the spring, pale rose, more discreet than the fiery whiteness of the knee half seen, or the flash of upper arm glimpsed up loose sleeve, frank rose, blood under satin, naked shoulders, naked hips, all a woman's nakedness, caressed by light, vivid rose, the budding blossoms of the bosom, the parting blooms of the lips as they draw in the scent of warm breath. And the climbing roses, vast growth with their downpour of white blossoms, enwrapped all these roses, all this flesh, in the lace of their sprays, in the innocence of their gossamer muslin, while here and there red wine lees roses, roses almost black, roses of blood, thrust the wound of fierce love deep into that purity of the bride. Wedding of sweet-scented coppices, bringing the virginities of May to the impregnation of July and August, first innocent kisses, culled like a posy of flowers on the marriage morn. Even in the grass underfoot, a froth of roses, roses in long high-necked gown of green cloth, awaited love. All down the ride, barred by rays of sunshine, flowers wandered, faces turned towards them, as the summoning zephyrs wafted them.

Brown's precision and phrasing goes to pieces at times but there is here a swelling mood of breathless excitement, the fine frenzy of being drowned in a voluptuous bed of flowers that softly kaleidoscopes into the limbs and torsos of perfumed women. Having caught your breath, now read Petrey's equally skilful rendering:

> The rose-bushes bloomed around them. It was the insane flowering of a lover, filled with red laughter, pink laughter, white laughter. The living flowers opened like naked flesh, like bodices revealing the treasures of breasts. There were yellow roses shedding the gilded skin of savage girls, straw roses, lemon roses, roses the color of the sun, all the subtle shades of necks bronzed by burning skies. Then the flesh softened, tea-colored roses hinted at exquisite moistness, spread hidden modesty, displayed the parts of the body which are not shown, possessing silken smoothness, made slightly blue by the body's veins. Next the laughing rose-life blossomed out: rose white, barely tinted by a spot of lake, white like a virgin's foot dipping into the water of a spring; pale rose, more discreet than the hot whiteness of a half-glimpsed knee, than the light with which a young arm illumines a wide sleeve; frank rose, blood under satin, naked shoulders, naked hips, all woman's nakedness caressed by light; lively rosebuds of a woman's breasts, half-open flowers of her lips, exhaling the smell of warm breath. And climbing rosebushes, large bushes raining white petals, dressed all these roses, all this flesh, in the lace of their clusters, in the innocence of their thin chiffon; while here and there, wine roses, almost black, bleeding, broke into this bridal purity with a passionate wound. Marriage of the scented forest leading May's virginity to the fertility of July and August; first ignorant kiss, picked like a flower on the wedding morning. Even in the grass, the moss roses, with their long dresses of

381

green linen, waited for love. Along the path striped by sunbeams strolled flowers, their faces bent forward, calling the gentle winds as they passed.

This version is far more controlled than Brown's breathless outpouring. There are the same attempts at alliteration: Brown has 'blossoms bronzed by blazing skies...in the lace of their sprays', while Petrey offers 'wine roses, almost black, bleeding, broke into this bridal purity...' Both are a long way short of perfection in poetic style, but if we look at the imagery, Zola's true preoccupation in this passage, it must be recognised that Brown's images invade the mind more readily than do Petrey's. 'With faint blue transparency of minute capillaries' is much more provocative to the senses than 'made slightly blue by the body's veins' and certainly more poetic. 'A virgin foot trying the waters of the spring' is an image; 'a virgin's foot dipping into the water' is reality. Herein lies the core of the problem of transposing Zola's imagery into English; for a poet to be read as a poet in another language, he needs a poet for his translator.

Both the modern translations, however, are highly recommended versions, which is more than can be said of the early English texts. Of these, Smyth's translation of 1904 is a quaint travesty of the original: in 'plighting his troth' Serge offers to carry out Albine's 'lightest behests', whatever they are. 'Was it to this, then, that his whole day had led up?' is typical of the style. In cutting the novel to 75,000 words it is amazing that the publisher still had to resort to euphemism, but the Victorians and post-Victorians never cease to astonish me. Luckily, this version is now a bibliophile's rarity.

The original Vizetelly translation of 1886 is a more conscientious effort and the translators themselves in a portion of a single, significant passage in which final effect is as stodgy as a plot of turnips. The novel was later edited by Ernest Vizetelly for Chatto & Windus, with dire results.

I think all that can be said about these various translations is summed up by the translators themselves in portion of a single, significant passage in which Zola shows Albine watching the sleeping Désirée, envious of her total rapport with nature. Here is Alec Brown's interpretation:

Motionless, Albine watched this other girl sleep, this lovely body finding its satisfaction by wallowing in straw, and she longed herself to be able thus to be languid, in the drowth of love, and slumber sweet from an orgasm reached merely by a few straws tickling her neck. She was envious of those powerful arms, that firm bosom, that utterly fleshly life lapped in the fertile warmth of a flock of farmyard creatures, that purely animal blossoming which made of that plump child the passive sister of the big white and red heifer in calf. She dreamed of being loved herself by a brown cock-bird and of herself loving naturally, without shame, as any tree grows, merely opening all her veins to the ejaculation of life's sap. It was the earth itself that satisfied Désirée when she wallowed on her back.

Petrey's version now, in which the translator obviously has the brake on the explosion of ideas and images evoked in the passage:

Albine, still motionless, was watching Désirée sleep, watching this beautiful girl who satisfied her flesh by rolling on straw. She wanted to be this tired and relaxed; she wished that she too could be put to sleep by enjoyment; she wanted straws to tickle her neck as well. She envied those strong arms, that hard chest, that completely carnal life in the impregnating heat of a flock of animals, that purely bestial expansion which made the plump child a peaceful sister to the red and white cow. She dreamed of being loved by the tawny rooster and of loving as the trees grow, naturally, without shame, opening every one of her veins to spurts of sap. It was the earth which made Désirée drowsy when she lay on her back.

It lacks earthiness, doesn't it, as though Petrey is a little ashamed at having to report such basic thoughts? Now for the original Vizetelly version in which you should immediately note some radical departures:

> Albine, who had remained perfectly still, watched Désirée sleeping, the pretty girl who could find a pleasure in rolling about in the straw. She wished that she, too, could slumber away so peacefully, tired out with pleasure, just because a few straws had tickled her neck. She felt envious and jealous of those strong arms and that well-developed breast, of all that fleshly vitality, and those purely animal emotions, which made that plump girl the tranquil easy-minded sister of the great red and white cow. She was dreaming there of being beloved by the yellow cock, and that she, too, loved, just as the trees send out shoots, quite as a matter of course, and with no feeling of shame, simply opening out their veins to the passage of the sap.

You'll note here that Albine dreams not of being 'loved' by the rooster, but 'beloved'. That the rooster is now yellow and not brown or tawny is a matter of interpretation; the original calls for *fauve*, or fawn-coloured. But the dramatic change is in the final sentence, where Albine should be dreaming of procreating like a universal mother, 'opening her veins to the ejaculation of life's sap'. Vizetelly intentionally misses the point, for the original is quite explicit. Finally, here is the Chatto & Windus version of the passage, retranslated by Ernest Vizetelly in 1900:

> Albine, who had remained perfectly still, watched the slumber of Désirée, that big, plump girl who found her great delight in rolling about in the straw. She wished that she, too, could slumber away so peacefully, and feel such pleasure, because a few straws had tickled her neck. And she felt jealous of those strong arms, that firm bosom, all that vitality, all that purely animal development which made the other like a tranquil easy-minded sister of the big red and white cow.

One aspect of translation which never ceases to present problems is the substitution of colloquialisms, usually in dialogue. In this regard Brown's version is a frequent offender with anachronistic slang. A cleric is described as a 'sky-pilot'; the folk of Artaud village are 'no cop' and bandits are 'gangsters'. Two of these slang terms are now double anachronisms; in the context of their meaning they could not conceivably have been used during the mid nineteenth century, the period of the novel, nor are they in use today.

Son Excellence Eugène Rougon

Serialised in *Le Siècle*, 25 January to 11 March 1876

| (29) *Clorinda: or the Rise and Reign of His Excellency Eugène Rougon* | Mary Neal Sherwood | 1880 | T.B. Peterson & Bros | Philadelphia |

(30)	*His Excellency Eugène Rougon**	for H. Vizetelly	1886	Vizetelly & Co.	London
(31)	*His Excellency*†	Alec Brown	1958	Elek Books Ltd	London

Alec Brown's attempt to render the political scene of the 1850's, written in 1876, into the modern English idiom, deserves some commendation. Unlike the previous novel, also translated by Brown, *His Excellency* makes few linguistic demands, and it hardly bristles with subtleties. The result is a craftsman-like interpretation of a straightforward narrative, only spoiled occasionally by inexplicable oddities like 'unbeknownst', 'deign' and 'a shudder seized her bosom'. The early translations are run-of-the-mill Victorian mannerist, and fortunately out of print.

L'Assommoir

Serialised in *Le Bien public*, 13 April to 7 June 1876; discontinued and resumed in *La Republique des lettres*, 9 July 1876 to 7 January 1877

(32)	*L'assommoir* (*sic*)	Mary Neal Sherwood	1879	T.B. Peterson & Bros	Phila-delphia
(33)	*Gervaise*	E. Binsse	1879	G. W. Carleton & Co.	New York
(34)	*The 'Assommoir'**	for H. Vizetelly	1884	Vizetelly & Co.	London
(35)	*L'Assommoir*†	Arthur Symons	1895	Lutetian Society	London
(36)	*The Dram Shop**	Ed. E. Vizetelly	1897	Chatto & Windus	London
(37)	*Drink*	S. J. A. Fitzgerald	1903	Greening & Co.	London
(38)	*The Dram Shop*	Gerard Hopkins	1951	Hamish Hamil-ton Ltd	London
(38a)	*The Gin Palace***	Buckner B. Trawick	1952	Avon Publications, Inc.	New York
(39)	*L'Assommoir*	Atwood H. Townsend	1962	New Ameri-can Library	New York
(40)	*L'Assommoir*	Leonard Tancock	1970	Penguin Books Ltd	London and New York

---

* Edited by Ernest Vizetelly and republished by Chatto & Windus, London, (1900).

† Published in America by Dufour Editions, Pennsylvania (1958).

* Both texts have been reprinted in various formats over the years, and in the U.S. by Alfred A. Knopf, New York (1924); and Walter J. Black, Inc, New York, (1928).

† Extensively reprinted; in England as *Drunkard* by Elek Books Ltd and Bestseller Library, London (1958); and in the U.S. by Boni & Liveright, New York (1924).

** Originally published in *World Literature*, Barnes and Noble, Inc. New York.

L'Assommoir, with its idiomatic dialogue and colourful slang, has always been a challenge to the translator. The difficulties, for example, in translating Cockney slang of a century ago into modern French, can be imagined. But that is just the problem *L'Assommoir* poses for the English translator. Leonard Tancock, in the introduction to his 1970 translation for Penguin, found that the task of rendering slang and obscenity 'is self-defeating in that the more exactly it hits off the tone of the original in the slang of the moment when the translator is doing it, the less durable it is likely to be, simply because the "in" or "with it" expression by its very nature never lasts and becomes incomprehensible in a very short time. On the other hand, a translation must speak the language of its own time and any attempt to reproduce "period" slang or popular language is bound to produce effects as grotesque as "Marry, thou art a scurvy knave"'.

Ideally, the aim of the translator of *L'Assommoir* ought to be to arrest the modern reader to the same degree Zola shocked his reader in 1876, with the blunt vernacular of its characters. Alas, this is neither practicable nor possible; we have, during the last couple of decades, been through the obscenity barrier and beyond, and most of us are immune from its shockwaves. The only solution, the compromise Tancock arrived at, is to use the guidelines of timelessness and universality when selecting slang expressions. Tancock has done this quite effectively, I think, but whether his translation will avoid the faded fate of many previous attempts only time will tell.

How well the various translators have captured the original force, colour and intention of the original is difficult to measure, but can be roughly demonstrated by comparing their renderings of a common passage. In the discussion of the novel in Chapter 8 the synopsis includes part of the laundry fight between Gervaise and Virginie excerpted from Symons's translation; the two Vizetelly versions are given in Chapter 15. Here is Gerard Hopkins's interpretation; Gervaise has just discovered that her husband, Lantier, has deserted her to live with Virginie's sister:

> 'All right, then, it *is* my sister...does that satisfy you?...Mad about each other, they are...you should just see 'em cuddling!...Oh, he's left you all right, you and your couple of byblows – nice pair of kids, I must say, with their scabby faces.... Copper got one of 'em on you, didn't he?...and there was three others you got rid of, because you wanted to travel light!...Your precious Lantier told us all about *that*, and a lot more, too! Had just about enough of your carcass, I sh'd say!'
> 'Whore!...whore!...whore!' shouted Gervaise, by now quite beside herself, and trembling from head to foot.
> She swung round, bent down and felt along the floor. But all she could find was a small pail of blue-bag. This she took by the legs and flung the contents full in Virginie's face.
> 'You filthy slut!' screamed the latter. 'Ruined my dress, that's what you've been and done!'

You'll notice that terms like 'whore' and 'filthy slut' replace Symons's 'jade' and 'dirty beast', while in the same contexts Vizetelly uses 'cow' and the rather sounding 'walking dungheap'.

The most modern translation, Tancock's, is also disappointingly restrained:

A titter ran round. Emboldened by the success, Virginie advanced two steps, drew herself up to her full height and screamed louder still:

'Just you come here and see. I'll settle your hash! We don't want you here, getting us down. Why, I don't even know the old cow! If she had caught me with that water I wouldn't half have pulled her skirt up! You'd have seen! What the hell have I done to her, anyway? What have I done to you, eh, you slut?'

'Don't you talk so much,' Gervaise stammered out. 'You know all right...my husband was seen last night...so shut your mouth or else I'll throttle you, and that's a fact!'

'Her husband! That's a good one, that is...the lady's husband! Just as though she could have had a husband, with a walk like that. It's not my fault if he's thrown you over. You don't think I've pinched him, do you? Search me. If you want to know, you got him down, he was too good for you. Had he got his collar on? Has anybody found Madame's husband? A reward is offered...'

More laughter. Gervaise could only go on muttering, almost inaudibly:

'You know all right, you know all right...It's that sister of your's, I'll strangle that sister of yours...'

'Right-oh, go and have it out with my sister,' sneered Virginie. 'Oh, so it's my sister, is it? It could be, at that – she's a damn sight better turned out than you are! But what's it got to do with me? Can't a woman wash her clothes in peace now? Leave me be, can't you? I've had enough.'

But she it was who started up again after five or six bangs with her beater, drunk with her own invective and carried away. Three times she stopped and started again:

'All right, it's my sister. There, are you satisfied now? They are madly in love. You should just see them billing and cooing! And so he's left you with your bastards? Sweet kids, with scabs all over their faces! You had one off a policeman, didn't you? And got rid of three others so as not to have excess luggage when you came here.... Oh yes, we got all that from your darling Lantier. He can tell some good ones, he can. He's had enough of your old carcass!'

'Bitch, bitch, bitch!' screamed Gervaise, beside herself and once again shaking all over.

She turned round and looked on the floor again, and finding nothing but the small tub of blue, she seized that by its legs and sloshed the stuff right in Virginie's face.

'The whore, she's done my dress in!' shrieked Virginie, who had one shoulder soaked and her left hand dyed blue. 'You wait, you slut!'

She seized a pail in her turn and emptied it over Gervaise. Then a battle royal was joined. They both ran along the rows of tubs, picked up full pails and ran back and threw the contents at each other's heads. Each deluge was accompanied by screams. Now Gervaise was answering back, too.

'One for you, you filthy bitch...you got that one all right. That'll cool your arse for you!'

In this version we seem to have made little advance on Vizetelly's, made almost a century before. There is also an odd incompatability between such terms as 'titter' and 'settle your hash' – the first from the schoolroom and the second from gangster movies. Nevertheless, none of the renderings can be judged a failure.

Then there are the idiomatic terms used as familiar endearments, as a barmaid's 'Same again, love?' or a mother's, 'Oh, you poor wee darling!' Zola's final paragraph, in which the drunken undertaker Bazouge fondly addresses Gervaise's corpse, is a good example, and a linguistically difficult one that presents demands few translators are apparently able to meet. Here is Symons's version of 1895, perhaps the most acceptable to our ears today:

'Now here...listen...it's me, Bibi-la-Gaieté, called the ladies' comforter.... Now you're all right. Sleep sound, my beauty!'

386

Hopkins's rendering has a Dickensian ring about it:

'Listen to what I tells yer... It's me, Bibi-la-Gaieté, more generally known as the Ladies' Comforter.... You're happy now...so, go bye-bye, my lovely.'

The early American translation by E. Binsse is an eye-moistening exercise in sentimentality:

'You know; listen well. It's me, Bibi-la-Gaieté, or the Gay Boy; yes, Dad Bazouge, the ladies' comforter. Go; you are happy! Rest, my darling!'

And, finally, extending the same sentimental strain, the version by S.J. Adair Fitzgerald:

'You know – now listen – it's me, Bibi-the-Gay, called the Ladies' Consoler. There, you're happy. Go to peepy-peepy, my beauty now!'

L'Assommoir attracted more translations than any other work of Zola's, and my list of nine is far from complete as it omits many turn-of-the-century cautionary tracts based on the novel. One of the earliest examples is *GERVAISE: A Story of Drink* by Henry Llewellyn Williams, one of a series of penny broadsheets published by Edward Asman, London, in 1878. An extremely scrambled rendition of the novel in five chapters, it contrives a happy ending, with Gervaise retreating from the awful abyss of alcoholism just in time; she finds happiness with her admirer Goujet: 'I'll try to live again!' says she. 'And a happy life this time,' Goujet adds, 'for Drink shall never enter our home!'

The fate of the Vizetelly translation has already been told in Chapter 15. The pre-1888 text was a fair enough interpretation and better than much of the product issued from Catherine Street, Strand; it shows none of the haste which spoils so many of Vizetelly's translations. The heavily expurgated version of 1895 is, however, quite another matter and it is unfortunate that it was the edited text that was so widely reprinted both in England and in America. Adding insult to injury, the Walter J. Black Inc. edition of 1928 cuts the text to half its length, from 180,000 words to 75,000. The disastrous effect of this wholesale amputation is evident in the marvellous chapter which describes the wedding party's visit to the Louvre, a short excerpt from which is given in Chapter 8. In the Black version this superbly comic scene is reduced to one paragraph.

The tragedy is that, until recent years, most English readers tasted Zola in this fleshless form; having only ever known spare ribs how could they ever visualise the original beast?

Drink – Zola's L'Assommoir done into English by S.J. Adair Fitzgerald – appeared in 1903 as a two-column sixpenny novel in the widely distributed 'Lotus Library' range. Companion volumes included Maupassant's *A Woman's Soul* and *When It Was Dark*, the phenomenal bestseller by Guy Thorne. Although edited to about half the length of the original, *Drink* displays quite a lot more animation in its prose than does Vizetelly's version.

There is not much between the modern translations, for, with the exception of Professor Buckner Trawick's corrupt, abbreviated and thoroughly dreadful text for Avon Publications, all are the products of skilled practitioners and all are immensely readable; Tancock, in particular, with several translations to his credit, can almost be considered a Zola veteran. But I cannot see that any of them offer an advance on Arthur Symons's (1865–1945) English text, still, fortunately, in print. It must rank as one of the finest translations of any Zola novel; with its cracking pace, economy and idiomatic rightness the reader is invariably jolted to discover that it was done as long ago as 1894. Symons's own career as a decadent poet was already deeply influenced at the time by the French symbolists, (Symons in turn influenced T.S. Eliot) and *L'Assommoir* undoubtedly benefited from his sympathy with Zola's symbol-laden and frank emotive prose.

Une Page d'amour

Serialised in *Le Bien public*, 11 December 1877 to 4 April 1878

(41)	*Hélène: A Love Episode*	Mary Neal Sherwood	1878	T.B. Peterson Phila-& Bros delphia
(42)	*A Love Episode*	for H. Vizetelly	1886	Vizetelly & Co. London
(43)	*A Love Episode*	Ed. E.A. Vizetelly	1895	Hutchinson London & Co.
(44)	*A Page of Love*	T.F. Rogerson	1897	Geo Barrie Philadelphia & Son
(45)	*A Love Affair**	Jean Stewart	1957	Paul Elek London

Under the title of *Hélène: A Love Episode*, this was the first of Zola's novels to be translated into English. Despite a warning by Henry James in the *New York Tribune* in 1876 about the 'crudeness' of the French author's language, the Philadelphia firm of T.B. Peterson & Brothers felt reasonably safe in publishing the innocuous *Une Page d'amour* in 1878. Even so it was considered judicious to hide the name of Mary Neal Sherwood, the translator, behind the masculine pseudonym of John Stirling. The book is now a rarity.

Henry Vizetelly followed with a much later translation in 1886, but notwithstanding the salubrious nature of the narrative and prose it fell victim to Ernest Vizetelly's surgery following the prosecution of his father. Hutchinson & Co. picked up the English translation rights in 1895, but dropped the passage describing the outcome of the assignation between Hélène and her lover Dr Deberle – perhaps one of the most genteel seductions in the history of literature. This version also appeared under the imprint of the Société des Beaux-Arts in England and America around the turn of the century.

* Published in the U.S. by Citadel Press, New York (1957); reprinted in Britain by Arrow Books Ltd, London (1967).

The Rogerson translation of 1897 is an inept shocker. When Hélène experienced an embarrassment, 'a rosy tint had mounted on her neck' or produced 'an empurpled countenance'; and her gentle breathing fails to 'swell the chaste line of her throat'. Even Vizetelly's expurgated version managed to ruffle the chaste repose of her bosom'! Accordingly the Rogerson translation need not concern us except as a museum piece. The current available translation is the excellent version by Jean Stewart which first appeared in 1957.

This novel places no extraordinary demands on a translator with the exception, perhaps, of the five 'word paintings' of Paris. These important mood passages take up a good deal of the text – each is a complete chapter – and obviously a translation must succeed in holding the reader's interest for several thousand words of lyrical prose. Most translators seem to have been conscious of this but only Jean Stewart manages to fire the visual imagination without being repetitious and boring. A single comparative example, a paragraph from the second view of Paris at sunset, indicates the problem. Here is Jean Stewart's rendering:

> But the sky had altered. The sun, sinking towards the slopes of Meudon, had parted the last clouds and shone out resplendent. The heavens were aflame with glory. On the far horizon the landslide of chalky boulders that lay across Charenton and Choisy-le-Roi had become a mass of carmine blocks edged with shining lacquer; the flotilla of small clouds swimming slowly in the blue over Paris put out crimson sails; while the film of white silk hung above Montmartre seemed all of a sudden to be a net of gold mesh, ready to catch the stars as they appeared. The city lay outspread under this blazing vault, yellow, streaked with long shadows. Below, on the huge square, cabs and omnibuses intermingled in a haze of orange dust, while the dark swarm of passers-by took on a paler glow, speckled with light...

Now compare the fluid brushstrokes of Jean Stewart's prose with Vizetelly's mechanical rendering and, even allowing for the dated style you will see at once the terrible fate that sometimes befalls descriptive passages in translation:

> But a change had come over the sky. The sun in its descent towards the Meudon hills had but a moment before burst through the clouds in all its splendour. The whole vault of heaven was illuminated; on the verge of the horizon a crumbling ridge of chalk-coloured clouds, that hid Charenton and Choisy-le-Roi in the distance, had their peaks tinged with carmine, edged with brilliant lace; the flotilla of smaller clouds floated slowly into the blue above Paris, and at once veiled themselves in purple; while the delicate network that seemed made of white silk thread, stretching over Montmartre, instantaneously assumed the appearance of golden tracery, the meshes of which were designed to snare the stars on their rising. Beneath the flaming vault of heaven Paris lay in yellow haze, striped with immense shadows.
> Far below, athwart its vast extent, cabs and omnibuses crawled in every direction through an orange-coloured mist, and the crowds of pedestrians, like some black swarm, glittered amidst the mass as the rays of light fell on them.

Nana

Serialised in *Le Voltaire*, 16 October 1879 to 5 February 1880

(46)	*Nana**	for H. Vizetelly	1884	Vizetelly & Co.	London
(47)	*Nana*†	Victor Plarr	1895	Lutetian Society	London
(48)	*Nana*	Joseph Keating	1926	Cecil Palmer	London
(49)	*Nana*	Charles Duff	1953	William Heinemann Ltd	Londo﹖
(50)	*Nana*	Lowell Blair	1964	Bantam Books	New York
(51)	*Nana*	George Holden	1972﹨	Penguin Books Ltd	London and New Yor﹖

By far the most widely circulated translation is that of the *fin-de-siecle* poe﹖ Victor Plarr (1863–1929), which was commissioned by the Lutetian Society i﹖ 1895, and while it is superior to Vizetelly's and Duff's it lacks the easy-pace﹖ style and readability of Holden's, which became available as a Penguin Classi﹖ in 1972.

Despite its reputation, *Nana* required very little bowdlerising for Victoria﹖ and Edwardian sensitivities, although odd quirks show up in some of th﹖ American versions. Thus, while every translation is fairly faithful in describin﹖ the lesbian scenes (Nana herself eliciting the typical response for the time; sh﹖ can't understand why, and pouts in disgust) Vizetelly baulks at a chamber-po﹖ preferring to call it a 'familiar utensil'. In the American versions of Plarr'﹖ translation, among them W.J. Black's of 1928 and the 1941 Book League o﹖ America edition, a seemingly inoffensive line is omitted from the passage i﹖ which Nana contemplates herself before a mirror: 'Then she unclasped he﹖ hands and slid them down her body as far as her breasts, and these she crushe﹖ in a passionate grasp.' American readers were allowed the slide, but not th﹖ squeeze. Many American versions of Plarr's translation also display a health﹖ fear of blasphemy, for when Nana, in the lesbian café, realises that one of th﹖ young men is really a woman and exclaims, 'Good Lord!' for American reader﹖ she says, 'Good lack!'

Most translators found difficulty with the passage describing Nana as th﹖ Golden Fly, unknowingly corrupting and poisoning Paris between he﹖ snow-white thighs, and 'curdling it just as women, every month, curdle milk﹖ As an old wives' tale this phenomenon seems to affect milk in different way﹖ Plarr has 'just as every month women turn the milk', while Duff's version is, '﹖ women every month cause milk to turn in churning'. An American editor o﹖ Plarr's translation rather gets himself churned up: 'churning it between he﹖ snow-white thighs as milk is monthly churned by housewives'! Vizetelly avoi﹖ the controversial subject altogether, and Keating drops the entire sequence.﹖

---

* Published in America by Alfred A. Knopf, New York (1922) and Pocket Books Lt﹖ New York (1958).

† Extensively reprinted: in Britain by Elek Books, London (1957); in America ﹖ Walter J. Black, Inc., New York (1928); Modern Library, N.Y. (1928); Mas﹖ Publishing Co., N.Y. (1931); Three Sirens Press, N.Y. (1933); Book League ﹖ America, (1941); World Publishing Co., N.Y. (1946) and Airmont Publishing C﹖ N.Y. (1970).

Holden is the only translator to reveal Daguenet's real reason for his nocturnal visit to Nana's bedroom after his wedding to Muffat's daughter. Some time before, he has promised Nana his 'innocence' before the bride, and all translations up to 1972 have Nana demanding a kiss from him. It hardly seemed likely that the thoroughly degenerate Daguenet would leave his young bride on his wedding night for a mere kiss, and this indeed is the case as Holden's version frankly reveals:

'Oh, Mimi, how funny you are...You remembered after all! And to think I'd forgotten all about it! So you got away – you've come straight from church. Yes, it's true, you still smell of incense...Come on, fuck me then! Oh, harder than that, Mimi! Go on, it may be the last time!'

Broadly, though, Nana hasn't been too cruelly de-sexed, except in the harshly edited paperback versions. Where some of the translations are deficient, however, is in the realm of style, and it is in the transcription of Zola's mood passages that the translator's skill is most severely tested. The long passage describing the breathless magnetism with which Nana draws out the lusts of the theatre audience wholly depends for its effect on prose of an equally magnetic quality, flowing and seductive, so that by the end of the paragraph the reader might imagine his own mouth prickly and dry. Holden's version, quoted in Chapter 9, comes closest in achieving this whereas the other translators interrupt the flow of the passage with spiky, ill-suited words, thus to a large extent breaking the spell.

A no less demanding passage, much shorter and impressively economical, describes how Nana's sensuality finally pierces a breach in Muffat's dammed-up passion. Holden interprets the attrition effectively, but compare his version (quoted in Chapter 9) with Vizetelly's:

In his sanguineous constitution, still in a state of virginity, inordinate desire, scourged by Nana's skilful tactics, was at length producing frightful ravages. That grave looking man, that chamberlain who traversed with such a dignified step the gilded salons of the Tuileries, would, at night-time, bite the bolster on his bed and sob aloud, carried away by his exasperation, and ever invoking the same sensual vision.

Poor old Muffat's desire is strangled in a string of verbal knots. Now compare the two passages with Plarr's:

Lust, which Nana's skilful tactics daily exasperated, had at last wrought terrible havoc in that sanguine, uncontaminated nature. The grave man, the chamberlain who was wont to tread the state apartments at the Tuileries with slow and dignified step, was now nightly driven to plunge his teeth into his bolster, whilst, with sobs of exasperation, he pictured to himself a sensual shape which never changed.

Although about as clumsy as Vizetelly's rendering it proceeds well enough until we come to the vision of Muffat plunging his choppers into the bolster, with its unintentional and unfortunate comic touch.

Nana has few of the idiomatic difficulties which characterised *L'Assommoir* although there are occasional traps which can lead the translator into phrases that stick out like a sore toe. When, during Nana's party in Chapter 4, the guests leave the overheated dining-room to take coffee in the adjacent drawing-room, one of them exclaims, according to Holden's translation, 'Crikey, it's a bit nippy in here!' Vizetelly's rendition is more genteel: 'Thank Goodness! it isn't so warm in here!'; Plarr uses the then current but now outdated, 'By Gum, it's less hot here.'; while Duff prefers the 'Love me' contraction: 'Lumme! It's not so hot in here!' All of them, even Holden's, read quaintly.

A far more difficult translatory problem arises with the childish, lisping sentences the tyrannical Nana forces Count Muffat to repeat during their bedroom games. Treating the Count like a child she demands, at one point, 'Say like me: "Shan't! Coco doethn't want to!"' which Holden judges to be closest to the author's intention. Plarr goes overboard with, 'Say as I do – 'tonfound it! Ickle man damn well don't tare about it!"' although the intention (to humiliate Muffat) is faithfully carried out; while Vizetelly completely misses the point with, 'Say like me: "And dash it all! Coco doesn't care"'.

The Keating translation is hardly worthy of discussion except perhaps as an example of extreme compression, for the 180,000 or so words of the original have been boiled down to 80,000. Great chunks of the narrative, even complete chapters, have been dropped, including the final humiliation of Muffat and many other passages vital to the story. Vandeuvres's spectacular suicide is mentioned in a single sentence, and the Grand Prix, over which Zola toiled for many days, is over at the first turn.

The sad fact is that, until George Holden's translation of 1972, the prose that has presented *Nana* to an English-reading public has had the ambient qualities of a faded sepia photograph rather than those of a *Playboy* spread which has been the showcase for any number of latter-day, would-be Nanas.

Pot-Bouille

Serialised in Le Gaulois, 23 January to 14 April 1882

(52) *Piping Hot!**   for H. Vizetelly   1885   Vizetelly & Co.   London
(53) *Pot-Bouille*†   Percy Pinkerton   1895   Lutetian Society   London

The dozens of paperback versions of this novel are invariably doctored and spiced-up rewrites of Vizetelly's translation, which has been undeservedly issued and reissued over a span of seventy years. Typical is the Pyramid Books edition, widely distributed throughout the world and seductively subtitled as *Zola's classic story of a young Frenchman in a Paris boarding house*. This and similar versions, which must have been bought and read by millions, are a travesty of the original and only a third of its length.

* Reprinted as *Lesson in Love* by Pyramid Books, New York (1953) and by World Distributors, London (1958).
† Reprinted by Boni & Liveright, New York (1924); as *Restless House* by Weidenfeld & Nicolson, London (1953); by Elek Books Ltd, London (1957); and by Farrar, Straus & Young, New York (1953).

The Vizetelly translator, unconsciously reflecting the very middle-class obliquity Zola so ruthlessly exposes in the novel, tiptoes cautiously through the text trying desperately not to offend. When Octave Mouret rapes his upstairs neighbour Marie, it takes place on the kitchen table and, in the violence, a dirty plate and a book fall to the floor. After the event, one of Marie's first impulses is to pick up the plate; but her brain is numbed, the action is mechanical, and she doesn't know what to do with it. It is this sort of detail, the sort Zola intuitively includes, that adds conviction to the incident and which compels the reader, whose eyes have been racing through the paragraph, to share a sense of stunned, post-injury shock. Pinkerton faithfully includes the detail but Vizetelly does not; nor does he have Marie even adjusting her rumpled skirts afterwards. The pulp versions, however, predictably include some additional erotic embroidery: 'Marie, running her hands through her tangled hair, quickly pulled down her petticoats, etc, etc.' Consequently, *Pot-Bouille* has been the victim of both the faint-hearted translator and the prurient publisher, and only Pinkerton's rendering, commissioned by the Lutetian Society, is at all readable today. Although its language is robust and straightforward, it lacks style and annoys with unnecessary, antiquated colloquialisms such as 'hugger-mugger' for 'secretly'. But at least Pinkerton calls a bum a 'behind', and not 'plumpness' as Vizetelly coyly refers to it.

But the most glaring omission from the Vizetelly translation (and therefore from most of the popular versions) is the heart-draining sequence in which the ignorant servant girl Adèle is forced to have her baby alone, in a freezing attic room by the dim light of a candle stump, afraid even to cry out in pain in case she is discovered and reported to the police. The vast gulf between her lonely misery in childbirth while her slightly indisposed mistress is being pampered with attentions downstairs was a culminating irony in Zola's exposure of the crass inhumanity of middle-class codes of conduct. It was unintentionally ironic that Zola's contemporary English readers were shielded from the knowledge of Adèle's pitiful distress by those same hypocritical codes.

Au Bonheur des dames

Serialised in *Le Gil Blas* from 17 December 1882 to 1 March 1883

(54) *Shop Girls of Paris*	Mary Neal Sherwood	1883	T.B. Peterson & Bros	Philadelphia
(55) *The Ladies' Paradise**	Frank Belmont	1883	Tinsley Bros	London
(56) *Ladies' Delight*†	April Fitzlyon	1957	John Calder	London

* Republished after editing by Vizetelly & Co., London (1886); and after further editing by Ernest Vizetelly, by Hutchinson & Co., London, (1897).
† Republished by Elek Books Bestseller Library, London (1960); and in the U.S. by Abelard-Schuman, New York (1958).

Au Bonheur des dames was the first of Zola's novels to be translated in England; after appearing as a magazine serial it was published in 1883 as a three-decker novel by Tinsley Brothers, in the Strand. The Tinsleys were an extraordinary couple who established their firm in 1854 and published George Moore and also Thomas Hardy until he asked them to better a £300 offer made for *Far From the Madding Crowd* which the penurious pair were unfortunately unable to do. The translation was made by Frank Belmont, the copyright for which was later purchased by Vizetelly & Co. who reissued the novel, considerably altered, in 1886.

This novel has never been popular with publishers despite its many-faceted appeal. The most modern version is that by biographer and broadcaster April Fitzlyon who, by comparison with the early efforts, captures the spirit of both the dialogue and the descriptive passages perfectly, and without sacrificing precision. There isn't really any excuse for Vizetelly's dun-coloured prose because there is nothing in the novel requiring the fashionable circumlocution of the time. His version merely reinforces the view that it was a tragedy that Zola's works ever fell into the hands of the Vizetelly family. For with this novel a successful translation boils down to transcribing the colour and vivacity of the many descriptive sequences which are its great strength, and this Vizetelly dismally fails to do.

La Joie de vivre

Serialised in *Le Gil Blas*, 29 November 1883 to 3 February 1884

(57)	*How Jolly Life Is!* for H. Vizetelly	1886	Vizetelly & Co.	London
(58)	*The Joy of Life* Ed. E. Vizetelly	1901	Chatto & Windus	London
(59)	*Zest for Life** Jean Stewart	1955	Elek Books Ltd	London

There isn't much choice here but fortunately Jean Stewart's translation is uniformly excellent, conveying both the sombre atmosphere and the dramatic incidents with equal skill. Vizetelley, too, found some *rapport* with the dark mood of the novel and the 1886 version is one of the best to be issued by that firm. There is, of course, the usual crop of evasions, a couple of which are worth noting as they throw some light on the reasons for the persistence of feminine ignorance during the late nineteenth century. In the early part of the novel we see Pauline grow through puberty and adolescence to young womanhood. During this process one event occurs which completely terrifies her, that of the onset of menstruation, for which she is quite unprepared. This conspiracy of ignorance, which frequently caused irreparable harm to young women, was a long-standing target of Zola's, and Pauline's disturbing

* Published in America by the Indiana University Press, Bloomington (1956).

experience is documented in some detail from which two very short extracts are given in Chapter 16. In Vizetelly's translation of 1886, though, the novelist's purpose is defeated by typical Victorian circumlocution. When Madame Chanteau hears Pauline's screams, she enters her room to find the girl on the bed, whitefaced with shock at the sight of the gush of blood which covers her parted legs. But this is not what we see from the account in the Vizetelly translation:

> Early one morning, just as Madame Chanteau was leaving her bedroom, she heard groans and sobs proceeding from Pauline's room, and she hastily went up to her in a state of alarm. The girl was sitting up in the middle of the bed, from which she had cast off the sheets and blankets, and, white with fear, was calling out ceaselessly for her aunt.
> 'Oh! aunt! aunt!'
> Madame Chanteau understood it at a glance.
> 'Oh! it's nothing, my dear. Make yourself quite easy and don't be frightened.'

There is no mention of blood at all, nor is any reason given why Pauline should be so terrified. Although Madame Chanteau draws back from illuminating the young girl about her condition, Pauline herself finds the answer by secretly searching through Lazare's medical books, stopping to gaze at 'every single organ' in the illustrations to Cruveilhier's *Descriptive Anatomy* with delight and wonder. So at least, in the 1886 edition, we have the satisfaction of knowing that Pauline's mind is put at rest. But no such satisfaction awaits us in the 1901 version of the same translation, extensively edited by Ernest Vizetelly. In it, the original three-page passage is reduced, with crass hypocrisy, to a few rewritten lines:

> She had developed, too, into a well-formed young woman, and with her healthy mind and love of knowledge it was with delight that she found herself reaching full growth and sunny ripeness.

The coyness about blood, birth and menstruation continues through the Vizetelly version to such an extent that any young reader must have been quite baffled by the periphrasis. Later in the novel, when Pauline returns alone to the house after the marriage of Lazare and Louise, she finds herself menstruating unexpectedly early. It is a cruel and ironical moment for her, for having lost perhaps her only chance to become a mother she now despairingly contemplates her wasted fecundity. A good part of this passage is quoted in Chapter 16, but here for comparison is the 1886 Vizetelly version:

> Alas! alas! the red dew of her puberty was trickling to-day like the vain tears of her virginity! Henceforth each month would bring with it this gushing forth of the ripened fruit, ready for the vintage; yet never would she be a wife, but would grow old in barren sterility!

It is curious that menstruating by a mature woman was considered mentionable, but not by a pubescent girl. I need hardly add that you will look for this passage in vain in the 1901 version.

The Victorians showed a similar lack of enthusiasm for the details of childbirth. The harrowing arrival into the world of Louise's child is the climax of the novel, and the pain which accompanies its entry is a vital part of Zola's message, and not without its educational aspects, either. But the long and detailed account of the birth, a triumph of descriptive prose, is reduced in the Vizetelly translation to just two lines:

> However, after a long and agonising period of suspense, a baby boy was born, and it was alive.

Germinal

Serialised in *Le Gil Blas* from 26 November 1884 to 25 February 1885

(60)	*Germinal*	Carlynne	1885	Belford, Clarke	Chicago & Co.
(61)	*Germinal**	Albert Vandam	1886	Vizetelly & Co.	London
(62)	*Germinal*†	Havelock Ellis	1894	Lutetian Society	London
(63)	*Germinal*	L.W. Tancock	1954	Penguin Books	London and New York
(64)	*Germinal*	Willard R. Trask	1962	Bantam Books	New York
(65)	*Germinal*	Stanley and Eleanor Hochman	1970	New American Library	New York

Germinal is, I think, about the most available translation of any Zola novel on both sides of the Atlantic. The Havelock Ellis translation has been continuously in print in the Everyman's Library edition since 1933 and the Penguin edition of Tancock's translation since 1954. In addition, the U.S. has been favoured with the popular Bantam Books version and, more recently, with the excellent Hochman translation published as a Signet Classic paperback.

The crucial aspect of *Germinal* is its *effect* upon readers, and a successful translation will have much the same effect on English readers as the original text has on the French, an aim which Dr E.V. Rieu has termed the 'law of equivalent effect'. In a note to his translation for the Penguin Classics, Leonard Tancock commented that he had kept this law in mind, 'the principle of fidelity to the *tone* of the original'. It is fair to say that all the modern translations achieve this very well, *Germinal* perhaps being one of those books which inspire translators, for no other work of Zola's can claim anything like this number of really good English-text versions.

There is, of course, the usual problem of slang and profanity, where the

---

* Zola sold the English serialisation rights to a Mr M.T. Madge, manager of *The People*, from whom Vizetelly acquired the book rights; these were subsequently purchased by Chatto & Windus, London, who published a version edited by Ernest Vizetelly in 1901.

† Extensively reprinted: Everyman's Library (J.M. Dent & Sons, London, and E.P. Dutton & Co., Inc., New York), 1933; revised (1946); Boni & Liveright, New York (1924), and The Nonesuch Press, London and New York (1942).

umsy selection of a substitute term can ruin the mood and effect of an entire
assage; and, in the case of this novel exclusively, the difficulty of rendering
ae technical vocabulary of the mining industry so as not to befuddle the reader
et not to lose the mining atmosphere, either. In both areas the post-war
anslations succeed fairly well.

Of the nineteenth-century translations, Vandam's and Carlynne's have
rious omissions. Carlynne flagrantly mistranslates so that many passages are
uite meaningless; *Montsou* is inexplicably spelled 'Montson' throughout and,
the episode where Maheude gives her husband his Sunday bath, the poor
iiner is denied his bit of fun afterwards. I mention this version only to
emonstrate again the appalling way in which Zola's greatest masterpieces
eached his avid, English-reading audience until relatively recently.

Vizetelly's unedited translation is a far more honest attempt, keeping in
iind that Victorian prudery had reached its zenith at the time of publication.
a this regard Vandam, the translator, had problems with many passages,
icluding one which is recognised as probably the most horrific in all of the
ovelist's work. This is the episode in which the shopkeeper Maigrat is
tacked, is killed while trying to escape, and has his corpse mutilated by the
omen. The frightful horror of this important and symbolic scene is expertly
iptured in the Havelock Ellis translation quoted in Chapter 12, but compare it
ow with Vizetelly's rendering:

> But the women had other vengeance to wreak upon him. They hovered round his
> corpse, sniffing like wolves. They were all seeking some outrage, some ferocious act
> which should give them satisfaction.
> Suddenly the Scorched-One's shrill voice was heard:
> 'Cut him like a tom cat!'
> 'Yes, yes! like a tom cat!' He deserves it, the swine!'
> La Mouquette was already tearing off his clothes, while La Levaque siezed him by
> the legs. And the Scorched-One with her bony old hands did the horrible deed,
> exclaiming as she laughed triumphantly:
> 'I've done it! I've done it!'
> A volley of imprecations greeted the abominable act.
> 'Ah! you filthy wretch, you'll leave our daughters alone now!'

What on earth is she doing? With the shuddering disgust inherent in the
etails of the act, which are included in all modern versions, Vizetelly was
erhaps wiser to leave it to the imaginations of his Victorian readers. Less wise,
ad even inexplicable, is the nineteenth-century treatment of the touching
assage which follows Maheu's death during the strike, when Etienne brings
ack the limp and unconscious body of Catherine to the house. Here, first, is
ae Hochman version:

> But one house more than the others, that of the Maheus, was especially dark and
> silent, overwhelmed by its mourning. From the time she had followed her husband's
> body to the cemetery La Maheude had not opened her mouth. After the battle she
> had permitted Etienne to bring Catherine, covered with mud and half-dead, back to
> the house; and while, as the young man stood there, she was undressing the girl to put
> her to bed, she had thought for a moment that her daughter too had been returned to
> her with a bullet in her belly, for her shift was spotted with large bloodstains. But she
> soon understood that it was the arrival of puberty, finally brought on by the shock of

397

that terrible day. Ah, another piece of good luck! – a fine gift that was, to be able t<
make children so the gendarmes could slaughter them later on!

Now the Vizetelly version; the translator recoils from mentioning Maheude'"
touching discovery:

> But there was one cottage above all – that of the Maheus – which remained mut<
> and sombre beneath the burden of its grief. Since she had accompanied her husban<
> to the cemetery, La Maheude had not opened her lips. After the battle, she ha<
> allowed Etienne to bring back Catherine, covered with mud and half-dead. Thoug<
> she undressed the girl, she never spoke a word to her any more than to Etienne.

Although done in 1894, the Havelock Ellis translation still stands, in my view
as the finest example of any rendering of Zola's fiction into English. 'That join
task has remained an abidingly pleasant memory,' was how Ellis recalled th<
winter and spring of 1894 when, in a Cornish cottage overlooking the sea, h<
translating aloud, his wife writing it down, they produced the first *complet*
English version of *Germinal*. The man who was shortly to become the world'
first authority on sex – his encyclopedic *Studies in the Psychology of Sex* appeare<
between 1898 and 1928 – was no stranger to public prejudice and this, with .
literary brilliance rarely revealed in his medical studies, and an admiration fo<
Zola's monumental achievement, made him the ideal collaborator to re-creat
this masterpiece in the English language.

Short of analysing a great number of passages from each of the moder<
translations my view on Ellis's superiority is probably difficult to prov<
especially as I have said that success should be judged on the total *effect* upo<
the reader. One of the chief devices behind the overall effect of the novel is th<
constant presence of symbolism and imagery which, in various ways, adds
range of emotive tones to both the descriptive and narrative passages, and a
least we can study some examples of these. Take the vital opening paragrap<
for instance, the Hochman version of which is quoted in Chapter 12. Here <
the Havelock Ellis translation:

> Over the open plain, beneath a starless sky as dark and thick as ink, a man walke<
> alone along the highway from Marchiennes to Montsou, a straight paved road te<
> kilometres in length, intersecting the beetroot-fields. He could not even see the blac<
> soil before him, and only felt the immense flat horizon by the gusts of March wind
> squalls as strong as on the sea, and frozen from sweeping leagues of marsh and nake<
> earth. No tree could be seen against the sky, and the road unrolled as straight as a pie<
> in the midst of the blinding spray of darkness.

Now Leonard Tancock's version of the same paragraph:

> On a pitch-black, starless night, a solitary man was trudging along the main road from
> Marchiennes to Montsou, ten kilometres of cobblestones running straight as a di<
> across the bare plain between fields of beet. He could not even make out the blac<
> ground in front of him, and it was only the feel of the March wind blowing in grea<
> gusts like a storm at sea, but icy cold from sweeping over miles of marshes and bar<
> earth, that gave him a sensation of limitless, flat horizons. There was not a single tre<

to darken the sky, and the cobbled highroad ran on with the straightness of a jetty through the swirling sea of black shadows.

It seems to me that the key words and phrases in the Ellis version are far more emotive than their equivalents in Tancock's: a 'starless sky as dark and thick as ink' is more indelible than 'pitch-black' with its connotations of hotness; 'a man walked alone' is more alone than a 'solitary man'; a 'blinding spray of darkness' has the impact of a bucket of ink in the face compared with a swirling sea of black shadows' which, while scary, is not so readily visualised. Additionally, Tancock obscures the feelings of flatness, broadness and distance by intruding the words *cobblestones* and *cobbled*, contrary to the original text which clearly calls for 'paved', so that our minds are on small, round stones rather than on a long, straight ribbon that bisects the plain. One also wonders how a single tree can 'darken the sky' which he has already described as pitch-black'. Ellis's rendering, 'No tree could be seen against the sky,' however, retains the ambiguity of the night.

Tancock's sense of the appropriate is uncomfortably deficient at times. When, for instance, the striker Maheu bares his chest and dares the soldier to impale him with his bayonet, he presses forward so that 'one point pricked him on the nipple'; the French text calls for 'chest'.

Finally, let us consider the question of interpretation. On occasions a translator will find himself at odds with a word in the original, the literal equivalent of which may reduce the effect he is striving for or cloud the author's intention. An interesting example occurs during the strike when thousands of miners and their women run undisciplined across the countryside. Caught in the path of this terrifying horde, some of the mine-owner families hide in a shed, and watch the passing mob through a gap in the plank wall. Here is a single paragraph from one of the most memorable crowd scenes Zola ever wrote:

The women had come into sight, nearly a thousand of them, dishevelled after their tramp, in rags through which could be seen their naked flesh worn out with bearing children doomed to starve. Some of them had babies in their arms and raised them aloft and waved them like flags of grief and vengeance. Others, younger, with chests thrown out like warriors, were brandishing sticks, whilst the old crones made a horrible sight as they yelled so hard that the strings in their skinny necks looked ready to snap. The men brought up the rear: two thousand raving madmen, pit-boys, colliers, repairers in a solid phalanx moving in a single block, so closely packed together that neither their faded trousers nor their ragged jerseys could be picked out from the uniform earth-coloured mass. All that could be seen was their blazing eyes and the black holes of their mouths singing the *Marseillaise*, the verses of which merged into a confused roar, accompanied by the clatter of clogs on the hard ground. Above their heads an axe rose straight up amidst the bristling crowbars, a single axe, the banner of the mob, and it stood out against the clear sky like the blade of the guillotine.

This is Tancock's rendering which may be compared with the Havelock Ellis translation of the same passage in Chapter 12. The effect in this masterly paragraph is cumulative: the shouting and arm-waving, the women and their

children, the vicious old crones – everything merges at the end of th
paragraph into a solid mob, as compact as a huge tank rumbling across th
countryside on a mission of death, which is presaged by the singing of th
'Marseillaise' and the erect axe, 'like the blade of the guillotine'.

Now nobody can justifiably pick fault with Tancock's translation, for
captures the atmosphere splendidly. But in the selection of a single key wor
Tancock – and all the other translators – lose out to Ellis. In the original, Zol
had the sabots' *claquement*, literally, clapping, over the frosty ground. Vizetell
had them clanking, the Hochmans have them clattering. But how inspired :
Ellis's choice of 'clang', preceding as it does the mention of the guillotine? Th
is surely poetic interpretation of a very high order, and examples of Ellis
superiority here abound throughout the novel.

Nonetheless, I must make it quite clear that all the modern translatio
mentioned here are of a uniformly high standard, and that the courage of the:
authors in attempting fresh translations with Ellis's formidable achievemer
sitting on their shoulders can only be admired.

One final point. In the Lutetian Society edition of Ellis's translation, *bougre*
transposed correctly as 'bugger' but in the Everyman's Library editior
variously as 'swine' and 'beggar'. There might have been an excuse for this i
1933 but not in the 1970s. After forty years of reprinting, surely the publishe
can now afford to reset this masterpiece and, in doing so, restore the force an
honesty of the original.

L'Oeuvre

Serialised in *Le Gil Blas*, 23 December 1885, to 27 March 1886

(66)	*The Masterpiece*	G. D. Cox	1886	T.B. Peterson & Bros	Phila-delphi
(67)	*His Masterpiece*	Albert Vandam	1886	Vizetelly & Co.	Londo
(68)	*His Masterpiece**	E.A. Vizetelly	1902	Chatto & Windus	London
(69)	*The Masterpiece*	Katherine Woods	1946	Howell, Soskin	New York
(70)	*The Masterpiece*	Thomas Walton	1950	Elek Books Ltd	London an New Yor

A serious translation which trims almost ten per cent from the narrative an
rearranges the chapters so there are twenty instead of twelve serious
jeopardises its integrity. Perhaps these regrettable innovations were directive
from the publisher, for otherwise Katherine Woods's rendering is a high
readable and sometimes sensitive translation. True, the shrinkage is achieve

* An edited version of the 1886 Vizetelly edition, with some new translation by Ern
Vizetelly.

by carefully shaving each paragraph, each sentence, even. But the erosion is annoying when it reduces significant passages – like the reminiscent rambling of Claude and Sandoz about their schooldays in Plassans, early in the novel – to a passing reference. The full text here is essential if we are to grasp the extent of the fond relationship which has grown up between the two men. Their school pranks and day-long country hikes, during which their youthful dreams began to shape into ambitions, are the cement of a stubborn bond that is vital to the story.

His Masterpiece was Vizetelly & Co.'s fourteenth translation, but the standard seems to be descending from bad to worse, the result of a desire, no doubt, to cash in on Zola's controversial novels as quickly as possible. One can also see the effects of pressure of another kind on Vizetelly, for he bends over backwards to twist anything promising into a moral. He translates the young friends' 'love of country walks', for example, as 'love of bodily exercise'; one expects, in subsequent editions, to have the cold tub and rough towel thrown in as well. These unctuous additions to Vizetelly's customary stiff verbosity – or at least that of the translators who worked for him – stamp this version as a Victorian curiosity, full of dun and darkness of the very kind the hero of the novel sets out to destroy.

Between the novelettish approach of Woods and the grey prolixity of Vizetelly, Walton's translation is a masterpiece by comparison; even the long, discursive passages and the arguments about aesthetics are rendered interesting and immediately understandable. Walton is also the only translator to successfully convey the tensions, as taut as gut in a tennis racquet, which thread their way through the narrative. Even on what was a joyful occasion for Claude – when Christine at last agrees to pose for him – there is an underlying tension, little understood by either of the characters, arising from what mounts to artistic rape. Walton's version was in Chapter 13; here for comparison is the translation of the first paragraph of the passage by Katherine Woods:

> She stood there very white before him, and understood every word of that prayer in his eyes. Without any hurry, she took off her hat and coat, as usual. Then she simply went on with the same tranquil movements: unfastened her bodice, dropped her petticoats, stepped out of her corset, unbuttoned the chemise that now slipped down over her hips. She had not spoken a word; she seemed to be somewhere else, as on those evenings alone when, lost in a dream, she would undress automatically, without paying any attention to what she was doing. Why should she let a rival give her body when she had already given her face? She wanted to be wholly there, to feel herself at home in his picture; and in her tenderness she understood at last the jealous disquiet this hybrid monster had been causing for a long time. Still without speaking, now entirely naked, she lay down on the divan and took the pose, one arm beneath her head, her eyes closed.

Compare the two and you must agree that in this version the tension is replaced by an inappropriate matter-of-factness. Towards the end of this significant paragraph, Zola has Christine 'nue et vierge', or as Walton translates, 'virgin in her nudity', a point ignored by Woods. But it is completely misconstrued by

Vizetelly who, rarely missing an opportunity to stress that the liaison between artist and model is sexless and pure, tells readers that Christine is 'silent, nude and chaste'. In the 1902 Chatto and Windus expurgation she is further purified: 'It was in silence and all chastity that she stretched herself on the couch...'

La Terre

Serialised in *Le Gil Blas*, 29 May to 16 September 1887

(71)	*The Soil* G.D. Cox	*c.* 1888	T.B. Peterson & Bros	Philadelphia
(72)	*The Soil** for H. Vizetelly	1888	Vizetelly & Co.	London
(73)	*La Terre†* Ernest Dowson	1895	Lutetian Society	London
(74)	*Earth*** Ann Lindsay	1954	Elek Books Ltd	London and New York
(75)	*Earth* Margaret Crosland	1962	New English Library	London
(76)	*Earth* George Holden (in prep)		Penguin Classics	London

The drama that followed in the wake of the first English translation of *La Terre* has already been recounted in Chapter 15. As it was completely withdrawn from sale in Britain after 1888, and because of its reputation among scholars another and more faithful translation was commissioned in 1894 by the Lutetian Society and published the following year in a privately issued edition of 300 copies. The same translation was reissued in an edition of 2,050 copies in 1924 by Boni & Liveright in America, and that seems to be the extent of the minuscule circulation of this novel in English until the Elek translation of 1954. At least two, and possibly three translators worked on the Vizetelly & Co edition and it is amazing that the text is as even as it is; nevertheless, it is little more than a repository of ossified prose and Victorian preciosity and thus hardly the ideal vehicle for conveying Zola's gutsy narrative. Ernest Dowson's translation is, on the other hand, quite remarkable for its time, although his talents as a poet are rather less in evidence here than his reputation for translating obscene French works for Leonard Charles Smithers, pornographic publisher who employed Dowson during the 1890s.

The 1954 Elek version by Ann Lindsay, wife of the Australian critic, novelist and biographer Jack Lindsay, is easily the most readable of the translations made to date, and is fortunately still in print. On her fine work *The Times Literary Supplement* was moved to say that in un-selfconsciously capturing the coarse earthiness and sweeping lyricism of the novel, 'it falls very little short of being impeccable.' The translation by Margaret Crosland, an accomplished biographer of Colette and Cocteau, appeared as a Four Square paperback in

---

* English text republished by Flammarion, Paris, (*c.*1890).

† Also published by Boni & Liveright, New York (1924).

** Reprinted by Arrow Books, London (1967).

1962. It honestly admits to being an abbreviated version, and readers are warned that the original 200,000 or so words have been reduced to a mere 75,000, achieved by sticking rigidly to the main story-line and omitting the activities of many of the supporting characters such as the Charles's and Jésus-Christ. It also concentrates on the more sensational aspects of the novel; the book was, according to the cover blurb, 'a ruthless portrait of peasant greed and brute sexual violence that shocked readers on both sides of the Channel. Zola's story and his manner of presenting it are startling even today when few forms of sordid and perverted behaviour are left unexplored...' Finally, to this list must be added the translation by George Holden (who translated *Nana* in 1972) to be issued by Penguin Books.

There are two elements in particular to watch for when comparing the various translations: the lyrical and often rhythmic treatment of the descriptive passages that bind the characters to the soil; and the earthy ribaldry which is the everyday language of the peasants.

In Chapter 14 I attempted to analyse the manner in which Zola modulated and accented his prose to add visual dimension and mood to the meaning he was trying to convey. As an example I translated the opening paragraph in the novel to show how the rhythmic phrasing harmonised with the actions of the sower in the field, as they were described. This is as good an instance as any to see how the various translators tackled this important aspect of Zola's prose style. Here is Vizetelly's version:

> That morning Jean, with a seed-bag of blue linen tied round his waist, held its mouth open with his left hand, while with his right, at every three steps, he drew forth a handful of corn, and flung it broadcast. The rich soil clung to his heavy shoes, which left holes in the ground, as his body lurched regularly from side to side; and each time he threw you saw, amid the ever-flying yellow seed, the gleam of two red stripes on the sleeve of the old regimental jacket he was wearing out. He strode forward in solitary state; and behind him, to bury the grain, there slowly came a harrow, to which were harnessed two horses, driven by a waggoner, who cracked his whip over their ears in long, regular sweeps.

Vizetelly's is a studious rendering which delivers our first view of the Beauce in stolid, measured phrases. Dowson's rendering is disappointing; for a nineteenth-century poet of some stature his rhythm falters badly in the first sentence and he never manages to pick it up again:

> All that morning, Jean kept open the pocket of the blue canvas wallet he wore tied in front of him, with the left hand, whilst with the right he took out a handful of corn every three paces, and with a long sweeping gesture scattered it around. As his body swayed regularly to and fro, his heavy shoes sank into the rich soil and caught it up, while at every cast, through the flying white seeds, there gleamed the two red stripes of a uniform that he was wearing out. He walked steadfastly forward, looking big in his loneliness, while behind him a harrow to bury the grain trundled slowly along, drawn by two horses. A waggoner drove them with long, regular strokes of his whip, which he cracked over their ears.

Now examine the deliberately condensed opening as translated by Margaret Crosland:

> Jean was sowing that morning, with his blue seed-bag tied round his waist; at every third step he took out a handful of corn and scattered it broadcast all at once. His rough shoes sank into the heavy, clinging soil as he swung along at a steady pace, and whenever he raised his arm the two red stripes on his old army jacket gleamed through the unending cloud of yellow grain. He walked on, tall in his solitude.

Inevitably the passage suffers from the extreme condensation, and our impression is of a landscape glimpsed through the blinkers of a passing horse. Finally, here is the same opening paragraph translated by Ann Lindsay:

> That morning, Jean was in the fields, holding open with his left hand a blue canvas seedbag knotted round his waist; with his right he brought out a fistful of corn and scattered it broadcast with a single flick of the wrist, every three steps. As he swung rhythmically along, his heavy clogs sank in the rich soil and came away thickly-caked. And at each throw, through the ceaselessly flying golden grain, gleamed the two red stripes on the sleeve of the army jacket he was wearing out. He strode on in solitary grandeur; and a harrow slowly followed, burying the seeds. Two horses, whom the waggoner urged on with long regular whipcracks over the ears, were harnessed to the harrow.

Again, this rendering also fails to capture the phlegmatic rhythms Zola so painstakingly worked into passages like this. While it must not be inferred that the deficiencies of a single translated paragraph are necessarily typical of the entire translation, this comparative example does indicate that the care with which Zola composed his novels was by no means imitated by his translators.

By far the most notable characteristics of *Earth* are its pervasive ribaldry and the explicitness of its language in both narrative and dialogue. Considering the hostile climate of the time, Vizetelly's translators struggled rather bravely with what Ernest Vizetelly termed 'Zola's outspokenness', but it was a hopelessly unequal fight and prudery won the day. Here's an example of the innocent, jokey ribaldry with which farmhands amuse themselves in the fields: a group of them are making hay when Françoise pauses to say:

> 'Oh, good gracious! There's something pricking me!'
> 'Whereabouts?'
> 'Under my petticoats; up here.'
> 'It's a spider. Hold hard! keep your legs together.'
> And the laughter grew louder, at improper jests that made them split their sides.... Victor, although he had left off hammering his blade, evinced no particular haste; and as La Trouille went by with her geese, he slily slipped off, and ran to meet her under shelter of a thick line of willows that edged the stream.
> 'Aha!' cried Jean; 'he prefers something else to mowing.'
> Françoise burst into a fresh guffaw.
> 'He's too old for her,' said she.
> 'Too old! Listen, and you'll hear them.'

This is Vizetelly's version of the vulgar banter, and if you detect the absence of the bucolic touch, you're right. For comparison, here's Ann Lindsay's translation of the same passage:

> 'O Lord, something's pricking me.'
> 'Where?'
> 'Under my skirt, up here.'
> 'It's a spider. Watch out – keep your legs tight together.'
> And there was louder laughter, a torrent of smutty jokes that made them rock....

404

Victor, no longer hammering his blade, seemed in no particular hurry; and when La Trouille passed with her geese, he slyly dodged away, slipping off to join her under a thick row of willows on the river-bank.

'Good,' cried Jean, 'he's got another tool to set now. The lady knife-grinder's there waiting ready for him.'

Françoise burst out laughing again at this allusion. 'He's too old for her.'

'Too old! Listen then if they're not grinding away together.'

Now the jokes begin to make sense; the allusive lewdness of the word-play on 'tool' and 'grinding' is completely lost in the Vizetelly translation. There are, unfortunately, endless examples similar to this, but there is little point in belabouring Vizetelly for something that was to a large extent outside his control.

What *is* worth examining, however, are the instances where really significant incidents are drastically altered, or even omitted. A good example is provided when Jean, his passions ablaze for Françoise, finally takes her behind a haystack:

Jean stopped talking. As he watched her lying defenceless on her back, his blood beat strongly in his veins. He hadn't planned the meeting and he tried to hold back, still thinking it shameful to take advantage of this child. But the loud thumping of his heart stupified him; he had longed so much for her. The image of possessing her gripped and maddened him, as it had in his nights of fever. He lay down beside her, satisfying himself first with one of her hands, then taking both her hands and crushing them between his own without even daring to lift them to his lips. She didn't pull away, she opened her faraway eyes with their heavy lids and looked at him, unsmiling, without a blush, her face tense with strain. And this mute almost sorrowful look was what suddenly made him brutal. He pushed under her skirts and grasped her thighs, just as the other man had done.

'No, no,' she stammered. 'Please, no, it's dirty...'

But she didn't fight. She only gave one cry of pain. It seemed to her that the earth was falling away under her; and in her giddiness she couldn't think clearly. Had the other man come back? She felt the same rough hands, the same acrid smell, drawn out by hard work in the sun. Her confusion was so great in the flickering darkness of her tight closed eyes that she let out some stammered words without thought.

'Please, no kid...withdraw...'

He jerked away. The human seed, diverted and lost, spurted into the ripe corn, on to the earth which never denies her body, gaping to take in all and any seed, eternally fecund.

In this extract, Ann Lindsay imaginatively preserves Zola's explicitness, for the novelist no doubt wished to stress that the peasants accepted love-making as an often brutal and uncontrollable outpouring of passion. But Jean is an outsider and not a born peasant, and therefore his behaviour here is a mixture of peasant brutality and – by withdrawing at Françoise's request – respect. Jean's action of ejaculating into the corn, incidentally, is a carefully planted piece of Zola's favourite fertility imagery: the sperm dies while the corn ripens, and the harvesting continues in the background.

Now let us compare Dowson's version of the incident. Here, you will notice, Françoise makes no specific demand for Jean to withdraw; instead, 'a few involuntary words escaped her unconsciously':

Thenceforward Jean too was silent. When he saw her thus, prostrate and yielding, the blood in his veins coursed fiercely. He had not counted on this meeting; he

405

resisted his temptation, thinking that it would be wrong to take advantage of this child. But the beating of his heart made him giddy; he had so greatly desired her. And a vision of possession invaded him, as during his nights of fever. He lay down beside her; he contented himself at first with her hand, then with her two hands, which he crushed together, not even daring to lift them to his lips. She did not withdraw them; she opened her vague eyes, with their heavy lids, and looked at him without a smile, or a trace of shame, her face drawn down nervously. And it was this silent, almost anguished glance which rendered him suddenly brutal.

'No, no,' she stammered; 'please don't. . .'

But she made no resistance. She gave one cry of pain. It seemed as though the earth gave way under her; and in her giddiness she lost all understanding; was it the other man who had come back? She found the same roughness, the same pungency of the male animal reeking from coarse work in the sun. Her confusion grew so great in the burning darkness which she inhabited – for her eyelids were obstinately shut – that a few involuntary words escaped her unconsciously. But the human seed, turned aside and wasted, fell amongst the ripe corn, upon the Earth, who has no refusals, whose womb is free to all men's sowing, fruitful eternally.

Vizetelly could not come to terms with the symbolism of this passage at all, for there is no request from Françoise, no withdrawal and no spilled seed in the harvest.

The confusion caused by the omission of significant detail is perhaps most apparent in the climactic rape of Françoise by Buteau towards the end of the novel; an extract of this horrifying incident, as translated by Ann Lindsay, is included in Chapter 14.

Reading between the lines of this passage in the Vizetelly version you are left in little doubt that Françoise has been raped. But what this passage doesn't explain is that it was no ordinary rape for, as Lindsay has it, 'when Buteau took her, she was carried away with such a spasm of keen ecstasy that she clung smotheringly to him with both arms and let out a long cry. The crows flying above were frightened.' In other words Françoise realised she loved Buteau at the moment of physical possession; it didn't dawn on her after the event. Denied this important clue, readers of Vizetelly's translation must have scratched their heads in disbelief when they were told, after this brutal assault, that Françoise suddenly found she was in love with her attacker. And see how much the passage loses by the omission of the frightened crows! If you have seen Van Gogh's paintings, those done near the end of his life, of black crows flying above a sun-drenched wheatfield, you will know instantly of the brooding apprehension evoked by the image.

Le Rêve

Serialised in *La Revue illustrée*, 1 April to 15 October 1888

(77) *The Dream** Eliza E. Chase 1893 Chatto & Windus London

The Dream was the first of Zola's novels many publishers felt they could safely tackle and in fact there was a race in America to bring out the first English-text edition; even before serialisation had concluded in France the novel became

* Also published by Everett & Co., Ltd, London (1912).

he subject of a bitter Supreme Court battle between Rand, McNally & Co. and
_aird and Lee over the translation rights. It is curious, therefore, that despite
he intense competition between publishers then, *The Dream* is today one of the
1ardest-to-find *Rougon-Macquart* novels in English, and no new translation has
1ppeared this century. The only translation available in England, also elusive,
s that by Eliza E. Chase, published by Chatto & Windus in 1893; the five-year
;ap between its appearance in Paris and London was a direct result of the
Vizetelly conviction.

With its complete absence of controversial ideas and embarrassing
:xpressions, *The Dream* lent itself perfectly to literal translation in the 1890s
1nd Miss Chase's version is straightforward and honest. Unfortunately,
hough, her interpretation tends to reinforce the sentimental elements in the
1ovel, and it is also spoiled for the modern reader by the impossibly stiff prose;
1t one point the uneducated Angélique says to her lover, 'Yet the moment that
[am reassured of your affection, all my martyrdom recommences...' – to give
ust one example. The novel is not quite as bad as many critics make out, and
vould benefit immeasurably from a fresh translation.

La Bête humaine

Serialised in *La Vie populaire*, 14 November 1889 to 2 March 1890

78)	*The Human Beast*	G.D. Cox	*c.*1891	T.B. Peterson	Phila-delphia
79)	*The Monomaniac*	E.A. Vizetelly	1901	Hutchinson & Co.	London
80)	*The Human Beast*	Louis Colman	1937	Julien Press	Newark, New York
81)	*The Human Beast*	Frances Frenaye	1954	Avon Publi-cations	New York
82)	*The Beast in Man*	Alec Brown	1958	Elek Books Ltd	London and New York

This novel was the first victim of the reaction against Zola's books that followed
he 1888 and 1889 prosecutions for pornography. Despite the adverse climate,
:rnest Vizetelly remained the novelist's most loyal supporter in England and
luring the years which followed the trials he waited for the opportunity to
estore Zola's – and his – fortune. But the English translation rights to *Le Rêve*
:eem to have been directly acquired by Chatto & Windus; *L'Argent* was
onsidered too unsensational; while *La Bête humaine* was rejected as being far
oo explosive. In the event Vizetelly resumed translating with *La Débâcle*, which
vas successfully published in 1892, whereas *La Bête humaine* had to wait until
901 before it was felt safe to place it in the hands of the English matron.

407

Hugo noted that the peculiarity of prudery is that it multiplies the guards in proportion as the fortress is less threatened, which is pretty much the case with this version of the novel. The text is so thoroughly laundered that the result is a travesty of the original. One might expect the unusual love-making of Jacques and Severine to be dropped, but the rigid excision of any mention or inference – even remote – of sex, bodies or bed reaches puritannical limits. When the insanely jealous Roubard is beating his wife to extract the confession from her that she and the old judge have been sexual partners – 'Confess you slept with him, you bloody tart!' – the Vizetelly version has: '"Confess that you did something wrong," said he'. And later in the book, when Severine confesses the murder of Grandmorin in all its gory detail to Jacques, interspersed with ecstatic love-making, not only is the whole point lost because Vizetelly omits to mention that all this makes Jacques sexually excited, but it all takes place in limbo because the translator dares not mention that they are in bed together! The squalid hypocrisy of late-nineteenth-century bowdlerism is nakedly revealed in the prurient blurb for this same translation: 'Every woman Jacques Lantier falls in love with, nay, every girl from whom he culls a kiss, or whose bare shoulders or throat he happens to catch a glimpse of, he feels an indomitable craving to slaughter!' Like iron maidens and slave bracelets this translation is simply a relic of a less enlightened age, and without any literary merit whatsoever.

Of the modern translations, Frenaye's and Colman's are abbreviated, the publishers obviously treating the work as a slick thriller. While there might have been some justification for this with Frenaye's version, which has been issued in cheap paperback editions in many countries, it is difficult to understand why Colman's corrupt text was originally published in an edition limited to a thousand copies. In 1948, however, it went into a much bigger edition under the imprint of the United Book Guild. Apart from the harsh editing, both these versions are intelligent translations.

When Alec Brown was commissioned to translate *La Bête humaine* in the late 1950s he must have shouted with joy for it had long been one of his favourite novels, read as a thriller in his youth and later, as he puts it, 'as one of the masterpieces of world literature'. The job of translation was for Brown not only an enjoyable intellectual exercise, 'but also emotionally absorbing, even terrifying'. It is no wonder, then, that his English version captures every nuance, every thrill and every intention of the original, and it is the definitive translation of this novel produced so far. I do, however, take exception to his occasional twee expressions. Jacques's love-making with Severine was necessarily clandestine, but did they have to be as quiet as 'two real little mousies'? And would Jacques, a tough railwayman, murmur, 'Shall us, pet, hush-a-bye?' Idiomatic terms of endearment as *Veux-tu? cherie, au dodo!* are nearly impossible to translate literally, but surely a more acceptable rendering would be, 'How about it, love? Coming to bed?' The invitation, as with other fondnesses, is better handled by the other translators, except Vizetelly, who omits it altogether.

L'Argent

Serialised in *Le Gil Blas*, 30 November 1890 to 3 March 1891

(83) *Money** E.A. Vizetelly 1894 Chatto & Windus London

Vizetelly's is the sole translation in English that I know of, and as with all of the Zola translations published after 1890 the text has been scrubbed, edited, condensed and rewritten in parts. While the single English version reflects both the book's dullness and the lack of public interest in it, a good case exists for a new translation, if only on its merit as a documentary of financial speculation of the nineteenth century.

La Débâcle

serialised in *La Vie populaire*, 21 February to 21 July 1892

84)	*The Downfall*	E.A. Vizetelly*	1892	Chatto & Windus London
85)	*The Downfall*	E.P. Robins	1898	The Cassell New York Company
86)	*The Downfall*	W.M. Sloane	1902	P.F. Collier New York & Son
87)	*The Debacle*	John Hands	1968	Elek Books Ltd London
88)	*The Debacle*	Leonard Tancock	1972	Penguin Books London Ltd

The veracity of a war novel, its effectiveness in conveying the confusion, noise and stark terror of front line combat, the bitter ironies of that no-man's-land between staying alive and being killed, rests to a large extent with the skill of the novelist in placing the reader right alongside the fighting man. There is little point in doing this, however, if the characters are not to be real; they must act and talk like men who must kill or be killed. In war conditions a man's speech undergoes a transformation, to a language that is primal, brutal and understandably blasphemous. New standards in the presentation of trench dialogue were set by *The Naked and the Dead, From Here to Eternity* and similar novels of World War II, and modern translations of older war novels like *The Debacle* are bound to take this into account. A translator would do Zola's story of the Franco-Prussian War no justice at all by perpetuating expressions used by Vizetelly in the 1890s like 'Dash it all!' and 'I don't care a fig!' In other respects, Vizetelly's version is a creditable effort although at times his own experience as a war correspondent during that same war proves to be his undoing. Writing in September 1892, he was justly proud of the intense and

* Reprinted by Gordon & Breach Inc, New York, 1976.
† Reprinted by Albert & Charles Boni, New York, 1925.

prolonged labour he put in to produce the English text of the novel, but it is pity that much of this industry was expended on dreary technicalities.

For the modern reader the horror of war diminishes somewhat when, in the Vizetelly translation, Maurice, after being captured by the Prussians, and starved and beaten to the point of desperation, says of a Prussian officer who has threatened him: 'Oh! How I should like to slap him!' This same passage illuminates the modern treatment of soldiers' language in the two most recent translations. Hands (1968) has Maurice say, 'Oh, what I'd give to hit that fellow in the face!' while Tancock's version (1 72) is, 'Oh, to give that one a clout' Neither seems to me to represent in the least what a captive soldier might say under such provocation. Tancock does hit the hard stuff occasionally though one character actually says, 'Fuck it!' – but it is inconsistent and unconvincing One can't have Jean saying, 'Oh, Lor!' and 'chuck yourself in the shit' in the same breath, and for an old soldier like Jean who also spent ten years with the brutish peasants in *Earth* to address the younger Maurice as 'my dear boy' is stretching credulity too far. Hands adopts a slightly more refined trench vernacular, and while it would be more at home on the rugger pitch of a public school it is at least consistent.

Another, no less important, challenge this novel presents to the translator lies in the descriptive passages, of which the book is rather overburdened. Vizetelly laboriously describes every nut and bolt and addes dozens of explanatory footnotes to his version, contributing further to its textbook tone Tancock, too, sacrifices style for precision and while his is the most literally correct modern translation, Hands's licence with the original results in a more readable narrative.

Le Docteur Pascal

Serialised in *La Revue hebdomadaire* from 18 March to 17 June 1893

(89)	*Doctor Pascal*	Ernest Vizetelly	1893	Chatto & Windus	London
(90)	*Doctor Pascal* *	Mary J. Serrano	1901	MacMillan Co	New York
(91)	*Doctor Pascal* †	Vladimir Kean	1957	Elek Books Ltd	London

When Zola wrote to Ernest Vizetelly in 1892 telling him of *Doctor Pascal*, he added, 'You may try to place an English serialisation of it, for it will not affect the modesty of your fellow countrymen.'

Alas, the novelist still could not come to grips with the stern moral stuff of which Englishmen were made, with the result that *Doctor Pascal* contains some of the most ludicrous bowdlerising of any English version of his novel

* Published in conjunction with the International Society of Newspapers & Authors New York.

† Published in America by Dufour Editions, Pennsylvania (1957).

Consequently, while English readers were allowed a distant whiff of this tragic and touching love idyll they were denied its essence. There is no point beating poor Vizetelly about the head over this because his hands were tied, as he indicates in his preface: 'Circumstances have constrained me to omit from this English version certain passages. . . I do not think that their omission will in any wise prevent the reader from understanding the drift of M. Zola's narrative. I may add that the suppressions in question have been made with the author's cordial consent.' If the author accepted that merely 'understanding the drift' was good enough for his English readers, then it is a black mark against Zola. Actually, the suppressions positively erode the force of the narrative by persistently omitting the underlying motivations and meaning. For example, the long and torrid dawn of Pascal's love for Clotilde, in which the older man's fears are broken down by the youthful, feverish force of the young woman's passion, is reduced to a few pointless lines. The couple aren't even in bed! And later on, this same Victorian fear of the bed demands, by the same disturbing black logic, the exclusion of Pascal's (Zola's) philosophy on procreation, one of the essential pillars of the story.

This is bad enough, but the first English version is totally damned by Vizetelly's awful, pedestrian prose. How it ever became a bestseller in the 1890s is not so much a mystery as a comment on Victorian tastes and standards; it is certainly unreadable today.

Fortunately, Vladimir Kean's translation for Elek, which is still in print, is intelligent, sensitive and a pleasure to read. There are a few falls from grace, however, one of which is worth noting. At the end of the episode in which Pascal and Clotilde consummate their love – which begins with a prelude of discovery, builds to a passionate crescendo and then fades on a long-held, rapturous note – the unfortunate choice of the word 'fertilizing' destroys, for me at any rate, the lyricism of the final paragraph:

> Her voice faded into an indistinct murmur. He laughed exultantly; they took each other again. The whole night was a miracle of beatitude, in that happy room, redolent of youth and passion. When the first faint flush of dawn began to light the sky, they opened the windows wide to let in the spring. The fertilizing April sun rose slowly in the immensity of the heavens in a cloudless sky, and the earth, aquiver with germinating life beneath it, celebrated their wedding.

The original has *le soleil fécondant d'avril,* and while 'fertilizing' might be correct in the narrow sense it is ill-used here. One of the novelist's favourite motif-words in the cycle is *fécondité* meaning fruitfulness, and in this sense it recurs throughout his work; either 'fecundating' or 'fruitful' would have conveyed the author's intention more accurately and certainly more poetically. More inept, though, is Kean's attempt to condense Clotilde's reiteration of Pascal's credo in the last chapter; a whole paragraph is missing. Even though it was less than profound, it deserved a better fate than abandonment.

411

LES TROIS VILLES (1894–8)

The Three Cities Trilogy 1894–1898

English interest in the Three Cities *novels has been such that no new translation have appeared since those made at the time of publication in France. There is little to sa about the quality of the translations.*

Lourdes

Serialised in *Le Gil Blas*, 15 April to 15 August 1894

(92) *Lourdes*   Ernest Vizetelly   1894   Chatto & Windus   London
                                           The MacMillan Co.   New York

Such was Zola's international reputation in the 1890s that the America serialisation rights to *Lourdes* were acquired by the *New York Herald*, which twenty years before had sent Stanley to Africa to find Dr Livingstone. With similar flair the paper paid 4,000 dollars for Zola's latest book. The novel wa well received in England, too, and went into many editions before World War before going out of print.

Lourdes is not without contemporary interest and deserves to be preserved i a form of English more readable than Vizetelly's fatiguing prose.

Rome

Serialised in *Le Journal*, 21 December 1895 to 8 May 1896

(93) *Rome*   Ernest Vizetelly   1896   Chatto & Windus   London
                                        The MacMillan Co   New York

Paris

Serialised in *Le Journal*, 23 October 1897 to 9 February 1898

(94) *Paris*   Ernest Vizetelly   1898   Chatto & Windus   London
                                         The MacMillan Co   New York

LES QUATRE EVANGILES

The Four Gospels Tetralogy (1899–1902)

Fecondite

Serialised in *L'Aurore*, 15 May to 4 October 1899

95) *Fruitfulness*   Ernest Vizetelly   1900   Chatto & Windus   London

As Marie Stopes in England and Margaret Sanger in America were to discover a decade or two later, the subject of birth control at the turn of the century was a closed book and there was no shortage of people determined to keep it closed. America's first birth control clinic wasn't opened until 1916, and then for only a few days before it was raided by police; in England, although Dr Stopes was not prosecuted she was mercilessly ridiculed. Understandably, then, Vizetelly was faced with a touchy situation, as he explains to the readers of his translation:

> When I first perused the original proofs of M. Zola's work I came to the conclusion that an English version of it would be well nigh impossible. Subsequently, however, my views became modified...and thus I at last reverted to the task from which I have turned aside almost in despair. For me the problem was how to retain the *ensemble* of the narrative and all the essence of the lessons which the work inculcates, whilst recasting some portion of it and sacrificing those matters of form to which exception was taken.

If *Fruitfulness* was not so much literature (even in its original language) as a tract for the times, Vizetelly's contraceptive editing removed its only remaining claim to exist at all.

Travail

Serialised in *L'Aurore*, 3 December 1900 to 11 March 1901

96) *Labor*   Anonymous   1901   Harper & Bros   New York
97) *Work*   E. Vizetelly   1901   Chatto & Windus   London

This appears to be the only novel in the *Les Quatre Evangiles* series to exist in two translations and the marked differences in a number of passages prompts the belief that the American publishers received proofs from Zola bearing many alterations and additions at variance with those sent to Vizetelly. Apart from this the Harper translation is considerably more straightforward in its use of language than Vizetelly's, especially in the dialogue. For example, where Vizetelly has Delaveau say to his wife: 'Come, there is something the matter with you; why don't you tell me what it is?', the American version puts it much more succinctly: 'What is the matter with you, love?' This straight talk is also carried into the narrative. When a character is 'striving to retain his *sangfroid*' in Vizetelly's translation, he is 'forcing himself to keep cool' in the American. If at times the prose in the Harper version is a little less lyrical than it might have been it is, by today's standards, far more readable than the Chatto text.

* Doubleday, Page & Co., New York, 1923.

413

Verite

Serialised in *L'Aurore*, 10 September 1902 to 15 February 1903

(98) *Truth* Ernest Vizetelly 1903 Chatto & Windus London

John Lane New York

Even *Truth* was not spared from the censorious hand of English hypocrisy
Zola's last novel suffered from many obliterations, mostly references to the
pederastic nature of the murder, but Vizetelly also took upon himself the task
of pruning some of the longer passages. Like the other novels in *Les Quatr*
Evangiles, it is an unlikely candidate for a fresh translation.

SHORT STORIES

These have been widely published in various collections, of which the following
English texts are representative:

Contes à Ninon was translated by Edward Vizetelly and published by William
Heinemann Ltd, London (1895). Selections from this collection and *Nouveau*
Contes à Ninon were translated by George Cox for T.B. Peterson & Bros
Philadelphia (1888). Vizetelly's text was used in a *Collected Works of Emile Zol*
published by Walter J. Black Inc, New York, in 1928; and in the *Best Know*
Works of Emile Zola by the Book League of America, New York (1941).

A Soldier's Honour, including Zola's famous war story, *The Attack on the Mill*
was also translated by Edward Vizetelly and published first by Vizetelly & Co
London, in 1888 and subsequently by Chatto & Windus in 1901. *The Attack o*
the Mill appears also under the Heinemann imprint (1892) and The Reader
Library (1905).

Other reprints and translations include Lafcadio Hearn's *Stories from Emil*
Zola, edited by Albert Mordell for the Hokuseido Press, Tokyo, 1935; separate
editions of the stories, translated by W.M. Foster Apthorp, were published b
Copeland & Day, Boston (1895); and various stories were published separatel
– *The Embezzler, The Flood, Shellfish, Death*, etc – by the Warren Press, New Yor
(1911).

The only modern translations of Zola's short stories are those by Rolan
Gant for The Vanguard Press, New York (1968) and Sphere Books Ltd
London (1969). This trio includes one story translated for the first time, *Voyag*
circulaire (*Round Trip*) which appeared in the posthumous collection publishe
in 1929 under the title of *Madame Sourdis*. Gant captures the Tati-esqu
humour superbly, indicating the need for another good look at Zola's shor
stories which for the most part exist – or, rather did exist – only in poo
translations.

* John Lane: The Bodley Head, New York, 1903.

PLAYS, CRITICAL AND POLEMIC WORKS

Zola's drama and critical writing has not found favour among English and American publishers. Of his plays, *Les Héritiers Rabourdin* was translated by A. Teixeira de Mattos as *The Heirs of Rabourdin* in 1893; and *Thérèse Raquin* is included in *Seeds of Modern Drama*, Dell Publishing Co., New York (1966); only critical works available in English are included in *The Experimental Novel and other Essays*, translated by Belle M. Sherman in 1893, and reprinted by Haskell House, New York (1964); and in *The Experimental Novel*, published by Harvest House, Montreal (1964).

23

In Retrospect:
Respect and Disrespect

Emile Zola's posthumous reputation, inside and outside France, was for many years linked to the decline of naturalism which had, even before his death in 1902, ceased to exist anywhere as a literary 'school'. In France this decline can be traced, though not attributed, to the *Manifesto of the Five against 'La Terre'* of 1887. Its young authors were rather more concerned with Zola's preoccupation with sex and violence than with his naturalist technique, but their public denunciation certainly drew attention to the disenchantment of the new literary generation with naturalism.

In the same vein, the *Echo de Paris* in 1891 conducted a survey among sixty prominent writers and critics on the question, 'Is Naturalism Dead?' The response was a resounding Yes. This exercise, however, was more a pointed rebuke to Zola than a detached enquiry, for by 1890 Zola had quietly abandoned most of the naturalist theories he'd formerly espoused, and in fact hadn't written on the subject for many years.

The critic and novelist Remy de Gourmont wrote that Zola's death was not the death of a writer, for he had given up writing ten years before, and had instead engaged in 'mixing humanitarian mortar'. But for twenty years during his life it could be claimed that Zola had symbolised the novel in France; he was fiction's spearhead; and the absence of this very vocal and argumentative giant from the literary scene left a pronounced vacuum during the 1890s and for some time after his death. More important, his death left the realist novel nowhere to go.

Naturalism suffered the same rise and decline in other European countries. Throughout the second half of the nineteenth century, French authors dominated the European literary scene, and Zola's naturalism was an influential French export. Oddly enough he was a best-selling author in Russia years before his escalation to fame in his own country; while writers like Tolstoy and Dostoevsky had to wait another decade for their works to be translated and published in France. In Germany, naturalism crossed the frontier during the 1880s when a group of young writers adopted the technique partly to break down the sterility of German literature and partly to shock the Philistinism of its critics. They succeeded in a spectacular manner. On the heels of political unification youthful Germans were ready and waiting for Zola's unflinching observations on the middle classes, government corruption and social evils; his novels fermented extremes of enthusiasm and censure and widespread controversy. But the forces of reaction were too strong, and by the 1890s Zolaism was synonymous with satanism; naturalism was 'pig literature'; the *Rougon-Macquart* books purveyed 'lust in its basest form'; Zola was a 'high-class degenerate and second-rate romanticist'. Of his methods, one German critic described them as 'darwinism gone mad, which transposes the physiology of heredity into the phantasmagoria of romanticism'. Another ran dangerously close to exhausting the store-house of epithets when he described Zola as having 'no kindness, love, gentleness or humour'; he was 'untrained, lacking in refinement, exploiting the public's sensual instincts, ugly, immoral, indecent and dangerous'.

Naturalism also came late to Spain and Portugal, on the wave of the international furore over the publication of *L'Assommoir* in 1877, but the Latins soon became avid readers and followers of naturalist works. The attractions of naturalism to Latin and Latin American writers were obvious; where dogmas and taboos needed to be broken down in countries lagging in social reform the young generation of writers had a ready-made technique with which to reflect and present reality.

With something like a seventy per cent illiteracy rate throughout Italy during the 1870s, it is not surprising that naturalism took some time to gain a hold there. But during the 1880s Zola gained many disciples of *verismo, realismo* and *naturalismo*, although they were to be notable more for polemic than literary attainment.

In all these European countries, naturalism was a spent force as a live literary movement by the turn of the century. There were many regional reasons for this, of course. From 1898 a particularly repressive regime in Spain discouraged the naturalist inclination to expose social injustice, and similar daunting obstacles faced naturalist writers in many other countries. Elsewhere, this great hope of fiction turned out to be merely fashionable, and the naturalist movement was discarded in favour of a more indigenous style.

But this hardly explains the sudden, universal collapse of the naturalist movement. For this, I think, one has to return to the fountainhead, to Zola himself. A decade before his death, Zola had taken naturalism to its furthermost limits, and even beyond it into the realms of symbolism and surrealism. As early as 1885 the American critic Hamilton Wright Mabie had written, 'Is there anything beyond Zola? He has pressed his theory so far that even his hottest adherents see no steps left for another to take. The energetic Naturalist – a man of great force and splendid working power – has left his followers not a single fig leaf to be plucked off the shameless nudity of the "bête humaine" – the human animal.'

Zola was a destructive rather than a liberating precursor, for he had explored and exhausted the whole potential of naturalism by himself. A writer of any talent at all soon realised he could not exist on the sparse and debilitating diet left for him, which explains why, after Zola, there were so few naturalist writers of any stature. In this regard it is useful to examine the experience of the Anglo-Irish novelist George Moore (1852–1933).

The naturalist movement made only a single direct crossing of the English Channel, in the mind and ambitions of George Moore. Moore had idolised Zola: 'He is to me a great epic poet, and he may be, I think, not inappropriately termed the Homer of modern life.' Moore found it difficult to understand 'how any man of average discrimination could speak with him for half an hour without recognising that he was one of those mighty monumental intelligences, the statues of a century, that remain and are gazed upon through the long pages of the world's history'. Moore's blind faith asserted itself in earnestly promulgating naturalist doctrines, and defending his hero's works when necessary. To him, Zola's great novel cycle had the properties of a mastodon: 'I believe that the gigantic skeleton of the *Rougon-Macquart* family will still continue to resist the ravages of time, and that western scientists will refer to it when disputing about the idiosyncrasies of a past civilisation.' Moore's propagandizing, however, made little headway in England, and he only wrote one truly naturalist novel, *A Mummer's Wife* (1885), overburdened with the mannerisms and excesses of the style, before abandoning naturalism.

George Moore's love affair with Zola is instructive for the light it throws on the reaction of an imaginative writer to the sterile, latter-day landscape of naturalism with its extravagances and shaky doctrines. Naturalism had brought the world face to face with the facts of life, but having banished the one faculty – imagination – which might penetrate these facts to reveal new insights, or to reaffirm eternal truths, or to create concepts undreamed of, the naturalist movement ground to an inevitable halt.

Thinking writers and readers were equally disenchanted with Zola's bright vision of the progressive, scientific Utopia presented in his later novels, which was shown to be a mere transient gleam by the philosophies of Kierkegaard and his followers. Reality to the individual, he argued, is not scientifically determinable but was and always would be ambiguous.

Zola's demotion from his position of literary messiah was inevitable, but as a powerful influence he has stubbornly refused to disappear, and pops up in some unexpected quarters. Naturalism was a child of its time, and it introduced a new method of representing reality. We have seen how documentary research was an essential element in Zola's art, but it was rarely *reported* in a form that could be described as factual or detached; instead it was distorted, coloured and often reshaped into symbols. By the time Zola emerged from a tour of a coal mine he'd undertaken before writing *Germinal*, it had become, in his imagination, a rapacious, living monster into whose black bowels poured a daily ration of human fodder. But in the 1890s the naturalist method had an important chock kicked from under it by the emerging science of sociology, whose researchers were far more suited to the objective study of social phenomena than novelists. Thereafter, fiction – a blend of observed fact, intuitive truth and pure imagination – was seen to be an inefficient vehicle for the purpose of exposing mankind's irregularities and injustices. Curiously, the wheel has almost turned full circle in the intervening eighty years, for factual documents have by their own proliferation and self-importance alienated the interest of the reading public. Not surprisingly, there is now a trend towards inserting fictional elements in otherwise factual accounts.

But Zola's main influence on subsequent fiction around the world was and is conveyed by the echoes of the naturalism he largely created, for despite the hostile forces massed against it, naturalism never completely expired. As a thrusting, virile movement, with the bugle blasts and battle cries that resounded during its early years, it certainly faded into eclipse; but its influence outside France was unstoppable. The echoes – unheard in England, except by Moore, Bennett and Galsworthy – were picked up with enthusiasm in America, to be recorded and amplified by successive generations of writers.

Theodore Dreiser (1871–1945) is the best-known early naturalist writer, often dubbed the 'American Zola' although he always insisted his adoption of the realist style was independent of outside influences. His *Sister Carrie* (1900) upset turn-of-the-century morality, and his publisher withdrew the book after review copies had been sent out. His last important novel, *An American Tragedy* (1925), deals with a character who is the helpless victim of devouring social forces. If Dreiser was the 'American Zola', Frank Norris (1870–1902) was just as frequently called the 'Boy Zola'. In his short literary life he wrote two of a trilogy of naturalist novels centred in the mid-west wheat belt: *The Octopus* (1901), which exposed the ruthless stranglehold the railroads had on the farmers; and *The Pit* (1903), which is the local name for the Chicago Wheat Exchange, the battlefield of the rural speculators. Both novels were considerably influenced by Zola. Two other Americans, contemporaries of Dreiser and Norris, also established their early careers with naturalist novels influenced by the French writer. Stephen Crane (1871–1900), despite his short career (he died in England, a close friend of Joseph Conrad), left brilliant poems, short stories and novels, including *The Red Badge of Courage* (1895), but his maiden work in fiction was *Maggie: A Girl of the Streets* which bears many similarities to Zola's *L'Assommoir*. Although he was shocked by the naturalism of Zola, Hamlin Garland (1860–1940) adapted it for his ruggedly real novels of farm life on the western plains.

This quartet was followed by what might be called a second generation of American novelists who were realists, although at least a proportion of their work owed a debt to Zola, as with Upton Sinclair's *The Jungle*, written in 1906. This powerful novel, set in the Chicago stockyards, caused a national furore and resulted in food law reform. Typically Zolaesque, Sinclair (1878–1968) was incredibly prolific – he wrote some eighty books – and concluded his career with a cycle of novels about world affairs, the first of which was *World's End* (1940). John Steinbeck (1902–68) is a member of this group with his magnificent *The Grapes of Wrath* (1939) and so is John Dos Passos (1896–1970), Sinclair Lewis (1885–1951) and James T. Farrell (b.1904) whose trilogy *Studs*

Lonigan, written between 1932 and 1935, reflects a late but clear echo of the naturalist technique.

Although the foundations of American naturalism were laid before Zola's death, the continuing loyalty to the style owed something to the imprimatur accorded it by Henry James in his article on the novelist in *Atlantic Monthly* in 1903 and in other critical pieces. Apart from George Moore, who by no means occupied the same lofty critical seat as James, Zola had no such champion in England. Almost without exception the little critical comment his work did attract was hostile in the extreme.

The mists of opprobrium which had surrounded Zola's work and life did not drift away in England upon his death. Just a month afterwards the critic of *The Fortnightly Review* attempted a retrospective view of the novelist's achievements while holding his nose: 'The task,' he wrote, 'is a noisome one, suggesting a quest for hidden treasures in a drain.' Perhaps the muck was a little too fresh for his sensitive membranes, for he went on to say that the 'obscenity of Zola is a thing apart, differing not in degree only, but in kind, from the obscenity of any other writer whose works have been accepted as literature'. It is not surprising, therefore, that the subscribers to this organ of advanced liberalism were treated to an uneven essay which, while admitting at the start that 'Zola was a great writer' then attempted to prove he wasn't. The article was a blend of untruths – 'Without wit, without pathos, without insight into human character, without even a natural turn for story-telling, he nevertheless always contrives to be effective'; half-truths – 'One can picture Zola, before sitting down to write a novel, making out a list of the ingredients, just as if he were going to make a pudding'; and near-truths – 'Religion, for him, was simply an hysterical hallucination, and love simply a sensual passion, the precursor of abominable crimes. The one enthusiasm that did at last lay hold of him was the enthusiasm for justice.' Yet woven into this collection of untruths, half-truths and near-truths were perceptive and original observations which tended to invest the quality of truth over the whole. In the receding tide of interest in Zola's work in the early part of this century such outbursts assumed an unwarranted prominence and thus were disproportionately influential on subsequent opinion, public and academic.

Of greater interest than the unrelieved hostility of the criticism of Zola and naturalism is the fact that there was so little of it. No major writer can ever have been so studiously neglected. We have already seen that the principal English objection to his work was a moral one, and it appears to have been upheld not only by readers, booksellers, libraries and the press, but also by the whole critical apparatus of the country. With hardly a responsible voice raised in his favour, Zola moved into a world of myth, superstition and rumour; he became some kind of bogey-man to the public. When, towards the end of the nineteenth century, his reputation emerged fleetingly from the pornographic bog to which it had been consigned in the previous couple of decades, it was promptly distorted by his involvement with the Dreyfus case and obscured by the mantle of morality hastily thrown over his shoulders by anxious publishers.

Zola then became many things to many people, but what he was not, to the population at large, was simply a novelist of genius. It was as a reformer, perhaps, that he made his greatest penetration into the public consciousness, mainly through the dozens of double-distilled versions of *L'Assommoir*. These were the years, of course, when the various temperance organisations were exercising their muscles; Zola's chilling account of Gervaise's tragic downfall accompanied by the demon drink was eagerly sanctified by the temperance leaders and it soon became the Bible of the teetotallers, to be used with such effectiveness that the story was paraphrased to popularise prohibitionist campaigns of another kind. In 1903, for example, there appeared *The Cigarette Smoker* by C. Ranger-Gull – 'A book of the Hour! The author deals with his subject in the same daring and realistic style as Zola did with alcoholism in DRINK!' Such was Zola's legacy to the Edwardians.

Unintentional contributions to temperance apart, far from conspiring to cause a breakdown of English morality, Zola and the naturalists were responsible for notable advances. It is true their novels tended to expose social cancers rather than cure them, and that their exposés led more to the disintegration of discredited conventions than the creation of desirable replacements. But for women especially, naturalism introduced some long-awaited illumination into the dark cave of sexual ignorance which generations of women had feared to enter. Prostitution, a wife's chattel-like subjection to her husband, the hypocrisy of the acceptance of mistresses, the seduction and corruption of poor working girls – all these nineteenth-century evils were courageously exposed for the malignant sores they were. Zola's novels, like the plain-speaking contraceptive tracts of Marie Stopes decades later, were feared by the middle classes and harangued from the pulpits. The tarring and feathering was so thorough and carried out with such maniacal fervour that to the vast majority of the English population the name of Zola was best forgotten.

Zola's penalty for outraging the established orders in France, England and America was near-total eclipse for half a century. From the time of his death until the 1950s only two or three new translations into English were added to the body of his work. Sales of his novels petered out before World War I, and when old copies were removed from libraries they were never replaced. For at least thirty years it became almost impossible for an English reader to buy or borrow any of his books. Scholarly and critical studies of his work sank out of sight, although there was a feeble revival in 1927 on the occasion of the twenty-fifth anniversary of his death. This interest, though, was exclusively continental; the *Rougon-Macquart* novels, for instance, were published in a new twenty-volume edition in Germany, but no equivalent enterprise was undertaken in England or America.

Instead, a formidable arsenal of hostile criticism was established to justify Zola's banishment, and it became fashionable to dismiss his work without any attempt to reassess or understand it. Zola was tendentious, rhetorical, heavy-handed, monotonous, dull. He always wrote the expected rather than

421

the unexpected. He was a mere book-keeper of life. His metaphors were commonplace and grotesque. Two generations of critics and academics could find nothing good to say about him. Two generations of writers turned their backs to him and while decrying his faults many ironically magnified them in their own work.

Much of this dismissive attitude resulted from the mistake of confusing the artist's life and beliefs with his work. As we have seen in so many instances, Zola's theories went one way while his creative energies went another. His lack of understanding of his own work was at times complete, enabling him to write some of the most surreal, lyrical prose in literature while believing he was simply setting down a logical sequence of sociological observations.

The banishment of Zola's work extended to schools and universities, thus effectively denying the opportunity for a reassessment by fresh minds. Studies of French literature intended for teaching pointedly omitted any useful discussion of his work. Typical of dozens of such books is *An Approach to French Literature* by Vincent Waite (Harrap, London, 1947) in which Zola is accorded just six lines in its 384 pages. These six lines indicate that the author had read few, if any, of Zola's novels: 'Emile Zola carried Naturalism to its worst extremes. Of his enormous series of novels planned under the title *Les Rougon-Macquart*, the best are *Le Ventre de Paris, L'Assommoir, Germinal* and *La Débâcle*. His studies of three towns, *Lourdes, Rome* and *Paris*, are interesting, but, like so much of Zola's work, unpleasant.' Selections from the writings of three of Zola's contemporaries, Daudet, Maupassant and Anatole France, take up eighty pages. Twenty-five years later the academic conspiracy against Zola, even in areas which ought to offer more enlightenment, is still active. In L. Cazamian's widely distributed *A History of French Literature* (Oxford University Press, 1971), Zola's magnificent literary achievement is derisively reduced to 'no more than the imposing mass of an ambitious but insecurely built monument'. This alarming academic prejudice is not confined to countries outside France, however. It was not until after 1952, and then only as the result of a long campaign, that *Germinal*, universally recognised as one of the greatest masterpieces of French literature, was placed by the universities on the syllabus for the *Agrégation*, the examination for secondary school-teachers.

In all this half-century of ostracism and persecution, there were only occasional cries raised in Zola's defence. André Gide, writing in 1932, named *Germinal* as one of the ten finest novels in the French language. He added that there was not a more personal nor a more representative French novelist than Zola, and considered that his disrepute was 'a monstrous injustice which does not enhance the credit of our contemporary literary critics'. The American critic Lionel Trilling, in *A Gathering of Fugitives* (Secker & Warburg, London, 1957) also stoutly defended Zola. Of *Pot-Bouille* he wrote, 'We read this book for the pleasure of its fierce energy, for the strange pleasure we habitually derive from the indictment of the human kind. The work has a reality beyond anything that might be proved of the Parisian middle class of 1882; it has the reality of the author's rage and disgust with human inadequacy.' But perhaps the most eloquent plea for the reinstatement of Zola to his rightful place in literature came from the Pulitzer Prize-winning American poet Edwin Arlington Robinson, who paid tribute to the novelist with this sonnet:

> Because he puts the compromising chart
> Of hell before your eyes, you are afraid;
> Because he counts the price that you have paid
> For innocence, and counts it from the start,
> You loathe him. But he sees the human heart
> Of God meanwhile, and in His hand was weighed
> You squeamish and emasculate crusade
> Against the grim domination of his art.——
>
> Never until we conquer the uncouth
> Connivings of our shamed indifference
> (We call it Christian faith) and we to scan
> The racked and shrieking hideousness of Truth
> To find in Hate's polluted self-defence
> Throbbing, the pulse, the divine heart of Man.

In the end it was the reading public, and not a small body of critical opinion, that broke through the barricades. A purely commercial publishing enterprise, which began in 1955 to issue old and new English-language versions of most of Zola's novels, and which continues to this day, has been resoundingly successful. Millions of copies, in hard covers and paperback, have been sold in many English-speaking countries of the world. The Penguin edition of *Germinal* has sold a quarter of a million copies in Britain alone and has been reprinted at least thirteen times – not bad for a novel written ninety years ago! Zola revivals have also gathered force in many other European countries, and in France Fasquelle, the novelist's publisher in later years, issues the entire *Rougon-Macquart* cycle in paperback. What almost amounts to a 'Zola industry' emerged, reaching its peak at the end of the 1950s with over eighty major studies of the novelist's life and work published during the decade.

The complex web of prejudice, conspiracy, addled morality and counter philosophies that exiled Emile Zola from the world of literature for three generations has now been largely removed; like Dreyfus, we are now thinking of letting him return from that lonely rock. Without Zola and the naturalists, we realise, there would not have been a Bennett, or a Steinbeck, a James Jones or an Arthur Hailey. There might not have been a Proust, either, or a Kafka, or a Joyce. For naturalism broke the traditional barriers which had shut out sordid reality as subject matter for fiction, and subsequently enlarged its sources and potential. Like any new movement in the arts it threw off one yoke to become another; thus naturalism is not a literary abberation to be dismissed and vilified, but an essential link in a logical progression. Today we accept the principles of naturalism as a matter of course, although we reject its extreme doctrines. We do not believe any writer can encompass the whole of life or the whole of truth; at best we may be privileged to have glimpses. But literature, most of us believe, remains firmly anchored to the world we live in, where, as Professor George Becker puts it, 'we still twist and turn on that hard bed, too belaboured and aching from the stones of fact to be able to escape into dreams.'

Sources and Further Reading

The definitive work on Emile Zola in English is *Emile Zola* by F.W.J. Hemmings (Oxford University Press, 1953, 1966). It deserves a special tribute for it remains the most concise yet exhaustively documented critical biography of this author in English since its first publication in 1953. Unusual for such a scholarly work it is written with style, insight and wit and, although all its references and excerpts are in French, if you only read one other book about Zola, this should be it. Professor Hemmings dominates contemporary Zola scholarship and criticism of French realist writing. Especially valuable are his *Culture and Society in France, 1848–1898* (Charles Scribner's Sons, New York, 1971) which sketches in the social background of the period in which Zola wrote; and *The Age of Realism* (Penguin Books, 1974), a survey, edited by Professor Hemmings, of realist and naturalist fiction in Europe; and *The Life and Times of Emile Zola* (Elek, 1977) with much new material about the author's life and with many hitherto unpublished photographs.

An excellent short introduction to Zola and his work is Angus Wilson's *Emile Zola* (Secker & Warburg, London, 1952) which is particularly illuminating on the emotional and sexual side of the author's life.

For a broad picture of French fiction, one of the best guides in print is the six-volume series *French Literature and its Background* (Oxford University Press, 1969) edited by John Cruikshank. This work surveys French writing from the Renaissance to the present day. Martin Turnell, in *The Art of French Fiction* (New Directions, New York, 1959), confines himself to seven novelists, including Zola, but his focus is sharper, especially with his analysis of style.

The Bibliography which follows lists the chief sources of this account of Zola's life, and of the quoted comments and assessments of his work. For a more detailed bibliography on the author I recommend that appended to Professor Hemmings's *Emile Zola* referred to above.

ALEXIS, Paul, *Emile Zola, notes d'un ami*, Charpentier, Paris, 1882

BARBUSSE, Henri, *Zola* (trans. M.B. and F. Green), E.P. Dutton & Co., Inc. New York, 1933.

BECKER, George J., *Documents of Modern Literary Realism* (ed.), Princeton University Press, New Jersey, 1973

BERNARD, Marc, *Zola* (trans. Jean Leblon), Evergreen Books Ltd, London; Grove Press, New York, 1960
BROWN, Calvin S., *Repetition in Zola's Novels*, University of Georgia Press, Athens, Georgia, 1952
BURCHELL, S.C., *Upstart Empire*, MacDonald, London, 1971
CARTER, Lawson A., *Zola and the Theater*, Yale University Press, New Haven, 1963
CEARD, Henri, *Lettres inédites à Emile Zola*, Nizet, Paris, 1958
CEZANNE, Paul, *Correspondance*, Grasset, Paris, 1937
CHAPMAN, Guy, *The Dreyfus Trials*, Granada Publishing, London, 1974
CRUIKSHANK, John, *French Literature and its Background* (ed.), Oxford University Press, 1969
CUNLIFFE, Marcus, *The Literature of the United States*, Penguin Books, London 1954
DE AMICIS, Edmondo, *Ricordi di Parigi*, Treves, Milan, 1879
Ritratti letterari, Treves, Milan, 1881
DREYFUS, Alfred, *The Diary of Captain Alfred Dreyfus*, Intro. Nicholas Halasz, Peebles Press, London, 1978
ELLIS, Havelock, *Affirmations*, Constable, London, 1898
FAIR, Charles, *From the Jaws of Victory*, Weidenfeld & Nicolson, London, 1972
FIELDING, Hubert, *The Life of Emile Zola*, Herbert Joseph, London, 1938
FLAUBERT, Gustave, *Correspondance*, Conrad, Paris, 1926-33.
FRIEDMAN, Lee M., *Zola and the Dreyfus Case*, Haskell, New York, 1966
GONCOURT, Edmond and Jules de, *Journal. Mémoires de la vie littéraire*, Editions de l'Imprimerie Nationale, Monaco, 1956
GONCOURT, Jules de, *Lettres de Jules de Goncourt*, Charpentier, Paris, 1885
GRAND-CARTERET, John, *Zola en images*, Librairie Felix Juven, Paris, 1905
GRANT, Elliott M., *Zola's 'Germinal': A critical and historical study*, Leicester University Press, 1970
GRANT, Richard B., *Zola's 'Son Excellence Eugène Rougon'*, Duke University Press, Durham, N.C., 1960
GRIEST, Gunivere, *Mudie's Circulating Library*, Indiana University Press, David & Charles, Newton Abbot, 1970
HEMMINGS, F.W.J., *Emile Zola*, Oxford University Press, 1966
Culture and Society in France, 1848-1898, Charles Scribner's Sons, New York, 1971
The Age of Realism (ed.), Penguin Books, 1974
The Life and Times of Emile Zola, Paul Elek, London, 1977
HOWE, Irving, *The Critical Point*, Horizon Press, New York, 1973
JAMES, Henry, *The House of Fiction*, Hart-Davis, London, 1957
JONES, Malcolm B., *Translations of Zola in the United States prior to 1900*, Modern Language Notes, Baltimore, 1940
JOSEPHSON, Matthew, *Zola and His Time*, The Macaulay Co., New York, 1928
KANES, Martin, *Zola's 'La Bête humaine'*, University of California Press, Berkeley, 1962

KLEMAN, M.K., *Emile Zola*, Khudozhestvennaya literatura, Leningrad, 1934
LANOUX, Armand, *Zola* (trans. Mary Glasgow), Staples Press, London, 1955
LE BLOND, Maurice, *La Publication de 'La Terre'*, Malfère, Paris, 1937
LE BLOND-ZOLA, Denise, *Emile Zola raconté par sa fille*, Fasquelle, Paris, 1931
LEVIN, Harry, *The Gates of Horn*, Oxford University Press, New York, 1963
LINDSAY, Jack, *Cézanne, his Life and Art*, Harper & Row, New York, 1972
LUKACS, George, *Studies in European Realism*, Hillway, London, 1950
MACDONALD, Arthur, *Emile Zola: A Study of his Personality*, Washington, D.C., 1898
MARX, Karl, *The Paris Commune, 1871* (ed. Christopher Hitchens), Sidgwick & Jackson, London, 1971
OWENS, Graham, *George Moore's Life and Art* (ed.), Oliver & Boyd, London, 1968
PATTERSON, J.G., *A Zola Dictionary*, Routledge, London, 1912
PEARSALL, Ronald, *The Worm in The Bud: The World of Victorian Sexuality* Penguin Books, London, 1971
PERRIN, Noel, *Dr. Bowdler's Legacy*, Macmillan & Co., London, 1970
ROOT, Winthrop H., *German Criticism of Zola*, Colombia University Press, New York, 1931
RUFENER, Helen B., *Biography of a War Novel: Zola's 'La Débâcle'*, King's Crown Press, New York, 1926
SALVAN, Albert J., *Zola aux Etats-Unis*, Brown University Press, Providence R.I., 1943
SHERARD, Robert H., *Emile Zola*, Chatto & Windus, London, 1893
STREET, Harry, *Freedom, the Individual and the Law*, Penguin Books, London 1972
TURNELL, Martin, *The Art of French Fiction*, New Directions, New York, 1959
VIZETELLY, Henry, *Glances Back through 70 Years*, Kegan Paul, Trench Trubner & Co., London, 1893
VIZETELLY, Ernest A., *With Zola in England*, Chatto & Windus, London, 1899
Emile Zola, Novelist and Reformer, John Lane: The Bodley Head, London 1904
WALKER, Philip *Emile Zola*, Humanities Press, New York, 1968
WILSON, Angus *Emile Zola*, Secker & Warburg, London, 1952
XAU, Fernand *Emile Zola*, Marpon et Flammarion, Paris, 1880
ZOLA, Emile *Oeuvres complets*, ed. Henri Mitterand, Cercle du Livre Précieux Paris, 1966–1969
Les Rougon-Macquart, ed. Henri Mitterand, Bibliothèque de la Pléiade, Paris 1960–1967

Appendix

Sales of Zola's Novels

The following table shows the accumulated sales of Zola's novels: the ordinary Charpentier and Fasquelle French editions to 1903; and English translations sold in Great Britain to 1911.

	Ordinary French Edition 1903	English Translations in Britain 1911
The Fortune of the Rougons	38,000	42,000
The Kill	50,000	57,000
The Belly of Paris	47,000	53,000
The Conquest of Plassans	34,000	39,000
The Abbé Mouret's Sin	52,000 (1)	62,000
His Excellency	36,000 (2)	36,000
L'Assommoir	151,000 (3)	162,000
A Love Episode	97,000	112,000
Nana	198,000 (4)	215,000
Piping Hot!	95,000	102,000
The Ladies' Paradise	75,000	85,000
Joy of Life	54,000	61,000
Germinal	110,000	132,000
The Masterpiece	64,000	71,000
Earth	135,000	162,000
The Dream	116,000	132,000
The Beast in Man	99,000	108,000
Money	89,000	96,000
The Debacle	207,000	229,000
Doctor Pascal	94,000	101,000
Lourdes	154,000	
Rome	106,000	
Paris	94,000	
Fruitfulness	94,000	
Labour	77,000	
Truth	—	

The French sales take no account of the sometimes huge illustrated and special editions: (1) plus 80,000 illustrated copies; (3) plus very large editions of illustrated copies; (4) plus over 200,000 illustrated copies. (2) Sales of this novel had reached 52,000 by 1927 and this increase of 50% also applies to most of the other novels.

Modern sales: Elek Books Ltd sell their hard cover editions at the rate of about 4,000 per year. This figure covers seventeen titles, with *Germinal* and *Nana* the most popular. Penguin Books Ltd have five titles on the market, each selling approximately 10,000 copies per annum.

Index

Newspapers, periodicals and painters are entered cumulatively under the appropriat headings.

429